START AND RUN
A PROFITABLE CONSULTING BUSINESS

START AND RUN
A PROFITABLE CONSULTING BUSINESS
A step-by-step business plan

Douglas A. Gray, B.A., LL.B.

Self-Counsel Press
(a division of)
International Self-Counsel Press Ltd.
Canada   U.S.A.

Printed in Canada

First edition: March, 1985; Reprinted: October, 1985
Second edition: August, 1986; Reprinted: August, 1987; 1988; November, 1989; July, 1990
Third edition: August, 1990; Reprinted: June, 1991

Canadian Cataloguing in Publication Data

Gray, Douglas A.
    Start and run a profitable consulting business

    (Self-counsel business series)
    ISBN 0-88908-897-7

    1. Consultants. 2. New business enterprises.
I. Title. II. Series.
HD69.C6G73 1990   658.4.'6'023   C90-091521-8

Self-Counsel Press
(a division of)
International Self-Counsel Press Ltd.
Head and Editorial Office
1481 Charlotte Road
North Vancouver, British Columbia V7J 1H1

U.S. Address
1704 N. State Street
Bellingham, Washington 98225

CONTENTS

INTRODUCTION   xvii

1 UNDERSTANDING THE CONSULTING BUSINESS   1
   a. What is a consultant?   1
   b. Who goes into consulting?   3
   c. Why do organizations use consultants?   4
       1. Temporary assistance   4
       2. Objective review   4
       3. Third-party request for problem identification and resolution 4
       4. Surviving a crisis   5
       5. Initiating change   5
       6. Obtaining funding   5
       7. Selecting personnel   5
       8. In-house education   5
       9. Dealing with internal personnel difficulties   5
      10. Delay tactics   5
      11. Executive assistance   6
      12. Government regulatory compliance   6
      13. Socio-economic and political changes   6
      14. Government excess funds   6
   d. Regulations affecting consultants   6

2 SELF-ASSESSMENT   8
   a. Introduction   8
   b. Assessing yourself and your marketable skills   8

3 SETTING UP YOUR BUSINESS   12
   a. Start-up costs and monthly expenses   12
       1. Start-up costs   12
       2. Monthly overhead expenses   13
       3. Personal expenses   13
   b. Selecting a name   13
       1. General considerations   14
       2. Fictitious name   17
   c. Selecting an office   17
       1. Home office   17
       2. Office outside of home   18
       3. Equipping an office   21
       4. Office supplies   22
       5. Personnel   23
   d. Selecting a telephone system   24
       1. A separate phone at home   24
       2. Business line terminating at answering service   24
       3. Business line terminating at home and answering service   25
       4. Overline   25

	5.	Measured business line	25
	6.	Shared line	25
	7.	Remote call forwarding	25
	8.	Telephone answering devices	26
	9.	Interconnect phone purchase	26
e.	Saving money on long distance phone calls		27
	1.	Direct distance dialing	27
	2.	Reduced long distance rates	27
	3.	800 service number	27
	4.	Wide area telephone service (WATS)	27
	5.	Some tips	28

4 LEGAL FORMS OF BUSINESS STRUCTURE   29
a.	Introduction		29
b.	Sole proprietorship		29
	1.	Advantages	29
	2.	Disadvantages	30
c.	Partnership		30
	1.	Advantages	31
	2.	Disadvantages	31
	3.	Partnership agreement	32
	4.	Kinds of partners	32
d.	Corporation		33
	1.	Advantages	33
	2.	Disadvantages	34
	3.	Corporate purposes	34
	4.	Shareholders' agreement	35
	5.	Maintaining the corporate protection	35
e.	Sub-chapter S (Sub-S) Corporation (U.S.)		37

5 SELECTING BUSINESS AND PROFESSIONAL ADVISORS   38
a.	General criteria for advisor selection		38
	1.	Recommendations	38
	2.	Credentials	39
	3.	Clientele	39
	4.	Fees	39
	5.	Technical competence and industry knowledge	40
	6.	Style and personality	40
	7.	Confidence	40
	8.	Communication	40
	9.	Commitment	41
	10.	Availability	41
	11.	Length of time in practice	41
	12.	Ability to aid growth	41
	13.	Small firm versus large firm	41
b.	Lawyer		42
c.	Accountant		42
d.	Banker		43

    e.   Insurance   44
    f.   Consultants   44
        1.   Private consultants   44
        2.   Consultants subsidized by government   44

6   PREPARING YOUR BUSINESS PLAN   46
    a.   Why prepare a plan?   46
    b.   Format   46
    c.   Estimating your start-up funds   60
        1.   Assessment of personal monthly financial needs   60
        2.   Estimated business start-up cash needs   60
    d.   Summary   60

7   HOW TO OBTAIN FINANCING   61
    a.   Types of financing   61
        1.   Equity   61
        2.   Debt   61
    b.   Sources of financing   64
        1.   Equity   64
        2.   Debt   65
    c.   Competition between lenders   66
    d.   Tips on approaching your lender   66
    e.   Why loans are turned down   67
    f.   Types of security a lender may require   68
        1.   Endorser   69
        2.   Co-maker   69
        3.   Guarantor   69
        4.   Promissory note   69
        5.   Demand loan   69
        6.   Realty mortgage   69
        7.   Chattel mortgage   70
        8.   Assignment of accounts receivable   70
        9.   Postponement of claim   70
     10.   Pledge of stocks or bonds   70
     11.   Assignment of life insurance   70

8   KEEPING RECORDS   71
    a.   Accounting and bookkeeping   71
        1.   Separate record-keeping   71
        2.   Double-entry and single-entry bookkeeping   72
        3.   One-write accounting system   72
        4.   Cash or accrual basis for records   73
    b.   Basic accounting records   73
        1.   Sales journal   73
        2.   Cash receipts journal   73
        3.   Accounts receivable ledger and control account   74
        4.   Accounts payable journal   74
        5.   Cash disbursements journal   74

		6.	Payroll journal	74
		7.	General ledger	75
	c.	Non-financial records		75
		1.	Personnel records	75
		2.	Tax records	75
		3.	Service records	76
	d.	Office systems		76
		1.	Handling new matters	76
		2.	Time records	76
		3.	Standard form engagement letters or contracts	80
		4.	Billing, credit, and collection	80
		5.	Calendars	80
		6.	Filing systems	80

9 HOW TO LEGALLY MINIMIZE PAYING TAX — 81
	a.	Tax avoidance and tax evasion		81
	b.	Cash or accrual method		81
	c.	Fiscal year-end		82
	d.	Corporations, proprietorships or partnerships		82
	e.	Maximizing deductible expenses		83
		1.	Home office	83
		2.	Automobile	84
		3.	Entertainment	84
		4.	Travel	85
		5.	Bad debts	85
		6.	Insurance	85
		7.	Professional development	85

10 INSURANCE — 86
	a.	Obtaining insurance		86
		1.	Agencies	86
		2.	Insurance brokers	86
		3.	Clubs and associations	86
	b.	Planning your insurance program		87
	c.	Types of business and personal insurance		88
		1.	General liability	88
		2.	Products or completed operations liability	88
		3.	Errors and omissions liability	88
		4.	Malpractice liability	88
		5.	Automobile liability	88
		6.	Fire and theft liability	89
		7.	Business interruption insurance	89
		8.	Overhead expense insurance	89
		9.	Personal disability insurance	89
		10.	Key person insurance	89
		11.	Shareholders or partners insurance	90
		12.	Business loan insurance	90
		13.	Term life insurance	90

	14.	Medical insurance	91
	15.	Group insurance	91
	16.	Workers' compensation insurance	91

11 PROFESSIONAL LIABILITY ... 92
a. Contract and tort liability ... 92
   1. Contract liabilty ... 92
   2. Tort liability ... 93
b. Reasons for claims ... 94
   1. Counterclaims ... 94
   2. Conflict of interest ... 94
   3. Conflicting interest of clients ... 94
   4. Delegation of part of contract to employee or
      sub-consultant ... 94
   5. Third party damages ... 94
   6. Unclear expectations by client ... 94
c. How to avoid professional liability and prevent losses ... 95
   1. Client control ... 95
   2. Cost estimates ... 95
   3. Carefully drafted contracts ... 95
   4. Free opinions ... 95
   5. Law ... 96
   6. Sub-consultants ... 96
   7. Records, systems, and procedures ... 96
   8. Continuing education ... 96
   9. Quality control ... 96
  10. Communication ... 96
d. Professional liability insurance ... 96
   1. Increase deductibles ... 97
   2. Comparing prices ... 97
   3. Changing the type of coverage ... 98
e. Practicing without insurance ... 98

12 CREDIT, BILLING, AND COLLECTION ... 99
a. Disadvantages of extending credit ... 99
b. Assessing the client ... 100
c. Avoiding client misunderstandings on fees ... 100
   1. Communication ... 101
   2. Written contract ... 101
   3. Invoice ... 101
d. Minimizing risk of bad debts ... 102
   1. Advance retainer ... 102
   2. Pre-paid disbursements ... 102
   3. Progress payments ... 102
   4. Regular billing ... 102
   5. Billing on time ... 103
   6. Accelerated billing ... 103
   7. Withholding vital information ... 103

    8.   Holding up completion of important stage of project   103

    9.   Personal guarantee of principals of a corporation   103

    10. Monitor payment trends of clients   103

    11. Follow-up of late payments   103

    12. Involving client in assignment   104

  e. Billing for services   104

  f. Why clients pay late   107

  g. Collecting late payments without legal action   108

  h. Legal steps if account remains unpaid   109

    1.   Collection agency   109

    2.   Small claims court   109

    3.   Lawyers   110

  i. Bad debts and taxes   110

13 SETTING FEES   111

  a. Daily billing rate (per diem)   111

    1.   Labor   111

    2.   Overhead   111

    3.   Profit   112

  b. Hourly rate   113

  c. Calculating a fixed price quotation   114

    1.   Determining a fixed price estimate   114

    2.   Tips on preparing fixed price estimates   114

  d. Fixed price plus expenses   116

  e. Contingency fee   116

  f. Percentage fee   116

  g. Project value fees   117

  h. Retainer fees   117

  i. Equity fees   117

  j. Utilization rate   118

  k. Varying your fees   118

  l. Increasing fees   118

  m. Increasing profits without increasing fees   119

14 DETERMINING MARKET OPPORTUNITIES   121

  a. Private sector opportunities   121

    1.   Individuals   122

    2.   Small businesses   122

    3.   Medium-size businesses   122

    4.   Large companies   123

  b. Public sector   123

    1.   Making contacts and obtaining information   123

    2.   Understanding the government approval system   124

  c. Grant consulting   125

15 MARKETING YOUR CONSULTING SERVICES   127

  a. Introduction   127

  b. Marketing plan   127

   c.   Marketing techniques   128

        1. Newspaper   128
        2. Advertising in trade or professional journals   129
        3. Directories   129
        4. Brochures   129
        5. Direct mail   130
        6. Contact network   132
        7. Membership in professional, trade or business associations   132
        8. Donating your services   133
        9. Attending public and professional meetings   133
      10. Lectures   133
      11. Teaching   134
      12. Seminars and workshops   134
      13. Free media exposure   135
      14. Radio and television talk shows   135
      15. Letters to the editor   136
      16. Writing articles   136
      17. Writing a book   137
      18. Have articles written about you   137
      19. Announcement columns   137
      20. Newsletters   138

16 THE CLIENT INTERVIEW AND CLIENT RELATIONS   139
   a.   Purpose of interview   139
   b.   Before the meeting   139
   c.   During the interview   142
   d.   After the interview   143
   e.   Why you should turn down business   143
   f.   How to turn down unwanted business   144

17 CONSULTING PROPOSALS   146
   a.   What is a proposal?   146
   b.   Private versus public sector proposals   146
   c.   Solicited versus unsolicited proposals   147
   d.   Simple and formal proposals   147
        1. Simple proposal   147
        2. Formal proposal   147
   e.   Guidelines and format for a successful proposal   148
   f.   Presenting your proposal   150
   g.   Proposal follow-up   151
   h.   What to do if your proposal is not accepted   151
   i.   How to avoid giving away free consulting   151
        1. Potential client interview or discussion   152
        2. Client need analysis   152
        3. Free detailed advice in written proposal   153
        4. Potential future benefit   153
        5. Additions to the original fixed price contract   153

		6.	Free consulting in a follow-up situation	154
		7.	Relatives, associates and friends	154
18	**CONTRACTS**			**156**
	a.	Essentials of a valid contract		156
		1.	Offer	156
		2.	Acceptance	156
		3.	Consideration	157
		4.	Competency	157
		5.	Legality	157
	b.	Why a written contract is needed		157
	c.	Structure of a formal contract		159
	d.	Types of contracts		162
		1.	Letter of agreement	162
		2.	Letter of agreement with general terms and conditions appended	162
		3.	Formal contract	162
		4.	Sub-consulting agreement	166
		5.	Agency agreement	174
		6.	Letter of retainer agreement	174
	e.	Preparing your own contract		174
19	**EXPANDING YOUR PRACTICE**			**176**
	BIBLIOGRAPHY			**179**
	APPENDICES			**189**
	#1 Sources of procurement and contracts information			189
	#2 Consulting associations in the U.S. and Canada			200
	#3 Free or nominal cost business publications			204
	#4 Proposal evaluation checklist			206

LIST OF SAMPLES

#1 Start-up expense checklist   14
#2 Monthly expense checklist   15
#3 Personal monthly expense checklist   16
#4 Business plan format   47
#5 Opening balance sheet   54
#6 Income and expense statement forecast   55
#7 Cash flow budget worksheet   56
#8 Personal net worth statement   57
#9 Statement of accounts receivable   59
#10 Prospective client sheet   77
#11 New consulting assignment sheet   78
#12 Time and service record   79
#13 General invoice   105
#14 Detailed invoice   106
#15 Fixed price costing sheet   115
#16 Proposal format   148
#17 Contract format   159
#18 Letter of agreement (prepared by consultant)   163
#19 Letter of agreement (prepared by client)   164
#20 Statement of general terms and conditions   166
#21 Consulting contract   168

LIST OF TABLES

#1 Major consulting subject areas   1
#2 Average start-up expenses   13
#3 Checklist of articles in a partnership agreement   33
#4 Detailed contract checklist   171

To Eleanor and Diana, the two women in my life.

INTRODUCTION

This book is designed primarily for the beginning or potential consultant, but consultants who have been in practice for a considerable time should also find it helpful. The purpose of the book is to provide essential information and practical step-by-step guidelines to assist you in starting and developing a successful and profitable consulting business. All the information necessary to set up and maintain your own business is included in this book.

The book is organized to reflect a typical consulting business, from getting the original idea to generating income sufficient for your needs and expectations. You will assess your consulting potential and determine your marketable skills in chapter 2. In chapters 3 through 13 you will learn all the basic steps you have to consider before starting your business. Chapters 14 and 15 deal with the marketing techniques essential to success. Without effective ongoing marketing, you simply will not succeed. The final chapters 16, 17, and 18 inform you how to negotiate a consulting assignment from the first interview to the proposal to obtaining a contract. Chapter 19 discusses ways of expanding your practice.

The tables, samples, and appendices have been provided to make the text as meaningful as possible. There are many good reference books that can assist you further; these are listed in the Bibliography and have been divided into various section headings for easy reference by subject area. A detailed source list of further information is contained in Appendix 1. Consulting is basically a knowledge industry, and access to ways of improving your knowledge should assist you in marketing your skill more effectively.

Each chapter in this book stands independently but is linked to the others. If you know little about consulting or being in business, you should read the chapters sequentially to appreciate the need for dealing with basic business considerations. Consulting is first of all a business, which can succeed or fail like any other business. Understanding and managing the business side of consulting is as essential as performing the consulting service.

Every year the demand for consultants increases as our society becomes more complex. Business, education, health care, government, military, labor unions, social services, churches, and volunteer organizations employ consultants on a regular basis. Consulting in North America has become a multi-billion dollar industry.

Consultants are people who are determined to succeed, who thrive on challenge, and who believe in themselves.

Consultants are entrepreneurs in the knowledge field. Consultants are individuals who believe that they are competent and capable of rendering a worthwhile service to others.

Consulting offers a continual challenge and can present opportunities for freedom, growth, and satisfaction far beyond those of employment or other forms of business. This book increases your chances of capitalizing on the opportunities and assisting your business success.

Note: This book aims to highlight common consulting practices accurately. However, the information is general in nature, and no legal, tax, or financial advice is given. If legal or other expert assistance is required, you should obtain the services of competent professionals.

Laws are constantly changing and neither the author nor the publisher can accept any responsibility for changes to the law or practice that occur after the printing of this publication.

1

UNDERSTANDING
THE CONSULTING BUSINESS

a. WHAT IS A CONSULTANT?

A consultant is someone who has an expertise in a specific area or areas and offers unbiased opinions and advice for a fee. The opinion or advice is rendered exclusively in the interests of the client and can cover review, analysis, recommendations, and implementation. A consultant generally works in conjunction with the resource personnel of the client, but uses employees, sub-consultants, or others as required for the specific project and in accord with the agreement.

A consultant is not an employee but an independent contractor, usually self-employed, contracted to perform a short-term or long-term task and paid on an hourly, daily or project basis or other fee arrangement.

There are numerous consulting opportunities in the private and public sector. Table #1 provides a brief summary of some of the major consulting areas. The consulting profession has grown extensively over the past 15 years and is now one of the major service industries in North America. The outlook for continued growth of consulting in the 1980s is very positive. Demand exceeds the projected supply.

TABLE #1
MAJOR CONSULTING SUBJECT AREAS

Acoustics	Construction services
Actuarial services	— Management
Advertising	— Heating/ventilating/air-conditioning
Architecture	— Inspection and estimates
Association management	Curriculum development
Audiovisual services	Data processing
Automation	— Computer hardware
— Office	— Computer software/programming
— Industrial	— Systems analysis
Building management	Direct marketing
Business administration	Economic research, analysis, forecasting
Business forms and systems	Editorial services
Cable television	Educational services
Career guidance	—Curriculum development
Communication	— School/camp selection
— Electronic	Electronics
— Interpersonal	Employee benefit planning
Community relations	— Pension planning
Conference and convention planning and management	— Profitsharing
	Energy management and conservation

TABLE #1 — Continued

Engineering
— Aeronautical
— Chemical
— Civil
— Electrical
— Electronics
— Environmental
— Industrial
— Marine
— Mechanical
— Mining
— Nuclear
— Petroleum
Estate planning
Executive development and recruitment
Exhibit planning and design
Financial management
— Banking
— Budgeting
— Investment counseling
Food facilities design
Food retailing
Food services
Foreign licensing
Forestry
Franchising
Freight transportation and shipping
Fundraising
Furnishings
Government relations
— Municipal
— State/provincial
— Federal
Graphics
Health services administration
Heating
Hospital administration
Hotel and motel management
House publications
Human factors engineering
Human relations
Human resources development
— Employee selection and training
— Employee surveys
— Industrial psychology
— Personnel productivity
Immigration and naturalization
Industrial/manufacturing services
— Industrial classification
— Industrial development
— Industrial testing
— Production management
Information storage and retrieval
Insurance

Interior design
— Color
— Furnishings
— Lighting
International business and trade
Inventory control
Labor relations
Land use planning
Landscaping
Leasing
— Equipment
— Transportation
Library design and services
Licensing
Lighting
Lithography
Mail order
Marketing programs and services
Marketing research and analysis
Marriage and family relations
Material handling
Materials science
Mergers and acquisitions
Microforms
Museum and exhibit planning and design
National security and defense
Naturalization
New product design
New product introduction
Nutrition
Office design
Office management
Operations research
Opinion polls
Organization analysis and development
Packaging
Personal image
Personnel
Planning (long range, strategic)
Political campaigning
Pollution control
— Air
— Noise
— Water
Product design
Professional practice management
Public relations
Publishing
Purchasing
Real estate
Records management
Recreation planning
Reliability and quality control
Religion

TABLE #1 — Continued

Relocation services	Social services
Research and development	Sports
Safety services	Standardization
— Accident investigation	Statistical services
— Expert witness	Stockholder relations
— Fire protection	Systems analysis
— Product liability	Taxes
— Program design and installation	Technology transfer
Sales	Telecommunications
— Forecasting	Television and radio
— Management	Traffic and parking
— Personnel recruiting	Transportation
— Policy and planning	Urban renewal
— Retail/wholesale	Utilities management
Salvage and reclamation	Venture capital
Sanitation	Wage and salary administration
Security (investigation and loss prevention)	Warehousing
Shipping	Women's issues and concerns
Small business development	

The consulting industry prospers in most economic conditions. The amount of income that a consultant can earn is, of course, related to many factors, including the field of knowledge and level of expertise in that field. The degree of profit is also directly related to how effectively time is managed and how efficiently the business is administered. New consultants spend a large portion of time managing the task, researching their field of expertise, improving on techniques, and marketing their expertise. Most of these tasks are essential but unbillable hours.

b. WHO GOES INTO CONSULTING?

Basically, consultants are people with a marketable skill, a perceptive mind, a need for independence and challenge, an ability to communicate with others and persuade them to follow advice, a desire to help others in an effective way, and a wish to be an agent of positive change. In general, the people who go into consulting include:

- People frustrated with their current careers, who see the solutions for problems but are unable to effectively influence decision-makers

- People who want a stimulating, dynamic, growing career that satisfies the need for personal development

- People dissatisfied with the lack of challenge, opportunity or creativity in their existing jobs

- People graduating from school with training but little experience who wish to work for a large consulting firm

- People who are between jobs and seeking new opportunities and careers

- People who see that they may be laid off and wish to establish themselves in a business to earn a livelihood; these people may start on a part-time basis while still employed

- Retired people who have expertise and wisdom to offer

- People who wish to supplement their present income by using their managerial expertise or technical or academic skills

- People with work experience and industry knowledge or other skills who want to combine a family life with work at home

- People who understand government operations and the contract process, or who have built up contacts in government, politics or industry over the years

c. WHY DO ORGANIZATIONS USE CONSULTANTS?

There are many reasons why the private and public sector need consultants for problem solving. Some of these reasons are discussed below.

1. Temporary assistance

Clients frequently wish to supplement skills in their organization by hiring trained, proven, motivated consultants on a short-term or long-term basis. Consultants may be hired on a project, seasonal or new funding basis.

By hiring consultants, clients do not have to contend with the training, instruction, and long-term commitment for salaries and fringe benefits entailed in hiring a skilled employee. Recruitment costs alone for a skilled employee can be considerable and cannot be justified for short-lived or cyclical need. Consultants are independent contractors and therefore no tax deductions or fringe benefits are involved.

2. Objective review

Consultants are retained as impartial advisors without any vested interest in the outcome of the recommendations. Internal staff may not be able to see the problems or may not be sufficiently objective. A consultant can perform a competent and thorough analysis of the issues. It is easier psychologically for personnel to adapt to external advice rather than the internal advice of someone who may be acting out of self-interest.

3. Third-party request for problem identification and resolution

Banks are naturally concerned about any signs of a problem that might put their investment at risk. A bank may need to know whether the problems are related to administrative, personnel, financial, market or product difficulties and how the problems can be solved. Only an outside consultant's opinion would be credible.

4. Surviving a crisis

A business owner suffering from serious business problems may seek an outside consultant to investigate causes and recommend solutions.

5. Initiating change

A consultant can act as a catalyst in stimulating ideas in a highly structured organization that otherwise might be resistent to change due to its size, bureaucracy and institutionalized nature.

6. Obtaining funding

Many non-profit organizations or small and medium size businesses need assistance in obtaining grants or loans for their continued survival. They may lack the expertise, ability or time to research the availability of funding and prepare a persuasive application. Consultants with an expertise in this area act as advisors or agents.

7. Selecting personnel

A client might hire a consultant for recruitment of key executives. The consultant is looked upon as being independent and unbiased with the expertise and time to selectively screen and recommend prospective candidates.

8. In-house education

Consultants are hired to provide in-house training to keep staff informed of new management and supervisory techniques or technical knowledge and to improve employee morale.

9. Dealing with internal personnel difficulties

Outside consultants are retained to review and make recommendations on internal structure, for example, consolidation of departments or services or elimination of redundant employees or executives. The consultant's report provides the rationale for making the decisions. The consultant then leaves and is not affected by the decision.

Consultants can also be used to resolve conflicts between various levels of management. The consultant plays an arbitrating or mediating role that permits frustrations to be expressed so that energy can be directed toward constructive resolution.

10. Delay tactics

Consultants can be hired to perform research studies which take the pressure off a company that is being exposed to public or government scrutiny. This also permits the organization to use the excuse of a consultant's study to justify a delay in decision-making. The consultant is frequently asked to take the brunt of any media attention by being the contact person, which reduces media attention toward the organization concerned.

11. Executive assistance

An executive who is aware of his or her personal limitations may request that a consultant review a problem situation, provide advice on how to deal with it, and possibly follow up with implementation.

12. Government regulatory compliance

Government regulations at all levels are constantly changing, and companies are frequently not prepared or trained to comply. Consultants may be retained to provide expertise to assist a company in complying economically, efficiently, and with the least amount of trauma to the organization.

13. Socio-economic and political changes

Socio-economic and political matters are always in a state of flux. These changes present opportunities for consultants. For example, pollution problems create a need for environmental protection experts, and fuel shortages create a need for energy conservation experts.

14. Government excess funds

Consultants benefit considerably from the expenditure of large amounts of government money. The government may be funding the private sector with the hope of stimulating the economy; there may be political reasons before an election; there may be a balance in a department's budget that is quickly spent before the end of the budget year, so as not to reduce the allotment requested by that department the following fiscal year. Governments also frequently hire consultants to assess needs and provide solutions, and to conduct in-house training.

d. REGULATIONS AFFECTING CONSULTANTS

Some professional organizations are empowered by legislation to exercise rights of practice, membership, and discipline. However, there is no government control or regulation of consultants as such. The term consultant is similar to the term accountant: anyone can use the word to describe his or her activity without credentials, experience, competence or accountability.

There are many consulting organizations for specific areas of consulting, but membership is voluntary. These organizations or associations have little power or authority to investigate complaints.

Management consultants can apply to become a member of the Institute of Management Consultants. This group provides guidelines for professional practice.

The benefits of membership in a consulting association include:

(a) Certification status if the consultant meets minimum acceptable standards of skill and knowledge

(b) Opportunities for self-development in seminars and workshops

(c) Interaction and networking with other consulting professionals

(d) Representation of the membership's areas of interest to government and other professional bodies

(e) A code of ethics and code of conduct

(f) Keeping current on issues in the area of consulting by means of a newsletter or other publication.

2

SELF-ASSESSMENT

a. INTRODUCTION

Many consultants open a business without ever doing a thorough, honest appraisal of their strengths and weaknesses. If you haven't identified your skills, attributes and talents, how can you determine your specialty areas and the target market? How are you able to package and sell your services and take advantage of opportunities? Without this awareness it is difficult to project the self-confidence necessary to operate your business and respond to questions a potential client might ask you.

Most consultants never go through the steps outlined in this chapter, and that gives you a distinct competitive advantage. To know yourself — your strengths and weaknesses — is to have power and a prescription for success.

b. ASSESSING YOURSELF AND YOUR MARKETABLE SKILLS

The following exercise is important to help you determine the direction you should take in your new consulting business. For the maximum benefit, take all the time you need to complete each stage. Be honest and candid with yourself. The material you are preparing is for your information and benefit only.

SELF-ASSESSMENT

1. Summarize your own autobiography. Review and detail all facets of your past, including work positions, projects you have done, education, credentials you have obtained, free time activities including hobbies and sports, family and personal relationships. Include all the work experiences performed during summers, weekends or holidays. Start with the most current time period and work backwards.

2. List all the areas of your special interest, achievement, knowledge, and personal satisfaction.

3. List all your skills, that is, things that you can do. Skills are developed or acquired abilities such as instructing, administering, researching, and problem-solving.

4. List all your talents. Talents are a natural endowment, often a unique "gift" or special, often creative, attribute. Frequently a talent is a combination of skills. Think of any evaluations that may have been made about you or comments made by your friends in which your talents were observed, for example.

5. List all your attributes. Attributes are inherent characteristics such as an analytical or inquiring mind, intuition or sensitivity. Various studies have found the following attributes essential to successful consultants:

- Good physical and mental health

- Professional etiquette and courtesy
- Stability of behavior
- Self-confidence
- Personal effectiveness and drive; that is, responsibility, vigor, initiative, resourcefulness and persistence
- Integrity, that is, the quality that engenders trust
- Independence; the successful consultant must be self-reliant and not conform to the opinions of others. The consultant must be able to form judgments in the areas of his or her competence and experience
- Intellectual competence
- Good judgment; the faculty of sound appraisal with complete objectivity
- Strong analytical or problem-solving ability; the ability to analyze, assemble, sort, balance, and evaluate the basic factors of problem situations of different degrees of complexity
- Creative imagination; the ability to see the situation with a fresh perspective
- Ability to communicate and persuade, with above-average facility, in oral, written and graphic formats
- Psychological maturity; the successful consultant is always ready to experience people, things and events as they really are with their unique individual characteristics; to view them in perspective and to take the action needed in a calm and objective manner without being diverted from a sound, logical and ethical course by outside pressure
- Skill in interpersonal relationships, including an ability to gain the trust and respect of client personnel, enlist client participation in the solution of problems, apply the principles and techniques of change, and transfer knowledge to client personnel; a receptiveness to new information or points of view expressed by others; and an orientation toward the people aspect of problems.
- Technical knowledge, which means an all-encompassing knowledge of the business and also recognizing lack of skill where it exists and seeking to acquire that skill or employing people with that skill

6. List all the skills and attributes you lack that you believe are necessary for a consulting business.

7. List the skills and attributes you lack related to being a consultant that you believe you can improve; write down how that will happen and how long it will take. Prioritize.

8. Of the skills and attributes that you believe you cannot improve, state how that will affect your consulting business choices, if at all.

9. Speak to friends, relatives or family members who know you well and whose judgment, candor, and goodwill you respect. Ask them to think about your strengths and weaknesses as they see them, and prepare a list. Also ask them to outline the skills, talents, and attributes they believe you possess and those you lack.

10. Update and modify the personal inventories you previously prepared.

11. Review your list of skills, talents, and attributes and provide specific examples where each trait was used that could have a marketing application in providing consulting services.

12. Prioritize the 10 activities that gave you the most pleasure and personal satisfaction. Outline how well you did these activities. Don't over-estimate or under-estimate your abilities.

13. List the top 10 skills or talents, starting with the most important, that you feel are basic to your consulting practice.

14. Imagine the type of consulting projects you would like to do and write them down in detail and why you would like to do them. Then review your notes and identify the skills, talents and attributes required to successfully complete these projects.

15. Imagine your personal life in the future. What direction are you currently headed in with your family and career, socially, financially, spiritually, and personally? What effect would a consulting business have on your existing lifestyle? Would the long hours and pressure of the first 6 to 12 months create strains in the family? Are you interested in marketing your abilities locally, regionally, nationally or internationally? What effect will these decisions have on you and the people in your life?

16. Think of all the consulting opportunities that might be available to you. Consultants sell themselves as people who have solutions to problems or needs, so look for problems/need situations. Focus only on existing or potential problem/need situations that relate to your area of interest and consulting expertise.

17. Increase your awareness of additional consulting opportunities by using the following resources.

(a) The Bibliography in this book

(b) Consulting newsletters will stimulate your ideas on managing your practice, marketing your skills, determining consulting opportunities and keeping current on events related to the consulting industry. A list of consulting newsletters is in the Bibliography.

(c) Magazines and newspapers; you should attempt to read everything you can relating to your specialty and general awareness of current events. Subscribe to trade journals related to your area of interest. Get on all the free mailing lists that are of interest or relevant to your specialty area. Read your local daily newspaper and, in Canada, *The Globe and Mail* and *The Financial Post;* in the United States, *The New York Times, The Washington Post* and *The Wall Street Journal.* There are other newspapers, of course, that you might prefer to read, but these provide a general indication of trends and interpretation of important events, all of which could have a bearing on opportunities for your business. There are numerous excellent business magazines which can stimulate further ideas and sources of contacts and information. Browse through your local international news outlet for an indication of the publications available. Another alternative is your public library.

(d) Consulting and professional associations; contact with the associations will provide you with an opportunity to obtain information related specifically to your specialty from newsletters, publications, meetings or other consultant contacts. A list of the major consulting associations is in Appendix 2.

If there is a local association of consultants, either of a general or specialized nature relevant to your needs, try to attend a number of meetings and ask a lot of questions.

The reference book, *Consultants and Consulting Organizations Directory,* available in public libraries, lists consultants in various specialties throughout the United States and Canada.

The SBA (U.S.) sponsors SCORE, which is an organization providing consulting for beginning businesses without charge. The FBDB (Canada) sponsors CASE, which is a program where consultants at a very nominal rate provide expertise and research skills to beginning small businesses. You may wish to take advantage of their expertise to assist you in the business side of consulting.

(e) Government agencies and publications; depending on the area of your interest, you may want to get on the mailing list of government organizations or departments that have regular publications distributed free or at a nominal charge to the public. The government, of course, is a major purchaser of consulting services, and very large sums of money are expended every year directly and indirectly for that purpose. Sources of procurement and contracts information are outlined in Appendix 1.

(f) Public and university libraries; there is a vast amount of information that is current and accessible to you for research or general ideas in your local public or university libraries. Most of the major libraries have the various directories listed in the Bibliography and Appendix 1.

(g) Continuing education courses and seminars; universities have continuing education courses pertaining to business and related services. The SBA (U.S.) and the FBDB (Canada) have small business seminars and workshops on an ongoing basis, as well as numerous publications pertaining to successful small business management.

(h) Competitors; attempt to identify the competitors in your specific field. Determine what their style and method of operation is, how long they have been in business, how they market themselves, what they charge, and who their clientele is, if possible. Try to ascertain why they are successful, if they are, and how you can best distinguish yourself and find your own niche in the market. You want to have your own unique style if comparisons are made between you and your other competitors by a prospective client.

18. Define the consulting service areas that you would like to provide (refer to Table #1 showing the major fields of consulting activity).

19. Identify who you believe could be possible clients and why.

20. Project how you would like to operate your consulting business. List the important stages and time frames of your business over the next year, three years, and five years.

21. List how you intend to market your services; that is, create a demand for your service and make potential clients realize that you exist. This question will be answered in another chapter, but it is helpful to go through the reflective exercise yourself.

You should now have a comprehensive, detailed and exhaustive guideline for your successful consulting business. Review it, update it and modify it on a regular basis. You should feel confident that you have developed a realistic framework for the next important stages of your business development.

3
SETTING UP YOUR BUSINESS

You have now assessed your skills, attributes, and abilities and have determined your area of interest and expertise. Various administrative matters have to be understood, considered and dealt with before embarking on your road to success.

This chapter and the next 10 chapters deal with the administrative fundamentals. The challenging and fun part — that is, successfully marketing your consulting — is explained later.

Before setting up your office and opening your doors to the public, many matters have to be considered. Your fee structures, marketing plan, and business plan, which includes your cash flow projections, will all determine how much revenue you must generate to pay your overhead. It is wise to be conservative on anticipated revenue and the lead time it will take to reach a breakeven point. Your legal, tax, accounting, and financial advisors will influence your initial decisions. These important aspects are covered in other chapters.

This chapter discusses how to establish the basics of an office while controlling your expenses. With thorough review and comparison of the costs of the key overhead areas, you should require minimal capital investment and keep your overhead and risk at a safe level.

a. START-UP COSTS AND MONTHLY EXPENSES

There are many factors that determine what your costs and expenses are going to be, such as whether you are going to use your own home or rent an office, whether you are going to buy, finance or lease new or used furniture and equipment, and whether you intend to hire staff or do the typing yourself. Your individual finances and needs and how shrewd you are in business and negotiating will clearly affect your overhead.

1. Start-up costs

Start-up costs vary widely depending upon your choices and circumstances. Table #2 lists average start-up expenses. Sample #1 is a start-up expense checklist as a guide for estimating initial costs of your business. It is important to keep a record of your estimated and actual costs during the start-up and first year of operation for overhead expenses as well as for your cash flow projections. The date to pay column should assist you in scheduling your cash flow or other funds to meet the initial expenses. You should be able to fill in the estimated costs schedule after you have thoroughly done your research. Further details on aspects of start-up costs are covered later.

TABLE #2
AVERAGE START-UP EXPENSES

Item	Price Range*		
Business licenses and permits	$ 20	to	$ 100
Business announcement or brochures	250	to	500
Supplies and stationery	100	to	250
Equipment (unless rented, then add rental charge)	500	to	3,000
Rental deposit on office (first and last months)	0	to	800
Utility and phone deposits	0	to	250
Insurance	100	to	300
Legal and accounting	500	to	1,500
Professional or business membership expenses	100	to	300
Answering service deposit (first and last months)	100	to	150
Miscellaneous	200	to	500
TOTAL START-UP COSTS	$1,870	to	$7,650

*Low range assumes the use of home office with outside secretarial service. High range assumes renting an office with one half-time secretary.

2. Monthly overhead expenses

Naturally, monthly expenses will vary widely depending upon the type of consulting service you are planning to operate. Sample #2 should assist you in planning and budgeting for your possible overhead expenses.

3. Personal expenses

Personal monthly overhead expenses obviously influence your cash flow needs and the amount of resources available to invest in your business. When you prepare your business plan, (see chapter 6), you will take into account your personal needs. It will be helpful, though, to consider your personal cash flow needs while planning your business expense outlay. See Sample #3 as a guide for detailing your personal expenses.

b. SELECTING A NAME

Selecting your name is an important decision both from an image and a legal perspective. It is essential to be aware of the implications of selecting your name to make it correct from the outset.

SAMPLE #1
START-UP EXPENSE CHECKLIST

Expense	Date to pay	Estimated cost	Actual cost
Business licenses and permits	_____	$ _____	$ _____
Business announcement or other initial business development including brochures	_____	_____	_____
Supplies and stationery	_____	_____	_____
Equipment/furniture	_____	_____	_____
Rental deposit on office (if outside home: first, second and last months)	_____	_____	_____
Telephone installation and deposits	_____	_____	_____
Utility deposits (if outside home)	_____	_____	_____
Insurance (health, life, liability, theft, etc.; unless paid monthly or quarterly)	_____	_____	_____
Legal and accounting	_____	_____	_____
Professional or business membership or expenses	_____	_____	_____
Answering service deposit (first and last months)	_____	_____	_____
Other	_____	_____	_____
Cushion for unexpected costs (contingency)	_____	_____	_____

1. General considerations

Many consultants do business under their own names, for example, "David R. Jones, Educational Consultant." The business card and letterhead stationery would also show the address and telephone number (with area code) and a brief description of the service. The description could read, for example, "Research studies and project management."

Many consultants prefer to use their own name because they are offering a personal service and promoting and selling themselves. The drawback of using your name is that it implies a one-person operation; this could cause a client to doubt your capacity to complete a project if you are ill or injured. For this reason, and by personal choice, some consultants prefer to use the phrase, "David R. Jones and Associates, Educational Consultants." This implies a business with more than one person and a resource base of skilled consultants.

Many consultants contract with sub-consultants as required, depending upon the job project. This cuts down on overhead, provides depth and flexibility,

SAMPLE #2
MONTHLY EXPENSE CHECKLIST

Expense	Date to pay	Estimated cost	Actual cost
Office rent (if outside home)	_____	$ _____	$ _____
Printing and supplies (not paid for by clients)	_____	_____	_____
Equipment (monthly payment and/or what you need to set aside for future cash purchases)	_____	_____	_____
Preparation of tax return and other accounting expenses (prorated, or if specific time owed then state)	_____	_____	_____
Legal services (projected and prorated)	_____	_____	_____
Typing and secretarial services	_____	_____	_____
Telephone	_____	_____	_____
Utilities (if outside home)	_____	_____	_____
Insurance costs (prorated over 12 months)	_____	_____	_____
Retirement contribution if applicable estimated costs prorated)	_____	_____	_____
Savings (for yourself and your business)	_____	_____	_____
Loan payment	_____	_____	_____
Taxes (including social security or pension plan prorated over 12 months)	_____	_____	_____
License renewal prorated	_____	_____	_____
Advertising	_____	_____	_____
Answering service	_____	_____	_____
Subscriptions	_____	_____	_____
Books and reference material	_____	_____	_____
Marketing	_____	_____	_____
Entertainment and promotion	_____	_____	_____
Automobile	_____	_____	_____
Travel (in town or out)	_____	_____	_____
Conventions, professional meetings, trade shows	_____	_____	_____
Professional development	_____	_____	_____
Salary (what you need to meet personal expenses)	_____	_____	_____
Miscellaneous	_____	_____	_____

SAMPLE #3
PERSONAL MONTHLY EXPENSE CHECKLIST

Budget for the month of _____

ITEM	BUDGET	ACTUAL	DEVIATION
Food	$ _____	$ _____	$ _____
Housing:			
Monthly payment	_____	_____	_____
Taxes (if owned)	_____	_____	_____
Insurance	_____	_____	_____
Clothing	_____	_____	_____
Auto:			
Payment	_____	_____	_____
Gasoline	_____	_____	_____
Repairs	_____	_____	_____
Insurance	_____	_____	_____
Utilities:			
Electricity	_____	_____	_____
Heat (if not electric)	_____	_____	_____
Telephone	_____	_____	_____
Other (water, gas)	_____	_____	_____
Personal spending (gifts)	_____	_____	_____
Credit cards (not covered elsewhere)	_____	_____	_____
Installment and other loans	_____	_____	_____
Life insurance	_____	_____	_____
Taxes	_____	_____	_____
Recreation	_____	_____	_____
Travel	_____	_____	_____
Investment, including saving	_____	_____	_____
Donations	_____	_____	_____
Medical and dental	_____	_____	_____
Education (family)	_____	_____	_____
Miscellaneous	_____	_____	_____
TOTALS	$ _____	$ _____	$ _____

and expands consulting contract opportunities. Other name variations include "Jones Educational Associates" or "Educational Consulting Associates."

It is important to describe the nature of the services you are offering, and not limit the future development of your consulting service. For example, if you are a hospital consultant, you may not want to state on your letterhead or business card "specializing in personnel development" if you could receive other spin-off consulting work outside the limits of description of personnel development. Don't use the word "freelance," as it may not project the professional image you want to create.

Some consultants prefer not to use their own name in the firm's name for a number of reasons. One reason is that the consultant does not want an employer to be aware that a consulting business is being operated part-time. Another reason is that if goodwill is developed under a company's name rather than an individual's, a higher price might be obtained if the consulting practice is sold.

If you decide to incorporate your business, you must have the name approved by the responsible government department and the name must end in Ltd. or Limited, Inc. or Incorporated, or Corp. or Corporation. Advantages and disadvantages of forming a corporation are discussed in chapter 4.

2. Fictitious name

If you are operating your proprietorship or partnership business under a name other than your own, you are required in most jurisdictions to register your fictitious name. Filing for fictitious names does not apply to corporations.

The procedures vary from area to area. The costs generally range from $10 to $75. Ask your lawyer about the requirements for your area. The procedure generally is to fill out forms disclosing the people behind the name and, in some cases, placing an ad in the local newspaper or legal gazette outlining the information in the filing documents.

c. SELECTING AN OFFICE

Most beginning consultants operate out of their homes. As the practice grows, the decision might be made to move into an office space.

Normally consultants go to the client's office, but occasionally clients wish to meet the consultant at the consultant's place of business.

1. Home office

There are several advantages to operating our of your home. You save money on gas and rent. The stress of commuting to work is reduced. You are able to deduct from income tax the portion of your home you are using for business purposes. (The tax deductions you can use when you have a home office are covered in chapter 9.)

Being close to the family is an important consideration for some consultants.

There are also disadvantages of having a home office. You may be distracted by your family members during the work day. Your presence may be distracting to your family members. The mix of home and office dynamics could negatively affect your private life. You could turn into a workaholic due to the proximity of your office. Your home might be distant from your clients' offices, which would make it difficult for your clients to visit you. If clients come to your home on occasion, you would want your home to present a positive impression so as not to detract from your professional image. Your home address on your stationery and business card could present a questionable image to prospective clients who may wonder about your business competence. Clients may view you as a freelancer, and be more likely to question your fees.

Due to the limitations of working out of your home, you may wish to consider a professional identity package provided by various office service businesses. This includes a mail drop address and telephone answering service, as well as other features you may desire.

The mail drop means having an address that is recognizable as a business and, depending upon the location, as a prestigious address. The staff at this location are able to receive or send out courier packages for you and receive envelopes or messages from clients who may stop by "your" office, etc.

These services can generally be found under "secretarial services" or "stenographers — public" in the yellow pages of the telephone directory. A post office box number has a negative effect in terms of your credibility and business reliability, and should be avoided if possible.

Having a personalized telephone answering service connected to your telephone at home allows you the freedom of knowing your telephone calls are being handled in a professional manner whether you are at home or out making calls. By keeping the answering service informed of your schedule for the day, your callers will receive the appropriate response and know when the call might be returned.

Generally, it's not a good idea to use an answering machine; they don't present a professional image, callers get the impression that you are a one-person operation (which, of course, you are), and you may be perceived as a freelancer, which has a negative connotation to some.

2. Office outside of home

You may wish to get an office outside your home when circumstances and finances justify it. Having your own office address increases credibility and stature when dealing with clients or prospective clients. Studies have shown that consultants are able to collect higher fees for performing the same work when operating out of an office.

When considering an office location, factors such as expense, image of business address, your proximity to clients, and referral possibilities should be examined.

Try to look at your long range goals over two years and imagine what your office needs might be. It is costly to pay for new office stationery and other start-up costs and several moves may create an image of instability.

(a) Office sharing arrangement

You may wish to look for an office with complementary professional or business tenants and prospective business clients. You have your own office and generally supply your own personal office furniture, but the rent expenses of the overall office and the receptionist's salary are shared on a proportional basis by the tenants. The secretarial expenses are negotiated depending upon use.

If you do seek out a pooling arrangement, try to have a minimal notice period to leave the premises. You may wish to leave due to expansion, inability to pay the rent or personality conflicts. It is fairly common to have a three-month notice provision. Make sure that the terms of your rental relationship are in writing and signed by the necessary parties before you begin your relationship.

As a general caution, avoid sharing space with a client. You could have a falling out or the client could attempt to use your time for free or look on you as staff.

(b) Sharing same private office

Two or more people may use the same office space. The parties agree on the costs of furnishing the office, unless it was already furnished, and an agreement would be worked in terms of the hours and days of use. Costs of this arrangement are negotiated on a per use basis.

(c) Office rental package

There are firms in the business of renting packaged office space. There can be anywhere from 5 to 50 tenants or more. Each tenant has a private office, and there is a common reception area.

The office package arrangement is a good source of potential contacts for networking or prospective clients, depending upon the mix of the tenants.

Frequently telephone answering and office furniture is included in the package price as well as a nominal number of hours of secretarial time per month. The rental arrangement may be a minimum two or three-month notice to vacate, or a six-month or one-year lease arrangement. Prices and terms of various office package arrangements may be negotiable if there is competition in that marketplace in your community.

There are several other advantages of an office package arrangement. Frequently other services are available which save you considerable money on staff and equipment. These include:

(a) Street mailing address — not a post office box number

(b) Postage metered . mail for prompt delivery and a professional appearance

(c) Typing — a variety of typestyles available on modern equipment for letters, reports, invoices, statements, etc.

(d) Dictaphone transcription

(e) Secretarial services, including letter composition and editing using correct business language and form

(f) Photocopying — a bond copier with various features including collating could be available to produce quality copies on your letterhead, transparencies or address labels

(g) Word processing services with the advantages of speed, efficiency, and storage and retrieval capacity.

(d) Occasional office

You can rent a board room or an office for as short a time as an hour, or half day or a day. The cost is negotiable. The occasional office space can be found through office rental package services described earlier. Some firms require that you have a telephone answering or professional identity package arrangement with them before you are able to rent occasional space.

(e) Leased space

Leasing space does have its disadvantages, and it is most important that you consult your accountant and a competent lawyer familiar with commercial leases before signing anything. You should shop around for space to make sure you have the best arrangement for your needs and to assist you in negotiating.

Leases are generally for a period of one to five years. There are basically three types of lease payment formulas. The terminology may vary, but the concepts are the same. The first type, called a "net" lease means that the base rent is the total rent. In other words, the flat negotiated rate is the only monthly payment you have to make.

The second type of rent, "double net," is similar to the first except you have to pay a pro rata share of any tax increases over the base tax period outlined in your lease. If the taxes increase substantially, you could have extra overhead you had not anticipated.

The third type, "triple net" rent, can be very expensive. The base rent is just the beginning. All other landlord costs, such as taxes, insurance, maintenance, repair, improvements, management and administration fees are passed on proportionately to the tenants. This could increase your monthly rent by 50% to 100%. The other problem with this type of rent structure is the uncertainty of not knowing for budgeting purposes your rental overhead expenses.

A variation of this third formula involves paying the landlord a percentage of your gross revenue. Naturally, for a professional consultant, this is an unacceptable arrangement.

Some of the clauses to be wary of when you are considering a lease include restrictions on your ability to sublet or assign your lease, liabilities and duties of the landlord and tenant, the use you intend for the premises, limitations on alterations or improvements to the premises, acceleration clauses in case of default, and a requirement for your personal guarantee if you are doing business as a corporation.

If you are still interested in signing a lease, attempt to negotiate as many attractive features as possible. All leases are negotiable and there are no standard clauses. Your lawyer can properly advise you and possibly negotiate the lease on your behalf.

Some tips on negotiating your lease include:

(a) Rather than negotiating a three-year lease, for example, try to negotiate a one-year lease with two additional one-year options. This way you minimize the risk in case you cannot afford the lease or in case you need to expand or the premises are otherwise unsuitable for your needs.

(b) Consider offering the last two or three months rent as a deposit. If you default the lease and leave before the end of the term, the deposit monies go to the landlord, and you are free of any further liability.

(c) Put in the lease that alterations or improvements you intend to make will be at the landlord's expense.

(d) Attempt to get the first few months free of rent as an incentive for you to lease the premises.

(e) Try to get out of paying the last month's security deposit rent, if possible. If it is not possible, try to negotiate with the landlord to pay you interest at a fixed rate on the security deposit money.

Another factor in leasing space is the additional expense for furniture and equipment for your office and reception area, plus the additional costs of a secretary or receptionist. All these additional costs have to be carefuly factored out to ensure there is sufficient cash flow to justify the commitment.

3. Equipping an office

Equipping an office is not too expensive if you buy secondhand furniture. You can obtain good used business furniture from bankruptcy sales, auction sales, or through the classified section in the newspaper. The type and quality of furniture that you select naturally will relate to your type of consulting clientele and the image that you want to project.

There are certain basic things you need for your office, including desk, chairs, tables, lamps, bookcases, file cabinet, typewriter, calculator, telephone answering device (optional), tape recorder (as a dictaphone, to record meetings, to record consulting or marketing ideas), card file and/or address file, clock, postage meter and briefcase.

4. Office supplies

The basic supplies you need include business cards, letterhead stationery and printed envelopes, brochures, records for bookkeeping, invoices, filing folders, and various types of calendars.

(a) Business stationery, cards, envelopes

Your business stationery is very important as it represents you, your image, and your business. It should present a professional and conservative image. It should state your name, your business name, the type of consulting (if applicable), address, postal/zip code and telephone number with area code.

All your stationery should correspond with the format and image of your business card. Choose a good quality paper stock. Purchase blank pages of your letter stock so that your second page will match the color of the first. Neutral shades for colors, such as beige, ivory or white, create a professional impression. You have a choice between litho (flat) or thermo (raised) ink. The thermo's raised, glossy appearance creates a richer effect. The cost of raised letter is not much more than flat, but extra time is required for printing. As the printing business is very competitive, be sure to compare rates.

Some consultants prefer to have a logo on their business card. Have a graphic artist prepare the logo or see *Design Your Own Logo*, another title in the Self-Counsel series.

(b) Brochures

Depending upon the type of consulting practice that you have and the nature of clientele you wish to attract, brochures may be part of your marketing plan. Naturally, brochures are less expensive by quantity. You may choose to request the services of a promotional writer to assist you in preparing the text for a brochure that will effectively outline the services you provide for your specific clientele or market. Such services can be found under the "sales promotion services" section of the yellow pages. For printing, check for competitive rates and allow yourself considerable lead time to obtain the best rate. One color ink on colored stock is less expensive than two inks and can be just as effective.

(c) Record-keeping documents, invoices, and file folders

These items are necessary for the orderly maintenance of projects, systems, and good business management. The types of record-keeping documents are outlined in chapter 8.

(d) Calendars

For recording appointments, telephone calls, and deadlines you should have a desk calendar, a wall calendar, and a daily diary that you carry with you. The time that you spend on client files must be recorded in detail for proper billing and for your protection in the event of a dispute.

5. Personnel

(a) Secretarial staff

Most beginning consultants do not have the workload or cash flow to justify hiring a secretary. Some consultants prefer to type the documents and correspondence themselves, but even if you are a good typist, you will make more money consulting or finding new clients than you will typing. Some consultants have a family member do the typing, but this can create strains on the family relationship.

It is far more cost efficient and practical to "rent" a secretary. In many cases, the typing costs related to a client file can be billed directly to the client, in addition to your fees. You then have verification from the typing service if there is any question on your account.

Find a professional typing service that offers temporary or one-time service. Ask how much lead time is required, what the turn-around time is, and what other services they offer. Interview several professional typing services and ask to see sample copies of their reports, newsletters, and correspondence so that you can judge the professional quality of the work.

It is essential that word processing services be available. As a consultant, you will be producing large quantities of material that require neat, clean, and correctly styled typing. A word processor can produce this quality, and store your contracts, proposals, form letters, reports, and mailing lists for retrieval.

A professional secretarial service can also look after all your correspondence and document needs including preparing invoices and reminder letters for your receivables. You can ask the secretarial service if one staff member will work on your file so that person will become familiar with your style. A dictaphone tape for transcription is a considerable benefit in terms of consistency and saving time when one person gets accustomed to your method of dictating.

(b) Retaining other consultants

Employing another consultant as an independent contractor, in other words, a sub-consultant, is a common technique to reduce overhead and increase your resource base and efficiency. There are times when you might need specialized skills or additional help to be able to satisfy a potential client contract. Try to develop a sub-contracting network of consultants you can call on when needed Many consultants take on projects they could not complete themselves and sub-contract portions to another consultant.

It is important to maintain your position with your client as the main source of information and communication. Your client need not know that you have sub-contracted out a part of the job.

d. SELECTING A TELEPHONE SYSTEM

Your telephone, in many ways, is your lifeline to a successful consulting practice. Many consultants start out using their home telephone number and a telephone answering device, but there are problems with this. Inexpensive alternatives exist. The important consideration is the impression your telephone system gives your clients or prospective clients and how effectively you receive incoming messages.

1. A separate phone at home

Many consultants operating out of their home prefer to have a separate line for their consulting practice apart from their personal line. This saves the frustration of having children answer your phone or family members tying up the phone with their personal calls.

2. Business line terminating at answering service

You may wish to have an office number that does not go to your home, but terminates at your answering service. Your answering service could then phone you at home (if those were your instructions) and advise you of a phone message.

Alternatively, you could telephone the answering service from time to time to pick up messages. You could then return calls on your personal line. The advantage of this system is that you save on the monthly line charges for a business telephone installed in your home, but have a telephone answering capacity.

When selecting an answering service, it is very important to consider the personal aspect of the service. An answering service that has only 40 to 60 lines will generally be more attentive, know your business better, and personalize the responses so that the caller is unaware it is an answering service. Compare various answering services and ask for references from their clients.

The quality of your answering service is vital to the reputation and goodwill of your business. In many cases the person answering the phone will be the first representative of your firm to the caller. A drawback of the larger answering service companies with trunk lines and hundreds of customers is that the switchboard operators are frequently very busy and therefore unable to personalize your phone messages. Another factor is the turnover that can occur in personnel. With the larger answering services, it is very difficult to hide the fact that it is an answering service.

3. Business line terminating at home and answering service

Your business line can pass through an answering service's switchboard. All calls may be intercepted by the answering service, if those are your instructions, or with a switch on your phone unit, you can decide to answer the phone yourself for certain periods of the day. The answering service staff can be told the appropriate procedures for incoming phone calls. There are additional monthly line charges for this system.

4. Overline

An overline feature allows an incoming phone call to come through on a second line while you are on the first line. This is an appropriate feature if you intend to use your business phone regularly, as your phone would otherwise ring busy for an incoming phone call if you just had one line. Too many busy signals give a negative impression, and may result in the loss of a prospective client. The other technique, as mentioned earlier, is to give out your business telephone number for incoming calls and use your personal phone for outgoing calls.

5. Measured business line

A measured business line can reduce your monthly phone charges for service in half. The reduced base rate has a limit of 50 outgoing phone calls per month. No limit is placed on the number of incoming calls. If you make more than 50 outgoing calls in a month, you are charged an additional fee per phone call (approximately 11¢, but it varies).

If you make many outgoing phone calls, this system is not economical. Some people use the measured line system for incoming calls and their personal phone for outgoing calls.

6. Shared line

A number of people may agree to share a common telephone number. Usually it is a feature offered through a telephone answering service for one of their unused lines. Telephone expenses are reduced considerably. The phone is answered "4444," "Suite 100" or some such non-descriptive phrase, or it can be answered "consulting office" if there are two or more consultants receiving calls on the same line.

7. Remote call forwarding

Remote call forwarding allows telephone calls to one number to be automatically redirected to another number without the caller being aware. For example, if you are going to be at a location other than your home office and want to receive all calls there temporarily, you can dial a predetermined code and the number you want calls redirected to. Anyone phoning your number may hear the phone ringing, but it is not ringing at your home or office, but at the number you designated the calls be redirected to. You therefore do not miss incoming or expected phone calls.

8. Telephone answering devices

The purpose of a telephone answering device (TAD) is to help you avoid losing critical calls if you are away from your office. It also acts as an efficient office screening agent. The TAD answers the phone, gives a message, and accepts a message from the caller on your behalf. After you have dictated your message into the machine, call your own number to listen with a critical ear to the impression of your message.

There are six basic kinds of answering machines. Due to the intense competition in this market area, comparative pricing is recommended if you are in the market for a TAD.

(a) *Announce only* answers the telephone with one or more pre-recorded announcements up to several minutes long

(b) *Announce/record* gives a pre-recorded message and allows the caller to leave a message.

(c) *Call screening* can help you avoid unwanted calls. By turning the volume higher, you can listen to caller's messages without their knowledge. If you wish, you can pick up the telephone, interrupt the regular answering cycle, and talk to the caller

(d) *Record* can record a conversation. This is useful if you need proof that you have communicated important information to another party. In many jurisdictions you are obliged to notify the other party that the call is being recorded. For this reason, these machines repeatedly emit a tone to remind both parties that the conversation continues to be recorded.

(e) *Dictation* allows you to dictate messages for subsequent transcription. You by-pass the normal use of the telephone answering machine and use features exactly like those of an office dictation machine.

(f) *Remote Control* allows you to transmit a signal from any other phone by means of a small device. The machine will automatically respond and play back over the phone any messages that have been recorded. This is convenient if you are out of town, but expecting calls at your office.

As mentioned earlier, the telephone answering device has its limitations. Some callers find it very annoying to talk to an answering machine; others refuse to leave a message or the message is unclear. The impression could be created that you are very much a beginner in business and still struggling.

9. Interconnect phone purchase

Private telephone equipment companies are now able to compete using the main telephone circuits. Rather than renting or leasing your phone from your telephone company, you have the choice of purchasing your phone. You still have to pay the monthly service charges and long distance charges, but you do not have to pay the monthly equipment charges. Your decision is a matter of comparing the breakeven point in purchasing your phone over renting your phone.

e. SAVING MONEY ON LONG DISTANCE PHONE CALLS

There are many occasions when consultants wish to make long distance phone calls for which no reimbursement can be expected from the client, for example, in marketing efforts, prospective client contacts, or a fixed price contract where your costs are built into the contract. Some of the ways of saving money on long distance calls are mentioned below.

1. Direct distance dialing

By dialing a number directly rather than asking for operator assistance or third-party billing, you save quite a bit. The amount of the savings varies but can be obtained from your telephone company.

2. Reduced long distance rates

There are specific times, which vary in different regions, that long distance rates are one-third to two-thirds less than the regular daily rates. This saving can be considerable especially when the time zones allow you to telephone at the cheapest rate but still during the business hours of the long distance call recipient.

3. 800 service number

There are many companies, including prospective clients, that have "800 service." This system allows the caller to phone long distance free to the 800 number. An "800 service" directory which lists the firms that have 800 numbers can be purchased through the phone company.

4. Wide area telephone service (WATS)

Many businesses and governments have incoming and/or outgoing WATS service lines available. This system is similar to the 800 system, if they have an incoming system. If the company you are calling only has an *outgoing* WATS system, then you may prefer to phone and leave a message for a return call.

If a prospective client or other party phones you long distance, have a policy of accepting the phone call if at all possible in case it is not appropriate to return the phone call collect or not possible to return the call on a WATS line.

5. Some tips

If you are placing long distance phone calls on behalf of a client, ask the operator to call you back with time and charges. This will allow you to record the call in your record system so that the expenses can be passed on as direct expenses to your client and on the next bill. If you do not adopt this system, you won't be able to render an account to a client for various long distance phone calls until you receive your telephone bill.

To limit your overhead for long distance phone calls on behalf of the client, you may wish to ask the client (and confirm it in writing) for the authority to third-party bill to the client's phone number any calls pertaining to your contract or consulting project.

A technique for saving money on long distance phone calls that are being done for information purposes or for marketing purposes is to place a long distance phone call person-to-person at 12:30 p.m. in the time zone of the recipient. In most cases, senior people are not in their offices at this time; a message is left by your operator with the recipient company, giving your name and phone number and operator call back number. Also leave a message through the operator about the time and day that you will be in to receive the phone call. State the recipient's time to eliminate confusion. It is very rare for the recipient caller in government or industry to return your call on a collect basis. You can make sure that you are in your office or home when the incoming call is expected, and you won't have to pay the long distance phone charges.

4

LEGAL FORMS OF BUSINESS STRUCTURE

a. INTRODUCTION

There are basically three forms of legal structure: proprietorship, partnership, and limited company. You should seek competent legal and accounting advice before deciding on your business structure, as there could be distinct advantages or disadvantages to each depending upon your situation.

Many consultants start out as a sole proprietor, as that is the easiest way to start a business. If additional skill or personnel is required on a specific project, sub-consultants may be retained as independent contractors by the proprietor.

In a partnership of two or more consultants, it is common to have problems and dissolve. In the field of consultancy in particular, a healthy ego is essential to sell yourself and your skills. Because of this, conflict is likely to occur when two or more consultants share joint decision-making but have individual dreams and goals.

Forming a corporation is a third option. The corporation can be owned by just one person (similar to a proprietorship) or two or more people (similar to a partnership).

This chapter discusses the factors that you and your professional advisors should examine when making a decision about your business structure.

b. SOLE PROPRIETORSHIP

A sole proprietorship is a business owned and operated by one person. To establish a sole proprietorship, you need only obtain whatever local licenses you require and open your business. It is the simplest form of business structure and operation.

1. Advantages

Ease of formation: There is less formality and few legal restrictions associated with establishing a sole proprietorship. You can start almost immediately. There are no complex forms to complete and no documentation required between yourself and any other party. In most jurisdictions, all that is legally necessary to operate as a sole proprietorship is to register the business and obtain the proper licenses. Licenses can be required by various levels of government.

Cost: Registering the business and obtaining licenses involves minimal costs. There are no partnership or corporate agreements required because you are the sole owner. Legal fees are reduced accordingly.

Lack of complexity: A sole proprietorship is staightforward. Unlike other forms of business, there is little government control and, accordingly, fewer reports are required to be filed with government agencies and departments. The owner and the business are taxed as one.

Decision-making process: Decisions are made exclusively by the sole owner, who has complete authority and freedom to move. The owner does not have to obtain approval from partners or shareholders or a board of directors.

Sole ownership of profits: The proprietor does not have to share the profits with anyone. The profits generated by the business belong to one person. The sole owner decides how and when the money will come out of the business.

Ease of terminating/sale of business: Apart from legal responsibilities to employees, creditors or perhaps clients, you can sell the business or close it down at your will.

Flexibility: You are able to respond quickly to business needs in day-to-day management decisions as governed by various laws and common sense.

2. Disadvantages

Unlimited liability: The sole owner's personal assets, such as house, property, car and investments, are liable to be seized if necessary to pay for outstanding debts or liabilities. As mentioned earlier, the proprietor and the business are deemed to be one and the same in law.

Less financing capacity: It is more difficult for a proprietor to borrow money than for a partnership with various partners or a corporation with a number of major shareholders. A lender, when looking for security and evidence of outside resources, can turn to other people connected with the business rather than just the one person in a proprietorship. A partnership or corporation can give an investor some form of equity position, which is not available in a proprietorship.

Unstable duration of business: The business might be crippled or terminated upon the illness or death of the owner. If there is no one appropriate to take over the business, it may have to be sold or liquidated. Such an unplanned action may result in a loss.

Sole decision-making: In partnerships or corporations, generally there is shared decision-making or at least input. In a proprietorship, just one person is involved, and if that person lacks business ability or experience, poor decision-making can cause the business to suffer.

Taxation: At a certain level of profit there are tax disadvantages for the sole proprietor.

c. PARTNERSHIP

A partnership is usually defined as an association of two or more persons to carry on a business in common with a view to making a profit. The partnership is created by a contract, either verbal or written, between the individual parties.

1. Advantages

Ease of formation: Legal formalities and expenses in forming a partnership are few compared to incorporating.

Pride of ownership and direct rewards: Pride of ownership generates personal motivation and identification with the business. The profit motive could be reinforced with more people having a vested interest.

Availability of more capital: A partnership can pool the funds of a number of people compared to a sole owner who has only his or her own resources to draw upon, unless loans are obtained.

Combination of expertise and talent: Two or more partners, by combining their energies and talents, can often be successful where one person alone would fail. This is particularly true if the business demands a variety of talents such as technical knowledge, sales ability, and financial skills. It is important that working partners bring complementary skills to the business, thereby reducing the workload of each partner.

Flexibility: A partnership may be relatively more flexible in the decision-making process than a corporation, but less so than a sole proprietorship.

Relative freedom of government control and special taxation: Compared to a corporation, a partnership is relatively free from many restrictions and bureaucratic red tape.

2. Disadvantages

Unlimited liability: The major disadvantage of a partnership is the unlimited liability. This unlimited liability is much more serious than in a proprietorship because all the partners are individually *and* collectively liable for all the debts and liabilities of the partnership. Each partner's personal assets are liable to be seized if necessary to pay for outstanding business debts.

Unstable duration of business: Any change in the partnership automatically ends the legal entity. Changes could include the death of a partner, or the admission or withdrawal of a partner. In each case, if the business is to continue, a new partnership agreement must be written.

Management difficulties: As mentioned, when more than one owner assumes responsibility for business management there is a possibility that differences of style, priorities, philosophy, and other factors will arise. If these differences become serious disputes and are unresolveable, the partnership may have to be terminated, with all the financial and personal trauma involved. It is difficult for future partners to foresee whether or not personalities and methods of operating will clash.

Relative difficulty in obtaining large sums of capital: This is particularly true of long-term financing when compared to a corporation.

Partnership agreement problems: The larger a partnership becomes, the more complex the written agreement has to be to protect the rights and identify the responsibilities of each partner. This can result in additional administration and legal costs.

Difficulty of disposing of partnership interest: To withdraw capital from the business requires approval from all the other partners. This takes time and involves legal and administrative expenses.

3. Partnership agreement

A partnership agreement, sometimes called articles of partnership, is absolutely necessary in a partnership relationship. The agreement normally outlines the contribution of each partner in the business, whether financial, material or managerial. In general, it defines the roles of the partners in the business relationship. Some of the typical articles contained in a partnership agreement are shown in Table #3.

If you are considering a partnership relationship, complete the checklist headings and then see your lawyer and accountant. By the time you have completed the checklist with your prospective business mate, the engagement could be off.

4. Kinds of partners

An *ostensible partner* is active in the business and known as a partner.

An *active partner* may or may not be ostensible as well.

A *dormant partner* is inactive and not known or held out as a partner.

A *secret partner* is active but not known or held out as a partner.

A *silent partner* is inactive (may be known to be a partner).

A *nominal partner* (partner by estoppel) is not a true partner in any sense, not being a party to the partnership agreement. A nominal partner, however, holds himself or herself out as a partner, or permits others to make such representation by the use of his/her name or otherwise. A nominal partner, therefore, is liable to third parties as if he or she were a partner.

A *sub partner* is a person who is not a member of the partnership but contracts with one of the partners to represent that partner by participating in the firm's business and profits.

A *limited or special partner* risks only his or her agreed investment in the business assuming that statutory formalities have been complied with. As long as he or she does not participate in the management and control of the enterprise or in the conduct of its business, the limited partner is generally not subject to the same liabilities as the general partner.

TABLE #3
CHECKLIST OF ARTICLES IN A PARTNERSHIP AGREEMENT

1. Name, purpose, and location of partnership
2. Duration of agreement
3. Names and character of partners (general or limited, active or silent)
4. Financial contribution by partners (at inception, at later date)
5. Role of individual partners in business management
6. Authority (authority of partner in conduct of business)
7. Nature and degree of each partner's contribution to firm's consulting services
8. Business expenses (how handled)
9. Separate debts
10. Signing of checks
11. Division of profits and losses
12. Books, records and method of accounting
13. Draws or salaries
14. Absence and disability
15. Death of a partner (dissolution and winding up)
16. Rights of continuing partner
17. Employee management
18. Sale of partnership interest
19. Release of debts
20. Settlement of disputes; arbitration
21. Additions, alterations or modifications to partnership agreement
22. Non-competition in the event of departure

d. CORPORATION

A corporation is a legal entity, with or without share capital, which can be established by one or more individuals or other legal entities. It exists separate and distinct from these individuals or other legal entities. A corporation has all the rights and responsibilities of a person with the exception of those rights that can only be exercised by a natural person.

1. Advantages

Limited liability of shareholders: Shareholders' personal assets are separate from the business and cannot be seized to pay for outstanding business debts incurred by the corporation. There are exceptions, dealing primarily with the issue of fraud.

Flexibility for tax planning: Various tax advantages are available to corporations that are not available to partnerships or proprietorships. Tax planning must be undertaken with the help of a professional accountant.

Corporate management flexibility: The owner or owners can be active in the management of the business to any desired degree. Agents, officers, and directors with specified authority can be appointed to manage the business.

Employees can be given stock options to share in the ownership, which can increase incentive and interest.

Financing more readily available: Investors find it more attractive to invest in a corporation with its limited liability than to invest in a business whose unlimited liability could involve them to an extent greater than the amount of the investment. Long-term financing from lending institutions is more available since lenders may use both corporate assets and personal guarantees as security.

Continual existence of corporation: A corporation continues to exist and operate regardless of the changes in the shareholders. Death of a shareholder does not discontinue the life of the corporation. Continual existence is also an effective device for building and retaining goodwill.

Ownership is readily transferable: It is a relatively simple procedure to transfer ownership by share transfer unless there are corporate restrictions to the contrary.

Draw on expertise and skills of more than one individual: This feature is the same concept as in a partnership, where more partners (shareholders) contribute diverse talents. However, a corporation is not required to have more than one shareholder.

2. Disadvantages

Extensive government regulations: There are more regulations affecting a corporation than a sole proprietorship or partnership. Corporations must report to all levels of government.

Activities limited by the charter and by-laws: Depending upon the jurisdiction, charters can be very broad or can severely restrict a company's activities.

Manipulation: Minority shareholders are potentially in a position to be exploited by the decisions of the majority of the company.

Expense: It is more expensive to establish and operate a corporation due to the additional documents and forms that are required compared to a proprietorship or partnership.

3. Corporate purposes

Some jurisdictions require that the articles of incorporation include a statement of the purposes of the corporation. When you provide a list of the purposes of the corporation, make sure that you define them expansively. Do not restrict the activity of your corporation. A general clause should be included allowing the corporation to expand into any business activity permitted by law. A competent lawyer can assist you in preparing this document to enable you to maximize your corporate options.

4. Shareholders' agreement

A shareholders' agreement involves the same concepts of protection as a partnership agreement. Many of the provisions outlined in the partnership agreement are also included in the shareholders' agreement. There are additional provisions frequently covered in the shareholders' agreement, including:

(a) A restriction on transfer of shares

(b) A buy-sell provision that sets out the formula for buying or selling shares in the company

(c) A provision on personal guarantees of corporate obligations

(d) A provision on payback by corporation of shareholders' loans

(e) A provision giving all shareholders the entitlement to sit as a director or nominate a director as their representative. This protects minority shareholders from lack of managerial information and provides them with a directorship vote or veto on corporate decisions. If you intend to be a majority shareholder, you may not wish to volunteer this provision.

Many shareholders believe that corporate by-laws set out the recipe for resolving problems within the corporation and between the shareholders, directors, and officers in some magical fashion. In most cases, the by-laws only cover formulas for resolving disputes in a few circumstances. It is the shareholders' agreement that expands the protections to resolve fairly any disputes between shareholders.

If you intend to incorporate and have one or more additional shareholders in your corporation, it would be wise to obtain your lawyer's advice on a shareholders' agreement to protect your interests.

5. Maintaining the corporate protection

One of the advantages of operating through a corporate entity is the protection against personal liability for the debts and liabilities of the corporation. This is assuming, of course, that you have not signed personal guarantees.

However, there are situations that could cause you to be personally liable for corporate debts. Generally, if it can be shown that a fraud was perpetrated through use of the corporation, or the director totally disregarded the corporate formalities, the advantage of the "corporate veil" can disappear.

When a court treats the corporation as a sham and imposes personal liability on the shareholders or directors, it is said to "pierce the corporate veil." Here is a list of precautions to follow, to prevent personal legal attack.

(a) *Meetings:* A corporation acts only when its employees (officers, directors, and shareholders) act. If a corporation holds no directors' or shareholders' meetings, the corporation may not really exist. Therefore, every corporation should hold at least one shareholders' and one directors' meeting annually and have that fact documented.

(b) *Corporate name:* A business operating in the corporate form must let the general public know that it is a corporation with limited liability by attaching either "Inc." or "Incorporation," "Corp." or "Corporation," or "Ltd." or "Limited" to its name, depending upon the form you selected at incorporation. You must specify the corporate designation everywhere the company name appears.

(c) *Acting as agent:* When a shareholder/employee executes a document or engages in a transaction, the person must make it clear that it is being done on behalf of the corporation. That is, when you sign a check or contract, you should write your corporate office title (i.e., president, secretary, etc.) after your name.

(d) *Tax returns:* The corporation must file an annual tax return and observe the rules for withholding on payroll taxes. You must make sure that all periodic reporting requirements are satisfied and that there is never any failure to pay to the taxing authorities all sums paid by or deductions from the corporate employees. Any sales tax collected must be remitted within the appropriate period.

(e) *Adequate capitalization:* If a corporation is inadequately capitalized so that there is insufficient capital investment to meet the claims by creditors, the courts may impose personal liability on the corporation's shareholders or directors for its business obligations. You should, therefore, be careful that your "equity" in the corporation does not become too diluted by loans from yourself and from third parties. As an arbitrary rule of thumb, a debt to equity ratio not exceeding 8:1 is reasonable. However, what is truly "inadequate" depends on the extent of actual corporate liabilities and the extent of assets to satisfy those liabilities.

The laws in Canada and the United States and within the individual provinces and states vary; these cautions may not be necessary or applicable in your area. Your lawyer can advise you properly.

(f) *Separate accounts:* Many shareholders of closely held corporations treat the corporation's assets as their own. They combine personal and corporate funds, use corporate funds to pay personal expenses, including medical bills and taxes, and generally disregard the corporate "formalities." By doing so, however, they run the risk that a court may also disregard the formalities and hold the person liable for the company's debts. The shareholders and directors, therefore, should maintain separate corporate and personal accounts, and use the company funds only for business needs.

(g) *Filing annual corporate forms:* Most jurisdictions require an annual report to be filed. The form requires that you list the shareholders, officers, directors and current business address of your company, as well as other incidental information. This document must be filed on time to avoid penalties and possible involuntary dissolution. This dissolution could mean that you would be held personally liable for debts of the corporation.

e. SUB-CHAPTER (SUB-S) CORPORATION (U.S.)

As a consultant you may wish to consider the advantages of a Sub-S corporation in the U.S. The purpose is to permit a small business corporation to treat its net income as though it were a partnership. One objective is to overcome the double-tax feature of taxing corporate income and shareholder dividends. Another purpose is to permit the shareholders to have the benefit of offsetting business losses incurred for the corporation against their income.

Only closely held corporations, that is with 10 or fewer shareholders may make the Sub-S election. All shareholders must consent to the Sub-S election, and only one class of outstanding stock is allowed. A specific portion of the corporation's income must be derived from active business rather than passive investments. No limit is placed on the size of the corporation's income and assets.

At some future point you may wish to revert to a full corporation for tax advantage reasons. This is permitted, but the corporation may not be able to re-elect the Sub-S vehicle for several years once the Sub-S election is reversed. This is to eliminate small corporations from changing frequently to maximize tax advantages. Since Sub-S forms of incorporation are not recognized in all states, you should obtain further information from your professional advisors.

5

SELECTING BUSINESS
AND PROFESSIONAL ADVISORS

Since you may be operating on your own, or with a few associates, you will need an extended management team to advise you in specialized areas where you lack knowledge, ability or interest. Your advisors are, in effect, your employees and associates, and should be considered an integral part of management decision-making.

Every business decision involves a legal decision or implication. Every business decision involves accounting, bookkeeping and, at times, tax considerations. The fatality rate of small businesses is enormously high. Statistically the odds are approximately ten to one that you as a small business person will not be in business three years after you begin your practice.

This chapter discusses the benefits of the effective use of business and professional advisors, how to selectively evaluate them, and how to use their skills to your advantage.

a. GENERAL CRITERIA FOR ADVISOR SELECTION

How well you select your professional and business advisors will have a direct bearing on your business success. Poor advisors or no advisors will almost certainly lead to your business downfall. Your main advisors are your lawyer and accountant, followed by your banker. You should see at least three different people from each of these three professions before you make your selection. It is important to have the comparative assessment.

The following general guidelines should assist you in the careful search and selection of your advisors.

1. Recommendations

One of the most reliable methods of finding an advisor is by a personal recommendation from your banker, your existing advisors or friends in business whose judgment and business sense you trust. Bankers and business advisors who deal on a regular basis with professional advisors are in a good position to pass judgment based on their business dealings. When lawyers, accountants or bankers refer each other, it implies a good working relationship and mutual trust.

Don't rely completely on any referral; make your own cautious assessment. You might also want to try the lawyer referral service in your area. For a nominal fee you can see a business or corporate lawyer for an initial consultation.

2. Credentials

In Canada all lawyers have an "LL.B." professional designation. In the United States, lawyers have either an "LL.B." or "J.D." professional designation.

Accountants in Canada have a professional designation such as "C.A." or "C.G.A." In the United States, look for the designation "C.P.A." The training requirements and public practice background of C.A.s, and C.P.A.s are similar if not identical.

Certification and credentials only ensure that the individual has passed a minimum standard of education. They do not ensure that the person is a dynamic, innovative or creative business advisor with a specific amount of experience relevant to your needs.

3. Clientele

Most professional advisors have a homogeneous client base. Some advisors have many small business clients, others emphasize personal clients, while others go after corporate business. An advisor with a good base of small to medium size commercial clients will probably be the most appropriate for your business needs.

4. Fees

Fees will often vary by the size of the community in which the professional practice is operated, the size of the practice, and the volume of business. You may find that advisors who charge fees in the middle range, edging toward the higher end of the scale, are often quality practitioners in high demand who are still aggressive and innovative in their business practice.

Advisors who are at the low end of the fee scale can be entrepreneurial types, but cut-rate pricing may also indicate a cut-rate, high volume approach to business which will not suit your objectives. Low prices are sometimes an indicator of low quality, low esteem or little experience.

Very high priced advisors tend to be more conservative, less aggressive and less willing to spend the necessary time with small business clients, as their priorities are the big firms. Fees vary and many professionals will negotiate them.

In a smaller or medium size community, a realistic hourly rate for a lawyer or accountant is approximately $50 to $75 per hour. Advisors in larger cities will be more expensive, perhaps $100 to $150 per hour. If you are given an estimate by your lawyer or accountant and that estimate is exceeded, it is not uncommon for your advisor to reduce the fee as a gesture of goodwill in order to keep your ongoing business. Lawyers in general are more agreeable to charging a fixed fee. In some jurisdictions a lawyer can charge a contingency fee. For example, a lawyer may sue on your behalf and recover $100,000 owing to you and receive a fee in the form of a percentage, say 35%, of that amount.

It is important to be very open when discussing fees and payment expectations.

5. Technical competence and industry knowledge

You must satisfy yourself that your advisor is competent in the areas of your greatest need. Ask him or her how much experience, and how comfortable, he or she is with your field.

A specific understanding of the problems, needs and issues of your type of business can enable your advisors to provide the exact assistance you require. This is different from technical skill competence. It has more to do with experience in a particular type of industry. If the advisor has provided guidance to other small business owners in similar situations, there is an increased possibility that the advisor will be able to provide you with more reliable assistance. For example, if you are a hospital consultant, a lawyer who specializes in or is very familiar with health or hospital law could be an asset to you.

6. Style and personality

A critical factor in the selection of advisors, beyond simple compatibility, is style. You can have greater confidence in the aggressive advisor who takes the initiative and offers advice before you request it. This style indicates an initiator rather than a reactor, a person who anticipates and performs before matters become serious. It also indicates a creator, an entrepreneur, and a person who can empathize with your problems and concerns. This kind of advisor is more likely to come up with creative solutions to problems, and be a complement to your planning function. This type of advisor will not only be a sounding board, but a true part of the management team.

7. Confidence

You should feel a sense of confidence when relating to your advisor, whether it be in the general sense or in dealing with a specific problem or issue. You should have a certain amount of personal compatibility with your advisor. If you don't, you will probably end up rejecting a fair amount of advice. In other words, if you do not feel that good chemistry exists with an advisor, seek a replacement as soon as possible. If you do not relate well to the advisor, you may hesitate to ask for advice, which could result in some poor management decisions.

Never allow your advisors to treat you in a condescending or paternalistic manner. You should consider them as equals with special knowledge offering a service in the same manner that you are offering a service to your clients.

8. Communication

You should select an advisor who communicates well, openly and free of jargon. Your advisor should explain the necessary concepts to you so that you understand the issues involved and the decisions that have to be made. Effective communication also means that your advisors forward to you any correspondence sent or received through their offices relating to your business.

9. Commitment

It is important to sense that your advisor is committed to your best interests and your success. An advisor who is involved with larger, more important or higher paying clients than you may become indifferent to your needs. You should be alert to this.

10. Availability

It is important for your advisors to be available when you need them. You are spending time and resources to develop a relationship that will enhance your business decisions. If your advisor is frequently out of town, or in the case of a lawyer, in court on a regular basis, you may not have the immediate access you need. Of course, if the advisor is of exceptional quality and ideally suited to your type of practice, some allowances should be made.

11. Length of time in practice

There is naturally a correlation between the degree of expertise and length of time in practice. You should therefore ask directly how many years of experience your advisor has in the area of your needs.

12. Ability to aid growth

A good professional advisor will have a history of assisting growth in other clients. The advisor would be able to anticipate growth problems in advance, and provide guidance to deal with them.

13. Small firm versus large firm

Choosing a small or large firm is in many ways a matter of your own personal style and the type of firm you relate to most comfortably. Larger firms tend to be in the central area of the city, which may involve parking problems. Their fees are higher. Generally, the larger firms do not have a small business orientation in their marketing and service priorities. The larger firms do have highly specialized advisors and a resource base of associate personnel. This degree of depth may or may not be necessary in your situation. It is not uncommon in larger firms to have small business clients passed over to junior associates or students in training as the more senior advisors handle larger clients.

Smaller firms generally deal with and relate to small business entrepreneurs. Selecting an advisor in a small or medium size firm of three to ten people provides you with a resource base if you need it. An advisor who is a sole practitioner may be very busy, too generalized in his or her areas of practice, and lack a referral resource base within the firm.

b. LAWYER

There are basically two types of lawyers that you should consider as your advisors. The same lawyer might be able to assume both roles.

You need a lawyer who specializes in small business. A lawyer who cares about small business clients assumes the same role and attitude toward your business health and survival as your physician to your personal health.

The other type of lawyer you need is one who specializes in contract law. You will need to have several "boiler plate" contracts prepared depending upon the type and style of service that you are providing. You can then modify these contracts on an individual client basis. There are times that you will need to have a specialized contract made up by a lawyer or have the lawyer review and advise you on a contract that has been prepared by the client.

If your business lawyer does not have the expertise in contract law, request that you be referred to someone within the firm or outside who does. For continuity and efficiency, you want to maintain your business lawyer for all matters that don't require additional expertise. You should be able to phone your lawyer as your needs arise, and feel confident that the unique aspects of your business are known and understood.

For your protection, you should retain a lawyer before you start up your business, as there are many legal pitfalls that can be encountered. There is a temptation to save money on legal fees in the beginning stages of the business when cash flow is minimal. Some people do their own incorporation to save on initial start-up expenses, but then continue the saving by never obtaining legal or accounting advice, an unfortunate example of false economy and bad judgment.

c. ACCOUNTANT

An accountant is the other essential business advisor on your management team. It is very important that you obtain a qualified accountant with the designations described earlier. A bookkeeper is not an accountant and, in most jurisdictions in Canada and the United States, there is no restriction from anyone using the name "accountant" and purporting to provide accounting services without any qualifications or training.

There are many essential services that an accountant can provide. Some of them are discussed below.

An accountant can advise on all start-up steps of a new business, including the tax and accounting considerations of various types of business organization. Normally an accountant will communicate with or coordinate work with your lawyer. The accountant considers such important matters as when your fiscal year-end should be and whether you should use cash or accrual method in keeping your books.

An accountant can advise on preparing a business plan for a loan application. This includes recommending the type of loan you should consider and how it is to be paid. Documents such as a profit and loss statement, a balance sheet, and a financial statement can be prepared by the accountant. He or she may refer you to a banker, which can have a positive effect on your loan application if the banker knows and respects the accountant.

An accountant can advise on all aspects of tax planning and tax-related business decisions which occur from time-to-time as well as file your tax returns.

An accountant can advise how to set up your office bookkeeping system. The accountant can have the bookkeeping done by someone in his or her firm, at a negotiated fee or you can hire an independent bookkeeper. Your accountant should be able to recommend some bookkeepers.

An accountant can analyze and interpret your financial information, point out areas that need control, and recommend ways of implementing the necessary change.

An accountant may be aware of various government grant programs that could be of interest to you.

An accountant can coordinate your personal and business affairs and advise you on investments, tax shelters, income splitting, and other matters.

An accountant can advise and assist you if you want to change your proprietorship or partnership into a limited company at some point. If the transfer is done correctly, you can minimize any negative tax consequences.

d. BANKER

Your relationship with your bank and banker is your financial lifeline. The process of selecting a bank and banker is a critical one, and substantial comparative shopping is necessary in order to obtain the optimal combination of personality and knowledge.

The qualifications of the banker should be considered along with the specific experience with your type of business, specific reputation for taking risk, and the demands that are made for security and for reporting results.

Find out the amount of the banker's loan approval limit. If your needs are less than the limit, the loan can be approved by that individual without further review by another loans officer. This means you only have to convince one person to approve your loan request, not additional anonymous people behind the scene. How well your relationship develops with the banker and how successfully your loans are approved will depend largely on the factors outlined in chapter 7 on how to obtain financing.

There are specific danger areas that can affect your banker's relationship with you. When the manager changes, there is always a period of risk and uncertainty. The new manager does not want to have any medium or high risk loans on the books to taint his or her record. During the first three or four months after a new manager takes over outstanding loans are reviewed and categorized within the criteria set by the new manager. This is the time when loans can be called or additional security requested or interest rates increased. You should develop a personal relationship with the manager when you take out a loan. If you hear that a new manager has taken over, make a point of quickly introducing yourself and briefly discussing your business in a positive way.

Bank policies change from time to time and your type of business could be looked upon as increasing in risk. For example, if real estate is in a slump in your region, a policy decision could be made by the bank to be very cautious about existing or pending loans related to real estate. If you are a real estate consultant, that decision could affect your loan. If you think the bank is concerned, prepare a realistic assessment of how you intend to deal with the situation in advance. You may have a diversified consultancy, not just related to real estate, or you may have other options available that you could explain to your banker.

Ask your accountant and lawyer which bank and banker they recommend. This is probably one of the most effective introductions. If the banker has an ongoing relationship with a professional who is advising you as a client, a less impersonal relationship will exist, and there is a better chance that decisions affecting your loans and your business will be made more carefully.

e. INSURANCE

It is important to select a professional insurance broker with experience and knowledge in the areas of insurance you require. An insurance broker can have various professional qualifications, and you may wish to find out what those credentials are. Insurance is covered in detail in chapter 10.

f. CONSULTANTS

1. Private consultants

You may wish to approach a practicing consultant for advice to assist you in your business. As previously discussed, consultants are not restrictively licensed like other professionals. To protect yourself, you should inquire about their expertise, qualifications, and length of experience. Obtain references and contact them.

Apply the general criteria for advisor selection. You will want to satisfy yourself that the consultant is personally successful. If the consultant has not been successful, how can he or she possibly offer advice that will help you? Consultant fees may range between $25 to $150 per hour or more, depending upon many variables.

2. Consultants subsidized by government

Both the Canadian and U.S. governments have consulting services available for small business.

(a) CASE (Counselling Assistance to Small Enterprises)

In Canada, the federal government, through the Federal Business Development Bank (FBDB), sponsors consultants in CASE. The counsellors are retired business experts who wish to remain active. They are able to identify areas of opportunity, solve problems, and help people manage more effectively. Businesses starting up, expanding, closing or just not making the kind of profit expected can benefit from the help of an experienced business person.

The requirements of the clients are matched with the background and expertise of available counsellors. The CASE coordinator selects the appropriate counsellor, reviews reports outlining recommendations submitted by the counsellor, and follows up on assignments. The hourly fee for the counsellor's time is nominal and includes meeting with the client, doing necessary research, and outlining recommendations in a written report to the client. The minimum charge of four hours is payable when the agreement is signed. Travel expenses of the counsellor are absorbed by the FBDB. Further information can be obtained from a local FBDB office.

The FBDB also sponsors small business management seminars and workshops. Contact your local branch to obtain further information and to place your name on their mailing list.

(b) SCORE (Service Corps of Retired Executives)

The American program is similar to the Canadian program, and is sponsored by the U.S. Small Business Administration (SBA). SCORE is composed of retired executives and active executives who share their knowledge, experience, and business counselling free of charge. Further information can be obtained from a local SBA office.

The SBA also sponsors small business management seminars and workshops. Contact your local branch to obtain further information and to place your name on their mailing list.

6

PREPARING YOUR BUSINESS PLAN

a. WHY PREPARE A PLAN?

Most consultants prefer to be a consultant first and a business owner second. But planning and good management skills are vital to business success. Those who do not plan run a very high risk of failure. If you do not know where you are going in your personal or business life, there is little prospect that you will arrive. A business plan is a written summary of what you hope to accomplish by being in business, and how you intend to organize your resources to meet your goals. It is an essential guide for operating your business successfully and measuring progress along the way.

Planning forces you to think ahead and visualize; it encourages realistic thinking instead of over-optimism. It helps you identify your customers, your market area, your pricing strategy, and the competitive conditions under which you must operate. This process often leads to the discovery of new opportunities as well as deficiencies in your plan.

Having clear goals and a well-written plan aids in decision-making. You can always change your goals, but at least with a business plan you have some basis and a standard comparison to use in evaluating alternatives presented to you.

A business plan establishes the amount of financing or outside investment required and when it is needed. It makes it much easier for a lender or investor to assess your financing proposal and to assess you as a business manager. It inspires confidence in lenders and self-confidence in yourself to know every aspect of the business when you are negotiating your financing. If you have a realistic, comprehensive and well documented plan, it will assist you greatly in convincing a lender.

Having well established objectives helps you analyze your progress. If you have not attained your objectives by a certain period, you will be aware of that fact and can make appropriate adjustments at an early stage.

Three or four hours spent each month updating your plan will save considerable time and money in the long run, and may even save your business. It is essential to develop a habit of planning and reassessing on an ongoing basis as an integral part of your management style.

b. FORMAT

The business plan format shown in Sample #4 is a starting point for organizing your own plan. The comments following the sub-headings should help you decide which sections are relevant to your business situations.

The business plan format normally consists of four parts: the introduction, the business concept, the financial plan, and the appendix.

The plan starts with an introductory page highlighting the business plan. Even though your entire business is described later, a crisp one- or two-page introduction helps capture the immediate attention of the potential investor or lender.

The business concept, which begins with a description of the industry, identifies your market potential within your industry and outlines your action plan for the coming year. Make sure your stated business goals are compatible with your personal goals and financial goals, your management ability, and family considerations. The heart of the business concept is your monthly sales forecast for the coming year. As your statement of confidence in your marketing strategy, it forms the basis for your cash flow forecast and projected income statement. This section also contains an assessment of business risks and a contingency plan. Being honest about your business risks and how you plan to deal with them is evidence of sound management.

The financial plan outlines the level of present financing and identifies the financing sought. This section should be brief. The financial plan contains pro-forma (projected) financial forecasts. These forecasts are a projection into the future based on current information and assumptions. In carrying out your action plan for the coming year, these operating forecasts are an essential guide to business survival and profitability. It is important to refer to them often and, if circumstances dictate, rework them.

The appendix section contains all the items that do not naturally fall elsewhere in the document, or which expand further on the summaries in the document.

SAMPLE #4
BUSINESS PLAN FORMAT

1. Introductory page
   (a) company name
       — include address and telephone number
   (b) contact person
       — consultant's name and telephone number
   (c) paragraph about company
       — nature of business and market area
   (d) securities offered to investors or lenders
       — outline securities such as preferred shares, common shares, debentures, etc.
   (e) business loans sought
       — such as term loan, operating line of credit, mortgage
   (f) summary of proposed use of funds

2. Summary
   (a) highlights of business plan
       — preferably one-page maximum
       — include your project, competitive advantage and "bottom line" needs

3. Table of contents
   (a) section titles and page numbers should be given for easy reference

4. Description of the industry
   (a) industry outlook and growth potential
       — outline industry trends — past, present and future — and new developments
       — state your sources of information
   (b) markets and customers
       — estimated size of total market, share and sales, new requirements and market trends
   (c) competitive companies
       — market share, strengths and weaknesses, profitability, trends
   (d) national and economic trends
       — population shifts, consumer trends, relevant economic indicators

5. Description of business venture
   (a) nature of consulting service
       — characteristics, method of operation, whether performed locally, regionally, nationally or internationally
   (b) target market
       — typical clients identified by groups, present consulting patterns and average earnings, wants and needs
   (c) competitive advantage of your business concept
       — your market niche, uniqueness, estimated market share
   (d) business location and size
       — location relative to market, size of premises, home or office use
   (e) staff and equipment needed
       — overall requirement, capacity, home of office use, part- or full-time staff or as required
   (f) brief history
       — principals involved in the consulting business or proposed consulting business, development work done, resumes and background experience of principals, resumes of key consulting associates if applicable

6. Business goals
   (a) one year
       — specific goals, such as gross sales, profit margin, share of market, opening new office, introducing new service, etc.
   (b) over the longer term
       — return on investment, business net worth, sale of business

7. Marketing plan
   (a) sales strategy
       — commission sales staff, agents, sub-consultants
       — sales objectives, sales tools, sales support
       — target clients
   (b) sales approach
       — style of operation and techniques
   (c) pricing
       — costing, mark-ups, margins, breakeven

(d) promotion
   — media advertising, promotions, publicity appropriate to reach target market
   — techniques of developing exposure, credibility and contacts
(e) service policies
   — policies that your consulting practice will adopt with regard to credit and collection, bidding, nature of clientele, etc.
(f) guarantees
   — service performance guarantees or other assurances will vary depending upon nature of consulting practice and type of contract or client
(g) tracking methods
   — method for confirming who your clients are and how they heard about you

8. Sales forecast
   (a) assumptions
      — one never has all the necessary information, so state all the assumptions made in developing the forecast
   (b) monthly forecast for coming year
      — sales volume, projected in dollars
   (c) annual forecast for following two to four years
      — sales volume, projected in dollars
   The sales forecast is the starting point for your projected income statement and cash flow forecast.

9. Costing plan
   (a) cost of facilities, equipment and materials (as applicable)
      — estimates and quotations
   (b) capital estimates
      — one time start-up or expansion capital required

10. Operations
   (a) purchasing plans
      — volume discounts, multiple sources, quality, price
   (b) inventory system
      — seasonal variation, turnover rate, method of control
   (c) space required
      — floor and office space, improvements required, expansion capability
   (d) staff and equipment required
      — personnel by skill level
      — fixtures, office equipment
   (e) operations strategy

11. Corporate structure
   (a) legal form
      — proprietorship, partnership or incorporation
   (b) share distribution
      — list of principal shareholders
   (c) contracts and agreements
      — list of contracts and agreements in force
      — management contract, shareholder or partnership agreement, service contract, leases
   (d) directors and officers
      — names and addresses, role in company
   (e) background of key management personnel
      — brief resumes of active owners and key employees

(f) organizational chart
— identify reporting relationships
(g) duties and responsibilities of key personnel
— brief job descriptions — who is responsible for what

12. Supporting professional assistance
(a) professionals on contract in specialized or deficient areas; would include lawyer, accountant, banker, insurance agent, etc.

13. Research and development program
(a) product or service improvements, process improvements, costs and risks

14. Risk assessment
(a) competitors' reaction
— will competitor try to squeeze you out? what form do you anticipate any reaction will take?
(b) list of critical external factors that might occur
— identify effects of strikes, recession, new technology, weather, new competition, supplier problems, shifts in consumer demand, costs of delays and overruns, unfavorable industry trends
(c) list of critical internal factors that might occur
— income projections not realized, client dispute or litigation, receivables difficulties, demand for services increases very quickly, key employee or consultant quits
(d) dealing with risks
— contingency plan to handle the most significant risks

15. Overall schedule
(a) interrelationship and timing of all major events important to starting and developing your business

16. Action plan
(a) steps to accomplish this year's goals
— flow chart by month or by quarter of specific action to be taken and by whom
(b) checkpoint for measuring results
— identify significant dates, sales levels as decision points

17. Financial forecast
If a business has been in operation for a period of time, the previous years' balance sheets and income statements are required, preferably for the past two or three years.
(a) opening balance sheet
— The balance sheet is a position statement, not an historical record; it shows what is owned and owed at a given date. There are three sections to a balance sheet: assets, liabilities, and owner's equity. You determine your firm's net worth by subtracting the liabilities from the assets.
— Your balance sheet will indicate how your investment has grown over a period of time. Investors and lenders typically examine balance sheets to determine if the company is within acceptable assets to liability limits.
— see Sample #5
(b) income and expense forecast statement (profit and loss)
— The income and expense forecast can be described as the operating statement you would expect to see for your business at the end of the period for which the forecast is being prepared.
— For a new business, the forecast would show what revenue and expenses you expect the business to have in its first year of operation.

— It is very useful, of course, to prepare a forecast for a period longer than one year. It is suggested that a detailed operating forecast be prepared for the next year of operation and a less detailed forecast for the following two years.

— Preparing an income and expense forecast for a new business is more difficult than preparing one for an existing business, simply because in a new business there is no historical record to go by. For this reason the preparation of this forecast is an even more essential, interesting and rewarding experience than doing it for an existing business, despite the time and effort required. The question will be answered by this analysis exercise, as to whether a profit will be made.

— The income statement (sales) is the most difficult because it is the most uncertain at the commencement of business. It is essential that a figure be projected on a conservative estimate.

— The main concern is to account for expenses accurately and in as much detail as possible. This will then provide a target or breakeven figure toward which to work.

— Some headings may not be appropriate for your type of consulting practice; other headings should be added.

— see Sample #6

(c)   cash flow forecast

— A cash flow budget measures the flow of money in and out of the business. It is critical to you and your banker.

— Many businesses operate on a seasonal basis, as there are slow months and busy months. The cash flow budget projection will provide an indication of the times of a cash flow shortage to assist in properly planning and financing your operation. It will tell you in advance if you have enough cash to get by.

— A cash flow budget should be prepared a year in advance and contain monthly breakdowns.

— see Sample #7

(d)   cash flow assumptions

When reviewing the cash flow plan, certain assumptions should be made:

— Sales: monthly sales (consulting service fees) that are expected to materialize

— Receipts: cash sales represent cash actually received; receivables collected represents the collection of amounts due for goods sold on credit; rental income is rent that will be collected in advance at the beginning of each month

— Disbursements: accounts payable to be paid in month following month of purchase

— Accounting and legal: to be paid upon receipt of bill, expected to be in the spring or after your fiscal year end financial statements have been completed

— Advertising: anticipated to be the same amount each month and paid for in the month the expense is incurred

— Automobile: anticipated to be the same amount each month and paid for in the month the expense is incurred

— Bank charges and interest: anticipated to be the same amount each month and monthly paid for in same month the expenses is incurred

— Equipment rental: to be paid for in monthly payments

— Income taxes: amount for taxes of the prior year and to be paid in the spring

— Insurance: annual premium to be paid quarterly, semi-annually or annually in installments of equal amounts

— Loan repayment: amount is the same each month and paid in accordance with the monthly schedule furnished by the lending institution

— Office supplies and expenses: to be paid in month following receipt of invoice and supplies to be purchased on a quarterly basis

— Taxes and licenses: to be paid for upon receipt of invoice, expected to be in January and July

— Telephone: to be paid for in month following the month the expense is incurred. Amount expected to be the same each month except in the last quarter when rates are expected to increase

— Utilities: expected to fluctuate with weather conditions and to be paid for in the month following the month the expense is incurred

— Wages and benefits: wages to increase at the beginning of the year. Amount considered to be the same each month and paid for in the month the expense is incurred

— Miscellaneous: expected to be the same each month and paid for in the same month the expense is incurred

— Bad debts: varies

(e) Breakeven analysis

— Your breakeven analysis is a critical calculation for every consulting business. Rather than calculating how much your firm would make if it attained an estimated sales volume, a more meaningful analysis determines at what sales volume your firm will break even. An estimated sales volume could be very unreliable as there are many factors which could affect revenue.

— The calculation of a breakeven point for every small business is one of the crucial pieces of information. Above the breakeven sales volume it is only a matter of how much money your business can generate; below the breakeven level of sales, it is only a matter of how many days a business can operate before bankruptcy.

— A breakeven analysis provides a very real and meaningful figure to work toward and might be required to be updated every few months to reflect your business growth.

— The breakeven point is where total costs are equal to total revenues.

— The calculation of total costs is determined by adding variable costs onto the fixed costs.

— Total costs are all costs of operating the business over a specified time period.

— Variable costs are those that vary directly with the number of consulting services provided or marketing and promotion activities undertaken. These typically include automobile expenses, business travel expenses, supplies, brochures, etc. Variable costs are not direct costs which are passed on to the client in the billing.

— Fixed costs are costs that do not generally vary with the number of clients serviced. Also known as indirect costs, these costs typically include salaries, rent, secretarial service, insurance, telephone, accounting and legal supplies.

18. Financing and capitalization
   (a) term loan applied for
      — the amount, terms and when required
   (b) purpose of term loan
      — attach a detailed description of the aspects of the business to be financed
   (c) owner's equity
      — the amount of your financial commitment to the business
   (d) summary of term loan requirements
      — for a particular consulting project or for the business as a whole

19. Operating loan
   (a) line of credit applied for
      — a new line of credit or an increase, and security offered
   (b) maximum operating cash required
      — amount required, timing of need (refer to "cash flow forecast")

20. Present financing (if applicable)
    (a) term loans outstanding
      — the balance owing, repayment terms, purpose, security and status
    (b) current operating line of credit
      — the amount and security held

21. References
    (a) name of present lending institution
      — branch and type of accounts
    (b) lawyer's name
      — lawyer's address and telephone number
    (c) accountant
      — accountant's name and address and telephone number

22. Appendix
    The nature of the contents of the appendices attached, if any, depends on the circumstances and requirements of the lender or investor, or the desire to enhance the loan proposal. It is recommended that the appendices be prepared for your own benefit and reference to assist your business analysis, and to be available if the information is required. The following list is a guide only. Some of the headings described may be unavailable or unnecessary.
    (a) personal net worth statement
      — includes personal property values, investments, cash, bank loans, charge accounts, mortgages and other liabilities. This will substantiate the value of your personal guarantee if required for security.
      — see Sample #8
    (b) letter of intent
      — potential orders for client commitments
    (c) description of personal and business insurance coverage
      — include insurance policies and amount of coverage
    (d) accounts receivable summary
      — include aging schedule of 30, 60 and 90 day periods
      — see Sample #9
    (e) accounts payable summary
      — include schedule of payments and total amounts owing
    (f) legal agreement
      — include a copy of contracts, leases and other documents
    (g) appraisals
      — fair market value of business property and equipment
    (h) financial statements for associated companies
      — where appropriate, a lender may require this information
    (i) copies of your brochure
    (j) testimonial letters from clients
    (k) references
    (l) sales forecast and market surveys
    (m) list of investors
    (n) credit status information
    (o) news articles about you and your business

SAMPLE #5
OPENING BALANCE SHEET (NEW BUSINESS)

DATE: _____

NAME OF COMPANY: _____

ASSETS

Current assets

Cash and bank accounts		$ _____
Accounts receivable		$ _____
Inventory		$ _____
Prepaid rent		$ _____
Other current assets		$ _____
TOTAL CURRENT ASSETS	(A)	$ _____

Fixed assets

Land and buildings		$ _____
Furniture, fixtures and equipment		$ _____
Automobiles		$ _____
Leasehold improvements		$ _____
Other assets		$ _____
TOTAL FIXED AND OTHER ASSETS	(B)	$ _____
TOTAL ASSETS (A + B = C)	(C)	$ _____

LIABILITIES

Current liabilities (debt due within next 12 months)

Bank loans		$ _____
Loans — other		$ _____
Accounts payable		$ _____
Current portion of long-term debt		$ _____
Other current liabilities		$ _____
TOTAL CURRENT LIABILITIES	(D)	$ _____

Long-term debt

Mortgages and liens payable (attach details)		$ _____
Less: current portion		$ _____
Loans from partners or stockholders (owner's equity)		$ _____
Other loans of long-term nature		$ _____
TOTAL LONG-TERM DEBT	(E)	$ _____
TOTAL LIABILITIES (D + E = F)	(F)	$ _____
NET WORTH (C - F = G)	(G)	$ _____
TOTAL NET WORTH AND LIABILITIES (F + G = H)	(H)	$ _____

SAMPLE #6
INCOME AND EXPENSE STATEMENT FORECAST
(NEW BUSINESS)

(Name of business)

For the period: _____ months ending _____ , 19 _____

PROJECTED INCOME

SALES _____ $ _____

_____ $ _____

TOTAL SALES $ _____

OTHER INCOME $ _____

TOTAL INCOME (A) $ _____

PROJECTED EXPENSES

Sales expenses
  Commissions and salaries $ _____
  Travel $ _____
  Advertising $ _____
  Automotive $ _____
  Other $ _____

TOTAL SELLING EXPENSES (B) $ _____

ADMINISTRATIVE AND FINANCIAL EXPENSES
  Management salaries (or proprietor/partner draws) $ _____
  Office salaries $ _____
  Professional fees $ _____
  Office expense and supplies $ _____
  Telephone $ _____
  Rent $ _____
  Interest and bank charges $ _____
  Inventory $ _____
  Bad debt $ _____
  Other $ _____

TOTAL ADMINISTRATIVE AND FINANCIAL EXPENSES (C) $ _____

TOTAL EXPENSES (B + C = D) (D) $ _____

OPERATING PROFIT (LOSS) (A - D) $ _____

  Add: Other income
  Less: Provisions for income taxes $ _____

NET PROFIT (LOSS) $ _____

SAMPLE #7
CASH FLOW BUDGET WORKSHEET

	January		February		March	
	Est.	**Actual**	**Est.**	**Actual**	**Est.**	**Actual**
Cash at beginning of month:	$_____	$_____	$_____	$_____	$_____	$_____
In bank and on hand	_____	_____	_____	_____	_____	_____
In investments	_____	_____	_____	_____	_____	_____
TOTAL CASH	$_____	$_____	$_____	$_____	$_____	$_____
Plus income during month:	_____	_____	_____	_____	_____	_____
Cash sales (include credit cards)	_____	_____	_____	_____	_____	_____
Credit sales payments	_____	_____	_____	_____	_____	_____
Investment income	_____	_____	_____	_____	_____	_____
Receivables collected	_____	_____	_____	_____	_____	_____
Loans	_____	_____	_____	_____	_____	_____
Personal investment	_____	_____	_____	_____	_____	_____
Other cash income	_____	_____	_____	_____	_____	_____
TOTAL CASH AND INCOME	$_____	$_____	$_____	$_____	$_____	$_____
Expenses during the month:	_____	_____	_____	_____	_____	_____
Rent (if applicable)	_____	_____	_____	_____	_____	_____
Utilities	_____	_____	_____	_____	_____	_____
Phone	_____	_____	_____	_____	_____	_____
Postage	_____	_____	_____	_____	_____	_____
Office equipment and furniture	_____	_____	_____	_____	_____	_____
Stationery and business cards	_____	_____	_____	_____	_____	_____
Insurance (health, fire, liability, theft, fire, etc.)	_____	_____	_____	_____	_____	_____
Answering service	_____	_____	_____	_____	_____	_____
Printing and supplies	_____	_____	_____	_____	_____	_____
Typing/secretarial service	_____	_____	_____	_____	_____	_____
Accounting and legal services	_____	_____	_____	_____	_____	_____
Advertising and promotion	_____	_____	_____	_____	_____	_____
Business licenses and permits	_____	_____	_____	_____	_____	_____
Dues and subscriptions	_____	_____	_____	_____	_____	_____
Books and reference materials	_____	_____	_____	_____	_____	_____
Travel: in town	_____	_____	_____	_____	_____	_____
Travel: out of town	_____	_____	_____	_____	_____	_____

	January		February		March	
	Est.	Actual	Est.	Actual	Est.	Actual
Conventions, professional meetings, trade shows	$_____	$_____	$_____	$_____	$_____	$_____
Continuing education	_____	_____	_____	_____	_____	_____
Entertainment	_____	_____	_____	_____	_____	_____
Contributions	_____	_____	_____	_____	_____	_____
Gifts	_____	_____	_____	_____	_____	_____
Salaries	_____	_____	_____	_____	_____	_____
Unemployment insurance	_____	_____	_____	_____	_____	_____
Pensions	_____	_____	_____	_____	_____	_____
Miscellaneous	_____	_____	_____	_____	_____	_____
Loan repayment	_____	_____	_____	_____	_____	_____
Other cash expenses	_____	_____	_____	_____	_____	_____
TOTAL EXPENSES	$_____	$_____	$_____	$_____	$_____	$_____
Cash flow excess or (deficit) at end of month	$_____	$_____	$_____	$_____	$_____	$_____
Cash flow cumulative (monthly)	$_____	$_____	$_____	$_____	$_____	$_____

SAMPLE #8
PERSONAL NET WORTH STATEMENT

Date: _____

Name: _____

Address: _____

GENERAL INFORMATION

Phone: Home _____ Business _____ Age _____ M or S _____

Dependents including spouse _____

Present employer _____ Position occupied _____ How long with this employer _____

Previous employer _____ How long _____

Landlord _____ Address _____ Monthly rental $ _____

Salary, wages or commission per annum $ _____   Other income per annum $ _____ Source _____

Guarantees on debts of others: Name _____ Amount _____

_____

ASSETS

Bank accounts _____

Stocks at cost (market value _____) _____

Bonds at cost (market value _____) _____

Life insurance (cash surrender value)

    Beneficiary _____

Automobile — year _____

            — make _____ _____

Home — registered _____

     — building size _____ Lot size _____

Other assets _____

                      TOTAL _____

LIABILITIES

Bank loan _____

Charge accounts _____

Policy loans on life insurance _____

Other loans _____

Installment purchases _____

Mortgages: Int. rate _____

    Term _____ Payments _____

    Taxes _____

Other liabilities _____

               SUB TOTAL _____

NET WORTH _____

               TOTAL _____

               (Name of company)

SAMPLE #9
STATEMENT OF ACCOUNTS RECEIVABLE

AS AT _____ 19 ___

Date: _____

_____
(Name of company)

Names of debtors	Total (Omit Cents)	Current	31 - 60 Days	61 - 90 Days	Over 90 Days & Holdbacks	Remarks

1. Sub totals .... $ _____

2. Aggregate of accts.
   under $ _____ $ _____

3. Number of
   accts. _____   No. _____ No. _____ No. _____ No. _____ No. _____

4. TOTALS .... $ _____

Percentage .... 100%   %   %   %   %

c. ESTIMATING YOUR START-UP FUNDS

1. Assessment of personal monthly financial needs

Personal expenses will continue in spite of the business, and therefore have to be taken into account when determining monthly cash flow needs. It is important to calculate personal expenses accurately so that appropriate decisions can be made in terms of funding and the nature of the start-up practice — whether it should start out on a part-time or full-time basis, using the home as an office or renting an outside office. See Sample #3.

2. Estimated business start-up cash needs

An estimate of the start-up cash required can be calculated by referring to Table #2. Naturally, each consultant's situation can vary considerably and therefore the worksheet is a guide only.

During your first few months you will probably not have enough sales revenue to finance your short-term costs. This usually occurs for one of three reasons: your sales are below projection, your costs rise unexpectedly, or you have not yet been paid for consulting work already performed (overdue accounts receivable). Many professionals experience accounts receivable problems during the early months of operation because clients tend to pay professionals after they have paid other outstanding bills. Your conservative cash flow analysis prepares you for this situation, and enables you to plan your cash needs.

d. SUMMARY

Before presenting your business plan to a lender or investor, have two or three impartial outsiders review the finished plan in detail. There may be something you overlooked or under-emphasized. After your plan has been reviewed by others, take your plan and financial statements to your accountant for review. You should also discuss with your accountant all the personal and business tax considerations that might be involved. You may wish to have your accountant come with you to the bank when you discuss your loan proposal. This is not uncommon and can create a very positive impression.

Discuss with your lawyer the security you are proposing. Your lawyer should explain fully before the plan is submitted the effect of your pledging collateral security and what the lender could do if you default. You should also seriously evaluate whether the security pledged is too excessive for the loan or risk involved and whether the risk is too great to pledge your personal assets.

Your familiarity with your business plan will increase your credibility and at the same time provide you with a good understanding of what the financial statements reveal about the viability of your business.

7

HOW TO OBTAIN FINANCING

Having completed your business plan and financial projections, you should now have a clear idea of your short-term and medium-term financial needs. You will want to be familiar with the types of financing available, the various sources, how to approach financial lending institutions, and the type of security that may be required. You should also be aware of the reasons that lending institutions or investors may turn down a request for funding. These matters and other issues are covered in this chapter.

a. TYPES OF FINANCING

There are two basic types of financing: equity and debt.

1. Equity

The money that *you* put into a company or business is equity. Initially all money must come from your own resources such as savings or personal borrowing from financial institutions, friends, relatives, or business associates. As time progresses, retained earnings in the business will increase your equity.

If you have formed a corporation, you can "buy" one or more shares and lend the rest of the money to the corporation as a "shareholder's loan." The advantages of a shareholder's loan are:

(a) Lenders consider these loans as equity as long as the money is left in the company.

(b) It is easier to repay the loan than sell shares back to the company or to other investors.

(c) Interest may be paid. For example, if you or your friends would like to earn a return on your investment, an interest rate may be established. The alternative is to pay dividends on shares when funds are available.

(d) Interest is tax deductible to the company.

2. Debt

A debt is a loan. It must be repaid, and the lender will charge interest on the money you have borrowed. With borrowed money, normally the principal and interest is paid back on a fixed monthly payment. You therefore have to include the principal and interest payments in a current business plan. Various forms of debt financing are discussed below.

(a) Short-term or operating loan (demand loan)

Short-term or operating loans are used for financing inventory, accounts receivable, special purchases or promotions, and other items requiring working capital during peak periods.

The main sources of short-term loans are commercial banks or similar financial institutions. Using a short-term loan is a good way to establish credit with a bank. This type of loan can be unsecured or secured by your personal or business assets.

Short-term loans are usually negotiated for specific periods of time; for example, 30, 60 or 90 days and frequently for periods up to a year or more. They may be repayable in a lump sum at the end of the period or in periodic installments, such as monthly.

Other characteristics of a demand loan include:

- Interest rate at time of signing may be lower than a term loan
- Fluctuating interest rate
- Repayment of the loan can be demanded at any time by the lender; usually only occurs when the account does not perform satisfactorily or in case of serious deterioration in the affairs of the business
- Can often be obtained more quickly than a term loan

(b) Line of credit

A line of credit is an agreement between you and the lender (a bank or similar financial institution) specifying the maximum amount of credit (overdraft) the bank will allow you at any one time for general operating purposes.

Credit lines are usually established for one year-periods, subject to annual renegotiation and renewal. Other characteristics of a line of credit include:

- Loan funds increase and decrease as you need the money or "revolves"
- Available from most banks
- Fluctuating interest rate
- Interest rate at time of signing may be lower than a term loan
- The lender uses accounts receivable, the money owed to you by customers, and inventory as the security. For accounts receivable, the lender may lend between 50% and 75% of the value, not including amounts over 90 days. For inventory, a lender may lend up to 50%
- Can often be obtained more quickly than a term loan
- Repyament of the loan can be demanded at any time by the lender or the line of credit can be reduced; usually this only occurs when the account does not perform satisfactorily or in a case of serious deterioration in the affairs of the business, or reduction in the value of the security provided

62

- The amount of credit granted is based on the lender's assessment of the creditworthiness of the company, its principals and the credit requested, among other factors.

(c) Term loans

A term loan is generally money borrowed for a term of one year up to fifteen years. A term loan is usually amortized. In other words, the regular loan payments include principal and interest and are for a fixed aggregate amount over the life or term of the loan agreement.

Term loans are commonly used to provide funds for the purchase of an **existing business**, to help finance expansions or capital expenditures, and to provide additional working capital for a growing business.

While the majority of term loans are secured by collateral such as fixed assets, or other chattels (cars, building, land, equipment, etc.), the lender places great importance upon the ability of the borrower to repay his or her indebtedness out of the business' earnings over the life of the loan.

The main characteristics of a term loan are:

- It may be repaid over a period of time generally related to the useful "life" of the assets; for example, car — 3 to 5 years; land and building —after 3 years.

- The lender will only give you a percentage of the value; for example, car — 80%; building — 75%. The other 20% or 25% of the cost of the asset must come from the equity you have in the company or new funds from shareholders or yourself.

- The company must be able to show the lender that future sales will generate enough cash to repay the loan.

- There are different lenders for different types of term loans. One consideration in the approval of your proposal is "leverage" or "debt to equity ratio." This is the ratio of the money you owe to the money you put in the business. Generally, the lender's assessment of this ratio is discretionary; but if you are a new business, or just building up a reputation, it is unlikely that the lender will want to go beyond 2:1 or even 1:1. Consequently, this may place an additional restriction on the amount that you can borrow.

- Interest rate at time of signing is slightly higher than a demand loan.

- Your payments, principal plus interest, are all the same.

- Repayment period of loan is specified and agreed upon in advance.

- It could take a longer time to obtain a loan approval than a demand loan.

(d) Trade credit or supplier financing

This is the most often used form of short-term financing. This means that a supplier will not insist on immediate payment for purchase of merchandise.

Terms can be arranged between both parties as to when payment will be made —generally 30 to 90 days.

(e) Renting or leasing

Renting or leasing assets is an alternative form of financing. Leasing companies will consider arranging a lease with option to purchase on virtually any tangible asset. Renting premises, as opposed to buying a building, is also a financing alternative. Assets such as typewriters, office furniture, personal computers or word processors, automobiles and telephone equipment, are examples. The advantages of leasing are:

- It frees up equity capital for investment in areas of greater return.
- It frees up borrowing power for the more critical areas of the business.
- There is no down payment requirement with leasing.
- Rates are usually fixed for a set term.
- The full payment is an allowable expense.
- Purchase options can be exercised at a later date at a pre-determined price.

There are also disadvantages. You should discuss the tax and financial considerations with your accountant before you make your decision.

b. SOURCES OF FINANCING

1. Equity

The most common source of equity capital is personal funds from savings. In exchange for the funds provided to the company, the owner obtains all the shares of the corporation or ownership of the business.

Equity can be further increased from the savings of friends willing to invest, or even from relatives. However, many small business people have created problems by bringing in friends or relatives as investors.

Conflicts generally occur if the business is not doing as well as everyone initially imagined, or if the terms and conditions of such loans are not clearly spelled out, or if the lenders or investors insist on becoming involved in day-to-day operations.

Any agreement should be documented in writing between the parties and signed in advance to eliminate any misunderstanding. Agreement should be reached on the rate of interest to be paid, when the loans will be repaid, any options you have to pay them back early, and the procedures that all parties will follow if the loans become delinquent. Consult competent legal counsel in advance to protect your interests.

An equity investment can be in the form of stockholder loans, or common stock or shares in the company or a combination of loans and shares. The investment structure will vary in each situation.

64

Generally speaking the advantage of money being invested as shareholder loans is that it can be paid back to lenders without tax, other than personal tax and interest you receive before the loan is paid off.

If the money is in the form of shares, it is much more difficult to withdraw since shares must be sold to someone else, and may be subject to capital gains tax.

Long-term debt investors may therefore place restrictions or conditions on when and how the company can pay off shareholder loans, redeem shares, or possibly even pay dividends on shares. These restrictions or conditions are imposed to protect the long-term debt invested.

The advice of a tax accountant is recommended since your personal tax situation and that of other potential equity investors could have a bearing on whether the shareholders' investment should be in the form of loans or purchase of shares.

2. Debt

Commercial banks are a major source of capital for new and continuing small ventures. Additional organizations that provide financing include insurance companies, pension companies, real estate investment, trust, commercial and mortgage banks, and even trust companies and credit unions.

(a) Small business administration (U.S.)

You may wish to consider the small business administration (SBA) in the U.S. The SBA was created by the federal government to assist entrepreneurs. Since 1953, the SBA has expanded to include many activities including finance and investment.

The SBA is organized in 10 regions and each region is subdivided, providing branch offices in many areas. SBA guidelines defining who qualifies for small business assistance vary, depending on the general classification of the enterprise. As the lender of final resort, the SBA tries not to compete with or replace the private banking system but to supplement it. There are three types of loans available from the SBA: guaranteed loans, immediate-participation loans and direct loans.

Since the SBA's loan regulations do change from time to time, you should verify current conditions by contacting your nearest branch of the SBA (listed in the telephone directory under U.S. Government) or write to: Small Business Administration, Washington, D C 20416.

(b) Federal Business Development Bank (Canada)

In Canada, the Federal Business Development Bank (FBDB) was established by the federal government especially to help those companies that could not obtain financing elsewhere. To obtain FBDB financing, the amount of your investment in the business must generally be sufficient to ensure that you are committed to it and that the business may reasonably be expected to be successful.

65

FBDB financing is available as loans, loan guarantees, equity financing, leasing, or any combination of these methods in whatever way best suits the particular needs of your business. If loans are involved, the interest rates are usually at slightly higher rates than chartered banks.

If you wish to obtain further information, contact your local branch of the FBDB or write to: Federal Business Development Bank, 901 Victoria Square, Montreal, Quebec H2Z 1R1.

c. COMPETITION BETWEEN LENDERS

There is considerable competition between banks and other financial institutions. Make comparisons between at least three different financial institutions to assess the most favorable loan package available.

All aspects of financial dealings are negotiable. Obtain the lending terms in writing before you sign. Have your outside advisors, such as your accountant or lawyer, review the terms. In addition, you may want to obtain the advice of your associates. Don't rush into a relationship with a financial institution without reasonably exploring all the other alternatives.

d. TIPS ON APPROACHING YOUR LENDER

When you approach a financial institution, you must sell the merits of your business proposal. As in all sales presentations, consider the needs and expectations of the other party — in this case, the loans officer. A loans officer will be interested in the following.

(a) Your familiarity with the business concept and the realities of the marketplace as reflected in your detailed business plan.

(b) Your ability to service the debt with sufficient surplus to cover contingencies, including carrying interest charges, and eventually repay the debt in full as demonstrated in your cash flow forecast and projected income statement.

(c) Your level of commitment as shown by your equity in the business or cash investment in the particular asset being purchased.

(d) Your secondary source of repayment, including security in the event of default, and other sources of income.

(e) Your track record and integrity as shown in your personal credit history, your business plan and business results or past business experience.

(f) Your approach. During the loan interview remember you're doing business the same as you do when you're with a client. Don't be subservient, overly familiar or too aggressive. Keep in mind that a lender is in business for the same reason you are — to make a profit. Keep the profit motive in mind during the interview. Don't try to appeal to a lender's social conscience. It won't work, since loans aren't granted for their social impact.

(g) Your judgment in supplying information. Be sensible with the number of documents you provide at the outset. You do not want to overwhelm the loans officer with too much material. For example, the introductory page, summary and financial plan sections provide a good basic loan submission if the amount requested is small. You should have all other documents prepared and available if requested.

(h) Your personal appearance. You should present yourself in a manner that projects self-confidence and success.

(i) Your mental alertness. What times during the day are you at your mental peak? This should be the time that you arrange for an interview with the loans officer.

(j) Your consideration in allowing sufficient lead time for approval. The lender needs a reasonable time to assess your proposal. Also, the loan may have to be referred to another level within the financial institution for review.

(k) Your credit rating. It's a good idea to review your credit rating periodically, as there may be errors to correct in your file. Note your positive and negative points, so you can discuss them when raised by the lender.

If your request for financing is approved, find out everything you need to know about the conditions, terms, payment methods, interest rates, security requirements, and any other fees to be paid. No commitment to accept the financing should be made until all this information is provided and understood and its impact on the proposed business analyzed. Ask your accountant and lawyer to assist you in the loan application in advance and review the bank's approval. Make certain you get the approval particulars in writing.

e. WHY LOANS ARE TURNED DOWN

If a request for financing is not approved, find out why. Use the lender's experience to your advantage. Lenders handle many requests for financing, and have experience in the financial aspects of many businesses, even if they do not have direct management experience.

If there is something specifically wrong with the financing proposal, see if it can be corrected and then re-apply. If not, use this knowledge when approaching other potential lenders or on future occasions when seeking funds.

Some of the causes of a loan rejection could be the following:

(a) The business idea was considered unsound or too risky. A lender's judgment is generally based on past performance of other businesses similar to the one you are proposing.

(b) Insufficient collateral. A lender must be satisfied that there are sufficient assets pledged to meet the outstanding debt if your business does not succeed financially. If you are just starting a business, a lender generally requires you to pledge personal assets, such as your home, car and other securities, against the loan. If you are borrowing funds under a corporate name, your personal guarantee will generally be requested and in some cases your spouse's guarantee as well, depending upon the circumstances. You may therefore not have sufficient security required for the amount of loan you are requesting or for the degree of risk, in the lender's opinion, that might be involved.

(c) Lack of financial commitment on your part. A lender will be reluctant to approve loan financing for business ventures if you are not fully committed. The lender does not want to foreclose or repossess and then have to sell assets to collect your money. The lender will therefore want to know how much personal financial capital you have made available to the business venture in order to assess your commitment to repay the loan. If you have not made any financial commitment and yet have security that you wish to pledge, the security alone may not be sufficient.

(d) Lack of a business plan or a poor business plan. A lender could reject your loan application if you have not prepared a detailed business plan or do not understand its significance.

(e) The purpose of the loan is not explained or is not acceptable. It is important that the specific use of the funds being borrowed be outlined in detail. It is also important that the purpose and amount of funds being requested be reasonable and appropriate. For example, it could be considered unreasonable for you to calculate a large draw or salary from your business in the first six months. If you intend to use the loan to pay off past debts or financial obligations, it may not be approved since the funds would not be directly generating cash flow for your new business venture.

(f) Your character, personality or stability can effect a lender's decision. It is important to appear confident, enthusiastic, well-informed, and realistic. If your personality is not consistent with the personality required for your type of business in the eyes of the lender, it could have a negative effect. If you are going through a separation or divorce proceedings or have declared personal bankruptcy or had business failures in the past, these factors could have an adverse impact on your loan application.

f.   TYPES OF SECURITY A LENDER MAY REQUIRE

Lenders primarily lend money to businesses that exhibit a strong potential to repay the loan. Nevertheless, they want to be covered in case of a default. Sometimes your signature is the only security the lender needs when making a loan. The kind and amount of security depends on the lender and on the borrower's situation. The most common types of security or collateral are: endorser, co-maker, guarantor, promissory note, demand loan, realty mortgage, chattel mortgage, assignment of accounts receivable, postponement of claim, pledging of stocks and bonds, and assignment of life insurance.

1. Endorser

Borrowers often get other people to sign a note in order to bolster their own credit. These endorsers are contingently liable for the note they sign. If the borrower fails to pay off the loan, the lender expects the endorser to make the note good. Sometimes the endorser may be asked to pledge assets or securities as well.

2. Co-maker

A co-maker is a person who takes on an obligation jointly with the borrower. In such cases, the lender can collect directly from either the maker or the co-maker.

3. Guarantor

A guarantor is a person who guarantees the payment of a note by signing a guarantee commitment. Both private and government lenders commonly require a personal guarantee from officers of corporations as security for loans advanced to the corporation. If the corporation defaults in its financial obligations, the lender has a choice of suing the guarantor or the corporation or both for the monies outstanding. Try to negotiate a limited guarantee to cover the shortfall in the security, if other securities have been pledged. Be very careful not to sign a personal guarantee for the full amount of the loan if at all possible. Recover your guarantee as soon as the business has paid off its obligation or can carry the debt on its own security. Resist having your spouse sign a personal guarantee of your debts. Your personal guarantee is often all you have left to negotiate with on another occasion.

4. Promissory note

A promissory note is a written promise to pay a specified sum of money to the lender, either on demand or at a specified future time.

5. Demand loan

A demand loan involves a written promise to pay the amount of monies outstanding to the lender upon demand.

6. Realty mortgage

A lender may require a mortgage against your property for the advancement of funds. It could be a first, second or third mortgage against your property, or a collateral mortgage to a guarantee or demand note.

7. Chattel mortgage

A chattel mortgage is on specific property, such as a car or boat, other than land and buildings. The title of the chattel remains in the name of the borrower, but a lien against the chattel is placed in favor of the lender.

8. Assignment of accounts receivable

A borrower may have to assign the business receivables to the lender to secure an operating line of credit or other loan. The borrower still collects the receivables, but in a default, the lender will assume collection. The assignment is supported by submitting monthly a list of the business receivables.

9. Postponement of claim

If there are any loans from shareholders, the lender may ask for an agreement that the company will not repay the shareholders until the lender has been repaid in full.

10. Pledge of stocks or bonds

The possession of stocks and bonds may be transferred to the lender, but title remains with the borrower. The security must be marketable. As a protection against market declines and possible expenses of liquidation, banks usually lend no more than 75% of the market value of "blue chip stock." On federal government or municipal bonds, they may be willing to lend 90% or more of their market value.

The lender may ask the borrower for additional security or payment whenever the market value of the stocks or bonds drops below the lender's required margin.

11. Assignment of life insurance

A lender may request that the borrower assign the proceeds of a life insurance policy to the lender up to the amount outstanding at the time of death of the borrower. Another form of assignment is against the cash surrender value of a life insurance policy. Banks generally lend up to the cash value of a life insurance policy.

8

KEEPING RECORDS

A consultant must keep accurate and thorough financial records covering all income received and expenses incurred. Records help in producing income, controlling expenses, planning growth and cash flow, keeping tax payments to a legal minimum, and complying with the multitude of regulatory requirements. This chapter explains the basic concepts and procedures of keeping records and outlines some of the issues you will have to discuss with your accountant and bookkeeper.

a. ACCOUNTING AND BOOKKEEPING

Accounting is the process of analyzing and systematically recording, in terms of money or some other unit of measurement, operations or transactions of the business. To capture these facts and figures, a system is necessary. Such a system usually consists of bookkeeping records which may be set up in journals, ledgers or other records.

A professional accountant can help design a system for recording the information each consultant needs in his or her particular circumstance. Some tips on selecting an accountant are outlined in chapter 5.

Bookkeeping is the process of classifying and recording business transactions in the books of account. A bookkeeper keeps the various records, journals and ledgers current and accurate.

Many consultants are not inclined or do not know how to maintain the books. A part-time bookkeeper can be employed to keep the books either at your home or place of business, or at the bookkeeper's office. It is highly advisable that a professional accountant establish a system for your books. You can then hire a bookkeeper recommended by your accountant or a business associate you trust.

Make sure the bookkeeper is competent to handle your specific type of records, as some bookkeepers specialize in certain areas. The costs of a bookkeeper are considerably lower than that of a professional accountant, and normally range between $10 to $20 per hour. Bookkeepers are not qualified to provide tax advice. Only an experienced tax accountant is able to provide you with the necessary tax planning information.

Different kinds of bookkeeping systems are discussed below.

1. Separate record-keeping

It is essential that your business books and records be kept separate from your personal books, records, and bank accounts. This is not only required by tax regulations, but is sound business management.

Separate records will allow you to control cash flow, budget for expenses, and draw up financial statements. A separate bank account for the business has the following advantages:

- Financial statements can be drawn and taxable income computed easily.

- When all income is deposited into the business account the income journal is maintained by the bank in the form of complete records of all receipts.

- Applications for financing for business purposes can be prepared more accurately with business records.

- All business expenses can be proven from one source.

- Personal draws can be budgeted carefully and completely controlled. Funds can be taken from the business account periodically and deposited into the personal account as draws or salary.

2. Double-entry and single-entry bookkeeping

Double-entry bookkeeping is usually the preferred method for keeping business records. Transactions are entered first in a journal, then monthly totals of the transactions are posted to the appropriate ledger accounts. The ledger accounts include five categories: income, expense, asset, liability, and net worth. Income and expense accounts are closed each year; asset, liability, and net worth accounts are maintained on a permanent and continuing basis.

Single-entry bookkeeping is not as complete as a double-entry method. This system, however, is relatively simple and records the flow of income and expense through a daily summary of cash receipts, a monthly summary of receipts, and a monthly disbursements journal such as a checkbook.

Your accountant will advise you about the appropriate system for your needs.

3. One-write accounting system

"One-write" is an accounting system where all the sales you make are automatically, through carbon paper, posted to a sales journal and monthly ledger card (for sending out statements) on the receivables side, and all the checks are posted to the proper expense journal on the payables side. The one-write system is also effective for showing the "aged" balance of receivables. In other words, it shows who owes you how much for 30, 60, 90 or over 90 days.

You may use either the receivable or payable system or both. It makes record-keeping very simple for you and your accountant, and is particularly useful if you write 50 or more checks and statements each month. If you are using the one-write system for payables, it automatically posts the checks written to a cash disbursement journal and all you need to do is summarize the sheet every 25 checks.

If you are interested in accounting systems, contact the suppliers under "accounting systems" in the yellow pages of the telephone directory.

4. Cash or accrual basis for records

Cash basis record-keeping is a method of recording transactions so that revenues and expenditures are reflected in the accounts in the period the related cash receipts or disbursements occur.

Accrual basis record-keeping is a method of recording transactions so that revenues and expenses are reflected in the accounts in the period they have been earned and incurred, whether or not such transactions have been finally settled. There are advantages and disadvantages of each system based on your circumstances. Tax advice will assist you in making the correct choice.

b. BASIC ACCOUNTING RECORDS

As previously discussed, informal records consist of evidence of business transactions such as sales slips, invoices, checks, etc. These informal records are then gathered into a more formal structure. For accounting purposes, these formalized basic records are referred to as "books of original entries" or as "journals."

1. Sales journal

A sales journal is a daily register of both cash and charge sales. The sales, both cash and charge, may be recorded by numbered invoices and accounted for. The total is then entered as the day's sales in the sales journal.

2. Cash receipts journal

This journal often combines the function of a sales journal along with a record of all transactions resulting in money coming into the business. When combined, this journal is referred to as a "sales and cash receipts journal".

In the cash receipts journal, all cash sales, charge sales, collections on account, and total deposits to the bank are entered. This is usually done in conjunction with the cash receipts journal. Referred to as a "daily summary of sales and cash receipts," it is both a summarizing vehicle as well as a form of reconciliation between cash on hand, cash receipts, charge sales, and total sales.

A sales and cash receipts journal briefly describes the transaction, whether it is a cash sale or a charge sale, whether the cash receipt came from a source other than a sale, and the amount of the total deposit.

In summary, the journal will show:

(a) Cash sale

(b) Bank deposit

(c) Receipts on account from a client

(d) Other receipts

3. Accounts receivable ledger and control account

These records are separate. The accounts receivable ledger contains separate cards or sheets for each charge client and records the sale with the invoice number or reference, the date, and the amount of the sale. When payments are made, the amount of the payment is deducted from the balance owing and is cross-referenced to the cash receipts journal.

The control account records in total all the charge sales and all the payments by charge customers which are detailed individually in the accounts receivable ledger. At any given time, the sum of all the individual charge account balances in the subsidiary ledger will equal the total net balance in the control account.

The accounts receivable aging schedule accompanies the accounts receivable ledger. This is a record of each charge customer that shows the balance owing and the age status of the charge — normally current, 30, 60, or 90 days.

In summary, each client has a ledger sheet that details: name, address, telephone number, credit information, date of sale, invoice number, date of payment, receipt number, balance owing.

Periodically the individual balances are added up (usually once a month), and the totals are reconciled to the accounts receivable balance in the general ledger.

4. Accounts payable journal

This journal is usually a subsidiary journal to the cash disbursements journal. The accounts payable journal records invoices for purchases, the amount and date, and when the invoice has to be paid. This journal's purpose is primarily a control over the payables. It allows you to correctly determine outstanding liabilities and when these obligations must be met.

5. Cash disbursements journal

This journal records, daily, all cash outlays for purchases, expenses, payroll, cash withdrawals, and loan payments. The payee or account is referenced, the check number is given, the amount is specified, and the purpose of the disbursement, by amount, is shown under the proper heading for each day. The purpose could be payroll, inventory purchased, accounts payable falling due, tax payments, etc. Any disbursements such as interest charges or withdrawals are also recorded.

6. Payroll journal

This journal consists usually of two records. The first is the record for the individual employee; it shows the pay period, the gross amount earned, the deductions (income tax, unemployment insurance, pension plan) made at source, and the net earnings. The second record is the "payroll summary" which, for the pay period, gives the total gross earnings, deductions, and net salaries paid to all employees. The total of the employees' salaries appears as an entry in the cash disbursements journal.

7. General ledger

The general ledger is the final book of entry in an accounting system. This record is required to complete even the most basic of bookkeeping systems. Every entry from the preceeding journals and ledgers is listed in the general ledger. The general ledger must always be kept in balance; that is to say, all debits and credits must be equal, so that the net additions and subtractions equal zero. The general ledger is to be used for preparing financial statements. Because it is the book of final entry, and a permanent record, none of the pages should ever be thrown away.

As it is important to understand the principles behind the bookkeeping records, it is recommended that you take various bookkeeping courses that are available through the FBDB (Canada), SBA (U.S.), community colleges, school board continuing education classes, and other educational facilities. Also see *Basic Accounting for the Small Business*, another title in the Self-Counsel series.

c. NON-FINANCIAL RECORDS

Administrative records can improve efficiency and profit. Non-financial records such as personnel records, tax records, and service records should be maintained.

1. Personnel records

Personnel records consist primarily of policies, benefits, and other matters pertaining to the general administration of the employees or consultants as a whole. Personnel records can also consist of individual records on each employee. These records contain all documents and correspondence relating to an employee from the time of applying for employment to termination. Individual employee records also include a summary of personal data, education and training, work history, and job and wage record.

2. Tax records

Tax records record details of sales taxes, income taxes, business taxes, and employee income tax deductions. Most businesses are regulated by a combination of federal, state/provincial, and municipal/county governments. The information for these records is obtained from different aspects of the business operations. For example, payroll deductions and service are obtained from the payroll records, and information on sales taxes collected comes from either the sales journal or the daily summary of sales and cash receipts.

Tax records detail assessments, rates, calculations, and remittances both by amount and date. Tax records also let you know when remittances must be made to avoid late filing penalties.

3. Service records

Service records are all the records associated with the provision of a service. Most importantly, these records are used to record, for each client, the cost of material, labor and overhead. These calculations are then used to determine a price when bidding on a contract or presenting a proposal, or assessing the profitability of a particular activity or product.

Service records can also keep track of employee efficiency to control non-chargeable time and to identify activities that are not performed to expected standards.

d. OFFICE SYSTEMS

Office systems should be implemented to reduce exposure to liability and to increase business awareness and sound decision-making.

1. Handling new matters

It is important that a form be developed to gather administrative information in a standard, consistent, and uniform manner to reduce the likelihood of an error or omission. The form should provide date and deadlines, as well as information that might give rise to potential conflicts of interest. You should have separate forms for prospective clients and new assignments. See Samples #10 and #11.

2. Time records

Maintenance of effective time records is critical in documenting what was done by the consultant or sub-consultant. Such records must be made as business is transacted.

Accurate time records are extremely important to ensure that clients are promptly charged, and that you have accounted for all billable time expended. It is easy to forget time expended if you don't write it down immediately. Time records also reflect the expenditure of time for the benefit received, and whether or not your efficiency and profit are improving or certain activities or clients should be reconsidered. See Sample #12.

SAMPLE #10
PROSPECTIVE CLIENT SHEET

File # _____

Name _____ Telephone _____

Address _____

_____

_____

LEAD

Date of inquiry _____

Person making inquiry _____

Source of referral _____

Nature of initial inquiry _____

Consultant contacted _____

Follow-up planned _____

Dates of:

Phone conversations _____

Meetings _____

Correspondence _____

Total time expended on client prior
to any proposal preparation _____

Status _____

PROPOSAL

Presentation date of proposal _____

Time required to complete proposal _____

Cost estimate _____

Consultant with primary
responsibility for assignment _____

Disposition of proposal _____

ASSIGNMENT

Starting date _____

Consultant(s) assigned _____

Primary client contact _____

Total billing _____

Completion date _____

SAMPLE #11
NEW CONSULTING ASSIGNMENT SHEET

File # _____   New client ( )
Consultant in charge _____   Old client ( )

Client _____   Date opened _____
Address _____

_____   Phone _____

Contact person(s) _____
Cross index _____
Assignment _____

. . . .

Type of work:

( ) Feasibility study   ( ) Marketing study   ( ) Research
( ) Grant acquisition   ( ) Organizational study   ( ) Speaking engagement
( ) Management study   ( ) Personnel/labor study   ( ) Training
Other _____

. . . .

Fees (costs additional):

Person/Class	Rate	Per	Range quoted $ _____	to	$ _____
_____	_____	_____	Minimum quoted		$ _____
_____	_____	_____	Time value		$ _____

Other fee arrangements (method of payment) _____
Costs (projected)   _____
Total fees and costs   _____

. . . .

Source of client contact _____

Promised completion date _____   Expected completion date _____

Opened by _____

. . . .

CLOSING INFORMATION
   Assignment completed on _____
   Time value $ _____   Total fee rec'd $ _____   Variance $ _____
   Client available for reference: Yes ( )   No ( )

78

SAMPLE #12
TIME AND SERVICE RECORD

Date	Client No.	Client name	Service	Service Code	Loc'n Code	Time		By
						Hours	Decimal Conv.	
					TOTAL TIME:			

Service codes

1 ADV	Advice	7 ENT	Entertain	13 REV	Review
2 AP	Appear	8 INT	Interview	14 SEC	Secretarial
3 AUD	Audit	9 INV	Investigate	15 TCF	Phone call from
4 CON	Confer	10 OF	Office	16 TCT	Phone call to
5 DIC	Dictate	11 PR	Promotion	17 TVL	Travel
6 DR	Draft	12 RES	Research	18 TR	Train

Local code

A In Town
B Out of Town
C Client's Office
D Other

Decimal
Conversion:

6 mins. = .1 hour   36 mins. = .6 hour
12 mins. = .2 hour   42 mins. = .7 hour
18 mins. = .3 hour   48 mins. = .8 hour
24 mins. = .4 hour   54 mins. = .9 hour
30 mins. = .5 hour   60 mins. = 1.0 hour

If there is a legal dispute, your time record and service documentation could make the difference between winning and losing. Keep your time records in a detailed fashion as if you had to introduce them as evidence into court. The odds are that at some point in your consulting career you will have to do so.

Consider using a "daytimer" type of system for time keeping. Carry it with you at all times and transfer all notations to your daily time record docket sheet. You should get into the habit of recording all your daily activities in your daytimer, whether client related or not so that you can graphically analyze how your time is spent. For example, make a note of hours spent on client entertainment, marketing, professional development, and research each day.

3. Standard form engagement letters or contracts

You should have your lawyer help you develop letters of agreement and contracts that you can use with modification in each particular situation. It is important that the services to be performed and fee to be rendered are clearly outlined in a written contract.

4. Billing, credit, and collection

Monthly or interim billing should be done wherever possible. This means bills can be sent close to the time the work was done. It also keeps your cash flow even and enables you to spot fee disputes while there is still time to remedy the problem. An effective record-keeping system for credit and collection is also needed. This system can include a standard credit application form, client account record, etc. This subject is covered in detail in chapter 12.

5. Calendars

Important dates and deadlines should be entered into an effective calendar system, which will provide a double-check on entries, adequate lead time for performance of tasks, deadlines, limitation dates, secretarial administration of the system, input by associates and sub-consultants as appropriate, and follow-up to ensure that the performance has occurred.

6. Filing systems

An effective filing system should be developed to eliminate the possibility of misplacement of client materials. A filing reference system should be designed for speedy retrieval of client information.

9

HOW TO LEGALLY MINIMIZE PAYING TAX

It is very important to obtain professional advice on tax planning. An accountant who specializes in tax should be retained before you start your business to advise you on all the various considerations. Tax legislation is changing constantly, and varies by jurisdiction.

At the time of writing, the Canadian government is proposing to implement a new goods and services tax (GST) on most services and products purchased in Canada commencing in January, 1991. Toll-free lines (accessible only from Canada) established by the Canadian government will provide you with further information. The English language number is 1-800-267-6620. The French language number is 1-800-267-6640. All consulting services provided in Canada are covered by GST legislation, although several options may be available to you in terms of the application and reporting requirements. As the details and regulations are still in flux, it is highly recommended that you ask an accountant to obtain current tax advice in your specific situation. It is essential that advance tax and administrative planning be done to minimize frustration and expense. If you are based in the U.S. but intend to provide consulting services in Canada, make sure that you obtain tax compliance advice from a Canadian accountant.

This chapter gives an overview of some of the key areas to consider when discussing your new business with your professional advisors. Your advisors will review the business plan that you will have prepared, your personal financial circumstances, and your anticipated profit, and recommend the correct approach for your needs.

a. TAX AVOIDANCE AND TAX EVASION

The distinction between tax avoidance and tax evasion should be made clear. Tax avoidance is the principle by which the consultant plans his or her transactions within the law using all available tax planning benefits to minimize the liability for paying income taxes.

Tax evasion is an action that is outside the law, and normally implies the receipt of monies without declaring them as income. Tax evasion is criminal in nature and can result in serious consequences including jail.

b. CASH OR ACCRUAL METHOD

Consultants have a choice about the method of accounting for financial transactions. Based on your individual situation, one method may be more attractive than the other. The cash basis of accounting is a method of recording transactions in which revenues and expenditures are entered in the accounts during the period in which the related cash receipts or disbursements occur.

The accrual basis of accounting is a method of recording transactions in which revenues and expenses are entered in the accounts during the period in which they have been earned and incurred, whether or not such transactions have been finally settled.

Tax planning is particularly difficult for cash basis consultants, because expenses are generally deductible in the period paid, and income is generally taxable as it is received. For accrual basis consultants, the problem is simplified in that cash does not need to exchange hands for the recognition of income, at least not within the tax period. For either type of method, the intent is that income and expenses be matched within like periods.

An example of tax planning for the consultant who reports on a cash basis is found in the timing of bill payment. Toward the end of the year, the cash basis consultant should maximize allowable deductions by paying all bills applying to that tax year, before the year closes. Accordingly, it is not wise to request advance payments from current clients before the year is closed.

c. FISCAL YEAR-END

The choice of fiscal year may depend on consideration of financial savings for accounting fees, tax deferral in the first year, and administrative convenience.

It is prudent to select a fiscal year distinct from the calendar year if you intend to retain accountants for annual audit or tax purposes. January through April is the busiest time for accountants, and you are likely to have better service and more attention paid to your financial affairs when your corporate fiscal year ends, for example, in July rather than in February.

If you experience seasonal changes in business volume, it may be wise to tailor a fiscal year-end along seasonal lines.

Ask yourself if you are particularly busy at a certain time of the year. For example, if you are a consultant who specializes in education, you will likely be busiest in the winter and relatively free during the summer months. If you are a consultant to the retail business, you may be the busiest during the period of time leading up to the holidays.

In these cases, you might benefit from structuring the fiscal year-end so that the highest concentration of income occurs in the beginning of the fiscal year. By doing this, you have the remainder of the year to plan for taxes, take care of business development for the next fiscal year, and regulate cash flow effectively.

d. CORPORATIONS, PROPRIETORSHIPS OR PARTNERSHIPS

The tax implications of a proprietorship and a partnership are the same. The net income or net loss from the proprietorship or your share of the partnership are declared on your personal income tax filings. Depending on your level of taxation, you could be paying more tax than if you were incorporated.

Your particular situation will determine whether or not it is best to incorporate for tax reasons. Factors to consider include your salary draw level, value of benefits a corporation would absorb, tax bracket, and projected growth patterns. The immediate and long range tax liability of the individual is a governing factor.

Remember, that in the U.S. an exception to the normal corporation exists which allows the consultant to have the advantages of a proprietorship and a corporation. The features of a Sub-S corporation are briefly discussed in chapter 4. Your accountant can better advise you in detail.

e. MAXIMIZING DEDUCTIBLE EXPENSES

It is very important for consultants to have a record-keeping system that keeps track of all expenses relating to the consultant's overhead as well as expenses that are directly payable by the client. For a specific project, you may have given a fixed price contract incorporating expenses that otherwise would be passed on to the client for separate payment.

Expenses are allowed if they are related to the operation of the business, are reasonable, are "ordinary" and "necessary," and if they are for items to be used within a period of one year. Your accountant can advise you in your situation.

If you are going to incur expenses that would be useful for more than one year, generally that expense cannot be fully deducted within the year the money is spent. The depreciation formula for expenses such as typewriters, desks, autos, etc., may be claimed for the useful life of the asset.

To ensure that you account for all expenses, keep all payment stubs, receipts, and vouchers, and maintain a record of entertainment and automobile expenses. The tax department can disallow claims for expenses without verification that the expense was indeed incurred and that it was related to your business and the generation of income.

Some of the areas you should discuss with your accountant to obtain advice and guidelines are discussed below. The examples given are general guidelines only. It is critical that you receive expert tax advice in advance on these and other expense deductions related to your consulting practice. As mentioned earlier, tax regulations and interpretations are constantly changing and tax court decisions alter the law on an ongoing basis. Only a tax accountant can properly advise you on the appropriate deductions in your individual situation.

1. Home office

It is quite common for consultants to operate out of their homes to keep overhead costs down. An office in the home is deductible, but the guidelines are very strict.

(a) The office must be necessary to the conduct of the business.

(b) A room or area must be used 100% of the time exclusively for the business.

(c) Deductions are allowed on a square foot percentage or other reasonable basis.

(d) Any deductions for an office in the home that are being claimed must be disclosed on the consultant's tax return.

It is important to keep an accurate account of home office expenses, as the potential for abuse in this area is well known. Deductible expenses are made on a percentage basis. For example, if 15% of the home's living space is used completely for the conduct of business, 15% of the following expenses are deductible:

(a) Interest paid on home mortgage

(b) Rent of home or apartment, home owner's or tenant's fire insurance

(c) Property taxes

(d) Reasonable expenses such as maintenance

(e) A portion of the telephone charges might also be deductible. Expenses related to the telephone should be itemized as applicable to business use rather than estimated as a percentage of the total. An alternative is for the consultant to install a corporate business telephone in the home office.

Your tax consultant can advise you about home office expense deductibility. It is necessary to maintain careful documentation of home office expenses to support deductions claimed on an income tax return.

2. Automobile

This is a potential problem area if one car is being used for both business and pleasure. A full deduction for business use is difficult to claim if you are using it personally at any time. A ledger record of business usage is essential.

A complete log should be kept of all mileage pertaining to business with a description about the purpose of the trip. In addition, a record of all tolls and parking expenses, repairs, purchases, and insurance payments should be kept. In some cases an estimate of business use for a jointly used car may be allowable if it seems reasonable in the circumstances. Because an estimation may be disallowed, good management requires accurate record-keeping.

If you have two cars, one for business use and one for personal use, it is easier to establish a case for full deduction of all the expenses related to one car.

3. Entertainment

It is difficult to claim a deduction for entertainment unless an accurate record is kept showing the date, amount, location of entertainment, who attended, connection to business, and the purpose of the meeting. As this area is one of potential abuse, it is looked at very carefully on an audit and may be disallowed. It is important, therefore, to mark on the back of the receipt the necessary information immediately after the entertainment function and before you forget.

4. Travel

This is another area in which potential abuse occurs, and it is therefore scrutinized very carefully. Travel that is strictly for business is deductible. This normally includes the cost of transportation; lodging of a reasonable nature; meals; transportation while away, such as taxis, rental cars and buses; tips; personal services, such as laundry; and telephone costs.

A personal trip cannot be written off as a business expense. Some consultants believe that a personal trip may be "converted" into a business trip if business is conducted while away from home. The key criterion is whether or not the trip was primarily personal in nature. If it was primarily personal in nature, this could exclude deductibility of any business expenses.

A careful distinction must be maintained where business expenses and personal expenses are combined. For example, a spouse may accompany a consultant on a business trip. The consultant is only able to deduct the portion of the expenses that relate directly to business. The primary purpose of the trip must be for business, not pleasure. All expenses pertaining to the spouse's share of travel, lodging or meals would not be deductible.

There are limitations on the number of business conferences and conventions that can be taken outside the country each year and be deductible. You must obtain specific advice on these points.

5. Bad debts

Income is recognized only as the cash is collected. Therefore, cash basis taxpayers cannot deduct bad debts for uncollected fees. However, the consultant can deduct returned checks as bad debts. If you are an accrual basis taxpayer and want to deduct bad debts, two important tests are required to determine if the debt can be declared "uncollectable." The criteria are the record of your attempt to collect the debt and the length of time the debt has been outstanding.

6. Insurance

Insurance premiums for all business related insurance policies are fully deductible. If coverage extends to both personal and business protection, only the business portion can be deducted.

7. Professional development

All the expenses related to professional development are deductible if they are directly related to your business and generating income, and if they are reasonable. Again, detailed documentation is required to support the deduction.

10

INSURANCE

Proper risk management means planning for potential problems and attempting to insure against them. You should be familiar with the numerous types of insurance available, the method of obtaining the insurance, the best way to reduce premiums, and the pitfalls to avoid.

a. OBTAINING INSURANCE

Insurance companies market their services chiefly through the methods discussed below.

1. Agencies

These are normally the smaller individualized operations that place home, car or other common types of insurance with several insurance companies to which they are contracted. In some cases, small agencies, to earn their commission, are under an obligation to place a certain volume of insurance with each company they deal with. Therefore, it is possible that you might be sold policies offered by companies which may not suit your needs and may not necessarily be placed on a competitive basis.

2. Insurance brokers

Insurance brokers claim to have complete independence from any insurance company and more flexibility than the common agencies. In comparison with agencies in general, brokers from the larger companies are more knowledgeable and flexible in the types of coverage and policies available, and they specialize in certain areas. Also, a broker should have no vested interest in placing insurance with any particular company, and will therefore attempt to get you the best price and the best coverage to meet your needs. You should make specific inquiries to satisfy yourself.

As in all matters of obtaining professional advice or assistance, you should have a minimum of three competitive quotes and an opportunity to evaluate the relative strengths and weaknesses of each. If the brokers are using the same insurance base for the best coverage and premiums, then all three brokers should recommend to you, in theory, the same insurance companies for the different forms of coverage you are requesting.

3. Clubs and associations

Ask your local Better Business Bureau and Chamber of Commerce about their group rates for insurance. These two organizations frequently have various types of insurance coverage available at a reduced group rate.

b. PLANNING YOUR INSURANCE PROGRAM

It is important to consider all criteria to determine the best type of insurance for you and your business. Your major goal should be adequate coverage, avoiding both over- and under-insurance. This is done by periodic review of risk, and by keeping your agent informed of any changes in your business that could potentially affect your coverage.

The following principles will help in planning an insurance program:

(a) Identify the risk to which your business is exposed.

(b) Cover your largest risk first.

(c) Determine the magnitude of loss the business can bear without financial difficulty, and use your premium dollar where the protection need is greatest.

(d) Decide what kind of protection will work best for each risk:

- Absorbing risks

- Minimizing risks

- Insuring against risks with commercial insurance

(e) Insure the correct risk

(f) Use every means possible to reduce costs of insurance:

- Negotiate for lower premiums if loss experience is low

- Use deductibles where applicable

- Shop around for comparable rates and analyze insurance terms and provisions offered by different insurance companies.

(g) Risk exposure changes, so a periodic review will save you from insuring matters that are no longer exposed to the same degree of risk. Conversely, you may need to increase limits of liability. Reviews can help avoid overlaps and gaps in coverage, and thereby keep your risk and premiums lower.

(h) If you are pleased with a particular broker who can handle your various forms of insurance, it is preferable to be selective and have just one broker company. An advantage of the larger broker firms is that they have a pool of insurance professionals expert in various areas as resource people for you.

(i) Attempt to keep your losses down in every way. Although your business may have adequate coverage, losses could be uninsurable, exempt from coverage, or have a large deductible. Problems with insurance coverage could seriously affect the survival of your business.

c. TYPES OF BUSINESS AND PERSONAL INSURANCE

The types of insurance you might need will vary widely as the risks vary widely according to the type of consulting practice you have. The following overview of insurance policies is provided to make you aware of what exists, and what might be appropriate in your situation. As mentioned earlier, these types of insurance are not necessarily recommended. Only you can make that decision after an objective assessment of your needs following comparative research in a competitive insurance market.

1. General liability

Most liability insurance policies encompass such losses as:

(a) Money you must legally pay because of bodily injury or damage to the property of others.

(b) All emergency, medical, and surgical expenses incurred from the accident.

(c) Expenses for investigation, your defense, settlements and a trial.

A general liability policy covers negligence causing injury to clients, employees, and the general public. The policy is normally written up as a comprehensive liability policy.

2. Products or completed operations liability

This policy offers protection against a law suit by a customer or client who used your product or service and, as a result, sustained bodily injury or property damage from it.

3. Errors and omissions liability

This coverage protects you and other professionals against litigation arising from losses incurred by your clients as a result of an error or omission in your advice to them.

4. Malpractice liability

This insurance protects you from claims arising from any losses incurred by your clients as a result of negligence or failure on your part to exercise an acceptable degree of professional skill.

5. Automobile liability

This coverage includes other people's property, other automobiles, persons in other vehicles, and persons in the insured automobile.

If you are using your car for business purposes, exclusively or occasionally, it is important that you have your premium cover business use. It is possible that your current motor vehicle insurance policy has just a premium based on personal use. Problems could occur if there were an accident and it was discovered that your car was indeed used for business purposes.

6. Fire and theft liability

You probably already have fire and theft insurance if you are working out of your home as a consultant. If you are working in an office or an apartment, it is important to make sure that you have satisfactory coverage.

7. Business interruption insurance

The indirect loss from a fire or theft can be greater than the loss itself. If your premises or files are destroyed, you can lose revenue. Certain expenses must still be met. Such a situation could put a severe strain on working capital and seriously affect the survival of the business.

Business interruption insurance is designed to cover the period between the time of the loss and the return to normal operating conditions. The insurance policy could also include the costs of temporarily renting other premises.

8. Overhead expense insurance

Consultants whose business income would cease if they were temporarily disabled by illness or accident may take out insurance to cover the cost to them of their fixed business expenses or overhead which have to be met even when they are unable to earn income.

9. Personal disability insurance

You could possibly be disabled for a short or long period of time. This insurance pays you a certain monthly amount if you are permanently disabled, or a portion of that amount if you are partially disabled, but capable of generating some income.

10. Key person insurance

The death of a key person could seriously affect the earning power of your consulting practice. For example, if you have an associate, or partner or sub-consultant who is critical to a particularly large project or your business as a whole, life insurance should be considered.

If the key person dies, the loss may result in a decrease of confidence by your existing or potential clients, leading to a loss of future contracts, loss of competitive position, loss of revenue, and the expense of finding and/or training a replacement. The amount and type of insurance will depend upon many factors, as designing an evaluation formula for a key person is difficult.

Proceeds of the key person policy are not subject to income tax generally, but premiums are not a deductible business expense.

11. Shareholders or partners insurance

If it is your intention to have a partnership in your consulting practice or a shareholder in your corporation, you may wish to consider shareholder or partnership insurance. Normally this type of insurance is part of a buy-sell agreement which allows for a deceased shareholder's or partner's interest to be purchased by the surviving partners or shareholders of the corporation.

In the absence of a buy-sell agreement funded by life insurance, the death of a partner could cause the immediate dissolution of the partnership in law. Unless there is an express agreement to the contrary, the surviving partner's duty is to liquidate the business, collect all outstanding accounts, pay off all debts, and account as trustee to the personal representative of the deceased partner for the value of the deceased's interest in the business.

In the case of a corporation, the deceased shareholder's interest would be considered an asset and would go to the beneficiary outlined in the will if a will existed. Naturally, the introduction of a new shareholder who owns an interest in the company, especially a majority interest could have a very traumatic effect on the shareholders and the company's continued operation.

In summary, the procedure is that each partner shareholder applies for a life insurance policy on the life of the other. The applicant is the beneficiary and pays the premiums on his or her partner's life insurance policy. When a partner dies, the funds from the insurance are received tax free by the beneficiary (the partner). These funds are then used to purchase the deceased partner's share of the business. The surviving partner retains control of the business, and the heirs of the deceased get cash for their interest.

12. Business loan insurance

In many cases your lender will be able to provide you with insurance coverage for the outstanding amount of your loan and then incorporate the premium payments into the loan. In the event of your death, the outstanding balance of your loan is paid off.

13. Term life insurance

This type of insurance insures a person for a specific period of time and then terminates. The most common period is five years. If the insured dies within the term of the policy, the insurance company pays the full face amount to the heirs. The costs of premiums are based on life expectancy for the person's age during the five-year period. Term life does not have a cash or loan value.

Because term life insurance can be written for various time periods, and because of inexpensive premiums, it is valuable to the businessperson. Such term policies are often used to provide collateral security for loans to the firm or for personal obligations. There is generally a reduced rate of approximately 10% for non-smokers.

It is highly advisable to have term insurance in the amount of at least your personal financial obligations and business financial obligations for which you have a direct or contingent liability. This area is frequently overlooked.

14. Medical insurance

It is important to take out sufficient medical coverage for your needs. If you are doing any consulting assignments outside the country, you should have extended coverage that pays for medical bills that may be incurred by injury or illness while you are out of the country.

15. Group insurance

You may be eligible for group insurance rates if you have four or more employees. The policies of insurance companies vary, but medical and dental plans are available for small groups.

16. Workers' compensation insurance

If you have a number of employees, you should make certain that you are covered by workers' compensation insurance if you are eligible. With this coverage, the insurer pays all costs that the employer is required to pay for any injury to the employee. The insurer also covers the employees for all benefits and compensations required by the appropriate laws.

If you have failed to pay your employer's portion of the insurance coverage, or have failed to meet your responsibilities adequately to your employees in terms of safety, is is possible that you as the employer could be held liable for any injury to the employee as determined by the common law as well as under workers' compensation laws. Employee coverage and the extent of the employer's liability vary considerably.

11

PROFESSIONAL LIABILITY

Consultants have the same degree of potential for law suits against them as other professionals, such as physicians, accountants, and lawyers do. The claims made against the consultant could be that the consultant was responsible for a wrongful act or omission or professional misjudgment. Professional liability claims may be brought by the client or by third parties, such as investors, creditors or lenders.

If the consultant is doing business as a proprietorship or partnership, liability extends to the consultant personally. It may also extend to the consultant's estate after death. Liability can also extend to persons who were the consultant's partners at the time of the alleged negligence. Claims may be made by the client long after the error or omission occurred. The statute of limitations in many jurisdictions will not begin until the claimant discovers or should have discovered, or knows or has reason to know of your alleged mistake.

As a consultant, you must weigh the degree of risk involved in your specific area of practice. Obtain expert legal and insurance advice about the proper methods of protecting yourself.

a. CONTRACT AND TORT LIABILITY

It is not uncommon for a consultant to be sued for both breach of contract and tort liability.

1. Contract liability

A claim made against a consultant by a client could be based on the allegation that the consultant failed to perform the services described in the contract in a reasonable and prudent manner. This liability involves only those who are parties to the contract, and it applies whether there is a verbal contract, implied contract or written contract.

For the client to succeed in the claim against the consultant, all of the following elements must be proven:

- There was a valid contract between the client and the consultant. This contract, as mentioned earlier, could be verbal or in writing.

- The consultant materially failed to perform his or her obligations under the contract.

- The client suffered damages as a result of the consultant's breach of obligation.

In actions brought under a breach of contract, it is irrelevant in most jurisdictions whether the consultant's breach was innocent, negligent or willful. The client need only prove that a material breach of contract occurred and that damages resulted. There are, of course, numerous defenses a consultant can raise depending on the particular circumstances. The amount of monies assessed against the consultant would be an attempt to restore the client to the position held if the contract had not been breached.

A consultant can be sued for breach of contract, for example, if the precise duties and responsibilities or services required under the contract were not met exactly as detailed in the contract. This is a good reason to make certain that a contract is written, not verbal. In a verbal contract it is difficult to establish exactly what the terms of the agreement were.

Another example is a consultant who signed a fixed price contract for a service to be provided by a certain date. If the consultant miscalculated the fixed price and abandoned the project before it was completed, he or she could be sued. This is not uncommon among new consultants unfamiliar with the skill required in preparing a fixed price proposal.

2. Tort liability

Tort liability is a violation of civil law rather than a breach of contract. Liability in tort is incurred toward the public at large. Any third party who has suffered through the direct or indirect actions of the consultant can make a claim against the consultant even if no contract existed with the consultant and the claimant had never met the consultant. For example, if a consultant submits a report with recommendations to a client and the client follows the recommendations, expends a large sum of money and subsequently loses the money, the clients creditors and investors and lenders could attempt to sue the consultant for losses suffered (damages) due to negligent advice of the consultant. It would have to be shown that the consultant knew or reasonably should have known that others would be seeing the report with recommendations, and they would be relying on that report before investing or lending money.

For the claimant to succeed in a claim against the consultant, all the following elements must be proven:

- The consultant owed the claimant a duty of care.

- The duty or standard of care was breached.

- Measureable damages resulted from the breach.

- There was a direct connection between the breach of duty and the damages that occurred.

In a suit based on tort, evidence introduced into court must establish that the consultant departed from the local custom and standard of practice. If a consultant is found to be negligent, the court will attempt to compensate the claimant for the damages incurred.

b. REASONS FOR CLAIMS

1. Counterclaims

In many instances when a consultant sues a client to collect overdue fees, the client will counterclaim. The client may have a valid reason for not paying the fee, but very often the countersuit is intended to create delay and act as a leverage mechanism for settlement.

2. Conflict of interest

A consultant could be liable if it can be shown that the consultant had a vested interest in the outcome of the recommendations. For example, a client requests a computer consultant to review existing hardware and make recommendations for replacement. The consultant recommends replacement equipment. At some later point the client learns that the consultant received a kick-back from the distributor of the product line for recommending a very large order. The client could sue the consultant for the undisclosed profit; and, if it could be shown that the recommended hardware system was not the appropriate system in the circumstances, additional liability on the consultant's part could be present.

3. Conflicting interest of clients

A consultant could be working for two clients who are in competition with each other. If it can be shown that confidential information was disclosed or the benefits of assistance to one client was at the expense of the other client, then possible liability of the consultant could be present.

4. Delegation of part of contract to employee or sub-consultant

The primary consultant is responsible for the work of employees or agents under the primary consultant's control. If the client maintains that the consulting work was not done, or not done properly by the employee or sub-consultant, legal action can be taken against the primary consultant.

5. Third party damages

If a third party such as a creditor, investor or lender suffers damages as a consequence of the recommendations of the consultant to a second party, a third party can sue in tort.

6. Unclear expectations by client

It is possible that a client has unclear or unrealistic expectations of the work to be performed by the consultant and the benefit to the client. This lack of clarity can be a basis for dispute if the performance was not perceived to be related to expectations.

c. HOW TO AVOID PROFESSIONAL LIABILITY AND PREVENT LOSSES

Although the possibility of being exposed to legal liability cannot be totally prevented, it can be substantially minimized by implementing effective administrative systems and procedures.

Many professionals concentrate on the technical aspects of their profession. Good management is equally important. Consideration must be given to proper staffing, training, credit and collection, and office procedures, such as keeping diaries, checklists and properly written records of every aspect and phase of the consulting business. As well, it is important to stay within the limits of your training, experience, and expertise. Do not take on work that is beyond your capability.

Some good management techniques that can help keep you out of trouble are discussed here.

1. Client control

Clients who habitually try to avoid paying fees by claiming that errors have been made, or clients who frequently resort to litigation can be costly for your business. Make sure that you have control over the areas for which you are responsible. In other words, do not assume responsibility for matters that your clients control.

You should implement a pre-screening process to select clients. Ways of pre-screening are covered in chapter 16.

2. Cost estimates

Avoid giving firm cost estimates for activities arising from your services if possible. Depending upon the type of consulting practice you have, you could be locked into a situation where a fixed cost has been given and the project suffers an overrun. Architects and engineers especially should avoid giving firm billing cost estimates.

3. Carefully drafted contracts

It is most important that a consultant operate with written contracts with clients. The contracts should be drafted carefully and based on competent legal advice. Contract ambiguities and misunderstandings are a major source of professional liability claims. Letters of understanding or contracts should be sent out to the client for acknowledgment and signature and returned by the client.

4. Free opinions

Be careful not to provide free opinions without knowing all the facts. You could be put in a position of being liable, even though you were not officially retained and had not received any fees. If it can be shown that someone relied on your advice and subsequently suffered because of your advice, you could be held liable.

5. Law

Make sure you understand the law pertaining to your specific work in the jurisdiction where the law would be interpreted. For example, if you are performing consulting assignments outside your home jurisdiction, different laws may apply that could create problems for you.

6. Sub-consultants

Sub-consultants should be carefully selected. Check to see that they carry adequate professional liability insurance. Make sure your insurance covers any work performed by a sub-consultant.

7. Records, systems, and procedures

Effective systems for your files, records, billing and office procedures are essential for any business. See chapter 8 for specific ideas on how to keep your records straight.

8. Continuing education

It is important that the consultant develop more expertise and training on an ongoing basis through various professional development and continuing education courses. This shows a professional attitude and desire for knowledge and current information.

9. Quality control

The consultant should set up some system for monitoring the activities and performance of employees or sub-consultants. If a system is in place, this will show that you have developed a high standard of care in the operation of your business.

10. Communication

Effective communication helps eliminate many client problems. This topic is covered in chapter 16.

d. PROFESSIONAL LIABILITY INSURANCE

The procedures outlined in the previous section, if implemented, should substantially reduce the risk of professional liability. However, professional liability insurance is necessary since the risk cannot be completely removed. Professional liability coverage should indemnify the consultant for losses and costs involved in the defense of claims.

The liability insurance coverage is limited to claims "arising out of the performance of professional services" including errors, omissions and negligent acts. If you provide a service outside the specified designation for your specialty, the insurance coverage could be voided.

There are two types of professional liability insurance coverage — claims made and occurrence. A claims made policy insures only against claims made during the policy period. Occurrence coverage provides protection against claims occurring during the policy period, even if the claims arise long after the occurrence and the policy period.

There are many provisions in the policy that should be thoroughly explained, and if you are not completely satisfied, alternative coverage should be considered. The seven most important factors that have to be reviewed in selecting or analyzing a professional liability insurance coverage are:

(a) Declarations

(b) Exclusions

(c) Insuring agreements

(d) Definitions

(e) Limits of liability

(f) Deductibles

(g) Policy conditions

Your premiums can be reduced in a variety of ways, some of which are discussed here.

1. Increase deductibles

The greater the deductible, the less expensive the policy premium should be. Check to see if the policy deductible applies to each separate claim or just once a year.

2. Comparing prices

There is competition in the marketplace for professional liability coverage. Make certain that the reduced premium presented to you does not reflect less attractive provisions in the policy that you may not understand. Professional advice should again be obtained from independent sources to satisfy yourself as to the nature of the coverage that you are getting. It is a prudent investment to have a lawyer who specializes in insurance law, review the proposed insurance terms and conditions.

3. Changing the type of coverage

Claims made policies are generally less costly than occurrence policies. The reason, as discussed earlier, is because the claims made policy covers just claims made during the policy term. The risk therefore to the insurance company is reduced compared to occurrence coverage.

In occurrence coverage the risk of the insurance company is considerable as a claim can be made against the insurance company many years after the negligence occurred and after your policy expired. The cost of settling a claim long after the event could be much higher than a settlement today. It is this risk and uncertainty on the part of the insurance company that is passed on to you in the form of higher premiums for occurrence coverage.

e. PRACTICING WITHOUT INSURANCE

Some consultants choose to conduct their business without any professional liability insurance. If the degree of exposure and risk is very low, this might be a viable alternative. If the consultant has very few personal assets and is effectively judgment proof, then personal bankruptcy may be an alternative in the most extreme circumstances if a claim is made.

Incorporating a company and conducting the consulting practice through the company should add some protection in a law suit if the company lacks any assets. The danger of operating a consulting business that has a risk element but no professional liability insurance is the uncertainty if problems occur. A client or third party could sue the consultant personally as well as the corporation and, until the trial, you would not know what the outcome would be. In the meantime you would have to incur the costs and pressure of the process. In other words, conducting a business through a corporation is not an automatic guarantee of personal protection. The other uncertainty is the nature and amount of damages that your advice caused your client or third parties. It may be very difficult to project at the time you are conducting a consulting assignment what the financial damages could be if your advice is in error.

If you do intend to practice without professional liability insurance, it is most important that you receive expert legal advice to maximize your protection in advance.

12

CREDIT, BILLING, AND COLLECTION

Many consultants starting out in businesses are more interested in performing their skilled service than developing a clear credit billing and collection policy. In many cases a consultant has had no previous business experience and does not realize the pitfalls that can occur.

A system rigidly followed is essential to your survival. It does not take many bad debts to completely eliminate the profit of the business for the whole year. In more serious cases, you could go out of business if a substantial debt owing by a client is not paid.

A number of common mistakes occur with beginning consultants. First, the consultant, wanting to build up a clientele and reputation as quickly as possible, takes on many clients, performs the service and incurs expenses, but allows the client to defer payment. Second, the new consultant may be too busy or too inexperienced to monitor receivables carefully. Third, unpaid bills are not followed up quickly with appropriate steps to collect funds. The effect of this sloppy approach can be disastrous.

This chapter outlines the pitfalls to be aware of and the procedures to adopt when reviewing your collection policy. If you develop the correct system for your needs, it will enhance your cash flow and profit and minimize stress, client problems, and bad debts.

a. DISADVANTAGES OF EXTENDING CREDIT

When you extend credit, the understanding is that the client intends to pay, is capable of paying, and that nothing will occur to prevent the client from paying. You assume that most clients are honest and acting with goodwill and in good faith. Many of these assumptions may not be accurate.

There are a number of potential disadvantages to extending credit.

Extending credit may take a great deal of your time, and the administrative paperwork — checking references, monitoring and following up on slow paying clients — may be tedious.

The expense of credit checking and collection could be more than you wish or are able to pay. Expenses could consist of credit reporting agency fees and memberships, collection costs, legal fees, and time lost that you could otherwise spend generating revenue.

You will need to increase your working capital requirements to keep your business in operation because receivables from your clients may or may not be paid when you expect or need it. You will be paying interest on the additional working capital that you may have to borrow to offset your decreased working capital.

b. ASSESSING THE CLIENT

It is important to be very careful about extending credit. Apply the following general guidelines to your business.

(a) Develop a clear credit policy for your business after consultation with your accountant and lawyer. Experienced professional advice is essential before you extend credit.

(b) Develop a credit application information sheet that has all the necessary information for your files.

(c) Consider joining a credit bureau as well as a credit reporting agency such as Dun and Bradstreet. Check into the past debt payment profile of your potential client in advance.

(d) Obtain references from your client if appropriate, and check the references. Ask about the client's length of time in business.

(e) Ask the client if consultants have been used before and the method of payment that was negotiated.

(f) Consider carefully the amount of credit being extended. The greater amount of money unpaid, the greater the risk for you.

(g) If the work you do is highly specialized, and you have very little competition, you have a lot of leverage in the nature of credit that you would be extending.

(h) If the client is a large institution or government, ask about the customary length of time for accounts rendered to be paid. Specify in your contract the exact terms of payment; government payments in particular can be delayed by bureaucracy for two or three months or longer.

(i) If the client requests deferred fees, you run a risk of default or other problems. Sometimes clients request a deferment of fees or payment because it is a large project, the client is suffering cash flow difficulties, or other considerations. If you are faced with a decision about deferral of fees, you should consider charging interest on the total amount, charging higher fees, requesting a sizeable retainer fee before you start the project, or obtaining collateral to protect yourself if your total fees are substantial.

(j) Consider the future benefit of a relationship with the prospective client. If there is a possibility of future contracts or sources of contacts with other prospective clients, you may wish to weigh the benefits against the risks.

c. AVOIDING CLIENT MISUNDERSTANDINGS ON FEES

Communication is vital to minimize client misunderstanding on fees. Many consultants feel uncomfortable discussing money matters during the first interview with the client. Or sometimes consultants become so involved in the client's problem that the fee is not discussed. It is important that the amount of money you expect is understood and agreed upon by the client before you commence work.

Three ways to eliminate misunderstanding on the issue of services performed for fees are through communication, written contract, and invoice.

1. Communication

Communication is a critical element to a satisfactory client relationship. It is important that the subject of fees be discussed openly at the time of the initial interview and resolved so that the client feels satisfied with the final bargain. Ask potential clients if they have hired consultants in the past, and the nature of the contract relationship that existed.

The interview should be followed by a letter of confirmation outlining the essence of the discussion about fees, among other matters. Progress reports should be sent to the client from time to time if the circumstances warrant it; copies of correspondence concerning the client should be sent to the client. If appropriate, try to involve the client with the project in some way so he or she feels a bonding to you in the project, and sees and appreciates the work you are doing on an ongoing basis. This should minimize the risk of a client disputing your fees for services.

2. Written contract

A written contract must be signed before work is commenced. The contract can take various forms as outlined later in chapter 18. Basically, a letter of agreement or formal contract explains the nature of fees involved and the method of payment — whether it is payment upon receipt, net 10 days or net 30 days.

Be very wary about financing a client; if at all possible, have payment upon receipt. This should assist your cash flow and minimize risk of late payments. The contract should also state the interest that will be added to the outstanding debt if it is not paid within the terms of the contract. The contract should spell out in detail the exact services that you will be performing for the fee.

In certain circumstances a stop work clause could be inserted in the agreement to the effect that if payment is not made within the terms of the contract that, at the option of the consultant, all work will stop.

Finally, the contract must be signed by the client decision-maker in authority. It is preferable that this individual be the same person with whom you negotiated the contract.

3. Invoice

To minimize misunderstanding on invoiced amounts, it is advisable to provide a detailed breakdown of the charges for services and expenses for the particular phase of the contract. If appropriate, reference should be made on the invoice to the contract agreement on fee structure and method of payment.

d. MINIMIZING RISK OF BAD DEBTS

There are several effective techniques to minimize the risk of bad debts. As discussed previously, most consultants cannot afford to have one or two non-paying clients without seriously affecting the viability of the business. The following general guidelines may not all be appropriate in a given client situation. Your judgment in each individual situation must dictate the appropriate approach.

1. Advance retainer

A client can be asked to pay a retainer or deposit of 10 to 25% or more of the total contract amount prior to the work being performed. This can be justified on the basis that you are very busy, and if you are going to schedule in a commitment to that client, it is your policy to require a advance commitment retainer.

This is also an effective technique for a potentially high risk client who has a reputation for non-payment or late payment, or who constantly argues about bills. This approach can also be considered when dealing with a new client who has not used consultants before.

2. Pre-paid disbursements

Depending upon the length of the job and the type of client, you may wish to request pre-paid disbursements if the disbursements are going to be sizable. You do not want to carry the client for out-of-pocket expenses at the risk of your own cash flow. You also do not want to run the risk of a non-payment or dispute of the overall account. As mentioned earlier, it is one thing to lose your time, it is another thing to also be out-of-pocket your own funds.

3. Progress payments

It is common for consultants to request funds by means of invoicing at specific points in the project. The stages at which progress payments are to be paid would be outlined in the contract.

4. Regular billing

Statements can be sent out on a weekly or monthly basis, depending on the circumstances. It is important to outline in the contract, if appropriate, your policy on the timing of billings. That way the client will not be taken by surprise. This also provides you with the advantage of knowing at an early stage in the consulting project if the client is going to dispute your fees, and at this point you can either resolve the problem or discontinue your services. It can be very risky to allow substantial work to be performed before rendering an account, or waiting until the end of the project.

5. Billing on time

Generally a client's appreciation for the value of your services diminishes over time. This is a common problem. It is important, therefore, to send your bill while the client can see the benefit of the service you have provided. Present your final bill at the completion of the project.

6. Accelerated billing

If you sense that the client may have problems paying the bill or other factors cause you concern, accelerate your normal billing pattern. You want to receive payment on your account before difficulties can appear.

The risk of rendering an account that states "net 30 days" is that the client is not legally overdue in payment to you until after 30 days. If you become aware of client financial problems, it is difficult to commence legal action or garnishee before the 30-day period has expired.

7. Withholding vital information

If you have documents, records, reports, and other material related to the client and the project, you may feel it appropriate, if circumstances warrant, to withhold returning all the necessary material to the client until your account has been paid, or other appropriate arrangements made.

8. Holding up completion of important stage of project

If client problems occur, you may wish to stop providing your services and resources at a critical stage until the matter has been resolved to your satisfaction.

9. Personal guarantee of principals of a corporation

Depending on the project and client, you may want to have the principals behind a corporation sign a formal contract as personal guarantors. Another variation is to have the contract in the name of the corporation and its principals as co-covenantors of the contract.

10. Monitor payment trends of clients

Record and monitor the payment patterns of clients so you can watch for trends that may place your fees at risk.

11. Follow-up of late payments

If you see an invoice is more than a week or 10 days overdue, begin the various steps of your collection system immediately.

12. Involving client in assignment

As mentioned previously, try to involve the client in some fashion during each step of the project. By making your client aware of your services, benefits, time and skill, you should minimize problems that could occur because of an unbonded or remote relationship.

e. BILLING FOR SERVICES

Billing requires a system that is carefully designed and effective. It is important to have a third party review your billing procedures before you open your business. Examine your billing procedures on an ongoing basis, especially during the first year, to make sure they are effective. This also gives you an opportunity to review your fee arrangements to make sure you are bringing in the appropriate cash flow for the time you are spending. As mentioned previously, it is important to monitor each client's file to see general trends in your client billing patterns.

Proper records must be maintained that detail the time and expenses incurred so that the bill can be prepared at the appropriate time. You should have an established procedure for regular billing so outstanding accounts are rendered on a regular basis, thereby minimizing collection disputes or bad debts.

When rendering a bill, make sure you send the account either directly to the appropriate person who has the authority to pay your account, or deliver the bill personally to the client. Your style, the client, and the circumstances will determine the most appropriate approach.

You may choose to send a general bill to your client outlining briefly the services performed, the number of hours, the expenses, and the total fee. A note on the bill might say, "detailed particulars are available upon request." See Sample #13 for a general bill and Sample #14 for a detailed bill.

Your bill should be rendered on your consulting firm's stationery showing your name, address, and telephone number. Always use stationery, not a blank piece of paper with your name typed on it. Prepare three copies of the bill. Send the original and a copy to your client and keep a copy for your files.

The wording on your bill should include the following:

(a) The date the bill is mailed

(b) The name and address of the person billed

(c) The phase of the project that has been completed

(d) A detailed outline of the services performed

(e) The consultants or other resource personnel who performed the services

John Smith & Associates

Consultants

123 Main Street
Anytown, Anywhere
(000) 123-4567

Date:
File reference:
Invoice number:
Terms: Net cash

TO: Superior Conglomerate Ltd.
789 Jones Street
Anytown, Anywhere

RE: South Branch Computing System Analysis

PROJECT CONSULTANT: John Smith

For professional services provided between July 15 and July 30, 198-:

Review, analysis and recommendations pertaining to
computing system:

26 hours @ $100 $2,600.00

Direct Expenses:

Photocopies, long distance telephone calls, and
automobile mileage   157.50

TOTAL FEES AND DIRECT EXPENSES DUE UPON RECEIPT $2,757.50

Detailed particulars supplied upon request.

Thank you.

Yours truly,

John Smith & Associates

DETAILED INVOICE

John Smith & Associates

Consultants

123 Main Street
Anytown, Anywhere
(000) 123-4567

Date:

File reference:

Invoice number:

Terms: Net cash

TO: Paul Roberts, President
Superior Conglomerate Ltd.
789 Jones Street
Anytown, Anywhere

RE: South Branch Computing System Analysis

PROJECT CONSULTANT: John Smith

Professional Services:

July 15	Attendance at South Branch site to review operations (4 hours)	$ 400.00	
July 17	Meeting with Mr. Roberts to discuss findings (3 hours)	300.00	
July 19	Attendance at South Branch site to analyze operations (5 hours)	500.00	
July 22	Preparation of report and recommendations (8 hours)	800.00	
July 26	Meeting with Mr. Roberts to review recommendations (3 hours)	300.00	
July 30	Prepare final report of recommendations (5 hours)	500.00	
Total professional services (28 hours @ $100)			$2,800.00

Direct Expenses:

Photocopies of 5 progress reports (400 pages @ 20¢)	80.00
Long distance telephone call of July 20 to Mr. Roberts	17.50
Automobile mileage (200 miles @ 30¢)	60.00

Total Direct Expenses: $ 157.50

TOTAL FEES AND EXPENSES DUE AND PAYABLE
UPON RECEIPT $2,957.50

Thank you.

Yours truly,

John Smith & Associates

(f)   The date services were performed, and the total hours worked

(g)   Total charges for services

(h)   Expense column separated and listed underneath the services column and then totalled

(i)   Total of fees and direct expenses payable by client

(j)   The date charges are due and payable (if appropriate, make a reference to "as per letter of agreement (or contract) dated (month/year)"

(k)   Use "thank you" or some other positive and appreciative closing remark

(l)   Your signature and title

f.   WHY CLIENTS PAY LATE

If you have established appropriate precautionary measures and a credit and billing policy, you should have very few overdue accounts. Overdue accounts will occur, though, in any practice and understanding your options should minimize your problems in this area.

There are several common reasons why a client might be late in paying for consulting services. The client could be indifferent to your deadlines. Some clients have a sloppy attitude about paying accounts due and are accustomed to being pressured or reminded frequently before they finally meet their obligations.

Institutional or government payment procedures sometimes involve a two or three month wait for accounts to be paid. This type of information is easily available by asking the right questions before you begin. Your account may be lost in the maze and require personal attention.

A client may deliberately delay payment in order to save money at your expense. You save the client interest on working capital if he or she can use your money for free. This is why you should have an interest factor for overdue accounts built into your initial contract as well as showing on the statement. If the overdue interest is high enough, that should act as an incentive for the client, to pay on time. If this is in the contract, the client cannot argue that there was no agreement on overdue interest. Rendering a statement with the interest factor noted on it is not in itself evidence of an agreement between the parties on the amount of interest on overdue accounts.

A client may prefer to give priority to other creditors, where pressure to pay is greater.

The client may not have the money. This does not necessarily mean that the client is going out of business, but is cash poor at the moment. The technique to handle this problem is discussed in the next section.

g. COLLECTING LATE PAYMENTS WITHOUT LEGAL ACTION

Because of the expense, time wasted, stress, and uncertainty of legal action, it is preferable to collect as much as you can from clients yourself. Some steps that you may wish to consider are:

(a) Send out a reminder invoice with a courteous comment that the invoice is "overdue and that perhaps it was an oversight or the check is already in the mail."

(b) The alternative to the above is to telephone the accounts payable department or the client directly to ask when the payment can be expected. Courteously ask if there was possibly a misunderstanding, or if they need further information or clarification on any matter. Make sure that you note in the client file the date and time, the person you spoke to at the client's office, a summary of the conversation, and when payment can be expected.

(c) If you have not received payment within a week of the preceeding step, send a letter stating that the account is in arrears and that it is to be paid on the terms of the contract. The alternative is to again telephone the client and ask about the reason for the delay.

(d) Another technique is to ask when the check will be ready. Say that you will be around to pick up the check or will arrange for a courier service to pick it up as soon as they telephone your office to advise that it is ready.

(e) If the client has still not paid, stopping work on the project is another option.

(f) If the client refuses to pay, then legal steps may be required immediately depending upon the size of the bill, the importance of the client, the reasons for non-payment, and the costs of legal action. Alternatively, you may decide to compromise with a client and settle for a reduced payment.

(g) If the client is unable to pay because of cash flow problems or other financial difficulties, you have to assess your options. If the client is not disputing the bill and wishes to have credit, there are basically three options:

- Installment payment plan: the client would agree upon definite dates for payment and would send you the amounts owing upon receipt of statements from you.

- Post-dated checks: you would receive post-dated checks from the client for the agreed period, and in the agreed amount.

- Promissory note: the client would sign a promissory note agreeing to the total amount of the debt and the date on which the debt would be paid. The note should be signed by the principals if the client is a corporation. Interest on the full amount of the debt should be built into the promissory note. It is negotiable whether or not interest is added onto the other two payment plans.

For more ideas and information on debt collection, see *Collection Techniques for the Small Business*, another title in the Self-Counsel series.

h. LEGAL STEPS IF ACCOUNT REMAINS UNPAID

If it is apparent that the client has no intention of paying you, or is objecting to your bill, or is unable to pay you, then legal action must be considered. It is critical that legal action be commenced as quickly as possible after it becomes apparent that you will not be paid by other arrangements. At this stage you are not interested in keeping the client for present or potential future business. You just want to salvage the best of a bad situation. There are basically three legal options available.

1. Collection agency

You may wish to assign the debt to a collection agency for which you will be charged between 25% to 50% of the amount collected. This is better than writing the account off as a total loss. Different agencies have different styles of collection, and one agency may achieve better results with your bad debts than another. If your client pays you directly during the period of the contract with the collection agency, you are obliged to pay the commission to the collection agency. Collection agencies are listed in the yellow pages of the telephone directory.

2. Small claims court

Small claims court is a relatively quick, informal, and inexpensive method of taking your client to court. If you are successful and obtain a judgment against your client, that does not necessarily mean you are going to collect on the judgment. There are additional steps you will have to take, such as garnisheeing the client or filing a judgment against the title of any properties owned by your client. Your client could turn out to be judgment proof.

3. Lawyers

Lawyers can be very effective in the collection of debts if you act promptly and select a lawyer who is experienced in the law and tactics of collecting. Lawyers generally bill on an hourly basis, and the more time expended on attempting to collect a debt, the more money it will cost you without any assurance that you will be successful at trial. If you are successful at trial and do obtain a judgment, your client could be bankrupt or judgment proof in terms of assets. As mentioned previously, the litigation process can be very protracted, uncertain, stressful, and expensive.

i. BAD DEBTS AND TAXES

Keep an accurate record of any bad debt accounts and the procedures you went through to attempt to collect. Generally you will be allowed to deduct bad debts from your other income, but this is a matter that should be discussed with your accountant as the laws and circumstances can vary.

13

SETTING FEES

There are many ways to set fees: by the hour, by the day, by the month or by the project. The most common fee arrangements (approximately 85% of them) are a daily rate (per diem), fixed price, and fixed price plus expenses.

This chapter discusses in detail how to determine the fee structure most appropriate for your situation and how to give an accurate quote to a prospective client.

a.   DAILY BILLING RATE (PER DIEM)

The daily billing rate has three components: labor, overhead, and profit.

1. Labor

The labor daily rate is obtained by taking the average of your most recent annual salary, your current annual salary, a recent job offer annual salary or the prevailing annual salaries in the marketplace for your type of work, and dividing the number by 261. The number 261 is the number of days in the year excluding weekends. For example, if your annual salary is $46,800, the daily labor rate is $46,800 divided by 261 days, equalling $180.

2. Overhead

Before calculating your daily overhead rate, it is important to understand a number of concepts pertaining to overhead and daily billing.

(a) Fixed and variable expenses

Fixed expenses are those expenses for overhead that are constant and do not change based on your volume of workload. Variable expenses are expenses that can change based on volume of workload; they include extra secretarial time to administer various aspects of your office operation, additional postage for promotional or marketing purposes, additional phone calls for promotional or marketing purposes, etc.

(b) Indirect and direct expenses

Indirect expenses are expenses you incur as overhead and the cost of doing business, and are not directly attributable to a specific client. Direct expenses are

111

expenses incurred on behalf of a specific client, and are charged directly to that particular client. These expenses can vary considerably from one consulting project to another. Some examples of direct expenses frequently encountered in consulting are:

- Computer time
- Printing and photocopying
- Postage
- Other consultant's time
- Long distance telephone calls
- Out of town living expenses such as meals, lodging, tips, etc.
- Air travel
- Car rental
- Parking and tolls

When quoting a daily rate, it is a common practice to state "plus expenses" after the daily rate. This includes all the direct expenses that have been outlined, plus any other direct expenses you might incur. If you are quoting your fee on a fixed price basis, direct expenses are incorporated within your estimate cost sheet.

(c) Calculation of overhead

Sample #2 in chapter 3 gave a checklist for determining your monthly overhead. Multiply that figure by 12 to get your annual overhead for the purpose of these calculations. Divide that figure by 168 to get your daily overhead. The number 168 represents the average number of billable days per year you have available. Although there are approximately 21 days a month of potential billable days, the norm is that one-third of that time is used for such non-billable functions such as vacation, sick leave, professional development, administration of the practice, and marketing. Studies have shown that approximately 15 to 20% of an experienced consultant's time is spent on developing and implementing various marketing plans.

The overhead rate is expressed as a per cent of your labor rate by dividing your daily rate for labor by your daily rate for overhead. For example, if $180 is your daily labor rate and your daily overhead rate is $130, the per cent factor is 72.2%, rounded out to 72%. This percent is a guide to the efficiency of your practice as well as a factor you would use for the overhead estimate in a fixed price contract.

3. Profit

Profit is the reason you are in business. It is your reward for taking business risks and the responsibility and pressures of ownership. It is above and beyond your salary for labor. Profit for consultants generally ranges from 10 to 30% of your salary, plus benefits, plus overhead. The amount of profit you decide to build in will depend on many factors, including your expertise, the demand for your services, and the competition in the marketplace.

To calculate your daily billing rate (or per diem), the formula is as follows:

Daily labor rate	$180.00
Daily overhead rate	130.00
Total daily cost	310.00
Profit (15% of $310)	<u>46.50</u>
Total daily billing rate	$356.50
(Rounded out to next highest $25)	$375.00

It is usual for consultants to calculate their daily or hourly billing rate rounded out to the next highest $25 amount. Recent studies have shown that the daily billing rates for all types of consultants range between $300 and $1,200 per day with an average of approximately $700 per day. There are many factors that will determine your rate, such as the economy, competition, experience, repeat business possibilities, and your financial needs.

In the example above, the daily billing rate would be quoted at $375.

When calculating per diem time, normally all time spent on the client project is billed out, including all time recorded for phone calls and travel. Your client should be advised in advance in writing that these charges will be passed on as direct costs. Many consultants prefer to charge the client directly for the time expended on travel on an hourly or per diem basis. Other consultants prefer not to charge directly for travel time. They may work on a client's project while travelling and charge out their work to the client as if working in the office. Another approach is to charge a higher billing rate for work the requires travel. For example, if your normal billing rate is $50 per hour, you may charge $65 per hour for work that requires travel, in addition to a minimum rate of a half-day or a full day for travel regardless of how much time is spent. You have to develop guidelines that meet your client's needs as well as your own.

b. HOURLY RATE

The hourly rate is calculated by dividing the daily rate by eight hours. Some consultants divide by seven hours or nine hours, depending upon their style of operation, but the average is eight hours. For example, a daily billing rate of $375.00 divided by 8 is $46.80 or, rounded out to the next highest $25 amount, $50. You quote your fee as $50 per hour.

Most consultants have a minimum number of hours (such as four hours) for any work contracted on an hourly basis. In addition to a minimum number of hours, some consultants prefer to add an extra factor onto the billing rate of 10 to 20% for the inefficiency of this type of fee arrangement. For example, at 20% extra, the hourly billing rate of $50 plus $10 equals $60 per hour. You should also charge travel time in addition to your hourly rate or minimum charge, depending on the circumstances.

c. CALCULATING A FIXED PRICE QUOTATION

1. Determining a fixed price estimate

Another method of quoting fees is to calculate a flat rate for the entire project. To calculate a fixed fee, a number of factors are determined, such as direct labor (that is, the cost of any consultants or secretarial or clerical staff), overhead (which is the per cent you have previously calculated of the total direct labor cost) and all direct expenses related to that specific consulting project.

The last factor in the formula of calculating a fixed rate estimate is the profit factor. In each situation you determine what you believe to be a fair profit for the risk, the time involved, the skill, the competition, your need for the job, and the ongoing work that might arise from this project. The profit is a per cent of the total of the preceeding expenses; that is, direct labor, overhead, and direct expenses. You then have calculated the total fixed price to quote to your client. Normally, your costing sheet is not shown to the client, only the total price. An example of a fixed price costing sheet is shown in Sample #15.

A fixed fee arrangement is often preferred by a client, as the total cost of the project can be budgeted and planned. The risk is the consultant's. If you have a budget overrun, you could lose a lot of money or go out of business. If you are very efficient and accurate in your costing of the fixed price and the management of the project, you could obtain the reward of an underrun which means a higher profit margin.

A fixed fee should only be used when you have effective cost control of the project, and are able to estimate your time and costs with a high degree of accuracy and experience. It is very risky to propose a fixed price contract for projects with which you have little experience, especially if the assignment is a unique or complex one.

If you are very experienced in a certain area, you would probably prefer a fixed price contract due to the efficiency of your mode of operation. In other words, because of your expertise and efficiency, you might not make as much on an hourly per diem basis as you could make by negotiating a fixed price.

2. Tips on preparing fixed price estimates

Because of the risk involved in a fixed price contract, many consultants avoid that type of fee arrangement if possible. In many cases though, a client requires a fixed price because that is their style of operation, or a government contract might be involved which frequently entails a fixed price arrangement. In order to minimize the risk of an overrun, that is, costs exceeding your revenue, and to increase your confidence in the preparation of estimates, the following guidelines are provided:

(a) A precise and specific definition of the project must be obtained. This is either obtained from the client, for example, in government projects where considerable detail is provided for costing purposes; or, the consultant must obtain as much information from the client as required to enable a detailed reconstruction of the entire project requirement. This involves having a checklist of questions that you ask the client to

SAMPLE #15
FIXED PRICE COSTING SHEET

DIRECT LABOR	
Senior consultant (15 days at $300)	$4,500
Senior consultant: B. Smith ($525 per day) 3 × $525	1,575
Junior consultant (7 days at $150)	1,050
Secretarial (12 days at $60)	720
TOTAL DIRECT LABOR	$ 7,845
DIRECT EXPENSES	
Air fares (5 x $191) (3 x $30) (1 x $61)	$1,106
Automobile mileage (550 x .22)	121
Entertainment	375
Postage	190
Printing and photocopying	550
Rental cars	430
Telephone	210
Miscellaneous	470
TOTAL DIRECT EXPENSES	3,452
SUBTOTAL	11,297
PROFIT (15%)	1,695
TOTAL FIXED PRICE	$12,992

ensure you have not forgotten any of the key components of the contract.

(b) It is helpful to draw a functional flow diagram (FFD) showing the interconnecting parts and stages of the project. This could be the same functional flow diagram you include in your proposal, or a less detailed one.

(c) Once you have determined the various skills and roles required of you for the project, list them all in order of sequential priority of the activities or stages. After you have listed each of the areas, do a breakdown of the stages within each of those areas. If you need more detail to assess the amount of time and direct expense, continue breaking down each of the sub-components into the various parts.

(d) Use a bid sheet when pricing a project. Each function of the project should be outlined and the direct labor and direct expense costs allocated.

(e) The advantages of the detailed costing, apart from a higher degree of accuracy, is the ability to be more flexible with your client. For example, if your client rejects your first fixed price proposal as being outside the budget allotted, you could reduce your estimate by reviewing your costing sheet in areas that still allow you to perform the overall project. You maintain your credibility with your client by not discounting your prices because of pressure from the client or your financial need. You are adjusting the price downward as a direct outcome of reducing the expense and time you will be putting into the project.

(f) Before you submit your bid to a client, make sure you have a person experienced in bidding in the area that you are doing your consulting work. Have your detailed costing sheet reviewed to find any areas you may have missed or that could be improved.

d. FIXED PRICE PLUS EXPENSES

A fixed price plus expenses fee arrangement is quite common; it is used when a fixed price is desired by both parties but expenses cannot be calculated with certainty. For example, you may have an estimate for the number of trips required, but there could be factors outside your control which could affect that financial outlay and therefore your costing. You should estimate the direct expenses for the benefit of your client, but the contract would clearly state that the client is responsible for all direct expenses.

e. CONTINGENCY FEE

In a contingency fee arrangement you do not receive any income unless you perform the objective successfully. The normal procedure is that you obtain a percentage of the final benefit that the client receives. For example, if you are skilled at appealing on behalf of a client a property reassessment tax, and you save your client considerable money, then you receive a portion of the saving.

The advantage to the client of this arrangement is the lack of risk — if taxes are not reduced, no fee is paid to the consultant. It is therefore an effective marketing device for clients who would otherwise not want to commit themselves to a consultant. From a consultant's viewpoint, considerable money can be made, much greater than the profit earned under the traditional consulting fee arrangements.

Many professional associations consider contingency fees unethical because of the risk of conflict of interest for the consultant. For example, if a consultant is retained to find a key executive for a client and performs an executive search, the final recommendation could be a biased one to obtain the commission payment.

f. PERCENTAGE FEE

A percentage fee is a common arrangement for engineers and architects on construction projects. Normally a uniform percentage is applied to the cost of the project. Percentage fees are not dependent on a successful result of the performance of a service, which makes them different from contingent fees.

g. PROJECT VALUE FEES

There are times when a consultant has unique and effective skills in a given situation, and thereby saves the client considerable money. The client is usually charged a substantially higher fee than a normal hourly rate. It is not uncommon for lawyers to apply this method. For example, a lawyer, through skill and experience and tactical negotiating techniques, might purchase a business at a considerable savings to the client. The lawyer may have spent only 15 hours at $150 per hour on the file, but saved the client $2 million. Because of the "value" obtained by the client the lawyer charges a substantially higher fee — possibly five or ten times more than the actual time spent.

h. RETAINER FEES

A retainer relationship, involves a consultant being "on call" either for continuing services, or to ensure that he or she is available when needed. The retainer is normally a fixed amount of money paid to the consultant every month. The consultant keeps track of the time spent and a running balance of the account, and bills for any excess. An account is rendered every month for extra time spent over and above the monthly retainer.

Another type of arrangement might involve not submitting additional accounts until the end of the retainer period, at which time any overage would be made up. A third variation could be that you are committed in your retainer arrangement to providing a certain amount of service every month. If you underestimated the amount of the monthly time involved, you would be then paid the extra time per month.

If you have an "on call" arrangement with the client, and therefore you are unable to commit yourself to other projects, the client would pay the fixed amount every month for the privilege of having you on call, whether or not your services were used. This could be whatever you negotiated; for example, 25 to 50% of your average monthly billable time. In addition to the on call retainer, when you perform services for the client you would bill out at your hourly or daily rate, depending upon the nature of your arrangement.

i. EQUITY FEES

If a client is having difficulty in a business venture and you have skills in obtaining financing or business management, a fee could be negotiated in the form of equity or percentage of the shares in the company. This is normally negotiated when the client lacks the financial resources to pay for your time. The risk for the consultant and the business is a high one so the equity arrangement would have to be very attractive to justify the risk, depending upon the situation.

117

The problem with an equity fee arrangement is that it changes your role from a consultant to a part owner. You could lose your ability to be an objective consultant due to your vested interest in the outcome of your advice. It would be prudent, due to potential conflict of interest, to remove yourself from the situation by either selling out your interest once you have received it, or resigning as a consultant.

j. UTILIZATION RATE

The utilization rate tells you how efficient you are; that is, the cost/benefit factor. It tells you the percentage of your total working hours that you bill to clients. To determine the utilization rate, divide the number of billable hours by the number of total working hours available. For example, if you assume a 40-hour work week and allow two weeks' vacation, you would have approximately 2,000 total work hours available each year. If you divide 1,000 hours of billing to clients each year by 2,000 you have 50% utilization rate. If you consult part-time at 12 hours per week and you bill for 4 hours each week, then your utilization rate is 33.3%.

Your utilization rate quickly informs you how much of your time clients are directly paying for and how much you must absorb as overhead. The fewer hours you bill, the more you must charge per hour, or reduce your overhead; the more hours you bill, the less you need to charge to maintain your profit level. You can see how important it is to keep an accurate record of how all your time is spent when operating a consulting practice, so that you can accurately and graphically see how efficiently (or inefficiently) you are operating.

k. VARYING YOUR FEES

The fees you quote a client can vary depending on various factors. As mentioned earlier, you should consider factors as: your experience, the ability of the client to pay, the future benefit of ongoing work the client might provide, your need for cash flow, and the different regional areas for which you are submitting a consulting proposal.

If you are submitting a proposal outside your region, you should check out the cost of doing business in that area. Is it more or less expensive than your own region? Check on your competitors and their rates within the region you are considering. If the local rates are higher, consider raising your rates to meet local schedules. If the rates are lower, consider reducing your rates, but only with a very clear analysis of the benefit and profit. The rates might be too low to be attractive. It is important that you go through these steps, as a prospective client will be able to detect inadequate preparation if your costing does not reflect local variances and customs.

l. INCREASING FEES

From time to time you will want to increase your fees. This could be based on your regular monthly, quarterly or other review of your cash flow statements, profit and loss statements or projected needs. Your utilization rate, as described earlier, is also a factor.

If you are considering increasing fees, it is tactically a good idea to do it at a fixed time every year, such as January 1. You should also attempt to notify your clients at least three months in advance, in writing, of your intention to increase your fees. Include a brief explanation about the reasons, such as an increase in costs, if appropriate. Invite the client to contact you if there are any questions. It is important, for obvious reasons, to keep the increase competitive.

m. INCREASING PROFITS WITHOUT INCREASING FEES

There are many ways you can increase your profits apart from raising fees. Naturally clients are not always going to appreciate your reasons for increasing your fees, so through careful tactics other effective methods could be used to increase your profits. Some methods you may wish to consider are as follows:

- Keep your overall fixed overhead down. Review all the ways of saving costs on space, telephone, and personnel discussed earlier.

- Use company cars, space, and supplies wherever possible.

- Obtain the client's agreement to supply necessary support services such as secretarial and clerical, mail rooms, postage, delivery service, and other support services and personnel. This will keep your administration costs down.

- Obtain approval to charge authorized purchases pertaining to the project to the client.

- Keep an accurate record of all out-of-pocket expenses incurred pertaining to the client's project, document them, and bill for them properly.

- Arrange with the client to pay you in advance for entertainment or travel expenses you anticipate. That way you can use the client's money and provide an accounting for any extra funds.

- If you are consulting on an hourly basis, attempt to arrange to be at your client's office or project for a full day if possible, rather than a portion of the day.

- Transportation costs and time of travel are not always accurately reflected in the adjustments with the client. Naturally you would attempt to spend the minimum number of hours at a higher hourly rate, but these factors may not cover your commuting time.

- Determine a minimum fee requirement. The time and costs of a proposal, and the administrative work required by a project, will dictate a minimum fee and profit before you make a proposal.

- Avoid giving away free consulting. There are techniques to avoid giving away your time, which is worth money. This will increase your effective utilization rate and therefore increase profits. The various ways of avoiding free consulting are covered in chapter 17.

- Increase your rates for work requested outside of regular business hours. A premium fee should be charged for work performed on the weekends or evenings or part of a day. This suggestion also applies when clients ask that their project be given priority over other projects.

- Consider obtaining advance payment on account for projected initial or total disbursements if they are considerable. The deposit can be collecting interest for your benefit. As discussed previously, you should consider negotiating in advance for a sizable deposit if your services are in demand and you are expending time for the client at the expense of other client work you could do.

- Review your credit policy regularly. If you extend credit, make sure your receivables are promptly collected; otherwise you will be paying more interest to the bank on your operating line of credit loan.

- Attempt to minimize bad debts by adopting the various procedures suggested in chapter 12, with modifications for your own situation and after your lawyer's advice. Eliminating bad debts is a very effective way of increasing your profits.

- Consider negotiating a bonus with a client for meeting contract needs. For example. if you complete a project for less than the amount allocated in the budget, you could negotiate a percentage of the saving. If your client has deadline schedules, you could agree to give the project priority, which would involve considerable overtime and other disruptions for you and negotiate a bonus for the number of days you are ahead of the deadline.

- Consider negotiating a "value of the project" fee or a contingency fee arrangement if the circumstances and the nature of your consulting practice make this approach feasible. You could therefore increase your profit without spending additional time by receiving a higher return due to your skill, knowledge of the industry or tactical or negotiating abilities.

14

DETERMINING MARKET OPPORTUNITIES

Before determining market opportunities and identifying clients with accuracy and success, various matters have to be considered.

You have to be very certain in your own mind of your area or areas of specialization. It is impossible to target your market without this basic information. Review the exercises in chapter 2 to determine your specific skills, talents, and attributes, and attempt to visualize the market that was suited to your abilities. It is important to avoid the tendency to be too restrictive in your view of the market for your services. Look for a wide spectrum to apply your services in vertical and horizontal markets and in both the public and private sector. Identify common themes and processes. Know why there is a demand for consulting services, so you can aim your marketing at those concerns when targeting prospective clients.

Thorough research is required to educate yourself and stimulate your mind on the wide range of possibilities. Read selected newspapers, magazines, and trade journals on a regular basis, and look for consulting opportunities created by political, economic, and social changes affecting your area of expertise and interest.

The next chapter discusses marketing techniques in more detail. This chapter is intended to provide a brief overview of the private and public sector markets and the possibility of market opportunities.

a. PRIVATE SECTOR OPPORTUNITIES

There are numerous opportunities in the private sector. By being aware of the issues and problems and solutions in your service area, it will be easier for you to identify and think of opportunities every time you are exposed to information through personal communication, television, radio, newspaper, magazines, trade journals or books. The habit of training yourself to be aware of marketing opportunities at all times is essential.

It is important to understand the motivating factors that will cause a potential client to want your services. You might be very aware of the needs of your service within your specialty area, but a client who does not recognize that your service is needed will not be receptive to your offer of assistance.

There are many reasons that motivate a client to retain a consultant, but three of the basic reasons are: to obtain information, to save time, and to save money. If you can visualize the ways you can save a client time and money, and provide the most current and accurate information in the client's area of interest and need, market opportunities in the private sector will be considerable.

1. Individuals

Individuals buy the services of consultants in a wide variety of fields. A walk through the yellow pages of your telephone directory should provide a good example. Advice on how to save money or how to make money is fairly common. In this instance, the target market is anyone in the higher earning bracket, including executives and professionals. Some examples of consultants in this area are tax consultants, financial consultants, investment consultants, and real estate consultants. Other consulting areas include interior design and fashion.

2. Small businesses

Small businesses provide an excellent client base for a new consultant. The failure rate of small businesses is very high. Lack of knowledge by the small business owner/operator in important areas of small business management is often a factor. If your skills include small business management and how to make money or save money for a small business owner, you can find a market. There are numerous books available on small business management that will provide ideas for you. Some are included in the Bibliography.

Various techniques can be used to attract small business clients. You can offer a fee based on percentage of savings or profits that occur as a result of your advice. Naturally, you would have to have a measurable basis for showing the positive benefits that your advice has created. A percentage fee is a good marketing device. It shows confidence in yourself, and it is a difficult offer to refuse as your payment is based on performance.

Another need of small businesses is to raise funds, either through the venture capital market, commercial banks or government grants and loans. Most small businesses go through growing pains. Wherever business growth occurs, problems occur, and wherever problems occur, a need exists for solutions.

3. Medium size businesses

There is a high demand for consultants in medium size businesses. Companies often hire experts as required instead of hiring staff. Staff involves the related costs of training, benefit packages, and long-term commitments for possibly short-term needs. Businesses are vulnerable to economic changes, and their survival is based on keeping overheads low and making a profit. Any areas of need you can identify to increase efficiency and productivity and sales, and decrease overhead and losses will create a demand for your services.

Medium size businesses, as well, are constantly going through various stages of growth with all the predictable problems involved.

The advantage of dealing with a medium size business is that projects tend to be more lucrative. There is also a greater chance of repeat business. Another advantage is that the decision-makers are generally more sophisticated, better able to see the need more readily, more accustomed to dealing with consultants, and able to respond more quickly on proposals.

122

4. Large companies

It is more difficult to obtain contracts from larger companies. Many large companies prefer dealing with large consulting firms or well-known consultants with considerable experience and contacts.

Because of the money available in larger businesses, consulting opportunities do exist, particularly in the area of temporary technical assistance. It is common for consultants to large companies to have developed their experience and confidence with smaller companies and medium size companies before marketing the larger companies.

b. PUBLIC SECTOR

Government is a major user of consulting services. Marketing opportunities are available in various forms in the public sector. You can submit a solicited or unsolicited proposal and attempt to get the contract directly. You can indirectly benefit from government by sub-contracting with other companies who have been awarded the main contract. An additional way of making money through government is as a grants consultant assisting organizations or businesses to obtain grants or subsidies.

If you are considering government as a source of business, you should be aware of the various ways of obtaining contacts or information to assist you. You should also have an understanding of the way the government approval system operates.

1. Making contacts and obtaining information

There are various steps you can take to obtain the necessary information and make the necessary contacts to assist you in your government dealings.

(a) Read government advertisements and publications pertaining to your areas of interest. Appendix 1 is an extensive summary of Canadian and U.S. government sources of information.

(b) Place your name on the government mailing list. There are numerous government departments and you can request that your name be placed on each list to receive all relevant information, including proposed procurements and contracts awarded relating to your field.

(c) Attempt to have your name placed on the government sourcing list as a consultant in various specialty areas. When the government is looking, your name should come to their attention. There are various computerized sourcing lists throughout the departments of government; make sure that your name is on all the ones that relate to your areas of interest.

(d) Contact government contract officers. Most government contracts are awarded at the department or agency level where the specific needs are best known and money has been allocated. The phone book has listings for various branches of government. The public library has updated lists of all the key government departments, individuals, their titles and phone numbers. Once you have obtained the correct department, ask to speak to the contract officer who can provide you with further background.

(e) Visit government departments and agencies. After you have submitted your resume to various government departments, you may wish to meet the person in charge of contracts approval and introduce yourself. This may or may not be appropriate or possible, depending on your geographic location and government policy. Keeping contact with the key person who could award a contract shows your interest in keeping your name current. It also demonstrates initiative and confidence. On the other hand, it could cause irritation or you could have a personality conflict.

(f) Contact large consulting firms that are the recipients of government contracts and require additional consulting assistance for those contracts.

(g) Contact other companies that have recently received a government contract. You can obtain government award publications, or view them in the public library. These are published weekly and announce all the contracts that have been awarded, who received the contract, and the amount and nature of the services to be performed. With this information, you can determine what sub-contracting opportunities might be available in your area of specialty, and immediately contact the companies concerned.

(h) If you have friends or acquaintances who work in government, tell them you are looking for consulting assignments in your specialty. You should also provide them with your resume and brochure if possible. They might be in a position to inform you if they hear of an agency in need of your services. You might therefore hear of a need before the department has advertised for services or selected a consultant. You can then submit an unsolicited proposal.

2. Understanding the government approval system

The government approval system is very formal and bureaucratic in its operation. Most government contracts are from solicited proposals, whereas in the private sector, submitting an unsolicited proposal is the most common method. The general procedure for government approval is given below. The procedure is the same for any level of government (i.e., municipal, state/provincial, federal).

(a) A government department head or agency requiring consulting service assigns personnel to an internal search to see if the service can be performed in-house.

(b) If no civil service employee is available to perform the work, a request for proposal is advertised, proposals are received, and the consultant is eventually selected. It is quite common that consultants are "pre-selected" before the closing date of the advertisement. This is because the consultant may already be on the source list and be known as best suited for the project. The advertisement is a required government formality.

(c) The government department drafts a contract and submits it to the consultant for review and signature.

(d) The signed contract is reviewed and approved again by the government's legal department.

(e) A contract is forwarded to the chief administrative officer of the division for approval.

(f) The contract and specifications are forwarded to a government purchaser for approval.

(g) The contract and fee schedule are forwarded to the government controller to verify that funds are available and have been set aside to honor the payment commitment.

(h) Notification of formal approval is sent to the consultant to begin the consulting services within the terms of the contract.

(i) Work begins and is completed.

(j) Payment is received at the end of the project or throughout the project, depending on the terms of the contract. Many government departments are slow in paying due to their bureaucratic nature and requirements within the system for approval before payment. As this may cause cash flow difficulties for you, you should make arrangements for progress payments if at all possible. If necessary you can get a bank loan for your cash flow needs based on the strength of a government contract.

c. GRANT CONSULTING

A grants consultant attempts to obtain grants, loans or subsidies for a client. The federal government and its various agencies award large sums of money to eligible applicants. The process followed by a grants consultant is as follows:

(a) The consultant learns as much as possible about the sources of funding, the amount of funding, the procedures required, and the key contact people. The consultant contacts the approval officer and obtains information on the appropriate or desired detail and format for successful applications.

(b) The consultant determines the potential target market and the names of the firms and individuals who could be future contacts.

(c) A personal letter with brochures is sent to the key people, followed by a telephone call and meeting, if possible.

(d) The consultant identifies the specific needs of the organization or company in the interview process. The interview process is similar to that described in chapter 16.

(e) The consultant advises the organization of the availability of government funds, and the consultant's expertise in obtaining them. Most organizations and businesses do not have people who realize that money is available or know how to effectively submit an application to obtain it. The consultant performs the analysis and all the necessary detail for documentation, and prepares the application for signature by an authorized representative of the organization or company.

(f) The consultant normally takes an administration fee which is a negotiated percentage of the amount awarded. The client therefore has an incentive to deal with the consultant, because the consultant's fee is based on performance only and paid from the funds received.

(g) The consultant could also be responsible for coordinating the implementation of the program on which the funding was based, if applicable.

(h) Once a grants consultant has succeeded with one group, marketing to all other organizations similar to that group can be effectively performed.

See Appendix 3 for a list of publications available on current government funding.

15

MARKETING YOUR CONSULTING SERVICES

a. INTRODUCTION

Marketing is an essential process for success in the consulting business. Marketing is a process that involves a wide spectrum of activities, ultimately directed at convincing prospective clients that their needs can be met and their problems can be solved through your specific services. Marketing is the stimulus that creates an awareness and demand for your services. Selling is a part of the marketing program. It is intended to result in a consulting assignment by means of personal interaction begun at the initial interview and maintained during and after the assignment.

The dynamics of the marketing/selling stages have to be clearly understood and carefully cultivated by the consultant. For example, when you are marketing yourself, you have to carefully calculate the image that you want to project when you are packaging your product, that is, yourself, and your services. You and your marketing efforts must project authority, confidence, friendliness, candor, expertise, competence, and leadership.

Many consultants fail, or maintain a marginal income because of poor marketing. Consultants frequently do not appreciate the necessity of marketing, do not know how to market, do not like to market, do not want to market or do not take the time to market.

This chapter will help you understand the various techniques required to build your image as an expert or authority, thereby creating a demand for your services. The next chapter will cover some of the personal selling techniques involved in the first interview. Once your marketing plan has stimulated the interest, the next step is to close the contract.

b. MARKETING PLAN

A summary of the factors that go into your marketing plan follows:

(a) Define your skills and services. This is covered in chapter 2. You should have a clear idea now of the nature of services you will be offering potential clients. You may have decided on just one particular area of interest and specialty, or you may have decided on several areas that you will promote as unique areas, either to the same client or to different categories of clients.

(b) Targeting prospective clients. Identifying possible client consulting opportunities is the next step in the marketing plan. This was covered in the last chapter.

(c) Make the public and potential clients aware of your services and create a demand. The various techniques required for this step are covered in the next section.

(d) Respond to inquiries with direct client meeting. Naturally, once interest has been shown by a prospective client due to your effective marketing, your next step is to quickly follow up on the lead, personally see the client, if possible, attempt to ascertain the client's precise needs and determine how to remedy the problem.

(e) Prepare a proposal. This step follows the preceeding one, confirms the client meeting and outlines what you intend to do, how, for how much, and when. You can only write a convincing proposal after you have had an opportunity to ascertain the client's needs and the benefits that you can provide.

(f) Perform the project. This is the purpose of the whole marketing exercise — to end up with a client so you can provide your service, generate revenue, and make a profit.

(g) Follow-up is the final step in the marketing plan. If you did not obtain a contract after your previous attempts to market, you should maintain some follow-up procedure in case the client needs your services in the future. Possibly there were budget restraints the first time.

If you were able to obtain a contract and provide a service, you should have a follow-up routine for that client to encourage repeat business. It is important to keep communication open with the client in various ways for goodwill and possible referral business.

c. MARKETING TECHNIQUES

The following suggestions describe traditional as well as unusual ways of marketing consulting services. Many of the techniques cost little or nothing except for your time. Whether you use just a few of the techniques or all of the techniques depends on your style, your priorities, the nature of your service and your type of clientele.

1. Newspaper

Most consultants do not use newspapers as a source of advertising for their services. It is looked upon as unprofessional by many. Most clients select a consultant by reputation. But it depends on the nature of your consulting business. For example, if you specialize in small business cash flow problems, and in your region there are small businesses with problems, you might put a tasteful, professional advertisement in the display ads in the business section or in the classified section to stimulate interest.

2. Advertising in trade or professional journals

The advantage of advertising in these publications is the very specialized market you reach as the readers could all be potential prospects. Therefore, the cost/benefit feature of this form of advertising can be low. You should attempt to get all the trade and professional journals related to your areas of skill and services, and familiarize yourself with the format and the nature of journal ads.

3. Directories

There are many excellent reference guides to technical, professional, and trade organizations and associations. Your public library might have the *Encyclopedia of Associations* and *The National Trade and Professional Associations Directory*. Many of the organizations listed in the directories publish annual directories of their memberships.

Of the organizations that have directories, approximately half of them will include your name in their directory free of charge as a consultant in that area of interest. Most of the other organizations have paid advertising available, which could be of benefit if the target group is read by a prime segment of your market.

For additional sources of information on directories, refer to the Bibliography and Appendix 1.

4. Brochures

Brochures are a very important part of marketing your practice. There are many ways to use a brochure.

(a) Leave the brochure with a prospective client after a face-to-face meeting.

(b) Mail the brochure after a written or formal request for further information.

(c) Send the brochure in a direct mail campaign targeted to prospective clients.

(d) Distribute the brochure at a seminar or presentation you are giving.

(e) Send the brochure out the next day to those attending a seminar or presentation as a form of follow-up communication.

Keep in mind that your brochure is probably the first contact a prospective client has with you and the services you offer. The reaction to the brochure may be positive or negative, depending upon its format, content, and quality. Following are some tips on preparing a brochure.

(a) As the first impression of the brochure is critical, it is important that the layout, graphics, and paper be of first quality. You want to stimulate a desire in the recipient to retain you as a consultant, or at least to inquire further.

(b) Use an 8½" x 11" size of paper that will have three folds and six panels. Obtain advice from typesetters and graphic artists and printers before you finish your draft. Seek out comparative opinions and quotes until you are satisfied with the quality and cost offered.

(c) The phrasing of the text should reflect a confident, positive, dynamic yet professional tone. Have the spelling, grammar, syntax, and style of your text reviewed by someone with skills in that area.

(d) The text should be concise, clear, and brief. Text in point form can be easily read. Refrain from using large or complicated words. Keep the words simple and direct. Focus on the benefits that a prospective client will receive from your services. Draft the text from the viewpoint of the client's needs.

(e) Provide information on the history of your business, the nature of your business, your clientele, and the type of services you perform. Explain why a particular service might be required. Explain or list the benefits that you can give to provide the service and meet the need or resolve the problem. Think of previous clients who benefitted from your advice and assistance.

(f) List your academic and professional achievements and experiences.

(g) Do not list your associates unless you have a long-standing relationship or know that they will be staying with you for an extended time. Refer to the resource base of talent your firm offers. You may wish to itemize the skills that are provided by key associates.

(h) If appropriate, a number of testimonials from clients, or a list of important clients, could be included in the brochure.

(i) Many consultants prefer not to have their photograph in the brochure, as a matter of personal choice and style. The reaction of a potential client to your photograph could be negative or positive based on your picture alone. The design of the brochure should be consistent with your stationery and business cards.

(j) Before you have the brochure printed, have a number of your friends, relatives, and business associates look at the draft copy of the brochure and obtain their candid feedback.

5. Direct mail

Direct mail can be a very effective means of making potential clients aware of and interested in your services. There are several advantages to direct mail: the cost is flexible, the sales message can be personalized to the needs of that particular target group, and the letters can be individually addressed to specific persons on a word processor. An important cost/benefit aspect is the controlled circulation to a very select audience.

An integral part of direct mail marketing is the development or rental of a mailing list. There are many sources of rental lists. The major ones are Standard

Rates and Data Service, and Dun and Bradstreet. Both these companies have extensive mailing lists available for the United States and Canada. The lists include names, addresses, and postal/zip codes broken down into specific categories and regions.

Mailing lists are generally rented for one-time use, and are "seeded" by means of fictitious companies or individuals to ensure you do not use the list more than the time contracted. For further information, look under "direct mail" in the yellow pages.

The various directories of organizations related to your specialty may also rent or sell mailing lists. The advantage of this type of mailing list is that prospective clients may be members of the organization that publishes the directory. You would therefore be targeting your services to your specific trade or interest market.

There are brokers who represent all the major direct mail marketing companies. For a fee, they will determine the best mix of mailing lists for your purposes, depending upon the amount of money you are prepared to budget for the purpose. The broker will obtain the best rates for you and charge you a fee.

It is important to keep a record of all contacts you make, and record the names and particulars. All clients should be added to your mailing list.

It is difficult to estimate with certainty, but approximately 1 to 4% of direct mail marketing ultimately ends up as consulting assignments. Many factors will determine your response rate, such as the type of consulting service you provide, the economic climate at the time, the cyclical or seasonal demand for your type of service, and the techniques and format you use in the direct mail approach.

There are various stages involved in direct mailing, all of which are equally important to obtain the desired objective. The basic steps are as follows:

(a) Your first mailing should be within the regional area you can realistically service. It is also an opportunity to test market and analyze the effectiveness of your mailings without spending a large sum of money.

(b) Your mailing should consist of a personalized cover letter (on a word processor if available) and sent directly to the key person who is the decision-maker. Use quality letterhead stationery to create a professional impression. Depending upon the circumstances, you might also enclose your business card. Enclose a copy of your brochure with your letter. Outline briefly the services you offer and the benefits that will be obtained by the prospective client. State that you will contact the client in 10 calendar (or business) days to answer any questions and discuss the matter further at that time.

(c) Keep an accurate filing system of all prospective clients you intend to follow-up. List all pertinent information on the card so you can review it and familiarize yourself with it before you contact the client. Note the date in your daily diary or calendar to remind you to contact the prospective client on that date.

(d) Follow-up with a telephone call 10 days after you mail the letter. This will create a positive impression with the client with regard to your administration and professionalism. Follow the phone call with a visit to the prospective client if circumstances allow. The next chapter outlines other procedures and techniques to follow before, during, and after the first meeting with the prospective client.

(e) If the response to your mailing is poor, thoroughly review all your techniques and format. This includes the direct mail target group, cover letter, brochure, telephone techniques, and meetings.

(f) Constantly revise, refine, and upgrade your mailing list with new prospects.

(g) Send out mailings on a quarterly basis (or more often), as your finances, marketing plan, and other circumstances dictate. This will remind people of your services and expertise, and the repetition ultimately does have an effect. When sending out repetitive mailings, consider enclosing a newsletter, which you could easily prepare, and copies of any articles or other papers pertaining to the industry that is your target base. You may want to have a tear-off feature in the newsletter offering a free subscription to the newsletter if a request is sent to be kept on the mailing list. This way you should be able to track the response. Over time, a large portion of qualified prospects should respond to regular and consistent promotional efforts.

6. Contact network

You need to develop a contact network for future prospects and mailing list purposes. It is a very effective way to acquire clients by referral. Studies have shown that a high percent of a consultant's clientele comes from referrals through a contact network or from satisfied clients. A contact network is a collection of relatives, associates, and acquaintances who will facilitate your prospects of being accepted by an organization or individual who needs your services.

You already have many and you can cultivate many more. A partial list includes past and present clients, employees, professional colleagues, business associates, bankers, lawyers, accountants, friends, neighbors, and relatives. Also included are contacts you develop in associations and religious, professional, trade, business or other organizations. If you sit down and list everyone you know who comes to mind as a potential contact, the list will be longer than you think.

Developing the contact network is the most effective and inexpensive way of increasing your exposure and credibility. Continually update your network by adding leads and other contacts to your mailing list.

7. Membership in professional, trade or business associations

Joining a group and then actively participating in meetings and other functions is an effective means of developing leads. Attempt to attend meetings on a regular basis and get involved in discussions. Evaluate a group or association on the basis of potential consulting prospects who are active in the association. You want to look for members who are likely to give you consulting opportunities. Because of the time commitment involved to develop your reputation within an organization, you must be very selective in your membership. Limit your memberships to one or two. You may wish to consider such civic or trade organizations or associations as the Chamber of Commerce, Rotarians, Kiwanis, or associations directly related to your service area. Obtain a list of all the members of the organization and review the list thoroughly. Most lists provide the name, position and company, type of business or profession of the member, and address.

8. Donating your services

You may wish to donate some consulting time and commitment to a worthwhile nonprofit organization as a gesture of goodwill. Naturally, you have to be very cautious about the time involved relative to the potential benefit, but your services without charge can enhance your image and result directly or indirectly in referrals.

9. Attending public and professional meetings

Consider attending meetings covering a subject directly or indirectly related to your field of expertise. You want to see and be seen. Plan to contribute your opinion, if appropriate, in a well-planned, concise, and intelligent fashion. Prospective clients could be attending the meeting. Attempt to identify and talk to people you believe are worthwhile contacts. There are many meetings held on an ongoing basis, such as city council meetings, federal commissions, public hearings on specific areas of concern, and appeal board meetings.

10. Lectures

Many organizations or associations need speakers for breakfast, luncheon or dinner meetings, conferences or conventions. Look in the yellow pages of your telephone directly under "associations" to obtain various names. Also, review directories of associations available at your local library. Two publications, in particular, are: *National Trade Professional Associations and Labor Unions of the U.S. and Canada* and *Directory of Associations of Canada.*

When you contact the program chairperson, offer your services for free, and advise him or her that you have a number of prepared talks you believe would be of particular interest to the membership. Mention that your subject areas are topical and interesting, and your talk can be between 10 and 30 minutes long. This is the normal range of time required for a speaker. Ask about the mix of membership and the number of members who normally attend meetings. Attempt to get in advance a list of members to review so that you can direct your comments more accurately toward your group.

It is helpful to have ready two or three 10 to 20 minute presentations with supporting material. You will then be available on short notice for any presentation.

The object of the presentation is not to make money, but to obtain contacts and increase your credibility and exposure for future consulting opportunities. Those who attend the presentation will probably tell their friends or acquaintances about you if your presentation is interesting. Make sure you tell the audience that you are a consultant. During your presentation you can give a number of examples or anecdotes based on your experiences. This will reinforce your image as an expert. People will remember you better by the examples or stories that you relate.

Books related to public speaking and effective presentations are listed in the Bibliography. You may also wish to consider Dale Carnegie courses, Toastmasters membership or public speaking workshops to enhance your communication ability.

11. Teaching

There are many opportunities to offer your services as a teacher for school board adult education classes or university or community college continuing education courses. You generally get paid for your time, but ideally the students who attend the course will be potential clients or will recommend you to friends or associates. Make sure that you teach adults only to maximize the potential benefit. You are primarily looking for credibility, exposure, and contacts. The preparation required to teach a course also keeps you current on your subject area.

12. Seminars and workshops

Depending upon your area of expertise and the size of your target market, you may wish to consider offering your own seminar or workshop. You can offer the seminar free, or at a nominal charge. The people who attend are excellent potential clients. You should try to select a subject that allows you to provide a practical overview of important tips and ideas within your specialty area. You can promote your seminar through your direct mail list. Allow four to eight weeks lead time to ensure that people can schedule in your seminar.

Other items to consider are the length of the seminar, the location, the time, whether day or evening, when refreshments would be served, if any, and the number of people you can accommodate. Make sure your announcement states that it is limited, advance registration only.

In your announcement you can request that registration be made by telephone one week in advance of the seminar. This will give you some idea as to the response, and assist you in the preparation of your material.

You may also wish to consider the free advertising possibilities in the local newspaper and other monthly or weekly publications. If you allow yourself enough lead time, you should be able to conduct the seminar at a cost of $100 to $500. Depending upon the number of people and the amount you are charging, you could break even on the seminar.

If you have a deadline for registration one week before the seminar, and not enough people appear to be interested, you can try to negotiate a cancellation arrangement with the hotel facility by paying a portion of the room rent, or possibly nothing at all if the hotel is able to rebook the facility.

Make sure you distribute your brochures, newsletters, and any other appropriate material at the seminar. Develop a seminar evaluation form with questions that will provide a good source of biographical information on the participants, opinions of you and your seminar topic through means of rating scales, and space for additional comments. Provide a coupon on the seminar evaluation form for participants to complete if they wish to be kept on your mailing list for newsletters. Also have a space on the form for asking what particular areas of interest or concern a participant might have. This should assist you in developing other seminars, or improving the existing one.

When a person phones in to register prior to the seminar, as well as on the day of the seminar, make sure that you get the full company name, address, phone number, and name and position of the person attending. You will want this information for your mailing list. For further information on conducting seminars and workshops, refer to the books outlined in the Bibliography.

13. Free media exposure

There are many devices for obtaining free media exposure. Exposure provides credibility for you, and develops an awareness in the public that you are an expert or authority in one or more areas. If a seminar or presentation is offered, either through your own company or through some other organization, consider preparing a news release. Send it in advance to the appropriate radio, television, newspaper or magazine contact person. Determine who the contact person is and call in advance so he or she will be expecting your letter or news release. It also gives you an opportunity to introduce yourself and to make sure that the approach you are adopting will obtain the desired free exposure.

Ask the contact person what format is preferred for the information they require. Spell out in your letter, and in your conversation, why you feel the topic of the presentation is of interest to the readers, viewers or listeners. The subject matter may be topical or controversial.

14. Radio and television talk shows

The previous point dealt primarily with announcements of upcoming presentations. An extension of that exposure is to appear in person on a radio or television talk show. The same approach applies as in free media announcements. Locate the appropriate contact person and sell them on the benefits to the listeners or viewers of you being interviewed on the program. If possible, try to be on the program a week before your seminar or presentation, in order to stimulate attendance. If the talk program is too distant from the seminar date, the listener may forget about it.

15. Letters to the editor

It is easy to get published in the "letters to the editor" section of a magazine or newspaper. Write a letter that is topical and relevant and reflects a controversial or divergent opinion. Refer to an earlier article if you are reacting to something previously published. Mention in the letter that you are a professional consultant in the field and have expertise in the subject area.

16. Writing articles

Writing is an effective way of developing exposure, credibility, and contacts. Once you have developed the format, style and discipline, you should be able to write three or more articles a year for various publications. All publications are looking for articles; many do not pay very much, if anything, for unsolicited articles — but they do frequently get published.

To locate magazines that have your target audience, look at a publication by Standard Rates and Data Service entitled *Business Publications Rates and Data*. You should be able to find this publication in your library or university, or through a local advertising agency.

Write an article about your area of expertise that you believe would be of particular interest to the readership of the publication. Use examples and stories in your article. The subject matter could deal with new trends, the effect of pending legislation, technical information, or any other angle that will enhance your image as an expert.

Contact the publishers of the magazines or journals and obtain free copies so you can review them and familiarize yourself with their style and length. If your article is accepted for publication, request a by-line and a brief biographical comment at the end of the article. Say that you are a consultant in your area of expertise, and invite questions or comments about the article. Not all publications will permit this.

There are numerous books on writing style. Some of them are listed in the Bibliography. Have your article reviewed by at least one, if not two, friends or relatives who will candidly comment. Submit a good quality 5" x 7" glossy photograph of yourself and a biography with the article. Submit the article one at a time to the editors of several trade journals and business magazines whose readership constitutes your potential target base. If your article is published, obtain extra copies from the publisher to distribute in your next direct mailing or presentation.

There is an additional benefit to writing articles. The research process is an excellent way to develop contacts and credibility. For example, you could carefully select 20 or 30 people to interview for background information for the article. These people could include key potential clients. Have a script ready before you phone them, ask open-ended questions, listen carefully and note their answers. Ask follow-up questions to their responses. This should show that you are knowledgeable and an intelligent communicator. When you contact the prospective client to be interviewed over the telephone, introduce yourself as a consultant writing an article. You can ask their opinion on such matters as the effect of pending legislation, unique problems they encounter in their field of interest, and major opportunities or trends they perceive.

Research implies analysis, and your analysis should be thorough. The telephone conversation can be followed by a letter on your stationery thanking people for their cooperation and assistance. Depending upon the responses to your questions, you may see that many consulting opportunities exist with the people contacted. They may have mentioned some of their problems. At a comfortable time in the future, you may wish to contact these sources and follow up with a personal letter and brochure. Depending upon the circumstances, you might feel it appropriate to say you will contact them 10 days later to ask whether you may be of service. Subtlety is essential.

17. Writing a book

Having a book published is another marketing technique to establish yourself as an expert in your field. There are a number of limitations though. You have to find a publisher for your book or publish it yourself, which can be quite expensive. Your book could be obsolete by the time it is published, as approximately one to one and a half year lead time is required before publication. The time you would have to spend on the book might not be justified in terms of the cost/benefit due to loss of income or potential income. It could be far more beneficial to spend the time writing articles rather than a book. Regular articles also keep your name in front of the public and reinforce your image as a specialist.

18. Have articles written about you

Every field of consulting has news value. By carefully cultivating relationships with editors and reporters, you could be looked upon as being an expert in your area. They might invite your opinion and quote you in an article on the topic. You could also have articles written about you, if you can demonstrate the newsworthy feature, topical benefit, or uniqueness. Attempt to look for news angles that could have a direct or indirect effect on the public at large or your target group in particular. Look at economic, social, political or legislative factors. Over time you could build up a reputation as an authority that will generate inquiries from prospective clients.

19. Announcement columns

Many professional, trade, or university alumni publications have sections devoted to announcements of interest about their members. Make a point of regularly updating information provided to these publications whenever you can find an excuse to justify it, if your style allows. Such things as having given a presentation, expanding the services that you provide, or announcing new associates or distinctions can get your name inserted. If you are giving a seminar or workshop, give yourself enough lead time for an announcement to be inserted, if possible, in these publications. Various publications of a daily or weekly nature frequently may have a free announcement section available.

20. Newsletters

Newsletters are a very common way for consultants to promote themselves. It is a subtle form of advertising that can give you credibility, as well as providing advice to readers. Most newsletters are distributed free, since they are used as a marketing device. Once you establish a reputation and a large mailing list, economics and demand may justify charging a fee for a subscription.

The important features of a newsletter are effective use of colors and layout, a professional appearance, and well-written articles on interesting subjects. Most potential clients who will receive your newsletter are very busy; unless the newsletter captures the attention and is easily readable, it will not serve the purpose that you intend. The newsletter should have tips, news and ideas, and possibly a question and answer column. The length should be two to six pages on regular 8½ x 11 size paper, and published on a regular basis, such as monthly, bi-monthly, quarterly or semi-annually. The frequency of your publication will depend on your finances and time.

A newsletter is distributed in the same manner outlined earlier for brochures. When sending out brochures with covering letters in response to an inquiry, you should also include a recent copy of your newsletter. As in the case of direct mail marketing and brochures, you should address the newsletter to the key people in target organizations.

16

THE CLIENT INTERVIEW
AND CLIENT RELATIONS

Your efforts at marketing have now been successful. The prospective client is aware of your services and a meeting has been arranged, requested by you or the prospective client. This will provide an opportunity for mutual assessment. The initial interview is a critical step before preparing a proposal and obtaining a contract. There are many important techniques that you will have to understand and adapt for your particular needs. This chapter covers the matters you should consider before, during, and after the client interview.

a. PURPOSE OF INTERVIEW

The purpose of the interview is primarily fact finding, followed by an analysis of the client needs and problem identification. After these steps, you are then able to prepare a proposal. The meeting, of course, has other purposes, such as assessing the prospective client's personality, ability to pay, and expectations. It also provides an opportunity for an interchange of ideas and mutual assessment. As negotiating skills are involved, you may wish to refer to the section on negotiating in the Bibliography. *How to Read a Person Like a Book* is of particular interest on non-verbal communication.

b. BEFORE THE MEETING

If the client contacted you, you know a need exists and the client has some confidence in you. You should not have an interview over the telephone if at all possible. You want to have a face-to-face talk. Do not quote your rates over the phone, as they could be misinterpreted and the prospective client may not wish to continue to the next stage of the interview. If you are asked about your rates, attempt to defer an answer until the time of your meeting by stating that your rates vary depending on various factors such as estimated time involved, the type of work required, and whether the client is a profit or nonprofit organization. None of these factors can be ascertained accurately before an interview. In addition, there are different forms of fee structure that can be negotiated. This response should satisfy any inquiry.

The initial interview is normally free, as a goodwill and marketing technique. Naturally, it depends on the circumstances. Once a specific date and time has been set for the interview, confirm it in writing beforehand so no misunderstanding occurs. If the consultation is to be without charge, state that. Send your brochure with the letter. Your brochure should describe your background, past experiences, nature of service and references, if you think that is appropriate.

There are specific steps to take to prepare for the interview.

Review the client's circumstances so you are familiar with them before the interview. Find out everything you can about the company, industry, and problems affecting the industry. Learn the client's jargon and way of doing business. You can obtain considerable information from business publications, annual reports, trade journals, newspapers, and other clients in similar industries.

Try to find out about the client's likes and dislikes, hobbies, memberships, sports, recreation, and travel. Look for clues of personal interest or accomplishment when you are in the client's office. If you can find common links, a basis for friendship can be quickly established.

Prepare specific questions to ask during the interview. Concentrate on client needs and problems. Some of the basic questions to ask include:

(a) Has the client used a consultant before? How long ago? What was the experience like? What was the purpose?

   If the client has not used a consultant before, you may need more time to convince the client, and there may be more problems to be aware of in working with the client. If the client has used a consultant before, and the relationship was a positive one, you should find out what particular aspects were considered favorable. If a previous consultant relationship was not satisfactory, you should find out the reasons for that from the viewpoint of the client.

(b) Has the project been attempted previously? If so, who attempted it and why was it abondoned? The assignment might be impractical or impossible to complete to the client's satisfaction.

(c) If a client had a past relationship with a consultant, what type of financial fee arrangement was negotiated? It is not necessary for you to know the dollar amount, just the type of contract. You can then ask if that type of arrangement was satisfactory. That will provide you with guidelines on the type of fee arrangement to present in your proposal. Naturally, you want to offer the same type of fee arrangement a client feels comfortable with. If you prefer a different type of fee arrangement, you will have to discuss the benefits of that with the client during the interview, if possible.

(d) What specific measureable results and benefits must be obtained for the client to feel satisfied? The nature of the change, what form it will take, and how long it will take must be clarified. It is essential that the expectations of the client be specific, measureable, attainable, and realistic.

(e) Has a time period for the proposed project been discussed, and is that possible within your time schedule and other commitments? Has the subject of the cost of the project in general terms been discussed? What was the client's tentative reaction? If the type of payment has been discussed, what are the terms?

(f) Has a discussion taken place about the client's responsibilities in matters such as availability of the client's personnel, equipment, and work area, etc.? Does the consultant report to a committee or to one person? Access to information resources is required in order to complete the project. Can that access be obtained and how? Has the client been effectively convinced of the consultant's role as an agent of change? Does the client demonstrate appreciation and respect for the consultant?

(g) Is travel involved?

(h) Do you feel confident that you are qualified and able to help the client?

(i) Do you feel comfortable that a clear understanding exists of the client's problem or need?

Try to understand and anticipate client fears or concerns in advance and deal with them. A client may have underlying biases about you as a consultant that could affect the interview and its outcome. By knowing in advance the fears that might exist, you can counter them directly during the interview and proposal stages. Studies have shown that the following anxieties often exist. They are listed generally in order of priority.

- A consultant may be incompetent.

- The client may be continually dependent upon the consultant once the first relationship begins.

- The consultant might assume or interfere with managerial control during the project.

- The consultant's fees are excessive relative to the services provided.

- The consultant may not be able to complete the project in time.

- The need for a consultant is an admission of failure on the part of management.

- The consultant might disclose confidential internal information.

- The consultant might have inaccurately analyzed the needs and therefore will give an improper diagnosis.

- The consultant will lack impartiality.

Normally, a consultant will meet a client in the client's office. The client feels comfortable in familiar surroundings and is therefore more relaxed. The advantage to the consultant is having the opportunity to view the client's offices and operations, and to leave diplomatically if the meeting is unproductive or continues too long.

Try not to have a meeting just before lunch, as the client could have a lunch commitment or be distracted by the time or feel hungry.

Attempt to arrange an appointment for the time that you are at your peak of mental clarity so that you will create the most positive impression.

Make sure you arrive on time. Being late automatically creates a negative impression and can destroy the client's desire to deal with you. A small matter such as being late for an important appointment could represent an attitude and management style, which could cause conflict during the consulting project.

c. DURING THE INTERVIEW

The day has now arrived. You made certain you were at the client's office 10 to 15 minutes prior to the appointment to relax and compose yourself. You are feeling self-confident and positive about the meeting because you have thoroughly prepared yourself and worked through in your own mind a role-play of events that are soon to occur.

Arriving early gives you an opportunity to observe the dynamics of the office and personnel, and the general tone of the company. If you are going to have a relationship with a client, these simple factors are important to know beforehand.

When the meeting starts, it is important to shake hands with a firm grasp. A less than firm grasp will betray an insecure personality or lack of confidence in your abilities, and that impression alone could lose a project. It is important to consciously project a confident personality, positive attitude, firm method of speaking, and an attentive and relaxed stance. Exhibit a sense of control and leadership. A client wants to associate with a person who projects himself or herself well.

During the interview, you should spend almost all the time asking questions and little time answering them. After the initial social pleasantries and after you have briefly exchanged backgrounds, control the meeting asking your prepared questions. It is helpful to advise the client that you will be taking notes as this is a fact-finding interview. Having a prepared checklist is evidence of efficient administration and an assurance that no questions will be overlooked and interview consistency will be maintained.

Ask for examples to illustrate general statements. Ask open-ended as well as very specific questions, and let the client do the talking. If a pause occurs, be prepared with the next question or other appropriate reaction. Listen intently to what the client says and how the client perceives the problem. If you want the client to continue elaborating on a situation, use questions starting with how, why, who, what, or where or state, "that's interesting, can you tell me more about that?"

Be aware of non-verbal communication in body posture, mannerisms, voice patterns and behavior. When forming an impression of a client's situation or opinion, restate it back to the client for confirmation.

If a client attempts to ask you a lot of questions, try to deflect the line of questioning back to the client. If the client asks specific questions about how you think the problem can be dealt with, or the various steps or stages that should be considered, don't answer the questions directly. Your first interview is a fact-finding stage and you should not get involved in speculation or offering advice. Tell the client that you will certainly give an opinion later, after you have had an opportunity to review and analyze the facts and determine the options. Say that it would be premature and unprofessional for you to provide an opinion at this early stage. You don't want to give away free consulting, especially based on incomplete information.

At the end of the interview, ask the client if he or she would like to see a proposal and whether it should be a simple or detailed one.

Throughout the interview, be aware of the fears and concerns that might be present. Try to make sure you have dealt with all of them to the client's satisfaction.

d. AFTER THE INTERVIEW

Once the interview is over, you should review the data while it is still fresh in your mind. Identify the problems as you see them, and analyze the needs. Then outline the possible solutions and draft a proposal. The proposal steps are outlined in the next chapter.

The normal steps that follow include writing a thank you letter to the client as soon as possible after the meeting and saying a proposal will follow as soon as it is complete.

e. WHY YOU SHOULD TURN DOWN BUSINESS

After your interview and assessment of the client and project and other factors involved, you may decide that it would be wise not to accept the project. That decision takes insight and foresight, and many consultants find it difficult to make. Consultants may be influenced by factors such as the need for cash flow, seeing a challenge in the project, seeing potential marketing opportunities, desiring some form of activity because of the lack of it, or wanting to help because a client is in need. Some of the reasons you should consider turning down business are as follows:

(a) A client looks as though he or she is on the verge of business failure. (Studies have shown that there are various reasons for business failure, such as management incompetence, imbalanced experience, lack of management experience, or lack of experience in the product or service line. Some of the danger signals may include: lack of a business plan, high overhead costs, low morale, lack of cash flow, lack of understanding of financial information, indecisiveness, backlog of commitments, inefficiency, poor communication, and general chaos. As a consequence, you do not want to be burdened with the stress of a client failure or the risk of not collecting your fee.)

(b) The reputation of a client is to pay late or not pay at all.

(c) The client has a bad reputation for other reasons, and you do not want to be associated with that client.

(d) You do not like the client personally

(e) A proposed project is illegal or unpleasant

(f) You are over-committed with other projects and unable to accept the work and perform satisfactorily and on time

(g) The potential job is too small for your time, priorities or cash flow

(h) The potential job is too large for your ability or desire to administer it

(i) You lack the expertise to perform the job to the standard that would be required

(j) You do not offer consulting services in that client industry area

(k) The client does not want to pay you the fee that you have requested, but wants to pay you less than you feel is fair to complete the project

(l) The project would involve you compromising what you consider to be your professional and ethical standards

(m) The client does not appear to fully appreciate your skills and abilities

(n) The client does not have any money.

f. HOW TO TURN DOWN UNWANTED BUSINESS

Once you have decided that you do not want the business at all, or in the form that is available, there are various tactics and techniques involved in turning down the business in such a way as to maintain goodwill and not hurt the client's feelings.

If the proposed project is simply unsuitable for you, you may wish to turn it down completely. There are different ways of rejecting projects directly:

(a) Tell the client that your present workload is very heavy and unfortunately you are unable to accept the job. This option makes you appear more attractive and desirable to the client for possible future projects.

(b) Tell the client you are unable to technically comply with the job specifications. This typically occurs with government agencies. If you are expected to take a government job because of previous projects, and you want to be considered favorably in the future, you could propose an approach that you feel the client will reject as it may be outside the stated or unstated guidelines.

(c) Tell the client that you do not perform the particular type of service being requested, either because you do not have the capacity, or it isn't your current field. If you normally perform that type of consulting, state that at the present time you are directing your talents and priorities in a slightly different direction.

(d) Bid the job too high. You can quote a fee much higher than you think the job is worth or that other competitors might bid. The risk here, of course, is that your bid might be accepted.

There may be occasions when you would accept a job if it was changed to meet your needs. Some of the techniques you could consider include:

(a) Accept only part of the proposed project. You could encourage other consultants to accept parts of the project you do not wish to handle.

(b) Redefine the project to meet your needs, and offer to conduct the assignment on your own terms. This approach only works if the client's goals, objectives, and expectations can be met without additional costs.

(c) Accept the job but act as project manager and employ other consultants to assist you in completing the job.

17

CONSULTING PROPOSALS

Most initial interviews result in a request for a proposal. The proposal plays a significant role in your ability to obtain consulting assignments. Because of the vital nature of writing and presenting successful proposals, you may wish to refer to the Bibliography for further references. This chapter covers some of the basic concepts and tactics required to succeed in your proposal.

a. WHAT IS A PROPOSAL?

A proposal is a letter or document that you prepare for a client describing your understanding of the client's needs. This is very important as your client, to have confidence in you, must be satisfied that you understand the problem as well as the client does. It states what you intend to do for the client, and indicates in specific terms the anticipated results and potential benefits to the client.

A proposal is a selling document. It is intended to be informative and appealing and convince the client to contract for your services.

b. PRIVATE VERSUS PUBLIC SECTOR PROPOSALS

Public sector proposals tend to be more formal than private sector proposals. When a client requests a proposal, the request is made on the assumption that anyone offering goods or services is properly qualified and equipped to do so. The government requires that you demonstrate your own competence and prove that your facilities, experience, resources and whatever else are adequate to handle the requirements. The client is evaluating not only the merits of the program you propose versus the merits of competitive programs, but also your credentials versus the credentials of your competitors. It is common for government agencies to require that you outline your personal qualifications. One reason government agencies request such information is that they are required by procurement regulation to make an objective evaluation of each proposal. Your qualifications provide one specific comparison.

Goverment agencies have various evaluation factors. An example of the criteria a government agency might use is shown in Appendix 4.

Private sector proposals are far more flexible in their selection requirements as they are not governed by legislation. Therefore, pragmatism and subjective factors have more of an influence on the final decision.

c. SOLICITED VERSUS UNSOLICITED PROPOSALS

Solicited proposals are those requests that are made by a prospective client from the public or private sector. An organization requesting a proposal has already identified some needs. Your proposal will be judged on its quality, timeliness, reliability, and effectiveness.

An unsolicited proposal is designed by a consultant who perceives a need and is confident that it can be met through the use of the consultant's services.

Solicited proposals generally involve a competition between large numbers of consultants who bid on the project. In an unsolicited proposal situation, you may be the only person being considered.

d. SIMPLE AND FORMAL PROPOSALS

1. Simple proposal

The simple proposal is simply a written statement, typed on the consultant's stationery, that includes the following items:

(a) A description of the work to be done

(b) The name of the consultant performing the work

(c) The services or personnel to be provided by the client

(d) The date work will begin and the length of time required to complete the assignment

(e) An outline of anticipated categories of costs to be paid by the client

(f) The fees to be paid for services rendered and the terms arranged.

The proposal is signed by the consultant and normally sent by mail or delivered in person to the client. If the proposal is agreed upon, the client should sign a copy of the proposal or letter. The letter of proposal and agreement constitutes a legal contract and is similar to a letter of agreement.

2. Formal proposal

A formal proposal is considerably more detailed in that all aspects of the project are spelled out in full. It is similar to a formal contract and offers protections to both the consultant and the client.

The proposal does not become a legally binding contract until the client agrees and signs the proposal document to that effect, or a covering letter referring to the proposal as a binding contract is signed, or a formal contract is drafted reflecting the contents of the proposal and signed by both parties. A sample format for a formal proposal is described in the next section.

e. GUIDELINES AND FORMAT FOR A SUCCESSFUL PROPOSAL

The basis for your written contract will be the matters that you discuss at the proposal stage. Make sure you expand on the need, outcome, benefits, and results. Do not expand on the process or methods. This protects you from a client rejecting the proposal, and performing the project in-house using your proposal as a guide or submitting your proposal to other consultants for estimates and then hiring someone else who uses the process you detailed.

Also keep in mind when you are preparing the proposal that your client might have some of the concerns and fears outlined in the preceeding chapter. Attempt to minimize any concerns in the content of your proposal.

You should consider having a number of standardized proposals if there is similarity in the type of services you offer. If the standardized documents are on a word processor, they can easily be adapted to include or exclude paragraphs and to make the document an original. It is also very easy to revise a document on a word processor. The standardized proposal contains all the basics of any proposal, leaving open those items that are specific to each project. Another advantage of a standardized proposal is your ability to deliver the completed proposal to the client within a short time after your initial meeting.

The sample proposal format and guidelines (Sample #16) is rather formal and detailed. It may include clauses that are not applicable or appropriate in all situations, as each project is unique.

SAMPLE #16
PROPOSAL FORMAT

---

1. **Table of contents:** Includes headings and page numbers

2. **Introduction:** It is important to persuade the client that you understand the project and the underlying factors that influence it. Briefly outline and analyze the factors that demonstrate the need. State that the matter is important and warrants professional outside assistance. Emphasize that you want to help and that you are the most appropriate source of help.

3. **Project purpose:** The purpose and goals of the engagement are outlined here in a clear and accurate fashion. State the purpose and goals in the client's own words so that the client can identify with the proposal. During your initial interview you attempted to elicit from the client what the client perceived as being the needs or problems and the means to resolve them. Detail the goals in such a way that you can refer to them as specific and measureable outcomes to have a reference point for measuring the progress of the project and satisfying the client.

4. **Project benefits:** Highlight the anticipated benefits the client will receive. Do not promise results you cannot guarantee, but the client has to be given some realistic hope of success. This is a particularly important section as the client has to clearly understand and recognize the benefits in order to justify the financial and administrative commitment. Your client may have to account to other directors or shareholders. You are assisting your client to assist you, the more detail you provide.

---

5. Approach, scope, and plan: Compare and contrast several possible approaches to the project, if appropriate. Explain how you will proceed in general terms. Define the scope and limits of the proposed consulting service. Divide the tasks into smaller segments that provide clear stages in the project as reference points for you and your client. As mentioned earlier, provide sufficient information to demonstrate your competence, but not enough about the process and techniques to provide a formula for the client to perform the project without you.

6. Project schedule: Determine the schedule and list the specific tasks required to attain the objectives. State the timing and sequence of tasks according to the various stages. A functional flow diagram might help to graphically assist the client's understanding and provide a reference point for progress.

7. Progress reports: It is important to maintain continual communication with the client. As explained in earlier chapters, the more information you provide your client, the more confidence the client will have in you, and the less risk there is of problems occurring. Progress reports are frequently made at specific stages, when interim bills are sent. A client is more disposed to pay if tangible benefits can be seen and specific problems have been resolved. The frequency and format of periodic progress reports should be specified.

8. Costing summary: Explain your fees, types of fee arrangement, billing procedures, and timing of bills. Detail the expected expenses that will be passed on directly to the client. Your client should understand that your estimate for time and costs is an estimate only. Provide sufficient detail about your fees, so that your client appreciates the correlation between the amount of time expended and the cost of your services. Outline any other terms and conditions or variables that could affect the final cost.

9. Personnel and qualifications: Provide a brief background history of your firm and the personnel who will be consulting on the project. If you have had experience solving problems similar to the client's, make reference to that. Select only those aspects of your background experience that related directly to the client and the proposal.

10. Sub-contracts: If you are sub-contracting or collaborating with other consultants, it is important to specify who they are and what duties they will perform. Specify whether you or the client is responsible for their technical performance to avoid any future problems.

11. Use of client personnel: It is important that the client understand what commitments and obligations will be his or her responsibility. If you are to delegate responsibilities or otherwise receive assistance from the client's staff or executives, you should make it clear that your fee estimate is based on the use of client personnel. Specify personnel duties and time required if possible.

12. Senior management support: Make the executives aware that their support is vital to the success of the project. It is important that support for the project be communicated throughout the organization to gain cooperation and compliance. If regular meetings are going to be held with senior executives, specify the purpose and frequency of such meetings.

13. Steering committee function, if applicable: A steering committee reviews, coordinates, assists, and implements the consultant's work. It provides momentum and organizational credibility and decision-making functions for the project. Detail the purposes, composition, and responsibilities of this committee.

14. Output material included: Describe any reports, surveys, instructional material or other products that are part of the proposal.

15. Management plan: Describe your approach to managing the overall project. Who will be the client contact person, and what will his or her management role and authority be pertaining to the project?

16. Disclaimers: If you have used disclaimers regarding the project, make sure that the reason is outlined. Your role is strictly that of advisor, not a decision-maker, and any benefits achieved is based on both your recommendations and the client's actions and decisions. If your client does not fulfill his or her obligations and support, your responsibility and choices should be outlined. Indicate who has ownership and control over any proprietary information that could develop from your services, for example, instructional material.

17. References: If requested, or if it is your style and wish to provide client references, make sure that you obtain written permission in advance from the references. Update them to make sure they still think highly of you.

18. Summary and closing of proposal: This should be a short restatement of your belief in the importance of the engagement. Mention your availability to answer questions. If you are prepared to begin the project within a short time after the client's acceptance, state that clearly. You want to stimulate the client's need and persuade the client that you can fulfill the need.

f. PRESENTING YOUR PROPOSAL

How you package your proposal is nearly as important as how it is stated. If possible, your proposal should be prepared on a word processor, as that reflects professionalism and quality secretarial resources. Your signature and the date should appear at the end of the proposal.

A covering letter should accompany your proposal thanking your client for the time and cooperation during the meeting and for the opportunity to submit a proposal. Highlight the topics discussed and state that you can help because you have had experience with this type of problem and would like to have the opportunity to be of service. You may want to flatter the client in some way by referring to his or her contribution in the meeting. Offer to answer any questions either by phone or at an arranged meeting. State that you will call within 10 business days to discuss the proposal further. Put that date on your calendar. If you have not heard from the client within that period, make sure that you contact the client on the 10th day.

You may wish to suggest in your covering letter if you didn't mention it in the proposal that references are available on request. You may wish to suggest that the client contact some of your other clients to discuss work you have performed. This should demonstrate your self-confidence and increase the client's trust and confidence in you.

g. PROPOSAL FOLLOW-UP

Your client may be slow in responding to your proposal. You do not want to appear to be pressuring the client, but you may have to take certain steps to clarify the situation or obtain a contract.

You stated in your covering letter that you would contact the client within 10 business days. It is appropriate, then, that you do contact the client on the 10th day to answer any questions. You may receive further questions at that point, or obtain a positive or negative response to your proposal.

If the reason for the delay appears inexplicable, you may wish to wait for a further five business days and then drop in to see the client in person to ask if a decision has been made. This approach may or may not be appropriate in a given situation.

If a client is waiting for a committee decision, determine when the committee will meet to discuss the proposal and follow-up by phone to the client the following day. You may also wish to consider giving an acceptance time limit in your proposal to encourage prompt consideration. In a given situation you might adopt the attitude that you would like to know one way or the other within a certain time. The client could construe the acceptance time limit in a positive fashion, as it could imply that you are in demand and have other projects available to you that require a decision.

h. WHAT TO DO IF YOUR PROPOSAL IS NOT ACCEPTED

It is helpful if you can determine why you received a rejection. It may not be appropriate, practical or possible for you to obtain the answer from the client. Budget restraints, other priorities, or lack of consensus could be reasons. Possibly another consultant was awarded the contract. If possible, find out who obtained the assignment and why that proposal was selected over your own. Rejected proposals can provide a good learning experience.

Regardless of the circumstances, write a thank you letter to the client expressing your appreciation for his or her time, interest, and cooperation, and mention that you would be pleased to submit a proposal for consideration in any future projects.

i. HOW TO AVOID GIVING AWAY FREE CONSULTING

At this stage you should know whether your proposal was rejected or accepted. If it was rejected, you may have provided too much information in your proposal to your client, who in turn used the information for his or her benefit. In other words, you gave away free consulting. If your proposal was accepted, and you now have a contract or a contract is being prepared, you should be aware of the various ways that clients can innocently or intentionally obtain your advice for free.

At times, you may decide to share your knowledge and ideas in an attempt to build goodwill with the client or prospective client. That is a judgment you will have to make at the time. But you are running a business, which requires income and profit. You cannot carelessly give away the only product you have, which is time and skill.

1. Potential client interview or discussion

A potential client may contact you and wish to discuss ideas and problems with you on the telephone, over lunch or at the client's office or your office. The potential client (referred to as "client" for convenience) wants to "pick your brains." You willingly cooperate due to your desire to obtain a consulting assignment.

The strategic solution is to confirm that you do provide service in the area concerned and you are available to the client on a professional basis and would be pleased to establish a relationship. Answer any concerns raised by the client by asking questions aimed at drawing out information. Do not offer solutions but imply that there are solutions to the problems discussed.

If answers are specifically requested, respond that you require far more information before providing an answer. State that it would be unprofessional for you to provide an opinion without sufficient information on which to base that opinion. Again, restate that you would be pleased to discuss the matter further on a professional basis if they so wish.

These deflective techniques are the same ones outlined in the preceeding chapter relating to the initial interview. Ask the client directly if he or she is interested in retaining a consultant to provide assistance in the specific area of concern. Clarify if the client would like you to submit a proposal to resolve the problem. Decide if the client is a serious enough prospect to spend the time on a proposal.

Make it clear throughout the discussion that you are paid for professional services and that you are capable of assisting the client on a fee for service basis.

2. Client need analysis

A client might perceive that a problem exists, but not understand the precise nature of the problem. The client implies to you that if an analysis of the needs is made with recommendations for resolution an attractive contract could immediately result. This teaser can entice unsophisticated or new consultants to provide a thorough diagnosis without fee.

A naive consultant can be easily exploited by this technique. The risk, of course, is that no subsequent contracts materialize or some other consultant is retained. One way of resolving this problem is to recommend that the client enter into a contract with the first stage to be a diagnostic stage. After the diagnosis is made, with recommendations, then the consultant could proceed to the next stage of contract and implement the recommendations. That way the consultant is protected by contract, and the sincerity of the client is assured.

152

An option can be inserted in the contract that if the client elects not to proceed with the recommendation, then the consultant is assured payment of an agreed sum in consideration for the time and energies spent during the diagnostic phase.

3. Free detailed advice in the written proposal

In your proposal you may write a complete, detailed formula with all the necessary instructions together with an outline of the methods and steps required to attain the objective. The client now has the prescription for resolving the problem and can give it to other consultants to submit an estimate or implement the detailed proposal with in-house personnel.

One approach to avoid this problem is to write the proposal highlighting in detail the need that exists, the objectives that must be achieved in order to resolve the client's problem, and the measurable, specific outcomes and benefits that will be attained at specific stages of the assignment. A functional flow diagram graphically illustrating the steps is an effective marketing tool. De-emphasize or omit information on the processes or methods to be used.

4. Potential future benefit

A client may try to convince you that some future benefit, such as goodwill or contacts, could occur if you performed the service. The condition is that you provide the service for free or a reduced amount as the price to pay for future opportunities and contacts.

This technique is normally exercised by larger or more influential clients who take advantage of a consultant's impressionable, desperate or opportunist nature. The client may attempt to blame the lack of financial recompense on budget allocations already spent, internal financial restraints being imposed, or a general hold on all project commitments. From a consultant's viewpoint, the mere association with an influential or prestigious client could be an inducement.

As long as you are aware of the business and psychological dynamics at work, you can make a responsible, pragmatic decision. The decision might be to accede to the client's overtures, resist them, or attempt to negotiate a more realistic package.

5. Additions to the original fixed price contract

You may be asked to perform additional work outside the original contract terms.

It is not uncommon for a client to request additional work, as all needs cannot be foreseen in advance or changing circumstances change the needs. Once you are aware that the request is outside the fixed price contract terms, you should contact the client, draw this fact to the client's attention in a polite fashion and suggest that a modified contract or addendum be negotiated to incorporate the additional work. You would then negotiate the amount and method of payment for the additional work.

This situation reinforces the importance of being specific in a fixed price contract as to the services that are to be performed. Ambiguity in terms could lead to a difference of opinion, an impasse, legal problems, and loss of goodwill as well as loss of a client.

Depending on the circumstances, a formal contract amendment may not be required; a confirmation letter outlining the amendments and signed by both parties may be enough. The method is a matter of style, nature of client, and other circumstances.

6. Free consulting in a follow-up situation

You can run into problems when you have performed your services as outlined in your contract, but the client continues to need your services for operating the project. For example, suppose you recommended a type of computer hardware that was subsequently installed in the client's premises, and the client's personnel had difficulty learning the new equipment. You might feel an obligation to assist the client by explaining the necessary matters to the personnel. You may then be continually phoned by the client requesting you to return to explain various features to the personnel. Unless you are aware of the process occurring, you could be providing considerable free consulting.

The obvious solution is to anticipate the situation in advance, and incorporate provisions for follow-up consultation fees into the original contract. The contract can specify the method of payment and terms. One option is a time retainer contract, which means that you perform a specified service regularly, (e.g., several specified hours or days per month). Another option is an availability retainer contract. This means you are "on call" for a fixed monthly fee as outlined in the terms of the agreement.

7. Relatives, associates, and friends

Relatives and friends may frequently come to you for advice. You must develop ways to maintain the relationship but clarify your role as a professional who provides service for a fee.

You can develop various subtle but effective approaches. One technique is to say that you have a policy of not advising family or friends because of possible conflict of interest or bias. Because you value the relationship and operate by professional standards, you feel it would not be appropriate or responsible or you would prefer not to provide professoinal advice that they might rely on.

Another approach is to say you are unable to provide advice because of incomplete information, and that it would be irresponsible, unprofessional, and unfair on your part to give an opinion based on incomplete facts.

You have choices. You can either decline to provide advice, provide advice for free, or establish your relationship in the context as a business one and negotiate a fee for service. It is also helpful to keep in mind that you can be exposed to professional liability and negligent claims if your advice is followed and problems occur even though you did not charge or get paid for your advice.

18

CONTRACTS

As a consultant, you will quickly become aware of the necessity of written contracts in all your business and client relationships. A contract is the framework within which your obligations, rights, remedies, and remunerations are clarified. There are oral, written, and implied contracts. You want to make sure that your consulting business assumes no commitments or financial outlay without the security of an agreement in writing. Many consultants and other small business people commence their business with the trusting attitude that a verbal agreement is sufficient. It only takes one bad experience to demonstrate the folly of relying on a verbal agreement. This chapter explores some of the important aspects of contracts.

a. ESSENTIALS OF A VALID CONTRACT

A contract is an agreement between two parties to perform mutual obligations. The most common forms of contract are the oral contract and the written contract. The problem with an oral contract is that if the parties disagree, unless there are reliable witnesses or part performance of the agreement, it is difficult to reconstruct what the original bargain was. A written contract simply records in a formal or informal manner the nature of the bargain. For example, if you send a letter to a client confirming your agreement and the five essential elements of a contract are present, you have a simple informal contract.

The five elements of a contract are as follows:

1. Offer

If you are submitting a proposal or a contract to a client, that constitutes your offer to the client to accept your proposal. Your offer, naturally, will be in writing and spell out the particulars in some detail.

2. Acceptance

Acceptance of your proposal must be clearly demonstrated. Normally this takes the form of your prospective client confirming in writing an acceptance of your proposal letter or document or contract, and acknowledging the terms you have outlined.

In certain situations an acceptance can be assumed and the contract made valid by part performance. In other words, it could be argued that your offer was accepted if your client permitted you to perform in part or in full the terms of your written proposal, even though a written acceptance had not been received.

Naturally, this is a high risk manner of doing business. Never begin a project without first protecting yourself in writing.

3. Consideration

Consideration is something of value being promised to you or given to you in exchange for your services. Valuable consideration normally refers to money or some other valuable assets, but a promise to pay money or provide some other benefit can be deemed to be consideration.

4. Competency

An agreement will not be considered binding if signed by persons lacking competence to understand the "nature and quality of their actions." This includes minors, the mentally infirm, or a person who is intoxicated at the time the agreement was accepted or signed. The age at which a person ceases to become a minor varies depending upon the jurisdiction. In some circumstances a contract signed by a minor is considered to be binding.

5. Legality

A contract created to perform an illegal act is void. For example, if a number of businesses signed an agreement to price fix in their area of product sales, and one of the parties failed to follow the agreement, the other parties to the agreement would not be able to sue for breach of contract, as the subject matter of the agreement was illegal.

b. WHY A WRITTEN CONTRACT IS NEEDED

There are many reasons why a written contract is essential. Some of the reasons are:

- *Projects professional image:* A written contract enhances your image as a responsible professional and businessperson.

- *Avoid misunderstandings:* It is difficult to remember complex details without having them in writing. Subsequent events and distractions can cloud the recall of earlier conversations. Both parties can have different assumptions and interpretations of what the bargain was on critical points of issue. It only makes sense to prevent this problem by the simple act of writing down the agreement.

- *Untruthful client:* It is not uncommon in verbal agreements for one party to reconstruct the agreement in a self-serving fashion at some later point. This could be to negotiate a more favorable contract or to get out of the contract obligations all together. If it is just one person's word against the other, it is difficult if not impossible for a court to attempt to reconstruct with certainty the original bargain. The time, delay, and expense of attempting to assert your rights eliminates any profit and possibly your business as well.

- *Death of either party:* If either party to the contract dies, the estate of the deceased would have difficulty determining the actual bargain. This could give rise to law suits against the estate of the deceased consultant if the client claimed damages had been suffered because of the death due to breach of contract. The estate of the deceased would be in a difficult position to defend any action, not knowing the exact terms and obligations of both parties.

- *Terms of payment outlined:* If you do not have specific terms of payment in writing, such as monthly or at specific stages in the project, the client could attempt to wait until the end of the job to pay you, claiming there was no other agreement to the contrary. You want to avoid this problem by having written agreement before you expend your time, energy, and resources.

- *Fee for service confirmed:* You want to make clear that you are being paid for your time, and that your efforts are not being supplied free as a marketing device or preliminary assessment.

- *Avoiding and limiting liability:* You want to protect your interests in writing by having provisions in the agreement to protect yourself from liability. For example, you may want to have a contingency clause to the effect that if events occur outside your control you are not to be held responsible. You might also consider a limited liability clause which sets a fixed amount of money that you would be responsible for if you are held liable. For example, you might have a clause stating that your liability is limited to $15,000 or the balance of the contract, whichever is less.

- *Preventing litigation:* If you do not have an agreement in writing, a client could claim that you acted improperly or that the work was not completely done. Unless an agreement in writing spelled out the nature of the services that you were going to provide, it would be difficult for you or your client to show exactly what you agreed upon. Because of this impasse on the terms and obligations of the agreement, litigation might be difficult to avoid.

- *Collateral for financing:* A written contract outlining benefits that you will receive for performing services is as good as money. You can pledge the contract at a bank as security for loan advances. This ability to lever your legal documents for working capital or cash flow purposes is just good business sense. No banker will lend money on the strength of your verbal assurance that you have a consulting agreement with a client.

- *Potential for increase of revenue:* If you have a contract that details the exact services and supplies you are providing, any variation would allow you to negotiate an addendum to the agreement. The problem with an oral agreement could be a dispute over the exact point at which your services and supplies are not included in the bargain.

- *Independent contractor status confirmed:* Without a written agreement specifying your independent status of operating, within the terms of the agreement, without direction or control, you could be considered to be an employee by the tax authorities. Make clear in the written agreement the nature of the roles of the parties. Also, the client might set down his or her own specifications, or question you in detail on an ongoing basis about what you are doing, thereby reducing some of your independence. To prevent this, take the initiative to specify the detail, nature, and form of the services you are going to provide.

- *Encourages contract acceptance:* Many prospective clients feel nervous about agreeing to have you perform a project unless they know the exact detail and terms of the relationship in writing. The person with whom you might be negotiating frequently has to explain the particulars to colleagues or superiors. Without a written contract in writing, you might not win the assignment.

- *Communication:* As mentioned previously, good communication is an essential ingredient for client satisfaction and goodwill. A well-written contract helps build client confidence.

c. STRUCTURE OF A FORMAL CONTRACT

A consulting contract can vary widely in its complexity depending upon the nature and value of the project being performed and the nature of the clients being served. Sample #17 describes the format for a formal contract and discusses clauses that are frequently included. Not all the clauses are necessarily appropriate or applicable in each case. A simple contract or letter of understanding does not need the same detail.

If a proposal letter or document exists, it can be referred to in the contract as part of the agreement and attached as an appendix.

SAMPLE #17
CONTRACT FORMAT

---

1. Parties involved: Name all parties involved in the contract and state the date the contract is signed.

2. Term of contract: The starting and completion dates of the contract are written here, or a reference is made to an appendix attached in which the dates and hours are described. The contract may state either the beginning and ending dates of an assignment, or both, or a maximum of hours within a fixed time period. The time period can either be closed or open. An open contract simply states that a specific job is to be performed, without giving a deadline for completion. Or, a contract might simply state that an ongoing relationship is commencing, the length of which shall be at the pleasure of both parties.

---

3. **Duties of the consultant:** Outline your proposed consulting in detail, by specific task and scope. Previous meetings have probably clarified services to be offered during the proposal stage, and the proposal letter or document spells out what you are offering. If this is included in the contract for practical, tactical or legal reasons, or choice of style, the following areas might be be covered:

- Services that you, as consultant, will provide
- The timing of the submission of various documents pertaining to the project
- The nature of reports to be furnished, if any, and the approximate dates when they will be completed
- Any special materials to be prepared, such as brochures, etc.
- The timing and nature of any consultant/client meetings, either on fixed dates or at specific stages in the project or upon mutual request
- Travel that might be required, the nature of compensation, when that is to be paid, and what is required to obtain payment
- Your authority to use client resources, office equipment, computer, files and records, and access to client's customers
- Your right to use third party information; for example, ledgers and journals and other financial information in the possession of the client
- A provision restricting you from performing services for the client's competitors (Be careful of this provision, especially if you intend to develop a clientele base within a certain industry.)

4. **Duties of the client:** Wherever a consultant requires access to information or to employees, customers, or advisors of the client, it should be specified clearly in the agreement that the client agrees and will have the responsibility of facilitating and performing in those specific areas. For example, if you require information from a third party, you should try to have the client responsible for obtaining the information for you. If the client does not or cannot cooperate and therefore impedes the project, how are you compensated?

5. **Payment for services:** This is an important section and should state the basis on which your fees will be paid; that is, per diem, fixed rate, fixed price plus expenses, or other form. Various types of fee structures are discussed in chapter 13. When and how the invoices will be rendered should be spelled out clearly, for example, invoices could be rendered at specific identifiable stages throughout the project. If the client is billing on an hourly or daily rate, it should be specified in the contract what that rate is. If a down payment (retainer) is required, that should also be specified.

6. **Expenses:** Any job-related expenses to be paid by the client are described here. In the case of a fixed price contract, your expenses are incorporated in the fixed price agreed upon. Most other forms of fee structure involve expenses to be paid by the client. Outline what is required for payment.

7. **Late payment:** The contract should specify when payment should take place — either at specified periods or upon receipt of invoice or 30 days after invoice, or whatever arrangement is agreed upon. A clause can be inserted in the agreement that if the invoice is not paid within the agreed upon billing period, interest on the overdue account will be added. The interest rate is normally slightly higher than the prevailing bank rate to act as an incentive to pay.

8. **Stop work clause:** This clause allows the consultant to cease providing services on the project until the oustanding fees and interest have been paid. Generally this clause is not applied until a certain period has elapsed and all other attempts at getting payment

through goodwill have been unsuccessful. Stopping work is a last resort. It is important that the basis on which you can discontinue your services be stated in the contract.

9. **Independent contractor:** State that you are an independent contractor and therefore not eligible to participate in any benefit programs or tax withholding obligations on the part of the client. This clause makes it clear that you are not an employee.

10. **Work delegation:** Outline the basis on which you are permitted to hire assistants and delegate work. Depending upon the nature of services you are providing, your personal service and expertise is probably desired by the client. If you plan to sub-contract out to other people, protect yourself by clarifying that in the contract.

11. **Additional work:** This clause allows a client to request a modification to the contract and add a provision for additional services. Any modification to the contract should be confirmed in writing with particulars and signed by both parties before any additional service work commences.

12. **Confidentiality:** State that any information disclosed to you pertaining to the project or any information that you become aware of during the period of the project will be kept strictly confidential.

13. **Ownership:** This clause covers ownership of materials or ideas resulting from your services. Many rejected ideas and plans could be useful for another project. Naturally, it is not in your best interests to have the client own this information. You should require that rejected plans or ideas are to remain your property.

14. **Limited liability of consultant:** You may wish to insert a clause saying any liability because of your mistakes or breach of contract is limited to the amount of the contract price, assuming that there is a fixed contract price, or the amount of loss, whichever is lower. If there is no fixed contract price, set a specific maximum to the loss. However, such a clause is difficult if not impossible to enforce. You should also take out professional liability insurance and errors and omissions insurance as a protection. (See chapter 11.)

15. **Contingencies:** This clause states that you have complete control of all services rendered, with the exception of events beyond the control of you or the client, such as accidents, delays, strikes or supplier problems. This clause attempts to protect both parties if the contract is not able to be completed.

16. **Advertising:** This clause restricts the use of the client's name for media release without the written approval of the client.

17. **Arbitration:** Outline the procedures to be followed in the event of disagreement by either party about the terms or interpretation of the terms of the contract. Normally, provision is made for a dispute to be settled by an independent arbitrator, the basis on which the arbitrator will be paid and by whom, and the criteria for selecting the arbitrator.

18. **Governing laws:** This clause simply states that the contract shall be governed by the laws of the jurisdiction in which it is written.

19. **Termination:** Either party is allowed to terminate services upon written notification a set number of days in advance. Outline the details and the reasons under which termination can take place.

20. **Agreement binding:** State that the written agreement is the total agreement between the parties and shall take the place of any previous contracts or verbal or written agreements. This clause normally states that any modification to the agreement must be in writing and agreed between the parties to be enforceable.

21. **Signatures:** The parties to the contract sign the agreement. It is very important that a representative of the client who sign has the authority to do so and the position is written on the contract. In some cases, corporate seals are required if corporations are involved.

d. TYPES OF CONTRACTS

There are several types of contracts frequently used in the consulting business. It is important to understand the options that are available to you as they involve various tactical and legal considerations. Following is a brief summary of the most common types of contracts.

1. Letter of agreement

This simple contract is in the form of a letter stating a summary of the agreement between the parties. This includes the nature of services to be performed, the method and time of payment, the starting date and duration of the contract, the resource materials and personnel to be supplied by the client, if applicable, and the consultants who will be involved on the project, if applicable.

The letter of agreement is normally prepared by the consultant and forwarded to the client for signature and approval. An example of a letter of agreement prepared by a consultant is shown in Sample #18.

Sample #19 shows a letter of agreement prepared by the client. Note the differences in tone and format between the two. The one prepared by the client has the appearance of a short formal contract.

2. Letter of agreement with general terms and conditions appended

Another option is to have a letter of agreement accompanied by a statement of standard terms and conditions (see Sample #20). The statement is a standardized form that you can use often for similar type of agreements. It includes such matters as fee structure, reimbursable expenses, sub-contracts, invoices and payments, warranty and limitation of professional liability. Other clauses can be included in this form based on your own needs and precautions. If you prefer this format, the letter of agreement attached to the terms and conditions need not be detailed. It can outline the specific, not general, terms of the agreement.

The letter of agreement and/or general terms and conditions form are frequently used if the client does not want a more formal contract. From a tactical viewpoint, you might feel that a client would be intimidated by a formally structured contract. Another factor might be your personal style of consulting practice. If the contract is not complex and the fee is low, you might favor the simpler contract format

3. Formal contract

A formal contract is preferred if the financial cost of the project is high, if the project is complex, if substantial financial commitment to suppliers or sub-consultants is involved, or if it is the style of the client to require such a detailed contract.

Normally when government contracts are involved, the government prepares the formal contract.

162

(Consultant's Letterhead)

_____, 198___

Mary Roberts, President
ABC Corporation
7890 Front Street
Anytown, Anywhere

Dear Ms. Roberts:

Re: Consulting Agreement

This letter will confirm our understanding concerning the terms of retainer and nature of services to be performed for ABC Corporation. These terms are as follows:

1. Term. This agreement will be for a period of _____ commencing on _____. Either of us may terminate this agreement with thirty (30) days' written notice to the other party. In the event of termination, I will be compensated for services rendered through the date of termination.

2. Duties. My duties will include:

    a. Review, analysis, and recommendations for changes in the systems and organizational structure of the research division.

    b. Preparation of weekly reports on the progress of the project.

    c. Preparation of a final report and oral presentation for the management of the company, with recommendations for implementing system and organizational improvements and related costing.

3. Compensation. The compensation for my services shall be at the rate of $450 per day, payable on receipt as billed. Other out-of-pocket costs, such as travel expenses and secretarial services will be billed separately.

Enclosed is a copy of this agreement for your records. Please sign the original and return it to this office in the enclosed envelope. If you have any questions, please contact me.

Sincerely,

David Jones
Consultant

Accepted and agreed to:

_____   _____
Mary Roberts, President   Date
ABC Corporation

SAMPLE #19
LETTER OF AGREEMENT
(Prepared by client)

ABC Corporation
7890 Front Street
Anytown, Anywhere

_____ 198____

Smith Jones & Associates
Consultants
1234 Main Street
Anytown, Anywhere

Dear _____ :

Re: Consulting Project

I am pleased to announce that your proposal to ABC Corporation has been accepted. The conditions of our acceptance are as outlined below.

1. **Term.** Your appointment as a consultant to ABC Corporation (hereinafter called "the Corporation") is confirmed for the period _____ to _____.

2. **Services.** You shall perform such work or services as are set forth in Exhibit A, attached hereto and specifically made a part of this Agreement. The work or services to be performed by you may be changed by the Corporation from time to time by letter requests sent to you. You shall keep the Corporation informed on the progress of any work being performed under this Agreement.

3. **Compensation and expenses.**

(a) The Corporation will pay you a total fee of $ _____ for all work performed hereunder on satisfactory completion of the work.

(b) Your compensation will be at the rate of $ _____ per month for all work performed hereunder. You will be paid at the same time you are reimbursed for approved expenses under paragraph 3(c) below.

(c) You will receive reimbursement for the actual cost of reasonable expenses arising out of the work performed under this Agreement (not to exceed $ _____), subject to the approval of the Corporation. You shall deliver an itemized statement to the Corporation on a monthly basis that shows fully the work being performed under this Agreement and all related expenses. The Corporation will pay you the amount of any authorized expenses within thirty (30) days of the receipt of the itemized statement of all expenses, submitted together with receipts for all hotel, car rental, air fare, and other transportation expenses for all other expenses of $25 or more.

4. **Working facilities.** You will be furnished with such facilities and services as shall be suitable for your position and adequate for the performance of your duties under this Agreement.

164

5. **Reports.** Any and all reports, manuscripts and any other work products, whether completed or not, that are prepared or developed by you as a part of the work under this Agreement shall be the property of the Corporation and shall be turned over to the Corporation promptly at the Corporation's request or at the termination of this Agreement, whichever is earlier.

6. **Independent contractor.** You shall exercise control over the means and manner in which you perform any work requested hereunder, and in all respects your relationship to the Corporation shall be that of an independent contractor serving as a consultant and not as an employee.

7. **Termination.** This Agreement may be terminated upon thirty (30) days' written notice by either party.

8. **Confidential information.** You agree that for the term of your appointment hereunder and for two (2) years thereafter, that you will not disclose to any person, firm or corporation any confidential information regarding the Corporation, its business, directors, officers and employees.

9. **Nonassignable.** This Agreement is personal in nature and is not assignable by you or by the Corporation.

10. **Arbitration.** Any controversy or claim arising out of the interpretation of this Agreement shall allow either party to submit the disputed clause to Arbitration under the Arbitration Act of (name of jurisdiction). The costs of such arbitration to be borne equally by both parties.

11. **Entire agreement.** This letter, including Exhibit A, contains the entire agreement of the parties. It may not be changed orally but only by an agreement signed by the party against whom enforcement of any waiver, change, modification, extension or discharge is sought.

I trust that the terms of this appointment meet with your approval. If so, please indicate this by signing a copy of this letter and returning it to the Corporation. An additional copy of this letter is enclosed for your records.

Very truly yours,

_____
Client signature

Accepted and agreed to this _____ day of _____, 198 ____.

_____
Consultant signature

Other situations where a formal contract might be considered, are if you have a new client, a client who has never used consulting services before, or a client who has a reputation for being difficult in general, or complaining about fees in particular. Naturally, in this latter case, if you have advance notice it would be very wise to reconsider any involvement with that client.

Sample #21 illustrates a formal contract. Table #7 is a checklist of provisions frequently covered in contracts with government or industry.

4. Sub-consulting agreement

This is an agreement between you and any sub-consultants you employ to undertake a part or all of a consulting project you have arranged.

SAMPLE #20
STATEMENT OF GENERAL TERMS AND CONDITIONS

1. FEE STRUCTURE

All time, including travel hours, spent on the project by professional technical and clerical personnel will be billed. The following approximate ranges of hourly rates for various categories of personnel are currently in effect:

Category	Hourly Rate
Principal	$ 70
Consultant	50
Analyst	40
Technician	30
Typist	15

Hourly rates will be adjusted semi-annually to reflect changes in the cost of living index as published by (state name of appropriate government department). If overtime for non-professional personnel is required, the premium differential figured at time and one-half of their regular hourly rate is charged at direct cost to the project. Unless otherwise stated, any cost estimate presented in a proposal is for budgetary purposes only, and is not a fixed price. The client will be notified when 75% of any budget figure is reached, and the budget figure will not be exceeded without prior authorization from the client.

2. REIMBURSABLE EXPENSES

The following expenses will be billed at direct cost plus 15%:

(a) Travel expenses necessary for the execution of the project, including air fares, rental vehicles, and highway mileage in company or personal vehicles, which will, be charged at _____ cents per mile. Air travel will be by tourist class; except when tourist class service is not regularly available.

(b) Telephone charges
(c) Postage
(d) Printing and reproduction
(e) Computer services, including word processing

(f)   Other expenses directly attributable to the project.

Subcontracts will be billable at cost plus 15%.

3. INVOICES AND PAYMENTS

Invoices will be submitted monthly and payment is due on receipt of invoice. A 2% per month service charge will be added to all delinquent accounts. In the event Consultant shall be successful in prosecuting any suit for damages for breach of this agreement, including suits for non-payment of invoices, to enforce this agreement, or to enjoin the other party from violating this agreement, Consultant shall be entitled to recover as part of its damages its reasonable legal costs and expenses for bringing and maintaining any such action.

Rates for foreign contracts are negotiable and the above rates do not apply.

4. WARRANTY

Our professional services will be performed, our findings obtained, and our recommendations prepared, in accordance with generally and currently accepted management consulting principles and practices. The warranty is in lieu of all other warranties either expressed or implied.

5. LIMITATION OF PROFESSIONAL LIABILITY

The Client agrees to limit any and all liability or claim for damage, for cost of defense, or for any expenses to be levied against Consultant to a sum not to exceed $15,000, or the amount of our fee, whichever is less, when such claim arises from any error, omission, or professional negligence on the part of Consultant.

6. OTHER DOCUMENTS

(e.g., Proposal letter dated _____) is hereby made a part of this document.

7. ACCEPTANCE BY CLIENT

Client, by signing below, hereby agrees to these general terms and conditions of Client except as noted below:

CLIENT (typed name of client)

BY: _____

(Signature)

(Name and Designation)

SAMPLE #21
CONSULTING CONTRACT

ABC Trainers Inc. (hereinafter called "the Company") desires to utilize the expert assistance of _____ (hereinafter called "the Consultant") in the field or fields in which the Consultant has professional qualifications.

1. Parties and relationships

The Company is a corporation engaged in the business of consulting and the provision of technical assistance and training to small business through the use of skilled independent contractors. The Consultant is a person who by education, training and experience is skilled in the provision of the service required.

2. Character and extent of services

(a) It is the mutual intent of the parties that the Consultant shall act strictly in a professional consulting capacity as an independent contractor for all purposes and in all situations and shall not be considered an employee of the Company.

(b) The Consultant reserves full control of his activities as to the manner and selection of methods with respect to rendering his professional consulting services to the Company.

(c) The Consultant agrees to perform his activities in accordance with the highest and best state of the art of his profession.

3. Period of service and termination

(a) The period of service by the Consultant under this agreement shall be from _____ through _____ and may be renewed upon the mutual agreement of the parties hereto.

(b) Either the Company or the Consultant may terminate this agreement by giving the other party 30 days' written notice of intention of such action.

(c) The Company reserves the right to halt or terminate the conduct of a seminar-workshop by the Consultant without prior notice or claim for additional compensation should, in the opinion of the Company, such conduct not be in the best interests of the Company.

4. Compensation

(a) Upon the Consultant's acceptance hereof, the Company agrees to pay the Consultant according to the following schedule:

(Insert compenstion rate or fixed fee and any allowance for or schedule of allowable expenses, if any.)

(b) In the event that the Company desires, and it is mutually agreed to by the Consultant, the Consultant's services may be used in the conduct of training/consulting programs not specifically identified in paragraph 4(a). In such cases, the Company agrees to pay the Consultant on the basis of the following schedule:

(Insert compensation rate or fixed fee and any allowance for or schedule of allowable expenses, if any.)

(c) In the event of special circumstances, variations to the fee schedule of paragraphs 4(a) and 4(b) will be allowed as mutually agreed to in writing by the parties hereto.

5. Notification

The Consultant will be notified by the Company in writing to begin his participation in specific training and/or consultation assignments to which the fee schedule of paragraphs 4(a) and 4(b) apply. Such notification will include a statement of the time(s) and place(s) of the intended training/consultation involvement with other necessary information.

6. Expenses

The Consultant, as an independent contractor, shall be responsible for any expenses incurred in the performance of this agreement, except as otherwise agreed to in writing prior to such expenses being incurred. The Company will reimburse the Consultant for reasonable travel expenses incurred with respect hereto.

(A specification of "reasonable" may be inserted here).

7. Method of payment

(a)   The Consultant shall be paid as provided for in paragraphs 4(a) and 4(b) hereof, on the basis of a properly executed "Claim for Consulting Service" form (sample attached).

(b)   The "Claim for Consulting Service" form is to be submitted at the end of the calendar month during which consulting services are performed. Exceptions to this arrangement are allowed with the written approval of the Company.

(c)   Payment to the Consultant will be made by check, delivered by certified mail postmarked no later than _____ days subsequent to receipt of the "Claim for Consulting Service" form as provided for in paragraphs 7(a) and 7(b).

8. Copyrights

(a)   The Consultant agrees that the Company shall determine the disposition of the title to and the rights under any copyright secured by the Consultant or his employee on copyrightable material first produced or composed and delivered to the Company under this agreement. The Consultant hereby grants to the Company a royalty fee, non-exclusive, irrevocable license to reproduce, translate, publish, use and dispose of, and to authorize others to do so, all copyrighted or copyrightable work not first produced or composed by the Consultant in the performance of this agreement but which is incorporated into the material furnished under this agreement, provided that such license shall be only to the extent the Consultant now has or prior to the completion or final settlement of this agreement may acquire the right to grant such license without becoming liable to pay compensation to others solely because of such grant.

(b)   The Consultant agrees that he will not knowingly include any copyrighted material in any written or copyrightable material furnished or delivered under this agreement without a license as provided in paragraph 8(a) hereof or without the consent of the copyright owner, unless specific written approval of the Company to the inclusion of such copyrighted material is secured.

(c)   The Consultant agrees to report in writing to the Company promptly and in reasonable detail any notice or claim of copyright infringement received by the Consultant with respect to any material delivered under this agreement.

9. Drawings, designs, specifications

(a) All drawings, sketches, designs, design data, specifications, notebooks, technical and scientific data, and all photographs, negatives, reports, findings, recommendations, data and memoranda of every description relating thereto, as well as all copies of the foregoing, relating to the work performed under this agreement or any part thereof, shall be subject to the inspection of the Company at all reasonable times; and the Consultant and his employees shall afford the Company proper facilities for such inspection; and further shall be the property of the Company and may be used by the Company for any purpose whatsoever without any claim on the part of the Consultant and his employees for additional compensation, and subject to the right of the Consultant to retain a copy of said material shall be delivered to the Company or otherwise disposed of by the Consultant, either as the Company may from time to time direct during the progress of the work, or in any event, as the Company shall direct upon the completion or termination of this agreement.

10. Confidentiality

(a) It is understood that in the performance of his duties, the Consultant will obtain information about both the Company and the Company's client, and that such information may include financial data, client lists, methods of operating, policy statements, and other confidential data.

(b) The Consultant agrees to restrict his use of such above-mentioned information to the performance of duties described in this agreement. The Consultant further agrees to return to the Company and to the Company's client upon the completion of his duties any and all documents (originals and copies) taken from either organization to facilitate the project described herein.

11. Non-competition

The consultant agrees that he will not perform his professional services for any organization known to the Consultant to be a client of the Company unless the Company has employed the Consultant for the provision of such services to the client. This restriction shall remain in effect for a period of two years after the termination of this agreement. For the purposes of this section, "client" is defined as any organization, which during the said period of restriction, has engaged the Company to promote:

(Provide a list of all the services/products provided by the Company).

12. Applicable law

The parties agree that this agreement is to be construed according to the laws of
_____ (state jurisdiction).

13. Assignment

The Company reserves the right to assign all or any part of its interest in and to this agreement. The Consultant may not assign or transfer this agreement, any interest therein or claim thereunder without the written approval of the Company.

14. Integration

This agreement, executed in duplicate, constitutes the entire contract between the parties and may be cancelled, modified, or amended only by a written supplemental document executed by each of the parties hereto.

IN WITNESS WHEREOF, the parties hereto have accepted and executed this agreement this _____ day of _____, 198 ____.

_____
John Smith, Consultant

ABC Trainers Inc.

by: _____
(Authorized signatory)

TABLE #4
DETAILED CONTRACT CHECKLIST
(Commonly used for government contracts)

GENERAL

1. Date of agreement

2. Identification of client and consultant, including transfer of responsibility to successors (if the client is a public body, the authority under which it acts and the source of available funds should be specified.)

3. Review of the background and brief definition of the project.

4. Scope of the assignment, including references to any detailed description incorporated in appendices

5. Effective date of commencement of work, when different from 1. and estimated or stipulated time for completion

6. Designation of individuals in client and consultant organizations responsible for policy decisions

7. Work Statement containing a description of the requirements in detail (The description should include the problem to be solved or the objective of the investigation, the approach or method to be used, and the extent or degree of work to be undertaken. The proposed statement of work should be sufficiently descriptive so as to become a usable yardstick).

8. Provision for changes in the work requirements

9. Provision for arbitration of disputes

10. Provision for termination by either party for "cause" or "convenience"

RESPONSIBILITIES OF THE CONSULTANT

1. Specify a project leader, professional help, services, and information to be supplied

2. Work schedule to be maintained

3. Personnel to be supplied (may be detailed in appendix).

4. Availability for conferences with the client

5. Reporting, including the schedule and nature of reports

TABLE #4 — Continued

6. Ownership of designs, blueprints, reports, etc., to be specified in the contract

7. Safeguarding of information supplied by client

8. Guarantee of performance, where required.

9. Limitation of liability of the consultant with regard to loss or damage of reports, third party use of reports, errors or omissions or professional negligence (this provision for the benefit of the consultant)

10. Right to cancel the contract upon written notice of (x) days, provided that nonperformance of the other party can be clearly documented and provided that the defaulting party has been given (x) days to make good nonperformance.

11. Provision for disposal of any or all materials used in the performance of work

RESPONSIBILITIES OF THE CLIENT

1. Information, services, and facilities to be provided

2. Availability for conference with the consultant

3. Number of days of staff support by client agency staff

4. Prompt review and approval of reports and products

5. Changes clause

DURATION OF CONTRACT

1. Stipulation of termination, either by stating a specific date, or by indicating the duration of the operation from the execution of the contract

2. Provision and mechanism for the modification of the specified date by mutual agreement

3. Provision for extension or renewal

4. Provision and mechanism for early termination by either party

5. Termination by reason of events beyond control of either party

6. Provision against delays

FINANCIAL PROVISIONS

1. Total financial commitment by the client

2. Method and schedule of billing by the consultant

3. Method of payment

4. Currency or currencies of payment and conversation rates

5. Guarantee of payment by the client

6. Payment of interest on delayed payments

7. What are patent requirements? Who has copyright in reports and other products? Who has publication rights and under what circumstances?

8. Payment shall be made within (x) days of billing, billing to be by arrangement

TABLE #4 — Continued

9.   Allowable costs or expenses to be billed separately from labor costs shall include but not be limited to:

Telephone
Postage and courier
Travel
Accommodation & miscellaneous
Photocopying and printing
Graphics
Special typing support
Translation
Miscellaneous special materials
Computer costs
Subcontractual services

It is quite common for consultants to sub-contract work out to other consultants. You may use sub-consultants to keep overhead low, or if you are unable to perform the task yourself because you lack expertise in the area, or because a large project requires a large number of support resource personnel.

Generally you need not explain to your client that you are using sub-contracting services, unless your client specifically asks. Sometimes a client would like to have the qualifications of a sub-contractor clarified. You are ultimately responsible for the quality of the work performed by your sub-consultants and therefore must be very selective. You should monitor and approve all work performed by the sub-consultant. All services performed by the sub-consultant are performed under your consulting company's name. All correspondence pertaining to the project is printed only on your stationery. In all outward respects, the sub-consultant is your employee under your direction.

Your sub-contracting agreement should clearly spell out that the relationship of the sub-consultant to you is one of an independent contractor. You should also seriously consider a non-competition clause in the contract restricting the sub-contractor from taking advantage of access to your clients to sell consulting services directly. A non-competition clause or restrictive covenant can vary depending upon the circumstances and the laws of your jurisdiction. Legal advice should be obtained before you complete any contract to be certain that the non-competition clause would be reasonably upheld as fair and appropriate if it were contested. The clause normally states that the sub-consultant shall not perform professional services independently of your firm to any of your clients past or present. The exception would be under your direct employ as an independent contractor. A two-year time period for the restriction is fairly common. The restriction covers a wide or narrow geographic base depending on the nature of your services.

A summary of the standard clauses that should be considered include:

(a) The parties to the contract

(b) Independent contractor status of sub-consultant

(c) The responsibilities of the sub-consultant fully specified

(d) Term of the contract

(e) Amount and method of payment for fees and expenses

(f) A cancellation provision in case the contract is cancelled

(g) The method and amount of remuneration to be paid to the sub-consultant up to the point of cancellation

(h) A confidentiality provision stating that all the client information accessible to the sub-consultant is to be held in strict confidence

(i) All documents obtained by the sub-consultant are to be returned to the consultant or client

(j) Provision that the contract cannot be assigned or duties delegated without the written consent of both parties

(k) Other "standard" or "unique" provisions

Sample #21 which shows a consultant contract can also be used as a format for a sub-consulting contract.

5. Agency agreement

An agency agreement is a contract that would be prepared if you were acting for a client as an external agent: for example, if you were selling a product on behalf of a client, or negotiating on behalf of the client with the government for funding purposes. The clauses in this type of contract vary considerably. Generally the client prepares the agreement for you to sign.

6. Letter of retainer agreement

This is an agreement that you outline in a letter. One form of retainer relationship is when you are available "on call" at the request of a client based on need of your services. The consultant charges the client for being "on call" and available, even though the consultant may not be used.

Another form of retainer relationship is if you provide a service on a periodic basis, for example, monthly or quarterly.

e. PREPARING YOUR OWN CONTRACT

You should consider having several standardized contracts with variations depending on the different types of consulting services you perform. Space can be left in the contract for inserting the unique features of a specific consulting project. If your contracts are stored on a word processor or a personal computer with word processing capabilities, each contract can easily be personalized in an original format for each consulting job.

The process of preparing your own contract is not difficult. Try to obtain as many sample forms of contracts as possible from your competitors and from contract books that are available from your local library or law school. Then refer to the various headings outlined in this chapter or shown in the sample contracts or checklists. Outline the areas that you feel are important for your particular type of consulting services or problems. As soon as you have completed this exercise, expand on the points in a descriptive paragraph and then sub-divide into clauses in a format appropriate to your needs and in a style you prefer.

Take your draft contracts to your lawyer to evaluate. It is to your benefit to save your lawyer's time and your money by preparing the documents yourself. You are most familiar with your work and the important factors of your projects. Your lawyer can review your draft contracts and rewrite them or add additional clauses if required.

Major companies or government frequently have their own standardized contracts and send them to you for signature. In some cases there is room for negotiation; in other cases no negotiation is possible. If you are presented with the contract, you should review it thoroughly yourself and mark the areas that cause you concern. Also, note the areas that are not in the contract that you would prefer to have covered. Then discuss the contract with your lawyer. If you have any doubts about the required provisions of the contract, it is best to either negotiate those provisions out if possible, or not accept the project. If a contract is not completely to your liking, the degree of risk or dissatisfaction on your part or your client's part is high.

If a client wants to make changes to your contract, it is better to make the changes rather than have them make up their own contract. A client-prepared contract could have clauses or conditions you do not want.

In summary, attempt to prepare all your own contracts. The client relationship will therefore be established on *your* terms. Your initiative and leadership in preparing the contract should have a positive effect on the dynamics of the relationship with your client.

19

EXPANDING YOUR PRACTICE

There are many ways of acquiring clients. The simplest way is to keep your existing clients happy and nurture the present and past clients well. Studies show that over 70% of a consultant's business is based on repeat business or referral business from existing clients. A marketing formula shows that the average person has over 200 contacts including friends, relatives, and associates. By carefully developing this client potential you can expand your practice rapidly.

For example, from one satisfied client you could obtain numerous projects sufficient to keep you busy on an ongoing basis. If your client gives you repeat work on a regular basis and also recommends you to 10 other business associates in the same industry and 5 of them become clients, your business will grow. Former employees of the first client or referral clients may go to work for other firms in the private or public sector. If they enjoyed working with you, they will request your services again or refer work to you. The possibilities are limitless.

An effective way of keeping your clients satisfied is to create client dependency. The more the client relies on you because of your specialty, the more repeat business you will generate. The more your client respects you for your knowledge and leadership, the more the client will look to you for guidance.

It is important that the client feel in control at all times. You must maintain your image as a unique commodity. Your role is to complement staff. You do not want to be perceived as just another person on staff.

If there are particular tasks that the client does not enjoy, and you can fill the void and have the skills and ability to perform the task, and the situation seems appropriate, this could create further dependency. If the outcome of a project is particularly successful and considerable positive feedback occurs, make a point of having your client share the glory with you. A satisfied client will appreciate your value, and provide you with more consulting contracts.

There are other ways of developing your practice. Expanding your line by adding additional services that are natural extensions of your first service is effective. If you have clients that retain you for one service, you are creating a potential two or three-fold growth pattern with all your clientele. Because you already have the credibility with the client for one project, it will be much easier for you to market your skills for the other services.

Sub-contracting is another way of expanding your practice. You can locate sub-contractors from your contract contact network and through referral. They can be effectively used to increase your earnings by providing depth and greater capacity for your business. You would be in a position to make proposals for larger or more complex projects using past, present or future clients as your base. If a client has been satisfied with your service on a smaller project or a particular service line, and you have additional service lines and a greater depth and capacity, the prospects are endless. Naturally, sub-contracting will involve more administration for you, but the independent contractor status of sub-consultants will allow you flexibility to hire them on a need basis.

Other ways of expanding your practice are to review all aspects of your operation on an ongoing basis, note the weak areas and develop a specific plan for dealing with them. Areas such as self-promotion and more efficient follow-up on leads can also enhance your clientele base.

A free brochure about seminars, mail order books, and tapes concerned with consulting practices is available upon request.

Please send your comments about this book, or your request for further information to:

Professional Development International
#310 - 1070 West Broadway
Vancouver, British Columbia
V6H 1E7

or

#200 - 15 Veteran Way
Oakland, California 94602

BIBLIOGRAPHY

a. GENERAL CONSULTING

Altman, Mary Ann & Weil, Robert I. *Managing Your Accounting and Consulting Business.* Matthew Bender, 1978.

Bailey, Geoffrey. *Maverick: Succeeding as a Freelance Entrepreneur.* Lester & Orpen Dennys, 1983.

Blake, Robert R. & Mauton, Jane S. *Consultation.* Addison Wesley, 1970.

Gore, George J. & Wright, Robert G. *The Academic Consultant's Connection.* Kendall-Hunt Publishing Co., 1979.

Guttman, H.P. *The International Consultant.* McGraw-Hill, 1976.

Holtz, Herman. *How to Succeed as an Independent Consultant.* John Wiley & Sons, 1983.

Johnson, Barbara L. *Private Consulting.* Prentice-Hall, 1982.

Kelley, Robert E. *Consulting: the Complete Guide to a Profitable Career.* Charles Scribner's Sons, 1981.

Lant, Jeffrey L. *The Consultant's Kit.* JLA Publications, 1981.

Lippitt, Gordon & Lippitt, Ronald. *The Consulting Process in Action.* University Associates Inc., 1978.

McGonagle, John J. *Managing the Consultant: a Corporate Guide.* Chilton Books, 1981.

Pickens, Judy E. *The Freelancer's Handbook.* N.J.: Prentice-Hall, 1981.

Pilon, Daniel H. & Bergguist, William H. *Consultation in Higher Education.* Council for Advancement of Small Colleges, 1979.

Shenson, Howard L. *Consulting Handbook.* Howard L. Shenson Inc., 1982.

_____ *The Successful Consultant's Guide to Fee Setting.* Howard L. Shenson Inc., 1980.

———————————— *How to Strategically Negotiate the Consulting Contract.* Bermont Books, 1980.

Spiro, Herbert T. *Financial Planning for the Independent Professional.* John Wiley & Sons, 1978.

Stanley, C.M. *The Consulting Engineer.* John Wiley & Sons, 1961.

Steele, Fritz. *Consulting for Organizational Change.* University of Massachusetts Press, 1975.

Smith, Brian R. *The Country Consultant.* Consultant News, a Division of Kennedy & Kennedy, Inc., 1982.

b. CONSULTING NEWSLETTERS

Consultant's News (monthly). Kennedy & Kennedy Inc., Templeton Road, Fitzwilliam, NH 03447.

Consulting Opportunities Journal (bimonthly), 1629 K Street, N.W., Suite 520, Washington, DC   20006.

Grantsmanship Center News (8 times a year). The Grantsmanship Center News, 1015 West Olympia Blvd., Los Angeles, CA 90015.

International Consulting News (semi-annually). International Consultants Foundation, 5605 Lamar Road, Washington, DC 20016.

The Professional Consultant (monthly). Howard L. Shenson Inc., 20121 Ventura Blvd., Woodland Hills, CA 91364.

c. GOVERNMENT CONSULTING

Bermont, Hubert. *The Successful Consultant's Guide to Winning Government Contracts.* Bermont Books, 1981.

Bermont, Hubert & Garnin, Andrew. *How to Win with Information or Lose Without It.* Bermont Books, 1981.

Cohen, W.A. *How to Sell to the Government.* John Wiley & Sons, 1981.

Gowan, Vincent Q. *Consulting to Government.* Ottawa: Infoscan Ltd., 1979.

Holtz, Herman. *The $100 Billion Market: How to do Business with the U.S. Government.* AMACOM, 1980.

_____ *Directory of Federal Purchasing Offices: Where, What, How to Sell to the U.S. Government,* John Wiley & Sons, 1981.

_____ *Government Contracts: Proposalmanship and Winning Strategies.* Plenum Publishing Corp., 1979.

Murphy, Harry. *Grantsmanship Consulting.* Howard L. Shenson Inc., 1981.

d. MANAGEMENT CONSULTING

Albert, Kenneth J. *How to be Your Own Management Consultant.* McGraw Hill Book Company, 1978.

Fuchs, Jerome H. *Making the Most of Management Consulting Services.* American Management Association, 1975.

_____ *Management Consultants in Action.* Hawthorne Books Inc., 1975.

Greiner, Larry E. & Metzger, Robert O. *Consulting to Management.* Prentice Hall, 1983.

How to Control the Quality of a Management Consulting Engagement. Association of Consulting Management Engineers, 1972.

Klein, Howard J. *Other People's Business: A Primer on Management Consultants.* Mason-Charter Publishing, 1977.

Kubr, M. *Management Consulting: A Guide to the Profession.* International Labor Office, 1982.

Kuttner, M. *Managing the Paperwork Pipeline.* John Wiley & Sons, 1978.

Schein, E. *Organizational Psychology.* Prentice-Hall, 1965.

Thompson, A.A. and Strickland, A.J. *Strategy Formulation and Implementation.* Business Publications, 1980.

e. MARKETING

Gray, Douglas A. and Cyr, Donald G. *Marketing Your Product.* Self-Counsel Press, 1987.

Hammeroff, Eugene & Nichols, Sandra. *How to Guarantee Professional Success: 765 Tested, Proven Techniques for Promoting Your Practice.* Bermont Books, 1982.

Holtz, Herman. *Winning Clients.* John Wiley & Sons, 1988.

Johnston, Karen and Withers, Jean. *Selling Strategies for Service Businesses.* Self-Counsel Press, 1988.

Kennedy, James H. *Public Relations for Management Consultants.* Consultants News.

Kotler, Philip and Bloom, Paul N. *Marketing Professional Services.* Prentice-Hall, 1984.

Lant, Jeffrey. *The Unabashed Self-Promoter's Guide.* Jeffrey Lant Associates Inc., 1983.

Mahon, J.J. *The Marketing of Professional Accounting Services.* John Wiley & Sons, 1978.

Marcus, Bruce W. *Competing for Clients.* Probus Publishing, 1986.

Shenson, Howard L. & Schacter, J. *Marketing Your Professional Services.* Howard L. Shenson Inc., 1981.

Todd, Alden, *Finding Facts Fast: How to Find Out What You Want to Know Immediately.* William Morrow & Company, 1972.

Watson, Dr. Ken, *The Consultant's Guide to Business Development.* Evaluation & Strategic Management Associates Ltd., 1984.

Webb, Stan. G. *Marketing and Strategic Planning for Professional Service Firms.* Amacom, 1982.

Weiner, Richard D. *Professional's Guide to Public Relations.* Richard Weiner Inc.

Wilson, Aubrey. *The Marketing of Professional Services.* McGraw Hill, 1972.

Withers, Jean and Vipperman, Carol. *Marketing Your Service.* Self-Counsel Press, 1987.

f.   NEGOTIATING

Coffin, R.A. *The Negotiator.* American Management Association, 1973.

Cohen, Herb. *You Can Negotiate Anything.* Bantam Books, 1980.

Fisher, Roger & Ury, William. *Getting to Yes: Negotiating Agreement Without Giving In.* Houghton-Mifflin, 1981.

Karrass, Chester L. *Give and Take: The Complete Guide to Negotiating Strategies and Tactics.* Thomas Y. Crawell Publishers, 1974.

Levin, Edward. *Negotiating Tactics: Bargain Your Way to Winning.* Fawcett Columbine Books, 1982.

Niremberg, Gerard I. *The Art of Negotiating.* Cornerstone Library, 1968.

——————————— *The Art of Creative Thinking.* Simon & Shuster, 1982.

——————————— *Fundamentals of Negotiating.* Hawthorn/Dutton, 1968.

——————————— *How to Give and Receive Advice.* Editorial Correspondents Inc., 1975.

Niremberg, Gerard I. & Calero, H. *How to Read a Person Like a Book.* Simon & Shuster, 1971.

——————————————— *Meta-talk: How to Uncover the Hidden Meanings in What People Say.* Simon & Shuster, 1973.

Schatzki, Michael. *Negotiation: The Art of Getting What You Want.* New American Library, 1981.

Warschaw, Tessa Alberta. *Winning by Negotiation.* McGraw-Hill, 1980.

g. NEWSLETTERS

Beach, Mark. *Editing Your Newsletter.* International Self-Counsel Press, 1983.

Holtz, Herman. *Successful Newsletter Publishing for the Consultant.* Bermont Publishing, 1983.

Hudson, H.P. *Publishing Newsletters.* Charles Scribners Sons, 1980.

The Newsletter on Newsletters. Newsletter Clearinghouse.

Shenson, Howard L. *How to Develop and Promote Your Own Newsletter for Profit and/or Personal Image Building.* Howard L. Shenson, Inc., 1980.

h. PRESENTATIONS AND PUBLIC SPEAKING

Boettinger, Henry M. *Moving Mountains: The Art of Letting Others See Things Your Way.* MacMillan.

Carnegie, Dale. *How to Develop Self-Confidence and Influence People by Public Speaking.* Simon and Shuster, 1936.

Dunckel, Jacqueline & Parnham, Elizabeth. *The Business Guide to Effective Speaking.* International Self-Counsel Press, 1984.

Leech, Thomas. *How to Prepare, Stage and Deliver Winning Proposals.* Amacom, 1982.

Lewis, David V. *Secrets of Successful Writing, Speaking and Listening.* Amacom, 1982.

Shenson, Howard L. *How Consultants Can Build a Lucrative Paid Speaking Business.* Howard L. Shenson Inc., 1982.

Spicer, Keith. *The Winging It Logic System.* Doubleday, 1982.

i. PROPOSAL WRITING AND REPORTS (see also Writing and Publishing)

Ammon-Wexsler, J. & Carmel, C. *How to Create a Winning Proposal.* Mercury Publications, 1978.

Bermont, Hubert. *The Successful Consultant's Guide to Writing Proposals and Reports.* Bermont Books, 1979.

Dunnigan, J.A. & Shenson, Howard L. *The Consultant's Guide to Proposal Writing.* Howard L. Shenson, 1981.

Ewing, D.W. *Writing for Results in Business, Government, Science and the Professions.* John Wiley & Sons, 1979.

Gallagher, William J. *Report Writing for Management.* Addison-Wesley, 1969.

Holtz, Herman and Schmidt, Terry. *The Winning Proposal: How to Write It.* McGraw Hill, 1981.

Kapp, R.P. *The Presentation of Technical Information.* Constable & Company Ltd., 1973.

Mandel, S. & Caldwell. *Proposal and Inquiry Writing.* MacMillan, 1962.

Program Planning and Proposal Writing. The Grantsmanship Center News.

Strunk, W. & White, E.B. *The Elements of Style.* MacMillan Publishing, 1972.

Watson, Dr. Ken. *Preparing Winning Proposals.* Evaluation & Strategic Management Associates Ltd., 1982.

j. SELF-EVALUATION AND DEVELOPMENT

Bolles, Richard N. *The Three Boxes of Life and How to Get Out of Them.* Ten Speed Press.

——————— *What Color is Your Parachute: A Practical Manual for Job-hunters and Career Changes.* Ten Speed Press, 1984.

Crystal, John C. and Bolles, Richard N. *Where Do I Go From Here With My Life.* Ten Speed Press, 1981.

Gray, Douglas A. *The Entrepreneur's Complete Self-Assessment Guide: How to accurately determine your potential for success.* International Self-Counsel Press, 1986.

Lakein, Alan. *How to Get Control of Your Time and Your Life.* The New American Library, 1973.

Molloy, John. *Dress for Success.* Warner Books, 1975.

Traxel, K. *Manager's Guide to Successful Job Hunting.* McGraw-Hill, 1978.

k. SMALL BUSINESS MANAGEMENT

Albert, Kenneth J. *How to Pick the Right Small Business Opportunity.* McGraw-Hill, 1977.

Armstrong, Michael. *Be a Better Manager.* International Self-Counsel Press Ltd., 1984.

Baumbeck, Clifford M. & Lawyer, Kenneth. *How to Organize and Manage a Small Business.* Prentice-Hall, 1979.

Brown, Beaner. *The Entrepreneur's Guide.* Ballantine Books, 1982.

Curtin, Richard T. *Running Your Own Show: Mastering the Basics of Small Business.* New American Library, 1982.

Dible, D. *Up Your Own Organization: A Handbook to Start and Finance a New Business.* The Entrepreneur Press, 1978.

Gray, Douglas A. and Gray, Diana L. *The Complete Canadian Small Business Guide.* McGraw-Hill Ryerson, 1988.

Greene, Gardiner G. *How to Start and Manage Your Own Business.* New American Library, 1983.

James, Jack. *Starting a Successful Business in Canada.* International Self-Counsel Press, 1986.

Mancuso, Joesph R. *How to Start, Finance and Manage Your Own Small Business.* Prentice-Hall, 1978.

_____ *Small Business Survival Guide.* Prentice-Hall, 1980.

Maumes, William. *The Entrepreneurial Manager in the Small Business.* Addison-Wesley, 1978.

Timmons, J., Smollen, L. and Dingee, A. *New Venture Creation: A Guide to Small Business Development.* Richard D. Irwin Inc., 1977.

l.   TIME/STRESS MANAGEMENT

Anderson, R. *Stress Power.* Human Science Press, 1978.

Benson, H. *The Relaxation Response.* Avon Books, 1975.

Bliss, E. *Getting Things Done.* Charles Scribners Sons, 197'6.

Friedman, M. & Rosenman, R. *Type A Behavior and Your Heart.* Fawcett Crest, 1974.

Lahaye, Tim. *How to Manage Pressure Before Pressure Manages You.* Zonderervan Publishing House, 1983.

Lakein, A. *How to Get Control of Your Time and Life.* The New American Library, 1974.

Mackenzie, R. Alec. *The Time Trap: How to Get More Done in Less Time.* McGraw-Hill, 1972.

McCay, James T. *The Management of Time.* Prentice-Hall, 1950.

McRae, Brad. *Practical Time Management.* Self-Counsel Press, 1988.

Neidhardt, E. J.; Weinstein, M. S.; and Conry, R. F. *Managing Stress.* Self-Counsel Press, 1985.

Rosen, G. *The Relaxation Book.* Prentice-Hall, 1977.

Selye, Hans. *Stress Without Distress.* New American Library, 1974.

Taylor, Harold L. *Making Time Work For You: A Guidebook to Effective and Productive Time Management.* General Publishing Co. Ltd., 1981.

_____ *Managing Your Memory.* General Publishing Ltd., 1982.

_____ *Personal Organization: The Key to Managing Your Time and Your Life.* Time Management Consultants Inc., 1983.

Warshaw, Leon J. *Managing Stress.* Addison-Wesley Publishing Co., 1979.

m. WRITING AND PUBLISHING (see also Proposal Writing and Reports)

Applebaum, Judith and Evans, Nancy. *How to Get Happily Published.* Harper & Row.

Bermont, Hubert. *The Successful Consultant's Guide to Authoring, Publishing and Lecturing.* Bermont Books, 1979.

Davidson, Marion and Blue, Martha. *Making It Legal: A Law Primer for the Craftmaker, Visual Artist and Writer.* McGraw Hill, 1979.

Ewing, David W. *Writing for Results in Business, Government and the Professions.* John Wiley & Sons, 1974.

Goodman, Joseph. *How to Publish, Promote and Sell Your Book.* Adams Press, 1980.

Mathiew, Aron. *The Book Market: How To Write, Publish and Market Your Book.* Andover Press, 1981.

The Writers Handbook. The Writer Inc.

Provost, Gary. *The Freelance Writer's Handbook.* New American Library, 1982.

Wilbur, Perry L. *How to Write Articles That Sell.* John Wiley & Sons, 1981.

_____ *How to Write Books That Sell.* Contemporary Books, 1979.

n. SEMINARS AND WORKSHOPS

Murray, Sheila L. *How to Organize and Manage a Seminar.* Prentice-Hall, 1983.

Shenson, Howard L. *How to Create and Market a Successful Seminar or Workshop.* Howard L. Shenson Inc., 1981.

Watson, Walter; Pardo, Luis & Tomouic, Vladislav. *How to Give an Effective Seminar.* General Publishing, 1978.

SOURCES OF PROCUREMENT AND CONTRACTS INFORMATION

a. SCIENCE PROCUREMENT INFORMATION NETWORK (CANADA)

This is a computerized "source information system" maintained by the Department of Supply and Services as a service to client departments. All consultants should ask for their capabilities to be entered on the system. This can take four to six months from the time of application.

Consultants' names are retrieved from the system by a "keyword" coding. The department has a book of keywords that covers location, industry groups, science fields, and specialization: *The Index of Science Procurement Key Words.*

Searches are normally done sequentially. First with a full list of desirable keywords, then, depending on the response, with less specific or demanding lists.

Write to:

Data Administrator
Science Procurement Information
    Network & Main Sourcing List
Supply and Services Canada
Place du Portage, Phase 3
Floor 10C1
11 Laurier Street
Hull, Quebec
K1A 0S5

Professional Services Branch
    Sourcing List (Canada)
Science and Professional Services Directorate
Place du Portage, Phase 3
11 Laurier Street
Hull, Quebec
K1A 0S5

b. THE R & D BULLETIN (CANADA)

The R & D Bulletin is published by the Canadian federal government in the second week of each month and contains three main sections:

(a) Projects for which proposals are expected to be invited

(b) Statistical summary

(c) Contracts awarded during the previous month

The first section describes selected research and development requirements for which the Science Centre of the Department of Supply and Services expects to solicit proposals. Organizations interested in submitting proposals may get further information from the science contract manager, listed against each requirement, at the following address:

Science Centre
Supply and Services Canada
Place du Portage, Phase 3
11 Laurier Street
Hull, Quebec
K1A 0S5

c. BULLETIN OF BUSINESS OPPORTUNITIES (CANADA)

This is a weekly listing of contracts awarded. Its only interest is perhaps the general one of seeing what other firms and departments are doing. Occasionally useful for identifying a subcontracting opportunity.

Information Services
Supply and Services Canada
Place du Portage, Phase 3
11 Laurier Street
Hull, Quebec
K1A 0S5

Program Export Market Development (Canada)
Department of External Affairs
125 Sussex Drive
Ottawa, Ontario
K1A 0G2

d. MULTILATERAL PROJECT INFORMATION SYSTEM (CANADA)

Each month Industry, Trade and Commerce (Canada) distributes project updates on multilateral projects worldwide. Distributed only to Canadian companies and organizations.

Office of Overseas Projects
Department of Industry, Trade and Commerce
Ottawa, Ontario
K1P 3X4

e. COMMERCE BUSINESS DAILY (U.S.)

The *Commerce Business Daily* (CBD) is published each weekday by the U.S. Department of Commerce. It identifies proposed defense procurements valued in excess of $10,000, and civilian agency procurements in excess of $5,000. It also lists contract awards over $25,000 for civilian agencies and $50,000 for military agencies. It is an essential source of information for the consultant.

The announcements are in a form similar to newspaper classified ads. A complete list of the classification headings is currently given on the back of the subscription form.

The principal sections of the CBD include:

(a) Business news: Announcements of procurement conferences, trade fairs, seminars, and small business assistance conferences.

(b) Procurement of services:

- Experimental development, test and research work
- Expert and consultant services
- Maintenance and repair of equipment
- Modification, alteration and rebuilding of equipment
- Technical representative services
- Operation and maintenance of government-owned facility
- Installation of equipment
- Medical services
- Architect — engineer services
- Housekeeping services
- Photographic, mapping, printing and publication services
- Training services
- Transportation services
- Lease or rental, except transportation equipment
- Miscellaneous
- New construction and major additions to existing buildings
- Maintenance repair and operation of real property

(c) Procurement of supplies, equipment and material

(d) Research and development sources sought

In order that potential sources may learn of research and development programs, advance notice of the government's interest in a specific research field is published here. Firms having the research and development capabilities described are invited to submit complete information to the purchasing office listed. Information requested generally includes: the total number of employees and professional qualification of scientists, engineers, and personnel specially qualified in the R & D area outlined, and description of general and special facilities, an outline of previous projects including specific work previously performed or being performed in the listed R & D area; statement regarding industrial security clearance previously granted; and other available descriptive literature. Note that these are not requests for proposals. Respondents are not notified of the results of the evaluation of the information submitted, but the sources deemed fully qualified are considered when requests for proposals are solicited. Closing date for submission of responses is 14 days from publication of the notice, unless otherwise specified.

(e) Contract awards

(Same subdivisions as earlier "procurements" section.)

(f) Trade leads

(Foreign construction and direct sales opportunities.)

CBD notices inform the reader whether response may be in the form of a request to be included among a list of possible contractors who will each be sent a formal request for proposal, or whether potential contractors should respond with a resume of experience, qualifications and capabilities to provide the advertised service, material or research. In the latter case, the RFP will be sent only if the qualifications are considered suitable for the proposed project.

(g) Numbered notes

As a space-saver the first issue of each week contains a definition for each of a series of numbered notes that are used in subsequent issues.

By the time a Request for Proposal appears in the CBD, the project will have been under active development within the government department for several months.

(h) Exemptions from publication in the CBD

Contracts of less than $10,000, classified contracts for reason of national security, and contracts resulting from an unsolicited proposal containing proprietary information.

A sole source procurement is published as an announcement for information only. This usually is a procurement where the government has been conducting research under contract with a certain firm and desires to extend the work for an additional period of time.

(i) Sources sought

A Sources Sought publication normally describes an area of research and development, rather than a specific program. It is used to cut down on the volume of synopses and to restrict those firms receiving copies of the Request for Proposal to only those actually qualified.

The information asked for will be equipment and facilities available, previous experience, resumes of key personnel, management ability, etc. It does not call for specific answers to specific problems but only for information to establish your capability to do research in the area of interest. It usually will have a response cutoff date and a prompt reply is

192

to your advantage. Sources Sought are published throughout the year, but usually during the summer to cover the coming fiscal year's program which begins October 1. After the responses to Sources Sought are evaluated, the respondents are not officially informed of their evaluation, but those found qualified are placed on a source list as a potential contractor in that area of interest. It is generally possible to confer with the evaluation team members concerning their assessment of your capabilities.

Government buyers are not allowed to give out either the size of the source list or the names of the sources. In all cases, the engineer and the buyer have the option, if they feel the firm is qualified, of adding firms to the source list even though those firms did not respond to the publication in the *Commerce Business Daily*.

(j) CBD subscription information

To order send remittance with full mailing address to:

Superintendent of Documents
Government Printing Office
Washington, DC 20402
(202) 783-3238.

Purchase order must be accompanied by payment. Make checks payable to Superintendent of Documents. Allow approximately six weeks for delivery of first issue.

f. COMMERCE CLEARING HOUSE REPORTS

Government Contracts Reports (U.S.) and numerous other U.S. and Canadian reports are available from:

Commerce Clearing House Inc. (U.S.)
425 13th Street, N.W.
Washington DC 20004

CCH Canada
6 Garamond Court
Don Mills, Ontario M3C 1Z5

g. FOUNDATION RESEARCH SERVICE (U.S.)

Foundation Research Service (F.R.S.), a subsidiary of Lawson & Williams Associates Inc., a management consultant firm, has dealt with the 1,000 largest foundations that account for 90% of all grants to all types of programs. They have introduced a new fundraising aid, called *The Foundation 500*. This publication is a cross-referenced system that matches foundations with 70 detailed subject categories such as arts, education, health, religion, international, science, welfare, etc. It also provides recipient-by-state categories showing what foundations have given in which of the 70 categories and in which of the 50 states and the District of Columbia.

Contact:

Foundation Research Service
c/o Lawson & Williams Associates, Inc.
39 East 51st Street
New York, NY 10022

h. THE CATALOGUE OF FEDERAL DOMESTIC ASSISTANCE

CFDA is the basic research tool for government grant seekers. Entries include complete information on numerous grant programs, and are cross-indexed.

Of special interest are Information Contacts and Related Programs. The former tells you where to find additional information on the program; the latter tells you where in CFDA you can find similar projects.

It gives information on grants, loans, loan guarantees, scholarships, mortgage loans, and insurance or other types of financial assistance. It also lists sources of assistance in the form of provision of federal property, facilities, equipment, goods, or services — including the donation of surplus, real, or personal property.

The CFDA is organized into three indexes: a functional index, a subject index, and an agency program index. Detailed program descriptions in the center portion of the catalogue are listed in the same order as the agency program index, alphabetically by name of the agency.

Continuous updating keeps the catalogue as current as possible, but the rapidity with which federal programs are wiped out and new ones established is such that it cannot be assumed that any listing is completely accurate at any given time.

The CFDA, a publication of the Executive Office of the President, Office of Management and Budget, may be ordered from:

Superintendent of Documents, U.S.
Government Printing Office
Washington, DC 20402

i. THE GRANTS REGISTER

The Grants Register is a broad research tool containing information on international granting programs as well as those conducted in the United States.

The Grants Register (current edition), Roland W. Turner (ed.), St. Martin's Press, Inc., New York, NY.

j. FUNDRAISING MANAGEMENT

This magazine has information about fundraising, such as computerized mailing lists, capital campaigns and whether you should use a window envelope for your direct mail piece. As one of the few commercial publications in the fundraising field, *Fundraising Management* is loaded with ads about direct mail lists, volunteer and donor recognition items, and conferences.

Write to:

Hoke Communications
224 Seventh Street
Garden City, Long Island, NY 11530

k. THE GUIDE TO FEDERAL ASSISTANCE (U.S.)

This is an information service on federal assistance programs, updated monthly. It includes consultation by "hot line" with staff. Write to:

The Guide to Federal Assistance
5791 Beaumont Avenue
La Jolla, CA 92037

l. THE FEDERAL REGISTER (U.S.)

The Federal Register, which is published every weekday by the U.S. Government, is a vital source of information about new programs and program changes. When legislation authorizing a program is signed into law, regulations implementing the legislation are supposed to be developed before funds are obligated. Those regulations must be published in the *Register*.

The Federal Register often contains valuable information on government contracts and/or grant programs described in *The Catalog of Federal Domestic Assistance*. Announcements related to programs usually deal with changes, expansions, or clarifications of programs already in existence. The *Register* is indexed monthly.

The Federal Register
Superintendent of Documents
U.S. Government Printing Office
Washington, DC 20402

m. LOCAL GOVERNMENT FUNDING REQUEST

Although oriented toward the concerns of local government, this newsletter may be of interest to consultants in that it offers fairly extensive coverage of developments in a number of policy and program areas. Write:

Government Information Services
752 National Press Building, N.W.
Washington, DC 20004

n. WASHINGTON RESEARCHERS (U.S.)

This information service provides clients with background reports, sources of information, expert opinions, documents from federal departments and agencies, facts and statistics, and Washington representation. The emphasis is on locating sources of information in the federal government. It includes:

- *The Information Report.* Quarterly. Free to clients.
- Sources of information on corporations
- List of country experts in the federal government
- List of industry analysts in the federal government
- List of foreign firms with U.S. affiliates
- Sources of information for selling to the federal government

Write to:

Washington Researchers
2612 P Street N.W.
Washington, DC 20007

o. PROFESSIONAL SERVICES MANAGEMENT JOURNAL

Contains a variety of information useful to consultants in the design, architectural, and engineering fields, including current developments in contracting, marketing, time management, quality control, and consulting.

Practice Management Associates Ltd.
Ten Midland Avenue
Newton, MA 02158

p. CONSULTING DIRECTORIES

(a) *Consultants & Consulting Organizations Directory (Gale Research Company)*

Edited by Paul Wasserman and Janice McLean. 1,034 pages; 5,314 entries. Cross index of subjects; subject index of U.S. and Canadian firms by location; index of foreign firms; index of individuals.

Entries cover 10 major points of information:
- Name of organization
- Address
- Telephone number
- Date founded
- Branch offices
- Principals: officials and titles
- Type of clients
- Non-profit or profit-making

- Description of services: type of consulting performed
- Code numbers for subjects in which firm is active

Entries cover 146 fields of activity (cross-referenced).

(b) *Who's Who in Consulting (Gale Research Company)*

Edited by Paul Wasserman and Janice McLean. Cross index of subjects; subject index of consultants by location. Contains 7,500 entries; each entry covers 9 points:

- Individual's name
- Addresses, business and home
- Date and place of birth
- Education: institutions attended, degrees and dates
- Career data
- Current position(s)
- Memberships in professional associations
- Consulting specialties
- Published works

Cross-referenced by subject area and geographic location

(c) *A Periodic Supplement to Consultants and Consulting Organizations Directory (Gale Research Company)*

Edited by Paul Wasserman and Janice McLean. Each issue contains approximately 250 new entries and two cumulative indexes:

- Subject index of firms by location
- Alphabetical index of individuals

(d) *Management Consultant's Bibliography (Institute of Management Consultants, N.Y.)*

q. NATIONAL TECHNICAL INFORMATION SERVICES

This division of the U.S. Department of Commerce offers a wide variety of reports and information services based on federally funded research. Subjects include technical information, business, industry, economics, government and health planning. NTIS, 5285 Port Royal Road, Springfield, VA 22161.

r. THE WORLD BANK: OPERATIONAL SUMMARY OF PROPOSED PROJECTS

The World Bank has launched a quarterly publication listing projects up for tender around the world. Besides giving details of the projects, worth in total billions of dollars each year, it states their current status: either identification, feasibility, appraisal, negotiation, approval or procurement.

The Johns Hopkins University Press
Journals Division
Baltimore, MD 21218

s. OTHER RESOURCE INFORMATION MATERIAL

1. Canada

Corpus Almanac and Canadian Sourcebook, Vol. 1 & 2, Gage Publishing, 1989.

Directory of Associations of Canada (4th edition), Micromedia, 1989.

Canadian Government Programs & Services CCH Canada, 1989.

Handbook of Grants & Subsidies of the Federal and Provincial Governments (Canada) STM Research & Publication, Montreal, 1989.

Canada: Trade and Commerce, *Selling to the Canadian Government*, Ottawa

Canada: Treasury Board, *Contracts for the Services of Individuals*, Ottawa

Canada: Treasury Board, *Fee Guidelines for Personal Service Contracts with Industries*, Ottawa

Canada: Supply and Services, *Selling Goods and Services to the Federal Government.*

2. United States

National Trade and Professional Associations and Labor Unions of the U.S. and Canada (23rd edition), Columbian Books, 1988.

Directory of Management Consultants, second edition, 1980. Available from publisher, Kennedy & Kennedy, Templeton Road, Fitzwilliam, N H   03447.

Encyclopedia of Professional Management, second edition, 1980. Kennedy & Kennedy, Fitzwilliam, NH.

Findex: Directory of Market Research Reports, Studies and Surveys. Offers a place to check for proposal-writing information. Information Clearing House, NY.

A Guide to Management Services, Dun and Bradstreet, New York, 1968. Describes numerous services that are marketed by consultants. Includes references for additional information.

How to Find Information about Companies. Identifies sources, such as public records, credit reporting and trade associations. Washington Researchers, Washington, DC

APPENDIX 2

CONSULTING ASSOCIATIONS
(U.S. AND CANADA)

AAHC   American Association of Hospital Consultants
         Suite 830 - 2341 Jefferson Davis Highway
         Arlington, VA   22202

AAMLC   American Association of Medico Legal Consultants
         2200 Benjamin Franklin Parkway
         Philadelphia, PA   19130

AAPBC   American Association of Professional Bridal Consultants
         42 Woodridge Circle
         West Hartford, CT   06107

AAPC   American Association of Political Consultants
         Suite 1406 - 1101 North Calvert Street
         Baltimore, MD   21202

ACCCE   Association of Consulting Chemists &
                  Chemical Engineers, Inc.
         50 East 41st Street
         New York, NY   10017

ACEC   American Consulting Engineers Council
         Suite 802 - 1015 15th Street, N.W.
         Washington, DC   20005

ACF   Association of Consulting Foresters
         Box 369
         Yorktown, VA   23690

ACME   Association of Consulting Management Engineers
         230 Park Avenue
         New York, NY   10017

AERC   Association of Executive Recruiting Consultants, Inc.
         30 Rockefeller Plaza
         New York, NY   10020

AFCCE
: Association of Federal Communications Consulting Engineers
525 Woodward Avenue
Bloomfield Hills, MI 48013

AHCC
: Academy of Health Care Consultants
Suite 3342 - 875 North Michigan Avenue
Chicago, IL 60611

AICPA-MAS
: American Institute of Certified Public Accountants,
  Management Advisory Services Division
1211 Avenue of the Americas
New York, NY 10036

APA
: American Psychological Association — Division of Consulting
  Psychologists
1200 17th Street, NW
Washington, DC 20036

APEC
: Automated Procedures for Engineering Consultants, Inc.
Miami Valley Tower, Suite M-15
Dayton, OH 45402

APMHC
: Association of Professional Material Handling Consultants
1548 Tower Road
Winnetka, IL 60093

APS
: Association of Productivity Specialists
One Illinois Center
Chicago, IL 60601

ASAC
: American Society of Agricultural Consultants
Suite 470, Enterprise Center
8301 Greensboro Drive
McLean, VA 22102

ASCA
: American Society of Consulting Arborists
12 Lakeview Avenue
Milltown, NJ 08850

ASEC
: Association of Consulting Engineers of Canada
Suite 616 - 130 Albert Street
Ottawa, Ontario
K1P 5G4

ASCP   American Society of Consultant Pharmacists
2300 9th Street, South
Arlington, VA 22264

ASCP   American Society of Consulting Planners
1717 North Street, NW
Washington, DC 20036

CABC   Canadian Association of Broadcast Consultants
2639 Portage Avenue
Winnipeg, Manitoba
R3J 9P7

CAMC   Canadian Association of Management Consultants
Suite 805
121 Bloor Street E.
Toronto, Ontario
M4W 3M5

FFCS   Food Facilities Consultants Society
135 Glenlawn Avenue
Sea Cliff, NY 11579

FCSI   Foodservice Consultants Society International
1400 Pickwick Avenue
Glenview, IL 60025

IABPC   International Association of Book Publishing Consultants
52 Vanderbilt Avenue
New York, NY 10017

ICCA   Independent Computer Consultants Association
Box 27412
St. Louis, MO 63141

IMC   Institute of Management Consultants
Room 810 - 19 West 44th Street
New York, NY 10036

NAFC   National Association of Financial Consultants
Suite 114 - 11059 East Bethany Drive
Aurora, CO 80014

NAMAC   National Association of Merger and Acquisitions Consultants
               Suite 282 - 4255 LBJ Freeway
               Dallas TX   75234

NAPCA   National Association of Pension Consultants & Administration
               Suite 300 - Three Piedmont Center
               Atlanta, GA   30305

NAPENA   National Association of Public Employer Negotiators and
                   Administrators
               1400 N. State Parkway
               Chicago, IL   60610

NCAC   National Council of Acoustical Consultants, Inc.
               66 Morris Avenue
               Springfield, NJ   07081

NICMC   National Institute of Certified Moving Consultants
               222 West Adams Street
               Chicago, IL   60606

NPC   National Personnel Consultants
               Suite 1702 - Pennsylvania Building
               Philadelphia, PA   19102

MCDAM   Managerial Consultation Division of the Academy of
                   Management
               College of Business
               University of Southern Florida
               Tampa, FL   33620

PMI   Project Management Institute
               Box 43
               Drexel Hill, PA   19026

PRSA   Public Relations Society of America, Inc.
               845 Third Avenue
               New York, NY   10022

RAAA   Relocation Assistance Association of America
               950 17th Street
               Denver, CO   80202

SMCAF   Society of Medical Consultants to the Armed Forces
             Box 4033
             Harrisburg, PA   17111

SPBC   Society of Professional Business Consultants
             221 North LaSalle Street
             Chicago, IL   60601

FREE OR NOMINAL COST BUSINESS PUBLICATIONS

a. UNITED STATES

1. Small Business Administration (SBA) Publications

A number of business publications are available from SBA. For copies call 800-433-7217 (in Texas call 800-729-8901) or write to:

Small Business Administration
P.O. Box 15434
Fort Worth, Texas 76119

There are publications available under these headings:

(a) Management Aids

(b) Small Marketers Aids

(c) Small Business Bibliographies

(d) Small Business Management Series

2. Internal Revenue Service

The IRS publishes many free pamphlets and guides to help the small business person. Request a complete list from your local IRS office.

3. Bank of America

Following is the list of business pamphlets from the *Small Business Reporter Series* available at nominal charge from the Bank of America. For copies, contact your local branch.

Beating the Cash Crisis

Avoiding Management Pitfalls

Business Management; Advice from Consultants

Cash Flow/Cash Management

Financing Small Business

Understanding Financial Statements

Equipment Leasing

Personnel for the Small Business

Steps to Starting a Business

Advertising Small Business

Marketing New Product Ideas

b. CANADA

1. Royal Bank of Canada

Following is the list of business pamphlets from the *Guide to Independent Business Series: Your Business Matters* available at no charge from the Royal Bank of Canada. For copies, contact your local branch.

Starting a Business

Market Planning

How to Finance Your Business

Planning and Budgeting

Control Over Direct Costs and Pricing

Good Management — Your Key to Survival

Advertising and Sales Promotion

Control Over Inventory Investments

Financial Reporting and Analysis

Credit Management and Collection

Evaluation and Management of Fixed Assets

Management of Liabilities and Equities

Pointers to Profit

Taxation

Management Audit

Managing Time for Profit and Growth

Exporting — Importing

Managing the Future

2. Federal Business Development Bank (FBDB)

Numerous publications, kits and other materials are available at no charge from the FBDB. Contact a local office for further information.

PROPOSAL EVALUATION CHECKLIST

a. GENERAL FACTORS

(a) Has the bidder responded with an appropriate technique or is he or she trying to fit the problem to a favorite technique?

(b) What priority will this project receive from the consultant? How important will it be to his or her firm?

(c) Does the proposal meet the Terms of Reference and the intended scope of the study?

(d) How useful or capable of implementation will the end product be?

(e) What degree of originality is present in the proposal?

(f) Are the submission of progress reports and presentation of interim briefings required? What progress reports and interim briefings are planned?

(g) What degree of direct consultant-client liaison is proposed? Does the consultant-client relationship include a training component for the client's personnel? What type of training is proposed?

(h) Is the proposed content of progress reports in accordance with the requirements of the client? Will progress reports contain a monthly statement of costs incurred, commitments, and, if necessary, a revised estimate of total costs?

(i) When the project is completed, how does the consultant intend to hand over the project?

(j) What degree of follow-up and/or debriefing is proposed? To whom do the relevant data belong and what happens to them when the project is completed?

b. PAST PERFORMANCE

(a) Is the usual business of the offeror closely related to the proposed work?

(b) Do the references to past experience include activities specifically related to the requirements of the proposed study?

(c) Has the proposer been honored by professional societies because of the performance in a specific professional area?

(d) What reputation does the firm hold in the area of the proposed study?

(e) Has the firm worked for this client before, and if so with what success?

(f) Are the statements of past performance worded in a meaningful way so you can identify what work was actually performed?

(g) Are there aspects of past performance that indicate particular weaknesses or strengths?

c. SCOPE OF WORK

(a) Has the proposal demonstrated an understanding of the problems to be solved?

(b) Is this research area new to the company?

(c) Has the offeror made an accurate assessment of the problem based on an interpretation of the requirements set forth in the work statement?

(d) Has the offeror presented an approach that will achieve the stated objectives?

(e) Is the proposed approach supported with justification of why it should achieve the evaluation objectives?

(f) Do you think the suggested approach will work?

(g) Has the offeror introduced unanticipated events which may result in a project overrun or an expanded scope of work?

(h) Does the proposal distinguish between the simpler and the more difficult performance requirements?

(i) Does the proposal convincingly show a depth of understanding of the problem?

(j) Are the technical problems clearly delineated or are they merely "parroted" from the proposal request?

(k) Have the limits of the problem been specified to show that the proposed study will be restricted to an appropriate scope?

(l) Is there a concise but adequate review of literature? Is the literature review merely an annotated bibliography or is it a scholarly critique?

(m) Are the specific objectives of the proposal clearly stated? Are these goals realistic in view of time, equipment, budget, and professional experience of the principal investigator?

(n) Does the plan, in fact, permit an unequivocal test of the stated hypotheses of research questions?

(o) Does the proposal represent a unique, imaginative approach?

(p) Is the technical program fully responsive to all written requirements and specifications?

(q) Are there any apparent discrepancies or omissions?

(r) Are "products" clearly defined and presented?

d. PERSONNEL

(a) Is it clear which tasks in the study specific personnel will be assigned to and for what amount of time?

(b) Are the personnel assigned to specific tasks qualified by training and experience to successfully perform the tasks?

(c) Is there a clear organization chart depicting project management? Is the apportionment of personnel level and time to specific tasks realistic?

(d) What assurances are made concerning the availability of personnel proposed? Was a contingency plan requested if certain personnel become unavailable?

(e) Have enough time and personnel been included to provide adequate administrative management of the study?

(f) Is the author of the proposal one of the key personnel?

(g) Does the success of the project depend, to a large degree, upon personnel not directly associated with the prospective firm?

(h) Do biographies relate specific experience of personnel to the specific needs of this project?

(j) Does the proposal show the capabilities of the management to handle a project of the size contemplated?

(k) Is the position of the program manager in the overall organization and the limits of his or her authority and responsibility shown?

(l) Are the type, frequency, and effectiveness of management controls and method for corrective action shown?

(m) Does the task organization integrate the overall organization in terms of effective lines of authority and communication, and in terms of effective integration of research, development, design, drafting, technical writing, and where appropriate test functions?

(n) Is it clearly demonstrated that top-level management will continue a high level of interest and assume responsibility for successful accomplishment of the program?

(o) Is the proposal dependent upon recruitment of key personnel?

e. PLANNING AND MANAGEMENT

(a) Has the work schedule been specified clearly, and is it realistic in terms of time and money? Does it fit with available personnel?

(b) If time of performance is important and is a competitive evaluation factor, is the proposed schedule supported by the technical proposal?

(c) Is the planning realistic? Does it follow recognized and accepted procedure?

(d) Does the proposal show that the delivery schedule will be met and how it will be met?

(e) Is sufficient detail regarding master scheduling, programming, follow-up, and other like functions given to reinforce the foregoing assurance?

(f) Are the various technical phases of the project detailed and realistically scheduled?

(g) Are effective review, evaluation, and control provided at specific checkpoints?

(h) Has the offeror allowed for all necessary clearances; e.g., OMB (U.S.), Statscan (Canada)?

f. FACILITIES

(a) Are the facilities and equipment needed for successful completion of the study specified in the proposal?

(b) How does the offeror intend to access facilities not at the contractor's site?

(c) Does the use of facilities outside of the contractor's firm require a subcontract? If so, is the proposed subcontractor specifically mentioned, along with an explanation of its required qualifications?

(d) Is the planned use of facilities, such as printing, data processing, etc., realistic?

(e) If computer services are required, are there controls built into the processing so corrective action can be taken at intermittent points if necessary?

(f) Is any government-furnished equipment required?

(g) Are the proposed laboratory and test facilities adequate for the requirements of the technical scope of work?

(h) Are resources overly committed?

g. COST

(a) Is the overall cost within range of your (the contracting agency's) budget?

(b) What is the relationship between the cost figures and equivalent items in the technical proposal?

(c) Are the personnel costs reasonable according to the tasks to be performed?

(d) Are the appropriate personnel assigned to perform the appropriate tasks?

(e) Have expenditures been set aside for subcontracting requirements, such as data processing?

(f) If a large-scale questionnaire must be mailed, has an adequate sum been set aside for postage?

(g) Have costs for development of instruments, purchase of materials, such as scoring sheets, etc., been included?

(h) Does the travel seem reasonable when compared to the tasks to be accomplished?

(i) If consultants or experts are included, is their daily rate reasonable and within the proper financial range? Is the proposed time reasonable?

(j) Is an appropriate type of contract requested?

(k) Is the schedule of payment acceptable?

(l) Have appropriate procedures been used to estimate costs?

OTHER TITLES IN THE SELF-COUNSEL SERIES

MARKETING YOUR SERVICE
A planning guide for small business
by Jean Withers, M.B.A. and
Carol Vipperman, B.A.

To effectively sell the service you offer, you must let people know that you exist and that you are better than your competition. Owners of service businesses are often inexperienced in marketing and unsure about how to market themselves in a professional manner.

This book explains what is necessary to develop a marketing plan that will work for service businesses ranging from law firms and dental practices to hair salons and auto repair shops. Whether your service is consulting or running a restaurant, you will profit from expanding your market.

The authors, consultants to service businesses, have provided 32 worksheets for you to develop your own specific marketing plan based on the procedures they describe. $12.95

Contents include:

- Stating your company mission
- Gathering the facts about your business
- Gathering the facts about outside influences
- Discovering problems and opportunities
- Setting goals and objectives
- Target markets and positioning
- Implementing the marketing action plan

SELLING STRATEGIES FOR SERVICE BUSINESS
How to sell what you can't see, taste, or touch
by Karen Johnston, M.A. and
Jean Withers, M.B.A.

Selling services requires new skills and challenges, and in this book the authors combine their nearly 20 years' experience to bring together the information you need to help you be more profitable and successful.

Diagrams, figures, and samples help illustrate the skills discussed, and 23 worksheets are provided for you to work out your own specific selling strategy. $12.95

Contents include:

- Styles of selling
- Overcoming resistance to selling
- Asking for what you're worth
- Setting sales goals
- Understanding why your clients buy
- How to find clients
- Overcoming phone-phobia
- Getting ready for the sales call
- Establishing rapport in the sales call
- Getting information from your client
- Talking about your service
- Handling your buyer's questions, concerns, and objections
- Getting a "yes"
- Follow-up, follow-up, follow-up

PREPARING A SUCCESSFUL BUSINESS PLAN
A practical guide for small business
by Rodger Touchie, B.Comm., M.B.A.

At some time, every business needs a formal business plan. Whether considering a new business venture or rethinking an existing one, an effective plan is essential to success. From start to finish, this working guide outlines how to prepare a plan that will win potential investors and help achieve business goals.

Using worksheets and a sample plan, readers learn how to create an effective plan, establish planning and maintenance methods, and update their strategy in response to actual business conditions. $14.95

Contents include:

- The basic elements of business planning
- The company and its product
- The marketing plan
- The financial plan
- The team
- Concluding remarks and appendixes
- The executive summary
- Presenting an impressive document
- Common misconceptions in business planning
- Your business plan as a tangible asset

UNDERSTANDING FINANCIAL INFORMATION
The non-financial manager's guide
by Michael M. Coltman, M.B.A.

Many small business people are frightened by the prospect of balancing ledgers, drawing up income statements and balance sheets, and comparing their current assets to their liabilities. However, this book takes the mystery out of accounting. In easy-to-understand language, this book takes you through the "after the basics" accounting procedure for the small business. $7.95

Contents include:

- An overview of accounting
- Financial statements
- Depreciation
- Income statement analysis
- Balance sheet analysis
- Internal control
- Cost management
- Fixed and variable costs
- Cost-volume-profit analysis
- Budgeting
- Cash management
- Long-term investments
- Leasing

BASIC ACCOUNTING FOR THE SMALL BUSINESS
Simple, foolproof techniques for keeping your books straight and staying out of trouble
by Clive Cornish, C.G.A.

Having bookkeeping problems? Do you feel you should know more about bookkeeping, but simply don't have time for a course? Do you wish that the paperwork in your business could be improved, but you don't know where or how to start?

This book is a down-to-earth manual on how to save your accountant's time and your time and money. Written in clear, everyday English, not in accounting jargon, this guide will help you and your office staff keep better records. U.S. edition $6.95, Canadian edition $7.95

Contents include:
- Your accountant
- On buying a business
- Sales, across the counter, in the mail
- Cash
- Receivables
- Payables
- The synoptic journal
- The general ledger
- Expenses
- The bank and you
- Payrolls
- Inventories
- Contents of a balance sheet
- What is "cash flow?"
- The general journal
- The trial balance
- The columnar work sheet
- Plus 30 samples of the various journals and financial statements

A PRACTICAL GUIDE TO FINANCIAL MANAGEMENT
Tips and and techniques for the non-financial manager
by Michael Coltman, M.B.A.

Good financial management is the key to high profits. It takes more than hard work and the right product to be successful in a small business. You must know how to manage your financial resources wisely and effectively. This book explains in easy-to-understand language how to get the most from every dollar you spend or save. It provides practical, realistic advice for those managers who do not have a background in finance, and it illustrates the many kinds of financial statements you should know how to draw up. $7.95

Contents include:
- Financial ratio analysis
- Working capital management
- Cash budgeting
- Equity financing
- Debt financing
- Short-term financing
- Intermediate - and long-term financing
- Sources of funding
- Financial plan
- Long-term asset management
- Leasing
- 21 samples

STANDARD LEGAL FORMS AND AGREEMENTS
Steve Sanderson, editor

This book provides a wide selection of indispensable legal forms and common business agreements ready to be copied and filled in with the particulars of the arrangement. It features a lay-flat binding and all samples are provided full-size in this large format volume so that no fussing with enlargements is necessary and copying is both easy and perfect quality. U.S. ed. $14.95; Canadian ed. $14.95

- New businesses — agreement of purchase — partnership agreement
- Services — engagement of services
- Employment — employment agreement — employee dismissal letter
- Buying — invitation to quote — cancellation of purchase order
- Selling — bill of sale — limited warranty
- Collections — request for payment — bad check letter
- Credit/Debit — personal credit application — guarantee
- Leases — commercial lease — agreement to cancel lease
- Assignments — assignment with warranties

ORDER FORM
All prices are subject to change without notice. Books are available in book, department, and stationery stores. If you cannot buy the book through a store, please use this order form. (Please print)

Name _____

Address _____

_____

Charge to:
❏ Visa   ❏ MasterCard

Account Number _____

Validation Date _____

Expiry Date _____

Signature _____

❏ Check here for a free catalogue outlining all of our publications.
IN CANADA

Please send your order to the nearest location:
Self-Counsel Press
1481 Charlotte Road
North Vancouver, B. C. V7J 1H1
Self-Counsel Press
#8 — 2283 Argentia Road
Mississauga, Ontario L5N5Z2

IN THE U.S.A.
Please send your order to
Self-Counsel Press Inc.
1704 N. State Street
Bellingham, WA 98225

YES, please send me:
_____ copies of **Marketing Your Service,** $12.95

_____ copies of **Selling Strategies for Service Businesses,** $12.95

_____ copies of **Preparing a Successful Business Plan,** $14.95

_____ copies of **Understanding Financial Information,** $7.95

_____ copies of **Basic Accounting for the Small Business** U.S. edition. $6.95 Canadian edition, $7.95

_____ copies of **A Practical Guide to Financial Management,** $7.95

_____ copies of **Standard Legal Forms and Agreements,** $14.95

Please add $2.50 for postage & handling.
WA residents, please add 7.8% sales tax.
In Canada, please add 7% GST to your order.

T2-CSE-520

RACE AND ETHNIC RELATIONS 96/97

Sixth Edition

Editor

John A. Kromkowski
Catholic University of America

John A. Kromkowski is president of The National Center for Urban Ethnic Affairs in Washington, D.C., a nonprofit research and educational institute that has sponsored and published many books and articles on ethnic relations, urban affairs, and economic revitalization. He is Assistant Dean of the College of Arts and Sciences at the Catholic University of America, and he coordinates international seminars and internship programs in the United States, England, Ireland, and Belgium. He has served on national advisory boards for the Campaign for Human Development, the U.S. Department of Education Ethnic Heritage Studies Program, the White House Fellows Program, the National Neighborhood Coalition, and the American Revolution Bicentennial Administration. Dr. Kromkowski has edited a series sponsored by the Council for Research in Values and Philosophy titled *Cultural Heritage and Contemporary Change*. These volumes include scholarly findings and reflections on urbanization, cultural affairs, personhood, community, and political economy.

A Library of Information from the Public Press

Cover illustration by Mike Eagle

**Dushkin Publishing Group/
Brown & Benchmark Publishers**
Sluice Dock, Guilford, Connecticut 06437

The Annual Editions Series

Annual Editions is a series of over 65 volumes designed to provide the reader with convenient, low-cost access to a wide range of current, carefully selected articles from some of the most important magazines, newspapers, and journals published today. Annual Editions are updated on an annual basis through a continuous monitoring of over 300 periodical sources. All Annual Editions have a number of features designed to make them particularly useful, including topic guides, annotated tables of contents, unit overviews, and indexes. For the teacher using Annual Editions in the classroom, an Instructor's Resource Guide with test questions is available for each volume.

Printed on Recycled Paper

VOLUMES AVAILABLE

Abnormal Psychology
Africa
Aging
American Foreign Policy
American Government
American History, Pre-Civil War
American History, Post-Civil War
American Public Policy
Anthropology
Archaeology
Biopsychology
Business Ethics
Child Growth and Development
China
Comparative Politics
Computers in Education
Computers in Society
Criminal Justice
Developing World
Deviant Behavior
Drugs, Society, and Behavior
Dying, Death, and Bereavement
Early Childhood Education
Economics
Educating Exceptional Children
Education
Educational Psychology
Environment
Geography
Global Issues
Health
Human Development
Human Resources
Human Sexuality

India and South Asia
International Business
Japan and the Pacific Rim
Latin America
Life Management
Macroeconomics
Management
Marketing
Marriage and Family
Mass Media
Microeconomics
Middle East and the Islamic World
Multicultural Education
Nutrition
Personal Growth and Behavior
Physical Anthropology
Psychology
Public Administration
Race and Ethnic Relations
Russia, the Eurasian Republics, and Central/Eastern Europe
Social Problems
Sociology
State and Local Government
Urban Society
Western Civilization, Pre-Reformation
Western Civilization, Post-Reformation
Western Europe
World History, Pre-Modern
World History, Modern
World Politics

Cataloging in Publication Data
Main entry under title: Annual editions: Race and ethnic relations. 1996/97.
    1. Race relations—Periodicals. 2. United States—Race relations—Periodicals. 3. Culture conflict—United States—Periodicals. I. Kromkowski, John A., *comp.* II. Title: Race and ethnic relations.
ISBN 0–697–31716–1   305.8′073′05

© 1996 by Dushkin Publishing Group/Brown & Benchmark Publishers, Guilford, CT 06437

Sixth Edition

Printed in the United States of America

Editors/ Advisory Board

To the Reader

In publishing ANNUAL EDITIONS we recognize the enormous role played by the magazines, newspapers, and journals of the *public press* in providing current, first-rate educational information in a broad spectrum of interest areas. Within the articles, the best scientists, practitioners, researchers, and commentators draw issues into new perspective as accepted theories and viewpoints are called into account by new events, recent discoveries change old facts, and fresh debate breaks out over important controversies.

Many of the articles resulting from this enormous editorial effort are appropriate for students, researchers, and professionals seeking accurate, current material to help bridge the gap between principles and theories and the real world. These articles, however, become more useful for study when those of lasting value are carefully *collected, organized, indexed,* and *reproduced* in a *low-cost format,* which provides easy and permanent access when the material is needed. That is the role played by ANNUAL EDITIONS. Under the direction of each volume's *Editor,* who is an expert in the subject area, and with the guidance of an *Advisory Board,* we seek each year to provide in each ANNUAL EDITION a current, well-balanced, carefully selected collection of the best of the public press for your study and enjoyment. We think you'll find this volume useful, and we hope you'll take a moment to let us know what you think.

The information explosion and expansion of knowledge about the range of diversity among and within societies have increased awareness of ethnicity and race. During previous periods of history, society was discussed in terms of a universal sense of common humanity. Differences between societies and the arrangements of economic production were noted, but they were usually explained in terms of theories of progressive development or of class conflict that was leading toward a universal and homogenized humanity. Consciousness of the enduring pluralism expressed in ethnic, racial, and cultural diversity that constitutes the human condition has emerged throughout the world. It appears, however, that the dimensions of diversity are significantly, if not essentially, shaped by social, economic, cultural, and, most importantly, political and communitarian processes. Creativity and imagination influence ethnic and racial relations.

The following collection of articles was designed to assist you in understanding ethnic and racial pluralism in the United States. Unit 1, for example, illustrates how the most basic legal principles of a society—and especially the U.S. Supreme Court's interpretation of them—are especially significant for the delineation of ethnic groups and for the acceptance of cultural pluralism. Subsequent sections include illustrative articles of ethnic interaction with and within American society. The immigration of persons, the focus of unit 2, into a relatively young society such as America is of particular concern, because the fragility of social continuity is exposed by the recognition of changes in the ethnic composition of American society.

The contemporary experiences of indigenous groups, including Native Americans, are arranged in unit 3. Discussion of the experiences of the descendants of the earliest and the most recently arrived ethnic populations and the legal framework for participating in America is extended in unit 4 on Hispanic/Latino Americans and unit 5 on Asian Americans. Unit 6 explores various dimensions of the African American experience. The experiences of these ethnicities form a cluster of concerns addressed in the traditional literature that focused on marginality, minority, and alienation. New voices from within these traditions suggest bridges to the topics included in unit 7, titled "The Ethnic Legacy," which exposes and articulates neglected dimensions of ethnicity derived from the industrial development of America. Unit 8, "The Ethnic Factor: International Challenges for the 1990s," broaches national and international implications of ethnic exclusivity and the imperatives of new approaches to group relations. Unit 9 focuses on understanding the origins of racialism and the ideas that shape consciousness of group affinities and, especially, the emergence of scientific claims of racialism in public affairs. This section ends with suggestions that religious and ethnic affinities may emerge as a forceful social influence and that our inability to bridge racial and ethnic gaps as well as our misunderstandings of the paradoxes of integration could impose heavy burdens on regional and national efforts to resolve differences. Our national and universal moral sensibilities compel us to search for new paradigms and new approaches that foster values of institutional and attitudinal inclusiveness.

The American experience, especially those legal protections that are most sacred, has been explained by many as the development of personal freedom. This focus is not entirely valid. For nearly eight decades, Americans have become increasingly aware of the ways that group and personal identity are interwoven, forming a dense network of culture, economy, polity, and sociality. This perspective on the American reality was fashioned from the experiences of the children and grandchildren of post–Civil War immigrants to the United States. Their valuation of a new form of pluralism—one beyond the dichotomous divide of white-Negro/freeman-former slave—became central to a new vision of American society. Thus, their language of ethnic relations aspires to refashion the dichotomous logic of social divisiveness that is historically derived from the race-slavery consciousness and institutional legacy of the English-American tradition. This reinterpretative project opts for a more complex matrix of ethnicities and cultures that constitute our common humanity.

Readers may have input into the next edition of *Race and Ethnic Relations* by completing and returning the prepaid article rating form in the back of the book.

John A. Kromkowski
Editor

Contents

Unit 1

Race and Ethnicity in the American Legal Tradition

Eight articles in this section include Supreme Court decisions that established the legal definitions of race, citizenship, and the historic landmarks of equal protection and due process, as well as discussions of civil rights doctrine and implementation and the rise of new critical legal theories that challenge traditional remedies.

To the Reader	iv
Topic Guide	2
Overview	4

1. *Dred Scott v. Sandford,* from *U.S. Reports,* 1856.   6
This case concerned Dred Scott, a slave who was taken by his owner to a free state, where he lived for several years until he was again taken back into a slave state. Dred Scott filed suit, claiming that because he had lived in a free state, he had lost his ***status as a slave.*** The U.S. Supreme Court ruled that Dred Scott was still a slave and that the U.S. Constitution did not protect African Americans—neither those free nor those held as slaves.

2. One Drop of Blood, Lawrence Wright, *The New Yorker,* 10
July 25, 1994.
This article explores the methods used to define ***racial and ethnic variety.*** The classification of racial and ethnic standards on federal forms and statistics proposed in 1977 by the Office of Management and Budget does not appear to be sufficient, and a reformulation of ***government data*** is currently under way.

3. *Plessy v. Ferguson,* from *U.S. Reports,* 1896.   17
In this case the Supreme Court examined the constitutionality of Louisiana laws that provided for ***the segregation of railroad car seating*** by race. The Court upheld this type of "Jim Crow" law, contending that segregation did not violate any rights guaranteed by the U.S. Constitution. In a bitter dissent, Justice John Harlan argued that "our Constitution is color-blind, and neither knows nor tolerates classes among citizens."

4. *Brown et al. v. Board of Education of Topeka et al.,* 24
from *U.S. Reports,* 1954.
In *Brown v. Board of Education,* the U.S. Supreme Court began to ***dismantle state-supported segregation*** of the nation's schools. In this landmark opinion, the court overturned *Plessy v. Ferguson,* which had legitimized racial segregation of public facilities. The Court ruled that "in the field of public education, the doctrine of 'separate but equal' has no place," for "separate education facilities are inherently unequal."

5. *University of California Regents v. Bakke,* from *U.S. Reports,* 1977.   27
In ***Regents of California v. Bakke,*** the U.S. Supreme Court addressed the question of whether or not a special admissions program to the medical school at the University of California at Davis that guaranteed admission for certain ethnic minorities violated the constitutional rights of better-qualified, ***nonminority applicants.*** In *Bakke,* a splintered Supreme Court upheld a lower court order to admit an applicant who had been denied admission on the basis of his race.

6. High Court Loosens Desegregation's Grip, Kevin Johnson 32
and Andrea Stone, *USA Today,* June 13, 1995.
These accounts of Supreme Court decisions trace ***a new line of argument and national policy*** that promises to shift governmental programs designed to end school segregation and discrimination in employment and in public contracting.

7. As Deadline Nears, Court Leaders Pin Hopes on "Holding 5," Joan Biskupic, *The Washington Post,* June 7, 1995.   34
Joan Biskupic explains what Supreme Court justices go through when writing majority rulings. Decisions are now being prepared in this term's cases, one involving how much race can be considered in drawing up congressional voting districts.

8. Court Grows Critical When Race, Law Intersect, Tony 36
Mauro and Tom Watson, *USA Today,* June 30, 1995.
This article and its maps review a cluster of cases in which the Supreme Court ruled that using race as a primary reason for redistricting, to remedy discrimination and to enhance the chances of minority representation, is unconstitutional.

The concepts in bold italics are developed in the article. For further expansion please refer to the Topic Guide and the Index.

Unit 2

Immigration: The American Experience in a New Era of Mobility

Seven articles in this section review the historical record of immigration and current concerns regarding patterns of immigration and the legal, social, cultural, and economic issues that are related to immigrants in the American experience.

Unit 3

Indigenous Ethnic Groups

Seven articles in this section review the issues and problems of indigenous peoples, and they portray the new relationship indigenous people are forging with concurrent governments and the processes that protect indigenous traditions within pluralistic societies.

Overview　　38

9. **A Nation of Immigrants,** Bernard A. Weisberger, *American Heritage,* February/March 1994.　　40
The author surveys *immigration* through periods of American history. America, he contends, is a nation of immigrants. The restrictionists' arguments have been heard before and will be heard again.

10. **Census Bureau Finds Significant Demographic Differences among Immigrant Groups,** Susan Lapham, *U.S. Department of Commerce News,* September 23, 1993.　　53
Susan Lapham's report on significant *demographic differences among immigrant groups* arrays an essential set of findings. Forecasts regarding the contributions of new immigrants to America can be derived from these findings.

11. **The Foreign-Born Population: 1994,** Kristin A. Hansen and Amara Bachu, *Current Population Reports,* August 1995.　　58
These social, economic, and geographic indicators establish a *quantitative framework and profile of the foreign-born populations* and an accurate baseline for discussion of current immigration issues.

12. **Is Latest Wave a Drain or Boon to Society?** Maria Puente, *USA Today,* June 30, 1995.　　63
Maria Puente offers an array of Immigration and Naturalization Service data from 1991 to 1993 on 2.2 million legal immigrants, the *geographic patterns of settlement,* and the results of a national poll of immigrants.

13. **Pride and Prejudice,** Brian Bergman, *Maclean's,* November 7, 1994.　　66
This reflection on *immigration in Canada* discusses the realities that are imposed by the movement of populations and the issues of settlement and group relations that challenge growing countries and attractive economies.

14. **Coping with Deportation—The Integration of Millions of Refugees,** Hans Klein, *Deutschland,* April 1995.　　68
Hans Klein explores *the consequences of immigration* and addresses the emergence of approaches to national unity that parallel the expansion of borders and the movement of peoples in Europe.

15. **The Limits to Cultural Diversity,** Harlan Cleveland, *The Futurist,* March/April 1995.　　70
This article ponders the *consequences of ethnic diversity* and prescribes a "cheerful acknowledgment of difference" as the imperative of a global civilization.

Overview　　74

16. **12th Session of UN Working Group on Indigenous Peoples,** Glenn T. Morris, *Fourth World Bulletin,* Fall 1994/Winter 1995.　　76
This report on the United Nations' structures, debate, and unresolved questions regarding *the rights of indigenous peoples* as well as the role of the U.S. government in shaping issues of self-determination indicates new horizons for the current politics of conflict resolution among peoples and states.

17. **Paupers in a World Their Ancestors Ruled,** Eugene Robinson, *Washington Post National Weekly Edition,* July 8–14, 1991.　　84
Eugene Robinson explains how deteriorated *the position of the natives* of South America has become. Many Indians continue to live in areas today where their ancestors flourished centuries ago.

18. **Struggling to Be Themselves,** Michael S. Serrill, *Time,* 88
November 9, 1992.
Michael Serrill's profiles of *indigenous populations* in Canada,
the United States, and Latin America indicate the commonalities
and differences that exist in this hemisphere and the relevance of
political order to the framework of land, culture, and social identity
that shapes the character of group relations.

19. **Return of the Natives,** Alan Thein Durning, *World Monitor,* 90
March 1993.
This account of the global tapestry of *indigenous peoples and
their relations to environmental issues* reveals the complex
character of ecological concerns and the impact of international
organizations and their responsibility for the protection of human
rights as well as their contentions regarding use and control of
natural resources.

20. **Why Did Chiapas Revolt?** Charles R. Simpson and Anita 94
Rapone, *Commonweal,* June 3, 1994.
This account of the origins and causes that drove the revolt of
indigenous people in Mexico exposes the strains between the
center and margin that exist in large territorial states, the need for
appropriate representation, and the potential for violence that challenges the process of large-scale political and economic integration.

21. **Towards Information Self-Sufficiency,** William B. Kemp 97
and Lorraine F. Brooke, *Cultural Survival Quarterly,* Winter
1995.
William Kemp and Lorraine Brooke describe the intersection of
information technology and ecology that has empowered *indigenous peoples,* with a focus on the Inuit of Nunavik.

22. **American Indians in the 1990s,** Dan Fost, *American* 101
Demographics, December 1991.
Evidence suggests that a growing number of *Americans are identifying with Indian culture.* Mainstream appetites for ethnic culture, the development of businesses on reservations, and the urge
to "go home" among middle-class Indians point to trends for the
1990s.

Unit
4

Hispanic/Latino Americans

Four articles in this section reveal the demographics of
Hispanic/Latino Americans as well as the economic and
political cultural dynamics of these diverse ethnicities.

Overview 106

23. **Specific Hispanics,** Morton Winsberg, *American Demo-* 108
graphics, February 1994.
Morton Winsberg, with Patricia Braus, reports on the stereotypical
groups that fall within the Hispanic category. Cultural and market
differentiations create a quilt of many borders with the various
ethnicities that are labeled *Hispanic/Latino American.*

24. **There's More to Racism than Black and White,** Elizabeth 115
Martinez, *Z Magazine,* November 1990.
This is an account of the Chicano moratorium against the Vietnam
War and the development of an ethnic ideology and grassroots
participation. Elizabeth Martinez traces a cluster of issues that are
pivotal to *coalition-building among racial and ethnic groups.*

25. **Born on the Border,** John Leland, *Newsweek,* October 23, 120
1995.
John Leland examines the meaning of singer Selena's music and
reflects on the emergent vibrancy of *Tejano* as *a fusion of ethnicities* and the passing of a multicultural icon that seared our
national consciousness with grief and loss.

26. **A Place of Our Own,** Kevin Coyne, *Notre Dame Magazine,* 122
Spring 1995.
This analysis of *Hispanic American parish life* exposes the interior weave within the fabric of ethnicity and religion in Hispanic
as well as other Catholic ethnic groups that are renegotiating religious and ethnic relationships.

The concepts in bold italics are developed in the article. For further expansion please refer to the Topic Guide and the Index.

Unit 5

Asian Americans

Four articles in this section explore dimensions of pluralism among Asian Americans and their issues related to the cultural, economic, and political dynamics of pluralism.

Overview 126

27. **Asian Americans Don't Fit Their Monochrome Image,** 128
Moon Lee, *Christian Science Monitor,* July 27, 1993.
Moon Lee notes that the "model-minority" image of *Asian Americans*—"hard-working, intelligent people who have made it in America"—is often misleading. Many "face widespread prejudice, discrimination, and denials of opportunity."

28. **A Migration Created by Burden of Suspicion,** Dirk 130
Johnson, *New York Times,* August 14, 1995.
Dirk Johnson profiles *Japanese Americans* and their resettlement throughout the country since their World War II internment and reveals the ongoing drama of pluralism.

29. **Asian-Indian Americans,** Marcia Mogelonsky, *American* 132
Demographics, August 1995.
Marcia Mogelonsky geographically locates migration patterns and profiles the linguistic, cultural, and market segments of the *Asian Indian* population of America, a growing and affluent component of Asian diversity in this country.

30. **Configuring the Filipino Diaspora in the United States,** 139
E. San Juan Jr., *Diaspora,* Fall 1994.
E. San Juan traces the relationship of Filipinos to the United States and critically reflects on the various attempts to fashion a meaningful narrative for *Filipino Americans* in the United States that includes the global dimensions of political claims extending to the future of the Philippines.

Unit 6

African Americans

Seven articles in this section review historical experiences derived from slavery and segregation and then explore current contexts and persistent concerns of African Americans.

Overview 146

31. **10 Most Dramatic Events in African-American History,** 148
Lerone Bennett Jr., *Ebony,* February 1992.
This article recounts meaningful episodes of American history that constitute the popular tradition of *African Americans.* Here are 10 distinctive stories profiling the shared memory of experiences that define the special sense of peoplehood of this ethnic group.

32. **Leader Popular among Marchers,** Mario A. Brossard and 152
Richard Morin, *The Washington Post,* October 17, 1995.
Mario Brossard and Richard Morin present a survey of opinions and attitudes of *participants in the Million Man March* of black men that captures the views, aspirations, energy, and interest of this stunning event.

33. **An Angry "Charmer,"** Howard Fineman and Vern E. 155
Smith, *Newsweek,* October 30, 1995.
This account of Louis Farrakhan written following *the Million Man March* focuses on his life, his future plans, and his anticipated "move into the mainstream of American politis."

34. **So You Want to Be Color-Blind,** Peter Schrag, *The American Prospect,* Summer 1995. 158
Peter Schrag presents six alternative principles for affirmative action that sharpen our attention to the core concerns that have thus far perplexed efforts to achieve fairness and public consensus regarding the legitimacy of *race preferences in public policy.*

35. **40 Years after *Brown,* Segregation Persists,** William 164
Celis III, *New York Times,* May 18, 1994.
This is a historical account and contemporary report on the legacy of the landmark Supreme Court decision outlawing *school segregation.* The author reveals the efforts of two generations to provide equal protection required by the decree that found segregated schools to be unconstitutional.

Unit 7

The Ethnic Legacy

Five articles in this section examine neglected dimensions of ethnic communities, their intersection with each other, and the influence of interethnic protocols within American society.

Unit 8

The Ethnic Factor: International Challenges for the 1990s

Five articles in this section look at the intersections of ethnicities and the impact of ethnic conflict and cooperation on international affairs and the prospect of peace.

36. **Affirmative Action: Four Groups' Views,** Kevin Johnson and Andrea Stone, *USA Today,* March 24, 1995.   **168**
This article reports the patterns of public **perceptions and assessments of affirmative action** that divide our opinions of this controversial attempt to end racial exclusion.

37. **Home Ownership Anchors the Middle Class: But Lending Games Sink Many Prospective Owners,** Scott Minerbrook, *Emerge,* October 1993.   **171**
Scott Minerbrook narrates the process as well as the consequences of practices and patterns that persist in the exchange of real estate and the ownership of property, which reveals **the extent of segregation that continues** despite laws and regulations that promise the end of **racial discrimination.**

Overview   **176**

38. **America's Dilemma,** Ellen K. Coughlin, *The Chronicle of Higher Education,* September 8, 1995.   **178**
Ellen Coughlin surveys the host of new books that address the ongoing discussion of race and racism. The topics range from backlash to the uses of ethnicity and race in the construction of social reality and the influences of this process on the formation of **personal identity and group relations.**

39. **The New Ethnicity,** Michael Novak, from *Further Reflections on Ethnicity,* Jednota Press, 1977.   **181**
This article explains the **origins and features of the new ethnicity.** Michael Novak proposes a generous and inclusive approach to understanding cultural diversity and the implications of ethnicity for those generations of Americans with roots in the large-scale immigration that ended in 1924.

40. **Italian Americans as a Cognizable Racial Group,** Dominic R. Massaro, *Italian Americans in a Multicultural Society,* 1994.   **187**
Dominic Massaro provides an account of the **Italian American** struggle to ensure full participation under and full protection of the law that supports guarantees for ethnic education and cultural rights.

41. **The Other and the Almost the Same,** Paul Berman, *Society,* September/October 1994.   **192**
Paul Berman reflects on **Jewish and African American relations** and searches for a wider interpretive framework from which the understanding of groups may emerge.

42. **The Arab American Market,** Samia El-Badry, *American Demographics,* January 1994.   **205**
Samia El-Badry provides information about **Arab Americans** that invites us to search for the causes of stereotypic images that defy social reality.

Overview   **210**

43. **Andrzej Szczypiorski: Poles and Germans,** Agnieszka Engelmann, *Deutschland,* April 1995.   **212**
This interview with a Polish author provides a historical glimpse into the relationship between the Poles and Germans. He discusses their process of rethinking **the terms of nationhood,** which, both individually and collectively, he believes, will form the core of the new European reality that began at the end of the cold war.

44. **The Ends of History: Balkan Culture and Catastrophe,** Thomas Butler, *The Washington Post,* August 30, 1992.   **214**
Thomas Butler's report on **the tragedy of Yugoslavia** uncovers the tangled roots of ancient conflict in the region. Current armed

The concepts in bold italics are developed in the article. For further expansion please refer to the Topic Guide and the Index.

misuse of cultural memories and religious traditions exposes savagery that cries out for reconciliation and peace.

45. The State of Bosnia-Herzegovina: Roots and Highlights of the Latest Balkan War, *USA Today,* December 5, 1995. **217**
This essay presents the numerous causative factors behind the present conflict in the Balkan Peninsula and investigates the latest turmoil of hatred that challenges the ***international community.***

46. Ethnic Conflict, Andrew Bell-Fialkoff, *The World & I,* July 1993. **218**
Andrew Bell-Fialkoff traces the modernity that attempted to implement a new social order designed supposedly to obviate the "primordial attachments" considered to be ***the source of ethnic and racial identities.*** The reemergence of ethnicities poses basic questions about the forms of social order that new governments will try to use in multiethnic societies.

47. Passions Set in Stone, Paul Goldberger, *The New York Times Magazine,* September 10, 1995. **224**
Paul Goldberger poses ongoing questions of ethno-religious relationships and the meaning of urban tolerance in the context of the Israeli-Palestinian peace process and accord that invite us to redefine what it means to be neighbors.

Overview **232**

48. Understanding Afrocentrism, Gerald Early, *Civilization,* July/August 1995. **234**
This essay articulates the elements of an idea-force that has emerged in the intellectual and cultural ferment caused by ***the insufficiency and inefficacy of Marxism.*** The author examines the challenges of gender and eugenic ideologies that seek our advocacy as educational and social guideposts in an arena fractured by disagreement and discredit.

49. Whose Peers? Richard Lacayo, *Time,* Special Issue, Fall 1993. **242**
Richard Lacayo discusses the question of racial balance in juries and especially the problems of creating multiracial juries.

50. Color Blinded? Race Seems to Play an Increasing Role in Many Jury Verdicts, Benjamin A. Holden, Laurie P. Cohen, and Eleena de Lisser, *Wall Street Journal,* October 4, 1995. **244**
The implications of ***jury trials in a multiethnic society,*** the warrants for so-called cultural defense strategies, and the variety of perceptions that are driven by an ethnic-racial rationality that may strain confidence in the justice system are explored in this report.

51. What Color Is Black? Tom Morganthau, *Newsweek,* February 13, 1995. **247**
According to Tom Morganthau, Americans remain ***preoccupied with race***: Race-based thinking affects our laws and policies, and blacks typically adhere to their role as ***history's victims,*** while whites grumble about ***reverse discrimination.*** Many continue to rank race relations as fair to poor.

Unit 9

Understanding Cultural Pluralism

Ten articles in this section examine the origins of misunderstandings regarding human variety, indicate the influence of race and ethnic opinions in selected contexts, and discuss the range of challenges that must be addressed to forge new approaches to understanding cultural pluralism.

The concepts in bold italics are developed in the article. For further expansion please refer to the Topic Guide and the Index.

52. **A Distorted Image of Minorities,** Richard Morin, *The* 249
Washington Post, October 8, 1995.
This article and its data regarding *race and ethnic perceptions*
are indicative of persistent attitudes and anxieties generated by
the present distorted methods of approaching and understanding
ethnic diversity in America.

53. **Three Is Not Enough,** Sharon Begley, *Newsweek,* Febru- 253
ary 13, 1995.
Sharon Begley addresses the rejection of *race as a biological
category* by many cultural and physical anthropologists. Scientists
are trying to explain the astounding diversity of humankind and its
conventional racial categories—black, white, and Asian.

54. **Goin' Gangsta, Choosin' Cholita: Teens Today "Claim"** 256
a Racial Identity, Nell Bernstein, *Utne Reader,* March/April
1995.
Nell Bernstein explores the fluid and self-selective character of
ethnic identities and the processes of self-definition that pluralism
and diversity induce.

55. **The Geometer of Race,** Stephen Jay Gould, *Discover,* No- 259
vember 1994.
This is a lucid account of the origins of the eighteenth-century
scientific climate of thought and the disastrous shift in the method
and mode of explanation that contributed to the racial misunderstandings that plague us today. The article reveals an important
feature of theory construction derived from insight into the *history
and philosophy of science.*

56. **Battling for Souls,** Carla Power and Allison Samuels, 264
Newsweek, October 30, 1995.
Carla Power and Allison Samuels trace the emerging force of religion in the shaping of character and consciousness and observe
that it appears to be influencing the direction of *race and ethnic
relations.*

57. **Bridging the Divides of Race and Ethnicity,** Martha L. 266
McCoy and Robert F. Sherman, *National Civic Review,*
Spring/Summer 1994.
This article illustrates the importance of face-to-face, *local initia-
tives* in forging opportunities for convergence of agendas among
the diverse backgrounds that exist in all communities.

Index 273
Article Review Form 276
Article Rating Form 277

The concepts in bold italics are developed in the article. For further expansion please refer to the Topic Guide and the Index.

Topic Guide

This topic guide suggests how the selections in this book relate to topics of traditional concern to students and professionals involved with the study of race and ethnic relations. It is useful for locating articles that relate to each other for reading and research. The guide is arranged alphabetically according to topic. Articles may, of course, treat topics that do not appear in the topic guide. In turn, entries in the topic guide do not necessarily constitute a comprehensive listing of all the contents of each selection.

TOPIC AREA	TREATED IN	TOPIC AREA	TREATED IN
Affirmative Action	5. *University of California Regents v. Bakke* 34. So You Want to Be Color-Blind 36. Affirmative Action: Four Views	**Demography (cont'd)**	19. Return of the Natives 23. Specific Hispanics 27. Asian Americans Don't Fit Monochrome Image 29. Asian-Indian Americans 35. 40 Years after *Brown* 38. America's Dilemma 42. Arab American Market 43. Poles and Germans 51. What Color is Black? 52. Distorted Image of Minorities 53. Three Is Not Enough 55. Geometer of Race
Asian-Indian Americans	10. Census Bureau 11. Foreign-Born Population 29. Asian-Indian Americans		
Arab Americans	10. Census Bureau 11. Foreign-Born Population 42. Arab American Market 47. Passions Set in Stone		
Canada	13. Pride and Prejudice 16. UN Working Group 18. Struggling to Be Themselves 21. Information Self-Sufficiency	**Discrimination**	1. *Dred Scott v. Sandford* 2. One Drop of Blood 3. *Plessy v. Ferguson* 4. *Brown v. Topeka Board of Education* 6. High Court Loosens Desegregation's Grip 7. Court Leaders Pin Hopes on "Holding 5" 8. Court Grows Critical When Race, Law Intersect 9. Nation of Immigrants 13. Pride and Prejudice 14. Coping with Deportation 24. There's More to Racism 31. 10 Most Dramatic Events 28. Migration Created by Burden of Suspicion 34. So You Want to Be Color-Blind 35. 40 Years after *Brown* 36. Affirmative Action: Four Views 37. Home Ownership 38. America's Dilemma 40. Italian Americans 41. Other and the Almost the Same 46. Ethnic Conflict 51. What Color Is Black? 54. Teens "Claim" Racial Identity
Chinese Americans	10. Census Bureau 11. Foreign-Born Population 27. Asian Americans Don't Fit Monochrome Image		
Civil Rights	1. *Dred Scott v. Sandford* 2. One Drop of Blood 4. *Brown v. Topeka Board of Education* 6. High Court Loosens Desegregation's Grip 7. Court Leaders Pin Hopes on "Holding 5" 8. Court Grows Critical When Race, Law Intersect 15. Limits to Cultural Diversity 16. UN Working Group 31. 10 Most Dramatic Events 34. So You Want to Be Color-Blind 35. 40 Years after *Brown* 40. Italian Americans		
Courts	1. *Dred Scott v. Sandford* 3. *Plessy v. Ferguson* 4. *Brown v. Topeka Board of Education* 5. *University of California Regents v. Bakke* 6. High Court Loosens Desegregation's Grip 7. Court Leaders Pin Hopes on "Holding 5" 8. Court Grows Critical When Race, Law Intersect 31. 10 Most Dramatic Events 35. 40 Years after *Brown* 36. Affirmative Action: Four Views 40. Italian Americans 49. Whose Peers? 50. Color Blinded?	**Economy**	9. Nation of Immigrants 10. Census Bureau 12. Is Latest Wave a Drain or Boon? 18. Struggling to Be Themselves 19. Return of the Natives 34. So You Want to Be Color-Blind 36. Affirmative Action: Four Views 37. Home Ownership
		Education	4. *Brown v. Topeka Board of Education* 6. High Court Loosens Desegregation's Grip 35. 40 Years after *Brown* 38. America's Dilemma 48. Understanding Afrocentrism
Demography	2. One Drop of Blood 9. Nation of Immigrants 10. Census Bureau 11. Foreign-Born Population 12. Is Latest Wave a Drain or Boon? 14. Coping with Deportation 17. Paupers in a World	**Family**	2. One Drop of Blood 9. Nation of Immigrants 12. Is Latest Wave a Drain or Boon? 26. Place of Our Own

TOPIC AREA	TREATED IN	TOPIC AREA	TREATED IN
Gender	25. Born on the Border 32. Leader Popular among Marchers 33. Angry "Charmer"	Prejudice (cont'd)	26. Place of Our Own 27. Asian Americans Don't Fit Monochrome Image 28. Migration Created by Burden of Suspicion 31. 10 Most Dramatic Events 34. So You Want to Be Color-Blind 38. America's Dilemma 39. New Ethnicity 40. Italian Americans 41. Other and the Almost the Same 44. Ends of History 46. Ethnic Conflict 49. Whose Peers? 51. What Color Is Black? 52. Distorted Image of Minorities 53. Three Is Not Enough 55. Geometer of Race 57. Bridging Race and Ethnicity
Germany	14. Coping with Deportation 43. Poles and Germans		
Japanese Americans	9. Nation of Immigrants 10. Census Bureau 11. Foreign-Born Population 27. Asian Americans Don't Fit Monochrome Image 28. Migration Created by Burden of Suspicion		
Jewish Americans	9. Nation of Immigrants 41. Other and the Almost the Same 47. Passions Set in Stone		
Mexican Americans	20. Why Did Chiapas Revolt? 23. Specific Hispanics 25. Born on the Border 26. Place of Our Own	Quotas	2. One Drop of Blood 5. *University of California Regents v. Bakke* 6. High Court Loosens Desegregation's Grip 9. Nation of Immigrants 24. There's More to Racism 34. So You Want to Be Color-Blind 36. Affirmative Action: Four Views
Migration	9. Nation of Immigrants 10. Census Bureau 11. Foreign-Born Population 12. Is Latest Wave a Drain or Boon? 14. Coping with Deportation 17. Paupers in a World 23. Specific Hispanics 26. Place of Our Own 27. Asian Americans Don't Fit Monochrome Image 29. Asian-Indian Americans 30. Filipino Diaspora	Refugees	9. Nation of Immigrants 10. Census Bureau 11. Foreign-Born Population 12. Is Latest Wave a Drain or Boon? 14. Coping with Deportation 15. Limits to Cultural Diversity 44. Ends of History
Polish Americans	9. Nation of Immigrants 10. Census Bureau 11. Foreign-Born Population 43. Poles and Germans	Religion	26. Place of Our Own 33. Angry "Charmer" 47. Passions Set in Stone 56. Battling for Souls
Population	9. Nation of Immigrants 10. Census Bureau 11. Foreign-Born Population 14. Coping with Deportation 17. Paupers in a World 22. American Indians 23. Specific Hispanics 27. Asian Americans Don't Fit Monochrome Image 29. Asian-Indian Americans 42. Arab American Market	Segregation	1. *Dred Scott v. Sandford* 2. One Drop of Blood 3. *Plessy v. Ferguson* 5. *Brown v. Topeka Board of Education* 6. High Court Loosens Desegregation's Grip 31. 10 Most Dramatic Events 35. 40 Years after *Brown* 37. Home Ownership 41. Other and the Almost the Same 46. Ethnic Conflict 57. Bridging Race and Ethnicity
Prejudice	2. One Drop of Blood 3. *Plessy v. Ferguson* 4. *Brown v. Topeka Board of Education* 9. Nation of Immigrants 13. Pride and Prejudice 15. Limits to Cultural Diversity 19. Return of the Natives 20. Why Did Chiapas Revolt? 24. There's More to Racism	Vietnamese Americans	9. Nation of Immigrants 10. Census Bureau 11. Foreign-Born Population 27. Asian Americans Don't Fit Monochrome Image
		Violence	20. Why Did Chiapas Revolt? 43. Poles and Germans 44. Ends of History 47. Passions Set in Stone

Race and Ethnicity in the American Legal Tradition

The legal framework established by the original U.S. Constitution illustrates the way the American founders handled ethnic pluralism. In most respects, they ignored the cultural and linguistic variety within and between the 13 original states, adopting instead a legal system that guaranteed religious exercise free from government interference, due process of law, and the freedom of speech and the press. The founders, however, conspicu-ously compromised their claims of unalienable rights and democratic republicanism with regard to the constitutional status of Africans in bondage and the indigenous Native Americans. Even after the Civil War and the inclusion of constitutional amendments that ended slavery and guaranteed equal protection of the laws to all, decisions by the U.S. Supreme Court helped to establish a legal system in which inequality and ethnic discrimination—both political and private—were legally permissible. In fact, it has been only recently that the Court has begun to redress the complex relationship between our constitutional system, our nation's cultural diversity, and ensurance of "equal justice under the law" for all persons.

Moreover, the history of American immigration legislation, from the Alien and Sedition Laws at the founding to the most recent statutes, establishes a legacy as well as a contemporary framework for governing the ethical, racial, and cultural populations in America. This legal framework continues to mirror the political forces that influence the definition of citizenship and the very constitution of ethnic identity and ethnic groups in America.

The legacies of African slavery, racial segregation, and ethnic discrimination established by the Constitution and by subsequent Court doctrines are traced in the following abbreviated U.S. Supreme Court opinions.

In *Dred Scott v. Sandford* (1856), the Supreme Court addressed the constitutional status of an African held in bondage who had been moved to a state that prohibited slavery. U.S. Supreme Court chief justice Roger B. Taney attempted to resolve the increasingly divisive issue of slavery by declaring that the "Negro African race"—whether free or slave—was "not intended to be included under the word 'citizens' in the Constitution, and can therefore claim none of the rights and privileges that instrument provides for and secures to citizens of the United States." Contrary to Taney's intentions, however, *Dred Scott* further fractured the nation, ensuring that only the Civil War would resolve the slavery issue.

In *Plessy v. Ferguson* (1896), the Supreme Court upheld the constitutionality of "Jim Crow" laws that segregated public facilities on the basis of an individual's racial ancestry. The Court reasoned that this "separate but equal" segregation did not violate any rights guaranteed by the U.S. Constitution, nor did it stamp "the colored race with a badge of inferiority." Instead, the Court argued that if "this be so, it is not by reason of anything found in the act but solely because the colored race chooses to put that construction upon it." In contrast, Justice John M. Harlan's vigorous dissent from the Court's *Plessy* opinion contends that "Our Constitution is color-blind, and neither knows nor tolerates classes among citizens."

In *Brown v. Board of Education of Topeka* (1954), the Supreme Court began the ambitious project of dismantling state-supported racial segregation. In *Brown,* a unanimous Court overturned *Plessy v. Ferguson,* arguing that "in the field of public education the doctrine of 'separate but equal' has no place," because "separate educational facilities are inherently unequal."

After the civil rights movement of the 1960s and 1970s, the process of incorporating and institutionalizing the legal reforms took many forms. The Office of Management and Budget (OMB) guided national data collection, and boards of education and ongoing litigation fostered the end of segregation and of limits on access to employment and public facilities. Remedies for changing public behavior and speech were included in the panoply of approaches designed to foster an integrated society. Articles in this section mirror both contemporary and future implications of the ongoing tensions that the legal tradition is invited to resolve.

However, this era of civil rights consensus embodied in the landmark actions of the Supreme Court has been challenged by contemporary plaintiffs who have turned to the Court for clarification regarding specific cases related to the significance of race and ethnic criteria in public affairs. The impact of these reconsiderations and of the remedies that should be applied will undoubtedly reverberate in a variety of ways. The implementation of the voting rights remedies through gerrymandering, which attempts to ensure minority election by contriving clusters of black, Hispanic, and Asian populations rather than increasing the number of legislative districts, has exacerbated racial and ethnic competition for public participation.

Another response to diversity that has emerged in legal scholarship despairs of universal norms and standards. Proponents argue for a critical reinterpretation of legality that privileges the particular experiences of racial, ethnic, gender, and class populations. They claim that the exclusion of such insights in the pursuit of justice in a pluralistic society has severely handicapped the expansion of equality, effective due process, and the exercise of legal rights.

Looking Ahead: Challenge Questions

Comment on the idea that the American political process has relied too extensively on the Supreme Court for doctrine and dogma regarding race and ethnicity.

The U.S. Congress is the lawmaking institution that authorized national policies of equal protection that are constitutionally guaranteed to all. What explains the disparity between the patently clear proclamation of equality and the painfully obvious practices of racial/ethnic discrimination?

DRED SCOTT V. SANDFORD

December Term 1856.

MR. CHIEF JUSTICE TANEY delivered the opinion of the court.

This case has been twice argued. After the argument at the last term, differences of opinion were found to exist among the members of the court; and as the questions in controversy are of the highest importance, and the court was at that time much pressed by the ordinary business of the term, it was deemed advisable to continue the case, and direct a re-argument on some of the points, in order that we might have an opportunity of giving to the whole subject a more deliberate consideration. It has accordingly been again argued by counsel, and considered by the court; and I now proceed to deliver its opinion.

There are two leading questions presented by the record:

1. Had the Circuit Court of the United States jurisdiction to hear and determine the case between these parties? And

2. If it had jurisdiction, is the judgment it has given erroneous or not?

The plaintiff in error, who was also the plaintiff in the court below, was, with his wife and children, held as slaves by the defendant, in the State of Missouri; and he brought this action in the Circuit Court of the United States for that district, to assert the title of himself and his family to freedom.

The declaration is in the form usually adopted in that State to try questions of this description, and contains the averment necessary to give the court jurisdiction; that he and the defendant are citizens of different States; that is, that he is a citizen of Missouri, and the defendant a citizen of New York.

The defendant pleaded in abatement to the jurisdiction of the court, that the plaintiff was not a citizen of the State of Missouri, as alleged in his declaration, being a negro of African descent, whose ancestors were of pure African blood, and who were brought into this country and sold as slaves.

To this plea the plaintiff demurred, and the defendant joined in demurrer. The court overruled the plea, and gave judgment that the defendant should answer over. And he thereupon put in sundry pleas in bar, upon which issues were joined; and at the trial the verdict and judgment were in his favor. Whereupon the plaintiff brought this writ of error.

Before we speak of the pleas in bar, it will be proper to dispose of the questions which have arisen on the plea in abatement.

That plea denies the right of the plaintiff to sue in a court of the United States, for the reasons therein stated.

If the question raised by it is legally before us, and the court should be of opinion that the facts stated in it disqualify the plaintiff from becoming a citizen, in the sense in which that word is used in the Constitution of the United States, then the judgment of the Circuit Court is erroneous, and must be reversed.

It is suggested, however, that this plea is not before us; and that as the judgment in the court below on this plea was in favor of the plaintiff, he does not seek to reverse it, or bring it before the court for revision by his writ of error; and also that the defendant waived this defence by pleading over, and thereby admitted the jurisdiction of the court.

But, in making this objection, we think the peculiar and limited jurisdiction of courts of the United States has not been adverted to. This peculiar and limited jurisdiction has made it necessary, in these courts, to adopt different rules and principles of pleading, so far as jurisdiction is concerned, from those which regulate courts of common law in England, and in the different States of the Union which have adopted the common-law rules.

In these last-mentioned courts, where their character and rank are analogous to that of a Circuit Court of the United States; in other words, where they are what the law terms courts of general jurisdiction; they are presumed to have jurisdiction, unless the contrary appears. No averment in the pleadings of the plaintiff is necessary, in order to give jurisdiction. If the defendant objects to it, he must plead it specially, and unless the fact on which he relies is found to be true by a jury, or admitted to be true by the plaintiff, the jurisdiction cannot be disputed in an appellate court.

Now, it is not necessary to inquire whether in courts of that description a party who pleads over in bar, when a plea to the jurisdiction has been ruled against him, does or does not waive his plea; nor whether upon a judgment in his favor on the pleas in bar, and a writ of error brought by the plaintiff, the question upon the plea in abatement would be open for revision in the appellate court. Cases that may have been decided in such courts, or rules that may have been laid down by common-law pleaders, can have no influence in the decision in this court. Because, under the Constitution and laws of the United States, the rules which govern the pleadings in its courts, in questions of jurisdiction, stand on different principles and are regulated by different laws.

This difference arises, as we have said, from the peculiar character of the Government of the United States. For although it is sovereign and supreme in its appropriate sphere of action, yet it does not possess all the powers which usually belong to the sovereignty of a nation. Certain specified powers, enumerated in the Constitution, have been conferred upon it; and neither the legislative, executive, nor judicial departments of the Government can lawfully exercise any authority beyond the limits marked out by the Constitution. And in regulating the judicial department, the cases in which the courts of the United States shall have jurisdiction are particularly and specifically enumerated and defined; and they are not authorized to take cognizance of any case which does not come within the description therein specified. Hence, when a plaintiff sues in a court of the United States, it is necessary that he should show, in his pleading, that the suit he brings is within the jurisdiction of the court, and that he is entitled to sue there. And if he omits to do this, and should, by any oversight of the Circuit Court, obtain a judgment in his favor, the judgment would be reversed in the appellate court for want of jurisdiction in the court below. The jurisdiction would not be presumed, as in the case of a common-law English or State court, unless the contrary appeared. But the record, when it comes before the appellate court, must show, affirmatively, that the inferior court had authority, under the Constitution, to hear and determine the case. And if the plaintiff claims a right to sue in a Circuit Court of the United States, under that provision of the Constitution which gives jurisdiction in controversies between citizens of different States, he must distinctly aver in his pleading that they are citizens of different States; and he cannot maintain his suit without showing that fact in the pleadings.

This point was decided in the case of *Bingham v. Cabot*, (in 3 Dall., 382,) and ever since adhered to by the court. And in *Jackson v. Ashton*, (8 Pet., 148,) it was held that the objection to which it was open could not be waived by the opposite party, because consent of parties could not give jurisdiction.

It is needless to accumulate cases on this subject. Those already referred to, and the cases of *Capron v. Van Noorden*, (in 2 Cr., 126) and *Montalet v. Murray*, (4 Cr., 46,) are sufficient to show the rule of which we have spoken. The case of *Capron v. Van Noorden* strikingly illustrates the difference between a common-law court and a court of the United States.

If, however, the fact of citizenship is averred in the declaration, and the defendant does not deny it, and put it in issue by plea in abatement, he cannot offer evidence at the trial to disprove it, and consequently cannot avail himself of the objection in the appellate court, unless the defect should be apparent in some other part of the record. For if there is no plea in abatement, and the want of jurisdiction does not appear in any other part of the transcript brought up by the writ of error, the undisputed averment of citizenship in the declaration must be taken in this court to be true. In this case, the citizenship is averred, but it is denied by the defendant in the manner required by the rules of pleading, and the fact upon which the denial is based is admitted by the demurrer. And, if the plea and demurrer, and judgment of the court below upon it, are before us upon this record, the question to be decided is, whether the facts stated in the plea are sufficient to show that the plaintiff is not entitled to sue as a citizen in a court of the United States. . . .

We think they are before us. The plea in abatement and the judgment of the court upon it, are a part of the judicial proceedings in the Circuit Court, and are there recorded as such; and a writ of error always brings up to the superior court the whole record of the proceedings in the court below. And in the case of the *United States v. Smith*, (11 Wheat., 172) this court said, that the case being brought up by writ of error, the whole record was under the consideration of this court. And this being the case in the present instance, the plea in abatement is necessarily under consideration; and it becomes, therefore, our duty to decide whether the facts stated in the plea are or are not sufficient to show that the plaintiff is not entitled to sue as a citizen in a court of the United States.

This is certainly a very serious question, and one that now for the first time has been brought for decision before this court. But it is brought here by those who have a right to bring it, and it is our duty to meet it and decide it.

The question is simply this: Can a negro, whose ancestors were imported into this country, and sold as slaves, become a member of the political community formed and brought into existence by the Constitution of the United States, and as such become entitled to all the rights, and privileges, and immunities, guaranteed by that instrument to the citizen? One of which rights is the privilege of suing in a court of the United States in the cases specified in the Constitution.

It will be observed, that the plea applies to that class of persons only whose ancestors were negroes of the African race, and imported into this country, and sold and held as slaves. The only matter in issue before the court, therefore, is, whether the descendants of such slaves, when they shall be emancipated, or who are born of parents who had become free before their birth, are citizens of a State, in the sense in which the word citizen is used in the Constitution of the United States. And this being the only matter in dispute on the pleadings, the court must be understood as speaking in this opinion of that class only, that is, of those persons who are the descendants of Africans who were imported into this country, and sold as slaves.

The situation of this population was altogether unlike that of the Indian race. The latter, it is true, formed no part of the colonial communities, and never amalgamated with them in social connections or in government. But although they were uncivilized, they were yet a free and independent people, associated together in nations or tribes, and governed by their own laws. Many of these political communities were situated in territories to which the white race claimed the ultimate right of dominion. But that claim was acknowledged to be subject to the right of the Indians to occupy it as long as they thought proper, and neither the English nor colonial Governments claimed or exercised any dominion over the tribe or nation by whom it was occupied, nor claimed the right to the possession of the territory, until the tribe or nation consented to cede it. These Indian Governments were regarded and treated as foreign Governments, as much so as if an ocean had separated the red man from the white; and their freedom has constantly been acknowledged, from the time of the first emigration to the English colonies to the present day, by the different Governments which succeeded each other. Treaties have been negotiated with them, and their alliance sought for in war; and the people who compose these Indian political communities have always been treated as foreigners not living under our Government. It is true that the course of events has brought the Indian tribes within the limits of the United States under subjection to the white race; and it has been found necessary, for their sake as well as our own, to regard them as in a state of pupilage, and to legislate to a certain extent over them and the territory they occupy. But they may, without doubt, like the subjects of any other foreign Government, be naturalized by the authority of Congress, and become citizens of a State, and of the United States; and if an individual should leave his nation or tribe, and take up his abode among the white population, he would be entitled to all the rights and privileges which would belong to an emigrant from any other foreign people.

We proceed to examine the case as presented by the pleadings.

The words "people of the United States" and "citizens" are synonymous terms, and mean the same thing. They both describe the political body who, according to our republican institutions, form the sovereignty, and who hold the power and conduct the Government through their representatives. They are what we familiarly call the "sovereign people," and every citizen is one of this people, and a constituent member of this sovereignty. The question before us is, whether the class of persons described in the plea in abatement compose a portion of this people, and are constituent members of this sovereignty? We think they are not, and that they are not included, and were not intended to be included, under the word "citizens" in the Constitution, and can therefore claim none of the rights and privileges which that instrument provides for and secures to citizens of the United States. On the contrary, they were at that time considered as a subordinate and inferior class of beings, who had been subjugated by the dominant race, and, whether emancipated or not, yet remained subject to their authority, and had no rights or privileges but such as those who held the power and the Government might choose to grant them.

It is not the province of the court to decide upon the justice or injustice, the policy or impolicy, of these laws. The decision of that question belonged to the political or law-making power; to those who formed the sovereignty and framed the Constitution. The duty of the court is, to interpret the instrument they have framed, with the best lights we can obtain on the subject, and to administer it as we find it, according to its true intent and meaning when it was adopted.

In discussing this question, we must not confound the rights of citizenship which a State may confer within its own limits, and the rights of citizenship as a member of the Union. It does not by any means follow, because he has all the rights and privileges of a citizen of a State, that he must be a citizen of the United States. He may have all of the rights and privileges of the citizen of a State, and yet not be entitled to the rights and privileges of a citizen in any other State. For, previous to the adoption of the Constitution of the United States, every State had the undoubted right to confer on whomsoever it pleased the character of citizen, and to endow him with all its rights. But this character of course was confined to the boundaries of the State, and gave him no rights or privileges in other States beyond those secured to him by the laws of nations and the comity of States. Nor have the several States surrendered the power of conferring these rights and privileges by adopting the Constitution of the United States. Each State may still confer them upon an alien, or any one it thinks proper, or upon any class or description of persons; yet he would not be a citizen in the sense in which that word is used in the Constitution of the United States, nor entitled to sue as such in one of its courts, nor to the privileges and immunities of a citizen in the other States. The rights which he would acquire would be restricted to the State which gave them. The Constitution has conferred on Congress the right to establish a uniform rule of naturalization, and this right is evidently exclusive, and has always been held by this court to be so. Consequently, no State, since the adoption of the Constitution, can by naturalizing an alien invest him with the rights and privileges secured to a citizen of a State under the Federal Government, although, so far as the State alone was concerned, he would undoubtedly be entitled to the rights of a citizen, and clothed with all the rights and immunities which the Constitution and laws of the State attached to that character.

It is very clear, therefore, that no State can, by any act or law of its own, passed since the adoption of the Constitution, introduce a new member into the political community created by the Constitution of the United States. It cannot make him a member of this community by making him a member of its own. And for the same reason it cannot introduce any person, or description of persons, who were not intended to be embraced in this new political family, which the Constitution brought into existence, but were intended to be excluded from it.

The question then arises, whether the provisions of the Constitution, in relation to the personal rights and privileges to which the citizen of a State should be entitled, embraced the negro African race, at that time in this country, or who might afterwards be imported, who had then or should afterwards be made free in any State; and to put it in the power of a single State to make him a citizen of the United States, and endue him with the full rights of citizenship in every other State without their consent? Does the Constitution of the United States act upon him whenever he shall be made free under the laws of a State, and raised there to the rank of a citizen, and immediately clothe him with all the privileges of a citizen in every other State, and in its own courts?

The court think the affirmative of these propositions cannot be maintained. And if it cannot, the plaintiff in error could not be a citizen of the State of Missouri, within the meaning of the Constitution of the United States, and, consequently, was not entitled to sue in its courts.

It is true, every person, and every class and description of persons, who were at the time of the adoption of the Constitution recognised as citizens in the several States, became also citizens of this new political body; but none other; it was formed by them, and for them and their posterity, but for no one else. And the personal rights and privileges guarantied to citizens of this new sovereignty were intended to embrace those only who were then members of the several State communities, or who should afterwards by birthright or otherwise become members, according to the provisions of the Constitution and the principles on which it was founded. It was the union of those who were at that time members of distinct and separate political communities into one political family, whose power, for certain specified purposes, was to extend over the whole territory of the United States. And it gave to each citizen rights and privileges outside of his State which he did not before possess, and placed him in every other State upon a perfect equality with its own citizens as to rights of person and rights of property; it made him a citizen of the United States.

It becomes necessary, therefore, to determine who were citizens of the several States when the Constitution was adopted. And in order to do this, we must recur to the Governments and institutions of the thirteen colonies, when they separated from Great Britain and formed new sovereignties, and took their places in the family of independent nations. We must inquire who, at that time, were recognised as the people or citizens of a State, whose rights and liberties had been outraged by the English Government; and who declared their independence, and assumed the powers of Government to defend their rights by force of arms.

In the opinion of the court, the legislation and histories of the times, and the language used in the Declaration of Independence, show, that neither the class of persons who had been imported as slaves, nor their descendants, whether they had become free or not, were then acknowledged as a part of the people, nor intended to be included in the general words used in that memorable instrument. . . .

ONE DROP OF BLOOD

Do ethnic categories protect us or divide us? The way that Washington chooses to define the population in the 2000 census could trigger the biggest debate over race in America since the nineteen-sixties.

LAWRENCE WRIGHT

WASHINGTON in the millennial years is a city of warring racial and ethnic groups fighting for recognition, protection, and entitlements. This war has been fought throughout the second half of the twentieth century largely by black Americans. How much this contest has widened, how bitter it has turned, how complex and baffling it is, and how far-reaching its consequences are became evident in a series of congressional hearings that began last year in the obscure House Subcommittee on Census, Statistics, and Postal Personnel, which is chaired by Representative Thomas C. Sawyer, Democrat of Ohio, and concluded in November, 1993.

Although the Sawyer hearings were scarcely reported in the news and were sparsely attended even by other members of the subcommittee, with the exception of Representative Thomas E. Petri, Republican of Wisconsin, they opened what may become the most searching examination of racial questions in this country since the sixties. Related federal agency hearings, and meetings that will be held in Washington and other cities around the country to prepare for the 2000 census, are considering not only modifications of existing racial categories but also the larger question of whether it is proper for the government to classify people according to arbitrary distinctions of skin color and ancestry. This discussion arises at a time when profound debates are occurring in minority communities about the rightfulness of group entitlements, some government officials are questioning the usefulness of race data, and scientists are debating whether race exists at all.

Tom Sawyer, forty-eight, a former English teacher and a former mayor of Akron, is now in his fourth term representing the Fourteenth District of Ohio. It would be fair to say that neither the House Committee on Post Office and Civil Service nor the subcommittee that Sawyer chairs is the kind of assignment that members of Congress would willingly shed blood for. Indeed, the attitude of most elected officials in Washington toward the census is polite loathing, because it is the census, as much as any other force in the country, that determines their political futures. Congressional districts rise and fall with the shifting demography of the country, yet census matters rarely seize the front pages of home-town newspapers, except briefly, once every ten years. Much of the subcommittee's business has to do with addressing the safety concerns of postal workers and overseeing federal statistical measurements. The subcommittee has an additional responsibility: it reviews the executive branch's policy about which racial and ethnic groups should be officially recognized by the United States government.

"We are unique in this country in the way we describe and define race and ascribe to it characteristics that other cultures view very differently," Sawyer, who is a friendly man with an open, boyish face and graying black hair, says. He points out that the country is in the midst of its most profound demographic shift since the eighteen-nineties—a time that opened "a period of the greatest immigration we have ever seen, whose numbers have not been matched until right now." A deluge of new Americans from every part of the world is overwhelming our traditional racial distinctions, Sawyer believes. "The categories themselves inevitably reflect the temporal bias of every age," he says. "That becomes a problem when the nation itself is undergoing deep and historic diversification."

Looming over the shoulder of Sawyer's subcommittee is the Office of Management and Budget, the federal agency that happens to be responsible for determining standard classifications of racial and ethnic data. Since 1977, those categories have been set by O.M.B. Statistical Directive 15, which controls the racial and ethnic standards on all federal forms and statistics. Directive 15 acknowledges four general racial groups in the United States: American Indian or Alaskan Native; Asian or Pacific Islander; Black; and White. Directive 15 also breaks down ethnicity into Hispanic Origin and Not of Hispanic Origin. These categories, or versions of them, are present on enrollment forms for schoolchildren; on application forms for jobs, scholarships, loans, and mortgages; and, of course, on United States census forms. The categories ask that every American fit himself or herself into one racial and one ethnic box. From this comes the information that is used to monitor and enforce civil-rights legislation, most notably the Voting Rights Act of 1965, but also a smorgasbord of set-asides and entitlements and affirmative-action programs. "The numbers drive the dollars," Sawyer observes, repeating a well-worn Washington adage.

The truth of that statement was abundantly evident in the hearings, in which a variety of racial and ethnic groups were bidding to increase their portions of the federal pot. The National Coalition for an Accurate Count of Asian Pacific Americans lobbied to add Cambodians and Lao to the nine different nationalities already listed on the census forms under the heading of Asian or Pacific Islander. The National Council of La Raza proposed that Hispanics be considered a race, not just an ethnic group. The Arab American Institute asked that persons from the Middle East, now counted as white, be given a separate, protected category of their own. Senator Daniel K. Akaka, a Native Hawaiian, urged that his people be moved from the Asian or Pacific Islander box to the American Indian or Alaskan Native box. "There is the misperception that Native Hawaiians, who number well over two hundred thousand, somehow 'immigrated' to the United States like other Asian or Pacific Island groups," the Senator testified. "This leads to the erroneous impression that Native Hawaiians, the original inhabitants of the Hawaiian Islands, no longer exist." In the Senator's opinion, being placed in the same category as other Native Americans would help rectify that situation. (He did not mention that certain American Indian tribes enjoy privileges concerning gambling concessions that Native Hawaiians currently don't enjoy.) The National Congress of American Indians would like the Hawaiians to stay where they are. In every case, issues of money, but also of identity, are at stake.

In this battle over racial turf, a disturbing new contender has appeared. "When I received my 1990 census form, I realized that there was no race category for my children," Susan Graham, who is a white woman married to a black man in Roswell, Georgia, testified. "I called the Census Bureau. After checking with supervisors, the bureau finally gave me their answer: the children should take the race of their mother. When I objected and asked why my children should be classified as their mother's race only, the Census Bureau representative said to me, in a very hushed voice, 'Because, in cases like these, we always know who the mother is and not always the father.'"

Graham went on to say, "I could not make a race choice from the basic categories when I enrolled my son in kindergarten in Georgia. The only choice I had, like most other parents of multiracial children, was to leave race blank. I later found that my child's teacher was instructed to choose for him based on her knowledge and observation of my child. Ironically, my child has been white on the United States census, black at school, and multiracial at home—all at the same time."

Graham and others were asking that a "Multiracial" box be added to the racial categories specified by Directive 15— a proposal that alarmed representatives of the other racial groups for a number of reasons, not the least of which was that multiracialism threatened to undermine the concept of racial classification altogether.

According to various estimates, at least seventy-five to more than ninety per cent of the people who now check the Black box could check Multiracial, because of their mixed genetic heritage. If a certain proportion of those people— say, ten per cent—should elect to identify themselves as Multiracial, legislative districts in many parts of the country might need to be redrawn. The entire civil-rights regulatory program concerning housing, employment, and education would have to be reassessed. School-desegregation plans would be thrown into the air. Of course, it is possible that only a small number of Americans will elect to choose the Multiracial option, if it is offered, with little social effect. Merely placing such an option on the census invites people to consider choosing it, however. When the census listed "Cajun" as one of several examples under the ancestry question, the number of Cajuns jumped nearly two thousand per cent. To remind people of the possibility is to encourage enormous change.

Those who are charged with enforcing civil-rights laws see the Multiracial box as a wrecking ball aimed at affirmative action, and they hold those in the mixed-race movement responsible. "There's no concern on any of these people's part about the effect on policy— it's just a subjective feeling that their identity needs to be stroked," one government analyst said. "What they don't understand is that it's going to cost their own groups"—by losing the advantages that accrue to minorities by way of affirmative-action programs, for instance. Graham contends that the object of her movement is not to create another protected category. In any case, she said, multiracial people know "to check the right box to get the goodies."

Of course, races have been mixing in America since Columbus arrived. Visitors to Colonial America found plantation slaves who were as light-skinned as their masters. Patrick Henry actually proposed, in 1784, that the State of Virginia encourage intermarriage between whites and Indians, through the use of tax incentives and cash stipends. The legacy of this intermingling is that Americans who are descendants of early settlers, of slaves, or of Indians often have ancestors of different races in their family tree.

Thomas Jefferson supervised the original census, in 1790. The population then was broken down into free white males, free white females, other persons (these included free blacks and "taxable Indians," which meant those living in or around white settlements), and slaves. How unsettled this country has always been about its racial categories is evident in the fact that nearly every census since has measured race differently. For most of the nineteenth century, the census reflected an American obsession with miscegenation. The color of slaves was to be specified as "B," for black, and "M," for mulatto. In the 1890 census, gradations of mulattoes were further broken down into quadroons and octoroons. After 1920, however, the Census Bureau gave up on such distinctions, estimating that three-quarters of all blacks in the United States were racially mixed already, and that pure blacks would soon disappear. Henceforth anyone with any black ancestry at all would be counted simply as black.

Actual interracial marriages, however, were historically rare. Multiracial children were often marginalized as illegitimate half-breeds who didn't fit comfortably into any racial community. This was particularly true of the offspring of black-white unions. "In my family, like many families with African-American ancestry, there is a history of multiracial offspring associated with rape and concubinage," G. Reginald Daniel, who teaches a course in multiracial identity at the University of California at Los Angeles, says. "I was reared in the segregationist South. Both sides of my family have been mixed for at least three generations. I struggled as a child over the question of why I had to exclude my East Indian and Irish and Native American and French ancestry, and could include only African."

Until recently, people like Daniel were identified simply as black because of a peculiarly American institution known informally as "the one-drop rule," which defines as black a person with as little as a single drop of "black blood." This notion derives from a long-discredited belief that each race had its own blood type, which was correlated with physical appearance and social behavior. The antebellum South promoted the rule as a way of enlarging the slave population with the children of slaveholders. By the nineteen-twenties, in Jim Crow America the one-drop rule was well established as the law of the land. It still is, according to a United States Supreme Court decision as late as 1986, which refused to review a lower court's ruling that a Louisiana woman whose great-great-great-great-grandmother had been the mistress of a French planter was black—even though that proportion of her ancestry amounted to no more than

three thirty-seconds of her genetic heritage. "We are the only country in the world that applies the one-drop rule, and the only group that the one-drop rule applies to is people of African descent," Daniel observes.

People of mixed black-and-white ancestry were rejected by whites and found acceptance by blacks. Many of the most notable "black" leaders over the last century and a half were "white" to some extent, from Booker T. Washington and Frederick Douglass (both of whom had white fathers) to W. E. B. Du Bois, Malcolm X, and Martin Luther King, Jr. (who had an Irish grandmother and some American Indian ancestry as well). The fact that Lani Guinier, Louis Farrakhan, and Virginia's former governor Douglas Wilder are defined as black, and define themselves that way, though they have light skin or "European" features, demonstrates how enduring the one-drop rule has proved to be in America, not only among whites but among blacks as well. Daniel sees this as "a double-edged sword." While the one-drop rule encouraged racism, it also galvanized the black community.

"But the one-drop rule is racist," Daniel says. "There's no way you can get away from the fact that it was historically implemented to create as many slaves as possible. No one leaped over to the white community—that was simply the mentality of the nation, and people of African descent internalized it. What this current discourse is about is lifting the lid of racial oppression in our institutions and letting people identify with the totality of their heritage. We have created a nightmare for human dignity. Multiracialism has the potential for undermining the very basis of racism, which is its categories."

But multiracialism introduces nightmares of its own. If people are to be counted as something other than completely black, for instance, how will affirmative-action programs be implemented? Suppose a court orders a city to hire additional black police officers to make up for past discrimination. Will mixed-race officers count? Will they count wholly or partly? Far from solving the problem of fragmented identities, multiracialism could open the door to fractional races, such as we already have in the case of the American Indians. In order to be eligible for certain federal benefits, such as hous-

ing-improvement programs, a person must prove that he or she either is a member of a federally recognized Indian tribe or has fifty per cent "Indian blood." One can envision a situation in which nonwhiteness itself becomes the only valued quality, to be compensated in various ways depending on a person's pedigree.

Kwame Anthony Appiah, of Harvard's Philosophy and Afro-American Studies Departments, says, "What the Multiracial category aims for is not people of mixed ancestry, because a majority of Americans are actually products of mixed ancestry. This category goes after people who have parents who are socially recognized as belonging to different races. That's O.K.—that's an interesting social category. But then you have to ask what happens to their children. Do we want to have more boxes, depending upon whether they marry back into one group or the other? What are the children of these people supposed to say? I think about these things because—look, my mother is English; my father is Ghanaian. My sisters are married to a Nigerian and a Norwegian. I have nephews who range from blond-haired kids to very black kids. They are all first cousins. Now according to the American scheme of things, they're all black—even the guy with blond hair who skis in Oslo. That's what the one-drop rule says. The Multiracial scheme, which is meant to solve anomalies, simply creates more anomalies of its own, and that's because the fundamental concept—that you should be able to assign every American to one of three or four races reliably—is crazy."

These are sentiments that Representative Sawyer agrees with profoundly. He says of the one-drop rule, "It is so embedded in our perception and policy, but it doesn't allow for the blurring that is the reality of our population. Just look at— What are the numbers?" he said in his congressional office as he leafed through a briefing book. "Thirty-eight per cent of American Japanese females and eighteen per cent of American Japanese males marry outside their traditional ethnic and nationality group. Seventy per cent of American Indians marry outside. I grant you that the enormous growth potential of multiracial marriages starts from a relatively small base, but the truth is it starts from a fiction to begin with; that is, what we think of as black-and-white marriages are not marriages between people who come from anything like a clearly defined ethnic, racial, or genetic base."

The United States Supreme Court struck down the last vestige of anti-miscegenation laws in 1967, in Loving v. Virginia. At that time, interracial marriages were rare; only sixty-five thousand marriages between blacks and whites were recorded in the 1970 census. Marriages between Asians and non-Asian Americans tended to be between soldiers and war brides. Since then, mixed marriages occurring between many racial and ethnic groups have risen to the point where they have eroded the distinctions between such peoples. Among American Indians, people are more likely to marry outside their group than within it, as Representative Sawyer noted. The number of children living in families where one parent is white and the other is black, Asian, or American Indian, to use one measure, has tripled—from fewer than four hundred thousand in 1970 to one and a half million in 1990—and this doesn't count the children of single parents or children whose parents are divorced.

Blacks are conspicuously less likely to marry outside their group, and yet marriages between blacks and whites have tripled in the last thirty years. Matthijs Kalmijn, a Dutch sociologist, analyzed marriage certificates filed in this country's non-Southern states since the Loving decision and found that in the nineteen-eighties the rate at which black men were marrying white women had reached approximately ten per cent. (The rate for black women marrying white men is about half that figure.) In the 1990 census, six per cent of black householders nationwide had nonblack spouses—still a small percentage, but a significant one.

Multiracial people, because they are now both unable and unwilling to be ignored, and because many of them refuse to be confined to traditional racial categories, inevitably undermine the entire concept of race as an irreducible difference between peoples. The continual modulation of racial differences in America is increasing the jumble created by centuries of ethnic intermarriage. The resulting dilemma is a profound one. If we choose to measure the mix-

ing by counting people as Multiracial, we pull the teeth of the civil-rights laws. Are we ready for that? Is it even possible to make changes in the way we count Americans, given the legislative mandates already built into law? "I don't know," Sawyer concedes. "At this point, my purpose is not so much to alter the laws that underlie these kinds of questions as to raise the question of whether or not the way in which we currently define who we are reflects the reality of the nation we are and who we are becoming. If it does not, then the policies underlying the terms of measurement are doomed to be flawed. What you measure is what you get."

SCIENCE has put forward many different racial models, the most enduring being the division of humanity into three broad groupings: the Mongoloid, the Negroid, and the Caucasoid. An influential paper by Masatoshi Nei and Arun K. Roychoudhury, entitled "Gene Differences between Caucasian, Negro, and Japanese Populations," which appeared in *Science*, in 1972, found that the genetic variation among individuals from these racial groups was only slightly greater than the variation within the groups.

In 1965, the anthropologist Stanley Garn proposed hundreds, even thousands, of racial groups, which he saw as gene clusters separated by geography or culture, some with only minor variations between them. The paleontologist Stephen Jay Gould, for one, has proposed doing away with all racial classifications and identifying people by clines—regional divisions that are used to account for the diversity of snails and of songbirds, among many other species. In this Gould follows the anthropologist Ashley Montagu, who waged a lifelong campaign to rid science of the term "race" altogether and never used it except in quotation marks. Montagu would have substituted the term "ethnic group," which he believed carried less odious baggage.

Race, in the common understanding, draws upon differences not only of skin color and physical attributes but also of language, nationality, and religion. At times, we have counted as "races" different national groups, such as Mexicans and Filipinos. Some Asian Indians were

counted as members of a "Hindu" race in the censuses from 1920 to 1940; then they became white for three decades. Racial categories are often used as ethnic intensifiers, with the aim of justifying the exploitation of one group by another. One can trace the ominous example of Jews in prewar Germany, who were counted as "Israelites," a religious group, until the Nazis came to power and turned them into a race. Mixtures of first- and second-degree Jewishness were distinguished, much as quadroons and octoroons had been in the United States. In fact, the Nazi experience ultimately caused a widespread reëxamination of the idea of race. Canada dropped the race question from its census in 1951 and has so far resisted all attempts to reinstitute it. People who were working in the United States Bureau of the Census in the fifties and early sixties remember that there was speculation that the race question would soon be phased out in America as well. The American Civil Liberties Union tried to get the race question dropped from the census in 1960, and the State of New Jersey stopped entering race information on birth and death certificates in 1962 and 1963. In 1964, however, the architecture of civil-rights laws began to be erected, and many of the new laws—particularly the Voting Rights Act of 1965—required highly detailed information about minority participation which could be gathered only by the decennial census, the nation's supreme instrument for gathering demographic statistics. The expectation that the race question would wither away surrendered to the realization that race data were fundamental to monitoring and enforcing desegregation. The census soon acquired a political importance that it had never had in the past.

Unfortunately, the sloppiness and multiplicity of certain racial and ethnic categories rendered them practically meaningless for statistical purposes. In 1973, Caspar Weinberger, who was then Secretary of Health, Education and Welfare, asked the Federal Interagency Committee on Education (FICE) to develop some standards for classifying race and ethnicity. An ad-hoc committee sprang into being and proposed to create an intellectual grid that would sort all Americans into five racial and ethnic categories. The first category was American Indian or Alaskan Native. Some members of the committee wanted the category to be called Original Peoples of the Western Hemisphere, in order to include Indians of South American origin, but the distinction that this category was seeking was so-called "Federal Indians," who were eligible for government benefits; to include Indians of any other origin, even though they might be genetically quite similar, would confuse the collecting of data. To accommodate the various, highly diverse peoples who originated in the Far East, Southeast Asia, and the Pacific Islands, the committee proposed a category called Asian or Pacific Islander, thus sweeping into one massive basket Chinese, Samoans, Cambodians, Filipinos, and others—peoples who had little or nothing in common, and many of whom were, indeed, traditional enemies. The fact that American Indians and Alaskan Natives originated from the same Mongoloid stock as many of these peoples did not stop the committee from putting them in a separate racial category. Black was defined as "a person having origins in any of the black racial groups of Africa," and White, initially, as "a person having origins in any of the original peoples of Europe, North Africa, the Middle East, or the Indian subcontinent"—everybody else, in other words. Because the Black category contained anyone with any African heritage at all, the range of actual skin colors covered the entire spectrum, as did the White category, which included Arabs and Asian Indians and various other darker-skinned peoples.

The final classification, Hispanic, was the most problematic of all. In the 1960 census, people whose ancestry was Latin-American were counted as white. Then people of Spanish origin became a protected group, requiring the census to gather data in order to monitor their civil rights. But how to define them? People who spoke Spanish? Defining the population that way would have included millions of Americans who spoke the language but had no actual roots in Hispanic culture, and it excluded Brazilians and children of immigrants who were not taught Spanish in

their homes. One approach was to count persons with Spanish surnames, but that created a number of difficulties: marriage made some non-Hispanic women into instant minorities, while stripping other women of their Hispanic status. The 1970 census inquired about people from "Central or South America," and more than a million people checked the box who were not Hispanic; they were from Kansas, Alabama, Mississippi—the central and southern United States, in other words.

The greatest dilemma was that there was no conceivable justification for calling Hispanics a race. There were black Hispanics from the Dominican Republic, Argentines who were almost entirely European whites, Mexicans who would have been counted as American Indians if they had been born north of the Rio Grande. The great preponderance of Hispanics are mestizos—a continuum of many different genetic backgrounds. Moreover, the fluid Latin-American concept of race differs from the rigid United States idea of biologically determined and highly distinct human divisions. In most Latin cultures, skin color is an individual variable—not a group marker—so that within the same family one sibling might be considered white and another black. By 1960, the United States census, which counts the population of Puerto Rico, gave up asking the race question on the island, because race did not carry the same distinction there that it did on the mainland. The ad-hoc committee decided to dodge riddles like these by calling Hispanics an ethnic group, not a race.

In 1977, O.M.B. Statistical Directive 15 adopted the FICE suggestions practically verbatim, with one principal exception: Asian Indians were moved to the Asian or Pacific Islander category. Thus, with little political discussion, the identities of Americans were fixed in five broad groupings. Those racial and ethnic categories that were dreamed up almost twenty years ago were not neutral in their effect. By attempting to provide a way for Americans to describe themselves, the categories actually began to shape those identities. The categories became political entities, with their own constituencies, lobbies, and vested interests. What was even more

significant, they caused people to think of themselves in new ways—as members of "races" that were little more than statistical devices. In 1974, the year the ad-hoc committee set to work, few people referred to themselves as Hispanic; rather, people who fell into that grouping tended to identify themselves by nationality—Mexican or Dominican, for instance. Such small categories, however, are inconvenient for statistics and politics, and the creation of the meta-concept "Hispanic" has resulted in the formation of a peculiarly American group. "It is a mixture of ethnicity, culture, history, birth, and a presumption of language," Sawyer contends. Largely because of immigration, the Asian or Pacific Islander group is considered the fastest-growing racial group in the United States, but it is a "racial" category that in all likelihood exists nowhere else in the world. The third-fastest-growing category is Other—made up of the nearly ten million people, most of them Hispanics, who refused to check any of the prescribed racial boxes. American Indian groups are also growing at a rate that far exceeds the growth of the population as a whole: from about half a million people in 1960 to nearly two million in 1990—a two-hundred-and-fifty-nine-per-cent increase, which was demographically impossible. It seemed to be accounted for by improvements in the census-taking procedure and also by the fact that Native Americans had become fashionable, and people now wished to identify with them. To make matters even more confounding, only seventy-four per cent of those who identified themselves as American Indian by race reported having Indian ancestry.

Whatever the word "race" may mean elsewhere in the world, or to the world of science, it is clear that in America the categories are arbitrary, confused, and hopelessly intermingled. In many cases, Americans don't know who they are, racially speaking. A National Center for Health Statistics study found that 5.8 per cent of the people who called themselves Black were seen as White by a census interviewer. Nearly a third of the people identifying themselves as Asian were classified as White or Black by independent observers. That was also true of seventy per cent of people who identified themselves as American Indians. Robert A. Hahn, an epidemiologist at the Centers for Disease Control and Prevention, analyzed deaths of infants born from 1983 through 1985. In an astounding number of cases, the infant had a different race on its death certificate from the one on its birth certificate, and this finding led to staggering increases in the infant-mortality rate for minority populations—46.9 per cent greater for American Indians, 48.8 per cent greater for Japanese-Americans, 78.7 per cent greater for Filipinos—over what had been previously recorded. Such disparities cast doubt on the dependability of race as a criterion for any statistical survey. "It seems to me that we have to go back and reëvaluate the whole system," Hahn says. "We have to ask, 'What do these categories mean?' We are not talking about race in the way that geneticists might use the term, because we're not making any kind of biological assessment. It's closer to self-perceived membership in a population—which is essentially what ethnicity is." There are genetic variations in disease patterns, Hahn points out, and he goes on to say, "But these variations don't always correspond to so-called races. What's really important is, essentially, two things. One, people from different ancestral backgrounds have different behaviors—diets, ideas about what to do when you're sick—that lead them to different health statuses. Two, people are discriminated against because of other people's perception of who they are and how they should be treated. There's still a lot of discrimination in the health-care system."

Racial statistics do serve an important purpose in the monitoring and enforcement of civil-rights laws; indeed, that has become the main justification for such data. A routine example is the Home Mortgage Disclosure Act. Because of race questions on loan applications, the federal government has been able to document the continued practice of redlining by financial institutions. The Federal Reserve found that, for conventional mortgages, in 1992 the denial rate for blacks and Hispanics was roughly double the rate for whites. Hiring practices, jury selection, discriminatory housing patterns, apportionment of

political power—in all these areas, and more, the government patrols society, armed with little more than statistical information to insure equal and fair treatment. "We need these categories essentially to get rid of them," Hahn says.

The unwanted corollary of slotting people by race is that such officially sanctioned classifications may actually worsen racial strife. By creating social-welfare programs based on race rather than on need, the government sets citizens against one another precisely because of perceived racial differences. "It is not 'race' but a *practice* of racial classification that bedevils the society," writes Yehudi Webster, a sociologist at California State University, Los Angeles, and the author of "The Racialization of America." The use of racial statistics, he and others have argued, creates a reality of racial divisions, which then require solutions, such as busing, affirmative action, and multicultural education, all of which are bound to fail, because they heighten the racial awareness that leads to contention. Webster believes that adding a Multiracial box would be "another leap into absurdity," because it reinforces the concept of race in the first place. "In a way, it's a continuation of the one-drop principle. Anybody can say, 'I've got one drop of *something*—I must be multiracial.' It may be a good thing. It may finally convince Americans of the absurdity of racial classification."

In 1990, Itabari Njeri, who writes about interethnic relations for the Los Angeles *Times*, organized a symposium for the National Association of Black Journalists. She recounts a presentation given by Charles Stewart, a Democratic Party activist: "If you consider yourself black for political reasons, raise your hand." The vast majority raised their hands. When Stewart then asked how many people present believed they were of pure African descent, without any mixture, no one raised his hand. Stewart commented later, "If you advocate a category that includes people who are multiracial to the detriment of their black identification, you will replicate what you saw—an empty room. We cannot afford to have an empty room."

Njeri maintains that the social and economic gap between light-skinned blacks

and dark-skinned blacks is as great as the gap between all blacks and all whites in America. If people of more obviously mixed backgrounds were to migrate to a Multiracial box, she says, they would be politically abandoning their former allies and the people who needed their help the most. Instead of draining the established categories of their influence, Njeri and others believe, it would be better to eliminate racial categories altogether.

That possibility is actually being discussed in the corridors of government. "It's quite strange—the original idea of O.M.B. Directive 15 has nothing to do with current efforts to 'define' race,' says Sally Katzen, the director of the Office of Information and Regulatory Affairs at O.M.B., who has the onerous responsibility of making the final recommendation on revising the racial categories. "When O.M.B. got into the business of establishing categories, it was purely statistical, not programmatic—purely for the purpose of data gathering, not for defining or protecting different categories. It was certainly never meant to *define* a race." And yet for more than twenty years Directive 15 did exactly that, with relatively little outcry. "Recently, a question has been raised about the increasing number of multiracial children. I personally have received pictures of beautiful children who are part Asian and part black, or part American Indian and part Asian, with these letters saying, 'I don't want to check just one box. I don't want to deny part of my heritage.' It's very compelling."

This year, Katzen convened a new interagency committee to consider how races should be categorized, and even whether racial information should be sought at all. "To me it's *offensive*—because I think of the Holocaust—for someone to say what a Jew is," says Katzen. "I don't think a government agency should be defining racial and ethnic categories—that certainly was not what was ever intended by these standards."

Is it any accident that racial and ethnic categories should come under attack now, when being a member of a minority group brings certain advantages? The white colonizers of North America conquered the indigenous people, imported African slaves, brought in Asians as laborers and then excluded them with prejudicial immigration laws, and appropriated Mexican land and the people who were living on it. In short, the nonwhite population of America has historically been subjugated and treated as second-class citizens by the white majority. It is to redress the social and economic inequalities of our history that we have civil-rights laws and affirmative-action plans in the first place. Advocates of various racial and ethnic groups point out that many of the people now calling for a race-blind society are political conservatives, who may have an interest in undermining the advancement of nonwhites in our society. Suddenly, the conservatives have adopted the language of integration, it seems, and the left-leaning racial-identity advocates have adopted the language of separatism. It amounts to a polar reversal of political rhetoric.

Jon Michael Spencer, a professor in the African and Afro-American Studies Curriculum at the University of North Carolina at Chapel Hill, recently wrote an article in *The Black Scholar* lamenting what he calls "the postmodern conspiracy to explode racial identity." The article ignited a passionate debate in the magazine over the nature and the future of race. Spencer believes that race is a useful metaphor for cultural and historic difference, because it permits a level of social cohesion among oppressed classes. "To relinquish the notion of race—even though it's a cruel

hoax—at this particular time is to relinquish our fortress against the powers and principalities that still try to undermine us," he says. He sees the Multiracial box as politically damaging to "those who need to galvanize peoples around the racial idea of black."

There are some black cultural nationalists who might welcome the Multiracial category. "In terms of the African-American population, it could be very, very useful, because there is a need to clarify who is in and who is not," Molefi Kete Asante, who is the chairperson of the Department of African-American Studies at Temple University, says. "In fact, I would think they should go further than that—identify those people who are in interracial marriages."

Spencer, however, thinks that it might be better to eliminate racial categories altogether than to create an additional category that empties the others of meaning. "If you had who knows how many thousands or tens of thousands or millions of people claiming to be multiracial, you would lessen the number who are black," Spencer says. "There's no end in sight. There's no limit to which one can go in claiming to be multiracial. For instance, I happen to be very brown in complexion, but when I go to the continent of Africa, blacks and whites there claim that I would be 'colored' rather than black, which means that somewhere in my distant past—probably during the era

of slavery—I could have one or more white ancestors. So does that mean that I, too, could check Multiracial? Certainly light-skinned black people might perhaps see this as a way out of being included among a despised racial group. The result could be the creation of another class of people, who are betwixt and between black and white."

Whatever comes out of this discussion, the nation is likely to engage in the most profound debate of racial questions in decades. "We recognize the importance of racial categories in correcting clear injustices under the law," Representative Sawyer says. "The dilemma we face is trying to assure the fundamental guarantees of equality of opportunity while at the same time recognizing that the populations themselves are changing as we seek to categorize them. It reaches the point where it becomes an absurd counting game. Part of the difficulty is that we are dealing with the illusion of precision. We wind up with precise counts of everybody in the country, and they are precisely wrong. They don't reflect who we are as a people. To be effective, the concepts of individual and group identity need to reflect not only who we have been but who we are becoming. The more these categories distort our perception of reality, the less useful they are. We act as if we knew what we're talking about when we talk about race, and we don't."

PLESSY v. FERGUSON

May 18, 1896
163 U.S. 537 (1896)

MR. JUSTICE BROWN, after stating the case, delivered the opinion of the court.

This case turns upon the constitutionality of an act of the General Assembly of the State of Louisiana, passed in 1890, providing for separate railway carriages for the white and colored races. Acts 1890, No. 111, p. 152.

The first section of the statute enacts "that all railway companies carrying passengers in their coaches in this State, shall provide equal but separate accommodations for the white, and colored races, by providing two or more passenger coaches for each passenger train, or by dividing the passenger coaches by a partition so as to secure separate accommodations: *Provided*, That this section shall not be construed to apply to street railroads. No person or persons, shall be admitted to occupy seats in coaches, other than, the ones, assigned, to them on account of the race they belong to."

By the second section it was enacted "that the officers of such passenger trains shall have power and are hereby required to assign each passenger to the coach or compartment used for the race to which such passenger belongs; any passenger insisting on going into a coach or compartment to which by race he does not belong, shall be liable to a fine of twenty-five dollars, or in lieu thereof to imprisonment for a period of not more than twenty days in the parish prison, and any officer of any railroad insisting on assigning a passenger to a coach or compartment other than the one set aside for the race to which said passenger belongs, shall be liable to a fine of twenty-five dollars, or in lieu thereof to imprisonment for a period of not more than twenty days in the parish prison; and should any passenger refuse to occupy the coach or compartment to which he or she is assigned by the officer of such railway, said officer shall have power to refuse to carry such passenger on his train, and for such refusal neither he nor the railway company which he represents shall be liable for damages in any of the courts of this State."

The third section provides penalties for the refusal or neglect of the officers, directors, conductors and employés of railway companies to comply with the act, with a proviso that "nothing in this act shall be construed as applying to nurses attending children of the other race." The fourth section is immaterial.

The information filed in the criminal District Court charged in substance that Plessy, being a passenger between two stations within the State of Louisiana, was assigned by officers of the company to the coach used for the race to which he belonged, but he insisted upon going into a coach used by the race to which he did not belong. Neither in the information nor plea was his particular race or color averred.

The petition for the writ of prohibition averred that petitioner was seven eighths Caucasian and one eighth African blood; that the mixture of colored blood was not discernible in him, and that he was entitled to every right, privilege and immunity secured to citizens of the United States of the white race; and that, upon such theory, he took possession of a vacant seat in a coach where passengers of the white race were accommodated, and was ordered by the conductor to vacate said coach and take a seat in another assigned to persons of the colored race, and having refused to comply with such demand he was forcibly ejected with the aid of a police officer, and imprisoned in the parish jail to answer a charge of having violated the above act.

The constitutionality of this act is attacked upon the ground that it conflicts both with the Thirteenth Amendment of the Constitution, abolishing slavery, and the Fourteenth Amendment, which prohibits certain restrictive legislation on the part of the States.

1. That it does not conflict with the Thirteenth Amendment, which abolished slavery and involuntary servitude, except as a punishment for crime, is too clear for argument. Slavery implies involuntary servitude—a state of bondage; the ownership of mankind as a chattel, or at least the control of the labor and services of one man for the benefit of another, and the absence of a legal right to the disposal of his own

From *U.S. Reports*, 1896. Opinion of the Supreme Court, May 18, 1896.

17

person, property and services. This amendment was said in the *Slaughter-house cases*, 16 Wall. 35, to have been intended primarily to abolish slavery, as it had been previously known in this country, and that it equally forbade Mexican peonage or the Chinese coolie trade, when they amounted to slavery or involuntary servitude, and that the use of the word "servitude" was intended to prohibit the use of all forms of involuntary slavery, of whatever class or name. It was intimated, however, in that case that this amendment was regarded by the statesmen of that day as insufficient to protect the colored race from certain laws which had been enacted in the Southern States, imposing upon the colored race onerous disabilities and burdens, and curtailing their rights in the pursuit of life, liberty and property to such an extent that their freedom was of little value; and that the Fourteenth Amendment was devised to meet this exigency.

So, too, in the *Civil Rights cases*, 109 U.S. 3, 24, it was said that the act of a mere individual, the owner of an inn, a public conveyance or place of amusement, refusing accommodations to colored people, cannot be justly regarded as imposing any badge of slavery or servitude upon the applicant, but only as involving an ordinary civil injury, properly cognizable by the laws of the State, and presumably subject to redress by those laws until the contrary appears. "It would be running the slavery argument into the ground," said Mr. Justice Bradley, "to make it apply to every act of discrimination which a person may see fit to make as to the guests he will entertain, or as to the people he will take into his coach or cab or car, or admit to his concert or theatre, or deal with in other matters of intercourse or business."

A statute which implies merely a legal distinction between the white and colored races—a distinction which is founded in the color of the two races, and which must always exist so long as white men are distinguished from the other race by color—has no tendency to destroy the legal equality of the two races, or reestablish a state of involuntary servitude. Indeed, we do not understand that the Thirteenth Amendment is strenuously relied upon by the plaintiff in error in this connection.

2. By the Fourteenth Amendment, all persons born or naturalized in the United States, and subject to the jurisdiction thereof, are made citizens of the United States and of the State wherein they reside; and the States are forbidden from making or enforcing any law which shall abridge the privileges or immunities of citizens of the United States, or shall deprive any person of life, liberty or property without due process of law, or deny to any person within their jurisdiction the equal protection of the laws.

The proper construction of this amendment was first called to the attention of this court in the *Slaughter-house cases*, 16 Wall. 36, which involved, however, not a question of race, but one of exclusive privileges. The case did not call for any expression of opinion as to the exact rights it was intended to secure to the colored race, but it was said generally that its main purpose was to establish the citizenship of the negro; to give definitions of citizenship of the United States and of the States, and to protect from the hostile legislation of the States the privileges and immunities of citizens of the United States, as distinguished from those of citizens of the States.

The object of the amendment was undoubtedly to enforce the absolute equality of the two races before the law, but in the nature of things it could not have been intended to abolish distinctions based upon color, or to enforce social, as distinguished from political, equality, or a commingling of the two races upon terms unsatisfactory to either. Laws permitting, and even requiring, their separation in places where they are liable to be brought into contact do not necessarily imply the inferiority of either race to the other, and have been generally, if not universally, recognized as within the competency of the state legislatures in the exercise of their police power. The most common instance of this is connected with the establishment of separate schools for white and colored children, which has been held to be a valid exercise of the legislative power even by courts of States where the political rights of the colored race have been longest and most earnestly enforced.

One of the earliest of these cases is that of *Roberts v. City of Boston*, 5 Cush. 198, in which the Supreme Judicial Court of Massachusetts held that the general school committee of Boston had power to make provision for the instruction of colored children in separate schools established exclusively for them, and to prohibit their attendance upon the other schools. . . .

Similar laws have been enacted by Congress under its general power of legislation over the District of Columbia, Rev. Stat. D.C. §§ 281, 282, 283, 310, 319, as well as by the legislatures of many of the States, and have been generally, if not uniformly, sustained by the courts. *State v. McCann*, 21 Ohio St. 198; *Lehew v. Brummell*, 15 S. W. Rep. 765; *Ward v. Flood*, 48 California, 36; *Bertonneau v. School Directors*, 3 Woods, 177; *People v. Gallagher*, 93 N.Y. 438; *Cory v. Carter*, 48 Indiana, 327; *Dawson v. Lee*, 83 Kentucky, 49.

Laws forbidding the intermarriage of the two races may be said in a technical sense to interfere with the freedom of contract, and yet have been universally recognized as within the police power of the State. *State v. Gibson*, 36 Indiana, 389.

The distinction between laws interfering with the political equality of the negro and those requiring the separation of the two races in schools, theatres and railway carriages has been frequently drawn by this court. Thus in *Strauder v. West Virginia*, 100 U.S. 303, it was held that a law of West Virginia limiting to white male persons, 21 years of age and citizens of the State, the right to sit upon juries, was a discrimination which implied a legal inferiority in civil society, which lessened the security of the right of the colored race, and was a step toward reducing them to a condition of servility. Indeed, the right of a colored man that, in the selection of jurors to pass upon his life, liberty and property, there shall be no exclusion of his race, and no discrimination against them because of color, has been asserted in a number of cases. *Virginia v. Rives,* 100 U.S. 313; *Neal v. Delaware,* 103 U.S. 370; *Bush v. Kentucky,* 107 U.S. 110; *Gibson v. Mississippi,* 162 U.S. 565. So, where the laws of a particular locality or the charter of a particular railway corporation has provided that no person shall be excluded from the cars on account of color, we have held that this meant that persons of color should travel in the same car as white ones, and that the enactment was not satisfied by the company's providing cars assigned exclusively to people of color, though they were as good as those which they assigned exclusively to white persons. *Railroad Company v. Brown,* 17 Wall. 445.

Upon the other hand, where a statute of Louisiana required those engaged in the transportation of passengers among the States to give to all persons travelling within that State, upon vessels employed in that business, equal rights and privileges in all parts of the vessel, without distinction on account of race or color, and subjected to an action for damages the owner of such a vessel, who excluded colored passengers on account of their color from the cabin set aside by him for the use of whites, it was held to be so far as it applied to interstate commerce, unconstitutional and void. *Hall v. De Cuir,* 95 U.S. 485. The court in this case, however, expressly disclaimed that it had anything whatever to do with the statute as a regulation of internal commerce, or affecting anything else than commerce among the States.

In the *Civil Rights case,* 109 U.S. 3, it was held that an act of Congress, entitling all persons within the jurisdiction of the United States to the full and equal enjoyment of the accommodations, advantages, facilities and privileges of inns, public conveyances, on land or water, theatres and other places of public amusement, and made applicable to citizens of every race and color, regardless of any previous condition of servitude, was unconstitutional and void, upon the ground that the Fourteenth Amendment was prohibitory upon the States only, and the legislation authorized to be adopted by Congress for enforcing it was not direct legislation on matters respecting which the States were prohibited from making or enforcing certain laws, or doing certain acts, but was corrective legislation, such as might be necessary or proper for counteracting and redressing the effect of such laws or acts. In delivering the opinion of the court Mr. Justice Bradley observed that the Fourteenth Amendment

"does not invest Congress with power to legislate upon subjects that are within the domain of state legislation; but to provide modes of relief against state legislation, or state action, of the kind referred to. It does not authorize Congress to create a code of municipal law for the regulation of private rights; but to provide modes of redress against the operation of state laws, and the action of state officers, executive or judicial, when these are subversive of the fundamental rights specified in the amendment. Positive rights and privileges are undoubtedly secured by the Fourteenth Amendment; but they are secured by way of prohibition against state laws and state proceedings affecting those rights and privileges, and by power given to Congress to legislate for the purpose of carrying such prohibition into effect; and such legislation must necessarily be predicated upon such supposed state laws or state proceedings, and be directed to the correction of their operation and effect."

Much nearer, and, indeed, almost directly in point, is the case of the *Louisville, New Orleans & c. Railway v. Mississippi,* 133 U.S. 587, wherein the railway company was indicted for a violation of a statute of Mississippi, enacting that all railroads carrying passengers should provide equal, but separate, accommodations for the white and colored races, by providing two or more passenger cars for each passenger train, or by dividing the passenger cars by a partition, so as to secure separate accommodations. The case was presented in a different aspect from the one under consideration, inasmuch as it was an indictment against the railway company for failing to provide the separate accommodations, but the question considered was the constitutionality of the law. In that case, the Supreme Court of Mississippi, 66 Mississippi, 662, had held that the statute applied solely to commerce within the State, and, that being the construction of the state statute by its highest court, was accepted as conclusive. "If it be a matter," said the court, p. 591, "respecting commerce wholly within a State, and not interfering with commerce between the States, then, obviously, there is no violation of the commerce clause of the Federal Constitution. . . . No question arises under this section, as to the power of the State to separate in different compartments interstate passengers, or affect, in any manner, the privileges and rights of such passengers. All that we can consider is, whether the State has the power to require that railroad trains within her limits shall have separate accommodations for the two races; that affecting only commerce within the State is no invasion of the power given to Congress by the commerce clause."

A like course of reasoning applies to the case under consideration, since the Supreme Court of Louisiana in the case of the *State ex rel. Abbott v. Hicks, Judge, et al.,* 44 La. Ann. 770, held that the statute in question did not apply to interstate passengers, but was confined in its application to passengers travelling exclusively within the borders of the State. The case was decided largely upon the authority of *Railway Co. v. State*, 66 Mississippi, 662, and affirmed by this court in 133 U.S. 587. In the present case no question of interference with interstate commerce can possibly arise, since the East Louisiana Railway appears to have been purely a local line, with both its termini within the State of Louisiana. Similar statutes for the separation of the two races upon public conveyances were held to be constitutional in *West Chester &c. Railroad v. Miles*, 55 Penn. St. 209; *Day v. Owen*, 5 Michigan, 520; *Chicago &c. Railway v. Williams*, 55 Illinois, 185; *Chesapeake &c. Railroad v. Wells*, 85 Tennessee, 613; *Memphis &c. Railroad v. Benson*, 85 Tennessee, 627; *The Sue*, 22 Fed. Rep. 843; *Logwood v. Memphis &c. Railroad*, 23 Fed. Rep. 318; *McGuinn v. Forbes*, 37 Fed. Rep. 639; *People v. King*, 18 N.E. Rep. 245; *Houck v. South Pac. Railway*, 38 Fed. Rep. 226; *Heard v. Georgia Railroad Co.*, 3 Int. Com. Com'n, 111; *S.C.*, 1 Ibid. 428.

While we think the enforced separation of the races, as applied to the internal commerce of the State, neither abridges the privileges or immunities of the colored man, deprives him of his property without due process of law, nor denies him the equal protection of the laws, within the meaning of the Fourteenth Amendment, we are not prepared to say that the conductor, in assigning passengers to the coaches according to their race, does not act at his peril, or that the provision of the second section of the act, that denies to the passenger compensation in damages for a refusal to receive him into the coach in which he properly belongs, is a valid exercise of the legislative power. Indeed, we understand it to be conceded by the State's attorney, that such part of the act as exempts from liability the railway company and its officers is unconstitutional. The power to assign to a particular coach obviously implies the power to determine to which race the passenger belongs, as well as the power to determine who, under the laws of the particular State, is to be deemed a white, and who a colored person. This question, though indicated in the brief of the plaintiff in error, does not properly arise upon the record in this case, since the only issue made is as to the unconstitutionality of the act, so far as it requires the railway to provide separate accommodations, and the conductor to assign passengers according to their race.

It is claimed by the plaintiff in error that, in any mixed community, the reputation of belonging to the dominant race, in this instance the white race, is *property*, in the same sense that a right of action, or of inheritance, is property. Conceding this to be so, for the purposes of this case, we are unable to see how this statute deprives him of, or in any way affects his right to, such property. If he be a white man and assigned to a colored coach, he may have his action for damages against the company for being deprived of his so called

property. Upon the other hand, if he be a colored man and be so assigned, he has been deprived of no property, since his is not lawfully entitled to the reputation of being a white man.

In this connection, it is also suggested by the learned counsel for the plaintiff in error that the same argument that will justify the state legislature in requiring railways to provide separate accommodations for the two races will also authorize them to require separate cars to be provided for people whose hair is of a certain color, or who are aliens, or who belong to certain nationalities, or to enact laws requiring colored people to walk upon one side of the street, and white people upon the other, or requiring white men's houses to be painted white, and colored men's black, or their vehicles or business signs to be of different colors, upon the theory that one side of the street is as good as the other, or that a house or vehicle of one color is as good as one of another color. The reply to all this is that every exercise of the police power must be reasonable, and extend only to such laws as are enacted in good faith for the promotion for the public good, and not for the annoyance or oppression of a particular class. Thus in *Yick Wo v. Hopkins*, 118 U.S. 356, it was held by this court that a municipal ordinance of the city of San Francisco, to regulate the carrying on of public laundries within the limits of the municipality, violated the provisions of the Constitution of the United States, if it conferred upon the municipal authorities arbitrary power, at their own will, and without regard to discretion, in the legal sense of the term, to give or withhold consent as to persons or places, without regard to the competency of the persons applying, or the propriety of the places selected for the carrying on of the business. It was held to be a covert attempt on the part of the municipality to make an arbitrary and unjust discrimination against the Chinese race. While this was the case of a municipal ordinance, a like principle has been held to apply to acts of a state legislature passed in the exercise of the police power. *Railroad Company v. Husen*, 95 U.S. 465; *Louisville & nashville Railroad v. Kentucky*, 161 U.S. 677, and cases cited on p. 700; *Daggett v. Hudson*, 43 Ohio St. 548; *Capen v. Foster*, 12 Pick. 485; *State ex rel. Wood v. Baker*, 38 Wisconsin, 71; *Monroe v. Collins*, 17 Ohio St. 665; *Hulseman v. Rems*, 41 Penn. St. 396; *Orman v. Riley*, 15 California, 48.

So far, then, as a conflict with the Fourteenth Amendment is concerned, the case reduces itself to the question whether the statute of Louisiana is a reasonable regulation, and with respect to this there must necessarily be a large discretion on the part of the legislature. In determining the question of reasonableness it is at liberty to act with reference to the established usages, customs and traditions of the people, and with a view to the promotion of their comfort, and the preservation of the public peace and good order. Gauged by this standard, we cannot say that a law which authorizes or even requires the separation of the two races in public conveyances is unreasonable, or more obnoxious to the Fourteenth Amendment than the acts of Congress requiring separate schools for colored children in the District of Columbia, the constitutionality of which does not seem to have been questioned, or the corresponding acts of state legislatures.

We consider the underlying fallacy of the plaintiff's argument to consist in the assumption that the enforced separation of the two races stamps the colored race with a badge of inferiority. If this be so, it is not by reason of anything found in the act, but solely because the colored race chooses to put that construction upon it. The argument necessarily assumes that if, as has been more than once the case, and is not unlikely to be so again, the colored race should become the dominant power in the state legislature, and should enact a law in precisely similar terms, it would thereby relegate the white race to an inferior position. We imagine that the white race, at least, would not acquiesce in this assumption. The argument also assumes that social prejudices may be overcome by legislation, and that equal rights cannot be secured to the negro except by an enforced commingling of the two races. We cannot accept this proposition. If the two races are to meet upon terms of social equality, it must be the result of natural affinities, a mutual appreciation of each other's merits and a voluntary consent of individuals. As was said by the Court of Appeals of New York in *People v. Gallagher*, 93 N.Y. 438, 448, "this end can neither be accomplished nor promoted by laws which conflict with the general sentiment of the community upon whom they are designed to operate. When the government, therefore, has secured to each of its citizens equal rights before the law and opportunities for improvement and progress, it has accomplished the end for which it was organized and performed all of the functions respecting social advantages with which it is endowed." Legislation is powerless to eradicate racial instincts or to abolish distinctions based upon physical differences, and the attempt to do so can only result in accentuating the difficulties of the present situation. If the civil and political rights of both races be equal one cannot be inferior to the other civilly or politically. If one race be inferior to the other socially, the Constitution of the United States cannot put them upon the same plane.

It is true that the question of the proportion of colored blood necessary to constitute a colored person, as distinguished from a white person, is one upon which there is a difference of opinion in the different States, some holding that any visible admixture of black blood stamps the person as belonging to the colored race, (*State v. Chavers*, 5 Jones, [N.C.] 1, p. 11); others that it depends upon the preponderance of blood, (*Gray v. State*, 4 Ohio, 354; *Monroe v. Collins*, 17

Ohio St. 665); and still others that the predominance of white blood must only be in the proportion of three fourths. (*People v. Dean*, 14 Michigan, 406; *Jones v. Commonwealth*, 80 Virginia, 538.) But these are questions to be determined under the laws of each State and are not properly put in issue in this case. Under the allegations of his petition it may undoubtedly become a question of importance whether, under the laws of Louisiana, the petitioner belongs to the white or colored race.

The judgment of the court below is, therefore,

Affirmed.

Mr. Justice Harlan dissenting.

By the Louisiana statute the validity of which is here involved, all railway companies (other than street-railroad companies) carrying passengers in that state are required to have separate but equal accommodations for white and colored persons, "by providing two more passenger coaches for each passenger train, or by dividing the passenger coaches by a partition so as to secure separate accommodations." Under this statute, no colored person is permitted to occupy a seat in a coach assigned to white persons; nor any white person to occupy a seat in a coach assigned to colored persons. The managers of the railroad are not allowed to exercise any discretion in the premises, but are required to assign each passenger to some coach or compartment set apart for the exclusive use of his race. If a passenger insists upon going into a coach or compartment not set apart for persons of his race, he is subject to be fined, or to be imprisoned in the parish jail. Penalties are prescribed for the refusal or neglect of the officers, directors, conductors, and employés of railroad companies to comply with the provisions of the act.

Only "nurses attending children of the other race" are excepted from the operation of the statute. No exception is made of colored attendants traveling with adults. A white man is not permitted to have his colored servant with him in the same coach, even if his condition of health requires the constant personal assistance of such servant. If a colored maid insists upon riding in the same coach with a white woman whom she has been employed to serve, and who may need her personal attention while traveling, she is subject to be fined or imprisoned for such an exhibition of zeal in the discharge of duty.

While there may be in Louisiana persons of different races who are not citizens of the United States, the words in the act "white and colored races" necessarily include all citizens of the United States of both races residing in that state. So that we have before us a state enactment that compels, under penalties, the separation of the two races in railroad passenger coaches, and makes it a crime for a citizen of either race to enter a coach that has been assigned to citizens of the other race.

Thus, the state regulates the use of a public highway by citizens of the United States solely upon the basis of race.

However apparent the injustice of such legislation may be, we have only to consider whether it is consistent with the constitution of the United States. . . .

In respect of civil rights, common to all citizens, the constitution of the United States does not, I think, permit any public authority to know the race of those entitled to be protected in the enjoyment of such rights. Every true man has pride of race, and under appropriate circumstances, when the rights of others, his equals before the law, are not to be affected, it is his privilege to express such pride and to take such action based upon it as to him seems proper. But I deny that any legislative body or judicial tribunal may have regard to the race of citizens when the civil rights of those citizens are involved. Indeed, such legislation as that here in question is inconsistent not only with that equality of rights which pertains to citizenship, national and state, but with the personal liberty enjoyed by every one within the United States. . . .

The white race deems itself to be the dominant race in this country. And so it is, in prestige, in achievements, in education, in wealth, and in power. So, I doubt not, it will continue to be for all time, if it remains true to its great heritage, and holds fast to the principles of constitutional liberty. But in view of the constitution, in the eye of the law, there is in this country no superior, dominant, ruling class of citizens. There is no caste here. Our constitution is color-blind, and neither knows nor tolerates classes among citizens. In respect of civil rights, all citizens are equal before the law. The humblest is the peer of the most powerful. The law regards man as man, and takes no account of his surroundings or of his color when his civil rights as guarantied by the supreme law of the land are involved. It is therefore to be regretted that this high tribunal, the final expositor of the fundamental law of the land, has reached the conclusion that it is competent for a state to regulate the enjoyment by citizens of their civil rights solely upon the basis of race.

In my opinion, the judgment this day rendered will, in time, prove to be quite as pernicious as the decision made by this tribunal in the Dred Scott Case.

It was adjudged in that case that the descendants of Africans who were imported into this country, and sold as slaves, were not included nor intended to be included under the word "citizens" in the constitution, and could not claim any of the rights and privileges which that instrument provided for and secured to citizens of the United States; that, at the time of the adoption of the constitution, they were "considered as a subordinate and inferior class of beings, who had

been subjugated by the dominant race, and, whether emancipated or not, yet remained subject to their authority, and had no rights or privileges but such as those who held the power and the government might choose to grant them" 17 How. 393, 404. The recent amendments of the constitution, it was supposed, had eradicated these principles from our institutions. But it seems that we have yet, in some of the states, a dominant race,—a superior class of citizens,—which assumes to regulate the enjoyment of civil rights, common to all citizens, upon the basis of race. The present decision, it may well be apprehended, will not only stimulate aggressions, more or less brutal and irritating, upon the admitted rights of colored citizens, but will encourage the belief that it is possible, by means of state enactments, to defeat the beneficent purposes which the people of the United States had in view when they adopted the recent amendments of the constitution, by one of which the blacks of this country were made citizens of the United States and of the states in which they respectively reside, and whose privileges and immunities, as citizens, the states are forbidden to abridge. Sixty millions of whites are in no danger from the presence here of eight millions of blacks. The destinies of the two races, in this country, are indissolubly linked together, and the interests of both require that the common government of all shall not permit the seeds of race hate to be planted under the sanction of law. What can more certainly arouse race hate, what more certainly create and perpetuate a feeling of distrust between these races, than state enactments which, in fact, proceed on the ground that colored citizens are so inferior and degraded that they cannot be allowed to sit in public coaches occupied by white citizens? That, as all will admit, is the real meaning of such legislation as was enacted in Louisiana.

The sure guaranty of the peace and security of each race is the clear, distinct, unconditional recognition by our governments, national and state, of every right that inheres in civil freedom, and of the equality before the law of all citizens of the United States, without regard to race. State enactments regulating the enjoyment of civil rights upon the basis of race, and cunningly devised to defeat legitimate results of the war, under the pretense of recognizing equality of rights, can have no other result than to render permanent peace impossible, and to keep alive a conflict of races, the continuance of which must do harm to all concerned. This question is not met by the suggestion that social equality cannot exist between the white and black races in this country. That argument, if it can be properly regarded as one, is scarcely worthy of consideration; for social equality no more exists between two races when traveling in a passenger coach or a public highway than when members of the same races sit by each other in a street car or in the jury box, or stand or sit with each other in a political assembly, or when they use in common the streets of a city or town, or when they are in the same room for the purpose of having their names placed on the registry of voters, or when they approach the ballot box in order to exercise the high privilege of voting. . . .

The arbitrary separation of citizens, on the basis of race, while they are on a public highway, is a badge of servitude wholly inconsistent with the civil freedom and the equality before the law established by the constitution. It cannot be justified upon any legal grounds.

If evils will result from the commingling of the two races upon public highways established for the benefit of all, they will be infinitely less than those that will surely come from state legislation regulating the enjoyment of civil rights upon the basis of race. We boast of the freedom enjoyed by our people above all other peoples. But it is difficult to reconcile that boast with a state of the law which, practically, puts the brand of servitude and degradation upon a large class of our fellow citizens,—our equals before the law. The thin disguise of "equal" accommodations for passengers in railroad coaches will not mislead any one, nor atone for the wrong this day done. . . .

I am of opinion that the statute of Louisiana is inconsistent with the personal liberty of citizens, white and black, in that state, and hostile to both the spirit and letter of the constitution of the United States. If laws of like character should be enacted in the several states of the Union, the effect would be in the highest degree mischievous. Slavery, as an institution tolerated by law, would, it is true, have disappeared from our country; but there would remain a power in the states, by sinister legislation, to interfere with the full enjoyment of the blessings of freedom, to regulate civil rights, common to all citizens, upon the basis of race, and to place in a condition of legal inferiority a large body of American citizens, now constituting a part of the political community, called the "People of the United States," for whom, and by whom through representatives, our government is administered. Such a system is inconsistent with the guaranty given by the constitution to each state of a republican form of government, and may be stricken down by congressional action, or by the courts in the discharge of their solemn duty to maintain the supreme law of the land, anything in the constitution or laws of any state to the contrary notwithstanding.

For the reason stated, I am constrained to withhold my assent from the opinion and judgment of the majority.

BROWN et al.
v.
BOARD OF EDUCATION
OF TOPEKA et al.

347 U.S. 483 (1954)

Mr. Chief Justice Warren delivered the opinion of the Court.

These cases come to us from the States of Kansas, South Carolina, Virginia, and Delaware. They are premised on different facts and different local conditions, but a common legal question justifies their consideration together in this consolidated opinion.[1]

In each of the cases, minors of the Negro race, through their legal representatives, seek the aid of the courts in   obtaining admission to the public schools of their community on a nonsegregated basis. In each instance, they had been denied admission to schools attended by white children under laws requiring or permitting segregation according to race. This segregation was alleged to deprive the plaintiffs of the equal protection of the laws under the Fourteenth Amendment. In each of the cases other than the Delaware case, a three-judge federal district court denied relief to the plaintiffs on the so-called "separate but equal" doctrine announced by this Court in *Plessy v. Ferguson*, 163 U.S. 537. Under that doctrine, equality of treatment is accorded when the races are provided substantially equal facilities, even though these facilities be separate. In the Delaware case, the Supreme Court of Delaware adhered to that doctrine, but ordered that the plaintiffs be admitted to the white schools because of their superiority to the Negro schools.

The plaintiffs contend that segregated public schools are not "equal" and cannot be made "equal," and that hence they are deprived of the equal protection of the laws. Because of the obvious importance of the question presented, the Court took jurisdiction.[2] Argument was heard in the 1952 Term, and reargument was heard this Term on certain questions propounded by the Court.[3]

Reargument was largely devoted to the circumstances surrounding the adoption of the Fourteenth Amendment in 1868. It covered exhaustively consideration of the Amendment in Congress, ratification by the states, then existing practices in racial segregation, and the views of proponents and opponents of the Amendment. This discussion and our own investigation convince us that, although these sources cast some light, it is not enough to resolve the problem with which we are faced. At best, they are inconclusive. The most avid proponents of the post–War Amendments undoubtedly intended them to remove all legal distinctions among "all persons born or naturalized in the United States." Their opponents, just as certainly, were antagonistic to both the letter and the spirit of the Amendments and wished them to have the most limited effect. What others in Congress and the state legislatures had in mind cannot be determined with an degree of certainty.

An additional reason for the inconclusive nature of the Amendment's history, with respect to segregated schools, is the status of public education at that time.[4] In the South, the movement toward free common schools, supported by general taxation, had not yet taken hold. Education of white children was largely in the hands of private groups. Education of Negroes was almost nonexistent, and practically all of the race were illiterate. In fact, any education of Negroes was forbidden by law in some states. Today, in contrast, many Negroes have achieved outstanding success in the arts and sciences as well as in the business and professional world. It is true that public school education at the time of the Amendment had advanced further in the North, but the effect of the Amendment on northern States was generally ignored in the congressional debates. Even in the North, the conditions of public education did not approximate those existing today. The curriculum was usually rudimentary; ungraded schools were common in rural areas; the school term

From *U.S. Reports*, 1954. Opinion of the Supreme Court, 1954.

was but three months a year in many states; and compulsory school attendance was virtually unknown. As a consequence, it is not surprising that there should be so little in the history of the Fourteenth Amendment relating to its intended effect on public education.

In the first cases in this Court construing the Fourteenth Amendment, decided shortly after its adoption, the Court interpreted it as proscribing all state-imposed discriminations against the Negro race.[5] The doctrine of "separate but equal" did not make its appearance in this Court until 1896 in the case of *Plessy v. Ferguson, supra,* involving not education but transportation.[6] American courts have since labored with the doctrine for over half a century. In this Court, there have been six cases involving the "separate but equal" doctrine in the field of public education.[7] In *Cumming v. County Board of Education,* 175 U.S. 528, and *Gong Lum v. Rice,* 275 U.S. 78, the validity of the doctrine itself was not challenged.[8] In more recent cases, all on the graduate school level, inequality was found in that specific benefits enjoyed by white students were denied to Negro students of the same educational qualifications. *Missouri ex rel. Gaines v. Canada,* 305 U.S. 337; *Sipuel v. Oklahoma,* 332 U.S. 631; *Sweatt v. Painter,* 339 U.S. 629; *McLaurin v. Oklahoma State Regents,* 339 U.S. 637. In none of these cases was it necessary to re-examine the doctrine to grant relief to the Negro plaintiff. And in *Sweatt v. Painter, supra,* the Court expressly reserved decision on the question whether *Plessy v. Ferguson* should be held inapplicable to public education.

In the instant cases, that question is directly presented. Here, unlike *Sweatt v. Painter,* there are findings below that the Negro and white schools involved have been equalized, or are being equalized, with respect to buildings, curricula, qualifications and salaries of teachers, and other "tangible" factors.[9] Our decision, therefore, cannot turn on merely a comparison of these tangible factors in the Negro and white schools involved in each of the cases. We must look instead to the effect of segregation itself on public education.

In approaching this problem, we cannot turn the clock back to 1868 when the Amendment was adopted, or even to 1896 when *Plessy v. Ferguson* was written. We must consider public education in the light of its full development and its present place in American life throughout the Nation. Only in this way can it be determined if segregation in public schools deprives these plaintiffs of the equal protection of the laws.

Today, education is perhaps the most important function of state and local governments. Compulsory school attendance laws and the great expenditures for education both demonstrate our recognition of the importance of education to our democratic society. It is required in the performance of our most basic public responsibilities, even service in the armed forces. It is

the very foundation of good citizenship. Today it is a principal instrument in awakening the child to cultural values, in preparing him for later professional training, and in helping him to adjust normally to his environment. In these days, it is doubtful that any child may reasonably be expected to succeed in life if he is denied the opportunity of an education. Such an opportunity, where the state has undertaken to provide it, is a right which must be made available to all on equal terms.

We come then to the question presented: Does segregation of children in public schools solely on the basis of race, even though the physical facilities and other "tangible" factors may be equal, deprive the children of the minority group of equal educational opportunities? We believe that it does.

In *Sweatt v. Painter, supra,* in finding that a segregated law school for Negroes could not provide them equal educational opportunities, this Court relied in large part on "those qualities which are incapable of objective measurement but which make for greatness in a law school." In *McLaurin v. Oklahoma State Regents, supra,* the Court, in requiring that a Negro admitted to a white graduate school be treated like all other students, again resorted to intangible considerations: " . . . his ability to study, to engage in discussions and exchange views with other students, and, in general, to learn his profession." Such considerations apply with added force to children in grade and high schools. To separate them from others of similar age and qualifications solely because of their race generates a feeling of inferiority as to their status in the community that may affect their hearts and minds in a way unlikely ever to be undone. The effect of this separation on their educational opportunities was well stated by a finding in the Kansas case by a court which nevertheless felt compelled to rule against the Negro plaintiffs:

> "Segregation of white and colored children in public schools has a detrimental effect upon the colored children. The impact is greater when it has the sanction of the law; for the policy of separating the races is usually interpreted as denoting the inferiority of the negro group. A sense of inferiority affects the motivation of a child to learn. Segregation with the sanction of law, therefore, has a tendency to [retard] the educational and mental development of negro children and to deprive them of some of the benefits they would receive in a racial[ly] integrated school system."[10]

Whatever may have been the extent of psychological knowledge at the time of *Plessy v. Ferguson,* this finding is amply supported by modern authority.[11] Any language in *Plessy v. Ferguson* contrary to this finding is rejected.

We conclude that in the field of public education the doctrine of "separate but equal" has no place. Separate educational facilities are inherently unequal. Therefore, we hold that the plaintiffs and others similarly situated for whom the actions have been brought are, by reason of the segregation complained of, deprived of the equal protection of the laws guaranteed by the Fourteenth Amendment. This disposition makes unnecessary any discussion whether such segregation also violates the Due Process Clause of the Fourteenth Amendment.[12]

Because these are class actions, because of the wide applicability of this decision, and because of the great variety of local conditions, the formulation of decrees in these cases presents problems of considerable complexity. On reargument, the consideration of appropriate relief was necessarily subordinated to the primary question—the constitutionality of segregation in public education. We have now announced that such segregation is a denial of the equal protection of the laws. In order that we may have the full assistance of the parties in formulating decrees, the cases will be restored to the docket, and the parties are requested to present further argument on Questions 4 and 5 previously propounded by the Court for the reargument this Term.[13] The Attorney General of the United States is again invited to participate. The Attorneys General of the states requiring or permitting segregation in public education will also be permitted to appear as *amici curiae* upon request to do so by September 15, 1954, and submission of briefs by October 1, 1954.[14]

It is so ordered.

NOTES

1. In the Kansas case, *Brown v. Board of Education*, the plaintiffs are Negro children of elementary school age residing in Topeka. They brought this action in the United States District Court for the District of Kansas to enjoin enforcement of a Kansas statute which permits, but does not require, cities of more than 15,000 population to maintain separate school facilities for Negro and white students. Kan. Gen. Stat. § 72–1724 (1949). Pursuant to that authority, the Topeka Board of Education elected to establish segregated elementary schools. Other public schools in the community, however, are operated on a nonsegregated basis. . . .

In the South Carolina case, *Briggs v. Elliott*, the plaintiffs are Negro children of both elementary and high school age residing in Clarendon County. They brought this action in the United States District Court for the Eastern District of South Carolina to enjoin enforcement of provisions in the state constitution and statutory code which require the segregation of Negroes and whites in public schools. . . .

In the Virginia case, *Davis v. County School Board*, the plaintiffs are Negro children of high school age residing in Prince Edward County. They brought this action in the United States District Court for the Eastern District of Virginia to enjoin enforcement of provisions in the state constitution and statutory code which require the segregation of Negroes and whites in public schools. . . .

In the Delaware case, *Gebhart v. Belton*, the plaintiffs are Negro children of both elementary and high school age residing in New Castle county. They brought this action in the Delaware Court of Chancery to enjoin enforcement of provisions in the state constitution and statutory code which require the segregation of Negroes and whites in public schools. . . .

2. technical footnote deleted.
3. technical footnote deleted.
4. technical footnote deleted.
5. technical footnote deleted.
6. technical footnote deleted.
7. technical footnote deleted.
8. technical footnote deleted.
9. technical footnote deleted.
10. technical footnote deleted.
11. K. B. Clark, Effect of Prejudice and Discrimination on Personality Development (Midcentury White House Conference on Children and Youth, 1950); Witmer and Kotinsky, Personality in the Making (1952), c. VI; Deutscher and Chein, The Psychological Effects of Enforced Segregation: A Survey of Social Science Opinion, 26 J. Psychol. 259 (1948); Chein, What are the Psychological Effects of Segregation Under Conditions of Equal Facilities?, 3 Int. J. Opinion and Attitude Res. 229 (1949); Brameld, Educational Costs, in Discrimination and National Welfare (MacIver, ed., 1949), 44–48; Frazier, The Negro in the United States (1949), 674–681. And see generally Myrdal, An American Dilemma (1944).
12. technical footnote deleted.
13. technical footnote deleted.
14. technical footnote deleted.

University of California Regents v. Bakke

428 U.S. 269 (1977)

MR. JUSTICE POWELL announced the judgment of the Court.

This case presents a challenge to the special admissions program of the petitioner, the Medical School of the University of California at Davis, which is designed to assure the admission of a specified number of students from certain minority groups. The Superior Court of California sustained respondent's challenge, holding that petitioner's program violated the California Constitution, Title VI of the Civil Rights Act of 1964, 42 U.S.C. § 2000d *et seq.*, and the Equal Protection Clause of the Fourteenth Amendment. The court enjoined petitioner from considering respondent's race or the race of any other applicant in making admissions decisions. It refused, however, to order respondent's admission to the Medical School, holding that he had not carried his burden of proving that he would have been admitted but for the constitutional and statutory violations. The Supreme Court of California affirmed those portions of the trial court's judgment declaring the special admissions program unlawful and enjoining petitioner from considering the race of any applicant.† It modified that portion of the judgment denying respondent's requested injunction and directed the trial court to order his admission.

For the reasons stated in the following opinion, I believe that so much of the judgment of the California court as holds petitioner's special admissions program unlawful and directs that respondent be admitted to the Medical School must be affirmed. For the reasons expressed in a separate opinion, my Brothers THE CHIEF JUSTICE, MR. JUSTICE STEWART, MR. JUSTICE REHNQUIST, and MR. JUSTICE STEVENS concur in this judgment.

I also conclude for the reasons stated in the following opinion that the portion of the court's judgment enjoining petitioner from according any consideration to race in its admissions process must be reversed. For reasons expressed in separate opinions, my Brothers MR. JUSTICE BRENNAN, MR. JUSTICE WHITE, MR. JUSTICE MARSHALL, and MR. JUSTICE BLACKMUN concur in this judgment.

Affirmed in part and reversed in part.

Opinion of Powell, J.
I‡

The Medical School of the University of California at Davis opened in 1968 with an entering class of 50 students. In 1971, the size of the entering class was increased to 100 students, a level at which it remains. No admissions program for disadvantaged or minority students existed when the school opened, and the first class contained three Asians but no blacks, no Mexican-Americans, and no American Indians. Over the next two years, the faculty devised a special admissions program to increase the representation of "disadvantaged" students in each Medical School class.[1] The special program consisted of a separate admissions system operating in coordination with the regular admissions process.

Under the regular admissions procedure, a candidate could submit his application to the Medical School beginning in July of the year preceding the academic year for which admission was sought. Record 149. Because of the large number of applications,[2] the admissions committee screened each one to select candidates for further consideration. Candidates whose overall undergraduate grade point averages fell below 2.5 on a scale of 4.0 were summarily rejected. *Id.*, at 63. About one out of six applicants was invited for a personal interview. *Ibid.* Following the interviews, each candidate was rated on a scale of 1 to 100 by his interviewers and four other members of the admissions committee. The rating embraced the interviewers' summaries, the candidate's overall grade point average, grade point average in science courses, scores on the Medical College Admissions Test (MCAT), letters of recommendation, extracurricular activities, and other biographical data. *Id.*, at 62. The ratings were added together to arrive at each candidate's "benchmark" score. Since five committee members rated each candidate in 1973, a perfect score was 500; in 1974, six members rated each candidate, so that a perfect score was 600. The full committee then reviewed the

From *U.S. Reports*, 1977. Opinion of the Supreme Court, 1977.

27

file and scores of each applicant and made offers of admission on a "rolling" basis.[3] The chairman was responsible for placing names on the waiting list. They were not placed in strict numerical order; instead, the chairman had discretion to include persons with "special skills." *Id.*, at 63–64.

The special admissions program operated with a separate committee, a majority of whom were members of minority groups. *Id.*, at 163. On the 1973 application form, candidates were asked to indicate whether they wished to be considered as "economically and/or educationally disadvantaged" applicants; on the 1974 form the question was whether they wished to be considered as members of a "minority group," which the Medical School apparently viewed as "Blacks," "Chicanos," "Asians," and "American Indians." *Id.*, at 65–66, 146, 197, 203–205, 216–218. If these questions were answered affirmatively, the application was forwarded to the special admissions committee. No formal definition of "disadvantaged" was ever produced, *id*, at 163–164, but the chairman of the special committee screened each application to see whether it reflected economic or educational deprivation.[4] Having passed this initial hurdle, the applications then were rated by the special committee in a fashion similar to that used by the general admissions committee, except that special candidates did not have to meet the 2.5 grade point average cutoff applied to regular applicants. About one-fifth of the total number of special applicants were invited for interviews in 1973 and 1974.[5] Following each interview, the special committee assigned each special applicant a benchmark score. The special committee then presented its top choices to the general admissions committee. The latter did not rate or compare the special candidates against the general applicants, *id.*, at 388, but could reject recommended special candidates for failure to meet course requirements or other specific deficiencies. *Id.*, at 171–172. The special committee continued to recommend special applicants until a number prescribed by faculty vote were admitted.

While the overall class size was still 50, the prescribed number was 8; in 1973 and 1974, when the class size had doubled to 100, the prescribed number of special admissions also doubled, to 16. *Id.*, at 164, 166.

From the year of the increase in class size—1971—through 1974, the special program resulted in the admission of 21 black students, 30 Mexican-Americans, and 12 Asians, for a total of 63 minority students. Over the same period, the regular admissions program produced 1 black, 6 Mexican-Americans, and 37 Asians, for a total of 44 minority students.[6] Although disadvantaged whites applied to the special program in large numbers, see no. 5, *supra*, none received an offer of admission through that process. Indeed, in 1974, at least, the special committee explicitly considered only "disadvantaged" special applicants who were members of one of the designated minority groups. Record 171.

Allan Bakke is a white male who applied to the Davis Medical School in both 1973 and 1974. In both years Bakke's application was considered under the general admissions program, and he received an interview. His 1973 interview was with Dr. Theodore C. West, who considered Bakke "a very desirable applicant to [the] medical school." *Id.*, at 225. Despite a strong benchmark score of 468 out of 500, Bakke was rejected. His application had come late in the year, and no applicants in the general admissions process with scores below 470 were accepted after Bakke's application was completed. *Id.*, at 69. There were four special admissions slots unfilled at that time, however, for which Bakke was not considered. *Id.*, at 70. After his 1973 rejection, Bakke wrote to Dr. George H. Lowrey Associate Dean and Chairman of the Admissions Committee, protesting that the special admissions program operated as a racial and ethnic quota. *Id.*, at 259.

Bakke's 1974 application was completed early in the year. *Id.*, at 70. His student interviewer gave him an overall rating of 94, finding him "friendly, well tempered, conscientious and delightful to speak with." *Id.*, at 229. His

faculty interviewer was, by coincidence, the same Dr. Lowrey, to whom he had written in protest of the special admissions program. Dr. Lowrey found Bakke "rather limited in his approach" to the problems of the medical profession and found disturbing Bakke's "very definite opinions which were based more on his personal viewpoints than upon a study of the total problem." *Id.*, at 226. Dr. Lowrey gave Bakke the lowest of his six ratings, an 86; his total was 549 out of 600. *Id.*, at 230. Again, Bakke's application was rejected. In neither year did the chairman of the admissions committee, Dr. Lowrey, exercise his discretion to place Bakke on the waiting list. *Id.*, at 64. In both years, applicants were admitted under the special program with grade point averages, MCAT scores, and benchmark scores significantly lower than Bakke's.[7]

After the second rejection, Bakke filed the instant suit in the Superior Court of California.[8] He sought mandatory, injunctive, and declaratory relief compelling his admission to the Medical School. He alleged that the Medical School's special admissions program operated to exclude him from the school on the basis of his race, in violation of his rights under the Equal Protection Clause of the Fourteenth Amendment,[9] Art. I, § 21, of the California Constitution,[10] and § 601 of Title VI of the Civil Rights Act of 1964, 78 Stat. 252, 42 U.S.C. § 2000d.[11] The University cross-complained for a declaration that its special admissions program was lawful. The trial court found that the special program operated as a racial quota, because minority applicants in the special program were rated only against one another, Record 388, and 16 places in the class of 100 were reserved for them. *Id.*, at 295–296. Declaring that the University could not take race into account in making admissions decisions, the trial court held the challenged program violative of the Federal Constitution, the State Constitution, and Title VI. The court refused to order Bakke's admission, however, holding that he had failed to carry his burden of proving that he would have been admitted but for the existence of the special program.

Bakke appealed from the portion of the trial court judgment denying him admission, and the University appealed from the decision that its special admissions program was unlawful and the order enjoining it from considering race in the processing of applications. The Supreme Court of California transferred the case directly from the trial court, "because of the importance of the issues involved." 18 Cal. 3d 34, 39, 553, P. 2d 1152, 1156 (1976). The California court accepted the findings of the trial court with respect to the University's program.[12] Because the special admissions program involved a racial classification, the Supreme Court held itself bound to apply strict scrutiny. *Id.*, at 49, 553 P. 2d, at 1162–1163. It then turned to the goals the University presented as justifying the special program. Although the court agreed that the goals of integrating the medical profession and increasing the number of physicians willing to serve members of minority groups were compelling state interests, *id.*, at 53, 553 P. 2d, at 1165, it concluded that the special admissions program was not the least intrusive means of achieving those goals. Without passing on the state constitutional or the federal statutory grounds cited in the trial court's judgment, the California court held that the Equal Protection Clause of the Fourteenth Amendment required that "no applicant may be rejected because of his race, in favor of another who is less qualified, as measured by standards applied without regard to race." *Id.*, at 55, 553 P. 2d, at 1166.

Turning to Bakke's appeal, the court ruled that since Bakke had established that the University had discriminated against him on the basis of his race, the burden of proof shifted to the University to demonstrate that he would not have been admitted even in the absence of the special admissions program.[13] *Id.*, at 63–64, 553 P. 2d, at 1172. The court analogized Bakke's situation to that of a plaintiff under Title VII of the Civil Rights Act of 1964, 42 U.S.C. § § 2000e–17 (1970 ed., Supp. V) see, *e.g.*, *Franks v. Bowman Transportation Co.*, 424 U.S. 747, 772 (1976). 18 Cal. 3d, at 63–64, 553 P. 2d, at 1172. On

this basis, the court initially ordered a remand for the purpose of determining whether, under the newly allocated burden of proof, Bakke would have been admitted to either the 1973 or the 1974 entering class in the absence of the special admissions program. App. A. to Application for Stay 48. In its petition for rehearing below, however, the University conceded its inability to carry that burden. App. B. to Application for Stay A19–A20.[14] The California court thereupon amended its opinion to direct that the trial court enter judgment ordering Bakke's admission to the Medical School. 18 Cal. 3d, at 64, 553 P. 2d, at 1172. That order was stayed pending review in this Court. 429 U.S. 953 (1976). We granted certiorari to consider the important constitutional issue. 429 U.S. 1090 (1977). . . .

V

A

It may be assumed that the reservation of a specified number of seats in each class for individuals from the preferred ethnic groups would contribute to the attainment of considerable ethnic diversity in the student body. But petitioner's argument that this is the only effective means of serving the interest of diversity is seriously flawed. In a most fundamental sense the argument misconceives the nature of the state interest that would justify consideration of race or ethnic background. It is not an interest in simple ethnic diversity in which a specified percentage of the student body is in effect guaranteed to be members of selected ethnic groups, with the remaining percentage an undifferentiated aggregation of students. The diversity that furthers a compelling state interest encompasses a far broader array of qualifications and characteristics of which racial or ethnic origin is but a single though important element. Petitioner's special admissions program, focused *solely* on ethnic diversity would, hinder rather than further attainment of genuine diversity.[50]

Nor would the state interest in genuine diversity be served by expanding

petitioner's two-track system into a multitrack program with a prescribed number of seats set aside for each identifiable category of applicants. Indeed, it is inconceivable that a university would thus pursue the logic of petitioner's two-track program to the illogical end of insulating each category of applicants with certain desired qualifications from competition with all other applicants.

The experience of other university admissions programs, which take race into account in achieving the educational diversity valued by the First Amendment, demonstrates that the assignment of a fixed number of places to a minority group is not a necessary means toward that end. An illuminating example is found in the Harvard College program:

> In recent years Harvard College has expanded the concept of diversity to include students from disadvantaged economic, racial and ethnic groups. Harvard College now recruits not only Californians or Louisianans but also blacks and Chicanos and other minority students.
>
> In practice, this new definition of diversity has meant that race has been a factor in some admission decisions. When the Committee on Admissions reviews the large middle group of applicants who are 'admissible' and deemed capable of doing good work in their courses, the race of an applicant may tip the balance in his favor just as geographic origin or a life spent on a farm may tip the balance in other candidates' cases. A farm boy from Idaho can bring something to Harvard College that a Bostonian cannot offer. Similarly, a black student can usually bring something that a white person cannot offer. . . .

In such an admissions program,[51] race or ethnic background may be deemed a "plus" in a particular applicant's file, yet it does not insulate the individual from comparison with all other candidates for the available seats. The file of a particular black applicant may be examined for his potential contribution to diversity without the factor of race being decisive when compared, for example, with that of an applicant identified as an Italian-American if the latter is thought to exhibit qualities more likely to promote beneficial educational pluralism. Such qualities could include exceptional personal talents, unique work or service experience, leadership potential, maturity, demonstrated compassion, a history of overcoming disadvantage, ability to communicate with the poor, or other qualifications deemed important. In short, an admissions program operated in this way is flexible enough to consider all pertinent elements of diversity in light of the particular qualifications of each applicant, and to place them on the same footing for consideration, although not necessarily according them the same weight. Indeed, the weight attributed to a particular quality may vary from year to year depending upon the "mix" both of the student body and the applicants for the incoming class.

This kind of program treats each applicant as an individual in the admissions process. The applicant who loses out on the last available seat to another candidate receiving a "plus" on the basis of ethnic background will not have been foreclosed from all consideration for that seat simply because he was not the right color or had the wrong surname. It would mean only that his combined qualifications, which may have included similar nonobjective factors, did not outweigh those of the other applicant. His qualifications would have been weighed fairly and competitively and he would have no basis to complain of unequal treatment under the Fourteenth Amendment.[52] . . .

B

In summary it is evident that the Davis special admissions program involves the use of an explicit racial classification never before countenanced by this Court. It tells applicants who are not Negro, Asian, or Chicano that they are totally excluded from a specific percentage of the seats in an entering class. No matter how strong their qualifications, quantitative and extracurricular, including their own

potential for contribution to educational diversity, they are never afforded the chance to compete with applicants from the preferred groups for the special admissions seats. At the same time, the preferred applicants have the opportunity to compete for every seat in the class.

The fatal flaw in petitioner's preferential program is its disregard of individual rights as guaranteed by the Fourteenth Amendment. *Shelley v. Kraemer*, 334 U.S., at 22. Such rights are not absolute. But when a State's distribution of benefits or imposition of burdens hinges on ancestry or the color of a person's skin, that individual is entitled to a demonstration that the challenged classification is necessary to promote a substantial state interest. Petitioner has failed to carry this burden. For this reason, that portion of the California court's judgment holding petitioner's special admissions program invalid under the Fourteenth Amendment must be affirmed.

C

In enjoining petitioner from ever considering the race of any applicant, however, the courts below failed to recognize that the State has a substantial interest that legitimately may be served by a properly devised admissions program involving the competitive consideration of race and ethnic origin. For this reason, so much of the California court's judgment as enjoins petitioner from any consideration of the race of any applicant must be reversed. . . .

NOTES

†. technical footnote deleted.
‡. technical footnote deleted.
1. technical footnote deleted.
2. technical footnote deleted.
3. technical footnote deleted.
4. technical footnote deleted.
5. technical footnote deleted.
6. technical footnote deleted.
7. technical footnote deleted.
8. technical footnote deleted.
9. technical footnote deleted.
10. technical footnote deleted.
11. technical footnote deleted.
12. technical footnote deleted.
13. technical footnote deleted.
14. technical footnote deleted.
50. technical footnote deleted.
51. technical footnote deleted.
52. technical footnote deleted.

Opinion of Marshall, J.

MR. JUSTICE MARSHALL.
I agree with the judgment of the Court only insofar as it permits a university to consider the race of an applicant in making admissions decisions. I do not agree that petitioner's admissions program violates the Constitution. For it must be remembered that, during most of the past 200 years, the Constitution as interpreted by this Court did not prohibit the most ingenious and pervasive forms of discrimination against the Negro. Now when a State acts to remedy the effects of that legacy of discrimination, I cannot believe that this same Constitution stands as a barrier.

I
A

Three hundred and fifty years ago, the Negro was dragged to this country in chains to be sold into slavery. Uprooted from his homeland and thrust into bondage for forced labor, the slave was deprived of all legal rights. It was unlawful to teach him to read; he could be sold away from his family and friends at the whim of his master; and killing or maiming him was not a crime. The system of slavery brutalized and dehumanized both master and slave.[1] . . .

II

The position of the Negro today in America is the tragic but inevitable consequence of centuries of unequal treatment. Measured by any benchmark of comfort or achievement, meaningful equality remains a distant dream for the Negro.

A Negro child today has a life expectancy which is shorter by more than five years than that of a white child.[2] The Negro child's mother is over three times more likely to die of complications in childbirth,[3] and the infant mortality rate for Negroes is nearly twice that for whites.[4] The median income of the Negro family is only 60% that of the median of a white family,[5] and the percentage of Negroes who live in families with incomes below the poverty line is nearly four times greater than that of whites.[6]

When the Negro child reaches working age, he finds that America offers him significantly less than it offers his white counterpart. For Negro adults, the unemployment rate is twice that of whites,[7] and the unemployment rate for Negro teenagers is nearly three times that of white teenagers.[8] A Negro male who completes four years of college can expect a median annual income of merely $110 more than a white male who has only a high school diploma.[9] Although Negroes represent 11.5% of the population,[10] they are only 1.2% of the lawyers and judges, 2% of the physicians, 2.3% of the dentists, 1.1% of the engineers and 2.6% of the college and university professors.[11]

The relationship between those figures and the history of unequal treatment afforded to the Negro cannot be denied. At every point from birth to death the impact of the past is reflected in the still disfavored position of the Negro.

In light of the sorry history of discrimination and its devastating impact on the lives of Negroes, bringing the Negro into the mainstream of American life should be a state interest of the highest order. To fail to do so is to ensure that America will forever remain a divided society.

III

I do not believe that the Fourteenth Amendment requires us to accept that fate. Neither its history nor our past cases lend any support to the conclusion that a university may not remedy the cumulative effects of society's discrimination by giving consideration to race in an effort to increase the number and percentage of Negro doctors. . . .

IV

While I applaud the judgment of the Court that a university may consider race in its admissions process, it is more than a little ironic that, after several hundred years of class-based discrimination against Negroes, the Court is unwilling to hold that a class-based remedy for that discrimination is permissible. In declining to so hold, today's judgment ignores the fact that for several hundred years Negroes have been discriminated against, not as individuals, but rather solely because of the color of their skins. It is unnecessary in 20th-century America to have individual Negroes demonstrate that they have been victims of racial discrimination; the racism of our society has been so pervasive that none, regardless of wealth or position, has managed to escape its impact. The experience of Negroes in America has been different in kind, not just in degree, from that of other ethnic groups. It is not merely the history of slavery alone but also that a whole people were marked as inferior by the law. And that mark has endured. The dream of America as the great melting pot has not been realized for the Negro; because of his skin color he never even made it into the pot....

It is because of a legacy of unequal treatment that we now must permit the institutions of this society to give consideration to race in making decisions about who will hold the positions of influence, affluence, and prestige in America. For far too long, the doors to those positions have been shut to Negroes. If we are ever to become a fully integrated society, one in which the color of a person's skin will not determine the opportunities available to him or her, we must be willing to take steps to open those doors. I do not believe that anyone can truly look into America's past and still find that a remedy for the effects of that past is impermissible.

It has been said that this case involves only the individual, Bakke, and this University. I doubt, however, that there is a computer capable of determining the number of persons and institutions that may be affected by the decision in this case. For example, we are told by the Attorney General of the United States that at least 27 federal agencies have adopted regulations requiring recipients of federal funds to take " '*affirmative action* to overcome the effects of conditions which result in limiting participation . . . by persons of a particular race, color, or national origin.' " Supplemental Brief for United States as *Amicus Curiae* 16 (emphasis added). I cannot even guess the number of state and local governments that have set up affirmative-action programs, which may be affected by today's decision.

I fear that we have come full circle. After the Civil War our Government started "affirmative action" programs. This Court in the *Civil Rights Cases* and *Plessy v. Ferguson* destroyed the movement toward complete equality. For almost a century no action was taken, and this nonaction was with the tacit approval of the courts. Then we had *Brown v. Board of Education* and the Civil Rights Acts of Congress, followed by numerous affirmative-action programs. *Now,* we have this Court again stepping in, this time to stop affirmative-action programs of the type used by the University of California.

NOTES

1. technical footnote deleted.
2. technical footnote deleted.
3. technical footnote deleted.
4. technical footnote deleted.
5. technical footnote deleted.
6. technical footnote deleted.
7. technical footnote deleted.
8. technical footnote deleted.
9. technical footnote deleted.
10. technical footnote deleted.
11. technical footnote deleted.

High Court
Loosens Desegregation's Grip

Ruling lands with force in Missouri

Kevin Johnson and Andrea Stone

USA TODAY

The Supreme Court has taken a giant step toward freeing local school districts from protracted desegregation orders.

In the 5–4 decision Monday, the justices ruled that desegregation plans ordered by federal courts can be terminated even if minority students continue to score below average on national tests—as long as a district has made a good-faith effort at compliance.

Student performance on standardized tests frequently is used to measure educational equity.

The ruling landed with the most force in the Kansas City, Mo., School District, whose desegregation program has been widely considered the most expensive effort in the nation's history.

The state had asked the court's help in stopping massive payments for Kansas City's desegregation plan.

Under the Kansas City plan, the district got $150 million from the state and $50 million from local taxes—out of an annual budget of $340 million—for desegregation efforts.

Much of that money has been channeled toward paying higher salaries for staff and supporting a magnet-school program designed to attract white students to the predominantly black district.

By siding with Missouri, the Supreme Court essentially said schools cannot be forced to guarantee equal levels of achievement for black and white students as long as schools provide pupils the same opportunities for success.

The justices also made it tougher to attract suburban white students to urban minority districts—like in Kansas City—saying such programs could be implemented only if both school systems showed effects of prior segregation.

"For all those school districts who want to return operations of their schools back to the community, and without court-ordered restraints, this is a win," says Missouri Attorney General Jay Nixon.

But in the Kansas City home of Rhonda Burnett, whose three children are enrolled in district schools, Nixon's words were as welcome as a bad report card.

"I'm sure Mr. Nixon is sitting by himself chortling right now," Burnett said of the lengthy and contentious case. "We were not under the illusion that desegregation funds were going to last forever, but now is not the time to end them. It would be a shame."

"We were leading the pack in changing the way we did business in education," Burnett said. "I don't see how they can think about gutting these programs now. It's bad news."

The Kansas City case was originally brought by a group of students represented by Kalima Jenkins, an African-American student who sued the state in the 1970s for not moving quickly enough to desegregate schools.

Attorney Arthur Benson, who represents the Kansas City Board of Education, refused to characterize the decision as a defeat. He said the district has at least a year to adjust to changes outlined in the court's decision.

However, Nixon said the state intends to act soon on the ruling, saying that continued state funding for school personnel salaries would become an immediate issue.

The ruling is expected to set off new debates in some of the 250 to 300 school districts governed by some form of court supervision where officials believe they have done all they can to comply with desegregation orders.

In Yonkers, N.Y., for example, school officials say they can now foresee a time when they will be freed from court orders that have governed the district since 1986.

Larry Thomas, attorney for the school district, said the decision emphasizes that court desegregation remedies would only be temporary.

"That's important," Thomas said. "It indicates that courts should look at returning schools to local districts."

Throughout the country, the Kansas City decision was interpreted as a mandate for gradual withdrawal of federal judges from schools.

• "It continues a trend in which the court has pulled back on judicial intervention in local school governnace," said Clint Bolick of the conservative Institute for Justice. "It demonstrates that desegregation orders cannot continue forever."

The court has never embraced equality of results as the touchstone for civil rights. It declined to do so again in this opinion. What civil rights is all about is equal opportunity and not equal results."

• George Washington University law professor Mary Cheh said the decision points to a time when "there has to be an end . . . of judicial supervision. The court has been slowly reacting to continued orders," she said. "It's becoming more generous in allowing school systems to come out from under court orders."

• David Armor, author of *Forced Justice: School Desegregation and the Law,* said the decision was first to deal with the school "achievement gap."

"It's an incredible burden on public schools to require equality of results," he says, adding that test score disparities are mostly caused by "things schools have no control over," including socio-economics and family relationships.

But at the National Association of State Boards of Education, Paul Houston was expressing more troubling concerns: 'I think people are fairly disappointed with this," Houston said.

"It's like somebody is trying to roll the clock back. You still have a lot of minority kids in inner-city schools, but are they going to get the same opportunities? This makes it more difficult to serve these kids."

A Look at Monday's Two Rulings

SCHOOL DESEGREGATION

THE CASE: *Missouri vs. Jenkins.* Black parents sued in 1977, arguing that their children were denied equal educational opportunities in Kansas City schools. A federal judge agreed and ordered a desegregation plan based on state-funded educational improvements, the voluntary transfer of white students from the suburbs to the city, magnet schools and district-wide capital improvements. The state sued to end its role in financing the plan.

THE VOTE: Justices ruled 5–4 in favor of the state, saying plans to attract white suburban students to mostly minority city schools can be used only if both city and suburban schools still show the effects of segregation. The court also said schools can't be forced to guarantee equal achievement by blacks and whites.

EXCERPTS

• **The majority opinion, written by Chief Justice William Rehnquist:** "In effect, the district court has devised a remedy to accomplish indirectly what it admittedly lacks the remedial authority to mandate directly: the interdistrict transfer of students."

• **Justice Sandra Day O'Connor, with the majority:** "Unlike Congress, which enjoys 'discretion in determining whether and what legislation is needed to secure the guarantees of the Fourteenth Amendment,' federal courts have no comparable license and must always observe their limited judicial role."

• **Justice Ruth Bader Ginsburg, dissenting:** "Given the deep, inglorious history of segregation in Missouri, to curtail desegregation at this time and in this manner is an action at once too swift and too soon."

AFFIRMATIVE ACTION

THE CASE: *Adarand Constructors Inc. vs. Pena, secretary of Transportation.* Randy Pech, owner of Adarand, sued the government in 1990 after a contract was given to a minority-owned company, even though Adarand had submitted a lower bid. Pech argued that the Transportation Department's policy was an unlawful set-aside based on race.

THE VOTE: Justices ruled 5–4 in favor of Adarand. The justices said federal affirmative action programs must meet a "strict scrutiny" requirement that allows race-based preferences only if they are narrowly tailored.

EXCERPTS

• **The majority opinion, written by Justice Sandra Day O'Connor:** "Indeed, the purpose of strict scrutiny is to 'smoke out' illegitimate uses of race by assuring that the legislative body is pursuing a goal important enough to warrant use of a highly suspect tool. The test also ensures that the means chosen 'fit' this compelling goal so closely that there is little or no possibility that the motive for the classification was illegitimate racial prejudice or stereotype."

• **Justice Antonin Scalia, with the majority:** "In my view, government can never have a 'compelling interest' in discriminating on the basis of race in order to 'make up' for past racial discrimination in the opposite direction."

• **Justice John Paul Stevens, dissenting:** "Ironically, after all of the time, effort and paper this court has expended in differentiating between federal and state affirmative action, the majority today virtually ignores the issue."

As Deadline Nears, Court Leaders Pin Hopes on 'Holding 5'

Majority Opinion Writers Must Maintain the Magic Number of Consenting Colleagues

Joan Biskupic

Washington Post Staff Writer

By now, the votes are in. All the Supreme Court justices know the likely outcomes of their final and biggest cases. But as they circulate drafts of their opinions, preparing them for release this month, the tricky part is "holding five."

Before the justices issue majority rulings—which require five votes—they go through several steps. Soon after oral arguments, they confer and take a preliminary tally. Ordinarily the justices stick with their votes.

In June, However, when the writing on the hardest cases comes to a head, some of the justices who voted with the majority may have second thoughts and the justice penning the court's opinion cannot hold on to the five votes.

Even the author has been known to change his mind.

Chief Justice William H. Rehnquist once yanked a "Majority" opinion from now-retired Justice Harry A. Blackmun following a conference vote "in view of the fact that your proposed opinion in this case has come out to 'reverse,' rather than to 'affirm.'"

The major Supreme Court cases awaiting decisions this term include:

ADARAND CONSTRUCTORS V. PENA: Tests the constitutionality of a federal affirmative action program that gives bonuses to highway contractors who subcontract with minority-owned firms.

BABBITT V. SWEET HOME CHAPTER: Tests how far the Endangered Species Act goes in stopping development on private lands that contain rare animal habitats.

CAPITOL SQUARE REVIEW V. PINETTE: Tests whether a state can deny the Ku Klux Klan a permit to put up a cross in a public square.

HURLEY V. IRISH-AMERICAN GAY, LESBIAN, AND BISEXUAL GROUP: Tests whether South Boston veterans can exclude gay and lesbian marchers from their annual St. Patrick's Day parade.

MILLER V. JOHNSON: Asks how much race can be considered by states drawing up congressional voting districts, testing a Georgia district.

ROSENBERGER V. THE RECTOR: Tests the constitutionality of a University of Virginia policy denying student activity funds to a student-run religious magazine.

VERNONIA SCHOOL DISTRICT V. ACTON: Tests whether an elementary school can require student athletes to submit to drug tests.

Justice John Paul Stevens, now the most senior member of the liberal-leaning justices, has joked about sometimes losing his colleagues once he began writing. He once refereed

to his "enviable record at writing majority opinions that end up in a tie."

It is rare for a justice to completely reverse his or her opinion and change the outcome of the conference room vote. More commonly, most justices who originally were in the majority will agree with the bottom-line ruling in a case but part company with an author on legal reasoning. In those cases, a justice will write a separate concurring statement, explaining his or her vote.

"When an opinion circulates in a close case, the justice who wrote it can find himself or herself waiting a long time for the expected fifth vote," said former Supreme Court law clerk Peter Rubin.

"You sometimes sense law clerks holding their breath, wondering whether the fifth vote is ever going to come. June is often the month when that question is answered."

This week the justices are negotiating decisions on cases involving affirmative action, school desegregation and voting rights.

They also have two important rulings to make on the constitutional requirements for separation of church and state. One involves the University of Virginia's denial of student activity funds for a student-run Christian magazine.

Overall, the court still has 26 cases to resolve; 57 signed opinions already have been handed down for the 1994-95 term. This week, the justices issued only one ruling. That's unusual for what is traditionally the last month of the term. Beginning next week, court watchers can anticipate an especially heavy rush of opinions; the court is expected to issue rulings about two days each week.

The ability of a justice to hold onto five votes for the final court opinion can influence a senior justice who assigns the opinion in a fractious case.

Justice Sandra Day O'Connor has a reputation for keeping five votes, and Rehnquist often asks her to write opinions on cases involving race-conscious programs such as affirmative action. O'Connor, the only former elected politician on the court (she was Arizona Senate majority leader), is known for her ability to write strategically, articulating compromises and avoiding bold statements of new law that could turn off a straddler.

Antonin Scalia, on the other hand, tends to say what he wants and can have a harder time holding a majority.

"I feel pretty good when I'm the fifth vote to decide the case," Justice Ruth Bader Ginsburg once told an audience. "I feel even better if I'm the fourth and I pick up a fifth vote based on the writing."

Rehnquist tries to run a tight ship and also rewards justices who finish their opinions quickly with good assignments.

"The chief thinks it is extremely important to get the opinions done before the beginning of July," said Maureen Mahoney, one of Rehnquist's former law clerks. "He makes serious efforts to keep the justices collegial and speaking to each other."

As the conference papers of the late Justice Thurgood Marshall show, when a justice is circulating an opinion, the most welcomed response memo is also the shortest: "I am still with you."

CREATIVE CARTOGRAPHY

The Supreme Court is considering challenges to black majority House districts in Louisiana and Georgia. Cases involving similar districts in North Carolina, Florida and Texas are making their way through lower courts.

In a preliminary ruling on the North Carolina case in 1993, Justice Sandra Day O'Connor focused on the "bizarre" shapes of black majority districts created to comply with the Voting Rights Act. Critics of her majority opinion in Shaw v. Reno *have charged other strangely shaped districts were drawn over the decades without much legal complaint.*

A review of House districts drawn since 1789 produced the following examples of creative cartography unrelated to either the Voting Rights Act of 1965 or the 1990 reapportionment. Most every unusual feature of the challenged districts has been used in the past to benefit while candidates of both political parties, a review of Congressional maps drawn since 1789 shows.

 **LOUISIANA 4 (1869–75)** was represented by Republicans during the Reconstruction. It encompassed most of the current 4th District under challenge before the Supreme Court and likewise followed the Red River in a diagonal across the state's midsection.

 **FLORIDA 4 (1915–37)** elected Democrats to represent a 500-mile stretch of the state's Atlantic coast from Jacksonville to the Keys. It was longer than any district cited in the five pending lawsuits. From 1875 to 1915, what was then the 2nd district was slightly longer, extending all the way north to the Georgia border.

 **OKLAHOMA 1 (1953–69)** elected Republicans during a era of Democratic domination of state's delegation. A single point, submerged under a state reservoir in 1964, connected Tulsa County to the anvil-shaped area along Kansas border. Plaintiffs have criticized such single-point connections in North Carolina districts.

 **NEW YORK 35 (1963–71)** was tailored by Republicans in an unsuccessful effort to oust a Democrat, Samuel S. Stratton. The district extended across most of upstate New York, nearly from Albany to Rochester, and was known around the Capitol as "the submarine."

 **ILLINOIS 6 (1973–83)** was represented by Republicans, including Judiciary Chairman Henry J. Hyde. The suburban Chicago district included three suburban islands completely surrounded by the 11th district of then-Rep. Frank Annunzio, a Democrat. A federal court drew a map based on a GOP legislative plan.

 OHIO 13 (1933–present) elected a Democrat, Rep. Sherrod Brown, to represent a barbell-shaped area west, south and east of Cleveland. Two distinct communities were connected only by the Ohio Turnpike in an effort to protect incumbent Democrats.

—Ken Cooper

SOURCES: The Historical Atlas of the United States Congressional Districts: 1789–1983, Almanac of American Politics, Politics in America

Court grows critical when race, law intersect

The majority now rejecting bias remedies

Tony Mauro and Tom Watson
USA TODAY

For the third time this month, the Supreme Court on Thursday said it was tired. Tired, that is, of the traditional approaches to remedying the national problem of race discrimination.

On June 12, the court's conservative majority voiced dissatisfaction with affirmative action and school desegregation. On Thursday, it was race-based redistricting that got the court upset.

Using race as the primary reason for creating a district, to enhance chances of electing a minority candidate, violates the constitutional guarantee of equal treatment of all races under the law, the court said.

That pronouncement, which throws hundreds of congressional, state and local districts nationwide into turmoil, must have given pause to retired Justice Harry Blackmun, who was in the courtroom Thursday to hear it.

It was 17 years ago that Blackmun penned the simple formulation that describes the underlying theory of the approach to civil rights that the current court is repudiating. "In order to get beyond racism, we must first take account of race," Blackmun wrote.

Under that banner, the court embraced affirmative action, which takes race into account by giving minorities prefer-

ences in contracts and employment. It endorsed special measures for minority students in schools and it encouraged remedies under the Voting Rights Act aimed at boosting the voting power of minorities.

But now, riding the same wave that brought the Republican majority to Congress last fall, the court seems to be saying that racial preferences are an idea whose time has passed.

In Baton Rouge, La., one of the areas affected by Thursday's ruling, opinion seems as divided as it is within the court.

A.J. Lord, owner of A.J.'s Restaurant, agrees it is important to have minorities in Congress. But he also believes other things are just as important, such as having members of Congress represent cohesive districts.

Louisiana's 4th District was drawn to create a majority-minority district, but it is so far-flung, says Lord, that many voters don't know who their congressman is.

"At some point, you have to weigh your objectives to elect black candidates to office, or have proper representation of a district," says Lord. "It's a balancing act and there's no easy solution."

Frank Ransburg, a political scientist at Southern University, a historically black school in north Baton Rouge, says abolishing the district now represented by Rep. Cleo Fields, who is black, would reverse important civil rights gains.

"There are some people in the state who don't feel that blacks should be allowed to fully participate in the political process," Ransburg says.

Most liberals say the court is too hasty in declaring the problem of racial bias solved, and that race-conscious remedies are no longer needed.

"The three decisions reflect unfortunate judicial resistance to reasonable efforts toward racial inclusiveness," says Harvard law professor Laurence Tribe. "The combined effect is to turn the clock back on an effort that is not yet completed."

The Rev. Jesse Jackson: "The court has authorized the country to unravel the legal fabric of social justice and inclusion that has been woven together over the last 41 years."

Jackson has special words of contempt for Justice Clarence Thomas, the court's only black justice, who was part of the 5-4 majority in all three cases. "It is especially painful that a descendant of slaves, in effect, stabbed Dr. (Martin Luther) King ... in the back, and is paving the way back toward slavery," Jackson says.

The idea of drawing districts to pull in pockets of minority voters developed in the last two decades in response to a political truth: Black candidates are rarely elected in districts where whites form the majority of the population.

"There are thousands of redistricting plans in the South and throughout the country in

How they voted on the cases

The justices continued their conservative march Thursday. But they didn't always agree.

Georgia redistricting

▶ **Against:** Chief Justice William Rehnquist and justices Anthony Kennedy, Antonin Scalia, Clarence Thomas and Sandra Day O'Connor

▶ **For:** Justices John Paul Stevens, David Souter, Ruth Bader Ginsburg and Stephen Breyer

Louisiana redistricting

▶ Set aside for technical reasons in a unanimous ruling

Other racially drawn districts may be challenged

The Supreme Court's ruling Thursday against a black-majority congressional district in Georgia is expected to prompt court challenges to similar racially drawn districts across the USA. Opponents say the districts, often oddly shaped, reduce the power of white voters. Georgia's 11th District and Louisiana's 4th District were both challenged in cases that went to the high court, but justices did not rule on the Louisiana case because the plaintiffs no longer live in the district. Also Thursday, the court agreed to hear arguments against three minority-majority districts in Texas and to rehear arguments against the black-majority 12th District in North Carolina. All of the districts were created after the 1990 Census to comply with the federal Voting Rights Act's mandate to increase minority political representation.

Georgia's 11th District

In September 1994, a federal appeals court ruled in favor of white voters who said in a lawsuit that it was unconstitutional to draw a district specifically to provide more black voters. The district is represented by Rep. Cynthia McKinney, a second-term Democrat and the first black woman elected to Congress from Georgia.

GEOGRAPHY
The district sweeps southeast from Atlanta suburbs 250 miles to Savannah. It includes parts of 22 counties, but 60% of the population is in three urban counties: De Kalb (east of Atlanta), Richmond (Augusta) and Chatham (Savannah). Between the urban pockets are miles and miles of agricultural acreage that was once Georgia's cotton belt but is now mainly corn, soybean and peanut farms.

DEMOGRAPHICS
Blacks are 64% of the population, and 60% of the registered voters, in this district of 586,195 people. It is one of three black-majority districts in the state. Comparing the district to Georgia by race:

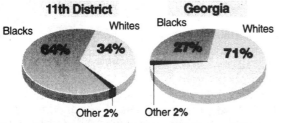

11th District — Blacks 64%, Whites 34%, Other 2%
Georgia — Blacks 27%, Whites 71%, Other 2%

Sources: USA TODAY research by Barbara Hansen, Mark Pearson and Brian O'Connell; *Politics in America*; *Congressional Quarterly*; U.S. Census Bureau, *Congressional Districts in the 1990s, a Portrait of America*.

Louisiana's 4th District

The district has been redrawn by the state twice since the 1990 Census. For the 1992 election, it zigzagged through all or parts of 28 parishes and five of the states largest cities to get its black majority. In December 1993, a federal three-judge panel threw out that plan. In 1994, the Louisiana Legislature redrew the district. The federal court again rejected the plan. The Supreme Court accepted the case in 1994. Democrat Rep. Cleo Fields, first elected in 1992 in the 'Z' district, was re-elected in 1994 in the redrawn district.

Louisiana — Blacks 31%, Whites 67%, Other 2%
4th District — Blacks 58%, Whites 41%, Other 1%

North Carolina's 12th District

In 1993, the Supreme Court used this black-majority district to rule that racial gerrymandering might violate the rights of white voters. The case was sent back to a lower court for further study. That court ruled last year that the 12th District was constitutional. Democrat Melvin Watt, in his second term, represents the district of 552,386 people.

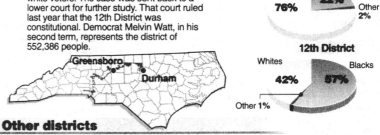

North Carolina — Whites 76%, Blacks 22%, Other 2%
12th District — Whites 42%, Blacks 57%, Other 1%

Other districts

Nationwide, there are 58 minority-majority districts and 62 minority members of Congress. Experts say these 18 districts could be at risk because of Thursday's ruling: Alabama's 7th; Arizona's 2nd; Florida's 3rd, 17th, 18th and 23rd; Georgia's 2nd and 11th; Illinois' 4th; Louisiana's 4th; New York's 12th; North Carolina's 1st and 12th; South Carolina's 6th; Texas' 18th, 29th and 30th; and Virginia's 3rd.

By Cliff Vancura, USA TODAY

---

which racial fairness was taken into account," says Lauglin McDonald of the American Civil Liberties Union. "All of these plans are presumed to be unlawful."

Others in the civil rights movement are more optimistic, especially after the court announced later Thursday that it would take up two new redistricting cases in the fall on related issues of race.

"They've muddied the waters, but they haven't yet turned 180 degrees," says Elaine Jones of the NAACP Legal Defense and Education Fund. "The issue has just begun."

Clinton administration civil rights chief Deval Patrick, whose department reviews redistricting plans under the Voting Rights Act, says, "It would be a tragedy if these decisions led to the resegregation of American democracy."

Immigration: The American Experience in a New Era of Mobility

The ever-growing influx of strangers to the Americas during the eighteenth and nineteenth centuries was probably perceived by its indigenous peoples as the intensification of conflict into the final stage of their conquest. Africans brought in bondage probably viewed the opening of America to the "wretched refuse" of Europe as a strategy designed to exclude them from prosperity and as a threat to their full enfranchisement.

To the European and Asian immigrant, America represented freedom from the constraints of state-bound societies whose limits could not be overcome except through emigration. Yet this historical pathway to liberty, justice, and opportunity came to be perceived as a "tarnished door" when the deep impulses of exclusion and exclusivity came to the fore. The victims were aliens who, ironically, achieved the American promise but were denied the reward of acceptance and incorporation into the very culture they helped to fashion. The following articles describe the immigrant experience and raise once again the issues that every large-scale multiethnic regime must address: How can unity and diversity be channeled into political, economic, and cultural well-being?

The history of immigration laws does not champion American ethnic groups. Immigration laws include the Chinese Exclusion Acts of the 1880s, the National Origins Quota System of the 1920s, the Mexican Repatriation Campaign of the 1950s, and the McCarran-Walter Act in 1952. A new era began with the inclusiveness of the mid-1960s. The findings of the 1990 U.S. Census indicate a range of demographic, economic, and social indicators in this most recent era of immigration in the United States. Both the immediate impact of present-day newcomers and the changes in America that can be attributed to the conflicts and contributions of previous immigrants appear to be facets of nearly every contemporary social issue.

The changing nature of immigration can be discerned more clearly through the experiences of recent immigrant families. The stories of new immigrants are aspects of a worldwide drama. Thus, the Canadian context discussed in this unit's context provides comparative perspectives on immigrant adjustment and their reception in other cultures and to offer support for arguments that immigrants need not be sources of fear and suspicion. Such change and growth pose great potential for the well-being and economic development of the United States. Nevertheless, the challenges that this large influx of persons and cultures brings requires awareness of our cultural diversity and common humanity as well as energy, mutual openness to talent, and participation of all in the experience of being and becoming Americans.

Full employment and social-economic mobility in countries from which persons are coming to the United States would decrease incentives for migration. Political and religious freedom in other countries would negate another cause for the movement of people from oppressive regimes to democratic and liberal societies.

Changes in the U.S. immigration laws in 1965 contributed to the growing number of Central American, South American, and Asian immigrants who have entered the country. The flow of population also includes persons who have entered without governmental authorization. Extreme violence and political turmoil have contributed to the number of refugees seeking asylum in the United States.

As the unit articles make clear, immigration not only impacts on the receiving country but also affects nations that lose the talents, skills, and loyalty of disaffected migrants. Immigration, moreover, contributes to an already-complex process of intergenerational relationships and the socialization of persons whose experiences of profound cultural change are intensified by competition, patterns of settlement, options for mobility, and the consciousness of ethnic traditions that conflict with dominant cultural and educational institutions.

Michael Piore's assessment of children born to immigrant workers suggests an interesting lens through which the following articles may be read. Dr. Piore writes:

> There is nothing in the immigration process that ensures that this second generation will be able to move up to the higher level jobs toward which they aspire. Indeed, historically industrial societies appear consistently to disappoint the expectations of the second generation in this regard. That disappointment has in turn been the source of enormous social tensions. The sit-down strikes in the late thirties which sparked the industrial unions movement in the United States may in large measure be attributed to the reaction of the children of pre–World War I European immigrants to their labor market conditions. Similarly, the racial disturbances in Northern urban ghettos in the middle and late 1960s may be looked upon as a revolt of the black migrants against a society bent upon confining them to their parents' jobs.

As a guide for your own study, the U.S. Commission on Civil Rights has noted that increased immigration

TO BE GIVEN TO
THE PERSON NATURALIZED

Petition No. 20179

Personal description of holder as of date of natu...
complexion Fair color of eyes...
weight 138 pounds; visible distinctive mark...
Marital status MARRIED
I certify that the description above giv...

Louis Raucci

group mobility strategies and ethnic succession in the workplace, especially in manufacturing, hospitals, restaurants, and maintenance and custodial positions. Some ethnic populations appear to have greater numbers of highly educated persons in professional or semiprofessional positions.

Institutional and societal barriers: The job preferences and discrimination against the ethnic enclave and persons in small communities that are isolated from mainstream English-speaking society suggest the value of second-language competencies. Mutual accommodation is required to minimize the effect of inadequate language skills and training and difficulties in obtaining licenses, memberships, and certification.

Exploitation of workers: The most common form is the payment of wages below minimum standards. Alien workers have been stereotyped as a drain on public services. Such scapegoating is insupportable.

Taking jobs from Americans: Fact or fiction?: The stunning fact is that immigrants are a source of increased productivity and a significant, if not utterly necessary, addition to the workforce as well as to the consumer power that drives the American economy.

Looking Ahead: Challenge Questions

In what respects are the historical experiences of America and Canada important in contemporary immigration issues and policies?

A decade ago, American national policy advisers discussed the claims of irredentist populations as an ethnic/political issue of comparison between Poland and Germany and the United States and Mexico. How has the globalization of the economy—NAFTA and the European Community—changed the relationships among states and their perceptions of one another?

Does the recent proposal of the Mexican government to allow dual citizenship—U.S. and Mexican—present a threat or an opportunity for ethnic group relations?

Why do periods of economic crisis appear to exacerbate tensions and strain relations among ethnic groups?

Which is better, clustering of ethnic populations in occupational groupings or a random mixing of persons in various occupations? Why?

What remedies for language diversity are acceptable in a democratic society?

How fruitful is discussion of immigration issues as if they were a matter of protecting American borders?

raises the following issues for both recent arrivals and Americans by birth:

Employment: The areas of occupation selected by or imposed upon various ethnic populations trace ethnic

A Nation of Immigrants

It's a politician's bromide—and it also happens to be a profound truth. No war, no national crisis, has left a greater impress on the American psyche than the successive waves of new arrivals that quite literally built the country. Now that arguments against immigration are rising again, it is well to remember that every single one of them has been heard before.

Bernard A. Weisberger

Bernard A. Weisberger, a contributing editor to this magazine, writes the "In the News" column.

The uproar over Zoë Baird has subsided by now, and readers with short memories may profit by a reminder that she was forced to withdraw as President Clinton's first nominee for Attorney General because she and her husband had hired two "illegal aliens" for babysitting and housekeeping chores. The episode put immigration into focus as a "live" topic for op-ed and talk-show manifestoes before it faded, only to return to the headlines when Clinton embraced the Bush administration's policy (which he had denounced during the campaign) of turning back boatloads of Haitian refugees before they reached the Florida shore. But in June of 1993 the front pages carried the tragic story of a freighter, ironically named the *Golden Venture,* that ran aground just outside New York City. Its hold contained a crowd of Chinese workers being unlawfully smuggled into the United States, a crude practice supposedly long obsolete. Ten of them drowned trying to swim ashore. Later in the summer several hundred more "illegal" Chinese, California-bound, were intercepted and imprisoned aboard their ships until the U.S. government persuaded Mexico to take them in and ship them back. So it is that immigration regularly returns to the news. It always has. It always does.

The question of what our policy toward the world's huddled masses should be is especially topical at this moment. The Statue of Liberty still lifts her lamp beside the golden door, but in a time of economic downturn, there is no longer an assured consensus that the door should be kept open very far. Restrictionism is back in fashion. For every journalistic article like that of *Business Week* in July 1992, which notes that "the U.S. is reaping a bonanza of highly educated foreigners" and that low-end immigrants "provide a hardworking labor force to fill the low-paid jobs that make a modern service economy run," there is another like Peter Brimelow's in the *National Review.* His title tells it all: "Time to Rethink Immigration?" The burden of his argument is that America has admitted too many immigrants of the wrong ethnic background (he himself is a new arrival from Britain), that neither our economy nor our culture can stand the strain, and that "it may be time to close the second period of American history [the first having been the era of the open frontier] with the announcement that the U.S. is no longer an 'immigrant country.'" In short, we're here; you foreigners stay home. Nor are journalists the only voices in the debate. Last August California's governor Pete Wilson got media attention with a proposal to amend the Constitution so as to deny citizenship to an entire class of people born in the United States, namely, those unlucky enough to be the children of illegal immigrants.

If, as I have, you have been "doing" immigration history for many years, you've heard the restrictionists arguments before and expect to hear them again. And you are under the obligation to answer back, because what is at stake in the argument is nothing less than the essential nature of the United States of America. We are different. We aren't the only country that receives immigration or that has to deal with resentment directed toward "aliens." The popularity in France of Jean-Marie Le Pen's National Front party and the surge of anti-foreign (and neo-Nazi) "Germany-for-Germans" violence in Germany are evidence of that. It's also true that in a world of swift intercontinental travel and instant global communication, immigration policy cannot really be made by separate governments as if they lived in a vacuum. Such problems as there are demand multinational solutions.

Only America takes special pride in describing its nationality as independent of race or blood.

Nevertheless and notwithstanding, the United States of America is different. Immigration is flesh of our flesh, and we need to be reminded of that. Some sneer at the statement that we are a nation of immigrants as a cliché; all nations, they assert, are made up of mixtures of different peoples. So they are, as new tribes and races displaced old ones by conquest or by random migration. But the United States was created by settlers who arrived from elsewhere, who deliberately and calculatedly invited and urged others to follow them, and who encouraged the process in ways that were unique. Of course, countries like Canada and Australia depended on immigration for survival and success, but only the United States made the acquisition of citizenship swift and simple; only the United States made it a matter of principle to equalize the conditions of new citizens and old; only the United States takes special pride in describing American nationality as, by definition, independent of race and blood—as something that is acquired by residence and allegiance regardless of birthplace or ancestry.

Confirmation of that statement is in the record, and the record needs to be reviewed. It is not a flawless one. Of course the people of the United States have not always extended an equal welcome to all races; of course there have been spasms of hostility like the current wave—in the 1790s, in the 1850s, in the 1920s. They are also part of the record, but on the whole the record is exceptional and ought to be known and understood before any new major changes in policy are made.

Every Passover Jews the world over sit down to the Seder table to retell the story of Exodus from Egypt in order to pass on to their children and renew in themselves their sense of who, what, and why they are. There was a time when the Fourth of July was an occasion for re-creating the days of the American Revolution, in order to serve the same purpose for Americans. (I hope that it makes a comeback, despite the assaults of a misguided "multiculturalism.")

Now is the proper occasion for retelling the immigration story. So let us begin at the beginning, with the statement that offends the new exclusionist.

IN THE BEGINNING: 1607–1798

"We are a nation of immigrants." It's a politician's generality at an ethnic picnic, a textbook bromide swallowed and soon forgotten. It is also, as it happens, a profound truth, defining us and explaining a good part of what is extraordinary in the short history of the United States of America. There is no American ancient soil, no founding race, but there is a common ancestral experience of moving from "there" to "here." Among the founders of this nation who believed that they were agents of destiny was an English preacher who said in 1669, "God hath sifted a nation that he might send choice grain into this wilderness." The grain has arrived steadily and from many nations. "Americans are not a narrow tribe," wrote Herman Melville; "our blood is as the flood of the Amazon, made up of a thousand noble currents all pouring into one."

We begin arbitrarily with a seventeenth-century English migration that produced the First Families of Virginia (founded in 1607) and Massachusetts's Pilgrim Fathers (1620). Arbitrarily because already in 1643 Isaac Jogues, a French Jesuit missionary visiting New Amsterdam, said he heard eighteen languages spoken in that seaport town, which probably included Mediterranean and North African dialects and the Hebrew of a small settlement of Sephardic Jews.

But the stock planted in the 1600s was basically English. In the eighteenth century it turned "British" as Scots and Irish arrived in significant numbers, then partly European through an influx of Germans, and African, too, through the thousands of involuntary black immigrants brought in on the hell ships of the slave trade.

Those initial colonial migrations to "British North America" illustrate forces that are still at work in 1993. The names, faces, and languages change, but the basics remain. Immigrants are pushed out of their original homes by war, upheaval, misery, and oppression. They are pulled toward America by the promise of economic betterment and a chance to breathe free. Sometimes they are lured by promoters who want their passage money or their labor and skills. Sometimes they have come in legal or actual bondage.

But whenever and wherever they have come, they have changed what they found. That was clear from the moment that seventeenth-century England sent the first immigrant wave. The land was ripe for mass exodus. Civil, religious, and class war raged from beginning to end of the century, encompassing in their course the execution of one king and the expulsion of another. Major changes in the economy drove small farmers off their subsistence plots in favor of sheep. "The people . . . do swarm in the land as young bees in a hive," said one clergyman. "The land grows weary of her inhabitants," said another—by name John

41

Immigration helped bring on the Revolution, and gave it a surprising new meaning.

Winthrop, soon to move with fellow Puritans to a place called Massachusetts Bay.

The London government planted colonies to help house-clean the surplus population. Some started under the rule of private corporations that looked for gold and silk and settled for the profits in fish, fur, and tobacco. Some were begun by like-minded religious seekers, some by individuals to whom the king gave huge tracts of wilderness to turn into profitable agricultural estates. All needed people to thrive, and got them. Some 378,000 Englishmen and women left for the Western Hemisphere during the century; 155,000 wound up on mainland North America. They came on the *Mayflower*; they came in groups brought over by colonial proprietors who got so many extra acres of land per head of immigrant. They came as indentured servants, under bond to work a term of years. Some came in fetters at the request of unchoosy colonial administrators, like the governor of Virginia who asked London in 1611 for "all offenders out of the common gaols condemned to die." There may have been, over the decades, as many as 50,000 of such "fellons and other desperate villaines."

They brought the imprint of England in their baggage. Without stinting other contributions, there isn't any question that constitutional self-rule, Protestant individualism, capitalism, and the work ethic were hammered into the national character in the seventeenth-century English. And yet English with a difference. "They ate the white corn-kernels parched in the sun," Stephen Vincent Benét wrote in 1943, "and they knew it not, but they'd not be English again." Autocratic rule was modified almost at once because London was far away—and freedom attracted new settlers. Virginia demanded and got a representative assembly in 1624; all the other colonies followed in due course.

It was an age of religious rigidity, but state-imposed conformity had to bend to the needs of settlement. In 1632 King Charles I gave his supporter Cecilius Calvert, Lord Baltimore, the future state of Maryland (named for the Catholic queen). Calvert saw to it that his fellow Catholics, under heavy pressure back home, were tolerated within its borders. In the 1680s a different king bestowed yet another colony on William Penn. The Quaker Penn opened Pennsylvania not only to other members of the Society of Friends but to "dissenters" of every description. In different colonies intolerance rose and fell, but more often fell as population grew and spread. "Here," reported New York's governor in 1687, "be not many of the Church of England, few Roman Catholics, abundance of . . . singing Quakers, ranting Quakers, Sabbatarians, Anti-Sabbatarians, some Anabaptists, some Independents, some Jews; in short, of all sorts of opinions there are some, and the most part none at all."

By the start of the eighteenth century, that latitude, along with virgin land and prospering towns, was exerting a magnetic force outside England itself: in France, where, in 1685, the king revoked an edict that had protected his Protestant subjects, thereby sending thousands of Huguenots—thrifty, skilled traders and artisans—to settle in America; in the many little German princedoms plagued by war, taxes, and rack rents, so that altogether there were some 225,000 colonists of German stock on the Revolution's eve, including groups like the Mennonites (ancestors of the Amish) and Moravians.

They spread through several colonies, but those in Pennsylvania became known as the Pennsylvania Dutch (a corruption of *Deutsch*), and their clannish ways at least once exasperated the usually tolerant Benjamin Franklin. "Why should the Palatine *Boors*," he asked (the Rhenish Palatinate was a German region that furnished many new Pennsylvanians), "be suffered to swarm into our Settlements, and by herding together, establish their Language and Manners to the Exclusion of ours? Why should *Pennsylvania*, founded by the *English*, become a Colony of *Aliens*?"

There was no language problem with the "Ulster" Irish or Scots Irish. These Scots, deliberately planted in the northern counties of Ireland in the 1600s to help subdue the native Catholics, were busy and productive farmers until, in 1699, English landowners got the door slammed on competitive agricultural imports. The ensuing distress sent as many as 12,000 a year of the Ulstermen and women to the colonies. They poured into the frontier regions, carrying with them strict Calvinism and a distaste for both Indians and speculators who cornered huge tracts to sell at high prices. It was, in their eyes, "against the laws of God and nature that so much land should be idle while Christians wanted it to labor on and raise their bread." They were the ancestors of such as Daniel Boone and Andrew Jackson.

The end of the French and Indian War in 1763 spurred a rush of migration to the now-secure colonial frontiers and the growing seaboard towns of Boston, New York, Philadelphia, Charleston. From 1763 to 1775 some 221,000 newcomers arrived: 55,000 Ulstermen, 40,000 Scots, 30,000 English, 12,000 Germans and Swiss—and 84,500 chained Africans. Perhaps a third of all the colonists in 1760 were either born abroad or had parents who were. The English government, once worried about overpopulation, now feared depopulation even more and cracked down on large landowners' seductive invitations to immigrants. Thus the charge in Jefferson's bill of particulars showing that the king sought an absolute tyranny over the colonies: "He has endeavoured to prevent the Population of these states; . . . obstructing the Laws for Naturalization of Foreigners; refusing to pass others to encourage their Migrations hither, and raising the Conditions of new Appropriations of Lands."

Immigration helped bring on the Revolution, and to give it a surprising new meaning. By 1782 the former English colonies were separate states, linked by common interests and a common culture that was more than simply English. Michel Guillaume Jean de Crèvecoeur, a French immigrant, put it this way: "What then is the American, this new man? He is either an European, or the descendant of a European, hence that strange mixture of blood, which you will find in no other country. I could point out to you a family whose grandfather was an Englishman, whose wife was Dutch, whose son married a French woman, and whose present four sons have now four wives of different nations. . . . Here individuals of all nations are melted into a new race of men, whose labours and posterity will one day cause great changes in the world. . ."

The immigrant generals and soldiers who fought on the American side in the Revolution (like Gen. Frederick Mühlenberg, the German-trained Lutheran pastor who would become the first Speaker of the House) would have agreed. So would Tom Paine, the English immigrant author of *Common Sense*, which, in 1776, called on the future United States to become an "asylum for mankind."

But when the Constitutional Convention came to consider naturalization laws and residence requirements for officials, a different point of view was evident. Even a sturdy democrat like Virginia's George Mason did not "chuse to let foreigners and adventurers make laws for us & govern us." Pierce Butler of South Carolina—born in Ireland—believed that aliens brought in "ideas of Government so distinct from ours that in every point of view they are dangerous." Gouverneur Morris, a gifted master of sarcasm from New York, applauded generosity to foreigners but counseled "a moderation in all things. . . . He would admit them to his house, he would invite them to his table . . . but would not carry the complaisance so far as to bed them with his wife."

Compromise prevailed; no person may be a representative who has not been a citizen seven years, or become a senator with less than nine years' citizenship. Presidents must be American-born. The issue blew up again in 1798 during stormy confrontations between Jefferson's Republicans and conservative Federalist opponents who feared an infiltration of radical immigrants full of dangerous ideas hatched by the French Revolution, then in full career. A Federalist-dominated Congress passed the Alien and Sedition Acts of 1798, which allowed the President to expel foreigners whom he deemed dangerous on suspicion of treasonable activities. Jefferson called the measure "worthy of the 8th or 9th cen-

tury," and when he and his supporters won the election of 1800, they let it die without renewal.

YOUNG REPUBLIC, 1815–60

Jefferson's optimistic vision of an always enlightened and open-minded America has survived as a hotly contested influence on the land. But his expectation that the nation would remain permanently agrarian was totally wrong. Half a century after he left the White House, steam power had transformed the country. Inventors and investors proved the truest American radicals. Steamboats and rail lines crisscrossed a Union that spread to the Pacific and boasted more than thirty states. Mills, mines, factories, distilleries, packinghouses, and shipyards yearly churned out millions of dollars' worth of manufactured goods.

And it was linked to mass immigration. Immigrants furnished much of the labor that made the productive explosion possible and many of the consumers who made it profitable. The same industrializing processes that were at work and opened jobs here uprooted millions in Europe whose handicrafts became obsolete or whose land fell into the hands of those who could farm more "efficiently." Two decades of Napoleonic warfare, followed by three more of suppressed democratic and nationalist revolution, created a new reservoir of suffering from which emigration offered an escape.

America was a major beneficiary. Europe's growing cities and new overseas dominions beckoned, but the United States was the special promised land as the nineteenth century took its dynamic course. Fewer than 8,000 immigrants per year landed on American shores between 1783 and 1815, but 2,598,000 came in the next forty-five years: 1,500,000 in the 1840s and 3,000,000 in the 1850s. The pre–Civil War period of immigration belonged predominantly to 1,500,000 Germans and 2,000,000 Irish. It was the Irish whose transplantation was most shadowed in tragedy. Unbelievably, Ireland—only a few hours by water from the very center of the modern world in England—was stricken by the oldest of Biblical scourges, famine.

Irish migration had begun early. The rich English absentee landlords who ruled the country left their peasant tenants to feed themselves on the potatoes grown on tiny plots. A visitor declared that "the most miserable of English paupers" was better off. Irish Catholics and Irish nationalists were equally despised and frustrated. There was little future, and thousands, early in the century, migrated to the United States to find pick-and-shovel jobs on the growing network of turnpikes, canals, and railroads. But in 1845 the stream of opportunity seekers was turned into a flood of refugees. The potato crop, smitten by a fungus, failed in three successive years. Mass starvation was the result. In the hovels inhabited by the "Paddies," rats gnawed on unburied bodies while others in their death throes looked on, too weak to move. "All with

To their contemporaries, the Germans seemed a model minority, the Irish a problem minority.

means are emigrating," wrote one official; "only the utterly destitute are left behind."

Victims of the "Great Hunger" were not through with their torments when they boarded filthy, overcrowded, and underprovisioned ships, where, said one witness, it was "a daily occurrence to see starving women and children fight for the food which was brought to the dogs and pigs that were kept on deck." En route 10 to 20 percent of them died of disease. In the United States, lacking capital and prepared only for low-level employment, they were crammed into the new urban slums. Some were housed, according to an investigation committee, nine in a room in windowless and waterless cellars, "huddled together like brutes without regard to age or sex or sense of decency."

It was a little better for the Germans. Many were professionals and scholars with some capital, political refugees rather than disaster victims. Some came in groups that pooled their money to buy cheap Western lands, and these founded towns like New Ulm in Minnesota or New Braunfels in Texas. So many of them became Texans, in fact, that in 1843 the state published a German edition of its laws. An American reporter visited a German farm in Texas in 1857. "You are welcomed," he told readers, "by a figure in a blue flannel shirt and pendant beard, quoting Tacitus, having in one hand a long pipe, in the other a butcher's knife; Madonnas upon log-walls; coffee in tin cups upon Dresden saucers; barrels for seats to hear a Beethoven's symphony on the grand piano."

German farmers spread through Illinois, Michigan, Missouri, Iowa, and Wisconsin. German brewers, bookbinders, butchers, musicians, and other craftspeople settled cohesively and proudly in cities from New York to New Orleans, St. Louis to Cincinnati. In 1860, 100,000 New York Germans supported twenty churches, fifty German-language schools, ten bookstores, five printing establishments, and a theater, in neighborhoods known collectively as *Kleindeutschland* (little Germany). To contemporaries the Germans seemed a model minority, the Irish a problem minority—a kind of generalizing that would, in time, be transferred to other peoples.

Besides these two major groups, there were Danes, Norwegians, and Swedes arriving in increasing numbers from the 1850s onward; French-Canadians moving into New England textile factories to replace Yankee workers of both sexes; Dutch farmers drifting to western Michigan; and in 1849 Chinese who had heard of the California gold strikes and came for their share of the "Golden Mountain," as they called America—only to be crowded out of the mining camps by mobs and restrictive laws and diverted into railway labor gangs, domestic service, restaurants, and laundries.

The immigrants helped push the United States population from 4,000,000 in 1790 to 32,000,000 in 1860. They built America by hand, for wages that were pittances by modern standards—$40 a month in Pennsylvania coal mines, $1.25 to $2 a day on the railroads—but tempting nonetheless. (In Sweden farmhands earned $33.50 *per year*.) They dug themselves into the economy and into the nation's not-always-kindly ethnic folklore. New England textile towns like Woonsocket and Burlington got to know the accent of French-Canadian "Canucks." So many Swedes became Western lumbermen that a double-saw was called a "Swedish fiddle." Welsh and Cornish copper miners in Michigan's Upper Peninsula, were known as Cousin Jacks.

There were exceptions to the geographical stereotypes—Dutch settlements in Arizona, a Swedish nucleus in Arkansas, a Chinese community in Mississippi—and Irishmen in Southern cities like Mobile and New Orleans, where they were employed on dangerous jobs like levee repair because they were more expendable than fifteen-hundred-dollar slaves.

American culture shaped itself around their presence. Religion was a conspicuous example. The Church of Rome in America was turned inside out by the Irish, whose sheer numbers overwhelmed the small groups of old-stock English and French Catholics from Maryland and Louisiana. The first American cardinal, John McCloskey, was the son of a Brooklyn Irishman. The second, James Gibbons, an Irish boy from Baltimore. German and Swiss Catholic immigrants added to the melting-pot nature of their church in the United States before the Civil War—and the Poles and Italians were yet to come.

German and Scandinavian Lutheran immigrants—free of state and ecclesiastical authorities—developed strong local leaders and new, secessionist bodies, like the German-dominated Missouri Synod and the Scandinavian Evangelical Lutheran Augustana Synod. Both of these were theologically conservative groups. On the other side Isaac Mayer Wise, a German immigrant rabbi, became the patriarch of Reform Judaism in America, to save the faith, in his words, from "disappearance" into "Polish-cabalistical . . . supernaturalism." All the "immigrant churches" in the United States built their own networks of social service agencies, parochial schools, and ministerial training seminaries without state help, blending the faith of their fathers with an American style of independent congregational activism. In the house of God, too, the American was a "new man."

Ethnic politics took root in immigrant-crowded city wards. Nowhere was it stronger than among the gregarious Irish, whose neighborhood saloons became political clubhouses. The Society of St. Tammany was an old-stock New York City association founded in 1789 to promote Jeffersonian ideas. Fifty years later the Irish had so infiltrated it that a writer quipped: "Ask an Irishman, and he will probably tell you that St. Tammany was a younger brother of St. Patrick who emigrated to America for the purpose of taking a city contract to drive all Republican reptiles out of New York." Patronage jobs handed out by the machine made Irish cops a stereotype for the rest of the century.

But the lower-class Irish in particular stung an American elite long steeped in anti-popery. Anti-immigrant feelings began to rise in the 1840s and focused especially on the Irish, who, like poor people before and after them, were denounced for not living better than they could afford. "Our Celtic fellow citizens," wrote a New York businessman, "are almost as remote from us in temperament and constitution as the Chinese." Bigotry can always find excuses and weapons. The handiest one in the 1840s was anti-Catholicism.

In 1834 a Boston mob burned a convent. Ten years later there were riots in Philadelphia after a school board ruled that Catholic children might use the Douay version of the Bible in school. "The bloody hand of the Pope," howled one newspaper, "has stretched itself forth to our destruction." A few years after that, anti-Catholic and anti-foreign feelings merged in a nativist crusade called the Know-Nothing movement. Its goal was to restrict admission and naturalization of foreigners, and among its adherents was Samuel F. B. Morse, the father of telegraphy, who cried aloud: "To your posts! . . . Fly to protect the vulnerable places of your Constitution and Laws. Place your guards. . . . And first, shut your gates."

Know-Nothings had some brief success but little enduring impact. Their drive got strength from a generalized anxiety about the future of the country on the eve of the Civil War. But Know-Nothingism cut across the grain of a venerable commitment to equal rights, and no one put his finger on the issue more squarely than Abraham Lincoln when asked in 1855 whether he was in favor of the Know-Nothing movement: "How could I be? How can any one who abhors the oppression of negroes, be in favor of degrading classes of white people? Our progress in degeneracy appears to me to be pretty rapid. As a nation, we began by declaring that *all men are created equal.*' We now practically read it, 'all men are created equal, *except negroes.*' When the Know-Nothings get control, it will read, ' all men are created equal, except negroes, and *foreigners and catholics.*' When it comes to this I should prefer emigrating to some country where they make no pretence of loving liberty—to Russia, for instance, where despotism can be taken pure, and without the base alloy of hypocrisy."

Three years later, on the Fourth of July, 1858, in debating with Stephen A. Douglas, Lincoln returned to the theme. What could the Fourth mean, he asked, to those who were not blood descendants of those who had fought in the Revolution? His answer was that in turning back to the Declaration of Independence, they found the sentiment "We hold these truths to be self-evident, that all men are created equal," that they "feel . . . and that they have a right to claim it as though they were blood of the blood, and flesh of the flesh of the men who wrote that Declaration and so they are. That is the electric cord . . . that links the hearts of patriotic and liberty-loving men together. . ."

Lincoln was unambiguous. There was no exclusively American race entitled to claim liberty by heredity. What held the nation together was an *idea* of equality that every newcomer could claim and defend by free choice.

That concept was soon tested to the limit with Lincoln himself presiding over the fiery trial. Foreign-born soldiers and officers served the Union in such numbers and with such distinction that the war itself should have laid to rest finally the question of whether "non-natives" could be loyal. It didn't do that. But it paved the way for another wave of economic growth and a new period of ingathering greater than any that had gone before.

HIGH TIDE AND REACTION: 1885-1930

After 1865 the United States thundered toward industrial leadership with the speed and power of one of the great locomotives that were the handsomest embodiment of the age of steam. That age peaked somewhere in the 1890s. By 1929 the age of electricity and petroleum was in flower. And the United States was the world's leading producer of steel, oil, coal, automobiles and trucks, electrical equipment, and an infinite variety of consumer goods from old-fashioned overalls to newfangled radios. The majority of Americans lived in supercities, their daily existence made possible by elaborate networks of power and gas lines, telephone wires, highways, bridges, tunnels, and rails.

And the foreign-born were at the center of the whirlwind. Expansion coincided with, depended on, incorporated the greatest wave of migration yet. In the first fourteen years after the Civil War ended yearly immigration ranged from 318,568 in 1866 to 459,803 in 1873, slumping during the hard times of 1873–77, and rebounding to 457,257 in 1880.

Then came the deluge: 669,431 in 1881; 788,992 in 1882. Seven times between 1883 and 1903 the half-million total was passed. The million mark was hit in 1905 with 1,026,499—and exceeded six times between that year and 1914. The all-time peak came in 1907: 1,285,349.

All told, some 14,000,000 arrived at the gates between 1860 and 1900; another 18,600,000 followed between 1900 and 1930. Almost all of them came from Europe, a transoceanic transplantation unmatched in history.

The "old" Americans—that is, the children of immigrants who had arrived earlier—watched the influx with feelings that ran from pride to bewilderment and alarm, for the "new" immigration was not from traditional sources. Until 1890 most new arrivals were from familiar places: the British Isles, Germany, the Scandinavian countries, Switzerland, the Netherlands. But now it was the turn of southern

Chicago once had more Germans than any of Kaiser Wilhelm's cities except Berlin and Hamburg.

and eastern Europe to swarm. Of the roughly 1,280,000 in the record-setting 1907 intake, 260,000 were from Russia, which then included a goodly portion of Poland. Another 285,000 were from Italy. Almost 340,000 were from Austria-Hungary, a doomed "dual monarchy" that included much of the future Yugoslavia and Czechoslovakia and another part of Poland. About 36,000 were from Romania, Bulgaria, and what was left of the Ottoman Turkish Empire in Europe. There were modest numbers of Greeks and Portuguese.

These new immigrants were palpably different. There were Eastern Orthodox as well as Roman Catholics, and Orthodox Jews. There were, at a time when ethnic labels were taken with great seriousness, Magyars, Croats, Slovenes, Slovaks, and people generally grouped as "Slavs" and "Latins" and sniffed at in suspicion and disdain. In 1875 *The New York Times* said of Italians that it was "hopeless to think of civilizing them, or keeping them in order, except by the arm of the law." A Yankee watching Polish farm workers was struck by their "stolid, stupid faces." An American Jewish journal, offended by the beards, side curls, and skullcaps of Polish greenhorns, wondered what could be done with these "miserable darkened Hebrews."

The immigration patterns had shifted with the course of modern European history. A rising demand for political independence in central Europe fed political turbulence. Russian nationalism spawned anti-Semitic outbursts and hard, impoverishing economic restrictions on Jews. Southern Italy was overwhelmed by agricultural poverty that was increased by policies of industrialization and modernization that favored the north. Europe was full of hopeful seekers of streets paved with gold.

And there were voices to entice them. The immigration bureaus of Western states distributed literature in several languages touting opportunities within their borders. Railroad companies with land grants wooed Russian and German farmers to come out and buy (on long-term credit) tracts on the Great Plains. The Great Northern line—which James J. Hill built without land grants—offered fares as low as thirty-three dollars to any point on the tracks that ran from Minnesota to Oregon, plus sweet deals on acquiring and moving machinery, livestock, lumber, fencing. Steamship companies were in the hunt too. Modern technology had reduced the dreaded transatlantic passage to ten or twelve days instead of months. Steerage accommodations were far from clean or comfortable, but

they cost as little as twenty-five dollars, and passengers were no longer likely to die on the way.

So the immigrants came. For the most part this was an urban migration. Millions went to the middling-sized red-brick towns dominated by the factory chimney and whistle. More millions went to the big cities, where they grunted and sweated in the creation of the skyscrapers, the bridges, the subways and trolley lines, the sewer and lighting systems —the guts of the metropolis. Or where, if they did not swing a pick or scrub floors, they sold groceries to those of their countrymen who did.

In the 1890s Chicago had more Germans than any of Kaiser Wilhelm's cities except Berlin and Hamburg; more Swedes than any place in Sweden except for Stockholm and Göteborg; more Norwegians than any Norwegian town outside of Christiana (now Oslo) and Bergen. Of some 12,500 laborers modernizing New York State's Erie Canal, fully 10,500 were Italians rounded up on the docks by Italian-speaking padrones and furnished to construction companies at so much per head. By 1897 Italians made up 75 percent of New York City's construction workers. Jews already dominated the town's once-German garment industry.

In Pennsylvania in 1900 almost 60 percent of white bituminous coal miners were foreign-born. In three anthracite coal mines in a single county, more than three-quarters of the work force was Slavic. Twenty-five languages were spoken in the textile mills of Lawrence, Massachusetts.

Ethnic monopolies of particular lines of work were established. In 1894 all but one of New York City's 474 foreign-born bootblacks were Italian, and Greeks dominated the confectionery business in Chicago until past the end of World War II.

For most, life in the golden land was potentially promising but actually brutal. Wages hung at or below the cost of living and far below the cost of comfort. Some parts of Chicago had three times as many inhabitants as the most crowded sections of Tokyo or Calcutta. A New York survey taker found 1,231 Italians living in 120 rooms. Single toilets and water faucets were shared by dozens of families. Uncollected garbage piled up in alleys. Privacy and health were equally impossible to maintain, and pulmonary diseases raged through the tenement "lung blocks."

Settlement-house workers took up residence in the worst neighborhoods, trying to teach the rudiments of hygiene. The American public school took on a new role. Authorities

In the 1890s, old New England families rallied to form the Immigration Restriction League.

regarded it as their mission to teach immigrant children not only basic skills but civic responsibility, respect for the flag, and the proper use of the toothbrush. In fact, the schools did produce millions of competent citizens. One alumna, Mary Antin, said that born Americans should be grateful for their role in "the recruiting of your armies of workers, thinkers, and leaders." But the precedent of having schools serve as agents of social policy—in this case of assimilation—would later haunt overburdened teachers and administrators.

The urban center of gravity of the new immigrants made it harder for them to be accepted. Most "native" Americans were encountering the basic problems of the big city—crowding, crime, graft, corruption, disease—for the first time. It was all too easy for them to associate these evils with the immigrants, who seemed always to be at the center of this or that dilemma. Sympathetic men and women like Jane Addams, Emily Balch, Hutchins Hapgood, and Horace M. Kallen did their best to explain immigrant culture to their fellow old-stock Americans and to guide the newcomers in acceptable American ways.

The immigrants themselves did not take on the role of clay awaiting the potter's hand. They organized their own newspapers, theaters, social clubs, night classes, and self-help societies. These, while keeping the old-country languages and folkways alive, steadfastly preached and practiced assimilation and urged members and readers to rush into citizenship and respectability, which the great majority of them did. Single men skimped and struggled to bring over families. Families sacrificed to send children to school. And the children found different paths to Americanization. Some joined political machines and parties; some worked in the union movement; others forged their own steps to success in business. (And some never graduated beyond the streets and dead-end jobs.)

Regardless of what they did, they were caught in the center of a steadily sharpening American debate over the "immigrant problem" that began in the early 1890s. It was a reprise of earlier nativist struggles. As early as 1882 Congress was prevailed upon to exclude Chinese from entry and citizenship. In the 1890s an Immigration Restriction League was formed. Its leaders were from old New England families who shared the fears of the writer Thomas Bailey Aldrich that through our "unguarded gates" there was pouring a "wild motley throng" of "Men from the Volga and the Tartar steppes."

Would the America of the future be populated, one restrictionist asked, by "British, German and Scandinavian stock, historically free, energetic, progressive, or by Slav, Latin and Asiatic races, historically down-trodden, atavistic and stagnant?" The call for an end to unchecked immigration was echoed by labor leaders like the AFL's Samuel Gompers (a Dutch-born Jewish immigrant from England in 1863), who complained that the "present immigration" consisted of "cheap labor, ignorant labor [that] takes our jobs and cuts our wages."

Bit by bit, curbs were imposed—first on immigrants with contagious diseases or serious criminal records, then on those who were "professional beggars" or anarchists or prostitutes or epileptics. In 1906 President Theodore Roosevelt got Congress to establish a commission to study the "problem." Chaired by the Vermont senator William Paul Dillingham, it labored for four years to produce a massive report that loaded the guns of a restrictionism based on invidious distinctions between the "old" and "new" immigrations. Among other things it marshaled data to "prove" that the most recent immigrants were "content to accept wages and conditions which . . . native Americans . . . had come to regard as unsatisfactory." It stated that "inherent racial tendencies" rather than poverty explained miserable immigrant living conditions and went on to say many other uncomplimentary things about the great-grandparents of some fifty million of today's Americans.

No action was taken on the report when it appeared in 1910. But racist feeling was on the rise. The Ku Klux Klan was revived in 1915. A hysterical drive for 100 percent Americanism during World War I and the Red scare immediately afterward fed a popular belief articulated by one congressman: "We get the majority of the communists, the I.W.W.'s, the dynamiters, and the assassins . . . from the ranks of the present-day immigrant."

In 1924 Congress passed the Johnson-Reed Act, which remained the cornerstone of national immigration policy for the next forty-one years. Starting in 1929, there would be an overall yearly limit of 150,000 on immigrants from outside the Western Hemisphere. The 150,000 was to be divided into quotas, assigned to nationalities in the proportion that they bore, by birth or descent, to the total population as of 1920.

What that meant was clear. The longer a national group had been here, the more of its descendants were in the population and the larger would be its quota. When the first shares were announced, half of all places were reserved for British residents, whereas only 5,802 Italians, 6,524 Poles, and 2,784 Russians could be admitted. Groups like Syrians or Albanians fared worse, with fewer than 100 places per year. And Asians were excluded altogether.

The national origins quota system of 1924 was a landmark, ending centuries of open admission. It was also a victory for ethnic stereotyping. Yet it was not without its ironies. For one thing, it did not impose limits on a Hispanic ingathering from Mexico and Puerto Rico that was just gaining steam. Nor did it deal with the internal migration of Southern blacks into Northern cities. Anglo-Saxon superiority was therefore left unprotected on two fronts.

And in the next and newest phase of the story, covering the final years of the twentieth century, there were dramatic changes in the "racial" composition of immigration that went far beyond anything that the Immigration Restriction League could possibly have anticipated.

THE THIRD WORLD COMES TO THE UNITED STATES: 1965–90

Like a good many pieces of social policy legislation, the Johnson-Reed Act began to be outdated from the moment it took effect. One of its objectives—cutting down on immigration overall—was brutally affected by the Great Crash. In the deepest year of the Depression, 1933, only 34,000 immigrants arrived to take their chances in a shuttered and darkened economy.

The totals did not rise dramatically in the next seven years, but they were important weather vanes of change. Fascist and Communist dictators, and World War II, gave new meaning to the word *refugee* and a new scale to misery. Millions of victims of history would soon be knocking at our closed gates.

First came those in flight from Hitler, primarily Jews. Their claim to asylum was especially powerful, considering the savagery that they were fleeing (and no one suspected yet that extermination would be the ultimate threat). This was a special kind of exodus, heavy with intellectual distinction. Thousands of scientists, engineers, doctors, lawyers, teachers, and managers were hit by the Nazi purge of independent thinkers in every part of German life. "Hitler shakes the tree," said one American arts administrator, "and I collect the apples." The choicest apples included such men and women as Bruno Walter, George Szell, Lotte Lenya, Paul Klee, Thomas Mann, and Hannah Arendt in the arts and philosophy. In the sciences the lists included the physicists and mathematicians Edward Teller, Leo Szilard, Eugene P. Wigner, and Enrico Fermi (in flight from Mussolini's Italy) who shared in the creation of the atom bomb. The weapon was first proposed to the American government by the superstar of all the refugees, Albert Einstein.

World War II came—and more signals of change. In 1943 the sixty-one-year-old Chinese Exclusion Act was repealed, because China was now an American ally. The gesture was small, and the quota tiny (105), and it could hardly be said to mark the end of anti-Asian prejudice when 112,000 American citizens of Japanese descent were behind barbed wire. But it was a beginning, a breach in the wall. The horrible consequences of Hitler's "racial science" were so clear that the philosophy of biological superiority underlying the national origins quota system received a fatal shock.

So the groundwork was laid for the future admission of nonwhite immigrants from the crumbling European empires in Africa and Asia—especially when, as it turned out, many of them were highly educated specialists.

Then the Cold War produced its worldwide tragedies and shake-ups, its expulsions and arrests and civil wars and invasions in China, Cuba, Korea, Indochina, the Philippines, Indonesia, Malaysia, Central Africa, the Middle East, Central America. A world in conflict was a world once more ready to swarm.

And in the United States an economic boom was reopening the job market. Attitudes toward immigration were changing as well. The children of the great 1890–1914 migration had come of age. They were powerful in the voting booths; political scientists credited them with a major role in supporting the New Deal. And the best-selling writers and dramatists among them were delving the richness of their experience in a way that wiped out the stereotypes of the old restrictionism.

So the walls began to crumble. First there were special enactments to clear the way for the wives and children of servicemen who had gotten married while overseas. Some 117,000 women and children entered under a War Brides Act of 1945—5,000 of them Chinese. In 1948 came the Displaced Persons Act, spurred by the misery of millions of homeless Eastern Europeans who had survived deportations, forced labor, bombings, and death camps. These were countries with the smallest national origins quotas. Congress did not repeal them, but it permitted borrowing against the future, so that at the end of the act's four-year life, for example, Poland's quota was mortgaged by half until 2000, and Latvia's until 2274. About 205,000 refugees entered under this law.

An attempt to overhaul the system in 1952 got entangled in the fear-ridden climate of McCarthyism, and the resulting McCarran-Walter Act kept the national origins quotas. Harry Truman vetoed it as "utterly unworthy of our traditions and ideals . . . our basic religious concepts, our belief in the brotherhood of man." It was passed over his veto, but time was on his side. Special emergency relief acts admitted refugees from China's civil war and Hungary's failed anti-Soviet uprising. Those who left Castro's Cuba needed no special relief, since there were as yet no limits on migration within the hemisphere, but they did get special help with resettlement. All told, in the 1950s immigration added up to some 2,500,000.

"Hitler shakes the tree," said one American arts administrator, "and I collect the apples."

It was a quality migration, lured by the promise of American wages and the consumer goods made visible in the films and television shows that America exported. And jet travel now put the promised land only hours away. Foreign governments ruefully watched their elites disappearing into the "brain drain" to the United States. Between 1956 and 1965 approximately 7,000 chemists, 35,000 engineers, 38,000 nurses, and 18,000 physicians were admitted. Between 1952 and 1961 Britain lost 16 percent of its Ph.D.s, half to the United States. Comparable losses were even more critical for developing states in the Third World or small European countries.

Yet there was still room at the bottom, for workers in the "service industries" and especially in the harvest fields of the Southwest. In 1951 growers got Congress to enact "temporary worker" programs that brought in thousands of Mexican braceros. Many who received green cards remained without authorization, joining imprecise numbers of illegal immigrants known as wetbacks after presumably swimming the Rio Grande to elude the Border Patrol. There were legal ways to stay too.

All we need is a gringuita
So that we can get married
And after we get our green card
We can get a divorce
Long live all the wetbacks.

So ran a popular Mexican ballad. Authorized and undocumented Mexicans alike became part of an enlarging Hispanic population, fed by migrants from Central America and the Caribbean. Great numbers of Puerto Ricans were part of it, but they did not count as immigrants because of the island's special status.

In 1965 the patched old system was finally discarded, and a brand-new act was passed. It mirrored the equal-rights spirit of the 1960s, modified by the political compromises that float bills through the riptides of congressional debate. The national origins quotas vanished, but there was no return to the wide-open days. Instead new quotas were established with three primary targets: reuniting families, opening the gates to refugees, and attracting skill and talent.

The new act mandated an annual limit of 170,000 immigrants from outside the Western Hemisphere, and 120,000 from within. These 290,000 were to be admitted under seven "preference" quotas. First and second preferences—40 percent of the total—were saved for unmarried grown sons and daughters of citizens and legally admitted alien residents. (Spouses, minor children, and parents of citizens came in free.) The third preference, 10 percent, went to "members of the professions and scientists and artists of exceptional ability." The fourth, 10 percent, went to adult *married* children of U.S. citizens, and the fifth, 24 percent, to brothers and sisters of citizens. The sixth, 10 percent, was held for "skilled labor in great demand" and "unskilled workers in occupations for which labor is in short supply," and the final preference, 6 percent, was for specifically defined refugees.

As Lyndon Johnson said when he signed the act at the base of the Statue of Liberty in October 1965, the new law was not "revolutionary." Yet, he added, it "repairs a deep and painful flaw in the fabric of American life. . . . The days of unlimited immigration are past. But those who come will come because of what they are—not because of the land from which they sprung."

The Immigration Act of 1965 was born in the year of Great Society programs and the Voting Rights Act. It fulfilled some of its authors' expectations and also carried some surprises—perhaps because 1965 was itself a turning-point year that also witnessed urban race riots and the first heavy and expensive commitments to combat in Vietnam. Johnson was wrong in one respect: The law's effects *have* been revolutionary, and are still with us every day. The twenty-five years of its existence have produced a major demographic turnaround.

Europe, the prime provider of new Americans for three centuries, fell off to little more than a 10 percent share of total immigration. The bulk of it now comes from Asia and the Western Hemisphere. In the decade from 1961 to 1970 some 3,321,000 immigrants arrived, and 1,123,000, less than 40 percent, were of European origin. Of 4,493,000 newcomers in the period 1971–80, only about 801,000 were Europeans. Between 1981 and 1990, when immigration totaled 7,338,000, the European contribution was only 761,550.

What of the other 85 to 90 percent? Of the 1,588,000 arrivals in the 1980s, 1,634,000 came from Asia (somewhat over one-third), 1,930,000 from North and South America, and 80,779 from Africa. The five major contributing nations were, in order, Mexico (640,300), the Philippines (355,000), Cuba (265,000), Korea (268,000), and China, both mainland and Taiwan (237,800).

Of the roughly 7,300,000 legal immigrants of 1981–90, 2,700,000 came from Asia, 3,600,000 from the Americas. The leaders—with numbers rounded—were Mexico at 1,656,000, the Philippines at 549,000, Vietnam with

281,000, the two Chinas with 98,000 and 346,000, and Korea with 334,000. Other heavy contributors were the Caribbean nations, with together 872,000; India with about 250,000, Laos at 112,000, Iran with some 116,000, Central America (Costa Rica, El Salvador, Guatemala, Honduras, Nicaragua, and Panama) with 468,000, and African nations with 177,000.

The rising Third World totals had two sources. One was the nature of the 1965 law itself, especially the fifth-preference brother-and-sister quota. Legally admitted and naturalized immigrants brought in their siblings, who went through the same cycle and then brought in *their* kin, and so on in a family tree of ever-spreading branches. When Congress endorsed family reunification, it had in mind the American 1950s model of two parents and two or three children. What it got was extended clans of Asians and Latins.

The other root of Third World influx was the bloody history of the 1970s and 1980s. The fall of Cambodia and South Vietnam in 1975 unleashed floods of refugees who were a special responsibility of the United States. Within the first six months we admitted some 130,000, and many more thousands under special quota exemptions in succeeding years. By 1990, counting their children born here, some 586,000 people of Indochinese origin were living in the United States.

The refugee problem was worldwide. It raised issues of what countries should share the burdens of admission. It sharpened agonizing questions of when repatriation might be justified: when a family was actually fleeing for its life and when it was only looking for a chance to go where air-conditioned cars and color television sets were the visible rewards of hard work (as if both motives could not coexist).

Congress made its own tentative answer with the first major modification of the 1965 law, the Refugee Act of 1980. It set up new offices within the federal government for handling refugee affairs and reshuffled the quota system. The old seventh (refugee) preference with its 17,400 slots was abolished in favor of an annual quota of up to 50,000 refugees that could be exceeded for "grave, humanitarian reasons" by the President in consultation with Congress. The overall limit was dropped to 270,000 as a trade-off. A refugee was officially defined as a person who could not go home again by reason of a "well-founded fear of persecution" on the basis of race, religion, nationality, or political opinion.

And as if to mock the effort to set boundaries around social revolutions, President Carter's signature was hardly dry on the act when 125,000 new Cuban refugees were knocking at the gates, released by Castro through the port of Mariel. Carter declared that he would admit them with open arms and an open heart, a sentiment not fully shared by some residents of the South Florida communities where the *Marielitos* at first clustered.

Society had changed greatly since the unstructured and unsupervised days of mass arrivals at Ellis Island (long deserted and shuttered). The newest refugees did not find unskilled jobs and low-rent tenements waiting for them. It was the age of big government and bureaucratic organization. With the U.S. Treasury providing funds, and church and social service agencies the personnel, programs were launched to help with health care, schooling, and other roads to citizenship. Until the immigrants dispersed themselves around the country, they were lodged in temporary camps, some of them former Army bases. What had been left between 1890 and 1914 to friends, families, padrones, *landsleit*, and political machines was now managed under guidelines set in Washington.

Washington's welcome was not universal. Cold War politics infiltrated refugee policy in the 1980s. Refugees from Communist nations were welcomed, but those from countries officially deemed "democratic," like El Salvador, got shorter shrift. So did those who were "merely" trying to escape harsh but non-Communist regimes or grinding poverty, like the Haitians. The Immigration and Naturalization Service held thousands of them in detention while their petitions for asylum were suspiciously reviewed. Nonetheless, thousands of Central Americans managed to escape the net and find work—usually low-paid and menial—and to melt into the underground economy of the Hispanic communities in Florida and New York.

General statements about this newest great migration are dangerous because it is tempting to lump its members together by race and nationality, as the old Dillingham Report did, rather than by class, education, experience, income, or other categories. To describe Colombian dentists and Mexican cotton pickers as "Hispanics" or Korean chemical engineers and Pakistani nurses' aides as "Asian" suggests nonexistent similarities.

But some broad observations fit most of the new immigrants: They get to this country swiftly and by air, they quickly fall into the consumerist culture familiar to them through television at home, and they are quickly integrated into the bureaucratic structure of entitlements that characterize life in the United States today.

Beyond that, all-embracing descriptions strain the facts. The Vietnamese, for example, include English-speaking professionals who worked for American corporations, Catholics educated during the period of French control, and people from the bottom rung: in the words of one writer, "cosmopolites, bourgeois provincials, and dirt-poor peasants . . . gifted intellectuals, street-wise hustlers and unworldly fisherfolk and farmers." The Koreans most visible to New Yorkers are the hardworking grocers who seem to have taken over the retail fruit and vegetable business completely from the Italians. But a survey shows that more than a third of all Koreans in the United States have completed four years of college.

Recent years have witnessed a new restrictionism, but it is based on some very old alliances.

Filipino immigrants are found in hospitals, as doctors and nurses and sometimes behind the counter in the basement cafeterias; Indians in the newsstands of New York City and likewise doing advanced biochemical or genetic research in its university laboratories. Middle Eastern Arabs, both Christian and Muslim, are heavily concentrated in Detroit, and many work in the American auto industry at both shop and managerial levels. Israeli and Soviet Jewish immigrants—some of them jobless Ph.D.s—drive taxis in Washington, Los Angeles, Chicago, and New York—and work as engineers in defense industries in the Southwest. Puerto Ricans, other Latinos, and Chinese fill the places in New York's declining garment industry once held by Italians and Jews.

Within the communities of Cambodians, Peruvians, Ecuadorians, Iranians, Russians, Israelis, Irish, and Puerto Ricans the old saga goes on as children learn new ways and move to new, unexpected disruptive rhythms. But in education the effect of the new immigration has been dramatically different from what it was prior to World War I. Then the public schools were on the rise and confident of their power and duty to unify *all* children behind the undisputedly correct symbols and rites of Americanism.

In the mood of the 1970s, however, things changed. Emphasis on ethnic pride and the power of the civil rights revolution dictated a new approach. Immigrant children were no longer to be thrown into English-speaking classrooms to sink or swim. Instead bilingual programs would help them in transit to a new system without their being stigmatized as stupid because they could not understand the teacher. Going further, some educators argued that preparing children for a multicultural society required exposure to many "life-styles" and building the self-esteem of "minority" students through appreciation of their own languages, customs, and cultures. So some states mandated bilingual (usually Hispanic-English) programs into the curriculum at every level.

Whatever the virtues of the theory (debatable in the light of evidence), bilingualism provoked a strong counterreaction, and by 1990 some organizations were insisting that new immigrants were not working hard enough to learn the common tongue that was so valuable a social binding agency. An English-only drive got under way to designate English, by constitutional amendment, if necessary, as the *official* language of the United States.

In actual fact, Spanish (and other language) newspapers, television stations, religious congregations, and social clubs were a re-enactment of what had gone before. In the early 1900s there had been a vigorous immigrant press, which, in time, died out. But the English-only movement drew strength from a sense of increasing discomfort over the increasing numbers of immigrants, a reawakening of the old idea that a "flood" of "unassimilated" newcomers was pouring in.

A new restrictionism was born, featuring some familiar alliances. Middle- and upper-class taxpayers believed that the immigrants, concentrated in certain areas, were a burden on schools, hospitals, and welfare and law-enforcement agencies. On the other hand, there were workers who were convinced that the immigrants took away low-level jobs that were rightfully theirs or depressed wages by working in sweatshops or permitting the employment of their underage children. Black Americans tended especially to believe that material assistance that had been denied to them was going to the refugees. They were now the bypassed "old Americans."

Resentment was fed by the widespread admiration of the academic and business success of Asian Americans, who were, in great numbers, advancing up the professional scale. They were described by some sociologists as a "model minority"—their delinquents and failures overlooked while the spotlight fell on those who succeeded.

A dread of the unknown and uncountable hovered over lawmakers. Undocumented aliens came in from the Mexico in annual numbers estimated from a few hundred thousand to many millions a year. The oft-repeated statement that we were "losing control of our borders" had a powerful psychological kick in a time of multiple American troubles. Had we, in fact, reached the limit our power to offer asylum? Was there truth in what Sen. Alan Simpson said in 1982: "We have to live within limits. The nation wants to be compassionate but we have been compassionate beyond our ability to respond"?

The evidence of the actual economic effect of immigration is inconclusive. The contribution of immigrant specialists to a high-tech economy has to be considered. Every working-age, well-trained immigrant who enters the country becomes a free resource, not schooled at American cost—a dividend from the brain drain. Even the "low-end" immigrants, including the "illegals" (or undocumented), may contribute as much in sales and other taxes and in purchasing power as they take out in services and schooling. The case has also been made that the undocumented aliens, fearful of discovery, rarely claim benefits due them. Thousands of employers likewise insist that without immigrants they could not staff the service industries or harvest the fields.

51

And the falling American birthrate suggests to some economists the possibility of labor shortages in the next century. They say that we can easily absorb half a million or so legal immigrants annually, perhaps more—though of what kind and for how long are left to debate.

But while debate went on, Congress did make a second change in the 1965 law. The Simpson-Mazzoli Act of 1986 tried to deal with two much-disputed issues. One was how to identify and count the unmeasured number of undocumented aliens already in the country without intrusive violations of civil liberties. The other was how to enforce immigration limits without a gigantic and costly expansion of the hard-pressed Immigration and Naturalization Service. The solution to the first problem was dealt with through an amnesty for pre-1982 immigrants; the second, by turning employers into enforcement agents. They would be "sanctioned" by fines if they hired undocumented aliens. The bill sparked bitter controversy in its career in three separate Congresses before final passage. Mexican-American organizations, for example, argued that employers, rather than risk sanctions, would simply refuse to hire Hispanic-looking or -sounding men and women. Employers complained about the cost and difficulty of checking credentials. But in the end a coalition for passage was established. It is still too early to tell how well the law is working.

It is not too early, however, to make some general predictions about the future course of the peopling of America. Immigration on the current scale, plus natural increase, will over time change the character of the people who inhabit these United States. Hispanic-descended men and women alone now constitute a little more than 22,000,000 in a population of about 248,000,000. By 2010 they are expected to number 39,300,000 in an overall population of about 282,000,000. In other words, their increase will account for 28 percent of the total population growth in that period. Another set of census projections for the period from 1990 to 2025 sees the white population declining from 84.3 to 75.6 percent, the black population percentage rising from 12.4 to 14.6, and the percentage of "other races" almost doubling, from 3.4 to 6.5. In some urban areas where the current crop of new immigrants clusters, the terms *nonwhite* and *minority* are no longer synonyms; in Los Angeles County, for example, only 15 percent of public school children are white.

We began with a reference to the many-tongued New York that Isaac Jogues found in 1643. It is appropriate to return for a look some 350 years afterward. The old tale continues. "Young Immigrant Wave Lifts New York Economy," runs a recent story in *The New York Times*. The paper found that the 2,600,000 foreign-born residents of the city (about one-third of the total population) had a positive effect. Their addition to the ranks of workers, small business owners, and consumers had probably kept New York from becoming "boarded up." No fewer than eighteen countries had sent 5,000 or more people to the hard-pressed metropolis from 1980 to 1986. At least 114 languages are spoken in the city's school systems. In one Queens school a sign directs visitors to register in English, Chinese, Korean, and Spanish. Among those photographed or interviewed for the article were a Serbian-speaking garment worker, a Romanian technician in a hematology laboratory, and an Albanian building owner who began as a superintendent.

And as in New York, so also in the other great cities of America in the 1990s—in Los Angeles (44 percent of adults foreign-born) and Miami (70 percent foreign-born), in Chicago, Dallas, Boston, in the ten largest cities of the land where increases in immigrant population offset the economic impact of the loss of other residents—and in the neighborhoods across the country where the new immigrants are working and raising their American children. For them the streets may not be paved with gold, but the dreams still glisten. What memories they will give their children, what gods they will worship, what leaders they will follow, what monuments they will create are all part of history yet to be written. It seems safe to say that, like the English, Scots, Irish, Germans, Swedes and Finns, Greeks, Poles, Italians, Hungarians, and Russians before them, they will neither "melt" into some undistinctive alloy nor, on the other hand, remain aloof and distinct from one another. Some kind of functional American mosaic will emerge. It is the historic way; the great Amazon that Melville described as America's noble bloodstream flows on undisturbed, into a new century.

CENSUS BUREAU FINDS SIGNIFICANT DEMOGRAPHIC DIFFERENCES AMONG IMMIGRANT GROUPS

Susan Lapham

A new report released today by the Commerce Department's Census Bureau on the nation's foreign-born population shows sharply varying levels of social-economic well-being among the various groups.

Susan Lapham, author of the report, *The Foreign Born Population in the United States: 1990 (CP-3-1)*, says, "An analysis of 1990 census information on recent immigrants (citizens and non-citizens) indicates that nearly 90 percent of African-born residents had a high school education or higher, compared with 76 percent of Asian-born and 46 percent of Central American-born residents. This report also shows that the per capita income of African immigrants was $20,117 in 1989, compared with $16,661 for Asian immigrants and $9,446 for foreign-born Central Americans. Family poverty rates for these same groups varied from 11.7 percent for foreign-born Africans to 13.1 percent for foreign-born Asians to 20.9 percent for foreign-born Central Americans.

The following additional highlights, extracted from the report's 400 pages of statistical tables, provide comparisons between foreign-born and natives:

- In 1990, about 20 million of the nation's total population were foreign-born and 229 million native-born. About 6 percent of immigrants entering the country between 1987 and 1990 were naturalized, compared with 10 percent of those entering between 1985 to 1986, 19 percent between 1982 to 1984, 27 percent from 1980 to 1981, and 61 percent before 1980.

- About 1 out of 5 adults, whether foreign born or native born, had a Bachelor's degree or higher in 1990. The ratio was 1 in 4 among immigrants who arrived after 1980 and 1 in 5 for those who arrived before 1980.

- About two-thirds of naturalized citizens had a high school diploma or more education in 1990, compared with slightly more than one-half of non-citizens. The gap was narrower for persons with a Bachelor's degree or more: 23 percent for naturalized and 19 percent for non-citizens.

- About 19 percent of families with a foreign-born householder had three or more workers in the family in 1990, compared with 13 percent among native-born families.

- About 19 percent each of naturalized and non-citizens had three or more workers in the family in 1990.

- Although the foreign born had a higher per capita income than the native born ($15,033 versus $14,367) in 1989, their median family income was almost $4,000 less than the native born ($31,785 versus $35,508).

- Although naturalized ($20,538) persons had a higher per capita income than non-citizens ($11,293) in 1989, their median family incomes were about the same at $31,754 and $31,943 respectively.

- The unemployment rate for foreign-born persons aged 16 and over was 7.8 percent in 1990, compared with 6.2 percent for the native born. Immigrants who entered since 1980 had an unemployment rate of nearly 10 percent, while those entering before 1980 had a rate of 6.4 percent.

- The unemployment rate for naturalized citizens (5.4 percent) was 4 percentage points lower than that for non-citizens (9.4 percent) in 1990.

- About 15 percent of families with a foreign-born householder were living in poverty in 1989, compared with nearly 10 percent of families with a native-born householder. Nearly 1 in 4 families with a foreign-born householder who entered the United

Reprinted with permission from *United States Department of Commerce News*, September 23, 1993, pp. 1-9.

States since 1980 were living in poverty—about twice the proportion (11 percent) of families with a foreign-born householder who entered before 1980.

- The poverty rate of families with a naturalized householder (8.7 percent) was 12 percentage points lower than that of comparable non-citizens (20.7 percent) in 1990.
- About 8 out of 10 of the foreign born (5 years and older) speak a language other than English at home. Nearly 9 out of 10 of those who have arrived since 1980 speak a language other than English at home, compared with 7 out of 10 of those who arrived before 1980.
- About 7 out of 10 naturalized citizens (5 years and older) speak a language other than English at home in 1990, compared with more than 8 out of 10 non-citizens.

Since data in this report are from the sample portion of the decennial census, they are subject to sampling variability.

Editor's Note: One-page demographic profiles (CPH-L-148) for 47 countries of origin and regions as well as tables that rank 38 of the countries by selected characteristics are available on request. In addition, a five-page summary of social and economic highlights for foreign-born persons now living in the U.S. who were born in Europe, the Soviet Union, Asia, North and South America, Africa or Oceania, also are available.

Other reports planned for release by the bureau in this series (CP-3) include ancestry, persons of Hispanic origin and Asian and Pacific Islanders.

The bureau has also started releasing, on a flow basis, subject summary tape files (SSTFs). The tapes include the same types of data shown in the reports, but provide additional geographic detail. These files are designed to meet the data needs expressed by users who have a special interest in selected subjects or subgroups of the population.

Media representatives may obtain copies of the report on the foreign population from the bureau's Public Information Office on 301-763-4040. Subject Summary Tape Files can be ordered from the bureau's Customer Services Office on 301-763-4100. Non-media orders for any of these products should go to the Customer Services Office.

born elderly than the respective native born populations.

More foreign born men than women have entered the country since 1980 resulting in a sex ratio of 110 males per 100 females. Foreign born who entered prior to 1980 had a sex ratio of 86 males per 100 females. Foreign born Africans have the highest sex ratio, 146 males per 100 females, while foreign born Canadians have the lowest sex ratio of 70 males per 100 females.

On average, foreign born women have 2,254 children ever born per 1,000 women, compared with 1,927 children ever born per 1,000 women for native born women.

Nativity, place of birth, and year of entry	Median age	Children ever born[1]	Sex ratio[2]
Native born	32.5	1,927	94.9
Foreign born	37.3	2,254	95.8
Entered 1980 to 1990	28.0	2,200	110.3
Entered before 1980	46.5	2,282	85.8
Naturalized	36.3	2,098	87.0
Entered 1980 to 1990	29.5	2,062	113.2
Entered before 1980	45.3	2,104	83.0
Not a citizen	38.0	2,371	102.3
Entered 1980 to 1990	27.8	2,230	110.0
Entered before 1980	51.2	2,512	90.3
Europe	53.2	1,865	77.8
Soviet Union	54.6	1,690	82.3
Asia	35.4	1,997	96.1
North America	33.2	2,718	104.2
Canada	52.9	1,772	70.3
Mexico	29.9	3,289	122.9
Caribbean	39.0	2,144	88.3
Central America	30.5	2,518	96.1
South American	35.1	1.931	93.4
Africa	33.9	2,202	145.6
Oceania	36.1	2,187	83.5

[1]Per 1,000 women 35 to 44 years old.
[2]Males per 100 females.

Source: Bureau of the Census, 1990 Census of Population and Housing, CP-3-1, The Foreign-Born Population in the United States: 1990.

Demographic Characteristics of the Foreign-Born

On average, the foreign born population is about 5 years older than the native born population. However, those who have entered the country since 1980 have a median age which is about 5 years younger than the median age for the foreign born.

About half the native born population is concentrated among the working ages (25 to 64 years old), compared with 64 percent of the foreign born. There are relatively fewer foreign born children or foreign

Language Ability of the Foreign Born

About 79 percent of the foreign born (5 years old and over) speak a language other than English in their homes and about 28 percent of the foreign born live in households which are linguistically isolated.

About 88 percent of those foreign born who have arrived since 1980 do not speak English at home, compared with about 72 percent of those who arrived before 1980.

Nearly 42 percent of the foreign born who have

arrived since 1980 are linguistically isolated, compared with only 18 percent of those who arrived before 1980.

Over 96 percent of foreign born Mexicans speak a language other than English at home, while about 60 percent of foreign born Europeans speak a language other than English at home.

Nativity, place of birth, and year of entry	Speak a language other than English	Do not speak English "very well"	Linguistically isolated[1]
Native born	7.8	2.3	1.2
Foreign born	79.1	47.0	28.2
Entered 1980 to 1990	88.0	59.9	41.6
Entered before 1980	72.4	37.2	18.0
Naturalized	70.6	32.7	16.8
Entered 1980 to 1990	86.9	49.9	31.8
Entered before 1980	67.6	29.6	14.1
Not a citizen	85.0	56.8	36.0
Entered 1980 to 1990	88.2	61.6	43.3
Entered before 1980	79.7	48.8	24.0
Europe	59.5	26.1	13.4
Soviet Union	81.1	52.1	39.9
Asia	91.6	49.9	30.0
North America	81.6	56.8	35.1
Canada	19.2	5.0	2.4
Mexico	96.1	70.7	43.5
Caribbean	67.8	42.8	25.5
Central America	92.7	63.3	41.4
South American	82.8	48.1	27.3
Africa	74.9	23.4	12.4
Oceania	46.1	17.5	7.3

[1]Linguistic isolation refers to persons in households in which no one 14 years old or over speaks only English and no one who speaks a language other than English speaks English "very well."

Source: Bureau of the Census, 1990 Census of Population and Housing, CP-3-1, The Foreign-Born Population in the United States: 1990.

Employment and Occupation Characteristics of the Foreign Born

The unemployment rate for native born persons 16 years and over was 6.2 percent, compared with 7.8 percent for the foreign born.

Foreign born who have entered since 1980 have an unemployment rate of nearly 10 percent. Those foreign born who entered before 1980 have unemployment rates more similar to the native born population.

Foreign born from the Soviet Union had the highest unemployment rate, about 13 percent, while foreign born Canadians had the lowest unemployment rate at 4.2 percent.

Just over 70 percent of the native born workers held skilled occupations, compared with 60 percent of foreign born workers.

Thirteen percent of families with a native born householder, compared with 19 percent of families with a foreign born householder had 3 or more workers in the family.

Nativity, place of birth, and year of entry	Unemployed	Employed in skilled occupations[1]	3 or more workers in family
Native born	6.2	70.5	12.8
Foreign born	7.8	59.5	18.5
Entered 1980 to 1990	9.6	51.2	16.6
Entered before 1980	6.4	65.3	19.4
Naturalized	5.4	69.6	18.5
Entered 1980 to 1990	7.5	56.7	18.6
Entered before 1980	5	72.1	18.5
Not a citizen	9.4	52.3	18.6
Entered 1980 to 1990	10	50.1	16.2
Entered before 1980	8.5	55.3	20.9
Europe	4.8	71.4	18.6
Soviet Union	13.3	76.7	10.2
Asia	5.6	71.8	19.1
North America	10.1	45.7	20.8
Canada	4.2	80.8	11.1
Mexico	11.3	34.3	23.5
Caribbean	9.4	59.7	18.6
Central America	10.2	43.2	21.9
South American	7.5	60.3	19.6
Africa	6.8	71.5	11.6
Oceania	5.5	70.5	14.6

[1]Skilled occupations include the general categories of managerial and professional speciality; technical, sales, and administrative support; and precision production, craft and repair occupations.

Source: Bureau of the Census, 1990 Census of Population and Housing, CP-3-1, The Foreign-Born Population in the United States: 1990.

Educational Attainment of the Foreign Born

One of every four foreign-born adults (25 years old and over) had less than a 9th grade education in 1990, compared with less than 1 of every 10 native born adults.

About 59 percent of the foreign born adults had a high school diploma or higher, compared with 77 percent of native born adults. However, foreign born and native born adults had nearly the same proportion who had a bachelor's degree or higher in 1990. And, the foreign born had a higher proportion than the native born of adults who had graduate degrees or higher, 3.8 percent versus 2.4 percent.

Estimated Resident Illegal Alien Population: October 1992

State of residence	Number	Pct.	Country or area of origin	Number	Pct.
U.S. TOTAL	3,200,000	100	N. America	2,100,000	66
			Asia	335,000	10
			Europe	310,000	10
California	1,275,000	40	S. America	200,000	10
New York	483,000	15	Africa	120,000	4
Florida	345,000	11	Oceania	15,000	–
Texas	320,000	10			
Illinois	170,000	5			
New Jersey	125,000	4	Mexico	1,002,000	31
Massachussetts	48,000	2	El Salvador	258,000	9
Arizona	47,000	1	Guatemala	121,000	4
Virginia	37,300	1	Canada	104,000	3
Georgia	28,000	1	Poland	102,000	3
			Philippines	101,000	3
Maryland	27,500	1	Haiti	98,000	3
Washington	26,200	1	Nicaragua	76,000	2
Pennsylvania	18,800	1	Colombia	75,000	2
Connecticut	17,000	1	The Bahamas	72,000	2
Oregon	16,600	1			
Nevada	16,400	1	Honduras	69,000	2
New Mexico	16,000	1	Italy	67,000	2
North Carolina	15,500	–	Ecuador	53,000	2
Colorado	14,500	–	Dom. Rep.	51,000	2
D.C.	14,500	–	Jamaica	50,000	2
			Trinidad	41,000	1
All other	136,700	4	Iran	37,000	1
			Ireland	37,000	1
Michigan, Oklahoma, Rhode Island, Utah, Louisiana, Ohio, and Hawaii.	6,000–9,900		Pakistan	33,000	1
			Portugal	32,000	1
			All other	681,000	21
Kansas, Wisconsin, Idaho, S. Carolina, Indiana, Minnesota, Tennessee, Missouri and Alabama.	3,000–5,500		India, Peru, Israel, China, Dominica, and Nigeria	24,000–30,000	
Nebraska, Arkansas, Iowa, Delaware, Alaska, Kentucky, Mississippit, and New Hampshire.	1,200–2,400		Yugoslavia, Lebanon, Guyana, Belize and France	15,000–19,000	
Wyoming, West Virginia, Montana, Maine, Vermont, North Dakota, and South Dakota.	100–700		All countries not listed above	Less than 15,000	

Source: INS Office of Strategic Planning, Statistics Division.

Foreign born Africans have the highest proportion of high school graduation or higher, 88 percent. This is about 12 percentage points higher than foreign born Asians, and about 15 percentage points higher than foreign born Canadians. Africans also have a higher proportion of bachelor's degrees or higher than any other immigrant group. Over 47 percent of foreign born Africans completed at least a bachelor's degree, compared with about 38 percent of foreign born Asians. On average, foreign born from Central American and Caribbean countries and Mexico were less educated than those from Africa, Asia, or Europe.

Nativity, place of birth, and year of entry	Per capita income	Median family income	Family poverty
Native born	$14,367	$35,508	9.5
Foreign born	$15,033	$31,785	14.9
Entered since 1980	$ 9,408	$24,595	23.4
Entered before 1980	$19,423	$35,733	11.0
Naturalized	$20,538	$31,754	8.7
Entered 1980 to 1990	$12,100	$29,257	18.0
Entered before 1980	$22,102	$36,028	7.5
Not a citizen	$11,293	$31,943	20.7
Entered 1980 to 1990	$ 8,954	$23,576	24.6
Entered before 1980	$15,274	$33,748	16.9
Europe	$20,904	$40,428	5.1
Soviet Union	$15,012	$28,799	18.5
Asia	$16,661	$39,395	13.1
North America	$11,225	$24,963	21.5
Canada	$21,904	$39,995	4.9
Mexico	$ 8,483	$21,585	27.4
Caribbean	$14,225	$29,464	16.4
Central America	$ 9,446	$23,587	20.9
South American	$14,955	$32,750	11.7
Africa	$20,117	$36,783	11.7
Oceania	$19,200	$39,775	11.6

Source: Bureau of the Census, 1990 Census of Population and Housing, CP-3-1, The Foreign-Born Population in the United States: 1990.

Nativity, place of birth, and year of entry	High school diploma or higher	Bachelor's degree or higher
Native born	77.0	20.3
Foreign born	58.8	20.4
Entered since 1980	59.4	23.7
Entered before 1980	58.5	18.7
Naturalized	65.4	22.5
Entered since 1980	65.6	23.6
Entered before 1980	65.3	22.3
Not a citizen	53.1	18.5
Entered since 1980	58.3	23.7
Entered before 1980	47.1	12.5
Europe	63.5	18.0
Soviet Union	64.0	27.1
Asia	75.8	38.4
North America	41.6	9.1
Canada	72.6	22.1
Mexico	24.3	3.5
Caribbean	56.9	13.6
Central America	45.7	8.5
South American	71.3	20.0
Africa	87.9	47.1
Oceania	77.0	24.2

Source: Bureau of the Census, 1990 Census of Population and Housing, CP-3-1, The Foreign-Born Population in the United States: 1990.

Income and Poverty of the Foreign Born

Although the foreign born have a higher per capita income than the native born population, their median family income was almost $4,000 less than the native born.

About 15 percent of families with a foreign born householder were below the poverty rate, compared with nearly 10 percent of native born families.

The per capita income of foreign born who have entered since 1980 is less than half the per capita income of foreign born who entered this country before 1980.

Nearly 1 of 4 families with a foreign born householder who entered the country since 1980 were living in poverty, compared with just over 1 of 10 families with a foreign born householder who entered before 1980.

The Foreign-Born Population: 1994

Kristin A. Hansen and Amara Bachu

Nearly 1 in 11 Americans are foreign-born

In 1994, 8.7 percent of the population of the United States was foreign-born — nearly double the percent foreign-born in 1970 (4.8 percent). While the percent foreign-born is at its highest level since before World War II, much greater proportions of the U.S. population were foreign-born during the early part of this century. From a high of 14.7 percent in 1910, the percent foreign-born declined to a low of 4.8 percent in 1970. Since that time, the percent has steadily increased.

One-third of the foreign-born live in California...

The foreign-born population is not distributed evenly throughout the country. California is home to 7.7 million foreign-born persons — more than one-third of all immigrants to the U.S. and nearly one-quarter of all California residents. New York ranks second with 2.9 million and Florida ranks third with 2.1 million foreign-born. Three other States have over 1 million foreign-born residents — Texas, Illinois, and New Jersey.

"Natives" are persons born in the United States, Puerto Rico, or an outlying area of the U.S., such as Guam or the U.S. Virgin Islands, and persons who were born in a foreign country but who had at least one parent who was a U.S. citizen. All other persons born outside the United States are "foreign-born."

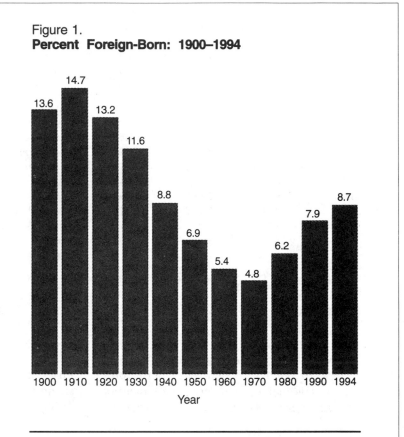

Figure 1.
Percent Foreign-Born: 1900–1994

13.6 14.7 13.2 11.6 8.8 6.9 5.4 4.8 6.2 7.9 8.7

1900 1910 1920 1930 1940 1950 1960 1970 1980 1990 1994
Year

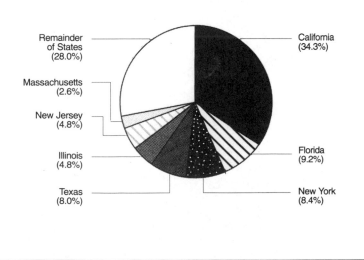

Figure 2.
Foreign-Born Population by State of Residence

Remainder of States (28.0%)
Massachusetts (2.6%)
New Jersey (4.8%)
Illinois (4.8%)
Texas (8.0%)
California (34.3%)
Florida (9.2%)
New York (8.4%)

From *Current Population Reports,* August 1995, pp. 1-5. Published by the U.S. Department of Commerce, Economics and Statistics Administration.

Year of entry

Twenty percent of the foreign-born population came to the U.S. in the last 5 years. Twice as many came per year during the 1990's than during the 1970's—4.5 million persons arrived in the 5-year period between 1990 and 1994 while 4.8 million came during the decade of the 1970's. Nearly as many came per year during the 1980's (8.3 million total) as in the last 5 years. The remainder of the foreign-born came to the U.S. prior to 1970.

Country of birth...

Of the 22,568,000 foreign-born persons living in the United States in March 1994, 6.2 million came from Mexico. Mexico was by far the country of origin with the largest number of immigrants. The next largest group was from the Philippines—1,033,000.

... by year of entry

Of the 4.5 million most recent immigrants, over a quarter (1.3 million) came from Mexico and an additional 243,000 came from Russia. Other countries with large numbers of recent immigrants include Vietnam, the Dominican Republic, the Philippines, India, and El Salvador.

During the 1980's, the largest numbers of immigrants came from Mexico (2,671,000) and the Philippines (424,000). China, Korea, the Dominican Republic, and Cuba also contributed large numbers. Prior to 1970, Mexico was still the most frequent country of origin (768,000), but the other top countries of origin were very different from today. They included Germany, Cuba, Italy, Canada, and England.

Citizenship

Foreign-born persons over the age of 18 can become "naturalized citizens" of the United States after they have lived here for a minimum of 5 years and have passed a citizenship exam. Spouses of U.S. citizens (and certain others) can become

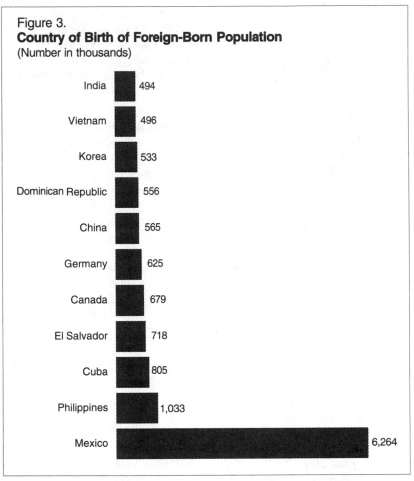

Figure 3.
Country of Birth of Foreign-Born Population
(Number in thousands)

Country	Number
India	494
Vietnam	496
Korea	533
Dominican Republic	556
China	565
Germany	625
Canada	679
El Salvador	718
Cuba	805
Philippines	1,033
Mexico	6,264

naturalized after 3 years and children who immigrate generally become citizens when their parents are naturalized. About 31 percent of the foreign-born population in the United States are naturalized citizens.

Foreign-born persons are older than natives....

The median age of all foreign-born persons in the United States (37 years) is higher than the median age for natives (33 years). But when the foreign-born population is divided into those who are naturalized citizens and those who are not citizens, a very different picture is formed. Only naturalized citizens are older on average (48 years) than natives.

... and younger than natives

Age and year of entry have obvious connections. The most recent immigrants are younger on average than natives. Those

who came to the United States between 1990 and 1994 have a median age of only 26 years.

Race and Hispanic origin

More than two-thirds of the foreign-born population are White, about 1 in 5 are Asian or Pacific Islander, and only 7.1 percent are Black. The remainder reported their race as either "American Indian, Eskimo, or Aleut" or "other race." Nearly half (45.5 percent) of all foreign-born persons are of Hispanic origin.

Nearly two-thirds of the Asian and Pacific Islanders in the United States are foreign-born and most of the immigrants (91.7 percent) entered this country since 1970. Although 38.5 percent of the persons of Hispanic origin in this country are foreign-born and most have lived in the U.S. long enough to qualify for naturalization, only 18.3 percent are naturalized citizens.

Fertility

In June 1994, there were 6.2 million foreign-born women 15 to 44 years old, representing 10.4 percent of all women in the United States in the childbearing ages. These women had borne 1.5 children each compared with 1.2 children borne to native-born women. About 68 percent of these women in childbearing ages immigrated to the United States after 1980. Women who became naturalized citizens had borne an average of 1.5 children each, not significantly different from the average reported by non-citizens.

Educational attainment

While it seems a paradox, the foreign-born are both more educated and less educated than natives. Recent immigrants 25 years and over are more likely to have a college degree than either natives or earlier immigrants. While 11.5 percent of recent immigrants have a graduate or professional degree, only about 7.5 percent of natives and immigrants in earlier years have such degrees. Recent immigrants are also more likely to have bachelor's degrees (20.9 percent) than either natives (14.7 percent) or earlier immigrants (13.9 percent).[1]

On the other hand, immigrants are also less likely to have graduated from high school than natives. Only 17.1 percent of natives over the age of 25 are not high school graduates while 36.0 percent of immigrants do not have high school degrees.

Labor force status

The foreign-born population has a higher unemployment rate than do natives (9.1 percent versus 6.8 percent, respectively). However, the unemployment

rate of naturalized citizens is no different statistically from that of natives. Foreign-born persons who are not citizens have the highest unemployment rate (10.7 percent).

Income in 1993

Foreign-born persons as a group had a lower median income in 1993 than natives ($12,179 versus $15,876) but this difference seems to be related to length of residence. Foreign-born persons who immigrated during the 1970's have median incomes no different than that of natives. Recent immigrants have the lowest median income ($8,393) of all immigrants by period of entry into the United States.

Receipt of public assistance

Recent immigrants are more likely to receive public assistance income than natives (5.7 percent versus 2.9 percent). The rates drop significantly for immigrants who have been here for 5 or more years. The rates for foreign-born persons who entered during the 1970's and 1980's are not significantly different from those of natives or recent immigrants. And immigrants who arrived before 1970 are less likely to be receiving public assistance (1.4 percent) than natives.

Aid to Families with Dependent Children (AFDC) is the primary source of public assistance income in the CPS data[2]; most natives and immigrants who are receiving some kind of public assistance are receiving AFDC.

Poverty status

While the data on income and receipt of public assistance are limited to persons ages 16 and over, poverty status is based upon family income and persons of all ages are tallied as to

whether or not they are in a family above or below the poverty line. The foreign-born are 1.6 times more likely to be in poverty that natives (22.9 versus 14.4 percent). And recent immigrants are over twice as likely to be in poverty (37.1 percent). Only persons who immigrated prior to 1970 are less likely than natives to be in poverty (10.8 percent).

Tenure

Homeownership is one indicator of economic well being. While over two-thirds of natives live in owner-occupied housing units, less than half of the foreign-born live in owner-occupied housing. Homeownership among immigrants increases with length of residence; while persons who immigrated before 1970 have homeownership rates higher than natives, only 17.5 percent of recent immigrants are living in their own homes.

Source of the data

The Current Population Survey began collecting monthly data on nativity in January of 1994. Each respondent was asked where they were born and the country of birth of each of their parents. Persons born outside of the United States were also asked their citizenship status and the year they came to the United States to live. Most of the characteristics of the foreign-born population shown in this brief report are from the March 1994 supplement to the Current Population Survey; the data on fertility are from June 1994.

The foreign-born population in this report include some undocumented immigrants, refugees, and temporary residents such as students and temporary workers as well as the legally admitted immigrants included in data from the Immigration and Naturalization Service.

---

[1]The percentages for natives and earlier immigrants are not significantly different from each other. Educational attainment by race and Hispanic origin and by country of origin are available in the detailed tabulation package.

---

[2]The CPS does not include the value of non-cash benefits, such as food stamps, as public assistance income.

Table 1. Selected Characteristics of Natives and the Foreign-Born Population by Citizenship and Year of Entry: 1994

(Numbers in thousands)

Characteristic	Native	Foreign born Total	Natural- ized citizen	Not a citizen	Before 1970	1970 to 1979	1980 to 1989	1990 to 1994
Age								
Total.......................	237,184	22,568	6,975	15,593	4,974	4,781	8,311	4,502
Under 5 years....................	20,160	298	28	270	0	0	24	274
5 to 17 years....................	47,118	2,190	245	1,945	0	88	1,203	899
18 to 24 years....................	22,839	2,636	383	2,253	1	533	1,196	904
25 to 29 years....................	17,034	2,592	412	2,180	106	402	1,410	673
30 to 34 years....................	19,643	2,677	599	2,078	251	578	1,324	524
35 to 44 years....................	37,006	4,522	1,489	3,033	662	1,528	1,757	575
45 to 64 years....................	45,245	5,014	2,193	2,821	2,088	1,359	1,069	498
65 years and over..................	28,139	2,640	1,626	1,014	1,864	293	328	154
Median age (years)	32.9	37.0	48.0	32.8	59.1	40.2	31.2	26.3
Sex								
Male	115,782	11,132	3,203	7,929	2,165	2,318	4,381	2,269
Female	121,402	11,436	3,772	7,664	2,810	2,463	3,930	2,233
Race and Hispanic origin								
White........................	199,793	15,428	4,749	10,680	4,313	3,058	5,190	2,867
Black........................	31,443	1,596	343	1,253	200	342	738	317
Asian or Pacific Islander	2,813	4,630	1,701	2,929	386	1,176	1,992	1,076
Hispanic origin[1]	16,376	10,270	1,879	8,391	1,560	2,334	4,404	1,971
Fertility[2]								
Women 15 to 44 years	53,849	6,239	1,439	4,801	620	1,366	2,752	1,501
Children ever born per 1,000.........	1,208	1,539	1,486	1,554	1,880	1,787	1,561	1,129
Educational Attainment								
Total 25 years and over........	147,067	17,445	6,319	11,126	4,972	4,161	5,887	2,423
Not high school graduate	25,166	6,274	1,538	4,736	1,590	1,574	2,302	807
High school grad/some college	89,382	7,147	3,085	4,062	2,402	1,667	2,245	831
Bachelor's degree	21,660	2,596	1,097	1,499	588	620	882	506
Graduate or professional degree......	10,859	1,428	599	830	392	300	458	279
Labor Force Status								
Total 16 years and over[3].......	176,607	20,559	6,764	13,795	4,974	4,748	7,334	3,504
In the civilian labor force	116,281	12,883	4,151	8,732	2,482	3,360	5,100	1,939
Employed.....................	108,402	11,706	3,905	7,801	2,342	3,077	4,583	1,703
Unemployed...................	7,880	1,176	245	931	140	283	517	236
Not in the labor force...............	59,411	7,635	2,580	5,056	2,485	1,363	2,223	1,565
Income in 1993								
Total 16 years and over........	176,607	20,559	6,764	13,795	4,974	4,748	7,334	3,504
Without income	10,540	2,802	380	2,421	210	504	1,144	943
With income	166,067	17,757	6,384	11,374	4,764	4,244	6,190	2,561
$1 to $9,999 or loss..............	57,416	7,283	2,064	5,217	1,759	1,478	2,614	1,429
$10,000 to $19,999	39,905	4,909	1,664	3,244	1,197	1,208	1,887	615
$20,000 to $34,999	36,994	3,067	1,361	1,707	938	825	1,001	303
$35,000 to $49,999	17,122	1,252	618	633	400	376	392	83
$50,000 or more	14,629	1,248	676	571	471	356	293	129
Median income (dollars)...........	$15,876	$12,179	$16,103	$10,930	$14,473	$15,121	$11,580	$8,393
Received Public Assistance[4].......	5,076	758	82	676	72	162	323	201
Received AFDC	4,082	550	63	487	57	121	257	116
Poverty Status[5]								
In poverty	34,086	5,179	707	4,472	535	778	2,195	1,672
Not in poverty	202,659	17,355	6,266	11,088	4,440	4,004	6,106	2,805
Tenure								
In owner-occupied unit	162,805	10,416	4,925	5,492	3,820	2,818	2,989	790
In renter-occupied unit..............	74,379	12,152	2,050	10,102	1,154	1,964	5,323	3,712

[1]Persons of Hispanic origin may be of any race. [2]Data from the June 1994 CPS. [3]Includes persons in Armed Forces, not shown separately. [4]Does not include non-cash benefits such as food stamps. [5]Persons for whom poverty status is determined.

More information

A package of tables showing detailed characteristics of the foreign-born by country of birth and selected states is available on floppy disk for $40 or on paper for $63 from Population Division's Statistical Information Office at 301-457-2422. The table package is also available on the Internet (www.census.gov); look for Foreign-born Data from the Population Division. Technical information about the collection, processing, and quality of the nativity data from the CPS is available in "Evaluation of Nativity Data from the Current Population Survey" by Gregg Robinson (forthcoming). Public Use Tapes of the Current Population Survey can be purchased from Customer Services at 301-457-4100.

Contacts

Nativity statistics —
Kristin A. Hansen
301-457-2454
KAHANSEN@CENSUS.GOV

Fertility statistics—
Amara Bachu
301-457-2449
ABACHU@CENSUS.GOV

The statistics in this report are subject to sampling variability, as well as survey design flaws, respondent classification errors, and data processing mistakes. The Census Bureau has taken steps to minimize errors, and analytical statements have been tested and meet statistical standards. However, because of methodological differences, use caution when comparing these data with data from other sources. For information on the source of data and the accuracy of estimates, including the use and computation of standard errors, see the "Source and Accuracy Statement" that accompanies the tabulation package.

Is Latest Wave a Drain or Boon to Society?

Critics want to focus more on skills, less on family ties

Maria Puente

USA TODAY

What once were private mutterings that immigrants are more a drain than a benefit to society have become bold public pronouncements.

Many politicians and ordinary citizens now say legal immigrants should be admitted only if they have good job skills, not because they happen to have a sister living in New York.

Some even say immigrants, arriving at near-record levels, are radically changing the ethnic and cultural balance of the country—and the country needs to change back.

The question before Congress and the people has become: Are immigrants still good for the country?

In a computer analysis of data on the 2.2 million people who became legal immigrants in 1993–93, USA TODAY illustrates how newcomers have changed the nation, bringing new colors and languages, a new vibrancy and vigor.

But the analysis also documents how densely immigrants from a few countries have clustered in some cities, bringing strained public budgets, community tension and, often, few marketable job skills.

Using current proposals to restrict immigration as its framework, the computer analysis finds:

• If job skills replaced kinship as the basis for immigration, it would greatly alter who gets into the country. The immigrant stream would become more European and Asian, less Hispanic and Caribbean.

In 1993, for example, 52% of immigrants from Mexico—by far the largest immigrant group—identified themselves as laborers, excluding homemakers, retirees and students. That compared to 7% from China and 1% from India.

By contrast, 0.3% of Mexicans identified themselves as engineers, compared to 25% of Indians.

Overall, more than half the 1993 immigrants of working age report low-skilled or unskilled occupations.

• If immigration of extended families had been restricted in 1993, 85% of the 880,014 people admitted to the USA would have gotten in.

Indeed, the analysis underscores the overwhelming family character of immigration. In 1993, almost two-thirds of immigrants were admitted solely because they were related—either closely or in an extended fashion—to someone already here.

• If a small but growing minority of restrictionists gets its way, future immigrants would be far different from those who actually arrived.

In 1993, about 80% of legal immigrants were from Latino, Asian, African and Caribbean countries, and just a few countries dominated the stream: People from Mexico, China, the Philippines, Vietnam and the Dominican Republic made up nearly 40% of all immigrants.

By comparison, 97% of immigrants who came 100 years ago were European or Canadian.

• If immigrants came for jobs instead of kinship, they likely would be scattered across the USA.

Between 1991–93, however, the nation's immigrant clusters stood out. Selected ZIP codes in New York City, Los Angeles, Chicago, Miami and Houston together averaged 206,000 new immigrants a year.

The cumulative effect of all these trends, experts say, has pushed so many social buttons that a nation of immigrants is wondering whether it should remain one.

There is "uneasiness over the scale of immigration," Nathan Galzer, a Harvard professor and immigration expert, says in a recent essay. "When this coincides with bad economic conditions, a majority of Americans will say, 'There is too much immigration.' "

Here is one fact: If immigration continues at the current rate of about 800,000 a year, more than 8 million newcomers will have arrived between 1990 and 2000—the highest decade-long number since 1900–1910.

59% FAVOR 'BLENDING IN'

For 30 years, since the 1965 Immigration Act opened the nation's doors to immigrants from around the world, the country's political and social culture has assumed that immigration is a positive force.

Many Americans are not feeling so generous these days.

"Now we're coming at (immigration) from a new perspective—what's in the best interest of American *citizens*," says Rep. Lamar Smith, R-Texas, head of the House subcommittee on immigration.

His counterpart in the Senate, Alan Simpson, R-Wyo., echoes that view: "The national interest is the interest of the majority of Americans, not the interests of those seeking to come here or (their) relatives."

Smith and Simpson argue the United States should reduce overall numbers and admit only those "who will contribute to our economy and our society"—meaning those who are educated, job-skilled, English-speaking and quickly naturalized.

A USA TODAY/CNN/Gallup Poll of immigrants—the first comprehensive, national poll of its kind—finds many immigrants agree.

"If we are not selective on immigrants, it will expedite the deterioration of this country," says David Chen, 30, an insurance adjuster in New York who came from Taiwan. "They have to be self-supportive."

Immigrants and natives also are in agreement about the need for immigrants to assimilate: 59% of both groups say "blending in" is better.

Luis Llanos, 25, a Colombian who immigrated in 1986 and now lives in New York, says he's eager to fit in.

"Some (immigrants) say they don't like it here, but I say to them, 'Nobody brought you here, you don't have to be here,' " Llanos says.

But there is a viable, vocal coalition of immigrant advocates led by Sen. Ted Kennedy, D-Mass., who say they'll fight to preserve the traditional view of immigrants.

"We live in a diverse world," says Kennedy, sponsor of the 1965 law. "The genius of America has been to take different traditions and draw on them (to) enhance the country."

'SENSE OF LOSS OF CONTROL'

In part, the drive to change the immigration system is a consequence of public resentment of unchecked illegal immigration, now estimated at about 300,000 people a year.

Few politicians can ignore the overwhelming passage last year of Proposition 187 in California, which denies illegal immigrants access to benefits, schools and health services.

"There is this sense of loss of control," says Bill Ong Hing, an immigration expert at Stanford University. "I don't think we have (lost control), but there's a sense of that."

Add to that the uncertainty caused by the economic restructuring of the '90s, both in high and low level jobs.

In Atlanta, for example, seeing sizeable immigration for the first time, an undercurrent of tension has developed over fears about jobs.

Some "see immigrants as a threat to their job opportunities," says Jeffery Tapia, director of the Latin American Association. "When you're looking to survive,

anyone who's a newcomer is seen as a threat."

But the impetus for change also may be based on a change in the immigrants themselves.

Today, Europeans make up just 18% of the immigrant stream, with 54% of newcomers from Asia, Africa and the Caribbean.

Most of these immigrants are not white, and some advocates say restrictionism is, at base, racism.

"A lot of their (arguments) are code words for, 'We don't want Mexicans or Asians,' " says Karen Narasaki of the National Asian Pacific American Legal Consortium.

A few restrictionists are blunt.

"Why this many? Why these particular immigrants? These questions are never addressed," says journalist Peter Brimelow, author of *Alien Nation,* a controver-

sial book about "America's immigration disaster."

But these questions are being addressed by the national Commission on Immigration Reform, which this month called on Congress to cut immigration to 550,000 a year, largely by eliminating some categories of immigrants and reducing others.

MANY WANT A 'TIME OUT'

Even assuming some change in immigration is necessary, there's no consensus on what kind. The various factions overlap on some important details but strongly disagree on others. Conservatives and liberals can be found on the same side:

• The *Alien Nation* faction argues there are too many immigrants and too many of the "wrong kind"—instead of skilled, white Europeans. They want a "time out" in immigration, and the highest priority to go to newcomers with skills.

Brimelow argues that immigration has changed the country "in a radical and rapid way unprecedented in history."

"Americans have the right to insist the government stop shifting the racial balance," he says.

Republican presidential candidate Patrick Buchanan supports this view, as do most restrictionist groups.

• Another faction argues that the system is mostly working, and the number of immigrants is acceptable, but that not enough is being done to "Americanize" them.

House Speaker Newt Gingrich is in this camp, along with GOP leaders Bill Bennett and Jack Kemp and many Democrats in Congress.

• Yet another faction favors even more generous immigration policies. Kennedy is a major voice here, along with a throng of advocacy groups. House Majority Leader Dick Armey, R-Texas, also is a philosophical ally.

"I'm hard-pressed to think of a single problem that would be solved by shutting off the supply of willing and eager new Americans," says Armey.

So far, President Clinton comes down somewhere in the middle, and backs the commission's proposals.

'WE HAVE TO DISCRIMINATE'

The profusion of immigration issues is bewildering, but these are some of the points of contention:

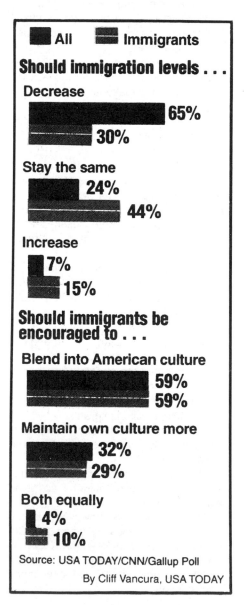

All   **Immigrants**

Should immigration levels . . .

Decrease
65%
30%

Stay the same
24%
44%

Increase
7%
15%

Should immigrants be encouraged to . . .

Blend into American culture
59%
59%

Maintain own culture more
32%
29%

Both equally
4%
10%

Source: USA TODAY/CNN/Gallup Poll

By Cliff Vancura, USA TODAY

The numbers. Because the commission is so influential, its recommendation for a relatively modest one-third reduction in the number of immigrants is likely to be adopted.

"Between the total restrictionists and the total open-border people, that's where we'll steer the boat," says Simpson.

Chain migration. The bulk of immigrants are spouses, children, grandchildren, siblings and parents of citizens or legal permanent residents. And once immigrants arrive, they may sponsor more relatives.

Wei Ming Wong, 41, an immigrant living in Los Angeles, can tick off 12 relatives who came to the USA thanks to one sister. "There is no one left" in Hong Kong, Wong says.

Cutting this chain migration is at the heart of the commission's proposals. It recommended immigration priority to go to nuclear families—spouses and minor children—and that the door be shut to siblings, their families and adult children.

These recommendations probably will be adopted by Congress.

Immigrant skills. Critics argue that immigration would best serve the nation if admissions were weighted on the basis of skills.

"We have to discriminate among people who want to come," says George Borjas, an economist at the University of California, San Diego, and a Cuban immigrant. "Choosing high-skilled workers is better."

Accepting that, the commission wants to eliminate 10,000 immigration slots now set aside for unskilled workers; Congress is likely to agree.

Immigrants and welfare. People cannot immigrate if they are likely to become a public charge. But courts have ruled that sponsorship "contracts" aren't enforceable.

Even advocates agree that's a huge loophole, and Congress is virtually certain to plug it. "We're going to look at sponsorship, set additional responsibilities," says Kennedy.

In addition, bills in Congress would cut off non-citizens from Supplementary Security Income—a program that provides aid to the poor and disabled. Non-citizens now make up about 30% of all SSI recipients.

The debate over all these aspects of immigration will begin in earnest this summer, and most experts are betting that the nation's door will close somewhat—but not entirely.

"The U.S. is largely what it is today because of our ability to draw and assimilate new peoples," says Arthur Helton, immigration expert at the Open Society Institute. "That has . . . resulted in displacement and conflict from time to time, but without it, we would not be America."

Pride and Prejudice

An immigrant author says multicultural policy creates ethnic ghettos

Montreal-based novelist Neil Bissoondath likes to tell the story of how four representatives of the federal multiculturalism department tracked him a couple of years ago to a citizenship conference in Ottawa, where he was giving a speech. Following his talk—in which the Trinidadian-born author repeated his oft-stated view that Canada's policy of official multiculturalism has served only to create ethnic ghettos—one of the federal officials took to the microphone to challenge Bissoondath. She told him, he says, that he should just "shut up" because all he was doing was "encouraging racists, like the Reform party." A hush fell on the room, Bissoondath recalls, "because it occurred to everyone that what we had here was a federal bureaucrat telling a Canadian writer to shut up."

The Ottawa officials clearly chose the wrong man to try to silence. At the urging of his publisher, the acclaimed 39-year-old novelist (*A Casual Brutality, The Innocence of Age*) agreed to venture into the realm of polemical nonfiction. The result is the provocatively titled *Selling Illusions: The Cult of Multiculturalism in Canada.* Released last month, the book is selling briskly. Moreover, as Bissoondath jets around the country giving readings and appearing on open-line programs (he is to tour Western Canada this week), the author has become the focal point of a passionate—and polarizing—debate over how immigrants and so-called "ethnic Canadians" should integrate into the larger society. "It's been remarkable," Bissoondath told *Maclean's* following a reading at Wilfrid Laurier University in Waterloo, Ont. "This book seems to be giving people permission to say in public what they've been thinking in private for a long time."

In *Selling Illusions,* Bissoondath dismisses the federal multiculturalism policy, introduced by Pierre Trudeau's Liberal government in 1971, as a cynical "instrument to attract ethnic votes." According to Bissoondath, the policy—and the millions of dollars that flowed from it to fund ethnic organizations and activities—have encouraged a generation of immigrants to believe that where they came from is more important than where they have settled. And instead of adapting to the shared values of Canadians, he contends, many immigrants have insisted on bringing the hostilities and prejudices of their homelands to Canada. "The psychology and politics of multiculturalism," he writes, "have made divisiveness in the name of

racial and ethnic rights socially acceptable. They have given legitimacy here to what was once deplored in racially segregated South Africa. Led by a policy apparently benign, betrayed by our own sensitivities, we have come a full and curious circle."

As that statement indicates, Bissoondath is not above resorting to hyperbole to make his case. But he has also put his finger on one of *the* hot-button issues of our times. The backlash against multiculturalism extends well beyond the smoky Legion halls where a handful of aging veterans have blocked entry to Sikhs wearing turbans. A Decima Research poll released last year showed that 72 per cent of Canadians surveyed said that ethnic or racial groups should adapt to the Canadian value system rather than maintain their differences. A significant minority (41 per cent) agreed with the statement: "I am tired of ethnic minorities being given special treatment."

Bissoondath contends that Canada's liberal elites are determined to ignore such popular expressions of discontent. He saves some of his most scathing criticism for the well-intentioned white liberals who have been among the staunchest defenders of all things multicultural. In *Selling Illusions,* he recounts the fractious debate within the Writers' Union of Canada over holding a conference exclusively for "writers of color" this past summer. "Throughout the mud-slinging and name-calling and self-pity," he writes, "one could hear the background swish of self-flagellation peeling the skin from white backs." In an interview, he elaborated on that theme: "Multiculturalism is one of those policies through which guilt-ridden white liberals feel that they are expiating the political sins of their forefathers."

As someone who considers himself "of the left, politically," Bissoondath is in the uncomfortable position of disagreeing profoundly with those who are his natural allies. And as a good liberal, he takes exceptional pains to disassociate himself from the Reform party. Before his reading at Wilfrid Laurier, he drew a round of smug laughter from students and faculty when he described Reformers as "at best, knowledge-challenged." Yet Bissoondath's position on multiculturalism and that of Reform are almost identical. Both say that Canadians should not be defined, or divided, along racial or ethnic lines. And both maintain that while it is fine for individuals and families to celebrate their cultural heritage, they should not expect the government to pick up the tab for doing so.

'White liberals feel they are expiating the sins of their forefathers'

Bissoondath traces his own skepticism about multiculturalism to his upbringing in Trinidad. About 80 per cent of the island nation's 1.2-million people are divided almost evenly between those of African and those of East Indian descent. Bissoondath, who was born into a well-to-do Indian faintly, recalls that the blacks and the Indians moved in separate social circles and even had their own political parties. "It was," he writes, "our island version of apartheid, as virile, as divisive, as insidious."

At the age of 18, a disillusioned Bissoondath immigrated to Canada. But after enrolling at Toronto's York University, he says he confronted many of the same racial tensions. In the student cafeteria, he moved uneasily among the tables that seemed to be separated according to race, with Chinese students in one corner, West Indians in another. He says such unofficial segregation was encouraged by the university, which provided many ethnic organizations with their own student lounges. Bissoondath avoided them all. "I had not come here," he says, "in order to join a ghetto."

Bissoondath now lives in Montreal with his companion, lawyer Anne Marcoux; the couple have a three-year-old daughter, Elyssa. The author says he hopes that when his dark-skinned daughter is asked her nationality in years to come, people will accept the one-word reply: Canadian. The alternative, he jokes, is quite a mouthful: a Franco-Québécoise-Indian-Trinidadian-West Indian-Canadian.

Bissoondath's critics say that he is being unduly alarmist. Sheila Finestone, the federal minister responsible for multiculturalism, told *Maclean's* that she was "quite exercised" by parts of the book. She said that, contrary to Bissoondath's assertions, the purpose of multiculturalism is to foster links and promote common values. Myrna Kostash, an Edmonton-based author who has written extensively about her own Ukrainian heritage (*All of Baba's Children, Bloodlines*), said she cannot understand why Bissoondath seems to think that ethnic identity presents a threat to national cohesion. "If I identify myself as a third-generation Ukrainian-Canadian, with certain things to say about that, how is that not being a Canadian?" she asks. "Who does he think is saying this, feeling this, if not a real Canadian?"

Others are even blunter, charging that Bissoondath favors a policy of forced assimilation. "If [Bissoondath] would like to revert to the colonial days, I'm sure there are a few countries that he could move to," says City of Toronto equal opportunity director Ceta Ramkhalawansingh, who, like Bissoondath, was born in Trinidad, and moved to Canada 30 years ago. Her voice then dissolves into laughter. "I'm sorry," she says. "I'm not taking this too seriously. I've decided I have to stop being angry about this stupid book."

For all his objections to multiculturalism Bissoondath's prescriptions for change are remarkably timid. In the final pages of *Selling Illusions,* he shies away from calling for the abolition of the federal multiculturalism department. Instead, he suggests that the department—which this year dispensed about $25 million in grants—should be placed at arm's length from the government, much like the Canada Council. Beyond that, he speaks vaguely about the need for Canadians to rediscover and define their common values—such as the national flair for conciliation—and insist that newcomers understand and abide by these. "It may sound nebulous," he admitted to *Maclean's.* "But I'm not a sociologist or a politician. I'm just trying to start the debate."

Mission accomplished.

BRIAN BERGMAN *in Waterloo*

Coping with Deportation – The Integration of Millions of Refugees

HANS KLEIN

After the Second World War, faith in God and in their own abilities enabled the Germans to rebuild their country, make restitution, and also to begin helping others. At the very start of this process stood an enormous act of solidarity, the system of compensation which helped reintegrate the millions of German deportees and refugees from central and eastern Europe who had lost everything. West Germans contributed a sum of over 140 billion marks to help new and fellow citizens who had suffered as a result of the war – a measure which proved to be a highly successful investment in a joint future. Shock at the total material and moral defeat, bewilderment and shame at the crimes committed, anger at the abuse of their willingness to make sacrifices and outrage at the experience of war, captivity, deportation, loss of rights, rape and murder in the course of flight and banishment – this particular historical experience was a catalyst, driving the Germans forward in the postwar decades.

Flight and deportation as well as their heinous counterparts, abduction and banishment, go back even further than the beginnings of written history. After the Second World War, according to the calculations of experts, a total of over 60 million people worldwide were on the move as a result of coercion, fear or hardship. In Europe, they included the Baltic Germans, Lithuanian Germans, East Prussians, Danzigers, West Prussians, Pomeranians, Lower and Upper Silesians, Sudeten Germans, Carpathian Germans, Germans from Hungary, Germans from Yugoslavia, Germans from Romania, and Germans from the Soviet Union. The vast majority of them managed to make their way to western Germany, a much smaller proportion arrived in the Soviet occupation zone, and a few hundred thousand eventually found themselves in Austria and other western states. Of the just under 19 million Germans in central, south-eastern and eastern Europe, only twelve million actually arrived at their destinations. Approximately four million were forced to stay in their countries of origin, and roughly three million met their deaths at the end of the war and immediately afterwards.

and how little attention is paid to the protection of minorities and the rights of ethnic groups.

In the course of the last century, European nationalism initially caused alienation and then hostile antagonism between Germans and their eastern neighbors. Advocates of the nationality principle employed all the means at their disposal, including misrepresentation, in their attempt to present a profound national history which frequently had nothing to do with historical reality. Professor Dr. Eugen Lemberg described this development in the following way: "The area to the east of the Oder and Neisse which had once been inhabited by Slav peoples thus appeared to the Poles as an illegally

Shock at the total moral and material defeat became a driving force in the postwar period

Mass deportations do not only represent one of the most brutal forms of human rights violations, they also clearly prove the correctness of the assertion that nothing is settled unless it is settled justly. The flight to the Ottoman Empire of approximately one million refugees after the Russians conquered the Caucasus in the 19th century has not brought peace to the Caucasus even today. Moreover, the current orgy of blood-letting in the Balkans is again demonstrating how unintelligently and irresponsibly the new order in Europe was constructed after the First World War,

confiscated territory which had to be 're-covered'. To the Czechs, the region inhabited by Germans became territory that had been lost to the Czech people through betrayal, national weakness, and a conscious or malicious process of Germanization, and as such was rightfully to be made Czech once again. By these and similar means, demands were justified for reclaiming the German – and in Hungary the Slovak, Romanian, Serbian and Croatian, and in Poland, among others, the Ukrainian and Lithuanian - population for the Czech, Hungarian and Polish peoples. From the perspective of the

Germans living in eastern central Europe, however, this whole development presented a completely different picture: they experienced the rebirth of the Czech, Hungarian and Baltic languages, their introduction as official languages, and the abandonment of German by increasingly broader sections of society as both a betrayal and an injustice."

The first years in the West were extraordinarily difficult. The owners of houses and flats had refugee families billeted on them. City-dwellers ended up living on farms, and farmers in bombed-out cities. Different dialects, different customs, different eating habits, membership of different churches – all these gave rise to considerable social friction.

Faith in the democratic restructuring of Europe, in liberty, and in reconciliation

---

These developments limited the ability of people on both sides to recognize their own culpable behavior. Such knowledge is, however, necessary in order to be able to assess the present attitude of our neighbors on the question of mass deportation, which has also been influenced by over 40 years of communist portrayals of history, and to appraise the behavior of the deportees themselves. Ignorance or maliciousness is demonstrated by those who simply judge the expulsions as punishment for Hitler's crimes.

Only a few weeks after the end of the war, an uncontrolled wave of deportations began which were accompanied by such inhuman incidents that, at the Potsdam Conference in July 1945, the victorious powers agreed that the "resettlement" of the eastern German population, the Sudeten Germans, and the Germans from Hungary should be carried out "in an orderly and humane fashion" and only after a deportation plan had been drawn up by the Allied Control Council.

Gradually, however, the more extreme nicknames for the newcomers were replaced by more moderate terms. The integration process began. It was completed when, for example, the German general public gave their wholehearted support to a swimmer from Silesia in the butterfly event at the Olympic Games in Helsinki, when young locals and newcomers married, or when these new citizens began to play a role in political parties. Bavaria's transformation from an agricultural state into Germany's most modern industrial location also owes a great deal to the efforts of Sudeten Germans.

On November 27, 1949, seventeen Sudeten German politicians, scientists and authors with different political views drew up the "Eichstätt Declaration". This document provided the impetus for the acceptance of the "Charter of German Displaced Persons" on August 5, 1950. Both these documents emphasize the need for a democratic restructuring of Europe. And here, for the first time, a declaration issued by deportees contains

the reconciliatory and forward-looking words: "We want justice, not retribution." This idea is also reflected in point one of the charter: "We renounce revenge and retribution. This decision is sacred to us in memory of the immeasurable suffering which the last decade has brought on mankind." This declaration did not prevent the states responsible for the deportations – during the period they were under communist rule – from denouncing the deportees as revanchist. Yet, the clear political position expressed in the charter refuted all doubts about the democratic convictions of the deportees in the Federal Republic of Germany. And their large numbers made them attractive to all political parties. Their basic anticommunist attitude, their significant involvement in entrepreneurial activity, and their intense patriotism resulted in voting behavior which largely benefited those parties that had no sympathies with the communist bloc, put their faith in a social market economy, and did not reduce German history to the twelve years of national socialist rule. This often made life difficult for the deportees, who, in the meantime, had organized themselves within a number of cultural associations, which had many members, but not a great deal of influence. This was particularly the case during the later decades of the East-West conflict when a considerable element of German public opinion found it easier to identify with ideas emanating from the communist propaganda headquarters than with the declarations of those who had been forced to leave their homes. Thomas Mann once coined the phrase: "When home becomes foreign, the foreign becomes home." Millions of deportees have experienced the truth of this statement. In recent years, many of them have been able to visit their former homes and birthplaces. They frequently find changed, even devastated landscapes, villages, and towns from which all traces of their childhood days have already faded. All that remains are a few external landmarks which rekindle images they carry inside them.

Their misfortune has been their master, and their achievement their answer to a historic challenge. The number of those who would be willing to abandon their new homes in favor of their old, now unfamiliar birthplaces is very small. All the larger, however, is the number of those who do not wish to tolerate injustice in addition to their long accepted but not forgotten misfortune.

11.7 million German expellees*, 1945 to 1950

Baltic states, Memel region	168,800
Danzig	283,800
Eastern Pomerania	1,431,600
East Prussia	1,935,400
Eastern Brandenburg	424,000
Poland	672,000
Silesia	3,152,600
Czechoslovakia	2,921,400
Romania	246,000
Hungary	206,000
Yugoslavia	287,000

*Numbers by region of origin. Those directly affected by forced expulsion from the eastern regions of the former German Reich and German settlement areas abroad. Census position Sep. 1950.
‡ West Germany without Saarland, including Berlin (West). Source: Federal Statistical Office

Arrived in Federal Republic‡

11.7 million Germans experienced deportation between 1945 and 1950. Most of them found a new home in western Germany

THE LIMITS TO CULTURAL DIVERSITY

Harlan Cleveland

Harlan Cleveland, president of the World Academy of Art and Science, is a former U.S. assistant secretary of state and ambassador to NATO. He is the author of Birth of a New World: An Open Moment for International Leadership, *which is available from the Futurist Bookstore for $25.95 ($23.95 for Society members), cat. no. B-1679. His address is 1235 Yale Place #802, Minneapolis, Minnesota 55403. Telephone 612/339-3589; fax 612/339-6230; e-mail address cleve004@maroon.tc.umn.edu*

I'm engaged just now in an effort to think through the most intellectually interesting, and morally disturbing, issue in my long experience of trying to think hard about hard subjects. I call it The Limits of Cultural Diversity. If that seems obscure, wait a moment.

After the multiple revolutions of 1989, it began to look as if three ideas we have thought were Good Things would be getting in each other's way, which is not a Good Thing. What I have called the "triple dilemma," or "trilemma," is the mutually damaging collision of individual human rights, cultural human diversity, and global human opportunities. Today the damage from that collision is suddenly all around us.

Ethnic and religious diversity is creating painful conflicts around the world. Finding ways to become unified despite diversity may be the world's most urgent problem in the years ahead.

In 1994, in the middle of Africa, ethnicity took over as an exclusive value, resulting in mass murder by machete. In ex-Yugoslavia (and too many other places), gunpowder and rape accomplish the same purpose: trampling on human rights and erasing human futures.

Even on the Internet, where individuals can now join global groups that are not defined by place-names or cordoned off by gender or ethnicity, people are shouting at each other in flaming, capital-letters rhetoric.

Look hard at your home town, at the nearest inner city; scan the world by radio, TV, or newspapers and magazines. What's happened is all too clear: Just when individual human rights have achieved superstar status in political philosophy, just when can-do information technologies promise what the U.N. Charter calls "better standards of life in larger freedom," culture and diversity have formed a big, ugly boulder in the road called Future.

"If we cannot end now our differences, at least we can help make the world safe for diversity." That was the key sentence in the most influential speech of John F. Kennedy's presidency: his commencement address at American University on June 10, 1963. That speech led directly (among other things) to the first nuclear test ban treaty.

For most of the years since then, we were mesmerized by the threat of strategic nuclear war. But now a big nuclear war has become the least likely eventuality among the major threats to human civilization. And that brings us face to face with the puzzle identified in Kennedy's speech: how to make diversity safe.

But is "cultural diversity" really the new Satan in our firmament? Or does it just seem so because "culture" is being used—as *Kultur* has been used in other times and places—as an instrument of repression, exclusion, and extinction?

An Excess of Cultural Identity

In today's disordered world, the collision of cultures with global trends is in evidence everywhere. Ethnic nations, fragmented faiths, transnational business, and professional groups find both their inward loyalties and their international contacts leading them to question the political structures by which the world is still, if tenuously, organized. The results are sometimes symbolic caricatures ("In Rome, can a Moslem minaret be built taller than St. Peter's dome?") and sometimes broken mosaics like the human tragedy in what used to be Yugoslavia.

More people moved in 1994 than ever before in world history, driven by fear of guns or desire for more butter and more freedom. (This was true even before a couple of million Rwandans left their homes in terror—and some were floated out of the country as cadavers.) This more-mobile world multiplies the incentives for individuals to develop "multiple personalities," to become "collages" of identities, with plural loyalties to overlapping groups. Many millions of people believe that their best haven of certainty and security is a group based on ethnic similarity, common faith, economic interest, or political like-mindedness.

Societies based on fear of outsiders tend toward "totalitarian" governance. Fear pushes the culture beyond normal limits on individuals' behavior. "To say that you're ready to *die* for cultural identity," said one of my colleagues at a workshop of the World Academy of Art and Science in Romania last year, "means that you're also ready to *kill* for cultural identity." Said another: "The ultimate consequence of what's called

'cultural identity' is Hutus and Tutsis murdering each other."

The fear that drives people to cleave to their primordial loyalties makes it harder for them to learn to be tolerant of others who may be guided by different faiths and loyalties. But isolating oneself by clinging to one's tribe is far from a stable condition; these days, the tribe itself is highly unstable. Differences in birth rates and pressures to move will continue to mix populations together. So ethnic purity isn't going to happen, even by forcible "cleansing."

Besides, cultures keep redefining themselves by mixing with other cul-

> ## "Ethnic purity isn't going to happen, even by forcible 'cleansing.'"

tures, getting to know people who look, act, and believe differently. In today's more-open electronic world, cultures also expose themselves to new faiths and fashions, new lifestyles, workways, technologies, clothing, and cuisines.

The early stage of every realization of "cultural identity," every assertion of a newfound "right" of differences, *does* create a distinct group marked by ethnic aspect ("black is beautiful"), gender ("women's lib"), religion ("chosen people"), or status as a political minority. But when members of a group insisting on the group's uniqueness do succeed in establishing their own personal right to be different, something very important happens: They begin to be treated *individually* as equals and tend to integrate with more inclusive communities.

Traditions of separateness and discrimination are often persistent, but they are never permanent and im-

mutable. The recent history of South Africa bears witness.

Before the fighting in Yugoslavia, the most-tolerant people in that part of the world were seen by their close neighbors to be the Serbs, Croats, and Moslems living together in Bosnia and Herzegovina, with the city of Sarajevo as a special haven of mutual tolerance.

The problem does not seem to be culture itself, but cultural overenthusiasm. Cultural loyalties, says one European, have the makings of a runaway nuclear reaction. Without the moderating influence of civil society—acting like fuel rods in a nuclear reactor—the explosive potential gets out of hand. What's needed is the counterforce of wider views, global perspectives, and more-universal ideas.

Post-communist societies, says a resident of one of them, have experienced a loss of equilibrium, a culture shock from the clash of traditional cultures, nostalgia for the stability of Soviet culture, and many new influences from outside. What's needed, he thinks, is cultural richness without cultural dominance, but with the moderating effect of intercultural respect.

Culture and Civilization

We have inherited a fuzzy vocabulary that sometimes treats *culture* as a synonym for *civilization*. At a World Academy workshop, my colleagues and I experimented with an alternative construct.

In this construct, *civilization* is what's universal—values, ideas, and practices that are in general currency everywhere, either because they are viewed as objectively "true" or because they are accepted pragmatically as useful in the existing circumstances. These accepted "truths" offer the promise of weaving together a *civitas* of universal laws and rules, becoming the basis for a global civil society.

What is sometimes called "management culture" appears to be achieving this kind of universal acceptance, hence becoming part of global "civilization." But nobody has to be in charge of practices that are generally accepted. For instance, the international exchange of money—a miracle of information technologies—is remarkably efficient, daily

WHOLENESS INCORPORATING DIVERSITY

By John W. Gardner

A vital community reconciles group purposes with individual diversity. On the larger scene the diversity is supplied not by individuals but by subgroups—national, ethnic, religious, linguistic, whatever. *In either case the goal is to achieve wholeness incorporating diversity.* That is the transcendent task for our generation, at home and worldwide.

To prevent the wholeness from smothering diversity, there must be a tradition of pluralism and healthy dissent. To prevent the diversity from destroying the wholeness, all segments must be committed to the common good—and there must be accommodation, coalition building, and well-developed practices of dispute resolution.

We must regenerate the sense of community from the ground up. Men and women who have come to understand in their own intimate settings—schools, congregations, neighborhoods—the principles of "wholeness incorporating diversity," the arts of diminishing polarization, the meaning of teamwork and participation, will be far better allies in the effort to build elements of community into the city, the nation, and the world.

In recent decades, much has been learned about the resolving of disputes, and it should be taught in every educational system. We

> The future of the 'community' depends on the ability of subgroups to unite without smothering each other.

have hardly begun to use all that we now know. The ethnic conflicts burning so fiercely in every corner of the world today teach us anew that the destructive possibilities of hatred are limitless. The ancient human impulse to hate and fear the tribe in the next valley, the ethnic group on the next block, those who are "not like us," is deep-seated.

That is why our interest in local community building leads us inevitably to a concern for *collaborative processes.* The diverse, some-

times mutually hostile, segments must learn the arts of communicating across boundaries and building consensus. The basic rules are that each group must be respected, *and each group must reach back toward the whole community.* We know that communities and the sense of community can be revitalized through collaborative problem solving, using well-tested techniques. □

About the Author

John W. Gardner is a philosopher-activist and chairman of the National Civic League. His address is Graduate School of Business, Stanford University, Stanford, California 94305. He has recently focused his attention on renewing the American community. The League is acting as convenor of The Alliance for National Renewal, a coalition of more than 90 organizations ranging from the American Association of Retired Persons to the National Urban League and Habitat for Humanity.

This article is drawn from his speech to the National Civic League in Philadelphia, November 12, 1994.

moving more than a trillion dollars' worth of money among countries. Yet, no one is in charge of the system that makes it happen. Recently, the puny efforts of governments to control monetary swings by buying and selling currencies have only demonstrated governments' incapacity to control them.

If civilization is what's universal, *culture* is the substance and symbols of the community. Culture meets the basic human need for a sense of belonging, for participating in the prides and fears that are shared with an in-group.

Both culture and civilization are subject to continuous change. In our time, the most-pervasive changes

seem to be brought about by the spread of knowledge, the fallout of information science and information technologies.

Civil society consists of many structures and networks, cutting across cultural fault lines, brought into being by their ability to help people communicate. They are not very dependent on public authority for their charters or their funding, increasingly taking on functions that used to be considered the responsibility of national governments.

Many of these "nongovernments" —such as those concerned with business and finance, scientific inquiry, the status of women, population policy, and the global environmental

commons—have become effective users of modern information technologies. In consequence, they are providing more and more of the policy initiative both inside countries and in world affairs.

Civilization is rooted in compromise—between the idea of a democratic state and a strong state, between a free-market economy and a caring economy, between "open" and "closed" processes, between horizontal and vertical relationships, between active and passive citizenship. The required solvent for civilization is *respect for differences.* Or, as one of my World Academy colleagues puts it, we need to learn *how to be different together.*

Civilization will be built by cooperation and compassion, in a social climate in which people in differing groups can deal with each other in ways that respect their cultural differences. "Wholeness incorporating diversity" is philosopher John W. Gardner's succinct formulation. The slogan on U.S. currency is even shorter, perhaps because it's in Latin: *E pluribus unum* ("from many, one").

Lessons from American Experience

We Americans have learned, in our short but intensive 200-plus years of history as a nation, a first lesson about diversity: that it cannot be governed by drowning it in "integration."

I came face to face with this truth when, just a quarter century ago, I became president of the University of Hawaii. Everyone who lives in Hawaii, or even visits there, is impressed by its residents' comparative tolerance toward each other. On closer inspection, paradise seems based on paradox: Everybody's a minority. The tolerance is not in spite of the diversity but because of it.

It is not through the disappearance of ethnic distinctions that the people of Hawaii achieved a level of racial peace that has few parallels around our discriminatory globe. Quite the contrary. The glory is that Hawaii's main ethnic groups managed to establish the right to be separate. The group separateness in turn helped establish the rights of individuals in each group to equality with individuals of different racial aspect, different ethnic origin, different cultural heritage.

Hawaii's experience is not so foreign to the transatlantic migrations of the various more-or-less-white Caucasians. On arrival in New York (passing that inscription on the Statue of Liberty, "Send these, the homeless, tempest-tost, to me"), the European immigrants did not melt into the open arms of the white Anglo-Saxon Protestants who preceded them. The reverse was true. The new arrivals stayed close to their own kind, shared religion and language and humor and discriminatory treatment with their soul brothers and sisters, and gravitated at first into occupations that did not too seriously threaten the earlier arrivals.

The waves of new Americans learned to tolerate each other—*first* as groups, only thereafter as individuals. Rubbing up against each other in an urbanizing America, they discovered not just the old Christian lesson that all men are brothers, but the hard, new, multicultural lesson that all brothers are different. Equality is not the product of similarity; it is the cheerful acknowledgment of difference.

What's so special about our experience is the assumption that people of many kinds and colors can to-

> ## "Equality is not the product of similarity; it is the cheerful acknowledgment of difference."

gether govern themselves *without* deciding in advance which kinds of people (male or female, black, brown, yellow, red, white, or any mix of these) may hold any particular public office in the pantheon of political power.

For the twenty-first century, this "cheerful acknowledgement of difference" is the alternative to a planet-wide spread of ethnic cleansing and religious rivalry. The challenge is great, for ethnic cleansing and reli-

gious rivalry are traditions as contemporary as Bosnia and Rwanda in the 1990s and as ancient as the Assyrians who, as Byron wrote, "came down like a wolf on the fold" but, says the biblical Book of Kings, were prevented by sword-wielding angels from taking Jerusalem.

In too many countries there is still a basic if often unspoken assumption that one kind of people is anointed to be in general charge. Try to imagine a Turkish chancellor of Germany, an Algerian president of France, a Pakistani prime minister of Britain, a Christian president of Egypt, an Arab prime minister of Israel, a Jewish president of Syria, a Tibetan ruler in Beijing, anyone but a Japanese in power in Tokyo.

Yet in the United States during the twentieth century, we have already elected an Irish Catholic as president, chosen several Jewish Supreme Court justices, and racially integrated the armed forces right up to chairman of the Joint Chiefs of Staff. We have not yet adjusted, as voters in India, Britain, and Turkey have done, to having a woman atop the American political heap. But early in the twenty-first century, that too will come. And during that same new century, which will begin with "minorities" as one in every three Americans, there is every prospect that an African American, a Latin American, and an Asian American will be elected president of the United States.

I wouldn't dream of arguing that we Americans have found the Holy Grail of cultural diversity when in fact we're still searching for it. We have to think hard about our growing pluralism. It's useful, I believe, to dissect in the open our thinking about it, to see whether the lessons we are trying to learn might stimulate some useful thinking elsewhere. We do not yet quite know how to create "wholeness incorporating diversity," but we owe it to the world, as well as to ourselves, to keep trying.

Indigenous Ethnic Groups

The contemporary issues of Native Americans as well as the descendants of all conquered indigenous peoples add their weight to the claims for cultural justice, equal protection, and due process in our hemisphere. As North and South America marked the 500th anniversary of Christopher Columbus's voyage of discovery, the indigenous peoples of the Americas explored their roots and new remedies for the conquest that turned many into a permanent underclass.

The following articles represent a cross section of the current experience of indigenous ethnic groups, their forced accommodation of a high-tech world, the environmental and cultural effects of rapid change, and the challenges to a renewal of their identifying traditions. The indigenous ethnic populations remember and invite us to recall their struggles, to find ways of shaping and sharing the new sense of pluralism offered within the American experience and the spiritual sources of ethnic identity that persons encounter as the legitimacy of ancient practices widens.

Indigenous ethnic communities have been plagued by a complex array of historical, social, cultural, and economic issues. As a result, in the late twentieth century, the traditions of indigenous ethnic groups have been renegotiated by yet another generation. The North and South American economies and pluralistic cultures are a challenging stage for their quest for self-sufficiency as well as their aspirations for the preservation of a unique cultural legacy. Current indigenous ethnic leaders challenge past perceptions. They find it increasingly difficult to strike a balance between traditional values and new demands. Native Americans' challenge of the American legal system is part of this current redefinition. Finally, however, they are challenging themselves to be themselves.

Ethnicity is built upon the truth and strength of a tradition. Senses of family and community, and an unwillingness to give up, have led to standoffs with many forces within America. In this light, this unit details ways in which an ethnic group retrieves its rights and heritage to preserve an ancient culture from amnesia and extinction.

The expansion and profitability of Native American gambling casinos, their attendant impact on state and local economies, and the tax exemptions enjoyed by these ventures appear to be headed toward contentions that may spill over into new issues of public order. On the international level, the discussion of human and cultural rights of peoples guaranteed in the United Nations and the traditional mode of state sovereignty indicates that a fragile accommodation between indigenous people and the mainstream societies at whose margins they exist may be entering a new phrase. Their unequal relationship began with the consolidation of large territorial political and economic regimes. Under scrutiny are personal rights, corporatist rights, pluralistic realms that ensure transnational solidarity, and cultural and religious challenges to those in authority fueled by the passion for power at those intersections between modernity and tradition—the large-scale institutional versus the local and culturally specific community.

Looking Ahead: Challenge Questions

How should commitments to the self-determination of people be ensured and enforced? What levels of tolerance are assumed by the UN Working Group? What value conflicts, if any, are beyond compromise? How does gaming affect the work ethic?

What are the most compelling issues that face indigenous ethnic communities?

What social, economic, and political conditions will affect the next indigenous ethnic generation?

Because of the strides of the current Native American community, will the next generation enter the middle class of America? Should that be a goal?

How will the American public and private bureaucratic systems address the challenges of pluralistic constituencies?

3

12th Session of UN Working Group on Indigenous Peoples

The Declaration Passes and the US Assumes a New Role

GLENN T. MORRIS

Glenn T. Morris is the Executive Director of the Fourth World Center for the Study of Indigenous Law and Politics, at the University of Colorado at Denver. He is also co-editor of the Fourth World Bulletin and Associate Professor of Political Science at CU-Denver.

After nearly nine years of debate, deliberation and revision, the United Nations Working Group on Indigenous Peoples (UNWGIP), at its 12th Session (25-29 July 1994), completed preparation of the Draft Declaration on the Rights of Indigenous Peoples and sent the document on to higher levels in the UN system. Over 160 indigenous peoples' organizations, forty two state members, nine specialized agencies of the United Nations, and dozens of interested non-governmental organizations, totaling nearly 800 individuals, participated in the 12th Session. The Declaration was forwarded to the UN Sub-Commission on Prevention of Discrimination and Protection of Minorities. At its 46th Session (in August 1994), the Sub-Commission agreed to transmit the Declaration to the UN Commission on Human Rights for discussion at its annual meeting in February 1995. For final adoption as an instrument of emerging international law, the Declaration must be ultimately be accepted by the UN General Assembly.

The 12th Session was notable for several important developments that this article reports in some detail. First, there was a significant debate about the Declaration's treatment of the right to self-determination; the ensuing discussion of the issue left momentous questions unresolved. Second, several other major issues that will have great bearing on the rights of indigenous peoples were postponed to future discussions in which they will be detached from the text of the Declaration. And third, the United States Government assumed a new and decidedly more dynamic role among the states that have actively participated in developing the Draft Declaration.

Self-determination

Discussion of the right to self-determination for indigenous peoples has always provoked passionate and oppositional controversy at Working Group sessions. In the initial drafts of the Declaration, the right was not mentioned explicitly at all. In subsequent drafts, at the insistence of indigenous peoples, the right was expressed, but was often accompanied by limiting language or provisions. At the 11th Session (1993), indigenous delegates proposed that reference to the right to self-determination for indigenous peoples should be modeled after the language already found in the International Covenant on Civil and Political Rights and the International Covenant on Economic, Social and Cultural Rights. That proposal was accepted, and Article 3 of the draft now reads:

> Indigenous peoples have the right of self-determination. By virtue of that right, they freely determine their political status and freely pursue their economic, social and cultural development.

Some states, notably the United States and Canada, have publicly opposed Article 3, and they can be expected to introduce dramatic revisions of it, or try to completely delete it in the future.

The major objection to self-determination stems from the fear by some states that explicit recognition of that right, in the language of the human rights covenants, will allow indigenous peoples and nations to exercise a right of political independence separate from the states that surround them. Through this exercise, states fear the dismemberment of their claimed territories and the emergence of new, independent indigenous states. This fear is especially pronounced in cases where indigenous enclaves are entirely surrounded by states or where indigenous territories contain valuable natural resources.

Most states assert that relations, especially territorial and jurisdictional relations, between themselves and indigenous peoples are internal, domestic matters that are beyond the scope of international law. The inclusion in the Declaration of a right that would allow indigenous peoples to be recognized to possess juridical character, with rights recognized in international forums, is viewed as an attack on the sovereignty and territorial integrity of current UN members.

Conversely, most indigenous peoples argue that they have never given their informed consent to be integrated into the states that came to surround them, that they have not been a party to the establishment of international legal principles to the present, and that they have been (and continue to be) denied the opportunity to decide for themselves their political status. In essence, they argue that they are in a state of internal colonial bondage, and they advocate an extension of international standards of decolonization to apply to their cases. In that regard, indigenous delegates have regularly stated that the right to self-determination is a major cornerstone of the Declaration, upon which other provisions of the document must rest.

Indigenous delegates have consistently argued that under the right to self-determination, complete independence is only one of several available options. They maintain that most indigenous peoples around the world do not aspire towards political independence, and would choose some variation of autonomy, short of independence, within the current state system. However, during the 12th Session, several states (Brazil, India, Myanmar) repeated their steadfast opposition to any recognition of a right to self-determination for indigenous peoples. Others, such as Denmark, expressed support for the self-determination provision.

Upon their arrival at the 12th Session, some indigenous representatives were surprised to find that the Declaration had been altered, without their consultation, from the form that had been concluded at the 11th Session. Of particular concern was the addition of Article 31, which recognizes "autonomy" or "self-government in internal and local affairs" as a specific form of the exercise of self-determination. Miguél Alfonso Martínez, the Latin American regional member of the Working Group and the author of Article 31, had reasoned that Latin American state governments were unlikely to accede to the open-ended interpretation of self-determination expressed in Article 3. He wrote and appended Article 31 to the Declaration in the hope that it would provide essential safeguards for Latin American indigenous peoples but not alarm the state governments of the region.

Serious discussion and disagreement developed over whether Article 31 would limit the right to self-determination expressed in Article 3. Some indigenous delegates (especially some Canadian and United States Indians, Native Hawaiians, Mapuches, Maoris, Nagas, and others) objected that the language of Article 3 was perfectly clear, and any attempt to modify the meaning (as they interpreted the intent of Article 31) might later be contrued as a limitation of the right to self-determination, that "autonomy" might result as the maximum (or at least the preferred) extent of the exercise of the right for indigenous peoples. They argued that Article 31 is therefore superfluous and should be deleted.

The opponents of Article 31 also suggested that certain states, notably the US and Canada, are hostile to Article 3 and can be expected to amend it significantly or even delete it from the Declaration, at future forums. If Article 3 is indeed eventually deleted, Article 31 will remain as the only articulation of what self-determination means. According to the opponents, Article 31, read alone, is an incomplete and inadequate protection of the right of self-determination for indigenous peoples.

The proponents of Article 31, on the other hand, maintained that the article should be read as an extension, not a limitation, of Article 3, and that local and regional autonomy would result as the *minimum* standard of self-determination that states must recognize for indigenous peoples. They suggested that for many indigenous peoples who must deal with states that fail to provide even minimal recognition of indigenous rights, Article 31 might provide a crucial safeguard against violations of fundamental human rights.

In future deliberations over the draft, the substance of the right to self-determination for indigenous peoples will remain of central importance. In the eyes of many indigenous peoples, the integrity of the entire instrument rests in the willingness of the international community to recognize the right of indigenous peoples to control their political, economic, social and cultural destinies. In contrast, the concerns of states over the freedom of indigenous peoples to exercise their right to self-determination is intimately linked to the belief that states possess a basic right to protect their own sovereignty and territorial integrity from competing indigenous claims. The ultimate success of the Declaration may therefore rest in the ability of the contending sides to assuage the fears of the other, by finding the common ground that satisfies the interests of all concerned.

Future Deliberations over the Declaration

According to modified UN rules of procedure, the discussion of the Draft Declaration at the Working Group level had been open to all UN members, all interested indigenous delegates, and all governmental and non-governmental organizations with an interest and a contribution to make to the efforts of the Working Group. With the conclusion of the Working Group's discussion, however, the Declaration was transmitted to the Sub-Commission and then to the Commission on Human Rights, where the procedures for participation are considerably more restrictive.

To participate at the Sub-Commission or the Commission, delegates must be credentialed by those respective bodies, and the application for credentialing must come through a non-governmental organization (NGO) that possesses consultative status within the UN Economic and Social Council (ECOSOC). To date, only twelve indigenous NGOs, primarily representing indigenous peoples of the Americas, have received consultative status.

During the 12th Session, both indigenous representatives and states expressed doubts that in future forums in which the Draft Declaration is discussed, indigenous peoples who are not affiliated with the recognized NGOs, or who are otherwise not credentialed, will be included in the discussions. This issue is of special concern to peoples from India and other parts of Asia and the Pacific, the Russian Federation, and Africa, because many of them are not currently members of credentialed NGOs.

The issue of who will be able to participate in future discussions becomes especially important when considering the probable course for the Declaration. According to a number of state observers at the 12th Session, once the Draft reaches the Commission on Human Rights, it will be sent to another working group, within the Commission itself. Unlike the discussions at the previous Working Group, which were directed by international legal experts (as opposed to delegates representing the interests of states), the Commission working group may well be directed by appointed delegates whose primary concern will be the protection of their governments' interests.

While the Draft is in the Commission's working group, it will be subject to a comprehensive review and reconsideration. Provisions that might seem problematic to states are susceptible to complete revision or removal. Indigenous representatives expressed concern that a limitation of their participation in this process may endanger the progress that has been made over the past ten years, and it may weaken the most important international legal instrument affecting indigenous peoples ever to appear.

Indigenous delegates have previous experience upon which to base their wariness. In 1989, during the debate over revision of International Labor Organization (ILO) Convention 107, only credentialed indigenous representatives could participate, and then only on a limited basis, while a number of important persons and perspectives were completely excluded. To many indigenous peoples, the ILO rules determining participation were totally arbitrary. Consequently, indigenous delegates now insist on more open participation at the Human Rights Commission and successive fora that deal with the Declaration.

Members of the Working Group itself have also recommended relaxation of the rules of procedure in the Human Rights Commission's discussion of the Draft. The Australian government promised that it would introduce a measure to allow indigenous participation, regardless of consultative status, and it proposed that any meetings of the Commission working group be convened immediately prior to the meeting of the Working Group on Indigenous Peoples, so as to maximize the opportunity for indigenous participation. Australia's proposals were endorsed by a few other countries, particularly Sweden, Denmark and Norway.

The Role of the US at the 12th Session and Beyond

The United States delegation to the 12th Session took a new and decidedly more active role in the deliberations of the Working Group and the discussion of the Draft Declaration. Until the 1994 meeting, the United States has participated mostly as an observer, relying on the lead of countries such as Canada and Australia to fashion and advance the interests of state members at the Working Group.

For several years, some indigenous delegates to the Working Group have become convinced that the most prominent governments from English-speaking countries (Australia, Canada, New Zealand and the United States) have coordinated their participation in international forums concerned with indigenous peoples' rights. Rudolph Rÿser, Director of the Center for World Indigenous Studies, has charted a succession of joint meetings between those governments. According to Rÿser's analysis, Canada has played a particularly active role, one that is considered by many indigenous delegates to be especially hostile toward any expanded recognition of

indigenous rights. Australia, conversely, has played a role that is publicly more sympathetic to indigenous claims, one that has even supported limited usage of terms like "peoples" and "self-determination." New Zealand and the United States, says Rÿser, have taken approaches that vary between those of Canada and Australia, while the US delegation's public posture has ranged from indifference to hostility.

Affirming Rÿser's analysis, the changing agenda of the United States has been revealed in an unclassified internal State Department memorandum of July 1993. In this document, State Department officials acknowledge that for the first dozen years of the Working Group's existence, the US "invested little effort in [it]." By 1993, however, the US attitude toward developments at the Working Group apparently had changed significantly. The memo explains that the Working Group and the Draft Declaration are now at a stage where it is important for the US to "try to shape the text [of the draft] to reflect US interests before it goes to the Commission [on Human Rights]."

Of major concern to the US is the question of what impact the application of the principles of collective rights and self-determination of indigenous peoples might have for the United States and international law. It is clear from the memo that the US opposes extending the right of self-determination, as it has been interpeted in the international human rights covenants, to indigenous peoples. The memo asserts that self-determination "is most commonly understood to mean the right to establish a sovereign and independent state, with separate personality under international law. Like many other countries, the United States could not accept the term in any contexts implying or permitting this meaning."

Addressing an issue closely related to self-determination, the State Department is critical of using the term "peoples" (with an "s" at the end) in conjunction with the word "indigenous." According to the memo, "the term [peoples] implies that such groups have the right to self-determination under international law." The document expresses concern about "the risks and uncertainties of extending the legal concept of self-determination to indigenous groups." It emphasizes that the recognition of indigenous collective rights expressed in the Draft Declaration is troublesome, because as a general rule, "the United States...does not recognize the existence of collective rights under international law..." and "we generally do not think it desirable to incorporate such rights into future legal instruments."

While the memo lends general support to the concept of a declaration for the protection of indigenous peoples, and while it even questions some basic assumptions about generally accepted notions in State Department circles (e.g., "recognizing carefully defined group rights need not *per se* be a BAD THING," and "should we oppose a tightly drawn treaty saying that a defined collective group has a defined legal right to practice their culture or religion opposable against their [sic] government?"), it also makes very clear that the security and integrity of the current state system is of preeminent importance.

The flavor of the 1993 memo was integrated into the US intervention at the 12th Session, where the use of the term "peoples" was deliberately avoided, and instead, the terms "people," "populations," "tribe," and "tribal," were used sixteen times. The delegation (led by Miriam Sapiro, from State's Legal Affairs Office, and John Crook, Counselor for Legal Affairs at the US Mission in Geneva) also provided further insight into the US position regarding indigenous self-determination. The memo suggests that US indigenous policy can be used as a working model for the effective implementation of indigenous rights on an international level, given that the essence and extent of self-determination for indigenous peoples should basically mean "self-governance and autonomy...within an existing state." Of course, this implies that US indigenous policy does not apply to "non-historic" or non-federally-recognized Indian nations, Alaskan or Hawaiian Natives,

Chamorros, Samoans, or other indigenous peoples that have never been given any pretense whatsoever in the realm of "self-governance" or "autonomy."

Equally revealing of the true US policy, at unofficial meetings during the 12th Session, Crook and Sapiro made clear that the semantic debates over such terms as "people" versus "peoples" were less important to them than was some resolution of the substance of the right to self-determination itself. Sapiro asked several times, "What does Article 3 mean?" And at one session Crook even called the semantic debate "stupid." However, the term proved important enough that the US delegation has made a conscious, deliberate decision to refuse to use the term "peoples" at all. The apparent implication is that if the term self-determination can be interpreted, in any

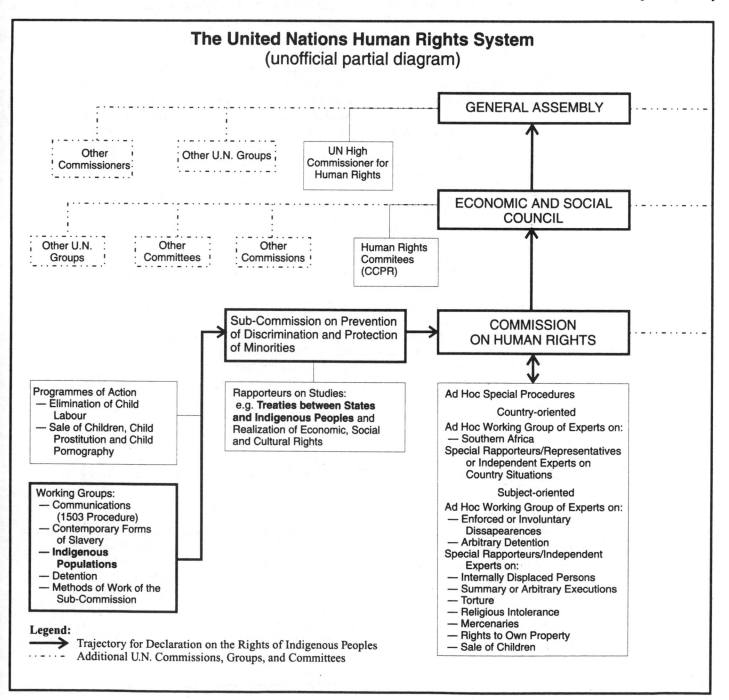

The United Nations Human Rights System
(unofficial partial diagram)

GENERAL ASSEMBLY

Other Commissioners

Other U.N. Groups

UN High Commissioner for Human Rights

ECONOMIC AND SOCIAL COUNCIL

Other U.N. Groups

Other Committees

Other Commissions

Human Rights Commitees (CCPR)

Sub-Commission on Prevention of Discrimination and Protection of Minorities

COMMISSION ON HUMAN RIGHTS

Programmes of Action
— Elimination of Child Labour
— Sale of Children, Child Prostitution and Child Pornography

Rapporteurs on Studies:
e.g. **Treaties between States and Indigenous Peoples** and Realization of Economic, Social and Cultural Rights

Ad Hoc Special Procedures

Country-oriented

Ad Hoc Working Group of Experts on:
— Southern Africa
Special Rapporteurs/Representatives or Independent Experts on Country Situations

Subject-oriented

Working Groups:
— Communications (1503 Procedure)
— Contemporary Forms of Slavery
— **Indigenous Populations**
— Detention
— Methods of Work of the Sub-Commission

Ad Hoc Working Group of Experts on:
— Enforced or Involuntary Dissapearences
— Arbitrary Detention
Special Rapporteurs/Independent Experts on:
— Internally Displaced Persons
— Summary or Arbitrary Executions
— Torture
— Religious Intolerance
— Mercenaries
— Rights to Own Property
— Sale of Children

Legend:
——▶ Trajectory for Declaration on the Rights of Indigenous Peoples
· · · · · Additional U.N. Commissions, Groups, and Committees

context, to recognize the right of indigenous peoples to independent political existence, then the United States will oppose it.

The current US position on the Declaration can be identified in a plank of the "Clinton-Gore Plan" (the campaign platform of 1992) and also in a statement by President Clinton on 29 April 1994, both of which affirmed "government-to-government" relationships between indigenous nations and the United States, while placing the treatment of indigenous self-determination solely within the domestic jurisdiction of the United States. Some indigenous delegates have observed that the use of the term "government-to-government" by the United States constitutes an attempt to reduce indigenous issues to "internal" status and to degrade the international (i.e., nation-to-nation) relationship that is embodied in the hundreds of treaties concluded between the US and various Indian nations. Others have observed that the quality of "self-determination" accorded to only the recognized "historic tribes" of the US is truncated by the language of the Indian Self-Determination and Education Act of 1975, which limits the exercise of self-determination to decisions concerning the allocation of appropriations distributed by the federal government.

Sapiro and Crook stated in the Session that the United States plans to play a more active role in the future of both the Draft Declaration and the Working Group. They appeared confident that the Draft would pass through the Sub-Commission in August 1994 (which it did), and that it would then be transmitted to a working group in the Commission on Human Rights, after February 1995. The delegation suggested that in future months very serious discussion and debate of the Draft will take place, especially over such controversial matters as collective rights, self-determination, control of territories and natural resources, and development matters, and that the US will play an active role in both the procedural and substantive aspects of these debates. The inference must be that, because the US and other states disagree with the wording of some key provisions of the Draft Declaration, significant changes might reasonably be expected at the Commission level.

In a briefing held in Washington DC, on 20 January 1995, John Shattuck, Assistant Secretary of State for Human Rights, reiterated that the US position regarding the Draft Declaration, at the February 1995 meeting of the UN Human Rights Commission, will be "supportive," and that the United States will follow Australia's lead in creating an open-ended working group within the Commission. Shattuck and his aides repeated that the US perceives human rights primarily pertaining to individuals, not to groups, that the US wants a clearer definition of "indigenous peoples," in order to determine to whom the rights in the Declaration apply. Shattuck also said that his office was committed to open discussions concerning the Declaration (to be held in the US), in various forums with indigenous groups and other NGOs.

The key features of US policy continue to be: that the US considers individuals and not groups to be the subject of human rights; that questions involving indigenous peoples are basically domestic matters to be negotiated between states and indigenous peoples; that the right to self-determination should be read more narrowly than it was in the past, and should not normally be read as a recognition of the right of independent political existence for indigenous peoples; and that any political and economic sovereignty rights of indigenous peoples are inferior and subordinate to the overarching sovereignty of existing states. Undoubtedly, the basic position of the United States on these questions will play an important and enduring role in the consideration of the Draft Declaration and in the future of the Working Group.

Whatever the role of the US in future deliberations of the Working Group, a serious amount of work remains unfinished and will have to be resolved in the coming years. These issues are, in summary, the scope and substance of the right of indigenous peoples to exercise self-determination, the international legal status of treaties between indigenous peoples and states, and the responsibilities of states and the United Nations in assuring that indigenous peoples and their territories are not sacrificed in the pursuit of national and international economic development.

Indigenous Self-Determination and U.S. Policy

Commentary

As explained in the [first part] of this issue article, there has recently been a major shift in the posture of the United States Government regarding the Draft Declaration on the Rights of Indigenous Peoples and the UN Working Group on Indigenous Peoples (UNWGIP). Some have applauded the U.S. awakening in the indigenous-rights arena, replete with its dubious interpretation of the language of "self-determination," as a welcome and positive change. Unfortunately, we are unable to share that optimism.

In our view, the position shift should be viewed cautiously as perhaps the latest reflection of a long tradition in U.S. policy, which is characterized by massive contradictions of legal and moral obligations. American Indians, more than any other indigenous peoples, should understand the implications of U.S. posturing on human rights. The possibility or probability that the U.S. will support or promote the Draft Declaration on the Rights of Indigenous Peoples can and should be measured in relation to the attachment of the U.S. to other, comparable pieces of international legislation on human rights.

It should be understood that the Declaration on Indigenous

Rights, even when finally concluded, will not create any immediately binding legal obligation on any state, because it is not a treaty. Subsequent to its adoption by the UN General Assembly, the Declaration may eventually be transformed into a Convention, just as the 1948 Universal Declaration on Human Rights was put into force in the form of two competing (or complementary) human-rights covenants, in 1976, but this development will take many years, if it happens at all. Present U.S. support for the Draft Declaration, therefore, can be understood to be virtually risk-free, as far as immediate legal obligations are concerned.

More importantly, the United States has consistently refused to participate in international human-rights institutions over the past fifty years. The U.S. Senate, which must ratify all treaties to which the country might become state-party, rejected all opportunities for the U.S. to accede to the 1948 Genocide Convention, until 1986. Similarly, it refused to ratify the 1966 International Covenant on Civil and Political Rights (which codifies that set of human rights expressed in the U.S. Bill of Rights itself), until 1992. Only last year, in 1994, did the Senate ratify the 1965 International Convention on the Elimination of All Forms of Racial Discrimination. But did ratification in these very few cases indicate that the United States would actually abide by the terms of the agreements? No, because whenever the Senate has ratified human-rights treaties, it has appended "provisions" and "reservations" that have made international laws subordinate to the laws of the United States. There is little reason to believe that the treatment of the Declaration on Indigenous Rights will be different.

The stated U.S. position should not be regarded as an insignificant policy change in an obscure area of international human-rights discourse, nor should it be viewed in isolation from the evidence of U.S. behavior when indigenous rights are obviously at stake. Rather, the policy statement should be viewed as intimately related to several other important foreign-policy areas that are implicated by past and present indigenous (or "nationality") conflicts around the globe. For example, the U.S. supported a Tibetan rebellion against Chinese occupation in the 1950s and 60s, but when President Nixon decided to play the "China card" against the USSR, in 1972, the Tibetans were abandoned to be slaughtered and exiled by the Chinese Army. Similarly, the U.S. supported Iraqi Kurds in their rebellion against Saddam Hussein, in 1973 (the prelude to the events of the Gulf War in 1991), but when U.S. interests in the region shifted, the Kurds, too, were abandoned to be slaughtered by the thousands. On the other hand, because of the strategic importance of Turkey, the U.S. virtually ignores the fate of Kurds in that country.

In another, similar policy contradiction, the U.S. supported and instigated Ukrainian secessionist rebellion against the USSR until 1991, when President Bush strangely attempted to persuade Ukraine *not* to seek independence, after all (of course, he was too late). Bush's address to the Ukrainians, in which he reversed forty-five years of policy to warn of the "excesses of suicidal nationalism," was labeled his "Chicken Kiev Speech" by *New York Times* columnist William Safire, marking the first evidence of a major dispute within the ranks

of U.S. conservatives on indigenous nationality policy generally and the policy applied toward Russia, in particular.

It is difficult to underestimate the cynicism of U.S. policy on human rights. At the Vienna World Conference on Human Rights, in July 1993, President Clinton and Secretary of State Christopher swore before the world that the United States was prepared to join the International Covenant on Economic, Social and Cultural Rights. That promise could not have been less believable, considering the fact that the ESC Covenant has always been understood as the major human-rights statement of socialist regimes, led by the former USSR, and so it hardly could have been expected ever to gain approval in the Senate. Clinton and Christopher also preached human rights to the Chinese government and threatened to withhold Most-Favored Nation (MFN) trading privileges unless China reformed its behavior according to Western precepts of "democracy" -- and then reversed themselves, when China indicated that it was not about to be pressured on human-rights issues.

Meanwhile, within the U.S. itself, indigenous human-rights issues go largely unacknowledged and unaddressed by the public, because of the myth that the U.S. is the world's leader in observance of human rights. This myth probably explains why, though people in western Europe, Russia, and elsewhere are aware that President Clinton has refused to deal with the worldwide campaign to grant clemency to the American Indian political prisoner Leonard Peltier, Americans themselves hardly know his name. The illusion that the U.S. alone is the hegemonic arbiter of good and evil may account for its pursuit of the forced relocation of Diné on the Hopi Partitioned Lands, while it forbids the UNWGIP to discuss that issue, lest the U.S. scuttle that forum.

As a measure of the current U.S. foreign policy on rights of indigenous/nationality peoples, Chechnya is an illustrative case, since Russia remains the "centerpiece" of U.S. foreign policy in the post-Cold War era. U.S. reaction to Russia's most recent invasion of Chechnya (there have been several over the past 300 years) has been typically full of contradictions. Although members of the Clinton Administration have condemned Russia's brutal military *tactics* against the Chechens, there has been virtually no challenge to the legitimacy of the basic Russian claim over Chechen territory. President Clinton is clearly supporting Yeltsin's regime, in its attempt to fend off opponents, including the fascistic Vladimir Zhirinovsky, who has no sympathy for Chechens and wants to re-establish a Russian empire. The Clinton Administration believes that Yeltsin represents the best present hope that Russia will become a pro-Western capitalist enterprise. That hope is contingent on territorial integrity, however, and Chechen secession would probably seal Russia's doom, by tapping the wellspring of endemic separatism in the complex Russian Federation. Such separatism could bring on a period of chaos and, given the genuine possibility of a military coup, precipitate another Cold War.

The absence of official criticism and opposition from the U.S. Government has been matched in the U.S. mainstream media. The *New York Times*, for instance, has repeatedly supported Russia's suppression of Chechen self-determination and encouraged Washington to "quietly counsel [Yeltsin] to apply force carefully," because the Chechen claims "cannot be allowed to stand" (*NYT*, 14 December 1994). This, despite the *Times*' own acknowledgment that the Russians have, in the past, occupied Chechnya but never subdued it — because the Chechens have resisted and rebelled continually against Russian domination, twice earlier in this century.

The U.S. State Department (the agency that is constructing the policy on indigenous peoples' rights) agreed with the *Times*, giving Russian territorial claims and military actions higher legitimacy than those of the Chechens. State Department official Mike McCurry succinctly stated the U.S. position on 14 December 1994 (also later affirmed by President Clinton and Secretary of State Christopher) that "Chechnya is an integral part of Russia, and events in Chechnya, because of that, are largely an internal affair." Vice President Al Gore underlined the Administration's stance by saying that the US is "not going to challenge Russian territorial integrity [on the Chechen question]" (Associated Press, 9 January 1995).

As the *Times* concluded, the U.S. statements gave "Mr. Yeltsin a green light for military intervention" (NYT, 28 December 1994). Apparently, neither the U.S. nor the *Times* will object to the general principle of an established state invading a stateless people's territory. The feeble concern that they do raise is rather that the invasion was bungled — it was not done quickly or quietly or effectively enough, and it was not executed cleanly out of television camera range.

Ironically, Zbigniew Brezinski (Jimmy Carter's National Security Adviser), recently joined a few Republican members of Congress and a smattering of conservative newpaper editors in condemning U.S. policy for complicity in the denial of Chechen self-determination, in a column in the *Washington Post* (8 January 1995). Brezinski claims that Chechnya "could become the graveyard of America's moral reputation," because the U.S. refuses to come to the assistance of a "freedom-seeking" people that "dared to reach out for independence." His defense of the "helpless Chechens... who are not Russian and do not wish to be Russian," while laudable under normal circumstances, rings hollow when one recalls his lack of defense of the freedom-seeking Tibetans against China, or of the freedom-seeking East Timorese against Indonesia, and the pounding of the freedom-seeking Kurds by Iran, Iraq, and Turkey, during his watch at the White House. His commentary represents the depth of contradictory sentiments within both conservative ranks and the policy community at large.

In a most telling distortion in his column, Brezinski claims that the U.S. vilification of an indigenous or nationality struggle (of the Chechens), and justification of oppression (by the Russians) "has never happened before." In addition to the cases mentioned above, Brezinski seems to have forgotten the decades of U.S. opposition to the African National Congress, the IRA, the Eritreans, the PLO, the Polisario Front in the Western Sahara, and the Naga Nation struggling for its independence from India. The list of freedom-seeking peoples engaged in nationality and indigenous struggles that have been opposed by the United States could fill pages. It is precisely the United States' own history of opposition to self-determination struggles that should give pause to those who

are watching the new U.S. agenda unfold on the indigenous-rights stage.

The justification applied by the U.S. to the Chechen case, that the survival of a state (Russia) and its territorial claims are more important than the survival of an indigenous people, can easily be observed in other serious cases at this very moment. The government of Myanmar (Burma) is waging a relentless and brutal military attack against the Karen Nation, killing hundreds and forcing tens of thousands of refugees to flee their homeland into Thailand. Not surprisingly, neither the United States, nor any other major power, has submitted any meaningful challenge to Myanmar's attacks. In November, just three months ago, the State Department claimed that it was taking a "conciliatory approach" toward the Burmese military regime, as far as human rights in general were concerned (especially the imprisonment of Nobel Peace Prize laureate Aung San Suu Kyi), but made no attempt to address the question of indigenous rights in particular. The U.S. maintains extensive trade relations with the Ne Win regime; the petroleum, natural gas, timber, weapons, and narcotics industries are all doing big business in Burma. Meanwhile, the U.S. supports, either actively or tacitly, the open relations between the Ne Win regime and China, Thailand, and Japan.

Rather than support the application of the principle of self-determination to the Chechens or the Karen—lest it set a precedent for other freedom-seeking peoples—the United States and other states of the world would prefer to protect the "sovereignty and territorial integrity" of the chauvinistic and human-rights-abusing governments of Russia and Myanmar out of political or economic expedience. Rather than examine the claims of the Karen or the Chechens, that they have never given their consent to be integrated into the Burmese or the Russian states, and that they have long-standing political and territorial claims of their own, the governments of the world side with the oppressor's invasion in the name of regional stability and order. Similar examples of expedience over principle can be cited from Chiapas to the Western Sahara, from Indonesia to Eritrea.

The self-determination of the peoples of Eritrea was ignored, even actively opposed, for over three decades by the major powers of the world, led alternately by the U.S. and the Soviet Union, in the interests of protecting Ethiopia's sovereignty. At the same time the U.S. was assuaging Israel's fear that the Red Sea might be completely bordered by states hostile to its existence. The Eritrean spirit of freedom prevailed despite prohibitive odds, surviving drought and over thirty years of military oppression from the Ethiopian government that was alternately supported by both the United States and the Soviet Union. Eritrea's seat in the United Nations, which can be celebrated as an enormous monument to the perseverance of the Eritrean people, should also serve as a constant source of shame to the world community that consistently rejected a legitimate claim of self-determination in favor of the territorial integrity claims of a corrupt Ethiopian government. Eritrea would still not be seated at the UN if it had to rely solely on the international community's embrace of high-sounding principles respecting the self-determination of peoples. Eritrea's seat would not exist had the Eritreans not mobilized the military might necessary to liberate their homeland and to defend and protect their claim to self-determination.

The lessons of the Chechens, the Karen, and the Eritreans should serve as important lessons to other indigenous peoples and nationalities. If the international community has a choice between the legitimacy of indigenous peoples' claims for territory, treaty rights, economic sustainability, or self-determination, versus the claims of a state, *any* state, for continued survival, indigenous peoples can be virtually certain that the statist claim will be supported consistently. For the United States, consolidating global hegemony is the preeminent national interest at this time. U.S. hegemony can be managed successfully only with a limited number of sovereign states in the system. The U.S., therefore, judges it imperative to forestall any possibility, real or imagined, of a wave of secessionism.

The United States clearly does not take international human-rights obligations seriously, despite its charade of being the world's bastion of respect for rights. Neither is it ever likely to accept the Declaration of Rights for Indigenous Peoples as a constraint on its own policy towards the indigenous peoples enclosed by its borders. At this point in history, there is no reason to believe that increased U.S. interest in indigenous peoples' rights is anything more than self-serving political posturing. The U.S. has made it clear that it opposes any meaningful recognition of the right to self-determination for indigenous peoples; it opposes any serious assertion of territorial or natural-resource control by indigenous peoples; it opposes recognition of the international standing of treaties between indigenous peoples and states; and its recommendation for the protection of indigenous rights rests solely within the domestic jurisdiction of the very states that have historically attacked, dismembered and sought to destroy indigenous peoples. Does this record bespeak an indigenous-rights policy that should be applauded?

Paupers in a World Their Ancestors Ruled

South American Indians still live under the thumb of the conquistadors

Eugene Robinson

Washington Post Foreign Service

LIMA, Peru—As South America prepares to mark the 500th anniversary of Christopher Columbus's voyage of discovery, the people he found when he arrived—and insisted on calling "Indians"—are at the bottom of the social and economic ladder, an underclass in lands their forebears ruled.

Throughout the continent, whites of European ancestry constitute the wealthiest and most powerful class, while Indians are among the poorest and most disenfranchised.

The gap is so wide, and dates so far back, that many people do not perceive it in those terms. Officials in South American countries talk of the need for programs to aid "peasants" or "poor people" in words that obscure the powerful role that race and ethnicity play in determining who is rich and who is poor.

"People like myths," says Maria Rostworowski, a noted Peruvian historian. "The Spanish had their myths; we have ours. To confront the reality of race is disturbing and at times painful. So people tell themselves stories."

One of the myths is that South American societies are mostly, if not entirely, colorblind—that after centuries of coexistence a truly hybrid culture has emerged, one that draws from both worlds.

"There has been a process of mixing, but there is also racism, discrimination and domination," says Jose Diego Condorcanqui, a leading Argentine advocate for Indian rights. Condorcanqui, 55, a self-taught sociologist and anthropologist, is a Kolla Indian born in the Andean province of Jujuy. Elders have named him an *amauta*, or guardian of his ancestors' cultural heritage.

"In the workplace, those of us with brown skin, no matter how qualified, have no real hope of advancement," Condorcanqui says. "Our young people go to the discotheques in Buenos Aires and find that if they do not look Italian or Spanish, they cannot get in. Our youth consider themselves Indian inside the home, but outside they have to abandon their identity."

The theme has regional variations. In Argentina, a country populated mostly by Europeans who arrived at the turn of the century, hundreds of thousands of Indians live out of sight, and out of mind, in the tropical northeast and mountainous northwest. There they endure grinding poverty and a rate of infant mortality twice that of the rest of the country.

Residents of cosmopolitan Buenos Aires can be overheard referring to people of Indian heritage, including the many who live in suburban slums, as "those blacks" or "those greasers."

As Indians in the rest of South America do, Argentina's estimated 3 million Indians enjoy full political rights but practically no representation on the national level. A comprehensive Indians' rights law passed in 1985 remains an empty shell. Its promises of land, development and better education for Indian communities have fallen victim to economic crisis. The government has yet to change an article of the constitution that commits leaders to "Christianize" indigenous populations.

In Brazil, forest Indian communities fight a losing battle against the steamrolling encroachment of the modern world. Their population of up to 5 million when whites arrived has been reduced to around 220,000 today. In the state of Mato Grosso do Sul, more than two dozen members of the Guarani-Kaiowa tribe, mostly young girls, have killed themselves over the past year in apparent despair over the invasion of their reservation lands by ranchers and farmers.

In Bolivia, the Indian majority in the high plains and valleys around La Paz, clinging to traditional clothing and customs, remains desperately poor and increasingly receptive to populist politicians trying to unite them into an electoral force. Last year [1990], hundreds of Indians from the eastern lowlands crossed the Andes on foot to demand that Bolivian officials recognize their claims for hunting and fishing lands.

In Ecuador, Indians fed up with centuries of ethnic discrimination have staged angry protests over the past year, blocking roads, occupying lands and attempting to sabotage elections.

In Paraguay, the racial pecking order exists as elsewhere, but there is more of an attempt to integrate Indian culture into the mainstream. Paraguay has two official languages—Spanish and Guarani, an Indian language—and more than nine out of 10 Paraguayans, including the president, speak both.

Nowhere are the issues of race more complex than in Peru. The seat of the mighty Inca empire, and later the proud headquarters of the Spanish viceroyalty, has been reduced to near-chaos by terrorism, disease, privation and economic catastrophe.

Cuzco, the Inca capital high in the southern Andes, once efficiently organized the care and feeding of millions. Today, the city is ringed by sad shantytowns populated almost exclusively by people of Indian descent—desperate people.

"We see malnutrition in 70 percent of the children under 5 in the shantytowns," says Jorge Silva Sierra, a psychologist who works with a government relief agency in Cuzco. "I spoke to a woman last week who sold her baby for adoption for $1,000."

The overwhelming majority of those struck by the cholera epidemic filling Peruvian hospitals are poor and dark. "Cholera is a poor person's disease," the director of a Lima-area hospital said recently. Up to 20,000 children, mostly Indian, die of diarrheal disease each year.

The streets of Lima are filled with at least a half-million *ambulantes*, or walking vendors, a brown-skinned army selling everything from socket wrenches to toilet paper in an attempt to eke out a living.

Estimates are that well over four-fifths of Peru's population of around 22 million are either Indian or *mestizo*, those of mixed blood. Here, as in other countries, numbers and even individuals are hard to pin down.

When Peruvians come from the countryside to Lima—as hordes have done, swelling the city's population from 700,000 to 7 million in the past 50 years—almost immediately they abandon the traditional rural costume. Long skirts and pigtails give way to stone-washed blue jeans, Michael Jackson T-shirts and curly permanents. Self-image also changes: Indians become mestizos.

The Peruvian state encourages this process of transformation. In a country where at least a third of the population grows up speaking a language other than Spanish—generally Quechua, the tongue of the Incas—there is essentially no bilingual education.

"When the Indian comes to the city and dresses like a mestizo, speaks Spanish instead of Quechua, goes to school and all that, he ceases being an Indian," says Diego Garcia-Sayan, head of the Andean Commission

of Jurists, a human rights lobby. "The Indian is forced to whiten himself. . . . This is just part of the discrimination that runs throughout the society."

In Peru and elsewhere on the continent, those ambiguities of racial identification have helped inhibit the development of any broad-based consciousness movement that might unite Indians into a coherent political force. But there are indications that in some places this may be changing.

Last year [1990], for the first time, racial consciousness—and anger—played a significant role in a Peruvian presidential election, helping political novice Alberto Fujimori defeat novelist Mario Vargas Llosa in a vote that sent analysts scrambling for answers.

Vargas Llosa had held a substantial lead throughout the campaign, but he came to be identified with the traditional elite—the fair-skinned Peruvian oligarchy. The monied classes backed him with their checkbooks and influence, helping Vargas Llosa's message of free-market sacrifice dominate the airwaves.

Fujimori, who is of Japanese descent, railed against "the little whites" who had selfishly run the country into the ground at the expense of the *campesinos* and the *pobladores*, code words for the dark-skinned majority. He told voters in the shantytowns around Lima and in the mountain villages that he would be "a president like you."

In working-class and poor neighborhoods, voters were almost gleeful as they cast their ballots for Fujimori, giving him an impressive victory. "Democracy has lost," television commentator Cesar Hildebrandt, a Vargas Llosa supporter, grumbled on election night.

Fujimori said after the election, "When I put on traditional dress, I look a lot more like most Peruvians than Mario Vargas Llosa ever will."

The racial divide is so striking that many have begun to see the Maoist insurgency called Shining Path—which has provoked the government into putting more than half the country under a state of emergency—as what amounts to an armed Indian revolt.

In reality, Shining Path is primarily led by whites and its doctrines pay little more than lip service to racial issues. About 90 percent of the guerrilla war's 20,000-plus victims over the past decade have been Indians and mestizos from the countryside or the shantytowns.

The Peruvian military is also commanded mostly by whites—just like the armed forces of other South American countries. Descending through the ranks, skin color darkens.

"Indians are just cannon fodder to Shining Path," says Garcia-Sayan, the human rights activist. "But Indians are also the army's cannon fodder. The myth of Shining Path as the voice of the oppressed Indian is simply wrong, but racial discrimination is so great that Shining Path is able to take advantage of the issue and use race to their advantage."

3. INDIGENOUS ETHNIC GROUPS

People like Antonia Saga are caught in the middle.

Saga, who is in her late forties, is from the mountain town of Huanta, just north of Ayacucho, the birthplace of Shining Path. The guerrillas moved into Huanta shortly after beginning their armed struggle in 1980, and attempted to establish a stronghold. The armed forces quickly followed in an attempt to root out the guerrillas. The battle for Huanta has been raging ever since.

Saga's husband, Alejandro Huanahuana, disappeared in 1983. Human rights advocates say there have been nearly 6,000 such disappearances over the past decade.

Frightened for her own safety and that of her eight children, Saga says, she moved to Lima, settling in Canto Grande, an archipelago of shantytowns stretching out from the city's northern suburbs. Like many other such *desplazados*, or displaced persons, she was unable to find work. She could not even afford to buy a cart to make money selling food in the street, she says, so she lived by the kindness of friends.

Last year, Saga says, she went back to Huanta to see what kind of life she could rebuild there. "My home had been searched and they had taken everything," she says. "I went to the army to report it, and they said I was a terrorist. They took me to jail."

She said she was released on condition that she join an antiguerrilla militia sponsored by the armed forces. It was an impossible position to be caught in: participate and become a certain target for Shining Path; refuse and be harassed by the army.

Saga says she fought the guerrillas for a while, witnessing several brutal killings by the militia of people suspected of being guerrillas—"they treat us like animals," she says—and then slipped away and came back to Lima.

"Now I am back in Canto Grande," she says. "The neighbors, bless them, give us food to eat. There is nothing for us, nothing."

Even in Lima, people who fled the highlands to get away from political violence find themselves caught in the middle. The shantytown of Huaycan, for example, has been infiltrated by Shining Path supporters who cover the walls with Maoist graffiti and occasionally drape the main street in red banners.

Whenever there is a high-profile terrorist attack in Lima, police raid places like Huaycan and arrest thousands of people, mostly brown-skinned young men. Citywide round-ups of 20,000 or more are not uncommon.

The flood of people like Antonia Saga coming to Lima has transformed the "City of the Kings," as named by conquistador Francisco Pizarro, from a European-flavored metropolis of wide boulevards and parks into something more Andean, more Indian.

Already, the social and political center of Lima is not the posh traditional suburbs of San Isidro and Mir-aflores, nor even the newer upscale residential redoubts such as Casuarinas—an exclusive, well-guarded hillside neighborhood that is home only to "white people and drug traffickers," in the words of one resident.

Rather, Lima's critical mass lies in the shantytowns that ring the periphery. The biggest and best-known of these in Villa El Salvador, which in less than 20 years has grown from a woebegone outpost clinging to the barren sand dunes south of the city into a makeshift community of more than 300,000 people.

Here, as in other such settlements, migrants from the same Andean region cling together—in social clubs and especially food cooperatives. Peru's economic crisis has forced families to band together to buy food and prepare meals. There are more than 1,000 such cooperatives in Villa El Salvador, comprising around two-thirds of the shantytown's population.

The sectors set aside for new arrivals are easily distinguished by the impermanence of the dwellings—most of them are made exclusively of straw mats—and by the sounds of spoken Quechua. Some older women still wear traditional long skirts and aprons, although immigrant youths quickly adopt the fashions of their city-born playmates.

But there is impermanence of a different kind in evidence in Lima's shantytowns of late—the fleeting dreams of immigrant Indians that a better life can be found in the city. The roads leading out of Lima are now full of return travelers forced by deprivation to seek their future in the places of their past.

"A great many people are having second thoughts," says Jose Rodriguez Aguirre, mayor of Villa El Salvador. "People came here believing that their problems of employment and housing would be solved. Now they realize that it just isn't so. We see an increasing number of people returning to the countryside, or trying to, after they see that Lima is no paradise."

But for many, such as Antonia Saga, a return to the highlands is impossible. Shining Path has extended its influence along the spine of the Andes, occupying some areas and forcing the government to turn others into armed camps.

One area that the armed forces have been able to keep relatively free from guerrilla influence is Cuzco, the gateway to Machu Picchu and focal point of Peru's tourism industry. Magnificent ruins attest to the glories of the past—but Cuzco's present is moribund. Neither Shining Path nor cholera is much in evidence in Cuzco, but nonetheless their specters have combined to keep the tourists away.

An hour outside the city is the Sacred Valley of the Incas, as Peruvians refer to the temple-filled valley of the Urubamba River. Some of the old traditions are still observed. In the town of Urubamba, an occasional house features a long pole crowned with a bunch of flowers or a puff of colored paper—a sign that the proprietor is offering *chicha*, Andean moonshine.

But the villages are shrinking. Some have seen their populations cut by half, as people moved to the shantytowns around Cuzco or Lima. On Sundays, some villagers dress in colorful traditional outfits and bring handicrafts to the town of Pisaq to sell at a weekly market, but it is an empty gesture as long as there are no tourists.

A few of the old Inca agricultural terraces are still in use, as is an old Inca salt mine. Inca bridges, fortresses, cemeteries and temples abound, most of them barely excavated and some completely untouched—there is little money for such undertakings.

At the end of the valley lies Ollantaytambo, perhaps the town in Peru most unchanged from the days when the Incas ruled. Here, amid narrow streets that lead uphill to an impressive fortress, the leader Manco Inca made a desperate stand against the Spaniards in 1536 before fleeing into the mountains. Today, barefoot children play among the ruins while their parents wait beside the road with trays of bargain-priced trinkets.

"This valley has a history that goes far back beyond the Incas," says Pedro Taca, who supervises the ruins at Ollantaytambo for the National Institute of Culture. "This is a heritage that we should all be proud of, that we should all celebrate. Sadly, we do not."

STRUGGLING TO BE THEMSELVES

MICHAEL S. SERRILL

ELIJAH HARPER, A CREE-OJIBWAY Indian and legislator in the province of Manitoba, became a hero to Canadian Indians and Inuit two years ago when he brought the machinery of national constitutional reform to a halt. His decisive no in the Manitoba legislative assembly not only doomed a complex pact designed to put the Canadian confederation on a new footing but also sent the country's political leadership back to the drawing board. Spurred in part by the Manitoban's stubborn stand, federal and provincial leaders agreed for the first time that a revised constitution must recognize native peoples' "inherent right to self-government."

But native rights lost ground when a broad majority of Canadians rejected the new constitution last week. Ovide Mercredi, chief of the Assembly of First Nations, warned of new confrontations as indigenous peoples sought redress through roadblocks and public protests instead. Still, Canada's attempts to codify native self-government was the latest sign that the struggle for political recognition by native peoples across North and South America is bearing some fruit. From the Yukon to Yuma to Cape Horn, indigenous peoples are using new strategies to recover some of the land, resources and sovereignty they lost in the past 500 years. They have negotiated, sued, launched international campaigns, occupied land and, in a few cases, taken up arms to press their cause, marking in their own way the quincentennial of Christopher Columbus' arrival in the New World—an event Native Americans rank as the greatest single disaster in their history.

History cannot be reversed, but historic change seems to be in the making. In Canada the commitment to native self-determination followed another major

CANADA

Native population: 1.5 million
Percent of total population: 6%
Number of bands: 633

Native peoples have made great strides in recovering their lands and political power. Since constitutional recognition has failed, they must seek self-government through legislation.

step: the creation of a self-governing entity called Nunavut out of the vast Northwest Territories, effectively turning a fifth of Canada's 4 million-sq.-mi. territory over to 17,500 Inuit. In the province of Quebec, persistent agitation by 10,000 Inuit and Cree Indians against the second phase of an $11 billion hydroelectric project at James Bay, which would flood thousands more acres of Indian and Inuit lands, has placed the enterprise's future in doubt.

In South America large areas of the Amazon Basin have been reserved for the exclusive use of Brazilian, Ecuadorian, Peruvian and Venezuelan Indians. The rights of tribes to conduct their own affairs, form their own councils and receive royalties for mining activities on Indian lands are gradually being recognized.

In the U.S., Indian tribes are trying to get government to honor promises of autonomy that go back 150 years. Some tribes fund the effort with dollars earned from gambling operations on Indian land, where state writ generally does not apply.

The fate of 40.5 million indigenous people—37 million in Latin America, 2 million in the U.S. and 1.5 million in Canada—has become a focus for discussion at the U.N. and in the councils of the European Community. Environmental groups have declared native peoples to be model conservators of the earth's increasingly fragile ecology. Native activism is entering a multinational phase. Over the past year, representatives of dozens of tribes in the hemisphere have held dozens of meetings to discuss common action to regain land and at least a measure of self-government. In some cases, they have called for recognition of their right to preserve their cultural identities.

Such assertiveness cannot come too soon for most of the Americas' original inhabitants, whose plight, more often than not, is desperate. The U.S.'s poorest county, according to the 1990 census, is the one encompassing the Pine Ridge Reservation of the Oglala Sioux in South Dakota, where 63% of the people live below the poverty line. Death from heart disease occurs at double the national rate; from alcoholism, at 10 times the U.S. average. Similarly, in Canada, aboriginals, as they are called, are among the poorest of the poor, afflicted by high rates of alcoholism and suicide. In Latin America the descendants of the Maya, Aztecs and Incas have been relegated to the lowest rung of society.

Neglect is not the worst that native peoples have suffered. "For centuries governments have often treated the rights of indigenous people with contempt—torturing and killing them in the tens of thousands and doing virtually nothing when others murder them," charges Amnesty International in a report issued last month. The depth of discrimination, poverty and despair makes some of the recent strides by the Americas' native peoples all the more remarkable:

CANADA. Sixty miles north of Vancouver, a group of 700 Sechelt Indians, self-governing since 1986, have established themselves on 3,000 acres of waterfront and forest land. They own a salmon hatch-

UNITED STATES

Indian population: 2 million
Percent of total population: 0.8%
Number of tribes: 515

Nominally autonomous since 1831, U.S. tribes have made real progress only in the past 25 years. They now control 40% of the Indian Affairs budget and fund some social programs through gambling.

---

ery and earn revenue from a gravel-quarrying business; the profits have helped build a community center and provide social benefits, including low-cost housing for the elderly. The Sechelt gained autonomy by giving up their claim to an additional 14,250 acres of British Columbia, for which they have asked $45 million in compensation. Though other natives have criticized the deal, Chief Thomas Paul, 46, says the settlement "will give us a large economic base to make us self-sufficient."

Canada's rejected constitutional changes would have given the natives a "third order of government," with status analogous to the federal and provincial governments. Indians would have gained full jurisdiction over such natural resources as oil and gas, minerals and forests, their own local or regional administrations, justice and education systems, and the administration of much of the $4.5 billion in federal social-welfare funds that flow to the tribes.

Such sweeping guarantees would have been an enormous step forward, but in practical ways Canada is already engaged in enormous land settlements and a broad transfer of local power to native peoples. In many cities as well as in the northern territories, administrative powers and tax money can be turned over to the natives, and Justice Minister Kim Campbell promised after the vote that this will be done. Although some Indians were just as glad the constitutional changes failed, both yes and no voters insisted that the referendum last week did not mean a permanent rejection of native rights.

THE U.S. On the Ak-Chin Indian reservation south of Phoenix, Arizona, self-government and self-sufficiency are taken for granted. The Ak-Chin broke away from the paternalistic U.S. Bureau of Indian Affairs, the federal agency that still controls much of Indian life from cradle to grave, in 1961 when the tribe insisted on farming its own lands rather than leasing them out to non-Indians for negligible revenues. Today the 600-member tribe takes in profits of more than $1 million a year by growing crops on 16,500 acres. About 175 Ak-Chins work on the land or in commu-

nity government; the tribal unemployment rate is 3%. The Ak-Chins accept federal funds only for housing loans. To become even more self-sufficient, the tribe has plans to start manufacturing operations and perhaps casinos.

On paper at least, the 2 million Indians and Eskimos in the U.S. have had more autonomy—and have had it longer—than their Canadian or Latin American counterparts; in 1831 the U.S. Supreme Court declared that the tribes were "domestic dependent nations" entitled to limited self-government. That status was largely fiction for the next 140 years, however; not until 25 years ago did an Indian-rights movement begin agitating to claim what had been guaranteed. Since then the movement has scored some notable gains:

▶ In 1971 Congress awarded the 60,000 native peoples of Alaska $962 million and 40 million acres to settle their land claims. Natives have used the funds to invest in companies involved in everything from timber to broadcasting.

▶ In 1988 the Puyallup Indians in Tacoma, Washington, received $66 million and 300 acres of prime land in the port of Tacoma based on an 1854 treaty. The tribe will build a marina and container-shipping facility on the land—and will celebrate each member's 21st birthday with a $20,000 gift.

▶ In 1990 the Shoshoni-Bannock people of the Fort Hall reservation in Idaho secured their right to use 581,000 acre-feet of water flowing through the Snake River under an 1868 treaty. The tribe will use the water for farming and sell any excess.

Ever since passage of the 1975 Indian Self-Determination Act, the tribes can take back from federal authorities the administration of education and other social programs; as a result, Indian governments now control about 40% of the Bureau of Indian Affairs' $1.9 billion budget. Self-government without development, however, has merely given many Indians the responsibility to administer their own poverty: they still have the shortest life-spans, highest infant-mortality rate, highest high school dropout rate and most extensive health problems of any U.S. ethnic group.

In some places that situation is changing slowly with the spin of roulette wheels. Empowered by a series of court decisions and a 1988 federal law, about 140 Indian tribes across the country operate 150 gambling operations. Revenue has grown from $287 million in 1987 to more than $3.2 billion and is making some tribes rich.

LATIN AMERICA. The protest was unlike anything Ecuadorians had ever seen. In June 1990, responding to a call from the Confederation of Indigenous Nationalities of Ecuador to demand title to their lands, more than half a million native Ecuadorians marched out of their isolated vil-

LATIN AMERICA

Indian population: 37 million
Percent of total population: 8%
Number of tribes: 589

Indians are demanding political rights and the return of lands lost centuries ago. Amazonian tribes have been most successful in obtaining millions of acres, but mineral rights and self-government are proving elusive.

---

lages to block roads, occupy churches and city halls, and stage noisy demonstrations. The sudden upheaval, which lasted a week and virtually shut down the country, shocked the European and mixed-race élites that have ruled Ecuador for centuries—but it also produced results. Last May, then President Rodrigo Borja agreed to hand over legal title to more than 2.5 million acres of Amazon land to 109 communities of Quichua, Achuar and Shiwiar peoples in the eastern province of Pastaza.

"We believe in our capacity to organize, not in the government's goodwill," says Valerio Grefa, leader of the Indians of the Ecuadorian Amazon. Similar sentiments have stirred tribes from Mexico to Chile and have even inspired some armed guerrilla movements that make the struggle for Indian rights part of their ideology. After initial anger and confusion, governments have begun to respond. In Peru, Amazonian Indians have reclaimed 5 million acres of traditional lands, using $1.3 million in assistance from Denmark. Colombia's 60 Indian tribes have won title to more than 2.5 million acres.

In Brazil, with 240,000 Indians in a population of 146 million, the government last year set aside 37,450 sq. mi. for 9,500 Yanomami, a fragile Amazon tribe whose way of life had been virtually destroyed by migratory gold miners. In the past 2½ years, Brasília has created 131 reserves covering 120,000 sq. mi. in 19 states that are home to 100,000 Indians. It is a beginning—but it does not come close to ending the threat to the tribes, whose lands are frequently invaded by aggressive miners and ranchers and who receive little help from the Indian-protection agency.

Cycles of destruction and rebirth are hardly unknown to the Americas' native peoples. The Aymara people of Bolivia have a word for times of war, enslavement and privation: *pachakuti,* or the disruption of the universe. But *pachakuti* also contains the assumption that the cosmic order will be restored, ushering in a period of peace and harmony, or *nayrapacha.* Though their struggle has a far way to go, the native peoples of the two continents are hoping that *nayrapacha* is within their reach. *—Reported by Nancy Harbert/*
Albuquerque, Ian McCluskey/Rio de Janeiro and
Courtney Tower/Ottawa

Return of the Natives

The Kayapó sell Brazil-nut oil to The Body Shop and use video
cameras to record politicians' promises. Just one
of the indigenous peoples who work with outsiders—and organize
themselves—to get off the world's endangered list.

Alan Thein Durning

Salmon from the Pacific Northwest
may be simply a passing pleasure for gourmets, but it is the very bedrock
of Native American culture in that rugged region. When non-Indians took
more and more salmon away from them, the Lummi, Tulalip, Muckleshoot,
and other Northwestern tribes faced the loss of what they held most dear.
Many peoples—among the world's nearly 5,000 distinct indigenous cultures—have faced similar losses, whether through commerce, disease, or
environmental degradation. A handful have found out how to save their

heritage. That handful includes the salmon tribes, who depend on the mysterious instincts of creatures that return from
years in the ocean and fight their way up
cascading rivers to spawn.

A century ago the US government demanded territorial concessions from the
Pacific Northwest Indians. In exchange,
the government promised them permanent access to their customary fishing
grounds, both on and off reservations.
But, starting early in this century, non-
Indian fishers began to take most of the
catch, leaving little for Indians.

ALAN THEIN DURNING ("Environment: What Sid
Did (and You Can Do)," WM, August 1992),
senior researcher at the Worldwatch Institute in
Washington, D.C., adapted this article from his
latest Worldwatch Paper, "Guardians of the Land:
Indigenous Peoples and the Health of the Earth."
His book "How Much Is Enough? The Consumer
Society and the Future of the Earth" was pub-
lished by W.W. Norton & Co.

The native fishing industry dwindled,
and by mid-century had almost died—
until the Indians organized themselves to
demand their rights. Eventually, in a series
of landmark legal rulings in the 1970s, US
courts interpreted the treaties as reserv-
ing half of all disputed fish for Indians.

Their rights secured, the tribes have
once again become accomplished fishery
managers—rejuvenating their traditional reverence for salmon and training themselves in modern approaches with the help
of supportive non-Indians. As stipulated
under the court rulings, state and federal fisheries regulators have agreed with
qualified tribes to manage fish runs jointly. Today those Lummi, Tulalip, Muckleshoot, and other Northwestern tribes are
managing the salmon runs that nourished
their ancestors.

All the globe's indigenous people—
hundreds of millions of them, from Africa
to Australia to the Philippines to the
Americas—have ancient ties to the land,

water, and wildlife of their ancestral do-
mains. All are endangered by the onrush-
ing force of the outside world. They have
been decimated by plagues and violence.
Their cultures have been altered by missionaries and exploited by entrepreneurs.
Their subsistence economies have been
dismantled by the agents of national development. And their homelands have
been overrun by commercial resource extractors and landless peasants.

It's not only in America's Northwest
that the future has begun to brighten. In
Ecuador, for example, Indians have
mounted a dramatic and effective campaign to claim their due. After centuries
of second-class citizenship, they want to
secure not only rights to the lands they
have worked since time immemorial, but
also constitutional recognition of their distinct cultures.

In June 1990, after decades of grassroots organizing, Ecuador's Indian federations called their people to march
peacefully on the cities, to blockade the
nation's highways, and to refuse to sell
food outside their communities. For three
days, a million Indians brought the country to a standstill. Enraged as they were,
the ruling classes had no choice but to
take heed as the Indians enumerated their
priorities. High on the list were 72 land
claims languishing in the bureaucracy.

Negotiations with the government, begun during that watershed week in 1990,
continued with little progress until a new
march began in 1992. This time 2,500

From *World Monitor,* March 1993, pp. 54-56, 58, 60, 62. Originally "Native Americans Stand Their Ground" from *Worldwatch,*
November/December 1991. © 1991 by the Worldwatch Institute, Washington, DC.

marchers set out from the jungle lowlands of Pastaza province, heading for the mountain capital of Quito. As the marchers gained altitude, they gained support, swelling to 10,000 when they reached the seat of government in April. There, with the weight of national opinion behind them, they won rights to almost 3 million acres of their forest homeland.

"The reason why in recent times the indigenous peoples have been having so much success is that indigenous peoples from many different places have come together and united to fight a common battle, to stand together," observes Albino Pereira Cece of the Kinikinau people of Brazil in a statement that applies equally to Ecuador.

A similar case can be found in Namibia, where most of the San (Bushmen)—after a century in which their population declined by 80% and their land base shrank by 85%—are now day laborers on cash-crop plantations. In the 1980s, however, some 48 bands of San, totaling about 2,500 individuals, organized themselves to return to the desert homes they had tenuous rights over. There they have created a modified version of their ancient hunting and gathering economy. With the help of anthropologists, they have added livestock and drip-irrigated gardens to the daily foraging trips of their forebears, fashioning a way of life that is both traditional and modern.

Perhaps because natural-resource rights are best recognized in the Americas, indigenous groups there are the furthest advanced in adapting traditional resource management arrangements to the modern setting.

• In northern Canada, the Inuvialuit people have created management plans for grizzly and polar bears and for beluga whales.

• In southern Mexico, the Chinantec Indians are gradually developing their own blend of timber cutting, furniture making, butterfly farming, and forest preservation in their retreat in the Juarez mountains.

• The Miskito Indians of Nicaragua's Atlantic Coast, meanwhile, are forming local management groups to police the use of forests, wetlands, and reefs in the extensive Miskito Coast Protected Area they helped create in 1991.

Another positive thrust comes from "alternative traders"—organizations committed to cultural survival and environmental sustainability. They now market millions of dollars worth of indigenous

peoples' products in industrial countries. The Mixe Indians of southern Mexico, for example, sell organic coffee to US consumers through the Texas-based alternative-trade organization Pueblo to People. The Kayapó sell Brazil-nut oil for use in hair conditioners to the British-based Body Shop chain.

By eliminating links from the merchandising chain, such alternative traders keep more of the product value flowing back to indigenous producers. The potential for alternative trade to expand is enormous, given the growing purchasing power of environmentally conscious consumers and the abundance of plant products hidden in indigenous lands.

Is all the effort to protect endangered cultures too little, too late—a case of closing the barn door after the barn has burned? Indigenous peoples get little attention in the mainstream media, and what little they get often implies that there are just a few remaining holdouts for a way of life that is, in any case, now largely gone.

Those perceptions are mistaken. Indigenous people are far from disappearing, and their cause is far from hopeless.

There are two compelling reasons for the world's dominant societies to heed the voices of indigenous peoples more seriously than they ever have. These reasons bear not only on the lives—and ways of life—of the threatened peoples, but on those of the dominant ones as well.

1. Indigenous peoples are the sole guardians of vast, little-disturbed habitats that modern societies depend on more than they may realize—to regulate water cycles, maintain the stability of the climate, and provide valuable plants, animals, and

They want rights to the lands they have worked— and to be recognized.

Indigenous cultures by region...

AFRICA AND MIDDLE EAST: Great cultural diversity throughout the continent. "Indigenous" share of land hotly contested. Some 25 million to 30 million nomadic herders in East Africa, Sahel, and Arabian peninsula include Bedouin, Dinka, Masai, and Turkana. San (Bushmen) of Namibia and Botswana and pygmies of central African rain forest, both traditionally hunter-gatherers, have occupied present homelands for at least 20,000 years. 2,000 languages spoken.

AMERICAS: Native Americans concentrated near centers of ancient civilizations: Aztec in Mexico, Mayan in Central America, and Incan in Andes. In Latin America, most farm small plots; in North America, 2 million Indians live in cities and reservations. 900 languages spoken.

ARCTIC: Inuit (Eskimo) and other Arctic peoples of North America, Greenland, and Siberia traditionally fishers, whalers, and hunters. Sami (Lapp) of arctic Scandinavia traditionally reindeer herders. 50 languages spoken.

EAST ASIA: Chinese indigenous peoples, numbering up to 82 million, mostly subsistence farmers such as Bulang of south China or former pastoralists such as ethnic Mongolians of north and west China. Ainu of Japan and aboriginal Taiwanese now largely industrial laborers. 150 languages spoken.

OCEANIA: Aborigines of Australia and Maoris of New Zealand, traditionally farmers, fishers, hunters, and gatherers. Many now raise livestock. Islanders of South Pacific continue to fish and harvest marine resources. 500 languages spoken.

SOUTH ASIA: Gond, Bhil, and other adivasis, or tribal peoples, inhabit forest belt of central India. Adivasis of Bangladesh concentrated in Chittagong hills on Burmese border; several million tribal farmers and pastoralists in Afghanistan, Pakistan, Nepal, Iran, and central Asian republics of former USSR. 700 languages spoken. Tribal Hmong, Karen, and other forest-farming peoples form ethnic mosaic covering uplands. Indigenous popula-

(continued next page)

tion proportional to distribution of forest: Laos has most forest and tribal peoples, Myanmar and Vietnam have less of each, and Thailand and mainland Malaysia have least. Tribal peoples concentrated at ends of Philippine and Indonesian archipelagoes. Island of New Guinea mostly indigenous tribes. 1,950 languages spoken.

...and how they tend their ecosystems

FOREST: Lacondon Maya of southern Mexico plant intricate tree gardens, mimicking the diversity of natural rain forests. Tribal peoples of India revere and protect certain trees as sacred. Gorowa of Tanzania, like the Gabra of Kenya, reserve ancient forest groves as sacred sites dedicated for coming-of-age rituals, men's and women's meeting places, and burials. Karen tribal elders in Thailand carefully regulate community use of forested watersheds.

GRASSLAND: Sukuma, south of Africa's Lake Victoria, rotate grazing on a 30- to 50-year cycle. Zaghawa of Niger move their camels and sheep north to wet-season Saharan pastures in separate, parallel paths, leaving ungrazed strips for the return trek. Fulani orchestrate the orderly return of thousands of head of livestock to the Niger delta in early dry season to avoid overgrazing.

WATERS: Temple priests in highlands of Bali distribute irrigation water to farmers through networks of channels, with synchronized rotation ensuring fairness, maximum yields, and minimum pest damage. In mountains of Iran, long-lived gravity-powered quanat system provides irrigation water through elaborate excavations and recharging of groundwater.

FISHERIES: In South Pacific, ritual restrictions based on area, season, and species prevent overfishing; religious events often open and close fishing seasons. In Marquesas islands, chieftains forbid the consumption of certain fish and enforce the ban, in extreme cases, by expulsion from island. Wet'suwet'en and Gitksan of Canadian Pacific believe salmon spirits give their bodies to humans for food but punish those who waste fish, catch more than they can use, or disrupt habitats.

genes. These homelands may harbor more endangered plant and animal species than all the world's nature reserves.

2. Indigenous peoples possess, in their ecological knowledge, an asset of incalculable value: a map to the biological diversity of the earth on which all plant, animal, and human life depends. Encoded in indigenous languages, customs, and practices may be as much understanding of nature as is stored in the libraries of modern science.

It was little appreciated in past centuries of exploitation, but it is undeniable now, that the world's dominant cultures cannot sustain Earth's ecological health without the aid of the world's endangered cultures. Biological diversity—of paramount importance both to sustaining viable ecosystems and to improving human existence through scientific advances—is inextricably linked to cultural diversity.

Indigenous peoples are "the 'miner's canary' of the human family," says Guajiro Indian writer José Barreiro. Their cultures, existing in direct and unmediated dependence on nature, are the first to suffer when it is poisoned, degraded, or exhausted. Yet in a world threatened by mass species extinction, catastrophic climate change, and industrial contamination of land, air, and water, no culture can afford to be complacent.

In the words of Guarani holy man Pae Antonio, whose Argentine village was burned to the ground in 1991 to make way for a casino, "When the Indians vanish, the rest will follow."

What are the conditions in which traditional systems of ecological management can persist in the modern world? Based on the diverse experience of indigenous peoples, three necessary conditions stand out.

1. Traditional stewardship's persistence depends on indigenous peoples having secure rights to their subsistence base—rights that are not only recognized but enforced by the state and, ideally, backed by international law. Latin American tribes such as the Shuar of Ecuador, when threatened with losing their land, have cleared their own forests and taken up cattle ranching, because in Latin America these actions prove ownership. If Ecuador had defended the Shuar's land rights, the ranching would have been unnecessary.

2. Indigenous ecological stewardship can survive the onslaught of the outside world if indigenous peoples are organized politically and the states in which they reside allow democratic initiatives. The Khant and Mansi peoples of Siberia, like most indigenous people in the former Soviet Union, were nominally autonomous in their customary territories under Soviet law, but political repression precluded the organized defense of that terrain until the end of the '80s. Since then, the peoples of Siberia have begun organizing themselves to turn paper rights into real local control. In neighboring China, in contrast, indigenous homelands remain nothing more than legal fictions because the state marginalizes all representative organizations.

3. If they are to surmount the obstacles of the outside world, indigenous communities need access to information, support, and advice from friendly sources. The tribal people of Papua New Guinea know much about their local environment, for example, but they know little about the impacts of large-scale logging and mining. Foreign and domestic investors have often played on this ignorance, assuring remote groups that no lasting harm would result from leasing parts of their land to resource extractors. If the forest peoples of Papua New Guinea could learn from the experience of threatened peoples elsewhere—through supportive organizations and indigenous peoples' federations—they might be more careful.

As they struggle to adapt their natural resource stewardship to modern pressures, indigenous peoples are beginning to pool their expertise.

• The Native Fish and Wildlife Service in Colorado, formed by a coalition of North American tribes, serves as an information clearinghouse on sustainable management.

• The Kuna of Panama—whose tribal regulations on hunting turtles and game, catching lobsters, and felling trees fill thick volumes—have convened international conferences on forest and fisheries management, with the aid of environmental funders.

• The Inuit Circumpolar Conference representing Inuit peoples from Canada, Greenland, Russia, and the United States, has developed an Inuit Regional Conservation Strategy that includes tight controls on wildlife harvesting and resource extraction, and collaborative arrangements for sharing ecological knowledge.

Such instances are still exceptional, but they blaze a trail for indigenous peoples everywhere.

A newer route to assuring indigenous peoples a basic income is through intellectual property rights—proprietary rights to ideas, designs, or information most commonly typified by patents and copyrights.

With the explosive growth in biotechnology since 1980, the demand for new genetic material is burgeoning. Many of the world's genes are in the millions of species in the endangered places known only to endangered peoples. Indeed, some indigenous leaders think of the rush to codify and exploit their people's knowledge of biological diversity as the latest in the long history of resource grabs perpetrated against them.

"Today," says Adrian Esquina Lisco, spiritual chief of the National Association of Indigenous Peoples of El Salvador, "the white world wants to understand the native cultures and extract those fragments of wisdom which extend its own dominion."

Still, supporters of indigenous peoples are developing legal strategies to turn the gene trade to native advantage by demanding recognition that indigenous communities possess intellectual property rights as valid as those of other inventors and discoverers.

Legal cases play an important part in native movements in places where the rule of law is strong. North American tribes now have a generation of talented lawyers who turn what they call "white man's law" to Indian advantage, winning back ancestral land and water rights. Maori organizations in New Zealand catalyzed the creation of a special tribunal to investigate violations of the century-old Waitangi treaty, which guaranteed Maori land rights. The tribunal is charged with sifting through claims that cover 70% of the country and many of its offshore fisheries.

All in all, from the smallest tribal settlements to the UN General Assembly, indigenous peoples' organizations are making themselves felt. Their grassroots movements have spread quickly since 1970, strengthening their political skills, recruiting ever more members, adapting their cultural techniques of self-defense to the political circumstances in which they find themselves.

Some indigenous movements have also mastered use of communications media. Brazil's Kayapó tribe takes video cameras to meetings with politicians to record the promises they make. Aboriginal groups in Australia publish newspapers reflecting their culture. And 2 million Aymara Indians in Bolivia, Peru, and Chile tune their radios to Radio San Gabriel for Aymara language news, music, and educational programming.

Regional and global meetings on the rights of indigenous peoples are now commonplace. In June 1992, for example, three separate conferences of native peoples were held in Rio, one preceding and two coinciding with the UN Conference on Environment and Development.

The longest-lived series of meetings, and perhaps the most important, has been the annual sessions of the Geneva-based UN Working Group on Indigenous Populations. Established by the UN Human Rights Commission in 1982, the Working Group is drafting a Universal Declaration on the Rights of Indigenous Peoples. The version of late 1992 stated: "Indigenous peoples have the collective and individual right to own, control and use the lands and territories they have traditionally occupied or otherwise used. This includes the right to full recognition of their own laws and customs, land tenure systems and institutions for the management of resources, and the right to effective measures by States to prevent any interference with or encroachment on these rights."

The end of the Cold War has unfrozen systems of governance, allowing a shifting of political authority from central governments both downward to local bodies and upward to international ones. It has also allowed the protection of the global environment to rise to a prominent place on the international agenda.

Some of the unfreezing of governance will undoubtedly play itself out in increased nationalism, as it has with tragic effects in the former Yugoslavia in the early '90s. Declarations of national independence have come at a frenzied pace in recent years, to the astonishment of most students of international affairs. Between 1988 and October 1992, the UN membership rolls added 16 new names, totalling 178.

Such a trend tends to reinforce itself. If Latvians, Czechs, and Eritreans deserve national recognition, peoples everywhere are bound to ask themselves, Why not us too? The Oromos of Ethiopia, the Tibetans, the Karen of northern Myanmar, and the Papuans and Timorese of eastern Indonesia have been struggling for autonomy or independence for decades. Scores of other peoples may eventually voice similar demands. Given the underlying cultural divisions that scar Africa and Asia in particular, the number of states could continue to rise swiftly for some time to come.

Such a scenario—involving the dissolution of China and various multi-ethnic African states—would have seemed farfetched in the late '80s. In 1993, it is at least conceivable.

A global tapestry of diverse cultures must still have some binding threads. The rapid degradation of the global environment suggests that one of these universal values should be the objective of passing on to future generations a planet undiminished by the present generation's actions. As this value gains political support worldwide, indigenous cultures could benefit. Their qualifications as stewards of ecosystems could increase their prominence and win them long-deserved respect. They may finally be seen as part of the future, as well as of the past.

These peoples also offer the world's dominant culture—a consumerist and individualist culture born in Europe and bred in the United States—living examples of ancient values that may be shared by everyone: devotion to future generations, ethical regard for nature, and commitment to community among people.

For environmentalists, indigenous peoples represent the best hope for preserving the vast, little-degraded habitats encompassed by ancestral homelands. For indigenous peoples, environmentalists are powerful allies, sometimes better skilled in the thrust and parry of modern resource politics. Both sides of this alliance are somewhat wary of the other, divided sometimes by culture, race, and priorities. Still, in the end, indigenous peoples and the environmental movement have much in common. In the words of a young man from the Banwa'on tribe of the Philippines: "Our skins might not be the same color, but our dreams are the same."

WHY DID CHIAPAS REVOLT?

THE MAKING OF AN EXPLOSION

CHARLES R. SIMPSON
ANITA RAPONE

CHARLES R. SIMPSON *and* ANITA RAPONE *are professors from the State University of New York doing research in Mexico for the year.*

n Mexico's state of Chiapas, the resistance to economic development without social development has found a popular voice. It is the voice of a Mayan peasant force, the Zapatista Army of National Liberation (EZLN), which appeared in San Cristóbal de las Casas and a handful of other places in Chiapas on January 1, 1994. In their Declaration from the Lacandon Jungle, which accompanied their appearance, the EZLN wrote:

> We are the product of 500 years of struggle: first against slavery, in the war of independence against Spain, then to escape being absorbed by North American expansion.... we have nothing to lose, absolutely nothing, no decent roof over our heads, no land, no work, poor health, no food, no education, no right to freely and democratically choose our leaders, no independence from foreign interests, and no justice for ourselves or our children.

> But we say it is enough! We are the descendants of those who truly build this nation. We are the millions of dispossessed, and we call upon all of our brethren to join our crusade, the only option to avoid dying of starvation!

In their declaration, and in their subsequent communications, the EZLN rejected a system of development where two of every three people in a population of over 3 million never complete primary school. It said "no" to electrification in which the rivers of Chiapas supply power to Mexico City, but a third of Chiapans are without electricity. It rejected a distribution of wealth in which 0.2 percent of the population—billionaires owning supermarket chains and speculators in telephone stock—are richer than half the people of Mexico combined, while half the people in Chiapas have houses with dirt floors. It deplored an economy in which 20 families in Chiapas monopolize the best land, exporting cattle to the United States, while 1,032,000 *Indigenas* possess 823,000 hectares, less than a hectare a person. It denounced a pay scale in which 80 percent of agricultural workers earn less than the minimum salary per day, under five dollars, resulting in 88 percent of indigenous children having growth retardation from malnourishment.

According to Major Sergio of the EZLN, "We want our children to study, to be able to leave, and go to the university." But in his part of the Selva Lacandon, the schools are closed eight out of ten months for lack of teachers. "The government was not going to respect us, and so the armed force began to grow. They obliged us to take the position we take. To meet our needs we must sell our land. And who will buy it? Those who have money. Our children are going to have to return to the slavery of the *finca* and the *patrones* who pay them only two pesos a day."

What has been the process of modernization in Chiapas?

Chiapas does not have a bucolic history. It is part of a region which was depopulated through recurrent plagues of European diseases from the sixteenth to the eighteenth century, a tragedy made worse by the *encomienda* system which granted Indian land to the Spanish and concentrated the indigenous population in villages obliged to pay taxes in crops and forced labor. In this roadless and mountainous terrain, both harvest and *ladino* landowners were carried on the backs of Indian porters, people being cheaper transportation than horses.

Nonetheless, the colonial period, whose racial caste system was unaltered by Mexican independence, left two positive results. The first was the identification of the Catholic church with the suffering of the indigenous population. The second was a solidarity among Indians which identified life with the continuity of community and culture, linking both to the fields which made life possible. Today, this syncretism can be seen in the Mayan crosses on Lacandon hills, a Christian cross with pine branches added as a reference to the four directions of Mayan cosmology. Such crosses, twenty and thirty feet high, are symbolic trees linking the earth to both an underworld and a spir-

From *Commonweal*, June 3, 1994, pp. 16-19. © 1994 by the Commonweal Foundation. Reprinted by permission.

it world, acting as an *axis mundi* around which nature and morality turn. And syncretism can be seen today in Catholic churches, such as the one at San Juan Chamula, where the images of saints take on a double identity as Mayan gods, becoming the object of indigenous as well as Christian ritual.

While the 1910 revolution did not alter economic and political domination by *ladinos* in Chiapas, it did reinforce Indian communal ownership of land through the *ejido* system, which made land ineligible for private sale. At present there are 1,714 communal agrarian communities in Chiapas, controlling 41 percent of the land. But they work their land without much capital or credit. Only 28 percent have farming structures, usually for pigs or chickens, and only 18.6 percent have tractors.

The post-World War II period brought a nationalist economic agenda to Mexico based on tariff protection of Mexican industry and an import-substitution program. Where development competed with rural land redistribution, the former took priority. In Chiapas, rivers were dammed for hydropower transmitted elsewhere. The dam at Angostura created Mexico's largest fresh water lake on land Indians considered to be among their most fertile.

At the same time, the internationalization of agricultural markets accelerated, with coffee and cattle coming to dominate export crops and providing an incentive for land consolidation in Chiapas. By 1980, about a hundred growers—0.16 percent of the 74,000 coffee producers—owned 12 percent of the land. Using impoverished migrant laborers from Guatemala, the large coffee producers have kept wages well below the Mexican legal minimum. Overall, 6,000 families own half the arable land in the state, using it largely for cattle production which produces few jobs.

Beneath these statistics lies a state political process tied to the ruling agricultural elite. This class, controlling the state organization of the near-monopolistic Institutional Revolutionary party (PRI), has systematically evaded the anti-latifundia laws, nominally dividing their estate lands into separate entitlements held in the names of others acting as fronts. For the past twenty years, the Chiapan state government has failed to prosecute *ladino* ranchers who illegally appropriate Indian lands, and who meet Indian resistance with violence. Instead, the state criminal justice system is used to repress Indians protesting the seizure of their lands. The absence of the rule of law has permitted the erosion of *ejido* lands, the growth of a labor surplus, and the maintenance of low rural wages.

As the fertile lower hills of Chiapas were converted to cattle ranches and coffee estates, unsustainable logging practices reduced the Lacandon rainforest to one-tenth its nineteenth-century size. Remaining forest land became the site of colonization, as the government sought to relieve the pressure for land by the poor without redistributing the land of the wealthy.

However inadequate and environmentally destructive this colonization process, even it ended by 1990, when Mexico's President Carlos Salinas de Gortari declared that the process begun in the 1910 revolution—the redistribution of land to the poor—had ended. Peasants, many of whom had waited decades for action on their petitions, now had no hope that the political process would end their landlessness. At the same time, the Salinas government eliminated the constitutional protection against the private purchase of *ejido* lands, permitting foreign investors to own and establish the market prices for Mexican land. In such a "free market" in land, a Mexican concession to the process of integrating markets and capital flows capped by the North American Free Trade Agreement (NAFTA), the Chiapan poor had no hope of a place.

As a voice calling for social development rather than inequitable economic growth, the Catholic church in Chiapas has played an important role. In the tradition of Bartolome de las Casas, Samuel Ruiz, the current bishop of San Cristóbal, facilitated an important meeting in 1974, the Indigenous Congress, which gave Indians a forum for their grievances. Employing the moral perspective of liberation theology, participants subsequently developed a variety of indigenous organizations. By 1980, three organizations merged to form the Union of Unions of Ejidos and Campesino Groups, whose 4,500 heads of families sought autonomy through alternative models of development. This "development from below" included establishing credit unions; utilizing their own processing, trucking, and marketing system to export organic coffee; and buying a commercial farm where they established a university. Other groups sought to organize coffee and cattle-ranch labor, and others led land invasions along the Chiapas coast. The success of indigenous organizing in the 1970s and '80s brought a backlash. Land takings, or retakings, were resisted by cattle ranchers in bloody confrontations. By the '80s, ranchers had organized a private security force, "white guards," to terrorize peasants. In 1988, the leaders of two indigenous peasant organizations were assassinated.

The underlying debate in Indian communities during the 1980s was over the tactics to be used to reclaim lands. These communities considered their inheritance from the ancient and sometimes recent past, and they discussed organizational forms for promoting Indian economic self-determination and for escaping from the day-labor system. One faction followed a strategy of autonomous economic development. But with the reluctance of the government to break up illegal agricultural estates, the jailing of land invaders, and the increase in "white guard" violence, a faction arguing the need for an armed resistance grew. This faction, rooted in the history of the land struggles of the indigenous communities, became the incipient EZLN.

The pressure on land increased in the 1990s as federal restrictions were placed on the remaining forest lands, much of it *ejido* property, prohibiting the ancient but sustainable practice of burning brush to clear and fertilize fields. According to *La Jornada* (January 14, 1994), by 1990 15,000 indigenous people were in prison on charges related to land conflicts, and in the last ten years over thirty peasant leaders have been assassinated. Conflicts between peasants and ranchers intensified near Ocosingo and Altamirano in early 1993, leading to the military occupation of several Indian communities.

3. INDIGENOUS ETHNIC GROUPS

According to EZLN spokesperson, Subcomandante Marcos, this was a decisive moment, with the Indians dedicating what they could from their 1993 harvest income to buy guns.

The January 1994 occupation of the towns of Ocozingo, San Cristóbal, and smaller communities was an act of "armed propaganda." Government buildings were taken over and federal food stores opened up for the poor. In openly displaying weapons, and what was to become their symbolic black ski mask, or *pasamontaña*, the EZLN asserted that the indigenous communities were already suffering from violence—disease, malnutrition, political exclusion, and economic exploitation—that was as real as and more pervasive than the sudden violence of war. While they did attack the military base of Nuevo Rancho and defended themselves fiercely against a government assault at Ocozingo, their appearance was essentially a dramatic gesture, aimed at redefining the direction of modernization. In placing themselves in a position to be killed by the far larger and better equipped Mexican army, they declared that since they already faced the extinction of the Indian community they had nothing to lose.

The Mexican government, initially unprepared, responded with the commitment of tanks and aircraft, bombed populated parts of San Cristóbal indiscriminately, and retook Ocozingo. The EZLN fell back to the forest where it defends a liberated zone of indigenous communities. Having regained control of the highway system and larger towns, the army set up road blocks and sweeps designed to deny the rebels outside aid. At a point where it appeared the army was waiting only for sufficient reinforcements to carry out a scorched earth policy, the church stepped in to prevent a massacre. Bishop Ruiz agreed to facilitate peace talks between the federal government and the EZLN. With pressure from Washington to downplay the Chiapas events as a regional disturbance unrelated to NAFTA—whose implementation began the day of the EZLN uprising and was explicitly cited in their list of grievances—the Mexican government decided to engage in peace talks with Ruiz as mediator. Following a second round of talks in April, the army has continued to hold itself more or less in place.

The situation, however, has not been static. Peasants, emboldened by the EZLN's armed posture and the legitimacy that the successful public relations campaign of Subcomandante Marcos gave to Indian grievances, seized an opportunity that might never be repeated to negotiate land redistribution from a position of possession. They initiated hundreds of land retakings throughout Chiapas, many far from the liberated zone of the Lacandon Selva. Their occupations were echoed by smaller occupations in other states. These repossessions are always community undertakings, usually involving lands petitioned for over many decades, sometimes to regain land seized by *ladinos* in the early nineteenth century. By early March, the peasant group CEIOC asserted that between 200,000 to 300,000 hectares had been occupied since the beginning of the year. Ranchers retaliated by assassinating peasant leaders and calling on the federal government to remove all foreign priests, close the Catholic hospital for Indians at Altamirano, and suspend Catholic church services in Chiapas until Bishop Ruiz was replaced.

There are those in the Mexican government, and in our own, who argue that the armed revolt of the Indian poor in Chiapas is a commentary, however unfortunate, on the *lack* of modernization in this part of Mexico. What is needed, they say, is more private enterprise: A swift opening of the repatriation of profits, state support of private business through public works, and job training. This is the standard neoliberal prescription for growth advocated by the World Bank and proposed by President Salinas. But with Mexico's poor exceeding half the population, a free market of land, resources, food, and labor is likely to bring disaster. Guatemala is clamoring to join NAFTA, adding to the pool of impoverished, surplus labor. There appears to be no floor to regional wage competition. Among the marginalized poor, one can only predict an increasingly desperate scramble for survival.

The revolt in Chiapas, we would argue, has presented a counter-definition of governmental responsibility. It is one based on cooperative responsibility among the members of grassroots communities, and it is based on the desire of these communities to sustain their integrity and cultures. That rebellion in Chiapas could be crushed militarily, and that Indian culture itself can be pulverized by conventional "development" is quite clear. Only the existence of heightened international scrutiny has prevented the first from taking place; only genuine self-determination for the region, a result not-at-all certain to come out of the peace negotiations, can prevent the second. What is less clear but just as critical is what the destruction of the indigenous perspective on place, time, and community would mean for Western society.

Towards Information Self-Sufficiency

The Nunavik Inuit gather information on ecology and land use

William B. Kemp and Lorraine F. Brooke

William B. Kemp and Lorraine F. Brooke worked with Makivik Corporation for 16 years. They now both work independently on issues related to indigenous environmental and ecological knowledge, cultural heritage and territorial rights.

> *There are many ways to be poor, but in today's world not having the right kind of information represents a certain kind of poverty. As long as outsiders decide what is important and are in a position to ask all of the questions, we will never be able to solve our own problems. Without information we are nothing at all and have no power to understand things or to change our life. If Inuit society is to develop we must be able to collect and use information according to our own terms.*
> **— a Nunavik Inuk, 1978**

In November 1975, the Inuit of Nunavik (northern Quebec, Canada) signed the James Bay and Northern Quebec Agreement, a document that would bring significant change to all aspects of the cultural, economic and political life of Nunavik. The signing of this document culminated a period of intense change set in motion by government programs initiated in northern Quebec with little consultation and with almost no understanding of the needs and priorities of Inuit. The negotiations leading up to the Agreement represented an information-based process, yet the Inuit still found themselves without access to, or control over, the critical information being used to chart their future.

The James Bay and Northern Quebec Agreement was the first comprehensive land claims settlement in Canada. For their part, the Inuit were granted lands in ownership, compensation funds, harvesting rights, participation in resource and land management regimes, control over education and cultural development and their own local and regional governments.

Immediately, the Nunavik Inuit had to face a staggering number of issues involved with developing their territory. New rights and responsibilities gave rise to new Inuit-controlled institutions with essential powers to manage, conserve and develop their territory and resources. From the very outset, it became apparent the Inuit needed appropriate information to make decisions and to influence the decision-making of others.

At first, the Inuit were concerned with equal access to scientific and other Western-based information concerning their territory and Arctic ecosystems. Very soon, however, it became apparent to them that this information was severely limited. It rarely showed changes over time, was far from complete, and failed to address many of the critical social, economic, political, environmental and educational issues confronting Inuit society. At this point the Inuit shifted to a concern with developing an entirely new information base.

3. INDIGENOUS ETHNIC GROUPS

The move towards information self-sufficiency was difficult and time-consuming. The Inuit of Nunavik were information-rich as a culture but data-poor as a political group. They were also skeptical about the importance of research and its role in the development of Nunavik. In those days, Inuit only met those researchers who came from the outside to collect information and then leave. Looking back on this time, many Inuit remain resentful about what happened to their heritage, to their traditional knowledge, and therefore to their intellectual and cultural property.

DEVELOPING THE DATA BASE

Makivik Corporation, the institution created to hold and invest the compensation funds from the Agreement on behalf of Inuit political and economic interests, decided to establish and fund a Research Department with the following mandate:

1. To identify the research needs and priorities of the Nunavik Inuit, to develop a relevant program of studies for meeting these needs and priorities, and to formulate principles and guidelines for Inuit participation in all phases of research;

2. To recognize both the intrinsic value as well as the scientific importance of Inuit knowledge to the future success of northern science and research;

3. To encourage Inuit participation in scientific work through programs of training and education, and to foster the exchange of knowledge and skills through the development of a cooperative working relationship between Inuit and non-native researchers;

4. To establish a scientific expertise within Makivik Corporation which can be called upon to inform decision-makers, help in the formulation of policies and programs dealing with scientific or research concerns, assist Inuit communities and other organizations, and play a leading role in establishing an effective consultation process with communities;

5. To place a major emphasis on the creation of a well-structured data base for all of Nunavik and to begin the development of a computer-based system for processing the information contained in this data base.

In order to fulfill its mandate, the Department concentrated on four main areas. The first was Inuit land use and harvesting: it decided to gather, review

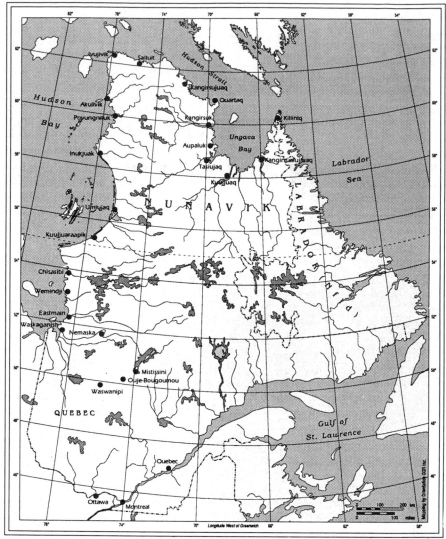

Nunavik, northern Quebec, Canada.

Orientation CGR Inc.

and continually update necessary information for a large geographical data base on past and present land use patterns and harvesting levels for all species, both on land and offshore. The second integrated Inuit knowledge about the environment, ecology and resources of Nunavik into the Nunavik data base. Studies of the wildlife resources of Nunavik would be a third area. Finally, the fourth area involves applying the results of the first three to planning and assessing social and environmental impact. Figure 1 on the following page lists the major outputs of the Department since its creation in 1975.

Of particular interest to this article is the Nunavik Inuit Land Use and Ecological Mapping Project. The first stage was to develop protocols and make methodological decisions in direct consultation with the Inuit communities involved. The protocols

established the rules guiding Inuit control, participation, and confidentiality of information. Maps were found to be essential for gathering the information, whether through individual or group interviews.

Maps were essential not only for recording data but also for animating the interview process. Each hunter could directly relate the visual language of the map to the specific types of data being recorded. Transcribing the hunter's information and knowledge onto a map also allowed them to evaluate its content and accuracy. Every interview is supported by a tape-recorded or written record, transcribing facts or interpretations that could not be mapped. (See Figure 2.)

All of the resulting information has been processed as part of a geographic information system developed specifically for this Project. The entire electronic

FIGURE 1

Major Research Projects Comprising the Nunavik Data Base

HARVESTING STUDIES

1975 - 1980	Harvest study - all communities
1976 - 1990	Development of annual monitoring studies on Koksoak River harvest
1978	Special study of "Weekend" Harvest - Kuujjuaq
1986	Follow-up marine mammal harvesting study - all communities
1988 - 1994	Beluga whale harvest monitoring - all communities

LAND USE AND ECOLOGICAL KNOWLEDGE STUDIES

1975 - 1976	Land use and ecological knowledge study - Koksoak River and Southern Ungava Bay
1976 - 1977	Collection of specific land use and ecological knowledge data - Kangirsujuaq, Quartaq and Kangirsuk
1977 - 1980	Collection of land use information as part of harvest calendar data
1978 - 1981	Special land use and ecological knowledge study - Salluit, Akulivik and Inukjuak
1982 - 1987	Beginning of systematic updating of land use and ecological knowledge studies - all communities
1989 - 1990	Supplementary data collection on land use - Kuujjuaraapik and Umiujaq
1990	Integration of land use and ecological knowledge derived from anthropological and geographical studies carried out in Nunavik prior to 1975, and primarily between 1961-1968

BIOLOGICAL AND ECOLOGICAL RESOURCE STUDIES

1976	First phase of biological monitoring - Koksoak River Fishery
1977 - 1990	Systematic annual biological monitoring - Koksoak River Fisheries
1980	Eider duck cooperative study, population biology of eider down production - Ungava Bay Coastal Survey
1980	Beluga whale cooperative study - Stock identity, assessment, biology and ecology - Ungava Bay and Hudson Strait
1981 - 1982	Beluga whale summer aerial surveys - Ungava and Hudson Bay; winter survey - Hudson Strait
1982	Beluga whale survey summer field stations - Nastapoka and Whale River Estuaries
1983 - 1984	Beluga whale sampling program for biological study
1983 - 1984	Arctic char biology and enhancement studies - Akulivik, Salluit (Deception Bay), Kangirsujuaq, Kangirsuk and Kangirsualujjuaq
1985 - 1990	Arctic char, continuation of enhancement studies
1985 - 1986	Eider duck, Southeastern Hudson Bay population, biology, down production, traditional knowledge
1987 - 1989	Arctic char, stream enhancement and habitat study
1989 - 1990	Marine mammal toxicity studies - Nottingham Island, Salluit and Kangirsualujjuaq

OFFSHORE FISHERY STUDIES

1979	Experimental fishery - Eastern Hudson Strait and Ungava Bay
1980	M/V Thalassa exploratory cruise
1984	Killiniq Fisheries Project - Phase 1
1986	Killiniq Fisheries Project - Phase 2
1987	Killiniq Fisheries Project - Phase 3
1987	Offshore Exploratory Program 1
1988	Offshore Exploratory Program 2
1989	Offshore Exploratory Program 3

ARCHEOLOGY

1979	Offshore Island, Southeastern Hudson Bay Survey
1980	Offshore Surveys - Sleeper and Adjacent Islands
1981 - 1982	Nearshore Islands and Inukjuak Survey
1984 - 1990	Archeological programs taken over by Avataq Cultural Institute

MANAGEMENT AND PLANNING PROGRAMS

1976	Development of coordinating committee for hunting, fishing and trapping
1978 - 1982	Development of community offshore/mainland management plans, community folios
1983	Creation and development of Anguvigaq resource management groups
1983	Kuujjuaraapik Hydro Development - study of impact on offshore hunting
1985	Feasibility study and community plan - new community at Taqpangayuk for Killiniq Resettlement
1985 - 1987	Airport infrastructure impact studies
1987	World Conservation Strategy for Sustainable Development - submission of program and plan for Nunavik
1989	Development of statements of claim to the offshore and Labrador
1991- 1994	Participation in the environmental assessment of the Great Whale River Hydro-electric Development Project

data base for Nunavik has been transferred to a Macintosh system running Micro Station software for processing electronic maps, Adobe Illustrator software for finished maps and graphics, Oracle software for managing the data base, and Power Draw for moving information between Micro Station and Illustrator. Written information is processed on Microsoft Word software, and statistical data on Microsoft Excel and Delta Graph Professional software.

The resulting electronic data base is essential for analyzing and evaluating cartographic information, since it enables all the data to be easily upgraded, expanded or integrated in different combinations to create new maps.

LESSONS LEARNED

The most important lesson learned from the Nunavik experience is that indigenous peoples must first and foremost control their own information. It has also become clear over the years that the knowledge base of indigenous peoples is vital, dynamic and evolving. Merely "collecting" and "documenting" indigenous environmental knowledge is in fact counterproductive. These knowledge systems have been under serious attack for centuries, and the social systems that support them have been seriously undermined. However, indigenous peoples must not just support "salvage" operations of what now is often referred to as "a rapidly disappearing knowledge base". It is not just a question of recovery and recording indigenous knowledge; it is one of respect and revitalization. This information has to remain current and not be considered a relic of the past. Indigenous peoples must also insist that their knowledge not be reduced to an interesting research topic for western science to explore.

On the technical side, the major lesson is that the process must be data-driven rather than technology-driven. Too often groups acquire complex computer hardware and geographic information systems without having made important methodological decisions concerning the information they wish to store and analyze and the type of data base they wish to develop. Computers are just a tool. The information base itself should be the core of any program.

FIGURE 2

Creating the Nunavik Inuit Land Use and Ecological Knowledge Database

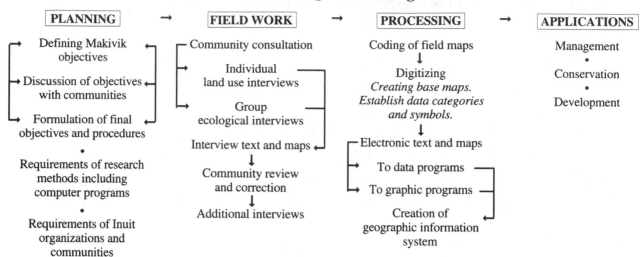

PLANNING	→	FIELD WORK	→	PROCESSING	→	APPLICATIONS
Defining Makivik objectives		Community consultation		Coding of field maps		Management
Discussion of objectives with communities		Individual land use interviews		Digitizing *Creating base maps. Establish data categories and symbols.*		Conservation
Formulation of final objectives and procedures		Group ecological interviews				Development
Requirements of research methods including computer programs		Interview text and maps		Electronic text and maps		
Requirements of Inuit organizations and communities		Community review and correction		To data programs		
		Additional interviews		To graphic programs		
				Creation of geographic information system		

Excerpt from a Land Use Interview with a Hunter

Interview: *HUNTER #040*
Topic: *CONTINUATION OF HISTORICAL LAND USE*

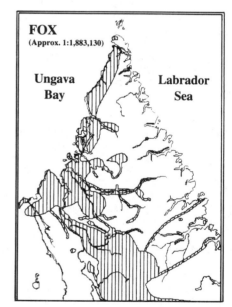

Example of a map, detailing land use and occupancy (specifically for fox) by the Inuit of Nunavik for the coastal and inland areas of Labrador.

ELDER DUCK: *"There are hardly any ducks around Nachvak Fiord, because the Nachvak Fiord has very high, steep cliffs which are impossible to nest on. There are only ducks once in a while. Ducks are usually moving north, in flocks. The cliffs were very steep. I know that there were eggs farther up the coast, though I didn't necessarily pick them. Ducks were found, as marked, around Kangalaksiorvik Fiord (the best area) and farther north."*

GEESE: *"There were hardly any geese before 1959. I travelled along the Koroc River Valley to Seven Islands Bay. Since that time, many geese are found along the Labrador coast. In those days, I didn't ever see sheets of paper like the one I am writing on. The Inuit children were writing in the sand instead. Sometimes I found soapstone around Kangalaksiorvik Fiord (across Alluviaq river) which could be used as slate or lead. These stones would be carried like pencils. Also, there were no matches in those days. They used white stone like a flint, and tinder from dried mosses to make a fire. Soapstone was also used for sharpening knives."*

FISH: *"I caught salmon in Komaktorvik Fiord. There were not too many salmon to be found in those days, in that area. When there were fish, they were caught with the kakivik or with rope from the company, woven into nets. Perhaps the salmon in the Komaktorvik was the only one in the whole province. Lake trout - I never tried to find out about Lake trout in the lakes. Brook trout - Brook trout were caught along the Koroc River. For catching them, I used a soapstone sinker, a small black hook from the company and sinew from the caribou to make the line. It was quite hard to fashion this equipment together."*

PTARMIGAN (GROUSE): *"Ptarmigan were found around Koroc. Also around the mouths of rivers, as marked, the West Wind river, Komaktorvik River, Palmer and Koroc River. Ptarmigan are found where there are bushes and small branches. Bullets were very valuable and I didn't take more than 10 bullets for hunting. I was trying to get fox even when I was hunting ptarmigan, because fox is valuable. If I had no bullets I used rocks to hit them instead. My parents would not let me use a gun if I didn't bring back any animals after a hunting trip. My parents were strict in the sense that they didn't like bullets wasted. Because I was short of real ammunition, I learned to use other sorts of things, like rocks, to get animals. I lived on the Koroc River where I learned to use bow and arrow, taught by my father. The bow was made from wood, the rope from braided caribou muscle, the arrow head (and arrow) was made out of bone, sharpened to a point."*

FOX: *"Fox are found in the same places ptarmigan are found, near the bushes along the West Wind River mouth, the Komaktorvik River, the Palmer and Koroc rivers."*

WOLF: *"I have heard of wolf being near Ramah and Saglek Fiords but I have not seen any there. I don't have time to do a map for the present day, but most of the places I went by dogteam are the places that I use by ski-doo nowadays."*

American Indians in the 1990s

The true number of American Indians may be unknowable, but a rapidly growing number of Americans are identifying with Indian culture. The Anglo appetite for Indian products is creating jobs on poverty-plagued reservations. Gambling and tourism are the most lucrative reservation businesses. Meanwhile, the middle-class Indian's urge to "go home" is growing.

D a n   F o s t

Dan Fost is a contributing editor of American Demographics *in Tiburon, California.*

When Nathan Tsosie was growing up in the Laguna Pueblo in New Mexico, he was not taught the Laguna language. The tribe's goal was to assimilate him into white society.

Today, Tsosie's 9-year-old son Darren learns his ancestral language and culture in the Laguna schools. He speaks Laguna better than either of his parents. "They're trying to bring it back," says Darren's mother, Josephine. "I'm glad he's learning. I just feel bad that we can't reinforce it and really teach it."

The strong bonds American Indians still feel to their native culture are driving a renaissance in Indian communities. This cultural resurrection has not yet erased the poverty, alcoholism, and other ills that affect many Indians. But it has brought educational and economic gains to many Indians living on and off reservations. A college-educated Indian middle class has emerged, American Indian business ownership has increased, and some tribes are creating good jobs for their members.

The census counted 1,878,000 American Indians in 1990, up from fewer than 1.4 million in 1980. This 38 percent leap exceeds the growth rate for blacks (6 percent) and non-Hispanic whites (13 percent), but not the growth of Hispanics (53 percent) or Asians (108 percent).

The increase is not due to an Indian baby boom or to immigration from other countries. Rather, Americans with Indian heritage are increasingly likely to identify their race as Indian on census forms. Also, the Census Bureau is doing a better job of counting American Indians.

Almost 2 million people say that their race is American Indian. But more than 7 million people claim some Indian ancestry, says Jeff Passel at the Urban Institute. That's about 1 American in 35.

"A lot of people have one or more ancestors who are American Indian," says Passel. "There's a clear trend over the last three censuses for increasing numbers of those people to answer the race question as American Indian. But it doesn't tell you how 'Indian' they are in a cultural sense.

"The strength of this identification in places that are not Indian strongholds is transitory. If it becomes unfashionable to be American Indian, it could go down."

People who try to count American Indians employ many different means that often confound demographers. Tribes keep tabs on enrollment, but the rules vary on how much Indian blood makes one a member. Some tribes are not recognized by the federal government. Local health services may keep one set of records, while federal agencies like the Bureau of Indian Affairs will keep another. Some Indians are nomadic; Navajos, for example, may maintain three residences. Rural Indians can be hard to find, and minorities are always more prone to census undercounts. A growing number of mixed marriages blurs the racial boundaries even further.

"I don't know what an Indian is," says Malcolm Margolin, publisher of the

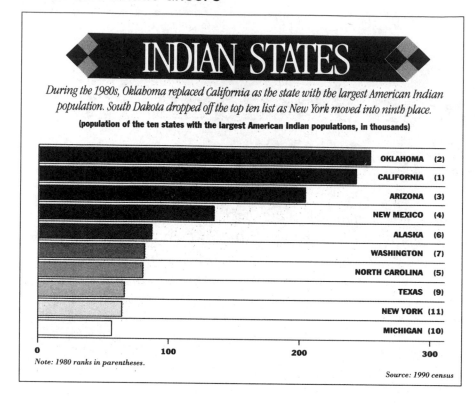

INDIAN STATES

During the 1980s, Oklahoma replaced California as the state with the largest American Indian population. South Dakota dropped off the top ten list as New York moved into ninth place.

(population of the ten states with the largest American Indian populations, in thousands)

OKLAHOMA (2)
CALIFORNIA (1)
ARIZONA (3)
NEW MEXICO (4)
ALASKA (6)
WASHINGTON (7)
NORTH CAROLINA (5)
TEXAS (9)
NEW YORK (11)
MICHIGAN (10)

0   100   200   300

Note: 1980 ranks in parentheses.

Source: 1990 census

monthly *News from Native California.* "Some people are clearly Indian, and some are clearly not. But the U.S. government figures are clearly inadequate for judging how many people are Indian."

Even those who can't agree on the numbers do agree that Indians are returning to their roots. "In the early 1960s, there was a stigma attached to being American Indian," Passel says. These days, even Anglos are proud of Indian heritage.

IDENTIFYING WITH INDIANS

When white patrons at Romo's restaurant in Holbrook, Arizona, learn that their host is half Navajo and half Hopi, they frequently exclaim, "I'm part Cherokee!" The host smiles and secretly rolls his eyes. More *bahanas* (whites) are jumping on the Indian bandwagon.

"In the last three years, interest in Indian beliefs has really taken off," says Marzenda McComb, the former co-owner of a New Age store in Portland, Oregon. To celebrate the sale of her store, a woman performed an Indian smudging ritual with burnt cedar and an eagle feather. Most of McComb's customers were non-Indian.

Controversy often accompanies such practices. Some Indians bristle at the sharing of their culture and spiritual practices with whites. But others welcome people of any race into their culture. And many tribal leaders recognize that Indian art and tourism are hot markets.

Anglos are not the only ones paying more attention to Indian ways. Indian children are showing a renewed interest in their culture. Jennifer Bates, who owns the Bear and Coyote Gallery in California, says her 9-year-old son has taken an independent interest in Northern Miwok dance. "It's nice, knowing that we're not pushing it on him," she says. "He wanted to dance and make his cape. It's up to us to keep things going, and if we don't, it's gone."

The oldest generation of California Indians "grew up among people who recalled California before the arrival of whites," says Malcolm Margolin. These people have "something in their tone, their mood, their manners—a very Indian quality." Younger generations are more comfortable in the white world, he says, but they sense "something very ominous about the passing of the older generation. It's the sense of the younger generation that it's up to them."

The Zuni tribe is trying to revive an-

cient crafts by opening two tribal-owned craft stores—one in their pueblo in New Mexico, and one on San Francisco's trendy Union Street. The most popular items are fetishes—small stone carvings of animals that serve as good-luck charms. "After *Dances with Wolves* came out, we weren't able to keep the wolf fetishes in stock," says Milford Nahohai, manager of the New Mexico store.

JOBS ON RESERVATIONS

Many Indians on and off the reservation face a well-established litany of problems, from poverty and alcoholism to unemployment. Many tribal leaders say that only jobs can solve the problem. Promoting Indian-owned businesses is their solution.

The number of Indian-owned businesses increased 64 percent between 1982 and 1987, compared with a 14 percent rise for all U.S. firms, according to the Census Bureau. "A whole new system of role models is being established," says Steven Stallings, president of the National Center for American Indian Enterprise Development in Mesa, Arizona. "Indians see self-employment as a viable opportunity."

In boosting reservation-based businesses, Stallings aims to create sustainable, self-reliant economies. In some areas, 92 cents of every dollar earned on a reservation is spent outside the reservation, he says. Non-Indian communities typically retain as much as 85 cents.

Stallings's center hopes to start by attracting employers to Indian country. The next step is to add retail and service businesses that will "create a revolving economy on the reservation."

This strategy is at work in Laguna, New Mexico. The Laguna Indians were hit hard in 1982, when the price of uranium plummeted and the Anaconda Mineral Company closed a mine located on their reservation. But the Lagunas have bounced back with several enterprises, including Laguna Industries, a tribal-owned manufacturing firm that employs 350 people.

Laguna Industries' clients include the Department of Defense, Raytheon, and Martin Marietta. Its flagship product is a communications shelter that U.S. forces

INDIAN INDUSTRIES

American Indian specialty contractors had receipts of $97 million in 1987.
But automotive and food-store owners may earn higher profits.

(ten largest industry groups in receipts for firms owned by American Indians and Alaska Natives)

rank	industry group	firms	receipts (in thousands)	receipts per firm (in thousands)
1	Special trade contractors	2,268	$97,400	$43
2	Miscellaneous retail	1,799	85,400	47
3	Agriculture services, forestry, and fishing	3,128	84,000	27
4	Automotive dealers and service stations	222	65,300	294
5	Food stores	301	54,300	180
6	Business services	2,532	48,600	19
7	Eating and drinking places	464	35,300	76
8	Construction	461	34,200	74
9	Trucking and warehousing	590	32,200	55
10	Personal services	1,719	26,500	15

Source: 1987 Economic Censuses, Survey of Minority-Owned Business Enterprises

INDIAN MARKETS

The 1990 census showed rapid increases among American Indians who live in large metropolitan areas. Some of the increases reflect an increasing willingness to declare one's Indian heritage.

(top ten metropolitan areas, ranked by American Indian, Eskimo, and Aleut population in 1990; and percent change in that population, 1980–90)

rank	metropolitan area	1990 population	percent change 1980–90
1	Los Angeles-Anaheim-Riverside, CA	87,500	5%
2	Tulsa, OK	48,200	41
3	New York-Northern New Jersey-Long Island, NY-NJ-CT	46,200	101
4	Oklahoma City, OK	45,700	82
5	San Francisco-Oakland-San Jose, CA	40,800	19
6	Phoenix, AZ	38,000	66
7	Seattle-Tacoma, WA	32,100	42
8	Minneapolis-St. Paul, MN-WI	24,000	49
9	Tucson, AZ	20,300	36
10	San Diego, CA	20,100	37

Source: 1990 census

used in the Gulf War. "It's pretty nice to see your own people getting involved in high-tech stuff," says welding supervisor Phillip Sarracino, 44.

Laguna Indians are given first priority for jobs at the plant, but several middle managers are white. Conrad Lucero, a plant group leader and former tribal governor, says that non-Indian supervisors are often retirees who lend their expertise until Indians can run things on their own.

"I have an 8-year-old daughter," says Sabin Chavez, 26, who works in the quality control division. "I'm hoping to keep this company going, so our kids can live on the reservation. It's a long shot, but we have to believe in long shots."

High morale at Laguna Industries is tempered by the risks of relying on the government. The Lagunas realize that their dependence on military contracts makes them vulnerable to cuts in the de-

fense budget. And in August 1994, the tribe's right to bid on minority set-aside contracts will expire—partly because the business has been so successful.

"We have to be able to meet and beat our competitors on the open market," Lucero says. The Lagunas may succeed: Martin Marietta Corporation has already awarded Laguna Industries a contract based on price and not minority status, says Martin Marietta customer representative Michael King.

Laguna Industries has not solved all the tribe's problems, however. Tribal planner Nathan Tsosie estimates that unemployment runs as high as 35 percent on the reservation. Much of the housing is substandard, water shortages could impede future development, and alcoholism still tears Indian families apart. But Tsosie has an answer: "We just need to develop more. People leave the reservation to get jobs. If there were jobs here, they'd stay."

GAMBLING AND TOURISM

Indians bring some real advantages to the business world. The Lagunas show that a cohesive community can be organized into an efficient production facility. Other reservations have rich natural resources. But the biggest benefit may be "sovereignty," or the suspension of many local, state, and federal laws on Indian territory. Reservations have no sales or property tax, so cigarettes, gasoline, and other items can be sold for low prices. They can also offer activities not permitted off-reservation.

Like gambling.

"Bingo is a way for tribes to amass funds so they can get into other economic development projects," says Frank Collins, a Mescalero Apache from San Jose who specializes in development.

Bingo can be big business. One parlor on the Morongo reservation, just north of Palm Springs, California, draws 5,000 people a week and employs more than 140 people. The Morongo tribe's main objective is to develop as a major resort destination, says bingo general manager Michael Lombardi.

Lombardi won't say how much money bingo generates for the Morongos. He will

THE BEST STATES FOR

Indians in Business

This table shows how the states rank on the basis of business ownership among American Indians. States in the South may offer the most opportunity for American Indians, while midwestern states may offer the least.

The number of Indian-owned businesses in a state is not closely related to the business ownership rate. Business ownership rates are calculated by dividing the number of Indian-owned businesses by the number of Indians and multiplying by 1,000. The top-ranked state, Alaska, is one of only five states with more than 1,000 Indian-owned firms. But the state that ranks last, Arizona, has the seventh-highest number of Indian-owned businesses.

Statistical analysis also indicates that the pattern of business ownership among American Indians is not driven by the rate of growth in a state's Indian population during the 1980s, or by a state's overall level of business ownership.

There appear to be strong regional biases in patterns of Indian business ownership. The business ownership rate was 12.2 Indian-owned firms per 1,000 Indians in the South, 10.3 in the West, 9.6 in the Northeast, and only 7.4 in the Midwest.

One clue to a state's business ownership rate among Indians could be the share of its Indian population living on reservations. The lowest-ranking state, Arizona, contains seven of the ten most populated reservations in the U.S., including a large share of the huge Navajo reservation (1990 Indian population of 143,400 in Arizona, New Mexico, and Utah). South Dakota, ranking 47th, contains the large and economically troubled Pine Ridge, Rosebud, and Standing Rock reservations. Indians living on a reservation have limited entrepreneurial opportunities. Another factor that may be related to the Indian business rate is the state's general economic health: several states near the bottom of the ranking, Ken-

William O'Hare is Director of Population and Policy Research Program, University of Louisville.

tucky, Nebraska, and Michigan, have experienced weak economic growth during the 1980s.

But the most powerful predictor is probably the business skill of a state's Indian tribes. Third-ranking North Carolina is home to one branch of the Cherokee tribe, which has large investments in lumber and tourism. And Alaska may rank first because its native American, Eskimo, and Aleut population received billions of dollars in a federal land claim settlement. These data do not contain businesses owned by Eskimos or Aleuts. But many of Alaska's Indians live in isolated towns where small businesses have a captive, all-native audience.

— *William O'Hare*

INDIAN OPPORTUNITY

(states with more than 100 American Indian-owned businesses in 1987, ranked by business ownership rate)

rank	state name	number of firms 1987	American Indian population 1987	business ownership rate*
1	Alaska	1,039	28,700	36.2
2	North Carolina	1,757	75,600	23.2
3	Texas	872	57,500	15.2
4	Virginia	188	13,300	14.1
5	Colorado	343	24,600	13.9
6	California	3,087	225,600	13.7
7	Louisiana	221	16,600	13.3
8	Massachusetts	132	10,700	12.4
9	Kansas	225	20,000	11.3
10	Florida	348	30,900	11.3
11	Maryland	123	11,300	10.9
12	Pennsylvania	139	12,800	10.8
13	Georgia	122	11,400	10.7
14	New Jersey	131	12,800	10.3
15	New Mexico	1,247	126,400	9.9
16	Illinois	182	19,600	9.3
17	Montana	405	44,700	9.1
18	Oklahoma	2,044	229,300	8.9
19	Oregon	306	34,500	8.9
20	North Dakota	208	24,300	8.6
21	Wisconsin	306	36,300	8.4
22	Ohio	149	17,700	8.4
23	Washington	602	72,300	8.3
24	Nevada	146	17,700	8.3
25	New York	425	54,800	7.8
26	Missouri	133	17,500	7.6
27	Minnesota	333	45,400	7.3
28	Michigan	304	50,900	6.0
29	South Dakota	267	49,000	5.5
30	Utah	109	22,700	4.8
31	Arizona	843	189,100	4.5

* Number of American Indian-owned firms per 1,000 Indians.

Source: Bureau of the Census, 1987 economic census, and author's estimates of 1987 Indian population

say that 113 reservations allow some form of gaming, and he attributes bingo's popularity to the effects of Reagan-era cutbacks in the Bureau of Indian Affairs budget. Lombardi says then-Secretary of the Interior James Watt told Indians, "Instead of depending on the Great White Father, why don't you start your own damn business?"

Indian culture also can create unique business opportunities. On the Hopi reservation in northern Arizona, Joe and Janice Day own a small shop on Janice's ancestral property. They swap elk hooves and cottonwood sticks, useful in Indian rituals, for jewelry, and baskets to sell to tourists.

The Days would like to credit their success to their shrewd sense of customer service. But they confess that the difference between profit and loss may be their wildly popular T-shirts, which read "Don't worry, be Hopi."

Not long ago, Hopis had to leave the reservation to go to school or find work. Today, the tribe has its own junior and senior high school and an entrepreneurial spirit. But small schools and small businesses won't keep people on the reservation. The Days still make a two-hour drive to Flagstaff each week to do their banking, laundry, and shopping. "The first Hopi you can get to build a laundromat is going to be a rich man," says Joe Day.

The Days lived in Flagstaff until their children finished high school. At that point, they decided to come "home." Janice's daughter is now an accountant in San Francisco, and she loves the amenities of the big city. "But who knows?" Janice says. "She may also want to come home someday. No matter where you are, you're still going to end up coming home."

THE URGE TO GO HOME

"Going home" may also mean renewing a bond with one's Indian heritage. While the population in 19 "Indian states" grew at predictable levels during the 1980s, the Urban Institute's Jeff Passel says it soared in the non-Indian states.

For example, Passel estimated the 1990 Indian population in Arizona at 202,000 (the 1980 population of 152,700, plus the intervening 58,600 births and minus the intervening 10,300 deaths)—a figure close to the 1990 census number (203,500). But in Alabama, a non-Indian state, Passel found a huge percentage increase that he could not have predicted. Alabama's Indian population grew from 7,600 in 1980 to 16,500 in 1990, a 117 percent increase. Higher birthrates, lower death rates, and migration from other states do not explain the increase.

Passel explains the gap this way: "The people who are Indians always identify themselves as Indians. They tell the census they are Indians, and they register their newborns as Indians." These people are usually found in the Indian states.

"People who are part Indian may not identify themselves as American Indians. But they don't do that consistently over time."

Today, for reasons of ethnic pride, part-Indians may tell the Census Bureau they

> "Instead of depending on the Great White Father, why don't you start your own damn business?"

are Indian. At the hospital, they may identify themselves as white to avoid discrimination. This is most common in non-Indian states, which Passel generally defines as having fewer than 3,000 Indians in 1950.

California ranks second only to Oklahoma in its Indian population, but its mixture of tribes is unique in the nation. Some Indian residents trace their roots to native California tribes, says Malcolm Margolin. Others came west as part of a federal relocation program in the 1950s. In California cities, Cherokees, Chippewas, and other out-of-state Indians congregate in clubs.

"What has happened is the formation of an inter-tribal ethic, a pan-Indian ethic," Margolin says. "People feel that America has a lot of problems. That cultural doubt causes them to look for their ethnic roots, for something they can draw strength from. And for Indians, it's right there. It's ready-made."

Hispanic/Latino Americans

The following collection of materials on Hispanic/Latino Americans is a composite of findings about ethnicities. The clustering of these ethnicities and nationalities, as well as their relationship to the Spanish language, seems to be sufficient evidence of the commonalities that constitute the shared expression of this complex of memory and contemporary politics. Yet the interchangeable use of "Hispanic" and "Latino" as nominative of their differentiation from the Anglo-American founding and their social expression as they search for a cultural and political terrain are but the surface of the process of intergroup dynamics in the United States.

The articles in this unit propose angles of vision that enable us to view the process of accommodation and change that is articulated in political practice, scholarship, advocacy, and art. The issues presented provocatively shift traditional perspectives from the eastern and midwestern mind-set toward the western and southwestern analysis of the immigration to the United States.

The Immigration Act of 1965 induced a process not unlike the period of large-scale eastern and southern European immigration between 1880 and 1924. This immigration includes scores of various ethnic groups. Cultural/geographic descriptions are not the clearest form of ethnic identity.

Hispanic/Latino Americans are not a single ethnic group. The designation of various ethnic populations whose ancestry is derived from Spanish-speaking countries by the words "Hispanic" and "Latino" is a relatively recent phenomenon in the United States. The cultural, economic, and political differences and similarities of various Hispanic communities, as well as the wide dispersal of these communities, suggest the need for care in generalization about Hispanic American populations.

The realities of these groups—whether they are political refugees, migrant workers, descendants of residents settled prior to territorial incorporation into the United States, long-settled immigrants, recent arrivals, or the children and grandchildren of immigrants—present interesting and varied patterns of enclave community, assimilation, and acculturation as well as isolation and marginalization. Hispanic/Latino American linkages to other Latin countries, the future of their emerging political power, and their contributions to cultural and economic change within the United States are interesting facets of the Hispanic/Latino American experience.

The Hispanic/Latino experience is a composite of groups seeking unity while interacting with the larger arena of ethnic groups that constitute American society. Convergent issues that bridge differences, as well as those that support ideological and strategic differences, bode a future of both cooperation and conflict.

What issues bind Hispanic groups together? What values cause cleavages among Hispanic populations? What does bilingualism mean? Is bilingualism a freedom-of-speech issue? Is bilingualism a concern of non-Spanish-speaking persons in the United States? What are the implications of establishing an official public language policy?

Competition and conflict over mobility into mainstream leadership positions are aspects of American society that may be exacerbated by the misuse of ethnic indicators. Nonetheless, indicators of social cohesion and traditional family bonds are apparently noncompetitive and nonconflictual dimensions of robust ethnic experiences. Thus, fears that Hispanic/Latino Americans may not relish competitive pressures are assuaged by the capacities of family and community to temper the cost of any such failure. This complex dynamic of personal and group interaction is a fascinating and fruitful topic for a society seeking competitiveness and stronger community bonds. Cast in this fashion, the American dilemma takes on a new and compelling relevance.

Looking Ahead: Challenge Questions

How does attention to historical background and its expression in current culture promote both understanding and tolerance?

Discuss whether or not the U.S. Census and its various publications regarding ethnic and racial issues foster understanding and tolerance.

What strengths and weaknesses do traditional bonds of ethnic communities possess?

In what respects is Hispanic/Latino American culture becoming part of mainstream American culture?

To what do you attribute the popularity of Mexican, Italian, and Chinese foods in the marketplace?

Specific Hispanics

SUMMARY Los Angeles, New York, Miami, Chicago, and Houston are well-known Hispanic markets. But just below the big five are dozens of smaller Hispanic centers. This first-ever look at 12 Hispanic groups reveals the top towns for Colombians, Brazilians, and others. The rapid growth of specific Hispanic groups is destined to attract attention from marketers.

Morton Winsberg

Morton Winsberg is professor of geography at Florida State University in Tallahassee.

Most marketers are familiar with the three biggest Hispanic-American groups. Since the U.S. census first counted Hispanics in 1970, those who identify Mexico, Puerto Rico, and Cuba as their country of origin have comprised about three-fourths of the total U.S. Hispanic population. Hispanics from other Latin-American nations and cultures are less well-understood, but they constitute one-quarter of an estimated $170 billion consumer market. And because Hispanics of all kinds often live together in small areas, each country of origin can form a visible and desirable target market.

Among all Hispanics, the share of Mexicans has fallen from 62 percent of all U.S. Hispanics in 1970 to 61 percent in 1990.

The Puerto Rican and Cuban shares have remained at about 12 percent and 5 percent, respectively. Hispanic Americans who don't have origins in these three countries are a small share of the nation's total Hispanic population, but they have been growing. Their numbers grew by slightly more than 2 million between 1970 and 1990. Immigrants of the new wave have been fleeing civil wars in Nicaragua, El Salvador, Guatemala, and Colombia. Others come for jobs or to rejoin family members already here.

The 1970 and 1980 censuses identified just four categories of Hispanics: Mexican, Puerto Rican, Cuban, and "other." The 1990 census provides much more detailed information, identifying 12 nations of Hispanic origin, as well as "other" Central Americans and "other" South Americans. These data provide the first opportunity to understand where specific Hispanic groups live.

Many of the smaller Hispanic subgroups never show up on marketers' computer screens. Language barriers and the lack of large ethnic neighborhoods can make it hard to reach them with specially designed messages. Also, many Hispanic immigrants do not plan to become U.S.

> **Immigrants have always settled in America's largest cities, and today's immigrants are not much different.**

citizens or permanent residents. But rapid growth will inevitably lead more businesses to target Hispanic diversity. In ten years, America's Little Havanas will get a lot bigger.

BELOW THE BIG FIVE

Immigrants have always settled in America's largest cities, and today's immigrants are not much different. Six of the 12 Hispanic subgroups identified in the 1990 census have more than 80 percent of their populations in the nation's 20 largest cities, and 3 others have between 70 and 79 percent.

Mexican Americans are the only exception to the urban rule, because many of their ancestors never immigrated. Many Mexicans became U.S. citizens in the 19th century following the acquisition of Mexican territory by the United States. Almost all of this land was and still is rural or small cities. Many Mexicans who immigrated to the U.S. in recent years have settled in these same southwestern states. Here they normally reside in cities both large and small, as well as in rural areas.

Hispanics, like immigrants who came earlier, tend to concentrate in one or two major urban areas. New York City and Los Angeles early became a popular destination for Hispanics, but more recently, many have chosen Miami, Washington, D.C., and San Francisco. An example of an unusually high concentration of a Hispanic group in one city is the 77 percent concentration of people of Dominican origin in the New York urbanized area. Greater New York also has 60 percent of the nation's Ecuadorians and 44 percent of Puerto Ricans. Los Angeles has 49 percent of the nation's Guatemalans and 47 percent of its Salvadoreans. Miami is home to 53 percent of Cuban Americans.

Several U.S. places have Hispanic populations that rival or even surpass the largest cities in their countries of origin. New York's Puerto Rican population is now more than double that of San Juan. New York also has the second-largest urban population of Dominicans in the world, and the third-largest Ecuadorian population. The Mexican, Salvadorean, and Guatemalan populations of urban Los Angeles are surpassed only by those of their respective capitals: Mexico City, San Salvador, and Guatemala City.

Eighteen percent of all Hispanic Ameri-

The most exotic place where Mexicans cluster may be Bay City-Saginaw, Michigan.

cans live in Los Angeles, and 12 percent live in New York. These two urban areas rank among the top-5 for 11 of the 12 Hispanic groups. Miami is on the top-5 list for 9 Hispanic groups, Washington, D.C., for 6, San Francisco for 5, and Houston and Chicago for 4.

The census also reveals many smaller areas with large and growing populations of specific Hispanics. For example, San Antonio and San Diego have the fourth- and fifth-largest Mexican-American communities in the nation, and Philadelphia has the third-largest Puerto Rican population. Tampa and Fort Lauderdale have the fourth- and fifth-largest concentrations of Cubans, and the Massachusetts areas of Boston and Lawrence have the third- and fourth-largest Dominican groups.

Chicago is the only midwestern urban area to come up on any of the top-5 lists, but it comes up a lot. Chicago has the country's second-largest Puerto Rican population, the second-largest Mexican population, and the third-largest Guatemalan and Ecuadorian populations. As a whole, Chicago has the fourth-largest Hispanic population of any urban area, at 4 percent of the national total.

TWELVE HISPANIC GROUPS

Laredo, Texas, is not big as urban areas go, with 99,258 people in 1990. But 94 percent of Laredo residents are Hispanic, and the overwhelming majority are of Mexican origin. The census count of Hispanics, also mainly Mexican, is 90 percent in Brownsville and 83 percent in McAllen, two other Texas border towns. Several border towns in other states have equally high shares of Mexican Americans.

Perhaps the most exotic place where Mexicans congregate in large numbers is in the Bay City-Saginaw metropolitan area in Michigan. Mexicans first came to Bay City-Saginaw to work on the local cu-

cumber farms. The descendants of these farm laborers now hold urban jobs, many in the local foundries.

Puerto Ricans began immigrating to the U.S. after World War II, and now they are a significant presence in the industrial cities of New York and southern New England. When older residents of these cities had achieved middle-class status and moved to the suburbs, they left behind entry-level jobs in manufacturing and service, and low-cost housing. The Puerto Ricans who took those jobs established the barrios of New York City.

While less affluent Puerto Ricans came to the U.S. for jobs, many middle-class Cubans fled their native country for political reasons. Cubans soon became closely identified with southeastern Florida, but now they are found in several other Florida towns. In the university towns of Gainesville and Tallahassee, for example, many second-generation Cuban Americans live as students.

Dominicans are a major Hispanic force in New York City and several New England industrial towns. They are only 2 percent of the nation's 1990 Hispanic population, but they are 15 percent of Hispanics in New York, 22 percent in Providence, and 35 percent in Lawrence, Massachusetts. Dominicans are flocking to the Northeast for the same reason Puerto Ricans did several decades ago: jobs. Hondurans and Nicaraguans, who have also immigrated largely for economic reasons, are settling in more bilingual areas on the Gulf of Mexico.

Hondurans are most numerous in New York, Los Angeles, and Miami, and Nicaraguans are most common in Miami, Los Angeles, and San Francisco. But both groups are dwarfed by the enormous numbers of other Hispanics in these large urban areas, so their largest concentrations emerge in unexpected places. Although Hondurans are less than 1 percent of the nation's Hispanic population, they are 20 percent of Hispanics in New Orleans. Nicaraguans are also well-represented among New Orleans Hispanics, and they are visible in nearby Baton Rouge and Port Arthur. Salvadoreans are just 3 percent of the

TWELVE FLAGS

Hispanics of all types cluster in New York a
Central Americans in San Francisco, Colombi

(top-five urbanized areas for H

OVER AMERICA

d Los Angeles. But you can also find lots of
ns in Chicago, and Peruvians in Washington.

ics by country of origin, 1990)

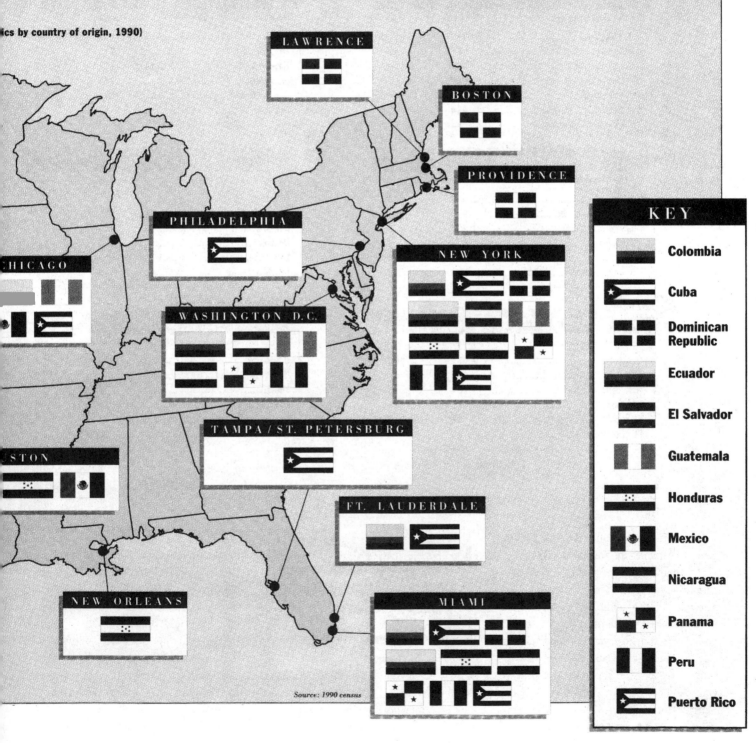

Source: 1990 census

KEY

- Colombia
- Cuba
- Dominican Republic
- Ecuador
- El Salvador
- Guatemala
- Honduras
- Mexico
- Nicaragua
- Panama
- Peru
- Puerto Rico

Little Quitos and Little

Mexico

top-five urbanized areas	population	share
U.S. total	13,393	100%
Los Angeles	3,066	23
Chicago	538	4
Houston	528	4
San Antonio	524	4
San Diego	414	3

El Salvador

top-five urbanized areas	population	share
U.S. total	565	100%
Los Angeles	265	47
New York	62	11
Washington, DC	52	9
San Francisco	43	8
Houston	39	7

Puerto Rico

top-five urbanized areas	population	share
U.S. total	2,652	100%
New York	1,178	44
Chicago	1,464	6
Philadelphia	107	4
Miami	68	3
Los Angeles	51	2

Dominican Republic

top-five urbanized areas	population	share
U.S. total	520	100%
New York	403	77
Miami	23	5
Boston	16	3
Lawrence, MA	12	2
Providence, RI	9	2

Cuba

top-five urbanized areas	population	share
U.S. total	1,053	100%
Miami	559	53
New York	154	15
Los Angeles	55	5
Tampa-St. Petersburg	32	3
Ft. Lauderdale	24	2

Colombia

top-five urbanized areas	population	share
U.S. total	379	100%
New York	152	40
Miami	53	14
Los Angeles	27	7
Ft. Lauderdale	12	3
Houston	10	3

nation's Hispanic population, but 25 percent of Hispanics in Washington, D.C.

Panamanians are perhaps the most geographically diverse of any Hispanic group. They are disproportionately represented in the local Hispanic population in towns near large military installations such as Fayetteville, North Carolina (Fort Bragg); Columbus, Georgia (Fort Benning); Clarksville, Tennessee (Fort Campbell); Killeen, Texas (Fort Hood); Seaside, California (Fort Ord); and naval installations in Nor-

The affluent Connecticut town of Stamford is particularly attractive to South Americans.

folk, Virginia; and Tacoma, Washington. Many who identified their ethnic origin as Panamanian in the 1990 census were military personnel once stationed in the former Panama Canal Zone.

People of South-American origin began moving in large numbers from New York City or coming directly from their homelands to coastal Connecticut towns during the 1980s, attracted to a growing number of service jobs that were not being filled by the local population. Housing was also more affordable than in New York City.

The affluent Connecticut town of Stamford is particularly attractive to South Americans. Its Hispanic population includes large proportions of Colombians,

San Juans

Mexicans are by far the largest Hispanic-American group, but 77 percent of Dominican Americans live in one urban area.

(top-five urbanized areas for Hispanics by country of origin, population in thousands; and share of segment, 1990)

Guatemala

top-five urbanized areas	population	share
U.S. total	269	100%
Los Angeles	133	49
New York	27	10
Chicago	15	6
San Francisco	11	4
Washington, DC	9	4

Peru

top-five urbanized areas	population	share
U.S. total	175	100%
New York	54	31
Los Angeles	27	15
Miami	16	9
Washington, DC	11	7
San Francisco	9	5

Nicaragua

top-five urbanized areas	population	share
U.S. total	203	100%
Miami	74	37
Los Angeles	37	18
San Francisco	25	12
New York	14	7
Washington, DC	8	4

Honduras

top-five urbanized areas	population	share
U.S. total	131	100%
New York	33	25
Los Angeles	24	18
Miami	18	14
New Orleans	9	7
Houston	5	4

Ecuador

top-five urbanized areas	population	share
U.S. total	191	100%
New York	115	60
Los Angeles	21	11
Chicago	8	4
Miami	8	4
Washington, DC	5	3

Panama

top-five urbanized areas	population	share
U.S. total	92	100%
New York	27	29
Miami	7	7
Los Angeles	6	6
Washington, DC	4	4
San Francisco	2	2

Source: 1990 census

Ecuadorians, and Peruvians. In nearby Norwalk, Colombians are 20 percent of the city's Hispanic population.

MARKETING ATTENTION

So far, few U.S. corporations have paid attention to the special needs of "other" Hispanics. Mainstream marketers "are resistant enough to work with Hispanic marketing in total," says Nilda Anderson, president of Hispanic Market Research in New York City. "They are not going to do focused marketing."

One problem is a lack of marketing information. Recent census results and private research have improved the data on smaller Hispanic groups, says Gary Berman, president of Market Segment Research in Coral Gables, Florida, but few data were available until the 1990s.

Another problem is that Hispanic immigrants are less likely than previous generations of immigrants to live in ethnic-specific neighborhoods. In Miami, for example, newly arrived Cubans are often neighbors to Nicaraguans, and Nicaraguans may live next to Venezuelans. The city's celebrated "Little Havana" neighborhood is defined by its Cuban-owned businesses, but census data do not show an extreme overrepresentation of Cubans living in the area adjacent to those businesses.

Whatever their nation of origin, most Hispanic immigrants quickly acquire two basic American tools: a car and a telephone. Miami's Cubans may go to Little Havana to shop, socialize, and eat, just as Miami's Nicaraguans go to the Sweetwater district to buy copies of *El Diario La Prensa* and loaves of *pan Nicaraguense*. But when the trip is over, they return to homes scattered all over the city.

Another problem is that many Hispanic immigrants are not interested in owning a home, buying a new car, or otherwise participating as full-fledged American consumers. New York City is home to about 10,000 foreign-born Brazilians, for example. But "most Brazilians are in New York only to save money for the return to Brazil," says Maxine L. Margolis, an anthropology professor at the University of Florida in Gainesville. In her book *Little Brazil*, Margolis tells the story of a local television news program called "TV Bra-

> **Whatever their nation of origin, most Hispanic immigrants quickly acquire two basic American tools: a car and a telephone.**

sil." When it began, Brazilian-owned businesses were eager to sponsor it. But the ads failed to attract new customers, she says, because many Brazilians spend only what they must and save everything else.

Perhaps the biggest problem is the size of "other" Hispanic groups. "TV Brasil's" producers tried to persuade the Coors Brewing Company to advertise by claiming that 200,000 Brazilians lived in New York City, according to Margolis. But Coors turned them down anyway, claiming that the market was too small.

These obstacles may scare most businesses away, but the few that do target "other" Hispanics are rewarded with a growing source of loyal customers. As the airline of Colombia, Avianca focuses its U.S. advertising on Colombians, says Alberto Gil, a marketing analyst for the airline in New York City. The city's five boroughs are home to about 86,000 Colombians, according to demographer Frank Vardy at the Department of City Planning.

Avianca advertising runs primarily on Spanish-language television, radio, and in newspapers circulated in New York. "We don't care so much about whether the [medium] has a high rating for all Hispanics, but for Colombians," he says. The airline gauges Colombians' interests by asking its customers to name their favorite publications, radio stations, and TV shows.

The airline also focuses on a 20-block area in North Queens that is the geographic heart of Colombian settlement in New York City. Travel agents in that neighborhood receive special attention from the airline, says Gil. "We are a sym-

bol for [Colombians]," he says. "We are Colombia in the United States."

Colombian politicians are well aware that New York-based expatriates form a powerful voting bloc. In past elections, polling places for Colombian elections have been established at the Colombian consulate and in Queens, says Javier Castano, a reporter for the Spanish-language newspaper *El Diario*. Colombian presidential candidates occasionally travel to New York City at election time, and politicians from many countries buy advertising in *El Diario* and other New York media.

Immigrants follow well-worn paths when they come to the United States, and these paths do not change rapidly. If immigration from Latin America continues at its current rapid pace, America's Little Havanas, Little San Juans, and other Hispanic enclaves will eventually grow to the point where targeting "other" Hispanics makes sense to mainstream marketers. Investing small amounts of time and money on specific Hispanics today could yield big payoffs tomorrow.

—*Additional reporting by Patricia Braus*

Behind the Numbers This study examines 1990 Hispanic populations in urbanized areas, defined by the U.S. Census Bureau as "one or more places (central place) and the adjacent densely settled surrounding territory (urban fringe) that together have a minimum of 50,000 persons." In 1990, the census identified 397 urbanized areas. For more information, contact the author at (904) 644-8377 or the Census Bureau at (301) 763-4040.

There's More to Racism Than Black and White

Elizabeth Martinez

The small brown woman with a serious face stood on the curb almost motionless as thousands of people marched by her in a line that stretched 22 blocks. Amidst huge banners and hundreds of big colorful signs, her hand-lettered words on corrugated paper had a haunting simplicity:

> *We were here*
> *We are here*
> *This was our land*
> *is still our land*
> *Stand up for your rights.*

It was August 25, 1990, in Los Angeles and people—mostly Mexican American—were marking the 20th anniversary of the Chicano Moratorium against the war in Vietnam. We assembled at the same park as we did two decades ago and marched the same route to the same park for a rally. As the *señora*'s sign indicated, the struggle goes on and in many ways conditions have worsened for Latinos—La Raza-over the past 20 years. At the same time, the Moratorium reflected important, complex, and often positive new developments. Finally, for the U.S. left in general, the event carried a message that cannot be ignored.

On August 29, 1970, some 20,000 mostly Chicano people came from all over the country to protest the Vietnam war and especially the fact that our casu-

alties were running at a much higher rate than the Mexican American proportion of the U.S. population. As the rally began around midday, a minor scuffle near the edge of the park served as the excuse for a massive police attack. Tear gas filled the air as 500 officers charged the youth, families, and elderly who had been sitting on the grass and drove out the panicked crowd. I remember running with a dozen other people into a nearby house to get away from the tear gas. Friends and relatives were scattered; my daughter, for one, could not be located until ten o'clock in the evening.

Three Chicanos died that day as a result of the police repression: Angel Diaz, Ruben Salazar and Lynn Ward. The best-known was journalist Salazar, who had been investigating and writing a series of articles on recent cases of police brutality for *The Los Angeles Times;* he had reportedly become radicalized in the process. After the attack in the park he had stopped with a friend at the nearby Silver Dollar cafe and was sitting at the bar. From the sidewalk outside, a sheriff's deputy fired a 10-inch tear-gas projectile into the cafe, which almost blew off Salazar's head. Later claiming they had received reports of an armed man in the bar, police said that before firing they had told all occupants to leave; witnesses said they heard no such warning.

That evening the sky over East Los Angeles turned black with smoke as protesters selectively torched many buildings. Sirens wailed for hours; barricades everywhere made "East Los," as it's called, look like an occupied territory. In the weeks that followed, the District Attorney refused to prosecute Salazar's killer despite an inquest damaging to the Sheriff's Department. Protesters demonstrated over the next few months; at one event, when officers again fired on the crowd with tear gas, some people hurled objects at them. Police killed one man, an Austrian student who looked Chicano, and left 19 wounded by buck-shot.

At this year's Moratorium police seemed to keep a relatively low profile. News reports said 6,000 people came, mostly from the Southwest with a sprinkling of Chicago and New York participants. It looked like more, and it certainly felt like more because of the high spirits and energized mood. Was it yet another Day of Nostalgia in the current era of 1960s anniversaries? Yes, but mostly no.

Moratorium organizers had said the day's goal was not just to commemorate a historic event but to protest conditions now facing the overwhelming majority of La Raza. The excellent, thoughtful tabloid *L.A. Moratorium,* published by the organizing committee, pointed to the elimination of Chicano studies, attacks on bilingual education, "English Only" laws, terror from police and immigration officers, attacks by the Klan and skinheads, youth killing one another, the dumping of toxic wastes in Raza communities, and CIA/FBI imported drugs. (One might add a recent statistic: the infant mortality rate among Latinos in Los Angeles County has risen by over a third since 1987.) At the same time, the tabloid said, "the ability of the Movement to defend its people's rights is extremely limited or nonexistent" and the lack of organization also prevents effective support for Native American struggles and against U.S. colonialism in Central America.

The rally program sustained these themes. Although activists with long histories of struggle were featured, like Dolores Huerta of the United Farm Workers and Professor Rudy Acuña, they never lingered on "the wonderful 1960s." This was no mere pep rally. Instead they and other speakers talked eloquently about domestic issues as well as U.S. militarism and intervention, democracy in Mexico, and opposition to the 1992 quincentenary to "celebrate" Christopher Columbus's arrival in 1492.

What about lessons to be drawn from the past, or a long-range strategy and developed vision for the future? The rally itself did not go much beyond calling for greater activism. Still something was being born, something new and very young was in the air.

About half the Moratorium participants seemed to be under 25, including many college as well as high school students. A major force in mobilizing the youth was MEChA (Movimiento Estudiantil Chicano de Aztlan, the Chicano Student Movement of Aztlan). Born

in 1969, its strength ebbed in later years. By 1985, according to one MEChA leader, much of the organization was splintered by ideological debate; activism revived in response to worsening socioeconomic conditions. Today divisions still exist on such issues as a strictly Chicano vs. broader Latino focus, and the merits of affiliation with nonstudent, left organizations. Still, MEChA has lasted far longer than most student groups and retains a certain moral authority.

Many of the Chicano youth marching on August 25 were not even born when the first Moratorium took place, and most schools teach little about the extraordinary struggles of the 1960s worldwide. At its best MEChA helps to fill this void, serving as a transmission belt from past to present, with faculty members who were 1960s activists sometimes providing continuity as well as inspiration. The youth on the march seemed to be learning their history and respecting it. You could feel a thrill ripple through the crowd when one speaker said: "20 years ago they tried to destroy the Chicano movement. 20 years later we are here to tell them that they failed!"

All that week and through September, events related to the Moratorium took place in Los Angeles: several days of extensive TV coverage; a photo exhibit; two plays, one of them a re-enactment of the killing of Salazar staged in the Silver Dollar itself and another called "August 29." A major exhibition, "Chicano Art: Resistance and Affirmation" (CARA) from 1965–1985 opened at the University of California, with many special cultural events scheduled around it.

"We want to pass on our history," said one student at the Moratorium and the spirit that visibly animated the youth that day was indeed nationalist. Dozens of times the 1960s cry of "Chicano Power!" rang out. But the words seem to have a different meaning today—more concrete and more complex than yesterday's generalized rhetoric.

"'Chicano Power' is different now because people realize we will be the majority in a few years," said a young Chicana from Fresno. "The next step will be to turn those numbers into political and economic power, to take over our communities. For example, in the valley in Fresno the people are 80 percent Chicano and Mexicano. The mayor and the school board should reflect that. When it happens, it will be a real affirmation of Chicano Power."

A second meaning of Chicano Power today lies in its implicit rejection of "Hispanic" as a label imposed by the dominant society and adopted by many Latinos themselves—specially those sometimes called Chuppies or Buppies—Chicano or Brown yuppies. "Hispanic" is a fundamentally racist term which obliterates the Native American and African American heritages of La Raza in favor of the white European component from Spain. The August 25 march countered this distortion with a contingent of Native Americans at the head of the line.

Others carried signs rejecting "Hispanic" and affirming "Chicano."

That message also came across while people assembled to march, when the group Culture Clash performed and "Slick Rick" did his bilingual Chicano rap songs. He chided: "Chicanos who are wearing blue contact lenses today—forget it, you're Chicano. Don't try to be white, they do it better!" And: "The 1980s were supposed to be the 'Decade of the Hispanic' but that turned out to be an event sponsored by Coors beer." In other words: the concept "Hispanic" emerged as a marketing tool to conveniently target all Spanish-speaking cultures at once.

The Chicano/Latino/Raza versus "Hispanic" debate is about more than terminology or even racism. It also concerns values, politics, and class: the Raza tradition of collectivity and sharing versus the individualism and consumerism that intensified during the 1980s. In that decade, for example, we saw one "Hispanic" art exhibit after another, often with corporate sponsors and usually apolitical in content. But the new exhibit, CARA, is consciously entitled "Chicano Art" and is not by chance much more political than its predecessors. CARA organizers also say they sought to avoid commercialization and cultural homogeneity. Further, the show was organized by means of an unusually collective approach—regional committees rather than a single curator—so as to promote the empowerment of community people rather than professional elitism.

In these and other ways, the nationalism that ran strong on August 25 has an implicitly or overtly anti-capitalist thrust. Any denunciation of capitalist exploitation brought strong cheers from the rally audience. The presence of organized labor at this year's Moratorium also seemed stronger than 20 years ago, in part because of militant struggles that have been recently waged by workers like Janitors for Justice. Mostly Central Americans, they have attracted wide support from many groups with their courage, determination, imaginative tactics—and by winning a major victory. The extremely brutal police attack on their peaceful demonstration at Century Plaza earlier this year further generated solidarity.

A NEW INTERNATIONALISM

Above all, the Moratorium emanated an internationalism much stronger than 20 years ago. Some of us had wondered if it would address current U.S. policy in the Persian Gulf. We need not have doubted. Signs everywhere, and not just from predominantly white left formations, called for an end to U.S. militarism in the Middle East. "The oil belongs to the people, not Texaco!" got some of the loudest applause at the rally.

There was also a much stronger Mexican presence than in 1970, which speaks to the ever-growing Mexi-

can population. Their numbers are rising so rapidly that formerly Chicano neighborhoods are now Mexican (the different terms here meaning, simplistically, born in the U.S. as opposed to born in Mexico). A well-known Mexican socialist leader, Heberto Castillo of the Democratic Revolutionary Party (PRD), spoke eloquently at the rally, stressing the crucial links between today's struggle for democracy in Mexico and action by Mexican-origin people here.

In another kind of internationalism not seen 20 years ago, a group from the Nation of Islam attended the rally and one of the best-received speakers came from the African People's Socialist Party. This spirit may be drawing encouragement from cross-cultural developments like the black-inspired Chicano rap music from Culture Clash, Kid Frost's *Hispanic Causing Panic* album, and other singers. Finally, a small Korean contingent marched in the Moratorium—a welcome sight.

The National Chicano Moratorium Committee, which worked on the event for many months at the national and regional levels, deserves much credit for its success. "The most democratic mobilization effort in my memory," Professor Rudy Acuña called it, despite having disagreed with members at times. Its commitment to combat sectarianism paid off well, judging by the wide variety of politics represented. The banner of the Mothers of East Los Angeles, a strong community organization, could be seen not far from a small sign proclaiming "Mao—hoy mas que nunca" (Mao, today more than ever). Although the "Principles of Unity" limited membership on the organizing committee to Chicano/Mexican organizations, anti-white feeling seemed absent.

When it came to gender roles, the committee showed little progress over 20 years ago. Women held the posts of—guess what—secretary and treasurer, plus one youth coordinator. All four media liaisons were men. Rally speakers had a better balance: far from equal but solid, and women's participation in the movement was not trivialized by tokenistic recognition. In addition to Dolores Huerta, Nita Gonzales of Denver (longtime community organizer and daughter of "Corky" Gonzales) spoke as did Juana Gutierrez of the Mothers of East Los Angeles and Patricia Marin of Orange County MEChA.

On the march itself you could see a Chicana women's consciousness that was absent 20 years ago. Signs like "Vote Chicano—Vote Chicana" may not have been numerous, but they wouldn't have been seen at all before. Activist women agree it's time for the decline of the "CPMG," a species identified by several Chicanas talking in the Silver Dollar after the Moratorium: the Chicano Person Movement Guy. The generation of women now in college may bring major changes. In recent years, for example, it has not been unusual to find a woman heading a MEChA chapter or women outnumbering the men on a MEChA board. A future Moratorium organizing committee should find more women with experience, in their 30s and 40s like much of the current committee, and ready at least to run more of the show.

HOW SHALL WHITE LEFTISTS RELATE TO A NEW MOVIMIENTO?

Some of us felt a new Chicano movement being born last Aug. 25. The day made it clear that sooner or later this will happen—a Latino movement, I would hope. An old question then arises: how will leftists relate to it? Past experience has been so poor that for many Latinos—not to mention other people of color in the U.S.—"the left" has often come to mean white folks. In the next era, will so much of the Anglo left continue to minimize the Mexican American struggle?

At the heart of the problem is a tendency to see race relations and the struggle against racism primarily or exclusively in terms of black and white. Every week articles or books appear that claim to address racial issues like Affirmative Action but contain not a single word about any population except the African American. In the histories of the 1960s by white authors, although the treatment of black struggle is never adequate one can at least find Martin Luther King, the Black Panthers, and a few other references. But in 25 such books reviewed by this writer, the massive Chicano movement of the 1960s and early 1970s might never have happened. (See "That Old White (Male) Magic," *Z*, July–August 1989.)

To criticize this blindness is not to deny the primacy of African American struggle: the genocidal nature of enslavement, the constant resistance by slaves, the "Second Reconstruction" of the 1960s and its extraordinary leaders, and today's destruction of black youth if not black males in general. Also, African Americans up to now remain the largest population of color in this country. I began my own political work in the black civil rights movement because it was so obviously on the cutting edge of history for all people of color, for the whole society. Many white progressives also gave support, sometimes even their lives, to that movement. But somehow, while combating the symbolism of blacks as "the Invisible Man" they overlooked new "invisible" men—and women—of other colors.

One apparent exception to the left's myopia about Mexican Americans surfaced during the party-building movement of the 1970s. A flurry of Marxist-Leninist position papers about Chicanos descended, telling us that we were a nation and should secede from the U.S. (wha?), or that we were a national minority whose goal should be regional autonomy (wha?), or that we were nothing more than part of the U.S. working-class (wha?), or that we were a racial but not a national minority (hunh?!). Those we called the Alphabet Soup

came to visit Chicano groups in New Mexico at different times. Their organizational positions were unrelated to the realities we knew, concoctions that seemed to have sprung full-grown from their heads, nourished by theory alone. This could only leave us feeling a lack of respect for our history, culture, and struggle.

Earlier the Communist Party had done better and provided courageous leadership to labor struggles involving Mexican or Chicano workers. But here too Raza who were in the party have their stories to tell of an alienating chauvinism. All in all, left organizations too often use that demeaning stock phrase: "African Americans and other minorities" or "African Americans and other Third World people" or "African Americans and other people of color."

Even when Anglo leftists do study Raza culture and history, the problem remains of demonstrating support for Latinos abroad rather than at home. Many Anglos have worked hard on solidarity with Central America and against U.S. intervention. They learn Spanish, embrace the culture, pass hard and often dangerous time in Central American countries. But, except for the issue of refugees and sanctuary, this has rarely translated into support for domestic struggles by Latino peoples—for example, Chicanos/Mexicans or Puerto Ricans in the U.S. Intentions aside, a romanticized and in the end paternalistic view of Latinos tends to prevail all too often.

Anglos are not alone in showing little effort to understand the history, culture, and struggles of Mexican Americans. Peoples of color can also be blind. Among blacks, for example, author Manning Marable is one of the few who regularly brings Latinos into his worldview. Even within the same population, class differences make some Chicanos want racism exposed, while others prefer to maintain a pretense of "No problem." Some will affirm their brownness proudly while others prefer to pass for white if possible.

Up to now the dominant society has had no interest in teaching our unknown histories to anyone and preferred to leave in place the melting-pot model. The burden then falls on the rest of us to work for internationalism inside—not just outside—U.S. borders. We have to teach and learn from each other, we have to develop mutual knowledge of and respect for all our cultures. A new kind of U.S. left will not be born otherwise, as activist/author Carlos Muñoz emphasized in a recent hard-hitting *Crossroads* article.

1992: A CHANCE TO SING "DE COLORES" AS NEVER BEFORE

The upcoming quincentenary offers a once-in-500-years chance to pull our colors together in common protest. Christopher Columbus's arrival on this continent has meaning, usually deadly, for all people of color and many others. In the face of what will be constant, repugnant official celebrations of 1492, we can together mount educational events and demonstrations of all kinds with great scope and impact. The symbolism begs for sweeping protest, a protest that will not merely say "No" to what happened 500 years ago but affirm the infinite treasure-house of non-European cultures and histories, then and now.

For Native Americans, of course, Columbus's arrival meant instant genocide. Today indigenous peoples all over the continent are already planning domestic and international actions. Europe's colonization also paved the way for the enslavement of Africans by the million, brought here to build vast wealth for others with their blood and sweat. At the same time, colonialism launched the birth—by conquest and rape—of a whole new people, La Raza, who combine the red, white, and black in what we may still call a bronze people.

On the backs of all these colors was constructed the greatest wealth ever seen in the world, a wealth that soon came to need more slaves of one kind or another. This time it drew them from the East: Chinese, Japanese, Filipino, Pacific peoples, and many others. Ultimately the whites failed to protect many of their own children from an inhuman poverty and contempt.

So we can come together on this, if we choose. We can make 1992 a year that THEY will remember. We can, in gentler terms, make it the year of "De Colores," of new alliances, in the spirit of the old song by that name: *"Y por eso los grandes amores de muchos colores me gustan a mi"* (*"And so the loves of many colors are pleasing to me."*)

MEXAMERICA

Born on the Border

Selena's music, Tejano, is the rollicking soundtrack to the border country,

fusing Hispanic culture to Anglo pop, connecting the present to the past

JOHN LELAND

AT THE CLUB SANTA FE IN CORPUS Christi, Texas, Pete Astudillo is working the crowd. The Santa Fe is a big, engulfing place—too big for Astudillo, maybe too big for a Wednesday night in this midsize city on the Gulf Coast. Until last year Astudillo had been a backup singer in Selena's band; now, with her family in support at the rear of the room, he is on his own. One by one, couples slip onto the dance floor: Anglo and Latin, twenty-somethings and middle-agers, easing or wrestling each other in a jaunty two-step as Astudillo sings songs of love in Spanish.

The accordion propels them, the joyous oom-pah that is the heart of Tejano music. It came to these parts with the Czech and German settlers of the 19th century and flourished in the cantinas of the Mexican working class. Now, as men in cowboy shirts swing their partners in front of him, its buoyant fluttering makes Astudillo silly. "Put your hands in the air," he chants, "and wave 'em like you just don't care." He has crossed not only to English, but to the English of rap music and the South Bronx, come down this way via MTV. As the polka beat barrels behind him, this is a perfect Tejano moment: a first-generation Mexican-American playing the past against the present, the cantina roots of the south against the video rootlessness of the north, while a bicultural audience drinks 50-cent beers and has a good time.

Literally, "Tejano" means Texan, not just the music but the people as well. It is the soundtrack to MexAmerica. "Tejano," says Abraham Quintanilla Jr., Selena's father and Astudillo's manager, "is a fusion, with all these influences: rock and roll, pop, country,

rap, jazz. We're Americans who happen to be of Mexican descent. When [the musicians] play a Mexican song, they infuse it with all the influences in their heads." Nurtured in the '30s and '40s, as a synthesis of the accordion-driven Mexican *conjunto* and the North American big-band sound, the music took root in the cantinas and speak-easies of south Texas. But as migrant farm laborers and later the Mexican-American factory workers moved north, the circuit followed. After a flash in the late '60s and early '70s, when rock-friendly acts like Freddie Fender and The Sir Douglas Quintet briefly crossed over to national attention, the music is now surging, driven by a battery of telegenic young stars. This summer Selena's posthumous album "Dreaming of You," with four songs in English, took a dramatic measure of this audience. Selling 175,000 copies in a day, it became the second fastest-moving album ever by a female performer. Tejano has become the fastest-growing market in Latin music, with annual revenues topping $100 million.

In Corpus Christi's working-class neighborhood of Molina, Lupe Lopez, 22, and her sister have decorated their modest family home as a shrine to the music. Promotional glossies of Tejano stars take their place beside family photos and religious portraits. Selena lived down the street, in a little brick house she shared with her husband, Chris Pérez; Selena's parents and her brother, A. B. Quintanilla, lived in the two houses next door. In her living room, piquant with the smell of cooking food, Lupe says she remembers Selena for her red Porsche, and for her humility: "You'd see her in Wal-Mart, you'd see her working in

the yard." After Selena was killed in the Corpus Christi Days Inn on March 31, just two weeks before her 24th birthday, Lopez spelled out SELENA in paper cups in the wire fence in front of her home. She had to give up on the cups—fans making the pilgrimage to Selena's house, as many as 1,000 a week, would take them as souvenirs. But she has kept up her brilliant blue sign reading HEAVEN NEEDED ANOTHER ANGEL. WE'LL MISS YOU.

For Lopez, as for many Tejanos, the music has always been around. Her parents and her aunt would sing at family gatherings; her cousin Albert Zamora is one of the rising stars of Tejano. But in the late '70s, Tejano lost a lot of young fans. Kids identified the music with their parents. The huge waves of recent Mexican immigrants wanted music that was more Mexican, like the horn-driven *banda* sounds that flourished in California. Like many young Mexican-Americans, Lopez didn't consider the music her own until the advent of performers like Selena: stars her own age who, like her, grew up in a mixed cultural environment. "The music has changed a lot," she says. "Kids can dance to it now. You could relate to [Selena]. All of a sudden you'd go to dances and you couldn't dance anymore, because there wasn't room." She beams as she says, "I feel a lot of pride in her."

'Too Mexican': For Bob Peña, the current Tejano revolution began in the early '80s. A massive man, Peña grew up with the Tejano industry; along with the Dallas Cowboys, it is his life. For 40 years, his father was a pioneering AM disc jockey in Alice, Texas, spinning Tejano in the morning and country in the afternoon. Now, at 39, Peña is program director at the station Club 98.3-FM in Corpus Christi. "Tejanos are fiercely proud of our culture," he says. "That's why we embrace the music so much. It's ours, it was born here. Most of our audience, their parents speak English in the house, but maybe their grandparents only speak Spanish. They flip back and forth." Around 1980, he says, groups like La Mafia and Grupo Mazz revolutionized the music, using synthesizers and bits of international pop sound. "In California, people are much more influenced by Mexican culture. We embrace that culture, but we don't mind the music changing. Banda would not survive here because it's too Mexican."

Scratch a Tejano, and chances are you'll find mixed roots. Peña says he "was a rocker until high school." Selena's first song, sung for her father when she was 6½, was "I Wanna Be Loved by You"; her father taught her Spanish only to further her career. Emilio Navaira, perhaps Selena's closest rival, says that when he started out in San Antonio, he wanted to sing country music, but that "it would have been hard to be a country band coming from the Hispanic part of my town." Now, after great success in the Tejano market, he has released an album of country songs in English, "Life Is Good." (He has also dropped his surname, for the benefit of Anglo disc jockeys.) Even Abraham Quintanilla, who had a middling career in the '60s and '70s with Los Dinos, originally saw their future as an American-style vocal group, in the manner of the Four Aces. "I told him, 'If you're going to make it, you'll have to record in Spanish'," says Johnny Herrera, a Tejano legend who recorded the Dinos' early work, and who himself had wanted to follow the style of Frank Sinatra. "'You can't compete with the big companies'."

Chris Pérez, Selena's husband, embodies many of the cultural contradictions facing young Tejanos. In his favorite restaurant, a Chinese place in a strip mall in south Corpus Christi, Pérez, 26, wears his black hair pulled back underneath a Lakers baseball cap. Since Selena's death, he has kept a low profile, quietly seeing friends and playing guitar in his home studio. "I just now started getting angry" about the murder, he says. "My main concern was what her last minutes were like." Before Selena's death, the two had put down money on a house, to move away from the family compound. "I let it go," he says. "I didn't need it." He says he dreams about his wife all the time. "I even dream that I dream about her. I dream that I wake up from the dream of what happened."

Tribute tour: With his deeply set dark eyes and classically handsome features, Pérez vaguely resembles a skinny Antonio Banderas. He first heard Tejano as a kid in San Antonio, when his grandmother came to baby-sit. "She'd pop that s--- on, I'd start crying." He laughs; across the table, his friend Rudy Martinez laughs as well. Rudy is the bass player in La Mafia. In their teens, Chris and Rudy played in rock bands—"My ceiling, wall to wall, was covered with Kiss posters," says Pérez—until a friend told them they could make $70 a night playing Tejano at weddings and debuts. Now, though they play in two of the most successful Tejano acts, they'd rather listen to Van Halen. After a scheduled tribute tour next spring, Pérez intends to return to rock.

At their most agile, Tejano musicians negotiate the boundary between two sometimes clashing cultures. The rocky juxtapositions and dislocations of MexAmerica

Taste of Tejano
Something old, something new: five CDs that give you the flavor

● **Conjunto Bernal** "*Mi Unico Camino*": vibrant, polished '50s *orquesta tejana*

● **Little Joe y Mi Familia** "*Para La Gente*": ambitious '70s classic, with strings

● **Los Alegres de Teran** "*La Traicionera*": simple, rootsy, festive

● **Emilio Navaira** "*Unsung Highways*": *conjunto* meets country

● **Selena** "*Dreaming of You*": her Latin hits, plus four songs in English

bubble up in the identities and styles of the musicians. Within the roots of the music there are conflicting messages, traditions of antagonism toward the north (fomented in the cantina traditions of *música norteña* and *corrida*), as well as those of genuine synthesis (which emerged in the jazzy Tex-Mex *orquesta tejana* of the 1950s). The music can hit both of those notes. As Gerard Béhague, a professor of ethnomusicology at the University of Texas, puts it, "It says, 'Yes, we are Americans but we speak Spanish and are very proud to be Americans'."

Selena worked the boundary perfectly: the powerful family bonds of Latin culture along with the economic possibilities and pop self-invention of the north. When she was criticized in Mexico for her weak Spanish, kids north of the border just loved her more; they got the same grief from their own relatives. Other acts, like Stephanie Lynn and High Energy, are still working to find their own niches along the border. "We're what you call coconuts," says Bob Rivera, in the family's San Antonio living room. "Brown on the outside, white on the inside." Stephanie Lynn, his sister, is not so sure. Her hair, her signature, is dyed a peroxide blond; like her brothers, she speaks Spanish only weakly. "To me Tejano is a symbol of the Mexican-American race," she says. "It reminds me of Motown. The mainstream wasn't available to many of us. Mexican-Americans couldn't be pop stars or jazz stars. So we made our own music and our own industry." At the same time, she admits, "we have confusion about who we are. Are we accepted by Mexicans? Are we accepted by Americans?"

This negotiation of identity runs through the airwaves and nightspots of MexAmerica, where musicians move nightly along a constantly changing cultural border. It invigorates the shifting lexicography of Spanglish, and the bilingual hustle of Tejano radio. It holds together the polka beats and the rap theatrics and the adversarial folklore of a heritage determined not to be swallowed.

At the Club Santa Fe, though, even on a slow night, the contradictions melt easily into the infectious, giddy rhythms of the accordion and the double-time drums. The music is weightless, Texan in its unwillingness to waste too much time in cultural accounting. It would rather make sure everyone has a cheap drink and a good time. At the lip of the stage, Astudillo poses for snapshots with a couple of young female fans, mugging ingratiatingly without missing a line in his singing. The music gets richer: elements of reggae creep in, a hint of the Caribbean *cumbia* favored by Selena. It has antennae as well as roots. On the dance floor couples take their spin around the parquet one more time, and one more.

A Place of Our Own

Despite strong ties to the Catholic faith, Hispanics have not always felt comfortable in the U.S. church. In some places that's changing.

Kevin Coyne

Kevin Coyne is a freelance writer in New Jersey and the author of DOMERS: A Year at Notre Dame, *published by Viking Penguin. Senia Torres Fix assisted with this article as a translator.*

As the 11:15 Mass at Saint Rose of Lima is about to begin, the last few worshipers slip quietly into the back of church, pushing through the heavy oak doors, stepping lightly past the baptismal font, finding a place in the last pew. The Sunday-morning sun slants sharply through the stained-glass windows high up on the wall of the nave. The altar table is draped with a red cloth in honor of the day's feast, Christ the King. The priest and the altar boys enter the sanctuary from the sacristy door, and the congregation stands to pray—just as congregations have been standing to pray in this sturdy, simple church for more than a century.

From the outside, Saint Rose looks much the same today as it did when it was consecrated in 1882 — a single-tower, carpenter-Gothic edifice of red brick and yellow terra cotta, surrounded by a web of close-packed, wood-frame houses, physically tied to the neighborhood by the kind of intimate proximity that zoning laws no longer allow. Inside, though, much has changed. As the priest offers the greeting this morning, a large, sunburst-colored mosaic of the risen Christ fills the wall behind him. The high and ornate white altar that once dominated the sanctuary is long since gone, a casualty of some post-Vatican-II house-cleaning. The dark, brooding ceiling murals are gone too, replaced by a stark, nubbly coat of cream-colored plaster that lends a vaguely Southwestern air to the church's interior. The vaulted sanctuary rises around the priest at the altar table now like a sparse desert cavern filled with light.

And when the congregation begins to recite the penitential rite, it becomes apparent that the changes aren't exclusively architectural. "*Yo confieso ante Dios todopoderoso,*" they say together in Spanish, "*y ante ustedes, hermanos, que he pacado. . . .*"

* * *

In stately old Catholic churches all over America — most of them built, like Saint Rose, to accommodate the waves of European immigrants and shaped to echo the ancient rhythms of the Latin Mass — the pews are now filling with more recent immigrants, and the language of worship is shifting to Spanish. More than a quarter of all the Catholics in the United States today are of Hispanic descent, and their numbers are rising faster than those of any other ethnic group; before long, some demographers estimate, they will account for almost half of American Catholics.

After decades of quiet growth, Hispanics are now beginning to assume a role within the church that more accurately reflects their numbers, and their influence can be felt in every corner of Catholic America—from huge Southwestern dioceses like San Antonio to small Northeastern towns like Freehold, New Jersey, the home of Saint Rose of Lima. If the last century belonged to the Irish, who now account for just 13 percent of American Catholics, the next century belongs to the Hispanics.

As the one parish in a one-parish town, Saint Rose has always been home to a variety of ethnic groups: Irish who came to work in the potato fields, Eastern Europeans who came to work in the factories, Italians who migrated down from Northern New Jersey and New York City. Mexicans are the most recent addition, a large and quick influx that, when added to the small, longstanding Puerto Rican population, has created a significant Hispanic minority in the parish. More than a decade ago, Saint Rose started offering one Mass in Spanish each Sunday, relying on the services of a patchwork network of visiting priests. By last year, the Hispanic population had grown large enough to warrant a Spanish-speaking priest of its own — and to start making ambitious plans for the future.

"*El Señor este con ustedes,*" Father Oran Ramirez says from the pulpit now, introducing the Gospel.

"*Y con tu espiritu,*" the congregation responds.

"*Lectura del santo Evangelio segun San Juan,*" intones the Colombian-born priest, who was sent here by the diocese to build a new and separate parish in town, a Spanish-speaking parish for Spanish-speaking Catholics.

"*Gloria a ti, Señor,*" the congregation answers. "*Glory to you, O Lord.*"

* * *

Each new Mexican immigrant welcomed into the parish, each new baby baptized, each new call for more Spanish services has confronted Saint Rose with the same basic question that, on a larger scale, confronts the Catholic Church across America: How best to serve a population it has sometimes served poorly.

Some of the first Catholics in America, of course, were Spanish — missionaries who evangelized the Southwest. Eventually overshadowed by immigrants from Europe, the Hispanics were relegated to the uncertain status of a small, foreign-tongued minority searching for a home in a church that neither spoke their language nor understood the trappings of their faith.

When European Catholics came to America they brought their own priests with them, priests who spoke German or Italian or Polish, who shared their culture and history, who built national parishes in ethnic neighborhoods, who helped ease the passage from the old world to the new. Hispanics, by contrast, came mostly alone and found few Spanish-speaking priests awaiting them. Even now there are only 2,000 Hispanic priests in America, just 3 percent of the total, stretched thin to serve 25 percent of the Catholic population.

What Hispanics did bring with them was a distinct tradition of Catholicism that didn't always mesh with the European-shaped American tradition. Many Hispanic immigrants — especially those from Mexico, with its long history of anticlericalism and its chronic shortage of priests — were used to a more personal kind of religion, centered less on the church than on the family. In villages without priests or regular Masses, they developed a sort of informal, lay-run church, mixing Catholic practices with folk customs. They might not go to Mass on Sunday (there might not be any Mass on Sunday) but they would devotedly join in the house-to-house procession on the Feast of Our Lady of Guadalupe, stage passion plays and celebrate saints' festivals. And they baptized, married and buried each other without the aid of clergy.

But in America, they soon learned, the priests were in charge. There were no processions and the Masses seemed colder and more distant than the worship rituals back home. The parishes were large, often forbidding, and the rules were rigid. Rather than bend to fit this unfamiliar form of Catholicism, many Hispanic Americans simply abandoned it, some for Protestant churches, some for no church at all.

As the defection rate among Hispanic Catholics climbed to alarming heights — 60,000 a year, according to Rev. Andrew Greeley, who calls it a "catastrophe" and "an ecclesiastical failure of unprecedented proportions"—church leaders finally came to realize that maybe it was the shepherd who should bend, not the flock.

* * *

The pulpit at Saint Rose, scaled to a taller man, accentuates Father Oran Ramirez's short stature, but as he thunders through his homily this morning, raising his arms and gesticulating toward heaven, he seems to grow to the size of his voice. He speaks in fiery, rhythmic cadences. His message is the primacy of Christ the King, the eternal leader who has outlasted so many temporal empires, and he delivers it with such force that the congregation, standing to recite the Profession of Faith when he finishes, is moved to raise its volume to match his.

"Creo en un solo Dios, Padre todopoderoso," their voices swell.

In the years before Father Ramirez's arrival, the average attendance at the Spanish Mass on Sundays hovered around 100. Some Hispanics were attending the local evangelical Protestant churches, where the religious practices seemed more welcoming: more Spanish-speaking ministers, more lay participation, a less rigid hierarchy and services that stressed emotion over structure. But Ramirez, with his passionate preaching, his knowledge of their culture and customs, his vision of an autonomous community, has lured them back. On this morning, maybe 300 worshipers are in the church.

"When he came, many people started coming, many new people," says Antonio Huerta, who sits with his family today in a pew near the front of the church. He, for one, comes to the Mass more now than he ever did in Mexico. "Many people want to help now."

Although he is just 42, Huerta is the elder statesmen of the Mexican community in Freehold. He arrived in 1976, a full decade ahead of the big wave, and worked for a tree nursery, as a dishwasher and finally as a mason earning paychecks large enough to make plans for buying a permanent home in America. He has also served as an unofficial, one-man resource agency for the Mexicans who followed him in the sudden migration, part of a huge influx all over the New York metropolitan area that started in the mid-1980s. "They all come to me," he says modestly, "for information, for work, for transportation, for anything."

He encouraged them to go to church too, but not many followed the advice. The weekly Spanish Mass alone, it turned out, was not enough to establish a lasting bond between the parish and the Hispanic community.

Like most parishes, Saint Rose has long since been assimilated into America, and it's had little recent experience in dealing with immigrants. Its intentions were good but the results were spotty. The main problem was a lack of stability, in both the congregation and the pulpit: The Mexicans often moved on to new jobs and new towns, and the Spanish-speaking priests shuttled through the parish like the itinerant pastors who served Saint Rose in the mid-19th century. There were priests from Ecuador, Colombia, Argentina, but none of them stayed very long and none of them lived in town.

As the Hispanic population in Freehold continued to grow but attendance at the Spanish Mass didn't, the diocese decided to take the next step. Last August it bought a five-acre wooded lot on the edge of town for $180,000. When Ramirez moved into the small house on the property, it was a significant milestone on the path to stability.

"We had to fix it up in a hurry, because Father was coming fast," says Antonio Huerta, who took a week off from work to help clean and paint the house. He is eager to volunteer his labor again on behalf of a church building. "It's not only for me, it's for my people. We need to go to church. When people don't, you see a lot of drinking and trouble."

When the early waves of Catholic immigrants arrived in America from Europe, one effective way to minister to their needs was to establish national parishes. When the more recent wave of Catholic immigrants arrived from Central and South America and the Caribbean, the church at first tried, with less success, a more assimilationist approach. Eventually it circled back toward the older strategy: establishing a new round of national parishes.

"When Italians moved into a neighborhood," says Notre Dame history professor Jay Dolan of earlier immigrant groups, "there would be special Masses for them in the basement of the church, and they really resented that to no end because the Irish were having their Masses upstairs." An expert on the national-parish phenomenon in America, Dolan is a former director of Notre Dame's Cushwa Center for the Study of American Catholicism and the editor of a three volume study, *Notre Dame History of Hispanic Catholics in the United States,* published last October by Notre Dame Press. " What's clear now," he says, "is that most Hispanic pastoral ministers want national churches."

Assimilation works well with some groups of Hispanics, especially English-speaking Puerto Ricans, and in some kinds of institutions, especially schools. Notre Dame, for instance, has seen a surge in Hispanic enrollment in recent years: from 10 Hispanic-American students in the 1970 freshman class to 130 in 1994. Notre Dame now appeals to first-generation American children of Mexican immigrants in much the same way it once did to first-generation children of Irish immigrants. "When you look at the natural evolution of Hispanics in America," says admissions director Kevin Rooney, "and the natural evolution of the church in America, then this is what should be Notre Dame's natural evolution as well."

But in parishes like Saint Rose of Lima, assimilation has been less successful. "Most of them who come here, they come to be richer, not to become better

Catholics," says Father Manuel Fernandez, the director of the Hispanic Apostolate for the Diocese of Trenton. "They may be Protestant for a while, but then they go back to the church they belong to."

What helps most, Fernandez has learned, is if their church also belongs to them. When he came to New Jersey in 1970 from his native Spain, after a brief detour to Texas, the Diocese of Trenton had only one Hispanic parish, the one he was assigned to. There are now 13, including one Fernandez built from scratch in a rehabbed old garment factory in the small coastal city of Long Branch.

Says Fernandez, "I'm not here to Americanize them." In describing the absorption of immigrants into American society, his preferred metaphor is the tossed salad, not the melting pot: "Every culture has value, and it would be a tremendous loss if they lose their ancestry and traditions."

* * *

When Father Ramirez steps out the back door of his small house to survey his new domain — the big yellow concrete block-garage, an auto repair shop in a previous life; the five acres reaching back to a high clearing surrounded by trees — he carries with him a plan for the future and a vision of the sort of transformation Father Fernandez wrought in that old garment factory in Long Branch.

"Maybe we could make this a small chapel now," says Ramirez. The flat ceiling of the garage, supported by a naked steel I-beam, rises tall and grimy above him. Lying jumbled in the rear corner are the disassembled pieces of an altar, salvaged from a nearby church renovation. He has a second altar stashed in the basement of the house. "then later maybe we could build something new and expand."

It requires a strong act of will, an act of faith really, to imagine this rough and worn property as the seat of a new parish, but Ramirez is accustomed to thinking in such terms. Born 50 years ago on a coffee farm in Colombia, he spent 16 years as a Redemptorist missionary shuttling from parish to parish in Venezuela. He was on vacation in New York when he met Father Fernandez and accepted his latest challenge.

Saint Rose has been generous in lending its church and some space in the grammar school, but it remains somebody else's parish, not the home Ramirez is looking for. In his view, a new church would be the center of a new community, a place where Hispanics could worship in their own way more than just once a week, a place that would be theirs alone.

But in America, he has found, it takes more than just faith to build a church. Standing in the way are questions about zoning variances, unhappy neighbors, site improvements, frontage requirements and other regulatory issues.

The new parish has a name already (Our Lady of Guadalupe), but for now its home is wherever Ramirez happens to be, whether at Saint Rose or at one of the churches in nearby towns where he also says Mass regularly. Although the proposed site of the new parish is just a mile from Saint Rose and a few blocks from the Mexican neighborhood, its jurisdiction will extend in a wide arc around Freehold and it will be open to any Hispanics in the region who don't find what they need in their own parishes.

While he waits for answers about the future, Ramirez spends almost as much time on the road as he did back in Venezuela. He visits other parishes, hospitals and the county jail just around the corner from his house. He is much in demand at Cursillo retreats. He takes every opportunity he can to make his presence known among the Hispanic community, but he lacks one forum here that proved particularly effective for spreading the word back in South America: the long novenas and wakes and funerals that accompany all deaths there.

"You can use that as a means of evangelization," he says. "You can reach more people that way." In Freehold, the Hispanic community is so young that death is still a stranger: In his first year here, Ramirez presided at only two funerals.

Baptisms are another story: He did 23 of those that year.

* * *

"Puedan ir en paz," Father Ramirez says from the altar of Saint Rose. *"Go in peace."*

Standing on the aisle in the first pew, Phil Martinez joins the congregation in answering, *"Demos gracias a Dios."*

As he turns to leave, Martinez holds in his hand his regular offering envelope for Saint Rose de Lima, which he plans to slip through the mail slot at the rectory next door. When the basket came around this morning on behalf of the new parish, he dug some money out of his pocket; but he wants also to make sure that the old parish doesn't get shortchanged. One of the original stalwarts of the local Hispanic community, a native of Puerto Rico who came to Freehold in the late 1950s and opened a small grocery store, Martinez and his wife lobbied for years to have a Spanish-speaking priest assigned here.

Now that their hopes have been realized, he finds his loyalties, like his offertory gifts, split. "I'd like to see it all together," he says. "We started as part of Saint Rose, and I'd like to continue that way."

Over four decades, Phil and Carmen Martinez have forged a strong bond with Saint Rose — they have buried one daughter, a young car-accident victim, seen another daughter married, and bought a burial plot for themselves in the parish cemetery. Their ties to the Hispanic community in the parish are equally strong: Through raffles, bake sales and dances, they have helped raise $25,000 over the years. On Sundays now, they alternate between the Hispanic Mass and what they call "the American Mass," at which Carmen sings in the choir.

"We really needed a full-time priest, because you found that people got sick and there was no one to give them last rites," says Carmen, who was asked by a priest at Saint Rose, back in 1965, to find out how many parishioners would be interested in a Spanish-language Mass. Going door-to-door, she compiled a list of 50 families. "Then I said, 'Where will we have these Masses?' and he said, 'Your house?' and I got mad. I figured, such a big church, why my house? I took the list and threw it away."

Within the Hispanic community, opinions about the proposed new parish range from enthusiastic to ambivalent. Some members, especially among the longer-settled, more assimilated Puerto Ricans, remain unconvinced of the need for a new parish, a view shared by the pastor of Saint Rose.

"The tendency in the community here is to be separate, and I'm not sure that's such a good idea," says Father Gerard McCarron, who holds a Ph.D. from Princeton Theological Seminary. He has earned high marks from the Hispanic community for the parish facilities he has made available to them and the respectful autonomy he has offered. "This is a decision they've made, and I'm helping them to the extent I can, but I don't want to be paternalistic about it. I support the decision, but now I've faded out of the picture and let them take a larger role."

* * *

For a long time after Mass, people linger in the church, chatting and mingling, swapping information about jobs and apartments. Children chase each other through the pews, their laughter a reminder of how young the congregation is and how fast it is growing. One girl runs her hand along the cool marble surface of the old communion rail, which is inscribed in memory of Saint Rose's first pastor, Monsignor Federick Kivelitz, the German-born priest who built the parish and anchored it for 58 years.

When Monsignor Kivelitz died in 1930, the mourners waiting to enter the church to view his body looked up at the cross atop the steeple and saw it glowing against the dusk sky — a strange, shimmering rose hue that some believers immediately took as a sign. The church itself, it seemed, was mourning its beloved pastor.

Thousands of people flocked to Saint Rose on subsequent nights to see the glowing cross, their pilgrimage halted only when a volunteer climbed the steeple for a closer look. The rose-colored hue, he found, was caused by nothing more miraculous than the copper surface of the cross itself, exposed when the gold leaf peeled away in several places.

This morning, a young Mexican woman leading her children to the back of the church stops to take a loaf of bread from the boxes of donated food that are placed there each week, a welcome gift in a hard season when jobs grow tight. She pushes out through the heavy oak doors.

As she starts walking toward home, leading her children and carrying her bread, the cross on the steeple above her is outlined starkly against the pale, cold sky, illuminated only by the small miracle of a peaceful Sunday in America.

Asian Americans

The following collection of articles on Asian Americans invites us to reflect on the fact that the United States is related to Asia in ways that would seem utterly amazing to the worldview of the American founders. The expansion of the American regime across the continent, the importation of Asian workers, and the subsequent exclusion of Asians from the American polity are signs of the tarnished image and broken promise of refuge that America extended and then revoked. The Asian world is a composite of ethnicities and traditions ranging from the Indian subcontinent northeastward to China and Japan. The engagement of the United States beyond its continental limits brought American and Asian interests into a common arena now called the Pacific Rim. The most recent and perhaps most traumatic episode of this encounter was the conflict that erupted in 1941 at Pearl Harbor in Hawaii. Thus, examining the Asian relationship to America begins with the dual burdens of domestic exclusion and war.

The cultural roots and current interaction between the United States and Asia form a complex of concerns explored in this unit's articles. Understanding the cultural matrices of Asian nations and their ethnicities and languages initiates the process of learning about the Asian emigrants who for many reasons decided to leave Asia to seek a fresh beginning in the United States.

The population growth of Asian Americans since the immigration reform of 1965, the emergence of Japan and other Asian nations as international fiscal players, and the image of Asian American intellectual and financial success have heightened interest in this ethnic group in the United States. Recent devastation of Korean American neighborhood stores in urban centers and the strategies of political, economic, and professional mobility chosen by Asian Americans are debated within these communities and in various public forums. This aftermath of conflict and resulting analysis have riveted attention to the ethnic factor.

The details of familial and cultural development within Asian American communities compose worlds of meaning that are a rich source of material from which both insights and troubling questions of personal and group identity emerge. Pivotal periods of conflict in the drama of the American experience provide an occasion for learning as much about ourselves as about one of the newest clusters of ethnicities—the Asian Americans.

One of the first large-scale interactions between the United States and Asia was with the Philippine Islands and its populations. This experience of war and empire and the attendant century-long process of military and defense relationships as well as the exportation of institutions and cultural change have forged a unique international-intercultural symbiosis. However, given the ongoing character of ethnogenesis and the significance of ethnic identity and ethnic group relations, it is not surprising that a redefinition of this relationship is well on its way. Even the name of this American ethnic population has changed, as has its relationship to the islands and its ancestry. There is new politicization of the future of both an Asian homeland and the diasporic remnant. Its aspiring leaders are fashioning a new consciousness that is meaningful for its time and is inspiring actions that will articulate a most worthy future.

Looking Ahead: Challenge Questions

The public passions generated during World War II have subsided, and anti-Japanese sentiment is no longer heard. Is this statement true or false? Why?

Under what circumstances and toward which nations could the snarls of ethnic hatred be renewed?

What are the attitudinal and institutional obstacles to inclusion?

How can inclusiveness as an American value be taught? What approaches are most promising?

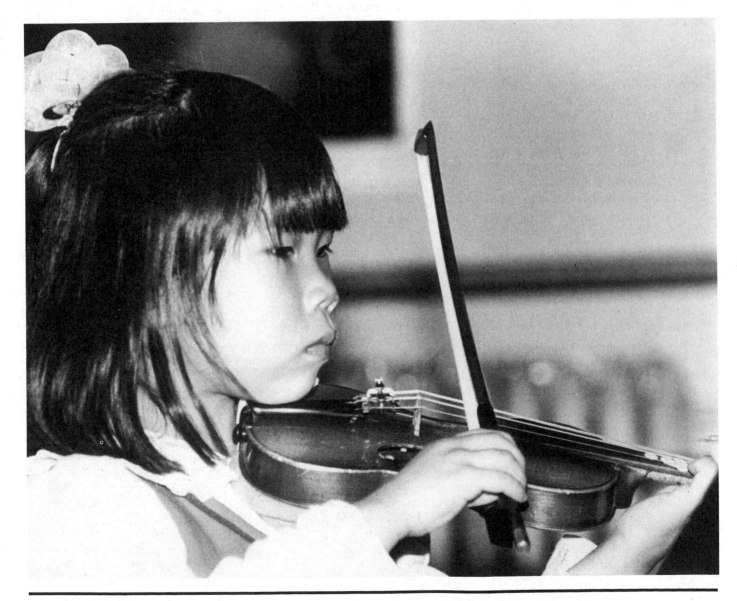

Asian Americans Don't Fit Their Monochrome Image

Moon Lee

Special to The Christian Science Monitor

BOSTON

Demographers project that by the year 2000, 10 million people of Asian and Pacific Islander descent will live in the United States. By 2020, the number is expected to reach 20 million. Yet many Americans know little about the fastest growing segment of the population.

Ironically, the relative invisibility of Asian Americans is exacerbated by their widespread image as the "model minority"—hard-working, intelligent people who have made it in America.

The model-minority image is often misleading, however. It is a myth that has hurt the Asian population, says J. D. Hokoyama, president of Leadership Education for Asian Pacifics (LEAP), a Los Angeles organization founded to develop new leaders in the Asian and Pacific Islander community.

A sizable percentage of the Asian American population is facing poverty, joblessness or underemployment, and lack of access to needed social services, according to a report this year by the LEAP Asian Pacific American Public Policy Institute and the UCLA Asian American Studies Center.

Asian Americans are not always treated in a model way. "Contrary to the popular perception that Asian Americans are a 'model minority,' . . . [they] face widespread prejudice, discrimination, and denials of equal opportunity," says a 1992 report of the US Commission on Civil Rights.

> *'Portrayal [of Asians as a model minority] has not been very fair because the community is so complex.'*
> —**Diane Yen-Mei Wong**

Monona Yin, director of development and public policy for the Committee Against Asian American Violence, based in New York City, says that 131 cases of bias-related crime against Asian Americans in New York were reported between 1987 and 1992. Many other hate-crime incidents go unreported, Ms. Yin says.

LEAP's Mr. Hokoyama sees, in part, a hidden agenda behind the positive stereotyping of Asian Americans. The model-minority image emerged, he contends, in the mid-1960s—a time of racial unrest, when some whites wanted to discredit the growing militancy and demands for social justice by African Americans.

"In general, the portrayal [of Asians as a model minority] has not been very fair because the community is so complex, and it's much easier to just resort to stereotypes than to deal with the reality of those complexities," says Diane Yen-Mei Wong, former executive director of the Asian American Journalists Association and a consultant to Unity '94, a coalition of four national minority journalism associations.

Stereotypes are always based upon some aspect of truth that is blown out of proportion, says Henry Der, a San Francisco activist and executive director of Chinese for Affirmative Action.

For instance, while it is true that many Asian American youths are successful in school, many other Asian students drop out, Ms. Wong says.

Phuong Do, leadership-program coordinator for the Indo China Resource Action Center, an advocacy and community-resource organization for Southeast Asian refugees in Washington, says schools do not pay attention to the needs of Asian students. "They don't see them as people in need," she says.

There are also differences in socioeconomic levels between the established Asian minorities and the recent immigrants and refugees, Hokoyama says.

Recent arrivals, such as the Southeast Asian refugees—Vietnamese, Cambodians, Laotians, and Hmongs—tend to be in a much more precarious economic and psychological state than established groups such as the Japanese, Chinese, Filipinos, and Koreans. Most members of the established Asian groups emigrated to America willingly, Hokoyama points out; whereas many members of the more recent groups fled to the US to save their lives, with only the possessions they could carry.

"Refugees have an even more difficult time . . . understanding this new system. It's the same as if we [Americans] had to move to Ethiopia," he says.

Yet both groups face the same problem when it comes to violence, Wong says. "Hit us with a baseball bat and it doesn't matter if you're a Japanese American, Korean American, or a foreigner, if you are a target of some kind of [anti-]Asian hatred."

Hokoyama says many people think that all Asians are the same. Yet the term Asian and Pacific Islander—a government classification—embraces 59 groups, each with its own language, customs, and culture, he notes.

Mr. Der says society has changed from 25 to 30 years ago, when Asians felt they had to assimilate in order to be accepted. The melting pot theory

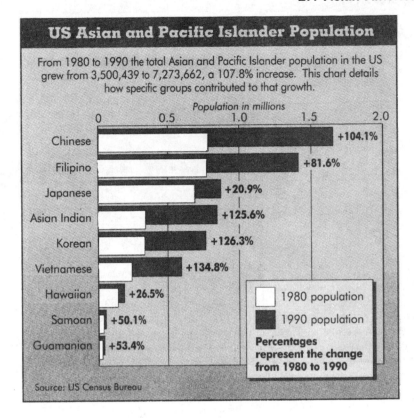

US Asian and Pacific Islander Population

From 1980 to 1990 the total Asian and Pacific Islander population in the US grew from 3,500,439 to 7,273,662, a 107.8% increase. This chart details how specific groups contributed to that growth.

Population in millions

Chinese	+104.1%
Filipino	+81.6%
Japanese	+20.9%
Asian Indian	+125.6%
Korean	+126.3%
Vietnamese	+134.8%
Hawaiian	+26.5%
Samoan	+50.1%
Guamanian	+53.4%

☐ 1980 population
■ 1990 population

Percentages represent the change from 1980 to 1990

Source: US Census Bureau

has "gone down the tube," he says. "To be an American, you don't have to shed your culture," he says.

Yet Hokoyama says that, although Asians have been in the US a long time, they are not considered American. The third-generation Japanese American says people ask him, "Where are you from?" When he answers, "Los Angeles," he says they ask again, meaning "What foreign country are you from."

A Migration Created by Burden of Suspicion

Dirk Johnson

CHICAGO, Aug. 13—When his fellow Chicagoans find out that Sam Ozaki is a native Californian, they almost always ask: "How in the world did you end up in this cold, windy city?"

The answer, the 70-year-old Mr. Ozaki explains, is rooted in war and racism.

On Feb. 19, 1942, after the outbreak of World War II, President Franklin D. Roosevelt signed an order sending more than 100,000 Japanese-Americans on the West Coast into internment camps scattered amid mountains and desert. They endured squalid living conditions behind barbed wire and the humiliation of being deemed suspect because of their ancestry. The nation was at war with Germany and Italy, as well as with Japan, of course, but there were no moves to lock up any European-Americans.

The internment did more than temporarily deprive Japanese-Americans of their freedom. It subtly changed the face of America, setting off an eastward migration of Japanese to places where few had lived before, like Chicago, Salt Lake City and Denver, because people released from the camps before the end of the war were not allowed to stay on the West Coast, and many chose not to return there.

In Chicago, there were churches offering help, and factories, short of labor during the war, offering jobs. Mr. Ozaki eventually became the first Asian-American principal in Chicago public schools, and he is now living a quiet retirement on the North Side. But 50 years after the end of the war, he recalls the burden of suspicion and the limited ways internees were able to escape the camps early. Many signed loyalty oaths and found sponsors inland, as required by the Government.

But Mr. Ozaki and thousands of other second-generation Japanese, or Nisei, chose another escape route from the camps: they volunteered to fight in the United States Army.

Some Japanese-Americans found new lives in the Midwest.

"There was a feeling that it was the only way we could prove our loyalty as Americans," said Mr. Ozaki, who served as an intelligence officer in a unit made up of Japanese-Americans, the 442d Regimental Combat Team. He worked as an interpreter—after a four-month crash course in Japanese in Camp Savage, Minn.

The 442d became one of the most highly decorated regiments in American military history. The 442d suffered huge casualties; Capt. Daniel K. Inouye, now a United States Senator from Hawaii, lost his right arm in battle. The team became famous for its rescue of the Texan "Lost Battalion," saving more than 200 men who had been surrounded by German troops.

By war's end, about 600 of the approximately 5,000 Nisei soldiers had lost their lives.

Less well known is the role played by Japanese-Americans who worked on the Pacific front as interpreters, interviewing prisoners of war, translating Imperial battle plans and deciphering secret codes.

One hero of the intelligence effort was Art Morimitsu, now 83, who interviewed wounded Japanese soldiers. "As they came to," he recalled, "they would look up and see this Japanese face, and there would be great relief and happiness." Then they would get a look at Mr.

Morimitsu's American uniform, and the relief would vanish.

Mr. Morimitsu is a bedrock American patriot who has served as a commander of an American Legion post. He was among the veterans who protested the original Smithsonian exhibit on the Enola Gay, the plane that dropped the atomic bomb on Hiroshima. "These revisionists make it look like the U.S. was the aggressor and Japan was the victim," said Mr. Morimitsu, who went into the carpet-cleaning business in Chicago after the war.

Yet he still runs into people who take him for a member of the enemy forces from 50 years ago, even though he was born and reared in Sacramento, Calif.

For Japanese-Americans, memories of the triumph in World War II is inextricably twined with memories of the camps and of being made to feel like traitors.

"For decades, there was silence in the Japanese-American community about the camps," said Prof. Ronald Takaki, who teaches history at the University of California at Berkeley and is the author of "Strangers From a Different Shore" (Little, Brown and Company, 1989). "It was seen as a shameful time."

It was not until the 1980's, when many Japanese-Americans who had been imprisoned began seeking reparations from the Federal Government, that more of them began to speak out. In 1988, President Reagan signed a law that apologized to Japanese-Americans for the internment and awarded each survivor $20,000 in damages. No case of espionage or sabotage by Japanese-Americans during the war has ever been documented.

For years before World War II, prejudice against Asian-Americans had been building. In 1882, Chinese were excluded from immigrating. In 1924, the Japanese were excluded from immigrating. They were also forbidden to own land or marry a white person in some states.

Mr. Morimitsu's wife, Virginia, recalled that on Dec. 7, 1941, she and her sister were attending a Christmas concert of Handel's "Messiah," at Santa Monica College. "Before we stood for the 'Hallelujah' chorus, it was announced that Japan had bombed Pearl Harbor," she said. "And it felt like all the eyes in the auditorium were placed on us."

In the weeks after the outbreak of war, Japanese-Americans anticipated a backlash. A headline in the San Francisco Examiner blared: "Ouster of All Japs in California Near!"

By February, signs were posted on telephone poles instructing all people with Japanese ancestry to prepare for evacuation.

The Morimitsus' daughter, Kathryn, a writer and computer consultant in Portland, said that her parents had never talked much about the internment camps but that she knew the experience had been 'incredibly traumatic.'

"My father's life," she said, "has been devoted to validating his part on the American scene as a patriot."

Being sent to the camps meant a loss of honor for people like her parents, who knew they were being tagged as second-class citizens, Mr. Morimitsu said. "And it's something that's subtly transmitted to my generation," she said. "So that while there is pride in our heritage, there is also a certain ambivalence."

In those frightening times, said Mrs. Morimitsu, who spent about a year at the Manzanar Camp in California, her mother destroyed all of her mementos from Japan, fearful that the authorities would see them as evidence of treason.

"Now I have nothing from my family's past," Mrs. Morimitsu said. "The Swedish ladies at my church will show me things handed down from their grandmothers, and I have nothing to show—nothing."

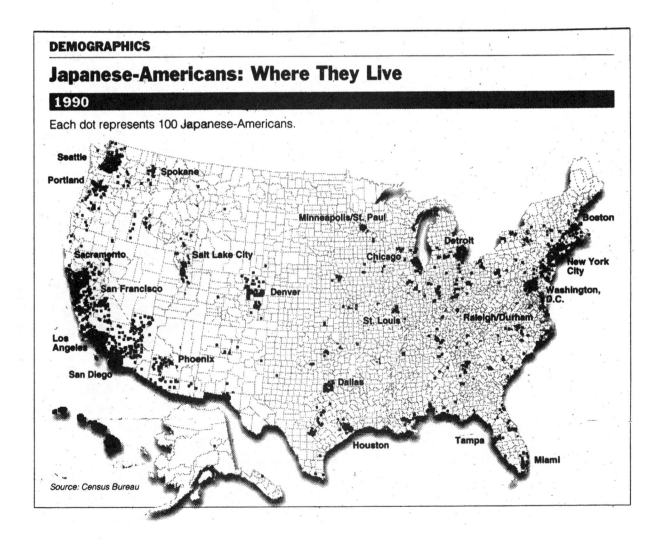

DEMOGRAPHICS

Japanese-Americans: Where They Live

1990

Each dot represents 100 Japanese-Americans.

Source: Census Bureau

Asian-Indian Americans

┌─SUMMARY

The Asian-Indian population of the U.S. is affluent and growing. Asian Indians often work as professionals and entrepreneurs. Marketers divide the group into three segments, but all Indians are keenly interested in financial security, good value, and shopping around. Although Asian Indians assimilate easily into U.S. culture, the best way to reach them is to support their communities and traditions.

> **Asian Indians are an especially strong presence in Middlesex-Somerset-Hunterdon, New Jersey.**

Marcia Mogelonsky

Marcia Mogelonsky is a contributing editor of American Demographics.

I magine a rapidly growing ethnic group of almost 1 million people who are generally well-educated and wealthy. Best of all, they speak English. Some may call this a marketer's dream. It also happens to be the general profile of Asian-Indian Americans, a segment of the population worth a closer look.

The number of Asian Indians immigrating to the United States increased rapidly after 1965, when amendments to the Immigration and Nationality Act made it possible for them to enter the country in greater numbers than ever before. Although the first sizable group of Asian Indians arrived in this country between 1907 and 1914, the population today is still primarily first-generation immigrants.

Although immigration data have been available for decades, the U.S. decennial census did not enumerate the Asian-Indian population separately from a miscellaneous category of "other Asians" until 1980. Furthermore, the population fluctuates as temporary residents arrive and leave as students, management trainees, and visiting technology specialists. As of 1990, however, the Asian-Indian population in the United States numbered 815,000, up 111 percent from 387,000 in 1980. While the increase may look small when measured against the 819 percent increase for Cambodians or the 1,631 percent increase in the Hmong population, it is impressive when compared with the 4 percent increase in non-Hispanic whites or 13 percent increase among blacks. Pakistani and Bangladeshi populations in the United States are much smaller, but have been growing even faster. The Pakistani population increased fivefold in the 1980s, from 16,000 to 81,000. Almost 12,000 people identified themselves as Bangladeshi in the 1990 census, up from a miniscule 1,300 in 1980.

Asian-Indian Country

More than three-quarters of Asian-Indian Americans live in ten states.

(top-ten states with largest Asian-Indian populations in 1990, population in 1990 and 1980, and percent change 1980-90)

1990 rank	state	1990 population	1980 population	percent change 1980-90
1	California	159,973	59,774	167.6%
2	New York	140,985	67,636	108.4
3	New Jersey	79,440	30,684	158.9
4	Illinois	64,200	37,438	71.5
5	Texas	55,795	23,395	138.5
6	Florida	31,457	11,039	185.0
7	Pennsylvania	28,396	17,230	64.8
8	Maryland	28,330	13,788	105.5
9	Michigan	23,845	15,363	55.2
10	Ohio	20,848	13,602	53.3
	TOTAL U.S.	815,447	387,223	110.6

Source: U.S. Census Bureau

Asians Indians traditionally have flocked to the Northeast, and primarily the urban portions of New York and New Jersey. But California led the states in 1990, with almost 159,000 Asian-Indian residents, up from 60,000 in 1980. Wyoming boasts the smallest population of Asian Indians—240—but it is also the first state in the nation to elect an Asian Indian to its legislature, Republican Nimi McConigley. Throughout the U.S., well-educated Asian Indians are assuming positions of power.

As with most recent immigrant groups, Asian Indians tend to live in and around major metropolitan areas. New York City, home to more than 106,000 Asian Indians in 1990 (1.2 percent of the city's population), had the largest population. It is followed by Chicago (54,000), Los Angeles-Long Beach (44,000), and Washington, D.C. (36,000). Asian Indians are an especially strong presence in Middlesex-Somerset-Hunterdon, New Jersey. They accounted for 2.3 percent of its population in 1990, the largest concentration of any metro area. They also made up 2.1 percent of the population of the Jersey City metro.

PROFESSIONALS AND ENTREPRENEURS

In many cases, the first wave of an immigrant group consists of affluent people. Asian Indians are a classic example of this rule. Among Asian Indians in the work force in 1990, 30 percent were employed in professional specialty occupations, compared with 13 percent of all U.S. employees. Twenty percent of foreign-born Indian professionals are physicians, 26 percent are engineers, and 12 percent are post-secondary teachers, according to the Washington, D.C.-based Center for Immigration Studies. Asian Indians are slightly overrepresented among managerial and sales/technical/clerical workers, and underrepresented among service and blue-collar workers, according to the 1990 census.

"The earlier immigrants came because of their qualifications. They had no trouble getting green cards or professional posts," says Dr. Madhulika Khandelwal of the Asian/American Center at Queens College in Flushing, New York. Indeed, foreign-born Indian professionals are highly qualified: more than 67 percent hold advanced degrees. And 21 percent of the 14,000 American-born Asian Indians aged 25 and older hold post-bachelor's degree accreditation.

"The more recent immigrants differ in two ways," says Khandelwal. "The professionals among them, those with master's degrees or even medical degrees or doctorates, are not always able to find jobs in their chosen professions in this country. They are faced with a choice—staying in India and working as professionals, or emigrating to America and working in trade or service jobs that may not suit their qualifications." This second wave also includes lower-middle-class Indians who tend to work in service industries, usually with members of their extended families, says Khandelwal.

United States immigration policy is based on family reunification, so it is not surprising that the qualifications of immigrants have changed over the past decade, according to the Center for Immigration Studies. Many find positions in family-run businesses or work in service industries such as taxi driving until they make enough money to pursue more lucrative ventures. More than 40 percent of New York City's 40,000 licensed Yellow Cab drivers are South Asian Indians, Pakistanis, and Bangladeshis. But most see their taxi-driving phase as a transitional period to acclimatize them to the U.S. and to give them the money they need to get started.

Many Asian Indians are self-employed. The number of Asian-Indian-owned businesses increased 120 percent between 1982 and 1987, according to the latest available Survey of Minority-Owned Business Enterprises released by the Census Bureau. Dollar receipts for these businesses increased 304 percent in the same five-year period.

"Asian Indians dominate in some trades, such as convenience and stationery stores," says Eliot Kang of the New York City-based Kang and Lee Advertising, which specializes in marketing to Asian minorities.

Kang points out that Asian-Indian retailers get an edge on competitors by pooling their resources and forming associations, which enables them to buy in bulk

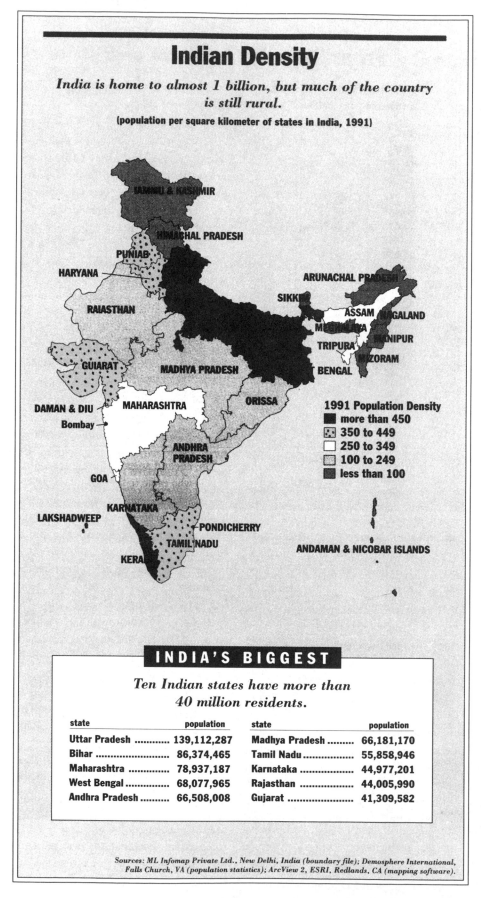

Indian Density

India is home to almost 1 billion, but much of the country is still rural.

(population per square kilometer of states in India, 1991)

1991 Population Density
- more than 450
- 350 to 449
- 250 to 349
- 100 to 249
- less than 100

INDIA'S BIGGEST

Ten Indian states have more than 40 million residents.

state	population	state	population
Uttar Pradesh	139,112,287	Madhya Pradesh	66,181,170
Bihar	86,374,465	Tamil Nadu	55,858,946
Maharashtra	78,937,187	Karnataka	44,977,201
West Bengal	68,077,965	Rajasthan	44,005,990
Andhra Pradesh	66,508,008	Gujarat	41,309,582

Sources: ML Infomap Private Ltd., New Delhi, India (boundary file); Demosphere International, Falls Church, VA (population statistics); ArcView 2, ESRI, Redlands, CA (mapping software).

and sell at lower prices. "Large family networks and family financing give these busi-

> **"Asian Indians dominate in some trades, such as convenience and stationery stores."**

nesses a chance to grow and expand. And because so many family members are involved, Asian-Indian businesses can flourish in labor-intensive service industries."

The Census Bureau tallied close to 30,000 Asian-Indian-owned service businesses in 1987. Retail establishments ran a distant second, at slightly more than 9,000. Asian-Indian ownership of hotels and motels is the standout example of Indian penetration into the service segment. In 1994, 7,200 Asian-Indian owners operated 12,500 of the nation's 28,000 budget hotels and motels, according to the Atlanta-based Asian American Hotel Owners Association.

ONE MARKET, THREE SEGMENTS

The median income for Asian-Indian households is $44,700, versus $31,200 for all U.S. households, according to the 1990 census. Not all Asian Indians are affluent, however. Dr. Arun Jain, professor of marketing at the State University of New York in Buffalo, divides the market into three distinct segments. The first, the majority of whom immigrated in the 1960s, is led by a cohort of highly educated men who came to this country because of professional opportunities. Most are doctors, scientists, academics, and other professionals who are now in their 50s and at the peak of their earning potential. Jain estimates that their average annual income may top $100,000. The

> **Asian Indians may save at least 15 percent of their income.**

wives of these high-powered professionals usually do not work outside of the home and are not highly educated. These women may have no more than a high school education, and a good portion do not speak English fluently, says Jain. Among this group, the majority of children are in college or about to marry and start families of their own.

The second segment includes immigrants who came to the U.S. in the 1970s. Like the first segment, the men are highly educated professionals. Yet unlike the first wave, many are married to highly educated women who work outside of the home. Their children are college-bound teenagers.

The third segment is made up of relatives of earlier immigrants who have been sponsored by established family members in this country. They are often less well-educated than members of the first two segments. This is the group most likely to be running motels, small grocery stores, gas stations, or other ventures. In this group, Jain also includes the majority of Asian-Indian Ugandans who fled that regime in the 1980s and have established themselves in this country.

Lifestyle and generational differences set the three groups apart, at least to some extent. People in the first segment are thinking about their children's marriages, while those in the second are about to put their children through college. Men in the first segment may be looking toward retirement, while the men and women in the third group are trying to establish themselves in successful businesses.

Generational distinctions are only part of the story, however. India has nearly 1 billion residents separated into 25 states and 7 union territories, speaking 15 official languages. "We are like Europe," says Pradip Kothari, president of the Iselin, New Jersey-based Indian Business Association, a not-for-profit organization linking the more than 60 small businesses that flourish in this heavily Indian enclave of Middlesex County.

SECURITY AND VALUE

Linguistic, nationalistic, and generational differences may divide the Indian popula-

tion, but they share a number of underlying principles and goals. Jain points out that all Asian Indians place great value in education. "Indians will do anything to further their children's education," he says.

Financial security is also important. Saving money is a major part of Indian culture, and targeted saving—for education or retirement—is especially emphasized. Jain estimates that the savings rate among Asian Indians in the U.S. is higher than the national average of 5 percent; he places it as high as 15 to 20 percent, similar to the rate in India. Asian-Indian Americans also place a high value on inheritance and prize investments that guarantee a secure future for children and grandchildren.

"When Indians get together, they will discuss such things as CD rates and which banks are offering the best value," says Eliot Kang of Kang and Lee Advertising. "They are savvy, informed, and conscious of getting value for their investments. They will compare and weigh information carefully and thoroughly before making a commitment."

Jain points out that investment bankers and financial institutions who reach out to this market stand to make substantial gains, particularly those in Asian-Indian communities. "We rely on local banks for local transactions," adds Pradip Kothari. "Because there are no foreign banks in New Jersey, we are forced to rely on Indian banks in New York City for international transactions. But we invest locally. We try to buy CDs at a bank that is interested in our community."

Asian Indians also find security in well-defined property and life insurance. "Indians love insurance," says Jain. "And they tend to buy policies with cash value." He points out another motivation for insurance companies to pursue this market. "Indians tend to carry little disability insurance. This is especially true of professionals who may be self-employed."

Asian-Indian merchants in the Oak Tree Road area of Iselin, New Jersey, favor Metropolitan Life and New York Life because these companies participate in

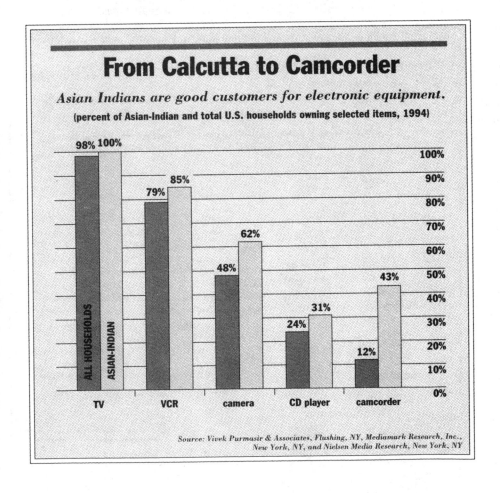

From Calcutta to Camcorder

Asian Indians are good customers for electronic equipment.
(percent of Asian-Indian and total U.S. households owning selected items, 1994)

ALL HOUSEHOLDS
ASIAN-INDIAN

TV: 98% 100%
VCR: 79% 85%
camera: 48% 62%
CD player: 24% 31%
camcorder: 12% 43%

Source: Vivek Purmasir & Associates, Flushing, NY, Mediamark Research, Inc., New York, NY, and Nielsen Media Research, New York, NY

THE INDIAN TOWER OF BABEL

Asian-Indian immigrants to the U.S. share the same mother country, but this doesn't mean they understand each other. India's constitution recognizes a total of 15 official languages, and a recent Indian census tabulated more than 500 mother tongues spoken within the nation's boundaries. These languages are similar to regional accents in the U.S., because they give clues to an Asian Indian's regional origin. This may in turn point to other cultural differences, such as religion or food preferences.

The languages of India are members of the Indo-Aryan branch of Indo-European, the family to which the majority of western languages belong. While some Indian languages are spoken by millions of people, others are common only to a handful. Each Indian state has its own official language or dialect, but residents may speak a host of other dialects, which form a sort of chain link with each other. This means that although neighbors who speak different dialects may understand each other, those who live a few dialects apart may not.

Almost 70 percent of Asian Indians aged 5 and older enumerated in the 1990 U.S. census reported speaking a language other than English at home.

The U.S. has 330,000 Hindi speakers, and a sizable number speak Gujarathi, Panjabi, Bengali, or Marathi. Some language groups are microscopic, however, such as the 18 people who speak Bihari and presumably hail from the northeastern Indian state of Bihar, where it is the official language. Fortunately for them, all 18 speak English well, as do the vast majority of all Asian Indians in the U.S.

Marketers don't necessarily need to speak 500 Indo-Aryan languages. But they do need to be aware of the diversity among their Asian-Indian customers.

—Marcia Mogelonsky

SPEAKING IN INDIAN TONGUES

English may be the only common language spoken by Asian-Indian Americans.

(five Indian languages spoken by largest numbers of Americans, number speaking language in U.S. in 1990, and Indian/Pakistani states where languages are spoken)

language	number of speakers in U.S.	Indian/Pakistani states where language is spoken
Hindi (Urdu)	331,484	Uttar Pradesh, Madhya Pradesh, Bihar, Haryana, Delhi, Rajasthan, Punjab, Himachal Pradesh, West Bengal, and Maharashtra, India
Gujarathi	102,418	Gujarat, Bombay district of Maharashtra, India
Panjabi	50,005	Punjab, northwest frontier province and Karachi, Pakistan; Haryana, Delhi, and Ganganagar district of Rajasthan, India
Bengali	38,101	Bangladesh, West Bengal, Tripura, and Assam, India
Marathi	14,755	Maharashtra and eight adjoining districts in three older states of India

Source: U.S. Census Bureau

the community, says Kothari. Metropolitan Life was a major sponsor of the local Navaratri, a religious festival that attracted some 100,000 participants from around New Jersey, New York, and even further afield. "It didn't take a lot. One of the chief executives of the company attended the festival, and the company took out a series of ads in the souvenir program. Now we feel that we should reward the company for taking an interest in us."

Indians do not have a "throw-away" mentality, says Jain. They expect value for their money and buy things with an eye to quality and durability. "Some West-

> **Asian Indians expect value for their money. They shop for quality and durability.**

erners may think it strange to see a doctor or engineer standing in line at a department store to get a broken appliance repaired. They may think, 'Wouldn't it be easier just to buy a new one?' But that is not the Indian way," says Jain.

Seeking value goes beyond durable goods. Many Asian Indians run up large long-distance telephone bills talking to extended family in India, so they actively price-shop among both major and smaller long-distance companies. These telecommunications companies are perhaps the most active in marketing directly to Asian Indians, with Indian-theme advertisements, Indian-language services, and highly competitive rates.

ASSIMILATING EASILY

The children of Asian-Indian immigrants set the tone for many purchases made outside the local Indian communities, especially for clothing and food. Second generation and "generation one-and-a-halfers," as Bryn Mawr College assistant dean Sonya Mehta describes Indians who came to the U.S. when they were young, may feel more American than Indian.

Asian-Indian children, like most second-generation Americans, are straddling two cultures. While they are as American-

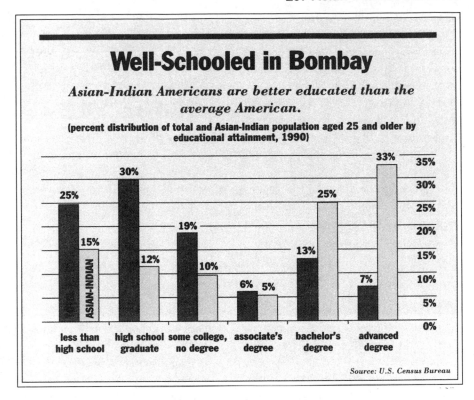

Well-Schooled in Bombay

Asian-Indian Americans are better educated than the average American.

(percent distribution of total and Asian-Indian population aged 25 and older by educational attainment, 1990)

	less than high school	high school graduate	some college, no degree	associate's degree	bachelor's degree	advanced degree
Total	25%	30%	19%	6%	13%	7%
Asian-Indian	15%	12%	10%	5%	25%	33%

Source: U.S. Census Bureau

ized as their schoolmates, they are strongly influenced by their parents' tradition and religion. They may listen to American pop music and watch American movies, but they are also comfortable with the popular music and movies of India. They also tend to follow the ways of their elders when it comes to such traditions as marriage and child-rearing.

This dual existence has found an outlet in a flourishing subculture of Indo-American magazines like *Masala*, *Onward*, and *Hum*. The magazines feature articles on drug use and prostitution among young Asian-Indian Americans, but they also review Indian art and dance exhibitions. Advertisers include long-distance telephone companies, airlines, Indian restaurants, and matchmaking/dating services.

Children in Asian-Indian American households carry a lot of weight when it comes to non-Indian food purchases. "My kids want American food. They don't like Indian food," says Pradip Kothari's wife Nandini. "And they want specific things— McDonald's, Coke, and things like that." SUNY Buffalo's Arun Jain points out that many Indian women, especially those who may not be particularly English-literate or educated in Western traditions, are not

familiar with many products found in the typical supermarket. He suggests that food manufacturers and retailers could enhance sales to this group by offering hints on how to adapt products to Indian recipes and the Indian palate, through cooking courses on cable TV or recipes in ethnic newspapers.

While children may influence food shopping choices, parents—especially fathers—are the primary decision-makers for most major purchases. Couples shop together, but the husband maintains veto power over purchases, according to Jain. This is especially true for older, less-wealthy shoppers. Even when husband and wife are both professionals, it is not unusual for the man to dominate purchase decisions.

The children of older Indian immigrants are now beginning to marry and start families of their own. Many proud parents are willing to spend a large amount of money on parties, gifts, honeymoons, and even down payments for houses or condominiums. At the same time, many of these parents are about to retire. This is another reason for parties and the myriad goods and services associated with them— banquet halls, caterers, printers, and other service providers. Asian Indians sometimes seek such services from other Indians who understand their culture, but not always. "Indians do not necessarily want to deal with other Indians," says Jain. "What they want is credibility, respect, and good service. Indians will patronize stores with good service."

Jain sees a burgeoning opportunity for the travel and tourism industries as this older generation reaches its retirement years. "Most people go to India to see their families, but as they age, there is less reason to travel, since there are fewer people left to visit in the old country. This is the time for Indian empty nesters to see the United States," Jain says. And while most non-Indians may assume that the only foreign trips Indians make are back to their home country, Nandini Kothari points out that her family does so only once every three or four years. "We go to see our families, but we don't go too often. It's usually too hot, the kids don't enjoy it, and there are so many family obligations that we don't get much of a chance to rest. We prefer to go to the Caribbean for our vacations."

REACHING ASIAN INDIANS

Although 68 percent of Asian Indians aged 5 and older speak a language other than English, only 21 percent do not speak English very well. Should marketers go out of their way to reach a group that has little problem accessing the information and advertisements already out there? "Most definitely," says Jain.

"If you want to win Asian-Indian customers, you have to participate in their communities," says Pradip Kothari. "You don't have to spend a lot of money for

> **"If you want to win Asian-Indian customers, you have to participate in their communities."**

name recognition—a little goes a long way." Rajiv Khanna, president of the New York City based India-America Chamber of Commerce, a national organization with more than 300 members, agrees. "Become involved with organizations such as ours. Advertise in community newspapers and on Indian cable TV. Network with Indian groups; sponsor Indian cultural events."

One way to contact Asian-Indian consumers is to get on the information highway. "The Internet is a wonderful resource for keeping informed about business affairs," says Bryn Mawr dean Sonya Mehta, who points out that there are more than a dozen newsgroups for Asian-Indian subscribers on the Net (see "Taking It Further").

Asian Indians also keep tabs on each other and informed about news at home through a host of Indian newspapers and magazines published in the U.S. The choices range from the 25-year-old weekly *India Abroad* to an array of glossy monthly magazines with cultural and business features. Iselin, New Jersey, has local cable TV geared to its large Asian community, and cable offerings on such networks as TVAsia, Eye on Asia, and Vision of Asia offer programming of interest to the market. Local radio programming is also important to Asian Indians as a vehicle for disseminating information about Indian culture and events.

"Targeted media are available," says SUNY Buffalo's Jain. "There are even specialty mail-order lists that target Asian Indians. But even more important than media advertising is the power of word of mouth. Indians talk to each other; they share information, recipes, news. They remember companies and organizations that sponsor Indian events. Reaching key opinion leaders will guarantee that your product or service quickly reaches the entire market."

TAKING IT FURTHER

For more information about the demographics of Asian Indians, see "Asian and Pacific Islanders in the U.S.: 1990, CP-3-5," available from the Government Printing Office at (202) 512-1800. Immigration data are available from the Immigration and Naturalization Service; telephone (202) 376-3066. *The Statistical Record of Asian Americans* ($105) is published by Gale Research, Inc.; telephone (313) 961-2242. *Foreign-Born Professionals in the United States*, by Leon F. Bouvier and David Simcox, is available from the Center for Immigration Studies; telephone (202) 466-8185. India-Net is an online communication service for people of Indian origin residing outside of India; for more information, contact Gaurang Desai, gdesai@megatest.com. Info-India is a volunteer-written digest of Indian newspapers; contact Vishal Sharma, vishal@spetses.ece. ucsb.edu. Prakash reviews about 60 Indian publications a day; contact Arvind Sitaram, asitaram@us.oracle.com. The Worldwide Indian Network lists useful documents for Indians in the U.S.; contact Biswanath Halder, bhalder@lynx.dac.neu.edu.

Configuring the Filipino Diaspora in the United States

E. San Juan, Jr.

The University of Connecticut, Storrs

An article by one Blanche d'Alpuget in the *New York Times Book Review* on Jessica Hagedorn's novel, *Dogeaters,* may have contributed to reviving an old impression of Filipinos as "dog-eaters" inhabiting an irredeemably debauched society where greed, corruption, and chaos rule. Hagedorn is, however, an American author who has never eaten dogmeat. A mestiza with Spanish, German, and Malayan blood, she spent her years growing up in California as part of the "Filipino national identity movement" (Pajaron 20) in the sixties. Later, as a student in the American Conservatory Theater, she would get roles only as maid or hooker. Her contemporaries—the writers included in one of the first Asian-American literary anthologies, *Aiiieeeeee!* (Chin)—bewailed "the years of racism, identity crises, and subsequent ethnic rejection" of the postwar milieu. Exposing the fraud of the "American Dream," these young Filipino-American (still hyphenated then) artists confessed how confused and dismayed they were at the "Oriental" Filipino back in the home islands ("brown faces with white minds") who adopted and imitated anything American. But how many have read their writings?

According to the 1990 census, the Filipino community is now the largest segment of Asian Americans, 21.5%, followed by the Chinese and the Vietnamese (Patel 112). By the year 2000, there will be over 2 million Filipinos in the United States. In recent surveys of Asian American literature sponsored by the Modern Language Association of America (MLA) and other professional organizations, however, there is a notable absence of any serious attention to Filipino writers, either born in the United States or self-exiled. In scholarly discourse and curricular offerings, "Asian American" usually designates Chinese (Kingston, Chin, etc.) or Japanese (Yamamoto, Okada, etc.) writers, or else Filipinos are tokenized with allusions to Carlos Bulosan or Hagedorn. At the turn of the century, William Dean Howells reviewed the novels of Jose Rizal, the national hero; Carlos Bulosan had to wait until World War II to be discovered. MLA president Houston Baker's edition of *Three American Literatures* privileged the Chinese and Japanese components of the category "Asian American," perhaps a form of editorial reverse discrimination repeated by A. LaVonne Ruoff and Jerry Ward's expanded survey *Redefining American Literary History.* This

has no doubt vitiated the honorably pluralist intent of an emergent canonizing, if revisionary, scholarship. Why were such well-known authors as Bulosan, Jose Garcia Villa, Bienvenido Santos, and others not considered on a par with Maxine Hong Kingston or Toshio Mori? Why this ethnic/multicultural marginalization or erasure?

In general, public perception in the United States cannot distinguish Filipinos from other Asians, or even from Latinos (the majority of Filipinos have Spanish names). The term "Asian American" continues to inflict semiotic violence on the Filipino, even as economic statistics confirm that Filipinos as a group receive the lowest income among Asians and occupy low-status jobs incommensurable with their advanced educational attainment (Nee and Sanders 85). Is this *either* a cause or a result of the failure of Filipinos to project their identity, to assert their ethnic uniqueness?

Apart from the usual scholarly exigencies and the endemic racism in the United States, I believe this is due to the historically unassimilable character of the Filipino cohort in the Asian American constituency. This unassimilability is a political effect. While the essentializing notion of "identity politics" has been quarantined by Asian commentators in favor of "heterogeneity, multiplicity, and nonequivalence" (Lowe 30–31), this has nevertheless generated the equally reprehensible binary opposition of "nationalism" versus "assimilation," in which nationalism seems reduced to a species of "fanatical nativism." Ri Radhakrishnan, for example, posits a binary world—"between the politics of an overarching and repressive Identity and the self-defeating strategies of 'difference' that lead to more and more painful fragmentations"—from which the only escape is what he calls "a carefully nuanced historical reading of the predicament of ethnicity" (112). From this "post-Marxist" perspective, however, all nationalisms are alike in their complicity with the elitist state. Either nationality is just one historical form like class, gender, sexuality, or else it is categorized as a negative, because totalizing, narrative of identity. Anthony Appiah even goes so far as to charge that Black Nationalists of the Sixties "responded to their experience of racial discrimination by accepting the racialism it presupposed" (11). In short, the nationalist response to racism in the United States of an oppressed ethnic group like Filipinos is bound to reproduce the evils of which it is the victim. The authors to whom I have alluded accept the primacy of historical specificity and the need for rich and complex negotiation with the contingencies of representation, power, and multiple spaces, but few honor these desiderata in practice.

Given the genuine historical, political, and cultural differences between the Filipino nationality and other Asian ethnic groups in the United States, one cannot help but discern how scholars have articulated "Asian American" in a selective and exclusivist direction, translating "Asian" as either Chinese or Japanese, rendering it useless as a totalizing signifier (for one, recent arrivals like Hmong refugees have had no participation in the disciplinary constitution of the term "Asian American" even if they are bureaucratically subsumed in it). Within the field of Asian Studies in the United States, the holy trinity of China, Japan (with Korea included in the space between the first two), and India still dominates, with Southeast Asian countries (mainly Indonesia) occupying the periphery. The Philippines then constitutes the margin or fold within the periphery, better known as the "Pacific Rim," despite the fact of its being the only Asian colony of the United States. Geopolitics, however, has superseded historical memory in the present realignment of historical capitalisms after the demise of the Soviet Union and Japan's economic ascendancy.

In line with the recent interrogation of the hegemonic claims of a unitary American common culture, I propose that Filipinos and their practice of cultural production no longer be subsumed under the rubric of Asian American (this has de facto taken place through exclusion anyway) and instead be recognized as distinct and different, even incommensurable. By the latter term I mean a "freak" or sport of historical circumstances. While this accords with what Charles Taylor calls a postmodern "politics of recognition" via difference (38–44), the fundamental rationale is that the Filipinos' homeland was an emergent sovereign territory when it was forcibly colonized (unlike China or Japan) by the United States and its "natives" were subjugated as aliens. They were then recognized or validated as "unfree labor." From 1898 to 1946, Filipinos in the United States thus were not immigrants in the conventional sense but colonial subjects whose bodies were transported or exiled from the periphery to the metropolis, their physiognomies studied and their cultures classified by the appropriate ideological apparatuses (including Protestant missionaries) in order to legitimate the supremacy of United States knowledge and power.

The entry of Filipinos into United States territory in sizable numbers began in 1908, when 141 workers were recruited by the Hawaii Sugar Planters Association. From then to 1946, when formal independence was granted to the islands, at least 125,000 Filipino workers exchanged their labor as commodity with the sugar planters (McWilliams 235). By 1930, there were 108,260 Filipinos all over the United States—though most were farmworkers concentrated on the West Coast. They had an indeterminate status; neither protected wards nor citizens, they were subjected to various forms of racist discrimination and exclusion, circumscribed by (among others) laws of antimiscegenation and prohibited from employment in government and ownership of land. Deterritorialized in this way, Filipinos in the process of affirming their human rights and dignity forged a culture of resistance linking their homeland and place of expatriation. Parallel to the incessant revolts of peasants in the colonized islands, Filipino workers organized one of the first unions in Hawaii in 1919, the Filipino Federation of Labor, which spearheaded industrywide multiracial strikes in 1920 and 1924. In 1934, the Filipino Labor Union was organized in California with 2,000 active members; it organized the historic strike of 1934 in Salinas, California, and set the stage for the Filipino Agricultural Workers Organizing Committee, which led the grape strike of 1965, matrix of the United Farm Workers of America (UFW) (CIIR).

In her chronicle *Asian Americans,* Sucheng Chan remarks on the changing landscape of the United States in the mid-1920s; due in part to the decline of the Japanese population, "Filipinos provided most of the agricultural labor force in the islands [Hawaii] and all along the Pacific Coast. Not surprisingly they became the main Asian immigrant group to engage in labor militancy" (87). Filipino males in vast numbers were admitted to the United States when Japanese labor was restricted by the Gentlemen's Agreement of 1908 and then barred in 1917 and 1924. But they did not blaze a new path of white toleration; they followed the beaten track of the Chinese (excluded in 1882) and the Japanese laborers. Even though they then numbered only about 30,000 in California, the Filipinos were seen by American nativists as an enigmatic horde with enormous sexual appetite, ready to impregnate Caucasian women and multiply. The locus of antagonism was the dance hall, where Filipinos congregated and patronized white women. Panicked at the prospect of Filipino fertility, the California legislature rushed to amend the antimiscegenation law to include "the Malay race" in the ban (Daniels and Kitano 67–68). This myth of Filipino sexuality departs from the Anglo-Saxon conception of "Oriental" male sexuality and can be traced to the media and popular identification of Filipinos with Americans during the Filipino-American War of 1898–1903. This perception of Filipino sexual aggressiveness accounts for the rabid anti-Filipino violence that erupted in 1928 in Yakima Valley, Washington, and in 1930 in Watsonville, California—to cite only two of numerous cases. Forbidden from owning land, refused government jobs, stigmatized by antimiscegenation laws, harassed and persecuted, these "nationals" from southeast Asia woke up in the thirties to find that, as Carlos Bulosan memorably put it in one of his letters, "[I]n many ways it was a crime to be a Filipino" in America since "we were stopped each time . . . patrolmen saw us driving a car. We were suspect each time we were seen with a white woman" ("Selected Letters" 144). With the 1934 passage of the Tydings-McDuffie Act promising eventual independence to the Philippines and the halting of Filipino immigration, the obsessive anxiety over Filipino sexuality dissipated—only to live an underground existence, metamorphosing into the shape of G.I. brides at the end of World War II and then in the commercialized "mail-order bride" syndrome that, beginning with the seventies, heralded the advent of a new racial dynamics of North-South relations.

The world system of the international division of labor thus mapped the libidinal economy of the Filipino psyche caught between two worlds: the underdeveloped hinterland and the center of finance capital. This hinterland, however, was haunted and saturated by a deeply rooted popular tradition of revolutionary resistance. United States domination of the insurgent Filipinos in the first three decades of this century required the harnessing of its entire knowledge-production apparatus to create the pacified subaltern subject. Social scientists in anthropology, political science, sociology, education, psychology, linguistics, literature, and other fields were mobilized for the purpose of constructing the appropriate disciplinary regimes to induce consensus and the consent to be ruled, at least from the native elite of landlords and comprador capitalists whose "nationalism" masked the client-patron relations between them and the imperial authority even as it sanctioned their legitimacy in the eyes of the compatriots they ruled. This "special relation" between the United States and the Philippines—democracy for the elite, backed by United States military and economic power guaranteeing the ascendancy of the propertied few and the poverty of 80% of the masses—has prevailed since then. This state of affairs was maintained through the "national security state" of the Marcos dictatorship (1972–86). It still remains the status quo, with the Philippines as a debtor nation largely managed by directives from the World Bank, the International Monetary Fund and major United States-based transnational corporations.

For about a century, Filipinos have remained subjugated bodies in a market-centered panopticon, dispersed as "warm body export" into the fetishized and fetishizing space of international commodity exchange, their memories of the injustice done to them temporarily suspended under the illusionary force of promised freedom and material success which that space imposes. But this amnesia is fast evaporating. According to *International Liberation,* the organ of the National Democratic Front of the Philippines, "Filipinos overseas are organizing themselves, studying the Philippine situation and are linking themselves with the progressive and revolutionary movement in the homefront" (Gomez 11). The Filipino diaspora is peculiar in this organic interdependency between the plight of contract workers abroad and the vicissitudes of workers at home, debunking the topos of postcoloniality by this spatial configuration of reproducing class antagonisms in the First World and doubling sub-alternity in enclaves of the Third World. The new term for this nomadic commodity is "overseas Filipino" and their occupation is labeled "alternative livelihood."

Exceptional throughout the world in the persistence of a nationalist and Marxist-inspired guerrilla insurgency rooted in the peasantry since the thirties, the Philippines remains a dangerous challenge to United States global hegemony (somewhat attenuated in the post-Cold War era). Most Filipinos in the United States resonate to the vicissitudes of this insurgency. During the Marcos dictatorship, Filipinos here periodically denounced Washington for its collusion with the atrocities committed by the Philippine military, which was managed by the Pentagon's "low-intensity warfare" experts. There are no Americans killed or endangered by guerrillas in China, Japan, Korea, or anywhere in Asia, but in the Philippines, "United States imperialism" and its local caretakers remain the enemy; hence Filipinos may be perceived as dangerous in proportion to the workings of this strangely postmodern dialectic in which the logic of dependency sustains the exodus of Filipinos from

Manila to Hawaii, San Francisco, Los Angeles, Seattle, Chicago, and New York City. If Filipinos indeed played the role of troublemakers in many strikes in Hawaii and California, and led the epoch-making 1965 grape strike in the West Coast, any recuperation of this communal history might serve as the redemptive *Jetztzeit* (to use Walter Benjamin's notion) that will blast the continuum of United States history. It might be better then (from the viewpoint of corporate capital) to stabilize the neocolony's political and economic conditions and to reinforce United States hegemony in the psyches of Filipinos in order to insure the "free flow" of global labor and surplus value.

Over 7,000 Filipinos joined the United States armed forces in World War II; those who survived and their families formed the second wave of Filipino immigrants (1945–1960). Their children were the politicized companions of Hagedorn in California and New York City. Almost twenty years divide that wave from Hagedorn's allegory of the Marcos era and the early stirrings of the Rainbow Coalition, a time when second-generation Filipinos initiated a process of self-conscientization in a racist society with a history of subjugating their parents and the community to which they belonged. In the seventies, amid the civil rights and antiwar movements, they discovered the lost world of the "Manongs," the generation of farmworkers and adventurous *Pinoys* (short for Fili*pinos*) memorialized by Manuel Buaken, Santos, and Bulosan. The 1972 reprinting of Bulosan's classic ethnobiography, *America Is in the Heart* (1946), was a catalyst in the education of a whole generation kept ignorant of the heroic struggles of Filipinos—from the resistance to American aggression in the Filipino-American War of 1899–1903 to the strikes of 1920 and 1924 against Hawaiian plantation owners, from the Salinas, California, strike of 1934 to the 1965 Delano grape sit-ins that led to the founding of the UFW. Bulosan captured both the shock of recognizing that it was "a crime" to be a Filipino in America and the pride he felt in 1942 in being a Filipino fighting in the ranks of the international popular front against fascism, as shown in his testimonial essay "My Education." The sacrifice of over a million Filipino lives in the resistance against Japanese fascism from 1941 to 1944 in fact engendered a fantasy of Filipino solidarity with America's rulers (registered in Bulosan's title) that weakened or sublimated the energies of the anti-United States imperialist resistance born from the Filipino-American War at the turn of the century.

The recent publication of Philip Vera Cruz's biography marks the end of that era of colonial subalternity. It not only reaffirms his fellow expatriate's vision of the Filipino inhabiting two worlds, the dependent/peripheral formation of his homeland and the imperial metropolis, but also extends it to a critique of the United States-supported Marcos dictatorship and the authoritarian leadership of the UFW (of which he was a founding member), which fell victim to manipulative bureaucratic temptations. The Marcos regime's bureaucrats offered material and political rewards for the UFW which Cesar Chavez was unable to refuse (Vera Cruz 112–17).

The Filipino community-in-the-making in the United States passed through three stages encompassed by Vera Cruz's autobiography. The first wave of migrants (1903–30) consisted chiefly of males, Filipino peasants recruited for agricultural and cannery work in Hawaii, Washington, and Alaska; a minuscule group of upper-class Filipinos given scholarships, called *pensionados,* returned home after taking their graduate degrees to fill the lower echelons of the bureaucracy. The second wave came by way of war marriages and naturalization through service in the United States Army and Navy during and after World War II. The third wave began to arrive after the 1965 liberalization of United States immigration law and is still continuing. With the influx of skilled workers and professionals through family reunification, this third stream of the Filipino diaspora has now reshaped the community as 70% foreign-born and 60% female, a demographic imbalance that may spell certain consequences in advocacy politics and cultural politics. Vera Cruz remaps familiar territory surveyed by Bulosan and encapsulated in sociological accounts written by Carey McWilliams, Emory Bogardus, Hi Brett Melendy, and others.

In particular, Vera Cruz reminds us of the enduring effects of antimiscegenation and other discriminatory laws dating from the time when Filipino men were virtually indentured by recruiters for the Hawaii plantations (from which they moved to the United States mainland). They lived in barracks, isolated from other groups, were allowed only the sociality afforded by taxi dance halls, gambling resorts, and the pool rooms of Chinatown, their ostracized lives punctuated by the terror of racist violence. It was not until 1946, after Philippine independence, that these pioneering survivors were allowed to petition for naturalization. The limbo of indeterminacy and the pathos of the Manongs' (*Manong* is the Ilocano term for "brother") decision not to reveal to their folks back home the pain of alienating work and exploitation by contractors and hustlers, or even their craft of survival, are distilled in the statement: "It was always an emergency and I was never ready to go back" (Vera Cruz 24). Though the growth of class consciousness is the theme of Vera Cruz's "remembrance of things past," this experience, a microcosm of the group's plight, is always rendered in historically complex and specific ways. This is the crucial lesson of his narrative of self-knowledge via solidarity with multiracial co-workers and associates, not just Filipinos. In this manner, the subject of the class-for-itself acquires concrete identity as a Filipino in that the dominant racist society perceives him as a "native," a colonized entity with non-Western "racial" peculiarities. *It is thus primarily through national and racial subjugation that class oppression becomes a lived experience,* inscribed within the disequilibrated power relations of a commodifying world system. From his committed position, Vera Cruz criticized Mexican chauvinism in the UFW (indeed, the privileging of the slogan "Viva La Raza" excluded blacks, Arabs, and Filipinos in the union) while acknowledging the irreplaceable contribution of Mexican workers and Euro-American supporters. For Filipinos like Vera Cruz, the *problematique* of difference-in-unity is thus not just a question of symbolic positionality or a rhetorical discursive pretext for postcolonial theorizing; it is a practice with enabling and disabling effects on bodies and psyches.

Vera Cruz's practice of internationalism, his belief in an egalitarian democracy (132), is firmly anchored in the habitus of a subjugated and dominated people, as the "Epilog" to his life history testifies. When he returns to the Philippines after 60 years of absence, he is dismayed to find his family completely apolitical. He is a "nobody" in his homeland; no one cares about what he presents or represents. This is due to what I have been characterizing here as the Filipinos' predicament of being unassimilable in the United States. Despite this, Vera Cruz reiterates the fact of his self-sacrifices for his family; he asserts that he made it "possible" for his brother and sister to keep ignorance and poverty at a distance. He hopes this knowledge can be communicated to them and others so that they also can make those sacrifices—"to use his or her intellect for the good of their people," especially for youth who need to get involved in the "issues of social justice" (146). Concluding his 1977 memoir, Vera Cruz hopes that his readers will "understand who I am and the things I stand for" (145). The fact that only a handful of Filipinos in the United States fully understand who Vera Cruz is and what he represents is symptomatic of the primitive level of ethical and political consciousness that afflicts the Filipino *ethnos* as a whole; a diagnosis of this malaise as a reflection of ethnic anomie in late capitalist society requires another occasion for full elaboration.

Vera Cruz's claim implicates not only his personal identity and principles but those of an entire community of two million people. If the Filipinos today count as the largest component of the Asian American category, and perhaps as one of the most marginalized and most misrecognized ethnic and racial constituencies in North America, it is because certain historical specificities of the Filipino incorporation into the United States racial formation (in particular the hegemonic domination of United States liberal ideology and cultural paradigms in individual Filipinos) distinguish the Filipino diaspora from its Chinese, Japanese, or Korean counterparts. Because the early armed resistance in the Philippines to United States colonial supremacy and persisting oppositional nationalism have functioned as a sedimented experience motivating Filipino initiatives in labor organizing and cultural practices, Filipinos as an oppressed nationality cannot just be lumped into the ethnic rubric of Asian American. A new representation of the Filipino community in the United States is needed to rectify years of misunderstanding based on assimilationist narratives and acculturation strategies now proved fallacious or untenable.

One of the sources of this misunderstanding may be traced to the United States academic and official producers of knowledge about the Filipino, of information and value judgments that have become the circulating doxa of public opinion or "common sense." Take, for example, an often reprinted article, "Anti-Filipino Race Riots," by Emory Bogardus. According to him, one of the causes of the 1930 Watsonville, California, vigilante attack on Filipinos was racial; the Filipino is an outsider, belonging to the "out-group" because of his "different color and culture" (59). Economic competitiveness and the preponderance of Filipino males were also causal factors; but Bogardus, undeterred by his tautologies, in the end faults the lack of "sane" Filipino leadership (61)! Since Bogardus premises his research on the assumption that human nature around the world is "one organic unity" (51), he fails to comprehend the differential power relations characterizing the Watsonville riots, in particular the ideology and practice of white supremacy materialized in state and civil society apparatuses that mediate and condense economic and political dimensions of social reality. To rectify this positivism, the antidote to date has been a phenomenological and even Weberian account of the lived experience of immigrant alienation by historians like Ronald Takaki and Barbara Posadas—a regress from the dialectic of class, nation, and race thematized by Bulosan, Vera Cruz, and other participant witnesses.

It is ironic to find Bogardus's account reproduced in a 1976 collection, *Letters in Exile,* whose chief merit is its attempt to restore a historical perspective to the study of the condition and status of the Filipino community in the United States. In the same volume, we find also a contribution by the leading producer/purveyor of knowledge about the Filipino in the United States, H. Brett Melendy. Melendy's entry on Filipinos in the *Harvard Encyclopedia of American Ethnic Groups* sums up his more detailed studies, found in *Asians in America* (1977) and elsewhere, and has become the source of most quotations regurgitated as unquestioned truths by Filipino and American scholars.

We cannot fault Melendy for lacking a historical perspective. But his version of history is an empiricist accumulation of "facts" culled from early and now dated anthropological reports. For example, he derives from the linguistic diversity of the Philippines a judgment about the inhabitants' political consciousness: "Local and regional identification are more important to members of these groups than the notion of being a Filipino; for some, a national identity is not even relevant; too often, such an identity has been superimposed on the Filipinos' other loyalties by outsiders unaware of linguistic and other ties among groups" (355). Here, Melendy employs a functionalist paradigm in order to explain the Filipino community's lack of unity and direction at the expense of historical veracity. This functionalist framework of knowledge production subordinates all elements, including the conflicts and tensions in any social formation, to a self-equilibrating order that legitimizes the norms of the ascendant group, in this case the Spanish and American colonizers. Hence the oppositional "deviations" of the natives, whose asymmetrical communities continued to resist foreign rule, are discounted as "lack of unity" and direction (362). Summarizing the *compadrazgo* or client-patron relations in the Philippines, Melendy uses this belief system pivoting around kinship and local alliances as a springboard to indict a whole people's "exclusiveness" (i.e., reluctance to assimilate to the individualist ethos of a market economy), the Filipinos' abstention from electoral politics, their civic inertia and political immaturity.

Melendy follows the mainstream social science methodology of diagnosing the behavior of the native/immigrant and its capacity for adaptation by superimposing on him the colonial structure that has determined the behavior. Thus he resorts to a crude determinism in his gloss on the alleged docility of Filipino workers in the Hawaiian plantations in the twenties: "For a long time the young Filipinos, separated from more militant groups and already indoctrinated to submission by the

barrio political system known as *caciquismo,* made no attempt to rebel against the plantation system" (358). Given this emphasis on system maintenance and value consensus, the only way for Melendy to account for the Filipinos' bold, militant initiative in the strikes is to allude to the influence of other national groups. "Disappeared" or forgotten is the centuries-long tradition of Filipino revolutionary opposition to colonial oppression and imperial exploitation.[1]

In conceptualizing the modality of Filipino behavior in the constrained parameters of plantations and other workplaces, Melendy remains unaware of his theoretical blind spots. For one, he forgets the crucial distinction between social exchange based on reciprocity and that based on complementarity. This point is worth underscoring: "Reciprocity is recognized as exchange where giving and receiving are *mutually contingent . . .* [and] *each* party has rights *and* duties. This mutuality is lacking in exchange based solely upon complementarity (as would be the case between master and slave or jailor and jailed) so that 'one's rights are another's obligations, and 'vice versa' " (Paine 8). This caveat also applies to the limitations of transactional, symbolic interactionist, and other ethnicity-centered research and policy programs that ignore the colony/metropolis asymmetry of power.

It may be instructive to emphasize here that the functionalist approach (as illustrated by Melendy) "conceives race relations as a problem of integration and assimilation or adaptation of minorities in a society that is fundamentally based on a widely shared system of common values" (Berting 183). By implication, the paradigm of ethnic assimilation to the dominant society and its normative code becomes the measure of group legitimacy and success. Studies like Antonio Pido's *The Pilipinos in America,*[2] a typical compendium of data and doxa, are vitiated by an inadequate theoretical grasp of the interplay of class, race, and gender in a history as conflicted as those of European settlers and Native Americans, Mexicans and Euro-Americans, and Euro-Americans and African-Americans. Pido's inconsistencies are symptomatic of empiricist and functionalist reductionism. One example may suffice: After asserting that "the Pilipino community in the country is more of a community of consciousness, located in social space, rather than a definite locality-based physical phenomenon," he immediately qualifies this "community" as true "only in the most abstract sense" because "intraethnic conflicts among Pilipinos and the tendency to identify with smaller groups [kinship or provincial factions] rather than with ethnicity, as well as the preimmigration heterogeneity of the Pilipinos, is still a basic reality" (121). However, another empiricist oriented study of Filipino group behavior today generates this thesis: "Factionalism [among professional Filipinos] arises where larger than personal relationships are at stake, where friendship and mutual respect end, and prestige and hierarchy begin" (Requiza 28).

I would argue then that given the mixture of banality and uncritical, one-sided assumptions informing such speculations on race relations, the sociology of minority-majority relations and the theory of immigration based on push/pull factors prove themselves unable to grasp the complex racialized subordination of the Filipino in the United States, and its articulations of race with class and nationality at specific conjunctures. In the same measure, they occlude the Filipino culture of resistance that has accompanied the process of subaltern incorporation or assimilation.

An attempt was made by Bruce Occeña and his associates in *Line of March* to render such articulations in an article entitled "The Filipino Nationality in the U.S.: An Overview." Occeña must be credited for his insistence in grounding the specific oppression of the different cohorts of Filipino immigrants in their race, class, and nationality determinants (for background data, see CIIR). Not only are Filipinos distinguished from other Asians by their collective experience at home of United States imperial oppression, but each wave of Filipino migration manifests distinctive characteristics rooted in the unequal relations of power between the Philippines and the United States. Occeña appropriately formulates the defining quality of the Filipino presence in the United States: "Taken as a group, Filipinos have been integrated into U.S. society on the basis of *inequality* and subjected to discrimination due both to their race and nationality" (31). My reservation regarding Occeña's inquiry concerns its naively economistic bias (defining the majority of the "third wave" as "concentrated in the lower strata of the U.S. working class" [31] does not automatically endow them with a proletarianized consciousness) and its neglect of gender and sexuality. As I have noted earlier, 60% of this new cohort of immigrants is female and endowed with a more sophisticated awareness of gender politics, if not feminist thinking (Beltran and De Dios; Evasco, De Dios, and Caagusan). Moreover, Occeña still clings to a static and monolithic conception of the extended family as constitutive of the social and political dynamics of the Filipino diaspora today.

Given the severely depressed economy of the Philippines today and the deteriorating condition of its resources, due to their unimpeded exploitation by transnationals assisted by World Bank International Monetary Fund conditionalities, over 40,000 Filipinos emigrate every year to the United States. The Philippine elite partly owes its continued supremacy to emigration and the artificial diaspora of redundant Filipino labor in that the latter's average earnings of over $3.5 billion a year (remitted to the homeland every year) serve to ease the balance of payments for more than $30 billion owed to the World Bank-International Monetary Fund and other financial consortiums. This allows the comprador bourgeoisie and its representatives in the state apparatuses (both coercive and ideological) to sustain their increasingly beleaguered exploitation of 66 million Filipinos (including five million Moros and about a million indigenous citizens). More than a million go back and forth to the Middle East, Europe, and Asia as contract workers, domestics, "hospitality workers" (Japan), and every conceivable kind of employment. The traffic in Filipino women as mail order brides proceeds unabated alongside sex tourism (more than 100,000 prostitutes were displaced when the United States military bases closed in 1992). At least 20,000 Filipinos work in the United States Navy—an anomalous situation for citizens of a sovereign nation-state. But this fact only functions as a synecdoche for the true geopolitics of United States-Philippines relations since Spain ceded the islands to the United States for twenty million

dollars at the Treaty of Paris in December 1898 without consulting the representatives of the first Philippine Republic. As long as this geopolitics of Philippine dependency dictates the contingencies of development for 66 million Filipinos, we can expect the transplantation of Filipino bodies into the United States to continue and with it the corresponding recolonizing of sensibilities for the complex needs of a service and information-oriented economy (San Juan, *Mapping the Boundaries*).

Census data indicate that the Filipino diaspora in the United States will total over 2.1 million at the beginning of the twenty-first century, with most of the new immigrants composed of professionals (nurses, scientists, technicians of all sorts) and skilled workers. Despite their educational achievement, they will not be spared the violence of a racial formation whose discourses and institutional practices have virtually segregated them into low-paying niches and accorded them a subordinate and tokenized status in the class and ethnic hierarchy (U.S. Commission on Civil Rights 17). I have argued that certain historical specificities of the Filipino nationality in the United States—in particular, the colonial/neocolonial position of the Philippines and the hegemonic power of the United States Imaginary (a network of fantasies programmed in Filipino psyches by a massive influx of United States media/ideological products) to promise the fulfillment of dreams for every Filipino—distinguish it from other Asian communities. I have also addressed here the heterogeneous, contingent forces that have contributed to the process of defining the emergent subjectivity (or subject position) of the Filipino nationality caught in the vicissitudes of United States racial politics. In the context of identity formation, this testimony from the establishment media attests to the power of a persisting libidinal *dispositif* or "desiring machine" (to use Deleuze-Guattari's term) attached to the American ethos:

> For most the climb is frustrating but ultimately successful. Antonio Cube, 49, a Filipino attorney, immigrated with his wife and two children in 1970. Accustomed to the services of three maids and a driver at home, but unqualified to practice law in the U.S., Cube found work instead as a computer encoder in a bank. "I almost went home," he says now. "But the bank sent me to technical schools and moved me up little by little. For five years my wife and I worked two full-time jobs." Today Cube is a supervisor for Seattle's Rainier Bank and owns not only his own home but three other houses in the metropolitan area. Two of them, now rented, are earmarked for his children, both university students. "We feel that life is about saving for the future," says Cube. "We live for our children." (Doerner 43)

Displaced and at the same time renewed by this fantasy is the Other tradition of resistance and revolt against this racist violence and the reassertion of a racial/ethnic subjectivity—prefigured by the undecidable protagonists of *Dogeaters,* by the spectacle of Moro rebels kidnapping American or Japanese businessmen in Mindanao, by the presence of women and Filipino priests leading the guerrillas of the New People's Army—that is just beginning to find articulation in the texts of young Filipino artists like Hagedorn and her contemporaries.

Other strategies of intervention by the uprooted and dispossessed people of a disintegrating nation-state may soon erupt in places that the diaspora has marked as sites of oppression and also of empowerment. After the war against Iraq, we have read stories of Filipino domestics defying their abusive Kuwaiti employers; one Lourana Crow Rafael is reported to have killed Sheikha Latifa Abdullah Al-Jaber Al-Sabah (a member of the ruling clan of Kuwait) in Cairo in February 1992 after she refused Rafael's request for permission to return to the Philippines (Kelley 1A). The ecology of the struggle for self-determination is much more complex and unpredictable than the limited texture of such incidents, but any mapping of the diasporic will is bound to implicate the volatile and highly surveilled urban spaces in the United States. Limitation of space does not allow me to explore the rise of a Filipino style of feminist and lesbian politics (see Urian), the active participation of Filipinos in the campaign for reproductive rights and a host of local issues (for example, the right to speak Tagalog in the workplace versus the campaign for English Only in some states). These all signify overdetermined traces of a genealogy of interventions marked within the last two decades by the 1977 campaign to defend Leonora Perez and Filipina Narciso, two nurses scapegoated for the mysterious deaths of patients in a veterans' hospital, and the successful prosecution of Marcos agents responsible for the murder of Seattle union activists Silme Domingo and Gene Viernes. One can also cite recent initiatives in electoral politics and in campaigns to stop the traffic in mail order brides and domestic labor (San Juan, *Racial Formations*).

We cannot understand the predicament and destiny of the Filipino diaspora here unless we place it both in its global context and in the unique historical specificity between United States hegemony and the resistance of a people struggling for national and popular self-determination. Analyzing the paradoxes, aporias, and duplicities of this relation, which offers opportunities for the exercise of popular democratic agency, remains the agenda for a future collective project.

NOTES

1. Unfortunately, even a recent dramatization of the worker's life in Hawaii, entitled *Istorya ni Bonipasyo [Bonipasyo's story: Hawaii Is Like Paradise]* (Cervantes and Felipe), although it foregrounds the workers' activism, fails to make the connection with the national-democratic resistance in the Philippines. As a symptom of the deeply sedimented "colonial mentality" of this "transported" peasant community, the play glorifies the hegemonic work ethic now ascribed as part of the natives' "cultural baggage"—a strange but revealing conflation!

2. The use of "P" instead of "F" for Filipino was introduced by some Filipino activists in the late sixties on the premise that the sound for "F" in English is not found in any of the Filipino languages and therefore a nationalist identity politics needs to revise the spelling of the designation for immigrants from the Philippines. But this practice did not really become popular. After 1987, however, the official term (as stipulated by the 1987 Constitution) for the emergent national language in the Philippines became "Filipino," not "Pilipino," in the interest of subsuming more than 70 languages and dialects used by the total population. For international communication, I opt for the more ecumenical "Filipino" instead of the symbolic, separatist "Pilipino" in the English usage.

WORKS CITED

Appiah, Anthony. "Racisms." *Anatomy of Racism.* Ed. David Goldberg. Minneapolis: U of Minnesota P, 1990. 3–17.

Baker, Houston, ed. *Three American Literatures: Essays in Chicano, Native American, and Asian-American Literature.* New York: MLA, 1982.

Beltran, Ruby P., and Aurora Javate De Dios, eds. *Filipino Women Overseas Contract Workers . . . At What Cost?* Manila: Goodwill Trading, 1992.

Berting, Jan. "An Appraisal of Functionalist Theories in Relation to Race and Colonial Societies." *Sociological Theories: Race and Colonialism.* Paris: UNESCO, 1980.

Bogardus, Emory. "Anti-Filipino Race Riots." *Letters in Exile.* Ed. Jesse Quinsaat. Los Angeles: UCLA Asian American Studies Center, 1976. 51–62.

Bulosan, Carlos. *America Is in the Heart.* New York: Harcourt, 1946. Seattle: U of Washington P, 1973.

—-. "My Education." *Selected Works and Letters.* Honolulu: Friends of the Filipino People, 1982. 31–37.

—-. "Selected Letters of Carlos Bulosan: 1934–1955." *Selected Writings. Amerasia Journal* 6.1 (1979) [Special issue devoted to Bulosan]. 143–54.

Chan, Sucheng. *Asian Americans.* Boston: Twayne, 1991.

Chin, Frank, et al., eds. *Aiiieeeeee! An Anthology of Asian-American Writers.* New York: Doubleday, 1975.

CIIR [Catholic Institute for International Relations]. *The Labour Trade.* London: CIIR, 1987.

d'Alpuget, Blanche. "Philippine Dream Feast." *New York Times Book Review* 25 Mar. 1990: 1, 38.

Daniels, Roger, and Harry Kitano. *American Racism: Exploration of the Nature of Prejudice.* Englewood Cliffs: Prentice-Hall, 1970.

Doerner, William. "To America with Skills." *Time* 8 July 1985: 42–44.

Evasco, Marjorie, Aurora Javate de Dios, and Flor Caagusan, eds. *Women's Springbook.* Quezon City: Women's Resource and Research Center, 1990.

Gomez, Alexander. "Filipinos for Sale." *Liberation International* 5.1 (1993): 9–11.

Kefley, Jack. "Kuwaitis Are 'Treating Us Like Animals.' " *USA Today* 21–23 Feb. 1992: 1, 1A.

Lowe, Lisa. "Heterogeneity, Hybridity, Multiplicity: Marking Asian American Differences." *Diaspora* 1 (1991): 24–43.

McWilliams, Carey. *Brothers Under the Skin.* Boston: Little, Brown, 1964.

Melendy, H. Brett. "Filipinos." *Harvard Encyclopedia of American Ethnic Groups.* Ed. Stephen Thernstrom. Cambridge: Harvard U P, 1980.

—-. *Asians in America.* New York: Hall, 1977. New York: Hippocrene, 1981.

Nee, Victor, and Jimy Sanders. "The Road to Parity: Determinants of the Socioeconomic Achievements of Asian Americans." *Ethnic and Racial Studies* 8.1 (1955): 77–93.

Occeña, Bruce. "The Filipino Nationality in the U.S.: An Overview." *Line of March* (1985): 29–41.

Paine, Robert. *Second Thoughts About Barth's Models.* London: Royal Anthropological Inst. of Great Britain and Ireland, 1974.

Pajaron, Ding. " 'Dogeaters' Is A Sumptuous Feast." *Katipunan* (1990): 17, 20.

Patel, Dinker. "Asian Americans: A Growing Force." *Race and Ethnic Relations 92/93.* Ed. John Kromkowski. Guilford: Dushkin, 1992.

Pido, Antonio J. A. *The Pilipinos in America.* New York: Center for Migration Studies, 1986.

Posadas, Barbara. "At a Crossroad: Filipino American History and the Old-Timers' Generation." *Amerasia* 13.1 (1986/87): 85–97.

Radhakrishnan, R. "Ethnicity in an Age of Diaspora." *Transition* 54 (1992): 104–15.

Requiza, Moreno. "Immigrant Adaptation of Filipinos in the Mid-Atlantic States." *Amauan Notebook* 2.1 (1981): 25–28.

Ruoff, A., LaVonne Brown, and Jerry Ward, eds. *Redefining American Literary History.* New York: Modern Language Association of America, 1990.

San Juan, E., Jr. "Mapping the Boundaries: The Filipino Writer in the U.S.A." *The Journal of Ethnic Studies* 19.1 (1991): 117–31.

—-. *Racial Formations/Critical Transformations.* New Jersey: Humanities P, 1992.

Takaki, Ronald. *Strangers from a Different Shore.* Boston: Little, 1989.

Taylor, Charles. *Multiculturalism and "The Politics of Recognition."* Princeton, NJ: Princeton U P, 1992.

Urian, Teresita. "Into the Light." As told to Mila de Guzman. *Katipunan* (1991): 10–11.

U.S. Commission on Civil Rights. *Civil Rights Issues Facing Asian Americans in the 1990s.* Washington: U.S. Commission on Civil Rights, 1992.

Vera Cruz, Philip. *Philip Vera Cruz.* With Craig Scharlin and Lilia V. Villanueva. Los Angeles: UCLA Labor Center, Institute of Industrial Relations, 1992.

African Americans

A 1988 *New York Times* editorial suggests an appropriate introductory focus for the following collection of articles about an ethnic group that traces its American ancestry to initial participation as "three-fifths" persons in the U.S. Constitution and to its later exclusion from the polity altogether by the U.S. Supreme Court's *Dred Scott* decision. The editors of the *Times* wrote in the article "Negro, Black and African American" (December 22, 1988):

> The archaeology is dramatically plain to older adults who, in one lifetime, have already heard preferred usage shift from *colored* to *Negro* to *black*. The four lingual layers

provide an abbreviated history of civil rights in this century.

Renaming this ethnic group "African American" may produce the fresh vision needed to understand and transcend the deep racism that infects society. The following glimpses of the African American reality, its struggles for freedom, its tradition and community, its achievements, and the stresses of building bridges between worlds reveal a dense set of problems. More importantly, they suggest pieces of authentic identity rather than stereotype. Becoming a healthy ethnic society involves more than the end of ethnic stereotyping. The basis of ethnic identity is sustained by authentic portrayal of positive personal and group identity. The cultivation of ethnicity that does not encourage disdain for and self-hatred among members and groups is an important psychological and social artifice.

Progress on issues of race involves examination of a complex of historical, social, cultural, and economic factors. Analysis of this sort requires assessment of the deep racism in the American mentality—that is, the cultural consciousness and the institutions whose images and practices shape social reality.

Discrimination and prejudice based on skin color are issues rarely broached in mainstream journals of opinion. Ethnic and racial intermarriage and the influence and impact of skin hue within the African American community raise attendant issues of discrimination and consciousness of color. This concern began in eighteenth- and nineteenth-century laws and practices of defining race that shaped the mentalities of color consciousness, prejudice, and racism in America. Other dimensions of the African American experience can be found in this unit's accounts of African American traditions and experiences of self-help and the family.

As this debate continues, patterns of change within African American populations compel discussion of the emerging black middle class. The purpose and influence of the historically black university, the reopening of the discussion of the separate-but-equal issue in the courts, and the renewed attention to Afrocentric education are clear evidence of the ambivalence and ambiguity inherent in the challenges of a multicultural society. Earlier dichotomies—slave/free, black/white, poor/rich—are still evident, but a variety of group relations based on historical and regional as well as institutional agendas to preserve cultural and racial consciousness have complicated the simple hope for liberty and justice that was shared by many Americans. Issues of race and class are addressed in this section, as are the ideological and psychological aspects of the complicated journey of African Americans toward full participation in the promises of liberty and justice—as well as the enjoyment of cultural freedom—in a multiethnic America.

Questions on the future state of American ethnic groups raise profound issues. For example, understanding of the changing structure of the African American family has stubbornly eluded researchers and parents who confront the realities of pride and prejudice. How does the continual redevelopment of an ethnic population enter public discussion, and what are the implications for public policy built upon alternative models of the family? Should public policy sustain an ethnic model of family or direct the formation of family life that is consonant with public purposes and goals?

The civil rights movement has been over for more than 20 years, but many African Americans still face challenges in housing, employment, and education. Changing circumstances within the larger American society and the civil rights agenda itself have been affected by success and failure, and once-clear issues and solutions have taken on more complex structural, economic, and philosophical dimensions. The growing gap between blacks and whites in terms of education, financial status, and class, and the growing crime and death rates of young black men paint a daunting picture of past policies and of this population's future. According to scales of mortality, health, income, education, and marital status, African Americans have emerged as one of the most troubled segments of American society. These problems also foreshadow grave difficulties for the African American family in the years ahead.

To be sure, African Americans have made advances since the civil rights movement of the 1960s. They have made dramatic gains in education, employment, and financial status. Unfortunately, they still are portrayed as being part of an urban underclass when only one-third of their population is considered part of this group. While not all African Americans are poor, those who are poor are in desperate situations. Will help come from the African American population that now constitutes part of the middle and upper classes of American society?

Scholarly differences of opinion concerning the composition of the urban underclass do not minimize the hardships that many endure. The growth of the underclass, its isolation from society, and society's inability to help it are tremendous obstacles that face our nation. Concrete strategies for improving this situation call upon both the public and the private sectors in areas of education, employment, and training. Suggestions for meeting future needs of this population and pragmatic policy responses also will help the general population.

Patent historical distortion and various forms of statistical evidence have been included in interpretations and rearticulations of race and ethnicity. The issues of race in the workplace and remedies for discriminating practices have been raised in the debate regarding the Civil Rights Act of 1991. Exploring ethnic and racial mobility and developing strategies that foster the breakdown of discrimination engage us in a web of baffling arguments and social, political, and institutional procedures.

Looking Ahead: Challenge Questions
What are the most compelling issues that face African American communities?

What social, economic, and political conditions have supported the expansion of an African American middle class?

What explains the persistence of an African American underclass?

What effect does the media have on shaping the consciousness of ethnic group identity?

In what respect is attention to pluralism diminished by the economic and social plight and isolation of African Americans?

Does the name "African Americans" augment the development of pluralism?

What did the Million Man March achieve?

What effect will the Supreme Court's deemphasis on remedies for segregation and on other initiatives that use racial preferences have on race and ethnic relations?

What relevance does the Nation of Islam have to the public dialogue that shapes relationships among racial and ethnic populations?

Comment on the idea that attitudinal change founded on achieving middle-class status could extend to the diminishing of interest in and the relevance of being an African American.

10 Most Dramatic Events In African-American History

Lerone Bennett Jr.

1. The Black Coming

A YEAR before the arrival of the celebrated *Mayflower*, 244 years before the signing of the Emancipation Proclamation, 335 years before *Brown* vs. *Board of Education*, a big, bluff-bowed ship sailed up the river James and landed the first generation of African-Americans at Jamestown, Va.

Nobody knows the hour or the date of the official Black coming. But there is not the slightest doubt about the month. John Rolfe, who betrayed Pochohontas and experimented with tobacco, was there, and he said in a letter that the ship arrived "about the latter end of August" in 1619 and that it "brought not anything but 20 and odd Negroes." Concerning which the most charitable thing to say is that John Rolfe was probably pulling his boss' leg. For no ship ever called at an American port with a more important cargo. In the hold of that ship, in a manner of speaking, was the whole gorgeous panorama of Black America, was jazz and the spirituals and the black gold that made American capitalism possible.* Bird was there and Bigger and King and Malcolm and millions of other Xs and crosses, along with Mahalia singing, Duke Ellington composing, Gwendolyn Brooks rhyming and Michael Jordan slam-dunking. It was all there, illegible and inevitable, on that day. A man with eyes would have seen it and would have announced to his contemporaries that this ship heralds the beginning of the first Civil War and the second.

As befitting a herald of fate, the ship was nameless, and mystery surrounds it to this day. Where did this ship come from? From the high seas, where the crew robbed a Spanish vessel of a cargo of Africans bound for the West Indies. The captain "ptended," John Rolfe noted, that he needed food, and he offered to exchange his cargo for "victualle." The deal was arranged. Antoney, Pedro, Isabella and 17 other Africans with Spanish names stepped ashore, and the history of Africans in America began.

And it began, contrary to what almost all texts say, not in slavery but in freedom. For there is indisputable evidence that most of the first Black immigrants, like most of the first White immigrants, were held in indentured servitude for a number of years and then freed. During a transitional period of some 40 years, the first Black immigrants held real property, sued in court and accumulated pounds and plantations.

This changed drastically in the sixth decade of the century when the White founding fathers, spurred on by greed and the unprotected status of African immigrants, enacted laws that reduced most Africans to slavery. And so, some 40 years after the Black coming, Black and White crossed a fatal threshold, and the echo of that decision will reverberate in the corridors of Black and White history forever.

2. The Founding of Black America

WHEN, on a Sunday in November 1786, the little band of Black Christians arrived at Philadelphia's St. George's Methodist Episcopal Church, the sexton pointed to the gallery. The Blacks paused and then started up the rickety stairs with downcast eyes and heavy hearts. To the leaders of this group, Richard Allen and Absalom Jones, this was the ultimate indignity—to be shunted from the first floor to the gallery in a church Black men had helped build.

The group had barely reached the top of the stairs when a voice from the pulpit said, "Let us pray." Without thinking, the men plopped down where they were—in the *front* of the gallery. Allen was praying as hard as he could when he heard loud voices. He opened his eyes and saw a white sexton trying to pull Absalom Jones from his knees.

"You must get up; you must not kneel down here!" the White sexton said.

"Wait until the prayer is over," Jones replied.

The voices echoed through the church, and people looked up and beheld the incredible scene of a Black Christian and a White Christian wrestling in the house of the Lord over the color of God's word.

"Get up!" the sexton said. "Get up!"

"Wait until the prayer is over," Jones replied wearily, "and I will not trouble you any more."

Four or five White Christians rushed to the sexton's aid, and the struggle spread over the gallery. Before the issue was resolved, the prayer ended. The Black men stood up then and, without a word, streamed out of the church in the first mass demonstration in Black American history.

Richard Allen added a mournful postscript:

". . . And they were no more plagued by us in the church."

They were no more plagued by Blacks in a lot of places. For the Philadelphia demonstration was the focal point of a national movement that created the foundations of Black America. On April 12, 1787, Richard Allen and Absalom

*The Shaping of Black America

Jones created the Free African Society which DuBois called "the first wavering step of a people toward a more organized social life."

Similar societies were formed in most major Northern cities. And on this foundation rose an intricate structure of independent Black churches, schools and cultural organizations. The movement climaxed in the 1820s and 1830s with the founding of Freedom's Journal, the first Black newspaper, and the convening of the first national Black convention.

3. Nat Turner's War

GOD was speaking, Nat Turner said later.

There was, he remembered, thunder and lightning and a "loud voice" in the sky. And the voice spoke to him, telling him to take up the yoke and fight against the serpent "for the time was fast approaching when the first should be last and the last should be first."

Nat Turner was numbered among the last. And although he was a slave in Southampton County, Va., it would be said of him later that he "made an impact upon the people of his section as great as that of John C. Calhoun or Jefferson Davis." A mystic with blood on his mind and a preacher with vengeance on his lips, he was an implacable foe of slaveholders. He had believed since he was a child that God had set him aside for some great purpose. And he decided now that God was calling him to rise up and "slay my enemies with their own weapons."

To this end, Turner, who was about 30 years old, chose four disciples and set his face towards Jerusalem, the county seat of Southampton.

On Sunday morning, Aug. 21, 1831, the disciples gathered on the banks of Cabin Pond on the property of Joseph Travis, who had married the widow of Turner's last master and who had therefore inherited Turner and death. Nat, who appreciated the value of a delayed and dramatic entrance, appeared suddenly late in the afternoon and announced that they would strike that night, beginning at the home of his master and proceeding from house to house, killing every man, woman and child.

At 1 a.m., Nat Turner and his army crept through the woods to the home of the luckless Joseph Travis. They were seven men, armed with one hatchet and a broadax. Twenty-four hours later, they would be seventy and at least fifty-seven Whites would be dead.

When, on Monday morning, the first bodies were discovered, a nameless dread seized the citizens. Men, women and children fled to the woods and hid under the leaves until soldiers and sailors arrived from Richmond and Norfolk. Some Whites left the county; others left the state.

Defeated in an engagement near Jerusalem, Turner went into hiding and was not captured until six weeks later. On Nov. 11, 1831, the short Black man called the Prophet was hanged in a field near the courthouse. Before climbing the gallows, he made one last prophecy, saying there would be a storm after his execution and that the sun would refuse to shine. There was, in fact, a storm in Jerusalem on that day, but Turner was not talking about the weather—he was predicting a major disturbance in the American psyche. The storm he saw came in the generation of crisis that his act helped precipitate.

4. Free at Last!

TO Felix Haywood, who was there, it was the Time of Glory when men and women walked "on golden clouds."

To Frederick Douglass, it was a downpayment on the redemption of the American soul.

To Sister Winny in Virginia, to Jane Montgomery in Louisiana, to Ed Bluff in Mississippi, to Black people all over the South and all over America, it was the Time of Jubilee, the wild, happy, sad, mocking, tearful, fearful time of the unchaining of the bodies of Black folks. And the air was sweet with song.

> *Free at last!*
> *Free at last!*
> *Thank God Almighty!*
> *We're free at last.*

W.E.B. Dubois was not there, but he summed the whole thing up in phrases worthy of the ages. It was all, he said, "foolish, bizarre, and tawdry. Gangs of dirty Negroes howling and dancing; poverty-stricken ignorant laborers mistaking war, destruction, and revolution for the mystery of the free human soul; and yet to these Black folk it was the Apocalypse." And he added:

"All that was Beauty, all that was Love, all that was Truth, stood on the top of these mad mornings and sang with the stars. A great human sob shrieked in the wind, and tossed its tears upon the sea— free, free, free."

Contrary to the common view, the emancipation of Blacks didn't happen at one time or even in one place. It started with the first shot fired at Fort Sumter. It continued during the war and in the Jubilee summer of 1865, *and it has not been completed.* For the slaves, who created the foundation of American wealth, never received the 40 acres of land that would have made freedom meaningful.

It was in this milieu that African-Americans embarked on a road called freedom. As the road twisted and turned, doubling back on itself, their enemies and their problems multiplied. But they endured, and endure.

5. Booker T. Washington vs. W. E. B. DuBois

THERE was a big parade in Atlanta on Wednesday, Sept. 18, 1895, and a huge crowd gathered in the Exposition Building at the Cotton States Exposition for the opening speeches. Several Whites spoke and then former Gov. Rufus Bullock introduced "Professor Booker T. Washington." The 39-year-old president of Tuskegee Institute moved to the front of the platform and started speaking to the segregated audience. Within 10 minutes, reporter James Creelman wrote, "the multitude was in an uproar of enthusiasm — handkerchiefs were waved . . . hats were tossed into the air. The fairest women of Georgia stood up and cheered."

What was the cheering about?

Metaphors mostly—and words millions of Whites wanted to hear. Washington told Blacks: "Cast down your buckets where you are." To Whites, he offered the same advice: "Cast down your bucket [among] the most patient, faithful, law-abiding and unresentful people the world has seen . . . ."

Suddenly, he flung his hand aloft, with the fingers held wide apart.

"In all things purely social," he said, "we can be as separate as the fingers, yet [he balled the fingers into a fist] one as the hand in all things essential to mutual progress."

The crowd came to its feet, yelling.

Washington's "Atlanta Compromise" speech made him famous and set the tone for race relations for some 20 years. One year after his speech, the Supreme Court rounded a fateful fork, endorsing in *Plessy* vs. *Ferguson* the principle of "separate but equal."

Washington's refusal to make a direct and open attack on Jim Crow and his implicit acceptance of segregation brought him into conflict with W.E.B. DuBois and a group of Black militants who organized the germinal Niagara Movement. At its first national meeting at Harpers Ferry in 1906, the Niagara militants said, "We claim for ourselves every single right that belongs to a freeborn American, political, civil, and social; and until we get these rights we will never cease to protest and assail the ears of America."

So saying, the Niagara militants laid the foundation for the National Association for the Advancement of Colored People which merged the forces of Black militancy and White liberalism.

6. *The Great Migration*

HISTORY does not always come with drums beating and flags flying.

Sometimes it comes in on a wave of silence.

Sometimes it whispers.

It was like that in the terrible days of despair that preceded the unprecedented explosion of hope and movement that is called The Great Migration.

This event, which was the largest internal migration in American history and one of the central events of African-American history, started in the cracks of history, in the minds and moods of the masses of Blacks, who were reduced to the status of semi-slaves in the post-Reconstruction period. Pushed back toward slavery by lynchings, segregation and the sharecropping systems, they turned around within themselves and decided that there had to be another way and another and better place. The feeling moved, became a mood, an imperative, a command. Without preamble, without a plan, without leadership, the people began to move, going from the plantation to Southern cities, going from there to the big cities of the North. There, they found jobs in wartime industries and sent letters to a cousin or an aunt or sister or brother, saying: Come! And they came, hundreds and hundreds of thousands. The first wave (300,000) came between 1910 and 1920, followed by a second wave (1,300,000) between 1920 and 1930, and

third (500,000) and fourth (2,500,000) waves, even larger, in the '30s and '40s.

In the big cities of the North, Blacks emancipated themselves politically and economically and created the foundation of contemporary Black America.

7. *Brown vs. Board of Education*

THE marshal's voice was loud and clear.

"Oyez! Oyez! Oyez! All persons having business before the Honorable, the Supreme Court of the United States, are admonished to draw near and give their attention, for the Court is now sitting."

The marshal paused and intoned the traditional words:

"God save the United States and this Honorable Court!"

It was high noon on Monday, May 17, 1954, and the Supreme Court was crammed to capacity with spectators. Among the dozen or so Blacks present was Thurgood Marshall, chief counsel of the NAACP, who leaned forward in expectation.

Cases from four states (South Carolina, Virginia, Delaware, Kansas) and the District of Columbia were before the Court, which had been asked by Marshall and his associates to overturn the *Plessy* vs. *Ferguson* decision and declare segregation in public schools unconstitutional. All America awaited the long-expected decision which would come on a Monday. But which Monday? No one knew, and there was no sign on the faces of the justices that the issue was going to be settled on this day.

The Court disposed of routine business and announced decisions in several boring cases involving the sale of milk and the picketing of retail stores. Then Chief Justice Earl Warren picked up a document and said in a firm, quiet voice: "I have for announcement the judgment and opinion of the Court in No. 1—*Oliver Brown et al. v. Board of Education of Topeka*. It was 12:52 p.m. A shiver ran through the courtroom, and bells started ringing in press rooms all over the world.

Warren held the crowd in suspense, reviewing the history of the cases. Then, abruptly, he came to the heart of the matter:

"Does segregation of children in public schools solely on the basis of race, even though the physical facilities and

other "tangible" factors may be equal, deprive the children of the minority group of equal educational opportunities?" Warren paused and said: "We believe that it does." The decision was unanimous: 9-0.

The words raced across the country and were received by different people according to their different lights. Southern diehards like Herman Talmadge issued statements of defiance and promised a generation of litigation, but the implications of the decision were so enormous that many Americans were shocked into silence and wonder. In Farmville, Va., a 16-year-old student named Barbara Trent burst into tears when her teacher announced the decision. "We went on studying history," she said later, "but things weren't the same and will never be the same again."

8. *Montgomery and the Freedom Movement*

IT was a quiet, peaceful day in Montgomery, Ala., the Cradle of the Confederacy—but it was unseasonably hot for December 1.

The Cleveland Avenue bus rolled through Court Square, where Blacks were auctioned in the days of the Confederacy, and braked to a halt in front of the Empire Theater. There was nothing special about the bus or the day; neither the driver nor the passengers realized that a revolution was about to begin that would turn America and the South upside down.

Six Whites boarded the bus at the Empire Theater, and the driver stormed to the rear and ordered the foremost Blacks to get up and give their seats to the White citizens. This was an ancient custom, sanctioned by the peculiar mores of the South, and it excited no undue comment. Three Blacks got up immediately, but Rosa Parks, a mild-mannered seamstress in rimless glasses, kept her seat. For this act of defiance, she was arrested. Local leaders called a one-day bus boycott on Monday, Dec. 5, 1955, to protest the arrest. The one-day boycott stretched out to 381 days; the 381 days changed the face and heart of Black America, creating a new leader (Martin Luther King Jr.), and a new movement. There then followed in quick succession a series of movements (the Sit-ins and Freedom Rides) and dramatic events (Birmingham, Selma, Watts, the March on Washington) that constituted Black America's finest hour and one of the greatest moments in the history of the Republic.

9. Little Rock

THE GIANT C-119 flying boxcars circled the field, like grim birds.

One by one, they glided into the Little Rock, Ark., airport and debouched paratroopers in full battle gear. There were, in all, more than 1,000 soldiers, Black and White; and they were in Little Rock to enforce the orders of a federal court. For the first time since the Reconstruction era, the United States of America was deploying federal troops to defend the rights of Black Americans.

Escorted by city police cars, a convoy of olive-drab jeeps and trucks sped to Central High School where a howling mob had prevented the enrollment of nine Black students. The troops deployed on the double to block all entrances to the schools, and signalmen strung telephone lines and set up command posts.

Wednesday morning, Sept. 25, 1957, dawned bright and clear, and nine Black teenagers gathered at the ranch-style home of Daisy Bates, president of the Arkansas NAACP. At 8:50 a.m., there was a rumble of heavy wheels. The teenagers rushed to the window.

"The streets were blocked off," Daisy Bates recalled later. "The soldiers closed ranks . . . Oh! It was beautiful. And the attitude of the children at that moment: the respect they had. I could hear them saying, 'For the first time in my life I truly feel like an American.' I could see it in their faces: Somebody cares for me—*America cares.*"

At 9:45, U.S. soldiers with drawn bayonets escorted six Black females and three Black males into Central High School, and the Rev. Dunbar H. Ogden, president of the Greater Little Rock Ministerial Association, said: "This may be looked back upon by future historians as the turning point—for good—of race relations in this country."

10. Memphis and the Triumph of the Spirit

THERE had never been a moment like this one.

Time stopped.
Everything stopped.

And every man and woman living at that terrible time would be able to tell you until the end of their time what they were doing and where they were on Thursday, April 4, 1968, when word came that Martin Luther King Jr. had been assassinated on the balcony of the Lorraine Motel in Memphis, Tenn.

The response in Black and White America was tumultuous. Performances, plays, meetings, baseball games were cancelled, and men and women walked aimlessly through the streets, weeping.

There were tears, rivers of tears, and there was also blood. For Black communities exploded, one after another, like firecrackers on a string. Some 46 persons were killed in uprisings in 126 cities, and federal troops were mobilized to put down rebellions in Chicago, Baltimore and Washington, D.C.

To counteract this fury, and to express their sorrow, Americans of all races and creeds joined forces in an unprecedented tribute to a Black American. President Lyndon B. Johnson declared a national day of mourning and ordered U.S. flags to fly at half-mast over U.S. installations at home and abroad. On the day of the funeral—Tuesday, April 9— more than 200,000 mourners followed King's coffin, which was carried through the streets of Atlanta on a wagon, borne by two Georgia mules.

Eighteen years later, the spirit and the truth of Martin Luther King Jr. triumphed when he became the second American citizen (with George Washington) to be celebrated in a personal national holiday.

Leader Popular Among Marchers

But Most Came to Support Black Family, Show Unity, Survey Finds

Mario A. Brossard and Richard Morin

Washington Post *Staff Writers*

The black men who came to Washington to march on the Mall were younger, wealthier and better-educated than black Americans as a whole, and they were far more willing to see Nation of Islam leader Louis Farrakhan assume a more prominent leadership role in the African American community, according to a Washington Post poll of participants in the Million Man March.

The survey of 1,047 march participants also found nearly three-fourths came from outside the Washington region—with about as many as from New York and New Jersey as from the District—and nearly half came with sons, fathers or another close family member.

The survey also found it was the message and not the march's most prominent messenger that brought these black men and a handful of women and whites to the nation's capital.

More than half said they had come primarily to show support for the black family or to support black men taking more responsibility for their families and communities. One in four came to demonstrate black unity.

"I'm here to join in solidarity with the black brothers here to send the message that we're all equal and want to be treated that way," said Lincoln Miller, 43, of Harlem, N.Y., who moved to the United States from Belize in the 1960s. "Being a foreigner, I also suffered prejudice from other black people. I'm here to show that before we unify with others, we have to have unity among ourselves."

Beyond yesterday's proclamations of goodwill and unity between the races, the survey also found an undercurrent of racial tension. Half of all march participants said they took part "to send a message to white people," although only a handful said this was the major reason they came to Washington. One in 10 said white reaction to the O.J. Simpson verdict was a major reason they marched. One in five said they had been unjustly accused of a crime in the last five years. And more than half had a close friend or family member who had been shot.

Nearly six in 10 blacks interviewed said they had an unfavorable impression of whites, and four in 10 said they held unfavorable views of Jews.

Some march participants dismissed the issue of antisemitism as a distraction. "The antisemitism has been blown out of proportion," said Michael Addison, 30, a physician from Hartsville, S.C. "I'm not concerned with Jewish people, or white people, or anybody else. Our major concern is to bring black people together."

Although most of the advance attention centered on Farrakhan, relatively few participants said they were responding simply to his call. A third of those interviewed said a major reason they came to the Mall was to "demonstrate support for Louis Farrakhan," but only 5 percent said Farrakhan was the biggest reason they made the trip.

Still, Farrakhan was clearly the star of yesterdays march—and perhaps an emerging force in national politics, the survey suggests. Nearly nine in 10 participants said they had a favorable impression of Farrakhan and a favorable view of the Nation of Islam. Nationally, fewer than one of three blacks expressed a favorable view of Farrakhan in the latest Washington Post survey, completed Sunday.

"Thomas Jefferson was a good man, but he owned slaves," said Leonard Richardson, 28, a D.C. physician. "We separate the message from the messenger in that case; why can't we do that now?"

Overall, the Post Survey of marchers found that Farrakhan is more popular than other prominent black political figures, including Jesse L. Jackson and Gen. Colin Powell. He was far more popular than President Clinton, who was elected in 1992 with the overwhelming support of black voters.

A large majority of the black men interviewed for the poll said there was a shortage of black leaders, and eight in 10 said the march would make Farrakhan more influential among blacks. Nationally, a new Post survey found black Americans overall are less enthusiastic about Farrakhan: Half expect him to become more influential in black affairs as the result of the march.

The survey was conducted for The Washington Post by Ronald Lester & Associates, an African American polling firm in Washington. A total of 62 black interviewers, positioned on and around the Mall and at nearby Metro stations, conducted interviews with randomly selected marchers. The survey's margin of sampling error is plus or minus 3 percentage points.

Overall, the Post survey suggests the march attracted much of its support from the growing black middle class.

Three out of four marchers surveyed were under the age of 45, compared with six out of 10 blacks nationally. And four in 10 were between the ages of 30 and 45.

More than two or three had household incomes of $30,000 a year or more, with nearly one in five making more than $75,000 a year—both considerably above the national average. Nearly three of four attended at least a year of college, with more than a third being college graduates.

Nearly half of those interviewed said they were single. More than four in 10 were married. Nearly two out of three said they had children, including a third of those who said they are single.

MILLION MAN MARCH POLL

What participants identified as the single most important reason they were participating in the Million Man March:

To show support for the black family.	29%
To show support for black men taking more responsibility for their families and communities.	25
To demonstrate black unity.	25
To demonstrate African American economic strength.	7
To show support for Louis Farrakhan.	5

Q. I'm going to read you a list of names and organizations. For each, please tell me if you have a favorable or unfavorable impression of that person or group, or perhaps you don't know enough to say.
(Shown: Percentage with a favorable view.)

Louis Farrakhan	87%
Benjamin Chavis	77
Colin Powell	73
Jesse Jackson	81
The Nation of Islam	88
Bill Clinton	54
White people	31
Jewish people	41
The criminal justice system	15

Q. Do you think there is a shortage of recognized black leaders who can speak about the concerns and issues that are important to most black people, or not?

Shortage of leaders	81%
Not a shortage of leaders	18

Q. As a result of the Million Man march, do you think Louis Farrakhan will become more influential in the African American community, or not?

	March Participants	Blacks Nationally
Yes	80%	47%
No	14	27

Q. As a result of the Million Man March, do you think Louis Farrakhan will become more influential among political leaders in Washington, or not?

	March Participants	Blacks Nationally
Yes	55%	34%
No	39	41

Q. Some people say the all-male march is acceptable because the idea is to emphasize the need for black men to take more responsibility for their families and communities. Others say women should have officially been included in the march as well. What about you, do you think women should have been included, or not?

	March Participants	Blacks Nationally
Should have been included	26%	69%
Should not have been included	59	26

The demographics of the Million Man Marchers:

Age

18–30	33%
30–44	42
45–60	20
61 and over	4

Q. What was the last grade of school you completed?

Less than high school	5%
High school graduate	22
Some college/college graduate	59
Post-graduate	14

Q. Are you from the Washington, D.C., area?/What state are you from?

Washington, D.C.	16%
Northern Virginia	5
Maryland suburbs	8
California	3
Illinois	4
Maryland	6
Michigan	5
New Jersey	6
New York	10
North Carolina	4
Pennsylvania	6
Virginia	4

Q. What religion do you consider yourself? Are you Protestant, Catholic, Muslim or some other religion?

Protestant	52%
Catholic	7
Muslim	6
Nation of Islam	5
None	14

Q. Are you married, single, divorced or widowed?

Married	42%
Single	46
Divorced	10
Widowed	1

Q. Are any other members of your family here today?

Yes	44%
No	53

Q. If you added up all the yearly incomes, before taxes, of all the members of your household for last year, 1994, would the total be:

Under $15,000	10%
Between $15,000 and $29,999	16
Between $30,000 and $49,999	33
Between $50,000 and $74,999	17
Between $75,000 and $99,999	11
$100,000 or more	8

Figures based on interviews with 1,047 randomly selected participants in the Million Man March. Margin of sampling error for the overall results is plus or minus 3 percentage points. Sampling error is only one of the many potential sources of error in this or any other public opinion poll. Interviewing conducted by Ronald Lester & Associates for The Washington Post.

6. AFRICAN AMERICANS

And they came with their children, their fathers and their grandfathers. According to the survey, more than four in 10 said they attended the march with immediate family members.

Kenneth Gandy, 33, of Charleson, S.C., came to Washington with his sons, Christopher, 7, and Brandon, 5, to "give them a legacy to identify with in future years."

"We as black men need to take more responsibility for our actions and the actions of others in our communities," Gandy said.

"It's a good father-and-son event," said Earl Wood, 51, a District resident who was attending the march with his 13-year-old son, Mackenzie. "It shows solidarity of all ages."

"It's important for black people, black men, to come together," Mackenzie said.

A voter registration drive was a featured march event, but the survey found eight of 10 participants already were registered. One out of four interviewed for the poll said they worked for local, state or the federal government. According to the survey, 5 percent said they were members of the Nation of Islam, while another 6 percent said they were Muslims but not members of the Nation. Half said they were Protestant, while 7 percent said they were Catholic. Six in 10 said they attended church or religious services at lest once or twice a month. Only one in seven said they were not religious.

More than half decided to attend the march more than a month ago, according to the poll. It was overwhelmingly a day for black men. Only 1 percent of those interviewed were white. And fewer than one in 10 marchers—9 percent—were women. Six in 10 survey respondents supported the decision to make black men the focus of the march.

"I'm disappointed with women's groups who came out against [the march]," said Jacqui Allen, 31, a Philadelphia radio personality. "It doesn't take anything away from us." "For a long time, women have stood up and been both mother and father," said Chris Mordecai, 24, a District lab technician. "It's time for black men to stand up."

An Angry 'Charmer'

Louis Farrakhan has always been a man of many faces. Now the calypso singer turned separatist wants to move into the mainstream of American politics. Even blacks are divided about his appeal—but they're listening.

HOWARD FINEMAN
AND VERN E. SMITH

As A YOUTH, LOUIS FARRA-khan was "The Charmer," a $500-a-week calypso singer who could transfix a night-club crowd with his ukulele and clever lyrics. But in the four decades since joining the Nation of Islam, he's become a spellbinding perform-er on another stage, and with a different instrument: his own deep hatred of the white-run power structure in America. He is king of an angry carnival.

So it wasn't easy for him to relax on the night after the Million Man March. It should have been a moment of triumph. At 62, he had just chanted his lyrics to the largest black audience ever assembled in America. Even critics had conceded that the event—if not his rambling speech—was a success. For dinner, he had invited politi-cal allies and lieutenants to join his family in the presidential suite of Washington's Vista Hotel. The widow of his beloved mentor, the late Elijah Muhammad, was there. So was D.C. Mayor Marion Barry, who had been busted in a drug sting five years ago, five floors below—and who had been re-elected with Farrakhan's help.

But Farrakhan is rarely offstage. He grew visibly perturbed as he watched what amounted to election returns: the television commentary. The official crowd count still infuriated him. It was a racist plot, he as-serted. The media were "so vicious," he declared. The talking heads, white and black, upset him. Whatever good the march may have done, said one pundit on "Mac-Neil/Lehrer," was outweighed by the "cen-tral role" Farrakhan plays "in creating divi-sions in our current society."

Farrakhan shook his head in disgust, ac-cording to one of his guests. *"Farrakhan has divided the nation?"* he said in mock astonishment. "It's the *whites* who have done the dividing in America." Another news show replayed Colin Powell's com-ments. The retired general, who had de-clined to attend the march, compared Farrakhan to Mark Fuhrman. Farrakhan reacted with bitter disdain—especially since, he later told NEWSWEEK, he'd had a "very warm" telephone conversation with Powell before the march. "Colin Powell," he said to his guests, "should have been here. He could have been validated by his brothers."

"Validated": a state of grace Farrakhan now thinks he's achieved. Let commenta-tors call him a "nut." Let them review his long history of verbal assaults on Jews, Koreans, Palestinian Arabs, homosexu-als—and whites in general. Yes, the NEWS-WEEK Poll shows that only 14 percent of blacks think he reflects the mainstream of African-American thought. But by holding their convocation on the Mall, the marchers made a series of political declarations, whether they intended to or not. One of them was this: there's no keeping Farra-khan from the national spotlight. "I am a reality in America," he declared. He now seems to want nothing less than to be the country's leading black political figure. "Farrakhan wants to be a plain old Ameri-can leader," says C. Eric Lincoln, a Duke sociologist who has known him since 1957.

Back home in Chicago, without a large audience to play to, Farrakhan talked at length to NEWSWEEK about what sounded like mainstream plans (page 36). Seated in the chandeliered dining room of the house Elijah Muhammad built in 1973 in a mid-dle-class neighborhood, Farrakhan careful-ly inched away from some tenets of the Nation of Islam: that politics is evil and the only course in America is "separation"—a black nation unto itself, built apart and paid for by white reparations for slavery.

In a "private setting," Farrakhan said, the Elijah Muhammad once conceded that the separatist dream was unrealistic. "'Per-haps I know that they will never give us eight or 10 states'," Farrakhan quoted his mentor as saying. As blacks and whites con-template "what alimony would look like if there is a divorce," Farrakhan told NEWS-WEEK, "that might be a strong incentive for the husband and wife to sit down and say 'Let's get it together'."

In previously eschewing politics, Farra-khan said, he was just following his leader's orders: "He disallowed us to register or to vote." He has voted only once, for Jesse Jackson in the 1984 Illinois Democratic pri-mary. Now he will dispatch his bow-tied army to register voters nationwide—and he'll vote in 1996. As for his policy agenda, Farrakhan envisions "a cooperative effort" to rebuild the inner cities, one that would join "government and corporate America" with an "alliance of black organizational, religious, political, civic and fraternal lead-ers." He hopes to play a major role in next month's "African-American summit."

It's A RADICAL AND, TO MANY, AN outrageous thought: Farrakhan goes mainstream. But his timing is good. Leadership in the black community, nurtured in the church-based civil-rights movement, is divided, confused, spent. Beset by economic fears and the chaos of the inner city, many blacks are ready for talk of go-it-alone self-help. Farra-khan fits the near-hysterical tone of public life today, in which versions of the "para-

---

41% of blacks view Louis Farrakhan unfavorably, and **41%** view him favorably; meanwhile, **60%** of whites have an unfavorable opinion of him.

FOR THIS NEWSWEEK POLL, PRINCETON SURVEY RESEARCH ASSOCIATES TELEPHONED 750 ADULTS, OCT. 18-20. THE MARGIN OF ERROR IS +/-4 PERCENTAGE POINTS FOR TOTAL SAMPLE, +/-9 FOR BLACKS. THE NEWSWEEK POLL © 1995 BY NEWSWEEK, INC.

The Man, the Movement

TORN BETWEEN HIS SEP-aratist ideology and his mainstream ambitions, Farrakhan tacks between anger and conciliation. Scenes from a black leader's battle for legitimacy:

1930: Elijah Poole meets Fard Muhammad, a silk salesman who's spreading a black Muslim gospel. After Fard Muhammad disappears in 1934, Poole claims his teacher was Allah incarnate. He then founds the Nation of Islam, calling himself Elijah Muhammad and preaching black self-sufficiency.

1933: Louis Eugene Walcott—later Farrakhan—is born in the Bronx, N.Y. Three years later, the family moves to Boston.

1953: His wife pregnant, Walcott drops out of Winston-Salem (N.C.) Teachers College. A talented musician since childhood, he becomes a calypso singer known as "The Charmer."

1955: Visiting Chicago, Walcott is converted by a speech by Elijah Muhammad and joins NOI as Louis X. Tutored by Malcolm X in Harlem, he becomes minister of NOI's Boston temple in 1957.

1964: Malcolm X, privately denouncing Elijah Muhammad's extramarital affairs, leaves NOI. Louis succeeds him as minister of Temple 7 in Harlem, and in December writes, "Malcolm shall not escape. . . . Such a man is worthy of death."

1965: Malcolm X is assassinated in February.

1975: Elijah Muhammad dies. His son, Wallace, moves Black Muslims toward mainstream Islam.

1978: After extensive travel in Africa and the Middle East, Louis, now Farrakhan, breaks from Wallace Muhammad and vows to revive Elijah Muhammad's original separatist teachings.

1984: Farrakhan supports Jesse Jackson's White House bid, but his entry into politics—and Jackson's campaign—is marred by a speech that seems to praise Hitler and remarks referring to Judaism as a "gutter religion."

1985: Libya's Muammar Kaddafi lends Farrakhan $5 million, interest-free, to finance POWER, a black economic-development project. At a POWER rally in New York, Farrakhan calls the city the "capital of the Jews."

1993: Farrakhan performs two violin concerts featuring the music of Jewish composer Felix Mendelssohn. The Congressional Black Caucus invites him to establish closer ties, but puts the reconciliation on hold when a Farrakhan aide makes a hate-filled speech at a New Jersey college.

1995: In January, Qubilah Shabazz, daughter of Malcolm X, is arrested for plotting to kill Farrakhan in retaliation for what she believed was his role in her father's death. In October, a shadow is cast over his Million Man March when reporters ask him to explain his earlier remark that Jews are "bloodsuckers."

noid style"—from Ross Perot to Pat Robertson to Pat Buchanan—are in fashion.

So what should we make of Farrakhan? Does he really want to be a "plain old American leader"? Even if he does, can he possibly be one? Will blacks accept him as something more than a megaphone for anger? Can whites ever tolerate him? It all depends on who the man behind the bow tie really is. "I know you do not know me," he said at a press conference last week, "but I know you will get to know me."

We will get to know a man who must overcome his own history. Farrakhan's hatred of what he calls the white-supremacist culture is both operatic and real. His life story is a catalog of resentments. In the neighborhood he grew up in, the political hero was Marcus Garvey, avatar of separatism. Farrakhan has spent his adulthood—since 1955—winning ferocious battles for dominance within a dictatorial organization he thinks he was divinely inspired to lead. Now he faces young radicals who may see his next steps toward "the mainstream" as a prelude to betrayal.

The parallels between Farrakhan's life and Colin Powell's are just close enough to be instructive. Both were born in New York in the '30s, light-skinned children of West Indian immigrants. Both love calypso. Both were model young members of the Episcopal Church. Both had opportunities to succeed in white society. But while Powell took advantage of his chance by joining an integrated U.S. Army, Farrakhan enlisted in the shock troops of racial separatism.

THE FATHER OF NINE CHILDREN by his wife of 41 years, Farrakhan came honestly to his belief in the traditional family: he didn't have one. He rarely talks of his lineage, but did so with NEWSWEEK. His mother, Mae Manning, was an immigrant to New York City from St. Kitts, then a British crown colony in the Caribbean. She married a man from Jamaica, Percival Clark, who soon disappeared. Mae fell in love with another West Indian, Louis Walcott, who fathered Farrakhan's older brother, Alvan

Walcott. Clark returned just long enough to get Mae pregnant with a second child.

Although Clark was her husband, Mae was distraught: Walcott was the man in her life. Years later, Farrakhan says, his mother confessed that she had tried to abort him three times with a coat hanger: "After the third time," Farrakhan recalls, "she decided she would go ahead and have the baby and face the consequences." Louis Eugene Walcott was born in 1933, given the name of a man who was not his father—and who later abandoned the family, too. "Gene" Walcott never met his real father.

There's more drama to the story: a matter of skin color. In a speech in Newark, N.J., last year, Farrakhan explained his mother's anguish. She and his brother were dark. She feared the baby would be light-skinned, and advertise her unfaithfulness. Speaking to African-American audiences, Farrakhan tries to laugh about the story. But he's always been self-conscious about his appearance, says Arthur Magida, who has interviewed Farrakhan and is writing an unauthorized biography. "He's been trying to

92% of blacks say race relations in the country today are only fair or poor;
84% of whites describe them the same way.

prove his blackness to himself and others all his life," Magida says.

Farrakhan had chances to move into white society, but it didn't happen. Reared in Boston's Roxbury, a thriving center of West Indian culture, he was gifted musically and began studying violin seriously at the age of 5. He was a good enough student to be admitted to Boston Latin, perhaps the nation's most prestigious public school. He enrolled in the seventh grade, but left after less than a year, lonely in a new place that was predominantly white. Farrakhan says he had hoped to attend Juilliard, but couldn't even think of applying. His mother was a domestic; the school was far away. "We were a very, very poor family," he says. Instead, after high school, Farrakhan attended a black teachers' college in North Carolina on a modest track scholarship.

Farrakhan fell back on his roots, literally. Marrying his high-school sweetheart, Betsy (now Khadijah), he left college and returned to Boston. His mother was a calypso fan, and so was he. The "kings of calypso"—men with grand stage names such as Lord Executioner, Growler, Attila the Hun and Black Prince—had visited his home in Boston. Their art was both musical and political, an outgrowth of a Lenten festival in Trinidad in which men competed to concoct clever put-downs of the powers that be. He had picked up the guitar and ukulele as a boy. Now he turned himself into "The Charmer," and hit the road to perform in clubs in the early '50s. Again: near success. The calypso craze was about to break, the first "black" pop music to enthrall white America. But it was Harry Belafonte who won the fame.

The next step—joining the Nation of Is-lam—wasn't hard for Farrakhan. Marcus Garvey, the Jamaican-born leader of the back-to-Africa movement, was a hero in Roxbury. Farrakhan's own mother was an admirer. The theories of Garvey and Elijah Muhammad were grounded in the same perception: that white America would never fully accept blacks in an equal society. In 1955, on a nightclub tour in Chicago, Gene Walcott heard Muhammad speak, and the calypso singer returned to Boston as Louis X. Years later he renamed himself Farrakhan. Muhammad became the surrogate for the father he'd never known.

Showmanship and music fueled Farrakhan's early rise. Within two years of joining the Nation, he had written, staged and starred in a play in Boston called "The Trial." Farrakhan played the "prosecutor." The defendant was a black man in whiteface, wearing a red wig and bright blue eye makeup. Farrakhan harangued the "white man." "I charge you with being the greatest liar on earth!" he bellowed. "I charge you with being the greatest fornicator on earth!" There was no suspense about the outcome, recalls C. Eric Lincoln, who saw the play. "The jury sentenced the defendant to death in about a half a second." Farrakhan wrote songs for the play, one of which he later made into a Nation of Islam calypso anthem: "The White Man's Heaven Is the Black Man's Hell."

There was more than stage anger. Farrakhan also rose by being willing to viciously condemn anyone who dared challenge the prerogatives of the Nation. When Malcolm X renounced the Nation's racist ideology, Farrakhan declared him to be marked for "death." Malcolm was assassi-nated soon thereafter. There is no evidence that Farrakhan was connected to the killings, but he's admitted to helping create the "atmosphere" that led to the murder.

The intervening 31 years have seen endless wrangles and occasional mayhem—with Farrakhan always surviving and rising. He's a controversial figure in the community at large. In the NEWSWEEK Poll, blacks divide evenly, 41 percent to 41 percent, on whether they view him favorably or unfavorably. Jesse Jackson, by contrast, is viewed favorably by 80 percent.

Still, Farrakhan can attract an audience like no other political performer. And he has been laying the groundwork for the march—and his entry into politics—more carefully than white America bothered to notice. He started in 1990 with a "Stop the Killing" tour aimed at highlighting urban violence. He drew huge crowds. In 1993, he spoke to 20,000 at the Javits Center in New York. He produced a video, and carefully maintained a list of volunteers he could use to make the march happen.

But Farrakhan also thinks the crowd on the Mall was a testament to his role as a messenger of God. In place of a wedding band, Farrakhan wears a giant gold ring emblazoned with 40 diamonds that form a silhouette of Elijah Muhammad. As the pope is wedded to Christ, Farrakhan says, "I am wedded to this man whom I believe is the Messiah." Pointing to the ring, he notes another detail—"a little tiny diamond where Mr. Muhammad's heart would be. I think that little, little bitty diamond represents Farrakhan." If grandiloquence alone is enough to make a leader, then America will have to deal with the "reality" of Louis Farrakhan for a long time to come.

So You Want to Be Color-Blind

Alternative Principles for Affirmative Action

Peter Schrag

Peter Schrag is editorial page editor of the *Sacramento Bee*.

By now, there's not much doubt that when Americans are asked yes-or-no questions about the legitimacy of race preferences in public-sector hiring, contracting, and education, the answer is likely to be a flat no. Roughly 60 percent of Californian voters say that they support the proposed California Civil Rights Initiative (CCRI), which would prohibit all consideration of race or gender in public employment, education, and contracting; only 35 percent oppose it. Those findings are consistent with a decade of other survey data showing overwhelming opposition, among both men and women and among member of both political parties, to race and gender preferences. They suggest relatively few Americans will be troubled, and many will be delighted, when Newt Gingrich and other Republicans try to write prohibitions against contract set-asides and other minority preferences into the federal budget this summer. By next year, when CCRI is expected to be on the California ballot, the undoing of race preferences could become a political and social avalanche. The people who will be living under that avalanche are called liberals.

Republicans are relishing the difficulties that the rollback of preferences will cause Democrats forced to choose between their civil rights constituencies and what left of their blue-collar support. Which, of course, is why even such Republicans as Senate majority Leader Bob Dole and California Governor Peter Wilson, not long ago regarded as among the steadfast supporters of affirmative action, flipped on the issue—and why they'd just as soon keep it a question of either-or: color conscious or color-blind. It's hard to think of a better political wedge to use on the Democrats next year. It could kill Clinton in California, a state indispensable to his re-election. It could make today's racial tensions look benign next to what follows.

> Are we prepared to accept the larger effects of an absolute ban on racial preferences?

But this ought not to be that kind of question; the issue is too complex, too nuanced, too circumstantial, too slippery in definition, too divisive. To debate it in such terms is almost certain to embitter and distort whatever outcome the nation chooses—and to assure a Democratic disaster.

Between Black and White

Affirmative action has produced some clearly unreasonable results. In San Francisco, for example, substantial numbers of high-achieving Chinese students are denied entrance to Lowell High

School, a selective public institution, to make room for blacks and Hispanics (and even some whites) with lower scores and weaker records. At the University of California Medical School at Irvine, the blacks and Hispanics who are accepted have lower average medical school admission test scores than the Vietnamese applicants who are rejected. It would be hard to defend either of these policies against the charge that it is both unfair and academically debilitating.

But does the effort to eliminate such distortions also justify an absolute prohibition against efforts of the police chief of Los Angeles (or Detroit or Chicago) to seek out and promote qualified minority officers to diversify their departments? Why should a school system, seeking more effective models, not give some margin of preference to teacher candidates from underrepresented minority groups? If such private firms as the Bank of America or Nynex regard it as good business practice to seek out minorities to work in ethnically diverse markets and communities, why shouldn't the state Department of Motor Vehicles or the city zoning board do so for the same reasons?

There's no end of questions. Are we prepared to accept the larger effects of an absolute prohibition on racial preferences in all public-sector activities? Would we create an even larger playpen for lawyers and consultants to file reverse discrimination suits on the grounds that some practices were not truly color-blind? How, absent a court order, could any employer voluntarily mitigate the effects of past discrimination? Would it be better for the federal government (a) to encourage its contractors to take reasonable steps to diversify their workforces; (b) to adopt a fiercely neutral position; or (c) to prohibit its contractors from in any way noticing gender and ethnicity?

So far, however, instead of asking such questions, the parties in this debate—liberals and Democrats in thrall to their minority constituencies, Republicans exploiting the liberals' panic—are usually talking past the central issue: To what extent should merit be compromised for the sake of inclusion? the defenders of race-based affirmative action insist that no such preferences are ever given to unqualified people—that the choice is only made among the qualified—and that if that principle is violated, somebody or something, probably the courts, will crack down in righteous remedy. They are also quick to remind critics of race preferences—correctly, for the most part—that such practices were and still are used to benefit WASP legacies in the Ivy League and other selective colleges long before they were ever applied in favor

of blacks and Hispanics. (What is not said is that the losers in both cases tend to be the same kinds of people: Jews and Asians.)

But what's the meaning of qualified? Some preferences clearly favor the less qualified. Under current law, contractors may win awards despite relatively high bids simply because they are black or Hispanic. In the ordinary sense, they are not as "qualified" as—and cost the taxpayers more than—lower (white) bidders passed over. But in trying to predict who will make a good cop or a good truck driver for the road crew, is there really any significant difference between the top three scores on the average civil service exam or perhaps even among the top ten? To what extent, indeed, are some affirmative action programs merely attempts to avert attacks on conventional hiring practices or university admission policies that are themselves based on shaky criteria and which, in any case, have never been fully disclosed, much less debated? The critics of affirmative action may have wildly exaggerated ideas of how much merit criteria are stretched in the cause of diversity. The defenders of race preferences may exaggerate how often relatives of union members get breaks in applying to apprenticeship programs, or how many alumni children get preferences in admission to Harvard or Princeton, but so far those institutions are not going out of their way to clarify what they do.

SHAKY FROM THE START

The foundations were always shaky. From the earliest presidential orders of the 1960s—Kennedy's, Johnson's, Nixon's—calling on federal agencies and contractors to use "affirmative action" to eliminate discriminatory racial practices, to the introduction of goals and timetables in industry training and hiring, to the Reagan-era attempt, largely unsuccessful, to dismantle affirmative action, the country was always tentative and uncomfortable about formal racial distinctions, even when invoked for the most noble purposes. This, after all, was what the whole civil rights fight had been about, what the movement had tried to teach the country, and what for the most part—despite continuing subtle (and sometimes not-so-subtle) racism—it succeeded in doing.

What made race preferences tolerable—and what the Supreme Court in crucial cases accepted—was the assumption that they would be marginal and temporary. When candidates for a job were equally qualified, the obligation to remedy the effects of past discrimination justified preferences for people from races—later expanded to gender and handicap—that had been victims of that discrimination. In 1965, the year of the great triumphs of the civil rights movement, it made sense to argue, as Lyndon Johnson did, that "you do not take a person who has been hobbled by chains, liberate him, bring him up to the starting line" and then tell him "you are free to compete with all the others." But the consensus for preferences was always tentative. In *Bakke,* where the Court sanctioned the use of race as one "plus factor" among many extra-academic characteristics (musical or artistic or athletic talent, geographic background, unusual experiences, public service) that might be considered in university admissions—Justice Powell called it "the Harvard plan"—Justice Blackmun spoke of the need for a period of "transitional inequality." Within "a decade at most," he hoped, the need would disappear. "Then persons will be regarded as persons and discrimination of the type we address today will be an ugly feature of history that is instructive but that is behind us."

But that was 1978, and in the meantime almost precisely the opposite has happened. Race preferences, justified as a choice among equally qualified candidates, have been institutionalized and have grown to the point where the University of Texas Law School argues that if it did not use two sets of criteria in admissions there would be virtually no blacks or Hispanics at all, and where the average SAT scores for preferred minority groups at universities like Berkeley are now between 200 and 250 points lower than they are for whites and Asians. (It's between 150 and 200 points elsewhere in the University of California system.) Yet even that was not sufficient for the California legislature, then controlled by Democrats, which took note of the unsurprising fact that UC's minority graduation rates were significantly lower than those of whites and Asians and in 1991 quietly approved an "education equity act" to put fiscal and administrative pressure on the state's universities not just to admit students in the ethnic proportions in which they were graduating from the state's high schools, but to graduate them from college in the same proportions. Only Pete Wilson's veto kept the bill from becoming law. (It was that bill, incidentally, that prompted Glynn Custred and Thomas Wood, the two conservative academics who wrote CCRI, to begin work on the initiative.)

Elsewhere as well, inches have become yards. Outreach in contracting has turned to tax breaks and set asides for women and minority-owned businesses, even when the owners are themselves multimillionaires, and (increasingly) into a scandalous use of dummy ownerships by white- or male-controlled enterprises. Pressure on businesses from equal opportunity bureaucrats wielding the club of rigid disparate impact standards has pushed "goals and timetables" toward de facto quotas. (In one case, the Equal Employment Opportunity Commission sued a Chicago company that employed only blacks and Hispanics, charging that it did not have enough blacks.) The guarantee of voting rights has led to racially gerrymandered districts and Republican control of most Southern congressional delegations. In the process, what had been an informal understanding to pursue a high moral objective through a combination of stringent rules against discrimination and marginal race preferences has evolved into a system of quasi-entitlements and rigid legal impositions governed by a complex structure of quietly enacted law, appellate court decisions, civil service rules, university and graduate school admissions practices, set-asides, hiring goals, and EEOC formulas managed by armies of counselors, contract compliance auditors, diversity trainers, affirmative action officers, experts in disparate impact studies, and layer upon layer of lawyers—a huge panoply of law, regulation, and administrative practice affecting virtually every sector of the nation's life.

RISING UP ANGRY

It's hardly surprising that there's growing anger about this unsightly landscape of entitlements and demands. Working-class Americans and a great many others face tightening economic prospects. Talk radio and other new media now legitimize attitudes that were regarded as offensive, if not unspeakable, not so long ago.

Yet economic fears and the angry voices on the radio are hardly the whole explanation. We are now thirty years beyond the searing consciousness of what things were like before the Civil Rights Act and the Voting Rights Act, even among the majority of black people. There is much dispute about who has gained from race preferences, but there's little doubt that where the original argument for affirmative action rested in passionately assimilationist demands for equal justice, its consequences, especially on university campuses, have been increasingly manifest in segregated programs with their own criteria, shape-up courses for blacks and Latinos, "theme" housing, student-administered speech codes enforcing political correctness with the threat of suspension, even separate graduation exercises—plus the long train of racial tension that comes with them. The moral case that had started with "We Shall Overcome" and Martin Luther King seems to be ending with gangsta rap, Ice-T, melanism, Louis Farrakhan, and Khalid Muhammad. It is hard to defend affirmative action for an in-your-face separatism that rejects the western values that underlie and represent the only justification for the whole effort.

But if there are moral problems, there are practical ones as well. The proliferating list of protected groups—blacks, Latinos, women (in some circumstances), Asians (in others), the handicapped (plus veterans and legacies)—makes the future of group preferences increasingly dubious. It was almost inevitable that CCRI, which sparked our current affirmative action fight, would arise in the nation's most heterogeneous state. California's multicultural population makes it increasingly difficult to draw legitimate distinctions between who's to be favored and who is not, or even to make reasonable decisions, as the Census Bureau is now pointing out, about how individuals should be counted. And as intermarriage proliferates among all those groups, who's to say how their offspring should be counted? Should the son of an Argentinian immigrant, now a corporate executive in San Diego (or a Cuban in Miami), get preference as a Latino? How do you classify a student with a hyphenated name, half Hispanic and half Jewish? Why do we give preference to the child of the black doctor and none to the child of the Appalachian coal miner?

Historian Hugh Davis Graham of Vanderbilt University points out that the most overlooked law of the civil rights era, the Immigration Reform Act of 1965, which ended the system of national-origins quotas in U.S. immigration policy, had enormous consequences that we still don't fully comprehend. Although its sponsors claimed that it would produce little significant increase in immigration, it brought to the country more than 20 million legal immigrants during the thirty years after its enactment, approximately 75 percent of whom "qualified upon arrival for minority-group preferences over Americans whose citizenship reached back many generations." Surely that was not justified by any effort to remedy past injustices. Surely that was not part of any tacit bargain to which the country ever agreed.

STRAINS OF AMBIVALENCE

But does even that certify the wisdom of a decision that would, virtually overnight, impose the across-the-board prohibitions on race preferences that the opponents of affirmative action are now demanding? Or does it make more sense—political, social, moral—to return to the limited (*Bakke*) version of affirmative action, messy as it often was, to which the country seemed to give its consent a generation ago—and which it may still be willing to accept? To return to polls for a moment: If the question is changed from an either-or choice about explicit race preferences to more general matters about affirmative action, the answers change as well. In a *USA Today*/CNN poll this spring, 73 percent said they favor companies "making special efforts to find qualified minorities and women." Similar answers are given to questions about special training programs for minorities and women. The vast majority of respondents, white and black, don't believe that the country has been purged of racial discrimination. On a general question about affirmative action programs on the *USA Today* poll, 31 percent favored expansion, 37 percent favored a decrease, and 26 percent thought they should be kept about the same.

It may be impossible to fully articulate that ambivalence, much less write it into policy. But with the stakes as high as they are on this issue, it surely deserves the effort. Considerations in the appointment of scholars for a research university may not apply to the hiring of heavy-equipment operators or postal clerks. What applies to contracting with small businesses, regardless of the race and gender of their owners, may not apply to large corporations. And what may apply to some colleges may not apply to others. Many states have created two- or three-tiered higher education systems to serve both merit and inclusion—a highly selective university combined with readily accessible junior colleges and moderately selective four-year state colleges. Why should that principle be compromised by tempering admission standards for the selective institutions in order to further inclusion there as well?

Which brings the issue back to a more basic question: What is merit and to what extent are existing criteria merit-based? In the past year there has been a bitter fight in Chicago over the promotion of a handful of black cops who were ranked high on "merit" even though they scored lower on the civil service exam than some officers over whom they were promoted. In that case, either the word "merit" is fatuous or it raises serious questions about just what the exam measures. Admissions officers at colleges raise the same issue when they defend affirmative action by arguing that test scores aren't good predictors of performance in college. But if that's the case, why use the test at all?

Chances are that it's not the case. As the neo-conservatives—some of whom defected from liberalism precisely over this issue—will tell you, the whole point of such tests was to foster merit against spoils systems at city hall and good-old-boy bias in the admission office at Yale. Ethnic spoils are no more acceptable now than the earlier varieties. In any case, nobody has yet shown what would be a better predictor of academic success for minorities.

And yet that hardly vitiates the general proposition: In many of the areas affected by public-sector racial preferences, there may be better ways of making choices than those we use now. If only court-ordered make-whole remedies to proven discrimination are permissible (which is what the opponents of race preferences advocate), how many more civil rights lawsuits would be filed that are now averted by voluntary action? Would any public employer, recognizing past discrimination, have to encourage a lawsuit before the victims could be made whole? Can race sometimes even be regarded—in practice, not in law—as part of the qualifications for certain jobs? If you seek out people not just for their technical knowledge, or their test-taking skills, but for their ability to deal with—and be trusted in—a community, why shouldn't ethnicity be a "plus factor" in the package?

The answers are hardly self-evident. None of these questions should suggest that it's proper for the police chief in Grosse Pointe to hire only white cops. This area doesn't lend itself well to across-the-board legal rules; it's better to build in flexibility and room to fudge. If there is a flat ban on any consideration of race in public policy, what happens to efforts to foster integration in elementary and secondary schools? John Bunzel, a former member of the U.S. Civil Rights Commission, now a fellow at the Hoover Institution and a sharp critic of the excesses of race preferences, has declined to support measures like CCRI which, he says, are too blunt; they simplify, and "I'm a complexifier." Shouldn't there be room at the margins, he asks, for ethnic diversity among all the other criteria? And that, of course is what the Supreme Court's *Bakke* decision, with all its flaws, sought to do.

Six Alternative Principles

It's not an easy task. Yet surely before the country is forced to a set of either-or choices, some alternative principles are worth considering:

1. *The more sophisticated the enterprise or skill for which candidates are chosen, the more important merit becomes and the weaker the claims for non-meritocratic criteria.* The kind of considerations we give in selecting people for blue-collar jobs should not be the same as the ones given to selecting graduate students in nuclear physics or brain surgery. The public junior college, by mandate, definition, and tradition, is more inclusive than the Institute for Advanced Study. Thomas Sowell makes a persuasive argument that the issue is not so much who should go to college but where. The frustration and tensions—not to mention the various distortions that have been created on many campuses to accommodate marginal students—result from the effort to bring people into academic situations for which they are not qualified. As a result, even those who are qualified are suspect and discredited.

2. *In public as well as private enterprises, diversity may well be a legitimate business consideration.* Where the choice is between candidates or contractors with similar bids or equal qualifications in skill, doesn't it make sense to consider first those who come from underrepresented groups and who will for that reason be more effective or make the enterprise more legitimate with clients and the community? In such choices, the lines of common sense, if they can be maintained, are better than the lines drawn by law.

3. *In college admission, economic disadvantage is a more legitimate extra factor for a borderline candidate than membership in a preferred racial group.* Why not shift the emphasis in affirmative action from minorities to children from families where no one has ever gone to college? Such policies may well result in smaller proportions of blacks or Hispanics at selective universities, at least in the short run, but it may have a far greater social impact. And unlike race preferences, economic disadvantage will not become a permanent entitlement. As such, it's far more consistent with the nation's historic principles. And to the extent that race preferences are forgotten, so will invidious assumptions about how minority students were accepted. What will become clear is the inadequate secondary school preparation, or worse, that causes the underrepresentation in the first place.

4. *All race preferences in public-sector activities—in contracting, hiring, and education—should be made fully public and subject to time limits and periodic public review by an objective, nonpartisan process.* We have already managed to do away with one of the most reprehensible practices: race-norming, the system of separately ranking candidates within their own ethnic groups on Labor Department job tests and hiring from the top of each list. The expectation ought to be that we will gradually do away with a great many more in coming years. An obvious way to

begin is to make affirmative action goals and the administrative definitions of disparate impact more flexible.

5. *Exclude all foreign-born residents, citizens, and aliens, and perhaps even the children of immigrants, from race preferences, excepting only children of American citizens who were living abroad.* There is no history of discrimination to justify such preferences. And they generate no end of resentment, as the passage of California's Proposition 187, the measure designed to deny social services to illegal aliens, has demonstrated.

6. *Vigorously enforce anti-discrimination law, not perhaps to the point of criminalizing discrimination as Shelby Steele proposes, but far more vigorously than we do now, and systematically review all public-sector merit systems to make certain that tests and other criteria are in fact appropriate to the tasks and positions for which they're used.*

This is hardly a complete list, much less an ideal one. But it recognizes that affirmative action—even race preference—has different meanings depending on the context, and that flexibility is critical. Affirmative action bears a heavy burden against the claims of real merit; where it favors rich over poor, strong over weak, it bears an insurmountable one. Yet rigid rules are likely to take us into a thicket of legal combat and social division more bitter than anything generated by the policies we have now. If the Democrats, rather than standing frozen in the headlights of the approaching disaster, were to try to articulate a third alternative, they might well reclaim some credibility on the issue.

The sense of a national moral imperative that once sustained affirmative action is rapidly eroding. It is only a matter of time before it's all gone. In those circumstances a soft landing—no phrase could be more appropriate in this context—would surely be better than a yes-or-no choice whose answer will almost certainly be no. But unless those who regard themselves as people of good will offer a third alternative, that's the answer we'll get.

40 Years After *Brown,* Segregation Persists

William Celis 3d

Special to The New York Times

TOPEKA, Kan.—Topeka Boulevard, a nine-mile-long stretch of commerce, fulfills most needs of the 120,000 people in this city on the plains. But the four-lane thoroughfare also serves an unintended purpose: dividing the races. Whites live to the west, blacks to the east.

Therein lies the problem for the city's public school system. The elementary schools, which were once deliberately segregated on school board orders, are segregated still, only now it results from housing patterns, not laws.

Those housing patterns have proved to be the implacable foe of school desegregation here and in some 1,200 school districts nationwide that are under Federal court desegregation orders. Such patterns have withstood busing programs that transported black children into predominantly white schools; they have withstood the creation of theme or "magnet" schools designed to lure white students from the suburbs to inner-city schools, and they have withstood the one-two punch of school consolidations and closings to achieve racial balance in the classrooms that remain.

Forty years have passed since the United States Supreme Court decided the landmark case, Brown v. the Board of Education of Topeka, Kan., that outlawed segregated education and marked this city as the cradle of the school desegregation movement. The board no longer designates which schools white students should attend and which are set aside for blacks. But 11 of Topeka's 26 elementary schools, a middle school and one high school are still as segregated as the neighborhoods that feed them.

Nationwide, nearly 70 percent of black students attend segregated schools, that is, schools with mostly black and Hispanic enrollments. In 1968, the first year in which educational data were collected, some 78 percent of black students and 54 percent of Hispanic students attended predominantly minority schools. The only difference the intervening years have made is that minorities are now more likely to attend segregated schools in the Northeast and the Midwest than in the South.

Other forces have also undermined the desegregation of schools: stubborn attitudes about race, and the rampant unemployment and underemployment that condemn many minorities to inner cities. Also blunting the effort, civil rights workers say, is the absence of a national will to embrace aggressive solutions like raising taxes or redistributing tax dollars to bring the budgets of poor districts up to those of rich ones.

"School desegregation was not supposed to be a cure-all," said Gary L. Orfield, director of the Harvard Project on School Desegregation. "There was supposed to be a housing act and job opportunities. Most of them have been beaten down. School desegregation is one of the last legs standing, although it is bruised and beaten."

But there are glimmers of hope, Mr. Orfield and other policy analysts said. Among them are these: Palm Beach County, Fla., which is encouraging homebuilders to racially mix their housing developments; Charlotte-Mecklenburg County, N.C., which has harnessed the diversity and financial strength of its large, countywide school district in the development of magnet schools, and Dade County, Fla., which has opened schools at the integrated sites where people work, not in the segregated neighborhoods where they live.

Topeka

Still Trying to Achieve Goal

In many ways, Topeka's experience is a microcosm of the history of desegregation nationally since 1954. Over the decades, the city became more integrated as employers offered good-paying jobs to black men and women, enabling them to enter the middle class and move their families into traditionally white neighborhoods. But whole neighborhoods were still inhabited by low-wage earners—blacks and, increasingly, other minorities, too.

In 1979, the American Civil Liberties Union reopened the Brown suit, asserting that the existence of 13 racially segregated schools on either side of Topeka Boulevard violated the 1954 High Court ruling. Signing on to the suit was Linda Brown Thompson, who was 11 when her father and other black parents brought the first Brown suit.

After years of legal maneuvering, in 1993 a Federal court agreed with the A.C.L.U. Now the Topeka district is proposing to close some of the segregated schools, bus more of its 15,000 students across neighborhood lines and create magnet schools, all in the name of integration.

But while several polls have shown that people support desegregation efforts nationally, they tend to fight it locally. Topeka is no exception. The school superintendent, Jeffrey W. Weaver, says he has received anonymous letters and calls with racial slurs from whites and blacks opposing the proposed plan, which was unveiled earlier this school year. He says the attitude among parents whose children will likely be affected by closings and busing is, "Why me?"

This was not the vision of Oliver L. Brown, a minister, or the 12 other parents who went to court in 1951 in an effort to end the city's system of segregating elementary school students by race. They had long recognized that separate was not equal, that the all-black schools their children attended were educationally inferior to the all-white schools down the road. They reasoned then, as research has now shown, that if black children, especially those living in poverty, were sent to well-financed, solidly middle-class schools, they were more likely to adopt middle-class values and get a better education.

"It was unrealistic to expect that we could overcome all these entrenched problems, even in 40 years," said Ted Shaw, associate director-counsel of the NAACP Legal Defense and Education Fund. "But it's not too late to turn this around. The question is whether the commitment is there."

Housing

Tackling Root of Segregation

The Civil Rights Act of 1968 gave members of minority groups the right to buy and sell property whenever they wanted. The notion was that creating integrated neighborhoods would lead to integrated schools.

More than 25 years later, the legislation has still not delivered on all its promises, in part because the Government has repeatedly subverted the plan. Even as Congress was approving the bill, the Department of Housing and Urban Development was building large public housing projects in inner cities, effectively concentrating huge numbers of minority families there. In the 1980's, the Reagan Administration's Justice Department allowed hundreds of complaints against biased real estate agents and landlords, filed under Federal fair-housing laws, to languish.

Battling against this history, the Palm Beach County district decided to attack school segregation at its roots. In 1991, the district unveiled an innovative program, which called on home builders to devise strong advertising campaigns for black newspapers and radio stations, with the aim of selling houses to a greater racial mix. Some of the county's 37 incorporated communities also altered their building codes, allowing builders to erect more modestly sized and priced homes in areas that previously restricted housing to large lots and structures.

In return for making these changes and attracting minority families, the school district rewarded builders by letting children living in the new developments attend neighborhood schools rather than be bused to achieve integration.

While 29 of the county's communities have signed agreements with the school district, which has 110,000 students across 2,500 square miles, success has been uneven. "In some communities, it has helped us," said Murray Harris, a district spokesman.

"But over all, it has not helped us in the way we thought it would."

The percentage of minority residents in communities has increased, sometimes significantly. In Crestwood, it rose to 12.3 percent in 1994 from 3.1 percent in 1991; in Riverbridge, it increased to 11.5 percent this year from 2.3 percent in 1991. But housing prices in some communities remain too high for many black and Hispanic families.

Palm Beach County, however, is no longer alone in taking aim at segregated housing patterns. The Department of Housing and Urban Development will embark this summer on a $70-million model program, Moving to Opportunity, that will involve 6,200 families in New York City, Baltimore, Boston, Chicago and Los Angeles.

The program will assist families as they search for new housing in suburbs and other neighborhoods where they would ordinarily not look. The intent is to break up concentrations of poverty.

But the program may also be a boon to education, since studies indicate that concentrations of poor families with children place a heavy burden on the local schools that must serve their educational, medical and emotional needs.

Magnet Schools

A Powerful Lure But Mixed Results

Build a curriculum around a special theme, like math or health. Lure the best teachers in those subjects to that school and invite students from all over the city to enroll in it.

The result is a type of public school, a magnet, that has been widely used to draw white students to predominantly black schools and black students to predominantly white ones. Such magnet schools are increasingly viewed as the most effective means to integration, because they give students and parents the freedom of choice. Still, they have a mixed record.

40 Years Since a Landmark Decision

1954 Brown v. Board of Education, Topeka, Kan. The United States Supreme Court rules, 9 to 0, that segregated schools are unconstitutional, overturning an 1896 Supreme Court decision, Plessy v. Ferguson, that said separate but equal facilities were constitutional.

1957 Gov. Orval Faubus of Arkansas orders the National Guard to prevent black students from enrolling in Central High School in Little Rock. President Dwight D. Eisenhower counters by ordering paratroopers to escort the students.

1964 Civil Rights Act of 1964 is approved by the Congress. The legislation includes Title VI, allowing the Federal Government to withhold education money to districts that fail to desegregate schools.

1968 Green v. New Kent County (Va.) Board of Education. The Supreme Court rules that desegregation applies not only to students but also to faculty assignments, extracurricular activities and transportation.

1968 Civil Rights Act of 1968, or Fair Housing Act, gives minorities the right to buy and sell property where they want.

1971 Swann v. Charlotte-Mecklenburg County (N.C.) Public Schools. The Supreme Court rules that all approaches to school desegregation, including busing, must be used to integrate schools.

1973 Keyes v. Denver School District. The Supreme Court applies standards of the Charlotte case to Northern states, ruling that they must desegregate schools when segregation was created by the school board.

1974 In Boston, rioting and burning of school buses over court-ordered busing illustrates the nationwide unpopularity of busing as a means to desegregation.

1974 Milliken v. Bradley (Milliken I). In first substantial defeat for civil rights in more than two decades, the Supreme Court severely limits lower courts' ability to order suburbs to join with inner cities in school desegregation plans.

1977 Milliken v. Bradley (Milliken II). The Supreme Court rules that if school districts are unable to integrate because of housing patterns, increasing resources to inner-city schools with mostly minority enrollment is a satisfactory remedy.

1978 In Topeka, the American Civil Liberties Union reopens the Brown suit, arguing that vestiges of segregation remain.

1990 Board of Education v. Dowell (Oklahoma City). The Supreme Court rules that districts under desegregation orders can be released from court supervision once they have taken all practical steps to eliminate the vestiges of legislated segregation.

1992 Freeman v. Pitts (Dekalb County, Ga.). In a ruling that civil rights advocates said further eroded the Brown decision, the Supreme Court ruled that Federal judges could stop supervising court-ordered school desegregation that they considered to have been achieved, even though full integration had not been achieved.

Kansas City, Mo., ringed by predominantly white suburbs, is struggling to make its magnets attract. By contrast, Montclair, N.J., has successfully used magnets to integrate its school-age population. New York City, the nation's largest school system and the home of the largest constellation of magnets, has also effectively used them as lures.

So has Charlotte-Mecklenburg, the nation's 29th largest school district, which has been desegregated largely as a result of magnet schools. But these were magnets established in a large and diverse countywide school district that sprawls over 527 square miles and serves 82,000 students. Twenty-seven of the North Carolina district's 115 schools have been turned into magnets since the program began in 1991 with 9 schools.

The percentage of blacks attending mostly black schools in Charlotte-Mecklenburg fell to 29 percent this year from 31 percent in 1991. Without magnets, district officials say, the percentage would have risen to 34 percent this year.

Suburban white parents in the Charlotte area say they embraced magnets because of the strong coursework it offered, even though attending a magnet school can sometimes require a bus ride of 1 hour and 45 minutes.

"I am more concerned about the quality of their education than who they are sitting beside at school," Brenda Emmons, a white parent, said of her children's participation in the program.

Still, the introduction of magnets there has not been tension free. As white students enrolled this year in Marie G. Davis Middle School, an inner-city magnet program with a communications theme and advanced classes for high-achieving students, "there was some wariness among the parents," said Gwendolyn Johnson, who is black and whose 11-year-old son attends the school.

But black and white parents have worked closely with each other this year, and next year Mrs. Johnson will share the presidency of the Davis

P.T.A. with a white parent, Deborah Holmes.

Charlotte, however, stands apart from much of the nation. Its enrollment mix of 60 percent whites and 40 percent minority has remained essentially unchanged for two decades, primarily because people can move to urban, rural and suburban areas without ever leaving the school district.

By contrast, the Kansas City district, which has labored under court-ordered desegregation since 1986, extends only as far as the city itself and its 37,000 students.

Kansas City has become increasingly black and Hispanic because of white flight to its suburbs and despite an expenditure of $1.2 billion—half from the state, the rest from the city—to improve curriculums and turn 58 of its 78 schools into magnets. A new Central High School was built at a cost of $32 million and old school buildings were upgraded, but the district's white enrollment has remained virtually unchanged at 24 percent.

The city's superintendent of schools, Walter L. Marks, who devised successful desegregation plans in Montclair and Raleigh, N.C., says Kansas City schools were so academically and structurally impoverished that it has taken more than $1 billion to right their course. Some $400 million was used simply to bring buildings up to code, Mr. Marks said.

"Progress is slow," he added, noting that the district's dropout rate tumbled to 39 percent this year from 52 percent in 1991 but remains far above the 11 percent national average.

Ultimately, the success of the Kansas City desegregation plan will depend upon the district's ability to persuade suburban parents like Brenda Gann of Lee's Summit, Mo., to transfer her two children from the Raymore-Peculiar School District south of the city into the city district. That will take quite a selling job. Raymore-Peculiar has a new high school and a rigorous curriculum, and the community offers a swim team for Mrs. Gann's 14-year-old daughter, Aubrey, who begins high school next fall.

"There's not much city schools can offer us," Mrs. Gann said. "We have everything we need out there."

Workplace Schools

Miami and Bases Point the Way

On the edge of the Miami International Airport is an elementary school for students from kindergarten through second grade. It is also integrated without the compulsion of a court order. The secret: the 78 pupils are children of the airport's employees, who are white, black, Hispanic and Asian.

By locating schools in or near work sites, some school systems, like that of Miami-Dade County, are having an easier time of integration than those whose educational institutions remain anchored in neighborhoods.

The airport school and four others at workplaces were conceived seven years ago by Joseph A. Fernandez, who was then county Superintendent of Schools.

Financed by the Dade County public school system, the workplace schools were not designed to achieve racial integration but to encourage Miami's business community and parents to participate in the education of the young. As a side effect, though, all five institutions have produced a lustrous ethnic and racial tapestry of students.

Nationwide, the 67 public schools operated on 16 military bases also have a rich student mix, thanks to both integrated workplaces and integrated neighborhoods.

At Ford Benning, Ga., an Army base with 23,592 residents, half of whom are families with children, Lieut. Col. Bruce Grant and his wife, Pat, both white, their three daughters and 3-year-old son live on Lumpkin Road, a street with 22 homes. Seven neighboring families are black; the rest are white.

This environment "teaches tolerance," Mrs. Grant said, "because we live next to one another, work with one another and go to school with another."

If the military is colorblind, so are some of the students in schools on bases, parents say. "When I talk to my children about their friends, I must admit the only way I know their color is when I see them," said Mrs. Grant, whose daughters attend Fort Benning schools. "I'm kind of proud of that."

Many others, parents as well as policy makers, remain hopeful that the task of school desegregation is coming to its slow but inevitable end.

"I'm not depressed because I've come from a long, long way," said Melba Pattillo Beals, who wrote the recently published "Warriors Don't Cry" (Pocket Books), her memoir as one of nine black students who desegregated Central High School in Little Rock, Ark., in 1957. "When you have fought your way up the stairs at Central High School, you know it can be worked out."

Affirmative Action: Four Groups' Views

Poll 'confirms the confusion' most people feel—until it becomes personal

Kevin Johnson and Andrea Stone

USA TODAY

In the gathering battle over affirmative action, there is no clear front line between white and black, male and female, Republican and Democrat.

A USA TODAY/CNN/Gallup Poll on the issue—the "most comprehensive" in two decades of polling, says John Barry of the Roper Center—instead finds a large middle that wants fairness, but opposes unfair advantages.

The poll is "a sober view of the complexity of this issue," says Gallup's David Moore.

From this debate is likely to come the future of affirmative action—under fire from Republicans in Congress, under review by the Clinton administration and certain to be an issue in the 1996 election.

The poll does show some general trends:

- Blacks are more sympathetic to the need for affirmative action than whites.
- Republicans oppose it far more than Democrats.
- Women are more supportive than men.

And while there is no strong call to eliminate affirmative action, there's even less support for expanding it.

"This is one of those issues that's tough to get a handle on," says Bob Roach, 30, a state worker from Jackson, Tenn. "Government should keep their hands off, let the cream rise to the top in business. But I know that when you do that, a lot of times you end up in court looking at some bad problems."

Howard University political scientist Ronald Walters agrees: The poll "con-firms the confusion. . . . The public is willing to accept something called affirmative action on the grounds of fairness, but not willing to accept hard quotas and set-asides, which have the same effect."

Beyond the traditional political, racial and gender fault lines, the poll shows the public split into four opinion groups, as identified by Gallup analyst Moore.

TRUE BELIEVERS

They are the backbone of support for affirmative action. Mostly Democratic, this group is nearly half women, many of

'TRUE BELIEVERS'	28%
They strongly favor affirmative action:	
How the group breaks down	
Minority women	18%
Minority men	15%
White women	45%
White men	24%
Republicans	29%
Democrats	63%

Source: Analysis of March 17-19 USA TODAY/CNN/Gallup Poll (Party affiliations include those who say they "lean" toward the party)

whom have benefited from the policies.

True Believers say that without government-mandated affirmative action programs, businesses and schools would not provide equal opportunities for women and minorities. And it is this group alone that supports quotas and favors an increase in preference programs.

Though not totally comfortable with quotas, Joseph Jones, 55, says if government opts out of affirmative action, so would businesses and schools.

"It always seems to start when the economy gets really bad, bad enough that whites start losing their jobs," says the black Chicago computer program-mer. "Then people start talking about how bad affirmative action is.

"You can't have all toys," Jones says. "If minorities and women get shut out, the game is over and then there is trouble. I wish affirmative action never had to be, but I don't think we'll ever get to the point where we can do without it."

There is little room for compromise on this point with Jones and others like him. Most True Believers say job discrimination remains a problem for blacks and Hispanics. In this group, Democrats outnumber Republicans more than 2 to 1—and almost a third are minorities.

This traditionally liberal group counts as its most articulate voices the National Organization for Women and the NAACP. And that may prove the biggest problem for President Clinton, who needs to retain his party's loyal voter base while not alienating the moderates he'll need to win re-election in 1996.

"The anti-affirmative action forces have controlled the dialogue and debate for many years," says Democratic pollster Mark Mellman. But his party has "done almost nothing to explain to the American public what it is and what it's good for. . . . Democrats have to defang the issue."

THE ANTAGONISTS

They are at the center of the current debate. Almost all white, mostly Republican and heavily male, affirmative action to this group means preferences, quotas and reverse discrimination. The Antagonists want no part of it.

They are also the force behind the proposed California Civil Rights Initiative, which would eliminate all preferences based on race or sex. They also report the highest incidence of reverse discrimination, making up the bulk of the 21% of white men who say they were denied a job or promotion, or failed to get admitted to a school, because of affirmative action.

For them, old-fashioned discrimination against women and minorities no longer is a problem.

"Affirmative action breeds distrust between the races," says Republican pollster Frank Luntz. "It takes real or perceived inequalities and rubs salt in the wounds."

A long time ago, Rodney Myer, 63, of Baton Rouge, La., worked as an affirmative action officer, but the white man wants no part of it now.

"It says you can't do the job on the merits so you have to do it another way," he says.

Antagonists aren't only angry white men, though.

Norma Stever, 62, a Spokane, Wash., medical transcriber, says she's "seen incompetent people get jobs who don't deserve them. . . . That kind of unfairness is very frustrating."

Says Loretta Lutman, an Ashboro, N.C., volunteer zoo worker: "When you talk about affirmative action, the standards start to drop for women and minorities and here sits the little ol' white man—left out.

"That really bugs me and I'm a woman," Lutman says.

It also bugs a tiny proportion of black men who say affirmative action casts a stigma on their qualifications and abilities.

"When you announce there are group preferences freely at work, people are going to perceive that to be the case, even when it isn't," says black conservative scholar Shelby Steele.

THE FLOATERS

Enter the great big muddy middle.

Talk-show rhetoric does not fuel extreme emotions here. There is healthy support for affirmative action, but the level of commitment is lukewarm. Floaters favor government contract set-asides for minority run businesses, gender and racial quotas in schools, and outreach programs. But they are divided on business quotas and race-based scholarships.

Only a quarter says existing programs should be pared. And many support specific measures to ensure broader participation by minorities and women in schools and business.

They go as far as to set aside some government contracts for minority businesses and favor minority hiring if they are as qualified as whites. There also is support for engaging in general outreach programs to benefit women and minorities.

But the group also exhibits a major contradiction: Despite the support for quotas and special programs, only 1 in 10 believe that discrimination is a major problem for minorities and women. An overwhelming majority says blacks have the same chance as whites of getting a job. And even without mandated affirmative action policy, Floaters say businesses and schools would still be fair to women and minorities.

Connie Sue Knuckols, 46, of Fredericksburg, Va., is a Floater. Her solution to the whole problem: simply change the way we deal with our children.

"Kids would be raised, not to look at the differences, but to look at what makes us the same," Knuckols says. "Affirmative action would be obsolete."

Though laced with contradiction, this middle ground perhaps best defines the perplexing nature of the issue, analysts say. For politicians seeking consensus, it is chockful of land mines and, analysts say, where Clinton has most at stake.

"The polarized debate is not where people are positioned," says Democratic strategist Brian Lunde. "If we allow Jesse Jackson and (Fund for the Feminist Majority president) Eleanor Smeal to define our affirmative action position, we'll lose."

THE DUBIOUS

Major divisions coexist here.

A majority says job discrimination against blacks and Hispanics persists, but the same number says blacks already have as good a chance as whites in the workplace.

While they overwhelmingly support job training, outreach and special education classes for minorities, they strongly oppose quotas, set-asides and special scholarships.

Patrick Green is among the Dubious. He wants a fair shot at a better job and believes affirmative action can help blacks like himself. But he is torn by a suspicion that the policy at its most extreme is misguided.

"No way could I support quotas or anything like that," says Green, 24, a Plainfield, N.J., data entry clerk. "That kind of thing can never help business be competitive."

Worse than that, Green says, "it does nothing to motivate minorities to be the best they can be. You tell me whether you would give your best effort if going into a job you knew that you got hired to fill a quota. It's demoralizing."

While there is strong resentment for anything smacking of mandated favoritism, the Dubious overwhelmingly support aggressive recruitment of minorities and women, employment training programs for the disadvantaged, and special education classes to help minorities and women enter schools.

A majority also believes that blacks already have as good a chance as whites in landing a job in their communities.

"Employers should have the right to pick and choose who they want and not have to hire based only on race or gender," says Pat James, a black Fulton County, Ga., government employee.

6. AFRICAN AMERICANS

"Sometimes, I think whites believe that the only reason you got the job is because you are black."

Exit the people, enter the politicians.

For them, the supreme test is finding consensus in this collision of principle and personal experience, because traditional political groupings only scratch the surface of the issue.

In that sense, the game could turn on simple semantics, says political analyst Stuart Rothenberg.

"It's a good political issue, ending affirmative action, if it's defined as quotas," Rothenberg says. "But Republicans have to make it clear if they want to use it in '96. They have to define it as preferences, advantages. If they do . . . they can tap that sensitivity."

Democrats, on the other hand, must redefine the debate if they are to prevail. Many are already trying to shift the focus away from race and toward gender, argu-ing that the biggest beneficiaries are not minorities, but women.

Still, despite all the philosophical hand-wringing over affirmative action, voters aren't likely to be riveted unless they feel their personal interests are at stake.

"If you only know it as an abstract you may not like it but it's not going to motivate you much," says political analyst Kevin Phillips. "But, if it becomes a job issue it simply becomes one of the most important issues."

Home Ownership Anchors The Middle Class

But Lending Games Sink Many Prospective Owners

Scott Minerbrook

It was the kind of house Donnell Cravens and his wife, Eugenie, had prayed for: a four-bedroom brick colonial with brown trim, hedges all around and an attached garage. They saw it for the first time in early July, and it was almost an apparition of earthly rewards. For him, a personnel director, there was a garden to raise corn, tomatoes and melons. For her, an accountant with the Detroit Symphony Orchestra, a green-sward of lawn manicured like a royal garden. True, West Bloomfield, Mich., didn't have many minority children for their kids to play with, but they'd somehow make do.

They almost didn't get it. They had $54,000 in the bank from the sale of their Detroit home and had been pre-approved for a $150,000 mortgage, complete with a letter of qualification from one financial institution. Then came the meeting with the seller's realtor. One look at the agent and Eugenie told Donnell, "She's going to give us trouble." The agent tried. She told the seller that the Cravens weren't qualified, even though she'd gotten a full rundown about the husband's finances — without his consent. The seller was about to pull out when the Cravens threatened to call in their lawyers. That seemed to do the trick. "It was a travesty," Donnell said. "I knew about the race game in real estate, but I wouldn't have believed it if I hadn't experienced it myself."

Welcome to the world of real estate, to seclusion and exclusion. It is a world where many minorities give up. Indeed, the very intent is to make minorities give up. "The ultimate humiliation for the black middle class is the denial of equal access to housing," said Charles Bromley, director for the Metropolitan Strategy Group in Cleveland, Ohio. For blacks, at all levels, the hoops are higher and smaller while for whites, they are wider and lower. It's discrimination with a smile."

For the black middle class, exclusion from better housing is the bitter fruit of a legacy of racial prejudice. In what scholars call the "inertia of segregation," millions of African-Americans who have climbed into the security of the middle and upper classes — about 12 per cent of all African-Americans now have earnings exceeding $50,000 a year — only to find that the dream of buying a home is a nightmare of miscues and obstacles. Nowhere is this fact of greater consequence than in the field of housing. Buying a home is not only part of the American Dream, it is essential to grasping it. But study after study reveals that those in the middle class are restricted in their choice of where to live and what to buy. They are treated differently by lending and insurance institutions simply because of the color of their skin. This has a profound impact on the wealth of generations to come.

More than two decades after the 1968 Fair Housing Act banned discrimination in the sale and rental of housing, blacks who try to move away from the disadvantages of city living often find themselves re-segregated into what sociologists call the "inner ring" or "near-in suburbs," such as Prince George's County or Silver Spring, in Maryland, which surround Washington, D.C. They find themselves hemmed in by housing practices that put them in close proximity to the poor and to lesser educational opportunities, despite the fact that they may be earning as much as their white counterparts. Steered there by discriminatory practices on the part of banks, insurance companies and realtors, middle-class blacks find themselves in areas where the demand for the houses they have purchased has already peaked, virtually ensuring a deflation in the value of their homes compared to those of the whiter suburbs beyond.

"The net result of segregation is that the black middle class loses the very freedom of movement that defines being in the middle class," said Douglas S. Massey, a sociologist at the University of Chicago.

Massey has a word for these collective experiences: hypersegregation. It is a term that defines the increasing spatial isolation of blacks from whites, not only in American cities, but in the suburbs that weren't built for blacks in the first place. In his recent book, *American Apartheid: Segregation and the Making of the Underclass*, Massey and his co-author, Nancy A. Denton, show just how deeply segregated America continues to be. A principal finding: Race, not class, is the main determinant of where blacks are allowed to live. According to the authors' data, a black person who makes $50,000 has fewer choices in where he or she can live and is more segregated than an Hispanic person earning $2,500. The authors say blacks earning $50,000 a year also experience the same degree of segregation as African-Americans earning $2,500 a year. And according to the National Research Council, it will take about six decades for blacks to achieve the minimal levels of economic security that integration with whites has already brought to Hispanics and Asians.

6. AFRICAN AMERICANS

"This is the penalty of race," said sociologist George Galster, of the Washington-based Urban Institute.

It is a reality so widespread that it is almost never challenged. The bottom line, Massey said, is that blacks in many big cities are less likely to move to the suburbs than either Asians or Hispanics and are more likely to live segregated lives once they are there. In the Chicago area, for instance, fewer than 16 percent of blacks live in the suburbs, compared to 27 percent of Hispanics and nearly half of the area's Asians.

The numbers are just as stark when Massey compares where blacks live to where whites live. By 1980, when black economic progress was beginning to stall because of resistance to affirmative action, 71 percent of all whites lived in northern suburbs. Blacks then composed less than a quarter of all suburban residents. In the South, the suburbs were 65 percent white and 34 percent black. In the North and Midwest, blacks were even less likely to live in the suburbs of Indianapolis, Kansas City, Milwaukee and New York — all of which had black residential rates of less than 10 per cent. In the suburbs of Los Angeles, Pittsburgh and St. Louis, the black residential rates didn't approach that of whites.

But even these numbers are potentially misleading. While blacks began moving into the suburbs in the '80s, Massey said, this didn't mean the neighborhoods where they lived were integrated. In fact, many black "suburbs" were often simply sections of declining municipalities, replete with all the problems that have hobbled the economic growth of central cities.

Even if an African-American moved to the suburbs, various studies show high degrees of segregation — of blacks closer to blacks and whites closer to whites — were usually the rule.

And this does not bode well for blacks living there. Those suburbs where the numbers of blacks have increased have followed the old rule of real estate: Where blacks are, white homeowners stay away, fearful that the value of their homes won't increase. This may or may not be racism *per se*, scholars say, since racial attitudes are often indistinguishable from economic ones. One expert has estimated that between 30 percent and 70 percent of racial segregation is the result of economic concerns, such as home value. In large measure it is perception that becomes reality. In most instances, whites are reluctant to move to areas where housing approaches a 20 percent black ratio. Once this level is reached, white demand softens even as black demand increases. This often leads to re-segregation of an area. So set are white home buyers in their identification of the suburbs as being "white" that a 1985 study of white voters in Detroit by the Michigan Democratic Party found that whites believed that not being black is what, by definition, constitutes being middle class and that "not living with blacks is what makes a neighborhood a decent place to live."

This generally has devastating effects on the areas that have become integrated. Proud and comfortable as they may be, weakening white demand means blacks will find themselves stuck with homes they can't sell. Median home prices in the city of Detroit tell this story over time. The median home value of a single-family home in that city dropped (in 1990 dollars) from $49,000 in 1970 to $36,000 in 1980 to $27,000 in 1990 — a 45 per cent drop in their equity as whites moved out over the 20-year period. As whites leave an area, a pattern of disinvestment that only hurts the areas where middle-class blacks are moving.

And that's for starters.

The inability of large numbers of blacks to buy homes in the suburbs reduces their ready access to jobs and increased income. Galster, at the Urban Institute, said that lack of access to markets in outlying areas where wages are higher than in the cities means lower savings rates, which diminish personal wealth.

Thus, the usual rule that has applied to virtually every immigrant European group — and now Asian — that political and economic power across generations can be secured through home purchase, has largely not been the experience of African-Americans. In 1970, 65 percent of whites owned homes. Today, that number is 69 percent. In 1970, 42 percent of blacks owned homes. That number increased to 45 percent in 1989, before falling back to 42 per cent two years later.

Instead of the crescendo of rising home values and economic viability, there is stagnation. "Realtors sense this weakness and begin offering forms of credit other than conventional mortgages," said Don DeMarco, executive director of the Fund for an Open Society, a Philadelphia-based fair housing group. "This tends to be a code for the fact that the neighborhood is no longer attractive to the majority population." Real estate agents jump into the breach by offering various federally-subsidized mortgage arrangements, including Veterans Administration and Federal Homeowners Administration loans that become a symptom of weakening market demand. And since the price of points and closing costs is generally higher for these deals, blacks who move into the neighborhoods offered are socked with a third whammy: neighborhoods of declining investment value where residents must deplete their funds to close, leaving less money to fix the homes.

The effect on black wealth is devastating. In 1988, the U.S. Census Bureau concluded that white families had 10 times the wealth of blacks in America. Crucially, 40 percent of that difference was the lack of home equity between black and white families. The latest numbers come from 1989. That year, the median value of home equity for all families—the vast numbers of whom were white—was $48,000. For blacks it was $37,000. Thus, while a white person can lean on their home-owning parents or relatives money needed for other investments—to buy a larger house the next time, to finance a child's education, a vacation—blacks do not enjoy this advantage. Some of this is the result of the historic legacy of segregation: since blacks have been barred in past generations from owning valuable homes, there is less money passed from the older generations to the new. "Wealth begets wealth and lack of wealth gets stuck," said Galster.

One of the most important consequences of these economic differences between blacks and whites, said Galster, is the number of blacks who would have enough money to cover the standard 10 percent down payment on a home and to finance a mortgage on a home at today's standard, about 9 percent. National figures show that 42 percent of white renters would be able to afford to purchase a typical starter home in a metropolitan area, while just 26 percent of blacks would be able to make that leap.

"What this means is that middle-class housing in America is bifurcated into two extremes," explained Bromley. "If you are white, you can trade up into a place in Chevy Chase [Md.], while a black family is sitting in a home in Shepherd Park in Northwest Washington, D.C., or in Silver Spring, Md., where demand isn't as great and the returns are low."

In 1989, *Money* magazine found that housing segregation tended to stifle the black middle class in its ability to build wealth through the appreciation of home values. The magazine illustrated the deflation in prices in black middle-class areas by comparing residential areas with the same income patterns. It found that price appreciation in middle-class black areas lagged behind those in white areas. For instance, in Washington, D.C.'s predominantly black Brookland/Catholic University area, housing prices rose 8 percent from 1985 to 1989. That was a 10 per cent drop in value (adjusting for inflation), the magazine reported. By comparison, in North Highland, which was 98 percent white, home prices increased nearly 100 percent. In Atlanta, prices in Ben Hill, about 97 percent black, appreciated 46 percent while those in North Highland, 93 percent white, jumped by 67 percent.

There are other costs to blacks as well. As a rule, blacks simply have far less wealth to give to their children. A 1984 Census Bureau study found that blacks who earned between $24,000 and $48,000 that year had net worths one-third as large as whites at the same income level. This means that whites will generally give their children a head start on blacks of the next generation. "That is generally the difference between going to the college of your choice and settling for a state or community college or no college at all," said Bart Landry, a sociologist at the University of Maryland and author of *The New Black Middle Class*.

In general, scholars are finding that these patterns of disparity and limitation of economic opportunity can be laid at the doorstep of racial discrimination by the real estate, banking and insurance industries. By far the most damaging evidence of discrimination by lenders is in how blacks and whites are treated when they try to obtain home mortgages. According to a study by the Federal Reserve Bank of Boston, published in 1989, even after accounting for differences in income and wealth, white neighborhoods received 24 percent more loans than black ones. The study looked at 3,000 mortgage application files from more than 300 lenders and found that people with identical credentials were rejected purely on the basis of race. Blacks were 56 percent more likely to be rejected than whites with similar credentials.

While whites were generally encouraged to learn about various mortgage plans, blacks were often discouraged through misinformation and lack of clear advice, for example, on how to clean up poor credit records.

The discriminatory behavior was not limited to the lending industry. Another study, by the Department of Housing and Urban Development, found widespread evidence of racially discriminatory practices in the real estate industry in 1989. The HUD report estimated that there were 2 million instances of housing discrimination annually against

Assets and liabilities

total net worth

$43,164 (white) $8,981 (black)

amount and type of wealth in 1988 (in 1990 dollars)

interest earning at financial institutions
white: 6,162
black: 735

regular checking
white: 234
black: 82

stock and mutual funds
white: 2,884
black: 97

equity in business
white: 3,846
black: 351

equity in motor vehicle
white: 2,434
black: 974

equity in home
white: 18,236
black: 6,068

equity in rental property
white: 3,412
black: 704

other real estate
white: 1,860
black: 272

U.S. savings bonds
white: 203
black: 245

IRA or Keoghs
white: 1,714
black: 1,859

source: U.S. Census Bureau

African-Americans and other minorities. Housing was systematically made more available to whites in 45 percent of all transactions in the rental market and in 34 percent of the sales market. Whites also received more favorable credit assistance in 46 percent of sales encounters and were offered more favorable terms in 17 percent of rental transactions.

In the sales market, the question of differential treatment boils down to behavior: how often a broker will call a buyer back; or if a buyer is called back, if the buyer be shown the preferred tree-lined streets and the cul-de-sacs.

"An agent will rely on code words, telling a white person, 'you wouldn't feel comfortable here,' while a black person will be told, 'there's nothing in your price range here,' " said Bromley. "Frequently, steering behavior consists of showing a black potential homebuyer a house priced at $150,000 after they've told the realtor to look for a house for no more than $125,000," Bromley said. "It's about the persistent feeling of being unwelcomed. It's about racism with a smile."

Often, the only time black home buyers get a chance to smile back is in the courtroom.

Under fair housing laws, any agent who has referred clients to banks or other lending institutions that discriminate, automatically become liable themselves. It was this leverage that Donnell Cravens used successfully when he threatened to sue the realtor and the banks in his attempt to buy a home in Bloomfield, Mich.

There are alternatives to the litigation threat for blacks who are seeking to break down the barriers of segregation. One of the best is offered by the Fund For An Open Society. It helped build a national model for resolution of the problems of segregation in Shaker Heights, Ohio, by trying to help address racial balance in both black and white communities. That unique approach allows individuals trying to find homes a low-interest loan as an incentive to integrate racially-segregated areas. Often, whites will be approached with the loan incentive to integrate black neighborhoods that appear to be in danger of losing their attractiveness because the density of black households is too high. Or, alternatively, the fund will approach blacks with the chance to integrate nearly all-white areas. Similar programs have been formed around the country, based on this model.

In the past, the real estate industry has been stuck in their basic way of thinking about human beings as economic objects. While whites have been encouraged to buy housing for its investment value because they are seeing them as "future-oriented people," blacks have been stigmatized by the industry which sees them as people who want to buy as much shelter as possible for the dollar, regardless of whether it is in an area that is losing its marketability to the majority population. One result is that blacks are forced to rely on mortgages from sources other than private lending institutions—falling back on government agencies such as VA and the FHA loans, where closing costs are higher, and additional points are required. "The result is that blacks are pushed by realtors into areas where private mortgages aren't even offered," Bromley said. "Breaking out of this pattern of inertia is difficult because there are so many higher costs."

The difficulty is overcoming the inertia of past generations. DeMarco said his program seeks to remedy this condition by involving the banks, real estate interests and home buyers in the process of keeping areas marketable through "integrative efforts." He explained, "You have to recognize that in this country, the majority simply has the money to determine supply and demand and unless minorities can link up with that system, they are in danger of losing out."

Massey proposed ending the crisis of inequality in black housing patterns by attacking racial discrimination in private housing markets, which comprise 98 percent of all dwellings in America. Public policies, he said, must interrupt the institutionalized process of neighborhood racial turnover, "which is the ultimate mechanism by which the ghetto is reproduced and maintained." That process depends on white prejudice and racial discrimination which restrict black access and channels black housing demand "to a few black or racially mixed areas." The federal government must insert itself into the housing markets, with HUD taking a greater role in enforcing Fair Housing Act directives, Massey said.

Whether the Clinton administration is willing to address the issue of housing segregation, meanwhile, is anybody's guess. There are strong indications that it may happen. HUD Secretary Henry Cisneros has promised stepped-up

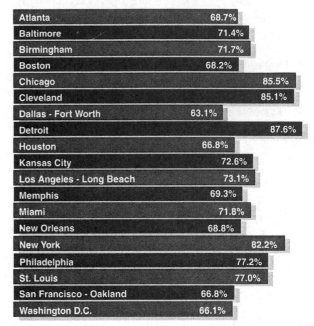

Percentage of blacks
who live in segregated neighborhoods in selected metropolitan areas.

Metropolitan Area	Percentage
Atlanta	68.7%
Baltimore	71.4%
Birmingham	71.7%
Boston	68.2%
Chicago	85.5%
Cleveland	85.1%
Dallas - Fort Worth	63.1%
Detroit	87.6%
Houston	66.8%
Kansas City	72.6%
Los Angeles - Long Beach	73.1%
Memphis	69.3%
Miami	71.8%
New Orleans	68.8%
New York	82.2%
Philadelphia	77.2%
St. Louis	77.0%
San Francisco - Oakland	66.8%
Washington D.C.	66.1%

source: Population Association of America, 1990

enforcement activities and the U.S. Justice Department appears to be increasing its monitoring of discriminatory practices in the real estate and banking industries.

But this isn't enough. One source of doubt about whether housing segregation will end any time soon comes from the black community itself, which appears to have lost faith in the benefits of integrated housing, despite widespread evidence that it is a powerful vehicle for joining the economic mainstream. There appears to be a kind of nostalgia that has settled in in many quarters of the minority community that support the idea that segregation in itself may not be such a bad thing. Even among African-Americans, who are most hurt financially by segregation, there appears to be little agreement on how to invest in the struggle against housing segregation with passionate commitment.

Recently, Massey was asked to discuss his book on a black Chicago radio station. He spoke of the problems blacks have with access to capital, about the real estate industry which blocks blacks from finding out how to exercise their options for a wider range of economically potent housing choices. "I was saying it was all about gaining access to greater opportunities, which basically means joining the mainstream, which means 'Are you willing to put up with white people to get what you want out of society?'"

A woman called the station and castigated those blacks who had moved out of the city. She said she didn't think blacks should be living near whites. The caller said blacks needed to "have pride in their communities." At another talk, Massey was confronted by a community activist who

Trends in black and white suburbanization
percentages of blacks and whites who lived in the suburbs in 1980 (the last year for which research was available).

whites   blacks

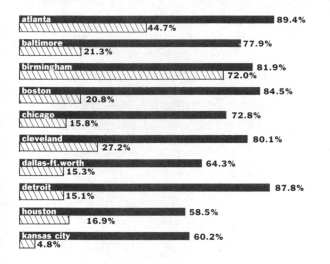
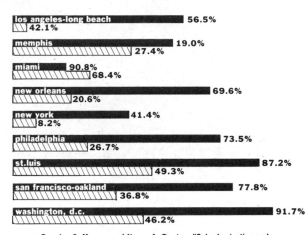

atlanta 89.4% / 44.7%
baltimore 77.9% / 21.3%
birmingham 81.9% / 72.0%
boston 84.5% / 20.8%
chicago 72.8% / 15.8%
cleveland 80.1% / 27.2%
dallas-ft.worth 64.3% / 15.3%
detroit 87.8% / 15.1%
houston 58.5% / 16.9%
kansas city 60.2% / 4.8%

los angeles-long beach 56.5% / 42.1%
memphis 19.0% / 27.4%
miami 90.8% / 68.4%
new orleans 69.6% / 20.6%
new york 41.4% / 8.2%
philadelphia 73.5% / 26.7%
st.luis 87.2% / 49.3%
san francisco-oakland 77.8% / 36.8%
washington, d.c. 91.7% / 46.2%

source: Douglas S. Massey and Nancy A. Denton, "Suburbanization and Segregation in U.S. Metropolitan Areas," American Journal of Sociology

told him that pursuit of integration by leaving the black ghetto was a dilution and betrayal of black political interests. Massey said he was stunned. "The bottom line is that I don't know of any story that begins with segregation and ends up with economic success. Segregation makes oppression easy and efficient. It allows disinvestment in the black community and it ultimately means the end of hope for the future."

FAIR HOUSING ADVOCATES:

NATIONAL FAIR HOUSING ALLIANCE
1400 I Street, N.W.
Washington, D.C. 20005
202-898-1661

FUND FOR AN OPEN SOCIETY
311 South Juniper Street, Suite 400
Philadelphia, Pa. 19107
215-735-6915

LEADERSHIP COUNCIL
401 South State Street, Suite 860
Chicago, Ill. 60605
312-341-5678

CINCINNATI COALITION OF NEIGHBORHOODS
6566 Montgomery Road, Suite 210
Cincinnati, Ohio 45213
513-531-2676

**FAIR HOUSING CONGRESS OF
SOUTHERN CALIFORNIA**
3535 West 6th Street, Second floor
Los Angeles, Calif. 90020
213-365-7184

D.C. FAIR HOUSING COUNCIL
1400 I Street, N.W.
Washington, D.C. 20005
202-289-5360

**TENNESSEE MID-SOUTH
PEACE AND JUSTICE CENTER**
P.O. Box 11428
Memphis, Tenn. 38111-0428
901-452-6997

**OAKLAND COUNTY CENTER
FOR OPEN HOUSING**
3060 Telegraph Road, Suite 1233
Bingham Farms, Mich. 48025
313-647-0575

The Ethnic Legacy

Ethnicity is often associated with immigrants and with importation of culture, language, stories, and foods from foreign shores. Appalachian, western, and other regional ethnicities are evidence of multigenerational ethnic cultural development within the American reality. The persistent, ongoing process of humanity expressed in unique and intriguing folkways, dialect-languages, myths, festivals, and foods displays another enduring and public dimension of ethnicity. As this unit's articles illustrate, ethnic experiences may be less foreign and alien than most imagine them to be.

The contributions and concerns of various ethnic immigrant groups over many generations provided a deep weave and pattern to the material and social history of America. Today we see a consciousness of ethnic tradition, exasperation and anger about stereotypes, and efforts to institutionalize attention to groups. Change and ethnicity are not contradictory, for each generation creates anew its ethnicity, which, alongside other affinities, affiliations, and loyalties, helps to guide our interactions. Present concerns of ethnic groups include language, preservation of neighborhoods, ethnic studies, and the rearticulation of historical claims to fairness, justice, and equity.

Perhaps the most obvious oscillation between celebration of achievement and concern about fairness is seen in the legacies of ancestry-conscious persons and groups. Should such populations be denied their distinctiveness through absorption into the mass of modernity, or can their distinctiveness accompany them into mainstream modern American identities? Their ethnicity is not a form of diminished existence; they are "Americans Plus"—Americans with a multicultural affinity and competencies in more than one culture.

The winds of political change in Ireland and England, the Middle East, and Eastern and Central Europe reveal the saliency of ethnicity and the varied textures of group relations. In America the ongoing affinity of ethnic populations to the nations of their origins is expressed in subtle as well as obvious ways. These articles explain the transmission of ethnic tradition in music and suggest linkages between religion and ethnicity. The story of the interaction of ethnicity and religion is curiously exposed in the etymology of the Greek word *ethnikos* (i.e., the rural, Gentile, or pagan people of the ancient Mediterranean world). Though such philological roots no longer drive our principal understanding of ethnicity, the experience of social affinity and cultural affiliation elaborated in the following articles about ethnics deepens our awareness and understanding of ethnicity—a changing yet persistent aspect of human identity and social cohesiveness.

Looking Ahead: Challenge Questions

How does ethnicity of an earlier era suggest the tension between worlds of meaning discussed in this section?

Comment on the idea that the legacy of multiple ancestral origins and ethnic identities of European Americans from an earlier era in America argues for the passing relevancy and their marginality to the central ethnic issues of our time.

What is a central ethnic issue? By what criteria do we decide the importance and preferential protection of one ethnic group vis-à-vis another group?

What lessons can be learned from the immigration and settlement experiences of Eastern and Southern Europeans?

America's Dilemma

New books attest to the intractability of 'the race problem'

Ellen K. Coughlin

THREE DECADES after the passage of the landmark civil-rights legislation of the 1960s, race is still the American dilemma.

As if proof of that were needed, this season will see a host of new scholarly books that testify to the continuing intractability of "the race problem." Taken together, they echo the cacophony of opinion on race and racism that reverberates through the public arena:

■ Racism is at the heart of the problems facing American blacks today. *Racism is an excuse that blacks should stop falling back on.*

■ The rise of the black middle class is a sign that the remedies of the civil-rights era were a success. *The rise of the black middle class is a myth.*

■ Affirmative action works. *Affirmative action is a failure.*

Race always has been a subject of intense interest for scholars and cultural critics; the social-science literature on race relations is vast. But the unusually large cluster of books to be published in the next several weeks suggests that race is, once again, the most pressing question on the public agenda.

It is also a question without an answer— or with so many answers as to make an ultimate solution seem elusive. On just two things do these authors form some rough consensus—that race in the new, multicultural America is still primarily a black-white issue, and that the parameters of that issue have changed.

"Race and racism are alive and well, but they have been transformed since the 1960s," says Manning Marable, a historian at Columbia University. "Almost no one, not even David Duke, steps forward today and says 'nigger.' "

'NEW PARADIGM FOR EMPOWERMENT'

Mr. Marable, who is also director of Columbia's Institute for Research in African-American Studies, is the author of the forthcoming *Beyond Black and White,* a collection of essays he has written in the past five years on contemporary race relations. He reflects on a variety of issues—university black-studies programs, the Clarence Thomas/Anita Hill hearings—but his key theme is the need to transform the way we think about race relations and racial inequities.

He believes, for example, that the civil-rights movement of the 1990s has to find what he calls a "new paradigm for empowerment," one that pays as much attention to cultivating grassroots leadership in the inner cities as it does to increasing the presence of blacks in Congress and corporate offices.

"You can't assume that 'a black base in a high place,' as we used to say, will be in blacks' interest," he says. "That strategy was flawed."

No one agrees with that last sentiment more, or takes the insight further, than Dinesh D'Souza, the young conservative writer who rattled American higher education four years ago with his *Illiberal Education,* a no-holds-barred attack from the right on the multicultural movement on the nation's campuses. Like Mr. Marable, he believes that the old civil-rights strategy is one whose time is past—but the two authors are hardly soul mates. Mr. Marable wants to combat racism; Mr. D'Souza wants to forget it.

"The cultural strategy that says that racism must be responsible is today a dysfunctional way of thinking," he says. "It's an obstacle to success."

DEBUNKING SACRED ASSUMPTIONS

In his new book, *The End of Racism,* Mr. D'Souza, a research fellow at the American Enterprise Institute, devotes most of his energy to debunking some of the most sacred assumptions embedded in civil-rights rhetoric: Slavery was not a racist institution, he argues. And most racial discrimination today is not racism, but a rational response to accurate generalizations about group differences.

At the heart of his book is Mr. D'Souza's contention that deficiencies in black culture, not racism, are mainly to blame for racial inequality. His targets here are not only the chronic poverty and crime of the inner city, but also what he sees as the tendency among many middle-class blacks to rely too heavily on government and to dismiss certain mainstream behaviors as "acting white."

SHIFT IN FEDERAL POLICY

If black people are to become competitive, he says, they have to stop blaming all their problems on racism and adopt the "cultural strategies" that make for success in America—everything from lots of homework to intact families to entrepreneurship.

He also believes that a shift in federal policy is in order, to allow private establishments to discriminate on the basis of race—so that, for example, black business owners would be free to hire their own, as entrepreneurs from other ethnic minorities tend to do. If that sounds like he is proposing to repeal the Civil Rights Law of 1964, he is.

Mr. D'Souza knows that a lot of people will find his book outrageous. In fact, his eagerness to point out its outrageousness

Race and Racism: Some of the Season's New Books

Beyond Black and White: Rethinking Race in American Politics and Society, by Manning Marable (Verso, 280 pages, $24.95).

Black Wealth/White Wealth: A New Perspective on Racial Inequality, by Melvin L. Oliver and Thomas M. Shapiro (Routledge, 236 pages, $22.95).

The Bubbling Cauldron: Race, Ethnicity, and the Urban Crisis, edited by Michael Peter Smith and Joe R. Feagin (University of Minnesota Press, 360 pages, $21.95).

The End of Racism: Principles for a Multiracial Society, by Dinesh D'Souza (The Free Press, 736 pages, $30).

Facing Up to the American Dream: Race, Class, and the Soul of the Nation, by Jennifer L. Hochschild (Princeton University Press, 395 pages, $29.95).

Killing Rage: Ending Racism, by bell hooks (Henry Holt and Company, 277 pages, $20).

Turning Back: The Retreat From Racial Justice in American Thought and Policy, by Stephen Steinberg (Beacon Press, 276 pages, $25).

suggests that he might be disappointed if they don't. But he insists that he is not trying to belittle the difficulty of being black in America.

"Blacks have been viewed differently. Their experience has been different," he says. "This experience has generated, out of oppression and reaction, patterns of behavior, an orientation, a culture that is historically adaptive—but is today dysfunctional."

Mr. D'Souza's book raises a question that scholars and writers have been asking at least since William Julius Wilson's 1978 study, *The Declining Significance of Race:* How much racial inequity in America today is due purely to race (or racism), and how much to class or culture?

Most commentators come out well to the left of Mr. D'Souza's answer, but the question of the potency of racism in U. S. society is still a matter of debate. For example, a collection of essays coming out this month—*The Bubbling Cauldron,* edited by Michael Peter Smith of the University of California at Davis and Joe R. Feagin of the University of Florida—offers, on the one hand, a catalogue of the continuing impact of racism in this country, and, on the other, an analysis by Martín Sanchez Jankowski, of the University of California at Berkeley, of the central importance of status in American race relations.

In another new book, one that is in some respects a mirror image of Mr. D'Souza's, Stephen Steinberg, a sociologist at Queens College of the City University of New York, traces what he calls the "retreat" from racial justice in the United States. *Turning Back* is an intellectual history of

Americans' ambivalence about race and race relations, even as the country was officially attempting to remedy racial injustices through anti-discrimination laws and affirmative action.

'SCHOLARSHIP OF BACKLASH'

Mr. Steinberg is particularly angered by what he calls the "scholarship of backlash," including Mr. Wilson's thesis about the declining significance of race and Cornel West's critique, in his 1993 book *Race Matters,* of the "nihilism" of poor black communities. "The whole pursuit of racial justice has been complicated by people on the left who have tended to subsume race into class," Mr. Steinberg says. "When they do that, they fail to address the distinctive nature and deep sources of racism, which has to be addressed on its own terms."

In his book, Mr. Steinberg attacks *The Bell Curve,* the 1994 study by Richard Herrnstein and Charles Murray suggesting that blacks are biologically inferior to whites in intelligence, as "the apogee of the backlash." He does not have much more patience for Mr. D'Souza's argument about the supposed deficiencies of black culture: "It takes those cultural responses at face value, instead of looking at the material conditions in which they exist. Plus, it fails to acknowledge the presence of old-fashioned racism."

Unlike Mr. D'Souza, who comes down hard on racial preferences, Mr. Steinberg argues fervently, if unfashionably, for affirmative action—"the only policy," he says, "that has chipped away at the structures of inequality."

How powerful a punch you believe racism still packs will affect where you stand on the vaunted subject of "black rage." Anger and alienation among poor inner-city blacks are easy to understand. But disaffection among middle-class blacks, who by most standards appear to have made it, has been much discussed in the press and often is dismissed by conservatives—Mr. D'Souza is one of them—as yet another instance of the tendency to use racism as an excuse. In the opinion of others, though, the rage is real enough.

In a new collection of her essays called *Killing Rage,* bell hooks, the cultural critic and literary scholar at C.U.N.Y.'s City College, writes of the anger that wells up in her when she encounters what seem to be racially motivated slights. Not all such indignities are necessarily racist, she says, but when you are black and on the receiving end, that's how they feel. "Domination breeds paranoia," she says.

Others see such anger in more practical terms. The success of the black middle class, they say, is not all it seems.

Blacks, Mr. Steinberg argues, are clustered in certain job sectors and are virtually absent from others. Black businesses tend to be located in black neighborhoods. "The black middle class is largely an artifact of public policy, especially affirmative action," he says. "It's not indicative of a relaxation of racial barriers in the job market."

FEW HAVE SUBSTANTIAL WEALTH

What's more, Melvin L. Oliver and Thomas M. Shapiro point out, while many blacks have achieved a respectable level of income—and a handful, like Bill Cosby and Oprah Winfrey, appear on lists of the richest people in America—few have any substantial wealth.

In *Black Wealth/White Wealth,* the authors—Mr. Oliver is a sociologist at the University of California at Los angeles, and Mr. Shapiro is a sociologist at Northeastern University—analyze the assets of blacks and whites in America. They find that, even when things like education and experience are taken into account, blacks have only 26 cents in assets for every dollar that whites hold. They attribute the difference to the long legacy of slavery and discrimination.

"Wealth is an intergenerationally transferred asset, one that blacks couldn't participate in until recently," Mr. Oliver says. "The economic racial divide is at the bottom of the issues endemic in the debate about race today."

But success is also counted in more subtle ways, and those also can divide black from whites. Jennifer L. Hochschild, a political scientist at Princeton University, looks at racial divisions in America by examining what people believe about the American dream.

TAKING THE CONCEPT SERIOUSLY

In *Facing Up to the American Dream,* she attempts to take seriously the concept, which many would consider a cliché, by drawing out the meanings that people attach to it. The American dream, she argues, is the central ideology of the U.S. society—simply stated, that all Americans have the opportunity to pursue their dreams, and, if they work hard enough, can hope to achieve a reasonable measure of success.

For her study, Ms. Hochschild analyzed survey data concerning what blacks and whites profess to believe about opportunity, success, and other aspects of the American dream. She found that middle-class blacks had little faith in the vision, far less than whites—and less, to her surprise, than working-class blacks.

Examining questions of equality and opportunity through the lens of the American dream gave Ms. Hochschild a clearer understanding of the rage that even many successful blacks feel. "The American dream is about dignity, respect, connectedness, belonging," she says. "They've achieved success in a narrow sense, but not in the wider sense of individual satisfaction and appreciation by the rest of society.

"They still can't get a cab at midnight in New York."

THE NEW ETHNICITY

Michael Novak

The word "ethnic" does not have a pleasing sound. The use of the word makes many people anxious. What sorts of repression account for this anxiety? What pretenses about the world are threatened when one points to the realities denoted and connoted by that ancient word? An internal history lies behind resistance to ethnicity; such resistance is almost always passional, convictional, not at all trivial. Many persons have tried to escape being "ethnic," in the name of a higher moral claim.

There are many meanings to the word itself. I have tried to map some of them below. There are many reasons for resistance to the word "ethnic" (and what it is taken to represent). Rather than beginning with these directly, I prefer to begin by defining the new ethnicity.

The definition I wish to give is personal; it grows out of personal experience; it is necessitated by an effort to attain an accurate self-knowledge. The hundreds of letters, reviews, comments, invitations, and conversations that followed upon *The Rise of the Unmeltable Ethnics* (1972) indicate that my own gropings to locate my own identity are not isolated. They struck a responsive chord in many others of Southern and Eastern European (or other) background. My aim was—and is—to open up the field to study. Let later inquiry descern just how broadly and how exactly my first attempts at definition apply. It is good to try to give voice to what has so far been untongued—and then to devise testable hypotheses at a later stage.

The new ethnicity, then, is a movement of self-knowledge on the part of members of the third and fourth generation of Southern and Eastern European immigrants in the United States. In a broader sense, the new ethnicity includes a renewed self-consciousness on the part of other generations and other ethnic groups: the Irish, the Norwegians and Swedes, the Germans, the Chinese and Japanese, and others. Much that can be said of one of these groups can be said, not univocally but analogously, of others. In this area, one must learn to speak with multiple meanings and with a sharp eye for differences in detail. (By "analogous" I mean "having resemblances but also essential differences"; by "univocal" I mean a generalization that applies equally to all cases.) My sentences are to be read, then, analogously, not univocally; they are meant to awaken fresh perception, not to close discussion. They are intended to speak directly of a limited (and yet quite large) range of ethnic groups, while conceding indirectly that much that is said of Southern and Eastern Europeans may also be said, *mutatis mutandis*, of others.

I stress that, in the main, the "new" ethnicity involves those of the third and fourth generation after immigration. Perhaps two anecdotes will suggest the kind of experience involved. When *Time* magazine referred to me in 1972 as a "Slovak-American," I felt an inner shock; I had never referred to myself or been publicly referred to in that way. I wasn't certain how I felt about it. Then, in 1974, after I had given a lecture on ethnicity to the only class in Slavic American studies in the United States,* at the City College of New York, the dean of the college said on the way to lunch, "Considering how sensitive you are on ethnic matters, the surprising thing to me was how American you are." I wanted to ask him, "What else?" In this area one grows used to symbolic uncertainties.

The new ethnicity does not entail: (a) speaking a foreign language; (b) living in a subculture; (c) living in a "tight-knit" ethnic neighborhood; (d) belonging to fraternal organizations; (e) responding to "ethnic" appeals; (f) exalting one's own nationality or culture, narrowly construed. Neither does it entail a university education or the reading of writers on the new ethnicity. Rather, the new ethnicity entails: first, a growing sense of discomfort with the sense of identity one is *supposed* to have—universalist, "melted," "like everyone else"; then a growing appreciation for the potential wisdom of one's own gut reactions (especially on moral matters) and their historical roots; a growing self-confidence and social power; a sense of being discriminated against, condescended to, or carelessly misapprehended; a growing disaffection regarding those to whom one had always been taught to defer; and a sense of injustice regarding the response of liberal spokesmen to conflicts between various ethnic groups, especially between "legitimate" minorities and "illegiti-

---

*This Slavic American course—in a happy symbol of the new ethnicity—is housed in the Program of Puerto Rican Studies, through the generosity of the latter.

From *Further Reflections on Ethnicity* by Michael Novak, published by Jednota Press, 1977. Originally from *Center* magazine, July/August 1974, pp. 18-25. © 1974 by Michael Novak. Reprinted by permission.

mate" ones. There is, in a word, an inner conflict between one's felt personal power and one's ascribed public power: a sense of outraged truth, justice, and equity.

The new ethnicity does, therefore, have political consequences. Many Southern and Eastern European-Americans have been taught, as I was, not to be "ethnic," or even "hyphenated," but only "American." Yet at critical points it became clear to some of us, then to more of us, that when push comes to shove we are always, in the eyes of others, "ethnics," unless we play completely by their rules, emotional as well as procedural. And in the end, even then, they retain the power and the status. Still, the stakes involved in admitting this reality to oneself are very high. Being "universal" is regarded as being good; being ethnically self-conscious raises anxieties. Since one's whole identity has been based upon being "universal," one is often loathe to change public face too suddenly. Many guard the little power and status they have acquired, although they cock one eye on how the ethnic "movement" is progressing. They are wise. But their talents are also needed.

The new ethnicity, then, is a fledgling movement, not to be confused with the appearance of ethnic themes on television commercials, in television police shows, and in magazines. All these manifestations in the public media would not have occurred unless the ethnic reality of America had begun to be noticed. In states from Massachusetts to Iowa, great concentrations of Catholics and Jews, especially in urban centers, have been some of the main bastions of Democratic Party politics for fifty years. The "new politics," centered in the universities, irritated and angered this constituency (even when, as it sometimes did, it won its votes). Thus there is a relation between the fledgling new ethnicity and this larger ethnic constituency. But what that relationship will finally be has not yet been demonstrated by events.

Those who do not come from Southern or Eastern European backgrounds in the United States may not be aware of how it feels to come from such a tradition; they may not know the internal history. They may note "mass passivity" and "alienation" without sharing the cynicism learned through particular experiences. They may regard the externals of ethnic economic and social success, modest but real, while never noticing the internal ambiguity—and its compound of peace and self-hatred, confidence and insecurity.

To be sure, at first many "white ethnics" of the third generation are not conscious of having any special feelings. The range of feelings about themselves they do have is very broad; more than one stream of feeling is involved. They are right-wingers and left-wingers, chauvinists and universalists, all-Americans and isolationists. Many want nothing more desperately than to be considered "American." Indeed, by now many have so deeply acquired that habit that to ask them point-blank how they are different from others would arouse strong emotional resistance.

For at least three reasons, many white ethnics *are* becoming self-conscious. As usual, great social forces outside the self draw forth from the self new responses. First, a critical mass of scholars, artists, and writers is beginning to emerge—the Italians, for example, are extraordinarily eminent in the cinema. Second, the prevailing image of the model American—the "best and the brightest" of the Ivy League, wealthy, suave, and powerful—has been discredited by the mismanagement of war abroad, by racial injustice at home, and by attitudes, values, and emotional patterns unworthy of emulation internally. The older image of the truly cultured American is no longer compelling. Many, therefore, are thrown back upon their own resources.

Finally, the attitudes of liberal, enlightened commentators on the "crisis of the cities" seem to fall into traditional patterns: guilt vis-a-vis blacks, and disdain for the Archie Bunkers of the land (Bunker is, of course, a classy British American name, but Carroll O'Connor is in appearance undisguisably Irish). The national media present to the public a model for what it is to be a "good American" which makes many people feel unacceptable to their betters, unwashed, and ignored. Richard Hofstadter wrote of "the anti-intellectualism of the people," but another feature of American life is the indifference—even hostility—of many intellectuals to Main Street. In return, then, many people respond with deep contempt for experts, educators, "limousine liberals," "radical chic," "bureaucrats"—a contempt whose sources are partly those of class ("the hidden injuries of class") and partly those of ethnicity ("legitimate" minorities and unacceptable minorities). The national social class that prides itself on being universalist has lost the confidence of many. Votes on school bond issues are an example of popular resistance to professionals.

In my own case, the reporting of voting patterns among white ethnic voters during the Wallace campaigns of 1964 and 1968 first aroused in me ethnic self-consciousness. Descriptions of "white backlash" often put the blame—inaccurately I came to see—upon Slavs and other Catholic groups. The Slavs of "South Milwaukee" were singled out for comment in the Wallace vote in Wisconsin in 1964. First, South Milwaukee was not distinguished from the south side of Milwaukee. Then, it was not noted that the Slavic vote for Wallace fell *below* his statewide average. Then, the very heavy vote for Wallace in outlying German and British American areas was not pointed out. Finally, the strong vote for Wallace in the wealthy northeastern suburbs of Milwaukee was similarly ignored. It seemed to me that those whom the grandfathers called "hunkies" and "dagos" were now being called "racists," "fascists," and "pigs," with no noticeable gain in affection. Even in 1972, a staff advisory in the Shriver "trip book" for a congressional district in Pittsburgh called the district "Wallace country," though the Wallace vote in that district in 1968 had been twelve per cent, and the Humphrey vote had been fifty-eight per cent. I obliged the staff member to revise his account and to call the district "Humphrey country." It is one of the most consistently liberal districts in Pennsylvania. Why send this constituency the message that it is the enemy?

Jimmy Breslin was once asked by an interviewer in *Penthouse* how, coming out of Queens, he could have grown up so liberal. Actually, next to Brooklyn, there is no more liberal county in the nation. A similar question was put to a liberal journalist from the Dorchester area, in Boston. The class and ethnic bias hidden in the way the word "liberal" is used in such interviews cries out for attention.

One of the large social generalizations systematically obscured by the traditional anti-Catholicism of American elites is the overwhelmingly progressive voting record in America's urban centers. The centers of large Catholic population in every northeastern and north central state have been the key to Democratic victories in those states since at least 1916. The hypothesis that Catholics have been, second only to Jews, the central constituency of successful progressive politics in this century is closer to the facts than historians have observed. (Massachusetts, that most Catholic of our states, stayed with McGovern in 1972.) The language of politics in America is, however, mainly Protestant, and Protestant biases color public perception. Protestant leadership is given the halo of morality and legitimacy, Catholic life is described in terms of negatively laden words: Catholic "power," "machine politics," etc.

There are other examples of odd perception on the part of American elites with respect to Catholic and other ethnic populations. The major institutions of American life—government, education, the media—give almost no assistance to those of "white ethnic" background who wish to obey the Socratic maxim: "Know thyself." One of the greatest and most dramatic migrations of human history brought more than thirty million immigrants to this land between 1874 and 1924. Despite the immense dramatic materials involved in this migration, only one major American film records it: Elia Kazan's *America! America!* That film ends with the hero's arrival in America. The tragic and costly experience of Americanization has scarcely yet been touched. How many died; how many were morally and psychologically destroyed; how many still carry the marks of changing their names, of "killing" their mother tongue and renouncing their former identity, in order to become "new men and new women"—these are motifs of violence, self-mutilation, joy, and irony. The inner history of this migration must come to be understood, if we are ever to understand the aspirations and fears of some seventy million Americans.

When this part of the population exhibits self-consciousness and begins to exert group claims—whether these are claims made by aggregated individuals or claims that are corporate—they are regularly confronted with the accusation that they are being "divisive". ("Divisive" is a code word for Catholic ethnics and Jews, is it not? It is seldom used of others: white Southerners, Appalachians, Chicanos, blacks, native Americans, prep-school British Americans, or others who maintain their own identity and institutions.) Earl Raab writes eloquently of this phenomenon in *Commentary* (May, 1974): "Modern Europe . . . never really accepted the legitimacy of the corporate Jew—although it was at its best willing to grant full civil rights to the individual Jew. That, for the Jews, was an impossible paradox, a secular vision of Christian demands to convert . . . [And] it is precisely this willingness to allow the Jews their separate identity as a group which is now coming into question in America." Individual diversity, yes; group identity, not for all.

The Christian white ethnic, like the Jew, actually has few group demands to make: positively, for educational resources to keep values and perceptions alive, articulate, and critical; negatively, for an equal access to power, status, and the definition of the general American purpose and symbolic world. Part of the strategic function of the cry "divisive!" is to limit access to these things. Only those individuals will be advanced who define themselves as individuals and who operate according to the symbols of the established. The emotional meaning is: *"Become like us."* This is an understandable strategy, but in a nation as pluralistic as the United States, it is shortsighted. The nation's hopes, purposes, and symbols need to be defined inclusively rather than exclusively; *all* must become "new men" and "new women." All the burden ought not to fall upon the newcomers.

There is much that is attractive about the British American, upper-class, northeastern culture that has established for the entire nation a model of behavior and perception. This model is composed of economic power; status; cultural tone; important institutional rituals and procedures; and the acceptable patterns of style, sensibility, and rationality. The terse phrase "Ivy League" suggests all these factors. The nation would be infinitely poorer than it is without the Ivy League. All of us who came to this land—including the many lower-class British Americans, Scotch-Irish, Scandinavians, and Germans—are much in the debt of the Ivy League, deeply, substantially so.

Still, the Ivy League is not the nation. The culture of the Ivy League is not the culture of America (not even of Protestant America).

Who are we, then, we who do not particularly reverberate to the literature of New England, whose interior history is not Puritan, whose social class is not Brahmin (either in reality or in pretense), whose ethnicity is not British American, or even Nordic? Where in American institutions, American literature, American education is our identity mirrored, objectified, rendered accessible to intelligent criticism, and confirmed? We are still, I think, persons without a public symbolic world, persons without a publicly verified culture to sustain us and our children.

It is not that we lack culture; it is not that we lack strength of ego and a certain internal peace. As Jean-Paul Sartre remarks in one of his later works, there is a distinction between one's identity in one's own eyes and one's identity in the eyes of others. In the United States, many who have internal dignity cannot avoid noticing that others regard them as less than equals, with a sense that they are different, with uncertainty, and with a lack of commonality. It is entirely possible that the "melting pot" would indeed have melted everyone, if those who were the models into which the molten metal was to be poured had not found the process excessively demanding. A sense of separate identity is, in part, induced from outside-in. I am made aware of being Catholic and Slovak by the actions of others. I would be sufficiently content were my identity to be so taken for granted, so utterly normal and real, that it would never have to be self-conscious.

The fact of American cultural power is that a more or less upper-class, Northeastern Protestant sensibility sets the tone, and that a fairly aggressive British American ethnocentricity, and even Anglophilia, govern the instruments of education and public life. Moreover, it is somehow emotionally important not to challenge this dominant ethnocentricity. It is quite proper to talk of other sorts of social difference—income, class, sex, even religion. To speak affirmatively of ethnicity, however, makes many uneasy. Some important truth must lie hidden underneath this uneasiness. A Niebuhrian analysis of social power suggests that a critical instrument of social control in the United States is, indeed, the one that dares not be spoken of.

In New York State, for example, in 1974 the four Democratic candidates for the office of lieutenant governor (not, however, for governor) were named Olivieri, Cuomo, La Falce, and Krupsak. It was the year, the pundits say, for "ethnic balance" on the ticket. But all four candidates insisted that their ethnicity was not significant. Two boasted of being from *upstate*, one of being a *woman*, one of being for "the *little* guy. " It is publicly legitimate to be different on any other account except ethnicity, even where the importance of ethnic diversity is tacitly agreed upon.

If I say, as I sometimes have, that I would love to organize an "ethnic caucus" within both the Democratic Party and the Republican Party, the common reaction is one of anxiety, distaste, and strained silence. But if I say, as I am learning to, that I would love to organize a "caucus of workingmen and women" in both parties, heads quickly nod in approval. Social class is, apparently, rational. Cultural background is, apparently, counter-rational.

Yet the odd political reality is that most Americans do not identify themselves in class terms. They respond to cultural symbols intimate to their ethnic history in America. Ethnicity is a "gut issue," even though it cannot be

mentioned. A wise political candidate does not, of course, speak to a longshoreman's local by calling its members Italian American and appealing to some supposed cultural solidarity. That would be a mistake. But if he speaks about those themes in the cultural tradition that confirm their own identity—themes like family, children, home, neighborhood, specific social aspirations, and grievances—they know he is with them: he does represent them. In order to be able to represent many constituencies, a representative has to be able to "pass over" into many cultural histories. He may never once make ethnicity explicit as a public theme; but, implicitly, he will be recognizing the daily realities of ethnicity and ethnic experience in the complex fabric of American social power.

According to one social myth, America is a "melting pot," and this myth is intended by many to be not merely descriptive but normative: the faster Americans—especially white ethnic Americans—"melt" into the British American pattern, the better. There is even a certain ranking according to the supposed degree of assimilation: Scotch Irish, Norwegians, Swedes, Germans, Swiss, Dutch, liberal or universalist Jews, the Irish, and on down the line to the less assimilated: Greeks, Yugoslavs, Hungarians, Central and East Europeans, Italians, Orthodox Jews, French Canadians, Portuguese, Latins and Spanish-speaking. . . . (The pattern almost exactly reflects the history and literature of England.).

Now it was one thing to be afraid of ethnicity in 1924, in confronting a first and second generation of immigrants. It is another thing to be afraid, in 1974, in confronting a third and fourth generation. Indeed, fears about a revival of ethnicity seem to be incompatible with conviction about how successful the "melting pot" has been. Fears about a "revival" of ethnicity confirm the fact that ethnicity is still a powerful reality in American life.

What, then, are the advantages and disadvantages in making this dangerous subject, this subterranean subject, explicit?

The disadvantages seem to be three. The first one on everyone's mind is that emphasis on ethnicity may work to the disadvantage of blacks. It may, it is said, become a legitimization of racism. It may "polarize" whites and blacks. Nothing could be further from the truth. Those who are concerned about the new ethnicity—Geno Baroni (Washington), Irving Levine (New York), Barbara Mikulski (Baltimore), Ralph Perrotta (New York), Steve Adubado (Newark), Otto Feinstein (Detroit), Stan Franczyk (Buffalo), Kenneth Kovach (Cleveland), Edward Marciniak (Chicago), and others—have given ample proof of their concern for the rights and opportunities of black Americans. Many got their start in the new ethnicity through their work among blacks. The overriding political perception among those concerned with the new ethnicity is that the harshness of life in the cities must be reduced by whites and blacks together, especially in working-class neighborhoods. Present social policies punish neighborhoods that integrate. Such neighborhoods should be rewarded and strengthened and guaranteed a long-range stability.

But fears about ethnicity require a further two-part response. Racism does not need ethnicity in order to be legitimated in America. It was quite well legitimated by Anglo-American culture, well before white ethnics arrived here in significant numbers, well before many white ethnics had ever met blacks. Indeed, there is some reason to believe that, while racism is an international phenomenon and found in all cultures, the British American and other Nordic peoples have a special emotional response to colored races. Not all European peoples respond to intermarriage, for example, with quite the emotional quality of the Anglo-Saxons. The French, the Spanish, the Italians, and the Slavs are not without their own forms of racism. But the felt quality of racism is different in different cultures. (It seems different among the North End Italians and the South Boston Irish of Boston, for example.)

In America, racism did not wait until the immigrants of 1880 and after began to arrive. Indeed, it is in precisely those parts of the country solely populated by British Americans that the conditions of blacks have been legally and institutionally least humane. In those parts of the country most heavily populated by white ethnics, the cultural symbols and the political muscle that have led to civil-rights and other legislation have received wide support. Liberal senators and congressmen elected by white ethnics—including the Kennedys—led the way. Even in 1972, both Hamtramck and Buffalo went for George McGovern. McGovern's share of the Slavic vote was fifty-two per cent. Nixon won the white Protestant vote by sixty-eight per cent.

It will be objected that white ethnic leaders like Frank Rizzo of Philadelphia, Ralph Perk of Cleveland, and others are signs of a new racism on the part of white ethnics in the Northern cities, of a retreat from support for blacks, and of a rising tide of anti-"crime" and anti-busing sentiment. The proponents of the new ethnicity perceive such developments as a product of liberal neglect and liberal divisiveness. The proponents of the new politics talk well of civil rights, equal opportunity, economic justice, and other beautiful themes. But the new politics, in distinguishing "legitimate" minorities (blacks, Chicanos, native Americans) from "less favored" minorities (Italians, Slavs, Orthodox Jews, Irish, etc.), has set up punitive and self-defeating mechanisms. The new politics has needlessly divided working-class blacks from working-class whites, in part by a romance (on television) with militance and flamboyance, in part by racial discrimination in favor of some against others, not because of need but because of color.

The second part of this response is that the politics of "the constituency of conscience" (as Michael Harrington, Eugene McCarthy, and others have called it)—the politics of the liberal, the educated, the enlightened—is less advantageous to blacks than is the politics of the new ethnicity. The new politics is less advantageous to blacks because it is obsessed with racial differences, and approaches these through the ineffectual lenses of guilt and moralism. Second, it is blind to cultural differences among blacks, as well as to cultural differences among whites; and sometimes these are significant. Third, it unconsciously but effectively keeps blacks in the position of a small racial minority outnumbered in the population ten to one.

By contrast, the new ethnicity notes many other significant differences besides those based upon race, and defines political and social problems in ways that unite diverse groups around common objectives. In Chicago, for example, neither Poles nor Italians are represented on the boards or in the executive suites of Chicago's top 105 corporations in a higher proportion than blacks or Latinos—all are of one per cent or less.* In Boston, neither white ethnics nor blacks desire busing, but this highly ideological instrument of social change is supported most by just those affluent liberals—in such suburbs as Brookline and Newton—whose children will not be involved.

The new ethnic politics would propose a strategy of social rewards—better garbage pickup, more heavily financed and orderly schools, long-range guarantees on home mortgages, easier access to federally insured home improvement loans, and other services—for neighborhoods that integrate. As a neighborhood moves from, say, a ten per cent population of blacks to twenty per-cent or more, integration should be regulated so that long-range community stability is guaranteed. It is better long-range policy to have a large number of neighborhoods integrated up to twenty or thirty per-cent than to encourage—even by inadvertence—a series of sudden flights and virtually total migrations. Institutional racism is a reality; the massive migration of blacks into a neighborhood does not bring with it social rewards but, almost exclusively, punishments.

There are other supposed disadvantages to emphasis upon ethnicity. Ethnicity, it is said, is a fundamentally counter-rational, primordial, uncontrollable social force; it leads to hatred and violence; it is the very enemy of enlightenment, rationality, and liberal politics. But this is to confuse nationalism or tribalism with cultural heritage. Because a man's name is Russell, or Ayer, or Flew, we would not wish to accuse him of tribalism on the ground that he found the Britons a uniquely civilized and clear-headed people, thought the Germans ponderous and mystic, the French philosophically romantic, etc. A little insular, we might conclude, but harmlessly ethnocentric. And if it is not necessarily tribalistic or unenlightened to read English literature in American schools, just possibly

*Cf. "The Representation of Poles, Italians, Latins, and Blacks in the Executive Suites of Chicago's Largest Corporations." The Institute of Urban Life, 820 North Michigan Avenue, Chicago, Illinois 60611.

it would be even more enlightened and even less tribalistic to make other literatures, germane to the heritage of other Americans, more accessible than they are.

The United States is, potentially, a multiculturally attuned society. The greatest number of immigrants in recent years arrives from Spanish-speaking and Asian nations. But the nation's cultural life, and its institutions of culture, are far from being sensitive to the varieties of the American people. Why should a cultural heritage not their own be imposed unilaterally upon newcomers? Would not genuine multicultural adaptation on the part of all be more cosmopolitan and humanistic? It would be quite significant in international affairs. The Americans would truly be a kind of prototype of planetary diversity.

Some claim that cultural institutions will be fragmented if every ethnic group in America clamors for attention. But the experience of the Illinois curriculum in ethnic studies suggests that no one school represents more than four or five ethnic groups (sometimes fewer) in significant density. With even modest adjustments in courses in history, literature, and the social sciences, material can be introduced that illuminates inherited patterns of family life, values, and preferences. The purpose for introducing multicultural materials is neither chauvinistic nor propagandistic but realistic. Education ought to illuminate what is happening in the self of each child.

What about the child of the mixed marriage, the child of *no* ethnic heritage—the child of the melting pot? So much in the present curriculum already supports such a child that the only possible shock to arise from multicultural materials would appear to be a beneficial one: not all others in America are like him (her), and that diversity, as well as homogenization, has a place in America.

The practical agenda that faces proponents of the new ethnicity is vast, indeed. At the heights of American economic and social power, there is not yet much of a melting pot. Significant ethnic diversity is manifested in the proportion of each group studying in universities, on faculties, in the professions, on boards of directors, among the creators of public social symbols, and the like. In patterns of home ownership, family income, work patterns, care for the aged, political activism, authoritarianism, individualism, and matters of ultimate concern, group differences are remarkable. About all these things, more information is surely needed. Appropriate social policies need to be hypothesized, tried, and evaluated.

Ethnic diversity in the United States persists in the consciousness of individuals, in their perceptions, preferences, behavior, even while mass production and mass communications homogenize our outward appearances. Some regard such persistence as a personal failure; they would prefer to "transcend" their origins, or perhaps they believe that they have. Here two questions arise. What cultural connection do they have with their brothers and sisters still back in Montgomery, or Wheeling, or Skokie, or Pawtucket? Second, has their personal assimilation introduced into the great American superculture fresh streams of image, myth, symbol, and style of intellectual life? Has anything distinctively their own—formed in them by a history longer than a thousand years—been added to the common wisdom?

The new ethnicity does not stand for the Balkanization of America. It stands for a true, real, multicultural cosmopolitanism. It points toward a common culture truly altered by each new infusion of diversity. Until now, the common culture has been relatively resistant to internal transformation; it has not so much arisen from the hearts of all as been imposed; the melting pot has had only a single recipe. That is why at present the common culture seems to have become discredited, shattered, unenforceable. Its cocoon has broken. Struggling to be born is a creature of multicultural beauty, dazzling, free, a higher and richer form of life. It was fashioned in the painful darkness of the melting pot and now, at the appointed time, it awakens.

Italian Americans as a Cognizable Racial Group

Dominic R. Massaro

Dominic Massaro is a Justice of the Supreme Court of New York. A "Grande Ufficiale della Repubblica Italiana," he is chairman emeritus of The Conference of Presidents of Major Italian-American Organizations. In 1991 his treatise, Cesare Beccaria—The Father of Criminal Justice: His Impact on Anglo-American Jurisprudence *(Prescia: International UP, 1991), garnered Italy's International Dorso Prize. Justice Massaro is the representative of the American Judges Association to the United Nations.*

Italian Americans are a cognizable racial group for purposes of the scope and application of civil rights laws. This view is confirmed by the sophistication of sociological definition and historical evidence, which is grounded in legal analysis and judicial interpretation. There are a number of citations, quotes, and references to which I will allude, including a limited amount of previous scholarship. Let me note at the onset that Italian Americans, more often than not, take umbrage at being defined as a minority group. Yet, a review of the relevant case law suggests that in no other manner can they hope for success in advancing legal claims that allege discrimination on the basis of national origin. Traditionally, civil rights legislation has provided virtually no protection against this form of discrimination. But the decision in *Scelsa v. the City University of New York* (CUNY) decided last November in Federal District Court in Manhattan—hereinafter referred to as *Scelsa*—accents the slow but steady erosion of the artificial distinction between "race" and "national origin" that has heretofore given rise to ethnic minorities, including Italian Americans, receiving "different treatment under the law, as written or applied."

As an aside, you should be aware of what lies behind my view of *Scelsa*. In my position [as] Human Rights Commissioner, and in response to a growing number of complaints, I threatened mandamus against CUNY in November 1971; that is, I mandated that it release a statistical breakdown of Americans of Italian descent employed throughout the university system. Twenty years later, while on the bench as a non-partisan choice, I

was invited to chair the Legislative Advisory Committee on Urban Public Higher Education. The Committee's central charge was to investigate and suggest redress for discrimination against Italian Americans at CUNY. Its final report, rendered 12 September 1991, contained a series of recommendations utilizing the special expertise of CUNY's Italian American Institute aimed at "underscor[ing] the University's commitment to the richness of diversity." Within a year, as the *Scelsa* Court observed that CUNY sought "to sever the outreach, counseling and research aspects of the Institute . . . [and] shunt aside its Director."

However, what I found particularly disturbing was that, despite two intervening decades, only negligible changes had been made to remedy the woeful underrepresentation of Italian Americans in the work force. The release of these earlier statistics became the underpinning for critical reportage, academic study, the designation of Italian Americans as an affirmative action category by CUNY (the so-called Kibbee Memorandum), and legislative inquiry. The latter culminated in public hearings and provided the backdrop for the establishment of the John D. Calandra Italian American Institute of CUNY in 1979.

From a purely legal perspective, *Scelsa* presents us with a precedent-making judicial grant of extraordinary relief to Italian Americans; not only did the case galvanize Italian-American organizations, it placed the Italian American Legal Defense and Higher Education Fund that handled the action in the forefront of civil rights activity. By its very nature, injunctive relief is an extraordinary remedy; it is grounded in equity; that is, it is responsive to the demands of justice and right conscience. The manner in which it was granted and the fact that it was granted by the *Scelsa* Court is significant. A colleague stated it rather succinctly; namely, that the decision "is a delight to those who are sympathetic to the plaintiffs' position and a nightmare to those favoring the defendants."

The petitioner, Dr. Joseph V. Scelsa, filed the action in both an individual and representative capacity (as director of the Calandra Institute). As dual plaintiff, he sought to bar CUNY from accomplishing three things: (1) "from employment discrimination against Italian Americans";

(2) "from relocating the Institute and transferring its operations to several different units of CUNY"; and (3) from removing him as the Institute's director. At the heart of his brief was the averment of discrimination in employment on the basis of national origin. The statutory prohibition against this type of discrimination is specifically proscribed by Title VII of the Civil Rights Act of 1964. Notwithstanding, the prohibition has been largely ignored by the courts and rarely used with success by plaintiffs seeking redress on this ground.

The *Scelsa* Court granted all three requests (or prayers as we say) by way of a preliminary injunction *pendente lite;* that is, pending trial, it barred CUNY from acting so as to prevent the further perpetration of a perceived wrong(s) until such time as the underlying issues are resolved. It concluded that the plaintiffs (Dr. Scelsa and the Institute) had "shown a balance of hardships tipping decidedly in their favor" and "irreparable harm" would otherwise follow. Significantly, the Court allowed Dr. Scelsa, equating his position as director of the Calandra Institute with representation of the Italian-American community of New York City, to cross the litigation threshold to test the merits of the case. In doing so, the Court relied not only on the so-called "disparate impact" theory of Title VII, wherein a discriminatory effect may be shown vis-à-vis employment patterns, but, *sua sponte:* by its own initiative, it also invoked Section 1981 of the Civil Rights Act of 1866, our nation's first civil rights statute for jurisdictional purposes.

This Reconstruction era statute is far wider in scope than Title VII. It concerns the right to make and enforce both private and public contracts and provides broad federal remedies for the enjoyment of all benefits of a contractual relationship. The Court noted that "in grant-[ing injunctive] relief to which the party in whose favor it is rendered is entitled," it may do so on such grounds "even if the party has not [specifically] demanded such relief in the party's pleading." Section 1981 was not pleaded in the moving papers. But the Court raised CUNY's two-decade-old awareness of Italian-American nonrepresentation and the university's pledge(s) to address and seek to correct this imbalance to the level of a contractual relationship with the Italian-American community. It noted:

A Section 1981 violation may be established not only via presentation of evidence regarding defendant's affirmative acts but also by evidence regarding defendant's omission where defendant is under some duty to act. . . . The Court must find that CUNY's current policy represents either an attempt to renege on the promises of the past or, by denying that such promises were ever made or intended to be kept, a reaffirmation of the original findings of discrimination against an under-representation of Italian Americans that motivated the original Kibbee Memorandum. . . .

Cited by the *Scelsa* Court is a case entitled *St. Francis College v. Al-Khazraj,* which was decided by the United States Supreme Court five years earlier in 1987. This also

is significant. Due to the representative conferral granted to Dr. Scelsa because of the Calandra Institute's wider purposes, the citation espouses, on a stage even larger than employment, an opportunity for Italian Americans as a group to redress harms arising out of national origin discrimination. Discrimination on the basis of national origin has always been, and sadly continues to be, a destructive force in American society. As such, it is indistinguishable from racial discrimination. Notwithstanding, modern day civil rights legislation expressly prohibiting discrimination based on "race, color, religion, sex or national origin," has not been interpreted either administratively or judicially to afford protection to these victims of national origin discrimination. The clear and unambiguous language set forth in Title VII as advanced in *Scelsa* states that failure by an employer because of national origin "to hire . . . or otherwise to discriminate against any individual with respect to his compensation, terms, conditions, or privileges of employment" is an unlawful employment practice. Yet the Act has a history of selective enforcement and it would appear that claims of national origin discrimination—either dismissed on procedural grounds or on the merits—have met with failure. A review of the regulations charting compliance with Title VII reveal that, notwithstanding the clear reference to "national origin," redress has primarily been defined within the context of racial classification for governmental purposes. Neither racial minorities nor ethnic minorities (including Italian Americans) have "melted" into Anglo conformity. Sociologists generally agree that thus far in the American saga, "acculturation" and not "structural assimilation" has proven to be the norm; and the diversity inherent in "cultural pluralism" has persisted well into the third, even the fourth generation. Public policy misconception of the process continues to ignore this reality, and the legal definition of minority continues for practical purposes to be synonymous with skin color.

In light of this, no governmental compilation of ethnic data is either required or taken; thus, legal writers rightly contend that is all but impossible to prove the existence of discrimination based on national origin. Therefore, Italian Americans who are victims of discrimination must try to prove their case without the benefit of officially compiled statistics—an overwhelming task given essential Title VII procedural requirements. The need for statistical analysis in order to fulfill the initial legal burden of going forward to establish what we term a *prima facie* case was noted in *Scelsa;* nor did CUNY, despite good faith promises extracted in the 1970s to do so, maintain ongoing data on Italian-American recruitment and employment for affirmative action purposes. However, and in view of this failure, two statistical studies compiled by the plaintiff, Calandra Institute, were deemed "the best available evidence" by the Court. The *Scelsa* Court went further. By adopting the conception of race set forth in *St. Francis College* under the 1866 law, it eased the way toward addressing not only employment but an array of civil rights violations alleging national origin discrimination against Italian Americans by CUNY.

The Civil Rights Act of 1866 was an enabling statute for the Thirteenth Amendment. This post-Civil War enactment intended to confer the equality "enjoyed by white citizens" of the time—the white majoritarian Anglo or Nordic "race" then populating the country, the standard control group, if you will—upon all other persons and in all respects. The Supreme Court's decision in *St. Francis College*, relying on the 1866 Act, significantly expanded the definition of "race" for purposes that can find and have found expression in the modern day search for equal protection under the law by those claiming national origin discrimination.

In *St. Francis College*, the Court held that a white person may be protected from racial discrimination. It based its holding on a broad construction of the original intent of Section 1981 of the 1866 Act. Section 1981 of the Act states: "All Persons . . . shall have the same right . . . to make and enforce contracts . . . and to the full and equal benefit of all laws and proceedings. . . ." The Court rejected the counter argument that a Caucasian was barred from suing other Caucasians under the statute. Instead, relying heavily on the legislative history of Section 1981 and on the general conception of race during the nineteenth century when the statute was enacted, it observed:

> [It] may be that a variety of ethnic groups . . . are now considered to be within the Caucasian race. The understanding of "race" in the nineteenth century, however was different. Plainly, all those who might be deemed Caucasian today were not thought to be of the same race at the time Section 1981 became law.

In support of this reasoning, the Court examined two strands of evidence from the nineteenth century: dictionary and encyclopedia definitions of "race" and the legislative history of Section 1981. In considering nineteenth-century definitions of race, Webster's dictionary of 1877 proved insightful: "[t]he descendants of a common ancestor; a family, tribe, people or nation, believed or presumed to belong to the same stock." The Court also listed "races" found in nineteenth-century encyclopedias: the *Encyclopedia Americana* (1858) and the *Encyclopedia Britannica* (1878) that *inter alia* referred to "Italians" and various other ethnic "races." Similarly, a review of the legislative history of Section 1981 proved convincing to the Court. It too was "replete with references to the universality of its application"; that is, to all ethnic "races." This, combined with the nineteenth-century concept of race as illustrated by reference materials of the period, formed the foundation for the Court's holding:

> Based on the history of Section 1981, we have little trouble in concluding that Congress intended to protect from discrimination identifiable classes of persons who are subjected to intentional discrimination solely because of their ancestry or ethnic characteristics. Such discrimination is racial discrimination that Congress intended Sec-

tion 1981 to forbid, whether or not it would be classified as racial in terms of modern scientific theory.

The Court's opinion specifically rejected reliance on genetics and/or physical characteristics:

> It is clear from our holding that a distinctive physiognomy is not essential to qualify for Section 1981 protection.

In making this finding, the Court defined the word "race" in its sociological, perhaps sociopolitical, rather than biological sense. "Race" in the sociological sense considers the concept that people differ from each other not primarily because of physical attributes, but because of differences rooted in culture. A review of the legislative history of the Act reveals that its supporters intended that its protection be liberally construed, encompassing the civil liberties of all persons without distinction as between race and national origin. Interestingly, the Court's research disclosed that only in this century have "races" been divided physiognomically, that is, "Caucasoid," "Mongoloid" and "Negroid," footnoting that many modern biologists and anthropologists . . . criticize [these] classifications as arbitrary and of little use in understanding the viability of human beings."

The *Scelsa* Court found that "[d]iscrimination on the basis of national origin is encompassed within the scope of activities prohibited by Section 1981." Italian Americans have benefited from this revised standard on a number of occasions prior to *Scelsa*, although not with the same potential for a sweeping remedy. The District of Maine in *DeSalle v. Key Bank of Southern Maine* in 1988 was the first Court to hold that Italian Americans are an identifiable class entitled to maintain an action under Section 1981 for purposes of discrimination. In *DeSalle*, the plaintiff had sued his former employer, alleging breach of contract and violation of civil rights on the basis of his Italian heritage. In accordance with *St. Francis College*, the Court held that discrimination based on a plaintiffs ancestry was actionable as a civil rights claim under Section 1981. The Court highlighted the references in *St. Francis College* to various ethnic "races." It concluded:

> The definition of race in the nineteenth century, when the legislative sources for Section 1981 were enacted, differed from the definition prevalent today; not all Caucasians were considered of the same race. . . . Section 1981 was designed to protect identifiable classes of persons, such as Italo-Americans, "who are subjected to intentional discrimination solely because of their ancestry or ethnic characteristics. . . ."

In one of the few cases where a plaintiff prevailed on the merits is a 1989 national origin discrimination case. The Ninth Circuit, which is based in San Francisco, held in *Benigni v. City of Hemet* that Italian Americans are protected against discrimination for purposes of a companion Section 1982 of the 1866 Act, which concerns the right to hold property. The plaintiff, an owner of a restaurant, had obtained a jury verdict claiming that the defendant's police officers had discriminatorily harassed his business and customers forcing him to sell his business at a loss. The Court of appeals, in upholding the verdict, agreed:

> Elements of an intentional discrimination claim . . . are present in this case because the evidence tends to show the discriminatory effect of greater law enforcement activity at [the plaintiffs business] than at other bars, and the discriminatory intent of singling out Benigni based on his Italian ancestry.

The Court cited *St. Francis College* for the interrelated proposition: "targets of race discrimination for purposes of Section 1981 include groups that today are considered merely different ethnic or national groups.

In another context, the Supreme Court has ruled that peremptory challenges in jury selection may not be used to further racially discriminatory motives. Under existing case law, a defendant must establish that he is "a member of a cognizable racial group" to make a *prima facie* or initial showing of discriminatory peremptory challenges. In 1989, *United States v. Biaggi* treated the issue. A motion to set aside a verdict on the ground that the prosecution had used its peremptory challenges discriminatorily to exclude Italian Americans from the jury was brought. In his moment of defeat, Mario Biaggi, the senior United States Congressman from New York City, provided yet another service to an Italian-American constituency that extended well beyond the confines of his congressional district. Relying on characteristic Italian names ending in vowels to make the claim, it was argued that the prosecution had exercised certain peremptory challenges solely to strike potential Italian-American jurors. The Court held that Italian Americans constitute a "cognizable racial group" for purposes of raising objections to this form of challenge. The *Biaggi* decision followed two strands of reasoning: The first traced the meaning of "racially cognizable group"; the second traced the meaning of this term in light of *St. Francis College*. As to the first strand, the Court found:

> Italian Americans are "recognizable" and "distinct." and appear to have been "singled out for different treatment under the laws, as written or applied. . . ." Italian Americans share a common ancestry in Italy, a common cultural and religious heritage here and there, and they often still share a common language. They are identifiable, in part, by their characteristic last names. The Court takes judicial notice that Italian Americans are considered in this district to be a recognizable and distinct ethnic group, commonly identified by their last names and by their neighborhoods. These qualities are sufficient to render Italian Americans no less cognizable than the other groups who have already been recognized for equal protection purposes.

The Court referred to three criteria useful in finding Italian Americans a cognizable racial group. They "(1) are definable and limited by some clearly identifiable factor; (2) share a common thread of attitudes, ideas or experiences; and (3) share a community of interests, such that the group's interests cannot be adequately represented if the group is excluded from the jury selection process."

Limiting its holding to the Eastern District of New York, which is based in Brooklyn, the Court held that Italian Americans satisfy these criteria to make "a sufficient showing to categorize [themselves] as cognizable." Moreover, it provided a detailed and illuminating discussion of its reasons for taking judicial notice of Italian Americans' cognizability:

> These observable, distinguishable names constitute a clearly identifiable factor separating Italian Americans from most other ethnic groups. These names emanate from Italian ancestors who immigrated to this country and who constitute a discrete resource from which Italian-American heritage has been passed down.
>
> Italian Americans share a common experience and background in their links to Italian families, Italian culture, and Italian group loyalties, and often share the same religious and culinary practices. The Court takes judicial notice that Italians have been subject to stereotyping, invidious ethnic humor and discrimination. (" . . . Italians . . . continue to be excluded from executive, middle-management, and other job levels because of discrimination based upon their religion and/or national origin"). . . . Like any group recently emigrated from a cohesive nation, Italian Americans share numerous common *threads* of attitudes, ideas, and experiences, often including largely intertwined family relations in the country of origin. Finally, Italian Americans have a community of interest; they generally share certain cherished values received through generations of Italian civilization and religion, including values relevant to moral culpability. Across the board exclusion of this group could not but impair the representation of these interests in juries.

Having concluded that Italian Americans are a cognizable racial group, the Court recounted *St. Francis College's* review of the nineteenth-century scholarly definitions of race and the legislative history of the 1866 Act. As to this second strand of reasoning, it found that the [l]egislative history of post-Civil War statutes provides corroborative support for the view that, at that time, "races" included "immigrant groups" coming from each foreign nation and, further, "[i]t can therefore be confidently concluded that . . . *cognizable racial groups* include[s] a variety of ethnic and ancestral groups subject to intentional discrimination, including Italian Americans."

The *Biaggi* decision has since been cited with approval. Although the Court did accept the prosecution's racially neutral explanations for exercising the peremptory challenges, and denied the motion to set aside the guilty verdict, the decision is still crucial. It admirably recognizes discrimination against Italian Americans in various aspects of American society. Additionally, it highlights for us that as an ethnic group, "Italian Americans are also shielded by the [Fourteenth Amendment's] equal protection clause's prohibition against discrimination because of ancestry."

In sum, Section 1981 grounds for seeking relief in cases of national origin discrimination illustrate a definite trend; namely, an expanded equal protection jurisprudence where race can be and, in fact, has been equated with ethnicity, or national origin. The Section provides an effective vehicle where injustice or inequity prevails against ethnic minorities. Moreover, Section 1981 filings are neither limited to the employment arena nor burdened with detailed procedural requirements that are a prerequisite to filings under modern-day civil rights legislation. Ethnics who have suffered discrimination as a result of their national origin in any area, would be well served in seeking judicial solicitude by alleging discrimination based on "race" under this statute—either alone or in conjunction with other statutory remedies.

In seeking social justice where right or entitlement within a sphere of cultural pluralism is denied, servitude in any form is alien to the espousal of a philosophy based on mutual respect and tolerance for differences. Indeed, it has been argued that the theory of Anglo conformity is inherently discriminatory: it requires assimilation into a majoritarian culture and inferentially emarginates other legitimate forms of cultural expression. Section 1981 relief, as we have seen from a reading of *Scelsa,* provides a wide avenue to redress this form of coercion. At the very least, it should suffice to assist plaintiffs who allege national origin discrimination in crossing the litigation threshold to test the merits of their cause before the Courts.

WORK CITED

Scelsa v the City University of New York, 806 F.Supp. 1126 (S.D.N.Y., 1992).

St. Francis College v. Al-Kharaj, 481 U.S. 604 (1987).

DeSalle v Key Bank of Southern Maine, 685 F. Supp. 282 (D. Me., 1988).

Benigni v. City of Hemet, 879 F. 2d 472 (9th Cir., 1989).

United States v. Biaggi, 673 F. Supp. 96 (E.D.N.Y., 1989).

The Other and the Almost the Same

Paul Berman

Paul Berman is a fellow of the New York Institute for the Humanities. He writes frequently on current social issues. He is editor of Blacks and Jews: Alliances and Arguments *for which this article serves as introduction; it was adapted from an article that appeared in the* The New Yorker.

The striking thing was the intensity. Khalid Abdul Muhammad, the "representative" and "national assistant" of Minister Louis Farrakhan and the Nation of Islam, arrived at Kean College in Union, New Jersey, on November 29, 1993, and rays of zeal and hatred beamed from his mouth. His topic was a book published by the Nation of Islam called *The Secret Relationship Between Blacks and Jews*. The national assistant said that the Jews were "impostor Jews," demonic liars who rejected Jesus. He said to the Jews, "Jesus was right. You're nothing but liars. The Book of Revelation is right. You're from the synagogue of Satan."

Muhammad outlined a Jewish conspiracy over the millennia. The Jews crucified Jesus. They dispossessed the Palestinians. They exploited the Germans: "Everybody always talks about Hitler exterminating six million Jews. But don't nobody ever ask what did they do to Hitler. . . . They went in there, in Germany, the way they do everywhere they go, and they supplanted, they usurped. . . . They had undermined the very fabric of the society." In the United States, they took control of the Federal Reserve and the White House. And they persecuted the blacks. They dominated the slave trade. They conspired against such great black leaders as Jesus, Marcus Garvey, and, today, Farrakhan. They participated in the civil rights movement in order to exploit the blacks. They set Hollywood against the blacks. The Jews and the Arab slumlords are "sucking our blood in the black community." The Jews support apartheid. They "raped black women," he said. "that the Jews did. What they did against Nat Turner. It's all

in here"—in *The Secret Relationship Between Blacks and Jews*. But the worst is their lies—the lie of the Jews, which is, in a sense, their essence. The Jews— "the hook-nosed, bagel-eatin', lox-eatin'" Jews—are not in fact Jews. Muhammad addressed his black audience: "For you are the true Jew. You are the true Hebrew. You are the true ones who are in line with Bible prophecy and scripture, so teaches the Most Honorable Elijah Muhammad and the Honorable Minister Louis Farrakhan."

The speech was venomous but not inarticulate. It outlined a coherent theological interpretation of black suffering: blacks as the people of God against whom the synagogue of Satan has conspired. It was the kind of speech that, with that same language about blood-sucking and the crucifixion, the Christian knights and priests of the First Crusade might have given in A.D. 1095, on their way to slaughter the Jews in the ghettos of Europe. The audience at Kean College cheered— though a lone, brave black student, when given the chance to ask a question, politely but firmly likened the speech to Hitlerism.

Then came a national response. On the op-ed page of *The New York Times*, A. M. Rosenthal banged his fist and, along with him, Roger Wilkins and Bob Herbert. The famous ad that was placed by the Anti-Defamation League—the ad that quoted Muhammad's speech below the words "You Decide"—filled an entire page in the *Times* and ran in other papers, too.

The Senate voted 97 to 0 to condemn the Kean College speech. The Congressional Black Caucus, having recently announced a "covenant" with Minister

Farrakhan, had reason to be embarrassed, and the whole weight of the black political establishment seemed to fall on Farrakhan—at least for a moment. Jesse Jackson and a variety of other political leaders denounced anti-Semitism and called on Farrakhan to act. Farrakhan conferred with Representative Kweisi Mfume, the chairman of the Black Caucus, and then summoned a press conference and demoted Muhammad and chastised him, and praised his "truths." And once again rays of hysteria and hatred beamed outward to the world, this time on CNN. Farrakhan held up with approval *The Secret Relationship Between Blacks and Jews*. He said that "Talmudic scholars" had caused blacks to suffer "the mental anguish of believing that we are black because of some distinct curse." He outdid even his own national assistant by saying that 75 percent of the black slaves in the Old South were owned by . . . Jews! He was raving—our American Zhirinovsky—which did not prevent the National Association for the Advancement of Colored People from declaring itself "satisfied" with Farrakhan's statement. The NAACP's director of communications said the part about slave owners in the South "may have exaggerated the historical fact," but that it is "a matter for academics to debate."

The counter-response was another full-page ad in *The New York Times*, this time placed by People for the American Way. There was shouting on the television talk shows and consternation at the colleges where Farrakhan's national assistant had been scheduled to speak. Then another counter-response: Does the world get upset every time some white person unleashes a racist remark about blacks? There was the case of the Jewish comedian Jackie Mason, who managed to make slurs sound funny. There was the argument that demanding a denunciation of anti-Semitism from every black leader in sight was deeply unfair, and that a controversy that had begun with anti-Semitism had turned—so *Time* magazine argued—into "just another kind of bigotry," namely, anti-black racism. To which, in yet another counter-response, A. M. Rosenthal replied—But why go on?

The intensity was startling, but it was nothing new. The same sparks and flames have been shooting upward every few years for more than a quarter of a century. The anger and the arguments were no different during the 1968 schoolteachers' strike in New York City, or in 1979, when Andrew Young left Jimmy Carter's administration. The intensity was the same in 1984, when Jesse Jackson made his first run for the presidency and employed Farrakhan's military-looking Fruit of Islam as his personal bodyguards

and, that time, pointedly declined to repudiate Farrakhan and instead complained about Jewish persecution. It was the same in Crown Heights in 1991, and again in 1992, after the failure to convict anyone for the murder of a man who had been killed by a mob yelling "Get the Jew!"

Yet during all those years what, exactly, has the argument been about—apart from the words themselves? Have the Jews and the blacks been fighting all this time over political spoils? Not especially. Over economic interests? Some people think so, but economic competition between blacks and Jews is strictly marginal. Has it been a war over neighborhoods? Sometimes, but not consistently. Is it a war between parties, Republicans and Democrats? Or between liberalism and conservatism? Not even that, for at the end of the day the blacks and the Jews have trooped off to the polls and in one national election after another they have, more often than not, voted for the same candidates. So what is it—this fire that burns without logs and never goes out?

Demanding a denunciation of anti-Semitism from every black leader in sight was deemed unfair.

One of Freud's first French translators was a man named Jankélévitch, whose son, Vladimir, fought in the French Resistance during the Second World War, taught philosophy for many years at the Sorbonne, was active in the political left and, by the time he died in 1985, had never stopped complaining bitterly about anti-Semitism. He had encountered it in the ranks of the Resistance. In the year A.D. 3000, Jankélévitch said, people will still be shouting, "Dirty Jew!" And from these several experiences—the Freudian background, the political engagement, the spectacle of anti-Semitism popping up even on the left—he fashioned a theory about hatred and nationality.

His theory was a variation on Freud's idea about the "narcissism of minor differences." Hatred between peoples comes in two varieties, Jankélévitch said. Racism—this is a truism—is a hatred you might feel for people who are different from you: for "the other." But the second kind of hatred is something you might feel for people who, compared with you, are neither "other" nor "brother." It is hatred for the "almost the same." In Jankélévitch's idea, relations with the other tend to be chilly—which does not make the hatred any less murderous, given the wrong circumstances. But relations between people who are almost the same tend to be highly charged. He invoked a passage in *Moses and Monotheism* in which Freud observes that "racial intolerance finds stronger expression, strange to say, in regard to small differences than to fundamental ones."

Freud's examples of populations in that kind of relation include the North Germans and the South Germans, the English and the Scots, and the Spanish and the Portuguese, who have everything in common and can end up hating each other even so. In the 1990s anyone can point to the mass insanity in the former Yugoslavia, where the warring groups resemble one another so closely that most of us in the world beyond the Balkans cannot detect any differences at all. Why do tensions between people who are almost the same heat up into uncontrollable hatred? It is a matter of self-preservation.

Economic differences between blacks and Jews have increased since the days of bedbug Jewish tenement poverty.

To the person whose resemblance to you is close, yet who is not really your double, you might easily end up saying, "You are almost like me. The similarity between us is so plain that in the eyes of the world you are my brother. But, to speak honestly, you are not my brother. My identity, in relation to you, consists precisely of the ways in which I am different from you. Yet the more you resemble me the harder it is for anyone to see those crucial differences. Our resemblance threatens to obliterate everything that is special about me. So you are my false brother. I have no alternative but to hate you because by working up a rage against you I am defending everything that is unique about me."

Since emotional relations fall under the star of irrationality, people who are almost the same might flip-flop into loving one another, bedazzled by their wonderful point of commonality. Or they might sink into confusion about the intensity of their feelings. "When you are in a state of passion, you don't know if you love or if you hate, like spouses who can neither live together nor live apart," Jankélévitch said.

Does anything in that analysis apply to the predicament of blacks and Jews in America? Not on the face of things. The American Jews and the African Americans have never looked or sounded alike, and the difference in economic conditions has become ever more pronounced since the days of bedbug-Jewish-tenement poverty. As for the shared history of having someone's boot press on their vulnerable necks, this experience has taken such different forms for blacks and for Jews as to be barely comparable. Any important element of Jewish and black almost-sameness, if it existed at all, would have to lie in the zone of the invisible, which is to say the psychological, where all is murk.

Still, I think a fateful trace of such an element does exist, and can even be described, if only vaguely. Many populations have suffered catastrophic defeats; but not all defeats have the same result. The French, having been conquered by the Germans in the Second World War, were subjected to every terrible thing that Jankélévitch and his Resistance comrades worked to destroy; but, even so, the French could think back on their golden centuries of glory, and on that basis they could picture a future of renewed freedom and national self-confidence maybe a bit chastened.

But there is a second kind of defeat from which you do not really bounce back. The calamity lasts too long; it is overwhelming. People who have undergone that second kind of experience can no longer remember a previous state of healthy self-confidence, except, maybe, in versions that are mythological or religious; and their lack of pleasant secular memories is matched by a lack of any place on earth they can confidently regard as uniquely theirs; and their lack of geography is matched by an almost physical discomfort with their own bodies.

Instead of a happy history or a home or a comfortable feeling about themselves, they carry around a memory of their own catastrophe—their "enemy-memory," in Shelby Steele's phrase. They look back and they shudder, and nothing is to be done about it. They might wish sometimes that the old injuries would fade and leave them in peace. But, in another mood, they might discover a treasure in that old frightening enemy-memory of theirs, a spur to all sorts of inventiveness, maybe to hypercreativity or superoriginality—which makes giving up the enemy-memory all the more difficult to do.

Anyone who wants to see an example of that plight in Europe today can wander into the main squares of the cities of Central Europe and contemplate the shabby-looking Gypsies. The majority populations passing on the sidewalk treat the Gypsies with contempt, and the Gypsies glower and skulk and are frightening in return. Let us say a political miracle took place and the oppressed Gypsies suddenly basked in the same rights and esteem as the majority populations, and the doors of opportunity flew open, and the days of Gypsy oppression were over. Just how quickly would the remembered accusations of their enemies stop ringing in Gypsy ears?

Steele, in his book *The Content of Our Character*, reminds us of how much harm these old memories can do—how they can leave people trapped forever in the worst moments of a bygone past, like someone huddling in an air-raid shelter long after the real-life planes have gone away. Yet if you think about the Gypsies it is easy to imagine that the ancient wounds have long ago inscribed themselves in the collective character, and around those wounds have grown all kinds of idiosyncrasies and compensatory works of originality—in music and dance, for instance, just to cite what all the world acknowledged long ago as expressions of a wholly admirable Gypsy genius. Why would the Gypsies want to abandon that? Obviously, the sound and healthy thing would be to adapt their enemy-memory to purposes that are strictly constructive, and to find a way to rid themselves of the hangdog look and the outlaw trades, as the Gypsies have done in the more enlightened democratic countries. But we can suppose that the Gypsies' room for maneuver is not unlimited—unless they want to stop being Gypsies altogether, which is inconceivable.

In the case of American Jews, a miracle did take place merely by the act of their fleeing from the Old World to the New. The era when superstitious Christians peered into the European ghettoes and interpreted the poverty and the stooped Jewish shoulders and the pasty complexions as signs of divine guilt for the long-ago murder of Jesus—this era, for American Jews, slips into the past at a rate that has come to seem positively amusing. "What is the difference between the ILGWU and the American Psychiatric Association?" Alfred Kazin once asked. And answered, "One generation."

Yet such is the enemy-memory that both the good and the bad in American society keep the last sparks of remembrance from going out. The styles of Jewish New World success follow patterns that were established in the Old World ghettoes, and the successes themselves are fated now and then to call up, out of the creepier depths of Christian civilization, the old paranoid accusations about conspiracies and evil.

Even the fat-and-happiest of American Jews has to shudder at the spectacle, which is always taking place, of some eminent person, not only spokesmen of the Nation of Islam, standing up to give the ancient libels a fresh new airing. Then there is the news about the surviving Jewish communities in the Slavic and Muslim worlds and elsewhere, which is never exactly designed to calm American Jewish nerves. Not that many years ago, a large, previously all-but-unknown Jewish tribe was discovered to be living in Ethiopia. Need it be added that the tribe was on the brink of starving to death? And between the memories of the past and what can be seen of the Jewish present outside the happy circle of Western democracy the predicament of the American Jews becomes ever more anomalous.

The styles of New World Jewish success follow patterns established in Old World ghettoes.

For the driveway may be long and circular, and the living room carpet may be thick, but the enemy-memory does not fade—except among the handful of Jews who choose to escape Jewishness altogether. And from the perspective of that memory, to prattle on about kinship between American Jewry and African Americans seems not so outlandish after all. For anyone can see that, if the Gypsies are a tragic people and the Jews are another, the African Americans are still another: marked by spectacular defeats; marked, too, by continuing accusations about other than fully human qualities; marked, even—and here the African-American conundrum is classic—by the compensatory feats of supreme cultural brilliance, which all the world has had to acknowledge, and which make the sufferings and the successes almost inextricable. And the whole phenomenon is, from the perspective of Jewish memory, all too familiar.

It is true that to detect invisible similarities you have to peer through a lens capable of revealing them. In a slightly sentimental mood, some American Jews like to imagine that Judaism itself is their lens. That seems to me a dubious aim. If Judaism per se had any such power of insight, there would be two or three hundred years of black-Jewish alliances in the United States by now. But history—real history, not the conspiracy fiend's version, shows nothing of the sort. During slavery times—when Jews counted for half of one percent, or even less, of the American population—a small number of Jews participated in the slave trade, along with vastly larger numbers of Christians and Muslims; and a small number of other Jews participated in the abolitionist movement; and the Jews failed to distinguish themselves either as slavers or as anti-slavers. Alternatively, it is sometimes said that the European Holocaust is the Jewish lens—though the Holocaust explanation stumbles over the same problem of historical dates. Probably the first important moment in the black-Jewish alliance was the founding of the NAACP, in 1909, long before the Nazi era in Europe. Yet that date—not the exact year but the turn-of-the-century era—does point, I think, to the series of ideas and sentiments that finally allowed a large number of Jews to notice similarities between themselves and the blacks.

The emancipatory liberalism of American Jews took an infinity of forms in the twentieth century.

No one can feel a boot in the neck for long without dreaming of removing it; but only after the American and the French revolutions did the Old World Jews have the chance to dream along lines of real-life practicality. The Old World Jews had been oppressed by superstition and bigotry, by Christian and Muslim desires to organize society according to religious principles, and by the feudal idea that dynastic landowners should dominate society. So the new political alternative promoted rationalism and education—against prejudice and superstition. It promised democratic, secular sovereignty—against theocratic domination. And it promised individual rights, equal for all, to be enforced by law—against an exclusively religious or ethnic vision of society.

Enlightenment liberalism was the new idea, and it sliced neatly through the knotty complication of being an unloved minority in a majoritarian world. For the basic unit in the liberal idea was not the exclusive group but the individual person, which opened to the Jews the appealing possibility of taking their place at last as members of a self-selected majority; namely, the grand, all-embracing majority of free and equal individuals. The French Revolution brought these ideas into the open air, and the French and German Jews took them up, and the ideas began a steady eastward push into regions where Jews were more numerous and prejudices more ferocious. The stronger the prejudices and the larger the Jewish population, the more ardent was the enthusiasm with which the new ideas were embraced, until by the time the emancipatory message finally arrived in darkest Poland and the

czarist empire, it was received almost in the spirit of a religious conversion.

It was the late-nineteenth century by then, which was precisely when the mass emigration of Eastern European Jews got under way. Thus America's Jewish population grew in numbers and in poverty but also in ardor. And this new ardor for an emancipatory liberal vision of a better society now became, circa 1909, the lens through which some of the American Jews began to notice those oddest of their new fellow citizens, the ones with no rights in the land of rights, the victims of majority hatred and outrageous prejudices, their fellows in tragedy: the blacks.

The origin of the Jewish attitude in liberal philosophy accounts, I think, for several of the quirks and oddities of the black-Jewish alliance that now began, very slowly, to emerge. The sympathy for blacks that certain Jews began to feel was not, by and large, a product of personal contact or cultural affinity—except, maybe, in the racially integrated bohemia of jazz and a few other places. The Jews who typically came in contact with blacks during the early and middle twentieth century—the old-time southern Jews and, around the country, the Jewish employers of black workers, the not very rich Jewish housewives who hired black housekeepers and were famous for a lack of genteel courtesy, the landlords and the storekeepers who lingered in northern Jewish neighborhoods after black populations had replaced the Jews—might feel no particular sympathy for the African-American cause. They might even be a little hostile, as a result of irritating face-to-face encounters or in conformity with mainstream American culture. Richard Wright drew quite a few Jewish portraits from the 1920s and 1930s in his autobiography, *Black Boy*, and the good, the bad, and the ugly were all represented.

When the Jews did sympathize, it was mostly as a result of abstract political reflection, and the people who indulged in the abstract reflection were not always in a rush to proclaim their own Jewishness. The emancipatory liberalism of the American Jews took an infinity of forms in the twentieth century, and only some of these movements flew a Jewish flag. Many Jews were more likely to proclaim a doctrine of purer universalism and to relegate Jewishness to the sphere of private life, or perhaps to the sphere of things to abolished some day, along with every other threat to village atheism. From the perspective of people with the universalist idea, humanism and liberalism, not what they conceived of as Jewishness, brought them to the cause of African America. There is an old and slightly peculiar Jewish custom of rebelling against

Jewishness by identifying with the most marginal of all possible groups, so as to rebel and still not assimilate into the mainstream; and this, too, played its part in attracting Jews to the black cause. A black person who judged from his own experience with Jewish storekeepers and with abstractly motivated civil rights supporters, who did not call themselves Jews, might easily suppose that Jewish support for black causes was, even in the mid-century heyday of the black-Jewish alliance, either spotty in the extreme or mostly a matter of elite arrangements by a handful of lawyers—and, in either case, not a large and popular tendency. That was how Jewish support did, in fact, begin.

The participation of a few Jews in helping to organize the NAACP, the devotion of some Jewish philanthropies to black education (which by the 1930s was benefiting up to 40 percent of southern black schoolchildren), the fraternal relations beginning in the 1920s between some top lawyers of the American Jewish Committee and of the NAACP—those were important steps, but they were taken by only a handful of people.

Support for black causes from the socialist party and its offshoots, during the years when socialism enjoyed a lot of popularity among poor immigrant Jews, had a bit more sidewalk visibility. Still, socialist friendliness to the black cause had its ups and downs. As for the communists, their own support for black causes, eager and important though it proved to be, was no end of peculiar. Even to mention communism among the currents of Jewish emancipatory liberalism may seem odd—except that, of course, a percentage of American Jews did, in the confusions of the Great Depression, turn to communism out of the same impulses that led a larger percentage to turn to movements that were democratic. And if out of the socialist and the communist movements, a genuine feeling for racial egalitarianism did emerge, and managed to survive the collapse of both parties into tiny sects, such that quite a few of the white liberal volunteers in the 1950s and 1960s heyday of the civil rights movement were actually Jews with backgrounds in the left-wing parties—even so, quirks and inconsistencies survived as well.

What were some of these peculiarities? Sometimes a Jewish snobbism played a part. One handsome check to the NAACP and a proper snob could look down forever on his ordinary American neighbors. It was possible to support black causes out of feelings that had more to do with Jewish origins than with black realities—out of a need to justify a bristly militant liberalism that no longer seemed to make much sense in relation to American Jewish causes.

The confusing quality of feeling oneself oppressed and poor yet anomalously burdened with prosperity sometimes led the more addled grandchildren of Polish and Russian peddler Jews to stand up and announce support for blacks on the basis of a largely imagined Jewish guilt. Jewish cynics who never did express much interest in black causes looked at this heap of contradictory impulses and were beside themselves with scorn. How sappy were the Jewish liberals, how softhearted and daft!

It was almost as if to be Jewish and liberal was, by definition, to fly a flag for black America.

Yet, for all these many twists and inconsistencies (and I could go on listing them, in a spirit of ethnic masochism), some aspect of that sympathy for black causes was authentic, and the aspect went on swelling, until the sentiments that had begun as spotty and unreliable and peculiar had become by the 1940s and 1950s a genuine popular enthusiasm among the large percentage of American Jews who considered themselves liberals. It was almost as if to be Jewish and liberal was, by definition, to fly a flag for black America—as if to embark on dangerous Freedom Rides into the Deep South were to live out a supremely Jewish sense of moral action. Jews accounted for almost two-thirds of the white volunteers who went south for Freedom Summer in 1964. Among the people who lacked that kind of physical courage, there was always the possibility of contributing money. Between half and three quarters of the money raised by the civil rights organizations at the height of the movement came from Jewish contributors, which is striking, considering that Jews made up by then less than 3 percent of the American population.

It was a matter of one population's recognizing another. The liberal Jew said to the black, in effect, "Among all the elements of American society, it is you who are most like me. The similarity between us is so plain that in my own eyes, if not in the eyes of the world, you are my brother. Slavery is Nazism; lynchings are pogroms and Jim Crow is czarist anti-Semitism, American style; Mississippi is Poland; bigotry is bigotry. I am with you! I understand your plight. I understand how it is a worse plight than most people can imagine. I understand it because of who I am, and who I am is someone who fights on behalf of people like you." There was passion in that statement. And if some kernel of practical self-interest lurked as well—if the higher-ups in the Jewish establishment always knew that people with sheets over their heads were no friends of Jewry, either, and blacks were a good ally to have that merely shows that idealism and self-interest need not be opposites, in spite of a cheap temptation to assume that they must be. Anyway, the Jewish young people who took up civil rights activism were not thinking of Jewish conditions. They were thinking of justice.

And the differences between the African Americans and the American Jews? The ones that matter, from a Jankélévitchian perspective, are not the big, obvious disparities but the little notes of disagreement, which, because they burrow within the similarities, are hardest to see. For, in dreaming of a better world, the African Americans likewise went tit for tat against their own oppression, and, since the horrors inflicted on the blacks resembled in many respects the horrors that had historically been inflicted on the Jews, the proposed black political alternatives naturally bore a resemblance to the liberalism of the Jews. But, just as the sufferings of the blacks were not, in fact, exactly those of the Jews, neither could the proposed alternatives be the same.

Black Americans had to fend against a society that was fundamentally liberal, except in connection with them.

African-American political thinking in the twentieth century is usually described as a series of mighty antinomies. Booker T. Washington stands against W.E.B. Du Bois, and Martin Luther King, Jr., against Malcolm X—which is interpreted to mean self-improvement versus the demand for rights, integration versus separatism, nonviolent protest versus what Malcolm coyly described as non-nonviolence. But deeper than all these, I think, lies a still mightier antinomy of African American political life, which is the conflict between emancipatory liberalism and the philosophy of global anti-imperialism, or Third Worldism.

By black emancipatory liberalism I mean the ideas of democratic socialists like A. Philip Randolph and Bayard Rustin, jurists like Thurgood Marshall, Christian activists like King—all of whom demanded that America live up to its liberal promise. The black liberals were always the people who won the

biggest victories for African Americans, and they were always the people who maintained the closest relations with the Jewish (and non-Jewish) liberals, fellow thinker to fellow thinker. Yet those same blacks always had to contend with a special American complexity, unlike anything in the experience of their Jewish counterparts. The Jews turned to liberalism as the negation of every feudal and theocratic thing that had historically kept them down. But the African Americans had to struggle against a society that was itself fundamentally liberal except in connection with them.

Out-and-out racism was always their main enemy. But in the land of Jefferson, the slave owner, racism comes dressed as often as not in a cloak of pieties. Slave masters did not necessarily defend bondage as such; they defended the democracy of states' rights. Segregationists did not necessarily defend Jim Crow as such; they defended an individual's right to choose his own associates. And so the black liberals faced a horrendous difficulty.

Liberalism in America ought in principle to have offered the blacks the same simple and cheering message that it always offered the Jews. But since in America the liberal words kept slipping away from their own obvious meaning, the black liberals were condemned to perform a task of excruciating subtlety: To bang the lectern in a demand for liberal justice while at the same time drawing surgical distinctions between true liberalism and the shoddy variant that was the African Americans' historic foe; to invoke what Jefferson should have said, and distinguish it from what he did say; to thunder while dissecting: a nearly impossible thing to do.

Third Worldism was simpler in every way. The idea of a worldwide revolution by the colonized and non-white populations against the European and white imperialists conveyed a good and encouraging message without having to make any delicate distinctions between the true and the shoddy. The message said, "You, the African Americans, are hopelessly outnumbered within the United States, and this unfortunate reality cannot be wished away by a lot of talk about liberalism and rights. But on a world scale you are no minority at all. The news for you is therefore encouraging. You are many, not few; strong, not weak; time will right your wrongs!"

It is true, for many years Third Worldist ideas among African Americans were mostly a cultural concept, with little prospect of becoming practical. Yet, just as the politics of Jewish America respond to developments abroad, so to the politics of African America, and, beginning with the anti-colonial revolutions after the Second World War, Third Worldism's practicality started to look more convincing.

Were Third Worldism and liberalism at odds with each other? You could look to the anti-colonial revolution as a way to achieve the liberal idea of democracy and universal individual rights, and be a liberal and a Third Worldist both. The skinny personage of Mahatma Gandhi incarnated the possibility. Yet liberalism and Third Worldism were not the same. Liberal movements in the Third World could stand up to European imperialism, but so could antiliberal movements. For the basic unit of the Third Worldist idea was not the individual but the group. It was the oppressed national entity, maybe the oppressed race. Dictators cannot fight for individual rights except by committing suicide, but they can fight splendidly on behalf of the group.

Anti-colonialism scored its victories around the world in the 1940s and 1950s and 1960s, and the Third Worldist inspiration did slip from the liberal to the authoritarian. Instead of Gandhi, there was Nasser; instead of individual rights, there were national rights. And, with these shifts going on in the Third World movement, the balance of argument at home in the United States between the black liberals and the black Third Worldists began to shift as well. In 1963, Bayard Rustin stood sufficiently central to African-American politics to serve as chief organizer of that year's historic March on Washington, but by the end of the decade the same person was deemed insufficiently black. And, whatever impact these developments had on African American circumstances as a whole, the effect on black-Jewish relations was extreme.

There was the matter of affirmative action, which emerged as a practical issue in the middle 1970s. The civil rights organizations came out in favor of affirmative action in order to give reality to the otherwise empty phrases about political equality which had just been adopted as national law—to forestall, in short, the traditional racial hypocrisy of American liberalism. But affirmative action was philosophically ambiguous. It could be supported on a pragmatic ground as a straightforward bit of social engineering, New Deal style. Or it could be interpreted to mean that people should be viewed primarily as members of groups, not as individuals.

The pragmatic interpretation ought to have been acceptable to the pure liberals, Jewish or otherwise. The second interpretation challenged liberalism at its core. But, because the ambiguity never did get cleared up, black activists could go on viewing the program as merely the proper next step for civil rights, regardless

of the philosophical intricacies, and could interpret the opposition to affirmative action on the part of certain (not all) leading Jewish groups as a sudden betrayal of the black cause. And the Jewish opponents of affirmative action could view the whole idea as a surprising and dangerous betrayal of liberalism. Affirmative action posed, at least in potential, a threat to all the civil rights achievements that had struck down the right to discriminate against Jews—most notably, the historic anti-Jewish quotas in the universities. So there was a lot of bad blood over affirmative action. And when the second great point of disagreement between a large number of blacks and Jews emerged—the argument over Zionism and the Palestinians—the bad blood turned worse.

The basic unit for the third-world idea was the group, not the individual.

In the early years after the Second World War, it was common to regard Israel as a mosquito version of the mammoth state created by Gandhi, distinguished by its democratic ideals and the previously miserable condition of its now liberated population. But, whereas India maintained its prestige, Israel was gradually redefined, within the ranks of the Third World movement, as a European-settler colony.

African Americans played no part in drawing up this new, unattractive image of Israel, and in the early years they displayed little interest in it, either. But in the 1960s the new image of Israel came to be accepted by revolutionaries around the world, and the American blacks who wanted to adhere to the Third Worldist idea really had no alternative but to accept at least some part of that view of Israel, and this was easy enough to do. In the rhetoric of Third World revolution, the African Americans figured among European imperialism's earliest victims, and the Palestinians among the latest. It was sometimes believed that Palestinian skin tone was darker than that of the Israeli Jews, as if in pigmental confirmation of the proposed new link between Palestinians and African Americans. And if any further sign of brotherhood between Palestinians and African Americans was needed there was the all too clear reality that, as the years wore on and the Arab boycott against Israel took hold, the old, warm relations between Israel and the newly independent countries of black Africa turned chilly, and one of the few African nations with which Israel did succeed in maintaining friendly exchanges was, of all unappealing countries, the land of apartheid. The link between Palestinians and African Americans (and between Israel and white South Africa) came to seem natural, not doctrinal.

The African American feeling of identification with the Palestinians cast a shadow over Jewish political motives. In Third Worldist eyes, any kind of principled or idealistic position on the Middle East had to mean support for the Palestinians against Israel. Yet, here were the same American Jews who claimed to support African American civil rights supporting Israel, too—quite as if Jewish liberalism were simply another version of the old American racial hypocrisy. Might not the Jewish support for black causes, given its seeming lack of idealism, conceal a deeper exploitation of blacks—or, if not exactly an exploitation, at least an appropriation of the black cause for other uses?

When a minority gains a bit of power, the majority will regard the achievement as an outrage against decency.

And, with one thing and another, a reasonable black person who began by subscribing to even the smallest portion of the Third Worldist logic could follow a chain of plausible analysis and conclude by saying to the liberal Jew, "You look like my brother—in some respects. You, too, have been persecuted and despised—though not much in this country. You have supported my cause somewhat. But if you were truly an idealist you would show enthusiasm for affirmative action here at home and for the Palestinians abroad—who are, in regard to racist oppression, my real brothers. Since you do not, your motives appear to be self-serving. And by advancing your interests while pretending to stand for the oppressed you are subtly undermining me. My own suffering has gone on for centuries with very little recognition from the world. Yet, whenever I speak up, you drown me out with your talk of Jewish suffering and your endless disquisitions on the benefits that you have bestowed on me. The more you speak about what we have in common, the harder it is for me to be heard. So you are my false brother. No, I don't hate you. But neither to I feel the ardor that you so strangely claim to feel for me. I am merely cool. Let us see coldly what my interests are, and what yours are, and if we happen to agree on some small point good."

From the perspective of Jewish liberalism, the argument over affirmative action was bad enough, but the black impulse to support the Palestinians was astonishing. Like the black Third Worldist, the Jewish liberal pictured his own doctrine as no doctrine at all but as simple reality. There might be much to complain about in Israeli policy. But to see Israel as a European colony and an agent of worldwide racism—no, that was inconceivable.

Imperialist? Israel was the self-defense of a tragic minority struggling to achieve a normal existence. White European? Jews were fleeing for their lives from hateful old Europe as well as from the Arab world, where Jewish skins were, by the way, not so light. An affliction to the Arabs? Zionism proposed to be the agricultural modernizer of the Middle East. Unsympathetic to black Africa? No country anywhere in the world had done as much for Africans as had Israel in airlifting the Ethiopian Jews to safety. Let the world's Christians and Muslims make even half that effort! But in the nature of things—so went the liberal-Jewish analysis—when an oppressed minority achieves a bit of power, majority populations everywhere will regard the achievement as an outrage to decency. And so it was when the oppressed Jews succeeded in winning for themselves their modest slice of the enormous region that had been ruled for so many centuries with such cruelty by the genuine imperialism of Christendom and Islam.

The contempt and enmity of the entire world pushed this new Jewish state into some of the ugliness that has always clung to the despised and the persecuted, and upon this ugliness all the bigotries of the ages had pounced, so that Israel in the age of anti-Zionism was now declared to be a kind of conspiracy for evil, just like the persecuted Jews in the past. Such was the liberal Jewish view.

And so the liberal Jews turned to the African Americans and said, in effect, "Naturally, we, the American Jews, understand that all over the world majority populations and the partisans of privilege will always look with contempt or outrage on Israel. But surely other peoples who are themselves tragic minorities will recognize in Israel their brother and will rally to its cause, and, weak as they may be in practical terms, will do everything they can to insure that Israel does not end up exterminated by its enemies, as could all too easily happen."

"Surely the African Americans will understand that Israel is the minority civil rights movement of the Middle East, and the terrorists and tyrants who oppose it are the majority enemies of justice. Surely the African Americans will understand how, just as poor whites in the American South are eager to attack the southern blacks, so are the poor Arabs in the Middle East eager to pounce on the Jews, and one can even sympathize with the poor Arabs, just as one can perhaps sympathize with the poor southern whites, to a degree. But surely we, the persecuted minorities, can appreciate each other's predicament. Surely the hearts of African Americans will beat for Israel!"

Those were the thoughts of the liberal Jews. And, of course, Bayard Rustin was not the only black liberal who did view Israel and the Jews in that way. But a sizable portion of black opinion shook its head in dissent. And at this the Jewish liberal felt almost dizzy with shock. It was the feeling that Jankélévitch defined as a "vertigo"—the vertigo felt by the Jews when they discovered that large parts of the left all over the world were suddenly shifting to an anti-Zionism that had always been the province of Arab monarchists and dictators and other traditional right-wingers. So the Jewish liberal said, in effect, "You, the African American, look like my brother, because you, too, have been spectacularly oppressed. But when you turn your eyes to the endangered minority population of the Middle East—the Jews—you see with the eyes of a majority oppressor. You are my false brother. And because you look like my brother but are actually my false brother you are undermining me. You are talking away my ability to summon the world's sympathy for the cause of an oppressed people."

"Your own sufferings have given you moral authority, but you are invoking this authority to counter my own. You are making other people think that I, a liberal, am instead merely a Jew, and that Jews are exactly what our enemies have always accused us of being—exploitative and tricky oppressors. You are helping to prepare the moral ground for what may someday turn out to be a new outbreak of anti-Semitic horror in the Middle East. And while you are doing that abroad you are undermining individual rights at home with your new notion of group rights. False brother, you are turning yourself into my enemy."

And now the real slide in relations between blacks and Jews, the avalanche, got under way—from both sides at once. There had always been a strain of folk anti-Semitism in African-American life. There had always been the Christian hostility to Judaism—a hostility that was white, not black, in its southern origins, yet that Richard Wright remembered being taught in a black Sunday school, too. But there was also the unique African-American theology from which Farrakhan's Nation of Islam has taken so many inspirations—the idea that African Americans are the Hebrews of the Bible, and that biblical epics of slavery

and redemption refer to blacks, not to whites. That was never a weak idea in African-American life. It was a beautiful idea; it was a reading of the Bible as living testimony to the present. How much hope and humanity must have clung to that idea in slavery times!

But, once the argument with the American Jews had begun, that ancient African-American theology blossomed into a conflict of identities beyond anything that Jankélévitch had described. For in the minds of the Nation of Islam, and perhaps among some Christians, too, the black was no longer saying to the Jew, "You appear to be my brother, but you are my false brother." The black was saying, "I am you, and you are an impostor. Your history is mine, not yours; and, insofar as people think that you are you, it is because you have stolen my identity. You are more than an enemy; you are a demon. Only Satan could do what you have done!"

The biblical epic of slavery and redemption was seen as referring to blacks not whites.

Something about those thoughts was touching, as well as despicable. There was a supreme degree of passion, as in the highest form of love: a feeling of complete identity, except in the form of hatred. And once those feelings were out in the open, and skilled orators were touring the college campuses bringing the message, and the idea was popping up in rap music—once that had happened, there was nothing to keep the wildest theories about the Jews from springing up from their ancient bed of myth, superstition, and theology.

The theories about Jews as a conspiracy to damage blacks via the slave trade and the movies, about evil Jewish doctors who infect blacks with AIDS (this was another theory that the Kean College speaker seemed to defend), about Jewish intentions to mis-educate black children through the public school system—all these gained a visibility they had never before enjoyed. And to combat those theories became, for anyone in the black community except a rigorous and consistent liberal, ever harder to do.

Even the great black majority who felt no hatred at all for Jews had to wonder if the wilder theories were really expressions of bigotry, as the liberals kept insisting. What is bigotry, after all, and whose definition should be followed? By a liberal definition, the views of a Farrakhan or a Leonard Jeffries are bizarre and reprehensible. But those same views are not at all bizarre or viewed as reprehensible in the intellectual atmosphere of Middle Eastern anti-Zionism.

Did not the United Nations itself declare that Zionism was in fact racism? So a cloud of Third Worldist confusion settled over these questions. Maybe the weird theories about Jewish evil were anti-Semitic, maybe not. But no one could doubt that to speak up against those theories was to break the solid front of black political protest, which some brave souls were always willing to do. But not every soul is brave. Or clear thinking. And so throughout the 1970s and 1980s the liberal voices within African America grew quieter, and the Third Worldist voices grew louder, and from within the third-worldist chorus could be heard the tones of old-fashioned prejudice; and prejudice led to prejudice, against Jews or against Asians; and the bigotries got ever more extreme, until a few lone loony voices were hitting the Hitlerian note, and the lone voices were authentically audible.

From within the Third World chorus could be heard the tones of old-fashioned prejudice.

"He was wickedly great," Farrakhan's national assistant said about Hitler—which was merely a quotation from Farrakhan himself. And whether that kind of language would excite a vigorous black response was hard to predict. For there had been an intellectual collapse. It was the collapse that made someone like Farrakhan's assistant a popular lecturer on the college campuses. It was, in the field of political thought, the equivalent of what had happened socially and culturally to the lower class in the poorest American ghettoes: a collapse into self-destruction and dangerousness, into hatred and self-hatred, which the black liberals were, at least for the moment, hard-pressed to restrain.

The Jewish version of the downhill slide was not exactly parallel. The growth of Jewish neoconservatism in the 1970s and 1980s was not itself an example of rightist extremism or of racist demagogy. Yet the Jewish neoconservatives did urge the liberal Jews to give up their pro-black sympathies. They endowed the Reagan coalition with a kind of intellectual sophistication that had never figured among the strengths of the southern California GOP. They became, in short, black America's political antagonists, and powerful ones, at that, which no important faction of Jewish

politics had been before. They never did win over a Jewish electoral majority. But they whittled away— from "above," let us say—at the old Jewish attitudes that had once done so much to support the African-American cause.

Another kind of whittling occurred from "below." Across the country, the modest neighborhoods of the working-class and lower-middle-class Jews turned out to be, of all the neighborhoods in a given city, some of the only districts that proved halfway receptive to black migration, for reasons that did not exclude the traditional liberalism of the old Jewish working class movements. So the blacks moved in, and the moment in which they moved was precisely the moment in which, for a thousand reasons having nothing to do with black-Jewish relations, the black lower class entered into its calamitous decline, and the Jewish poor and not so poor, the school teachers and the shopkeepers who remained behind, found themselves beset by the violence of the social disaster. And, between the neoconservative criticisms from "above" and the sidewalk experiences from "below," the old liberal ideas underwent the kind of silent evolution in which the words remain the same but the tone of voice turns cold. Then came the discovery about black anti-Semitism, and the experience was devastating.

Jews who still called themselves liberals ended up obsessing about black street crime, whether the crime statistics were up or down. Every phrase uttered by a black writer or leader on Jewish topics even when the phrase was intended to be friendly—came to feel like a dagger thrust. A litany of invidious comparison took the place of the older litany of sympathetic comparison. We got over our original poverty, went the new Jewish argument, and we took advantage of the public schools and colleges, and we flourished, and we are the cat's meow. Why aren't you? And in these ways the differences between the American Jews and the rest of the white population regarding race began to narrow, even if the narrowing was not expressed at the polls.

It is a little unfair to take the 1991 fighting in Crown Heights as a symbol of the larger dispute. The Lubavitcher Jews of Crown Heights are members of a peculiar sect that never did join in the mass Jewish embrace of liberal ideas, and the blacks of Crown Heights are in large numbers immigrants from the Caribbean with no background in the history of black and Jewish alliances in America. Still, a shocking scene is a shocking scene. A murderous black mob dashing through the streets shouting slogans in favor of Hitler is no small thing to contemplate. A mob of

Hasidic Jews marching around the neighborhood dressed in the costumes of eighteenth-century Poland, chanting (peacefully—but still) in Yiddish-inflected accents that blacks should go back to Africa: that does make a piquant tableau. The faces above bigotry's most vulnerable necks were howling bigotry's favorite phrases.

It was a Jankélévitchian moment. And, with rage and idiocy awash in the Brooklyn streets, blacks and Jews everywhere in America not just the crazies or the religious sectarians could say, as if in chorus, except with fingers pointed at each other's chests, "You look like an oppressed minority. But it is I who belong to the true minority. You are yourself part of the oppressive majority. It is I who deserve the sympathy of others. But it is you who receive it. Not only are you oppressing me; you are making it harder for the world to appreciate the cruelty that has historically been done to me. And, because my tragic history is a crucial part of who I am, you are denying me my recognition as a human being. You are turning me into nobody. The war between us is therefore total."

The first stage of the relation described by Jankélévitch was an acknowledgment of similarity, and the second stage was an acknowledgment that similarity contains a difference, thereby funneling a broad passion into a narrow spout of rancor. Now we enter a third stage, which turns out to follow Jankélévitch's analysis exactly, except that its causes have more to do with outer events than with inner dynamics. The revolutions of 1989/91 around the world were liberalism's greatest moment of triumph probably in all history. But triumph meant exhaustion. And these two factors—liberalism and fatigue— are almost guaranteed, as I see it, to transform the black-Jewish relation. Without Soviet backing, the air went out of the Third Worldist revolutionary idea in a matter of months.

The international pressures that made it more or less mandatory for African Americans, if they wanted to take their place within the Third World revolutionary movement, to endorse or, at least, abide the anti-Zionist cause disappeared almost overnight. The evolution in Jesse Jackson's descriptions of Zionism—from "a kind of poisonous weed" (in a speech to an American Palestinian group in 1980) to an estimable "liberation movement" (in a speech to the World Jewish Congress in 1992)—no doubt reflected a personal development, but man and zeitgeist have always been intertwined in the person of Jesse Jackson. And, with Third Worldism in defeat, the radical criticism of liberalism, not just on the question of Israel but on

all questions, lost its force. I do not question that outright anti-Semites will keep turning up among black campus lecturers or that the old animosities will linger among the sidewalk booksellers and among some of the less distinguished black studies departments, or that the chain of influence which descends from anti-Semitic professors through demagogic street activists to the young kids with knives in the poor neighborhoods will still be visible.

But there was a time when these things looked like a wave of the future. Today they seem like a strange misshapen thing left over from the past. Already, in the early 1990s, a new generation of liberal black intellectuals began to make itself heard. Here and there a liberal politician began to speak up a bit louder. There was reason to hope that liberalism was reviving, a little shakily, perhaps. But even the shakiest liberalism, if it goes on growing, will eventually allow larger numbers of African Americans to look on their old, frustrating Jewish allies of the past with less anger and prejudice in the future, if not in every case with warmth.

Socialism, as a worldwide movement, did not deliver universal emancipation.

Will liberalism among the American Jews similarly become a little stronger? Many regimes collapsed when the Soviet Union collapsed, and Jewish neoconservatism was among them. But then, among the American Jews, political emotions in the future are likely to remain a little cool. The twentieth century was not only the worst century in the history of the Jews but also, within the Jewish world, one of the most passionate centuries, and the passions have been expended chiefly on projects of emancipatory liberalism, not just for the Jews, that have proved to be less than successful. Socialism as a worldwide movement did not deliver universal emancipation. Communism turned out to be a fiasco in which the Jews themselves ended up prominent among the victims. In the Middle East, Zionism's loftiest dream was obliged to sink to the undreamy level of merely surviving, no matter what the price.

The effort of the Jewish liberals in the United States to perfect American democracy by supporting the cause of African Americans was just one more among these several universalist campaigns, and it ended with some success but also with a pathetic aspiration that went no further than the hope that anti-Semitism among blacks could be contained. And, in the wintry atmosphere that has followed on these failures, the old-fashioned ideas of emancipatory liberalism are not about to burst into renewed bloom among Jews in America or anywhere else, and the moral grandeur of the Jewish political movements of the twentieth century is not likely to be matched in the twenty-first. What, then, will be the ground for either hostility or fraternity between African Americans and American Jews in that century? I can guess. The blacks and the Jews will remember their old alliances and their old fights. They will forgive some old injuries, forget none.

But there is a little joke at the end of this story. Judaism allows divorce, and the mainstream black church, in its Protestant denominations, likewise permits it. But the relation between Jews and blacks does not allow divorce. The American Jews and the African Americans are who they are because of long centuries of a past that can be put to different uses but cannot be overcome. It was the past that made the blacks and the Jews almost the same, and the past has the singular inconvenience of never going away.

Jankélévitch knew this. His idea of almost-the-same populations pictured "spouses who can neither live together nor live apart." That is the situation today. Separate beds, separate rooms; the same house. Love, hatred; a wobbling back and forth from one to the other. A slightly irrational relation, as all emotional relations are irrational. An intensity that never quite evaporates—all of it destined to go on as long as polyglot America goes on.

The Arab-American MARKET

SUMMARY **Americans of Arab origin are more educated, younger, and more affluent than the average American. The vast majority are citizens, and they are likely to hold sales jobs and executive positions. Arab Americans are also likely to be entrepreneurs, so they are particularly important for business-to-business marketing.**

by Samia El-Badry

Samia El-Badry is president of International Demographic and Economic Associates (IDEA) of Austin, Texas.

Real Arab Americans don't fit into media stereotypes. They are people we know and respect, like consumer advocate Ralph Nader. Singer Paula Abdul and deejay Casey Kasem prove that Arab Americans can be as American as rock and roll. Heart surgeon Michael De Bakey and Heisman Trophy winner Doug Flutie place Arab Americans among our heroes. Secretary of Health Donna Shalala, Senate majority leader George Mitchell, and many other Arab Americans rank among our leaders.

The vast majority of Arab Americans are citizens. They are much like other Americans, except younger, more educated, more affluent, and more likely to own a business. The demographics of Arab Americans make them an important consumer market.

According to the Census Bureau's definition, Arab Americans are people who trace their ancestry to the northern African countries of Morocco, Tunisia, Algeria, Libya, Sudan, and Egypt, and the western Asian countries of Lebanon, occupied Palestine, Syria, Jordan, Iraq, Bahrain, Qatar, Oman, Saudi Arabia, Kuwait, United Arab Emirates, and Yemen. While these nations vary somewhat in their cultures and traditions, the common ground is an "Arabic heritage" and the Arabic language.

Arab Americans may be olive-skinned, white, or black. Some have blue eyes; others have brown. Some are Moslems, some are Christians, and a small share are Jews. They can dress in traditional attire, but most favor Western garb.

Arab immigration to the U.S. began in the late 19th century. Early arrivals were mostly Christians from Syria and Lebanon who established themselves as merchants. The U.S. then curbed immigration substantially between 1925 and 1948 when

> **Many postwar Arab immigrants attended Western schools, speak fluent English, and hold professional jobs.**

it suffered through a lengthy economic depression and world war.

Since World War II, Arab immigration has been characterized by people from capitalist classes, landed gentry, and influential urban families fleeing from countries where the leadership was overthrown. Many postwar immigrants were Palestinians displaced when Israel was established in 1948. Others were Egyptians whose land was taken by the Nasser regime, Syrians fleeing a country overthrown by revolutionaries, or Iraqi royalists escaping republican regimes. Many immigrants attended Western or western-

TOP TOWNS FOR
ARAB AMERICANS

Twenty metropolitan areas are home to 48 percent of Arab Americans.

(top-20 metropolitan areas for Arab Americans, and number and percent of total Arab-American population, 1990)

rank	metropolitan area	number	percent of all Arab Americans
1	Detroit, MI	61,065	7.0%
2	New York, NY	58,347	6.7
3	Los Angeles-Long Beach, CA	56,345	6.5
4	Washington, DC-MD-VA	28,148	3.2
5	Chicago, IL	26,770	3.1
6	Boston, MA	22,391	2.6
7	Anaheim-Santa Ana, CA	15,662	1.8
8	Bergen-Passaic, NJ	15,580	1.8
9	Houston, TX	15,389	1.8
10	Cleveland, OH	14,005	1.6
11	San Diego, CA	13,055	1.5
12	Pittsburgh, PA	12,141	1.4
13	San Francisco, CA	11,973	1.4
14	Miami-Hialeah, FL	11,344	1.3
15	Philadelphia, PA	10,345	1.2
16	Riverside-San Bernardino, CA	10,291	1.2
17	Nassau-Suffolk, NY	8,837	1.0
18	Oakland, CA	8,668	1.0
19	Minneapolis-St. Paul, MN-WI	8,155	0.9
20	Phoenix, AZ	7,719	0.9
	TOTAL U.S.	870,000	100.0%

Source: 1990 census

ARAB-AMERICAN
AFFLUENCE

In eight of the ten metros where they are most numerous, Arab Americans have high incomes.

(1989 median household income for Arab-American and all households, by top-ten metro areas by Arab-American population, 1990)

rank	metropolitan area	Arab-American median income	total median income
1	Washington, DC-MD-VA	$53,577	$46,884
2	Boston, MA	50,000	40,491
3	Bergen-Passaic, NJ	48,050	45,040
4	Los Angeles-Long Beach, CA	45,750	34,965
5	Cleveland, OH	39,011	30,560
6	Chicago, IL	38,505	35,265
7	Houston, TX	36,700	31,473
8	Anaheim-Santa Ana, CA	36,000	45,922
9	New York, NY	35,000	31,659
10	Detroit, MI	32,325	34,612
	TOTAL U.S.	$39,111	$30,056

Source: 1990 census

ized schools, spoke fluent English, and identified themselves as members of a professional class.

Immigration from the Middle East picked up dramatically in the 1960s. In fact, more than 75 percent of foreign-born Arab Americans in 1990 had immigrated after 1964, compared with 52 percent of the total foreign-born U.S. population. The largest share (44 percent) came to the U.S. between 1975 and 1980, compared with just 24 percent of all foreign-born persons. This recent flood is due in large part to the Immigration Act of 1965, which ended a quota system that favored immigrants from Europe. Most post-1965 Arab immigrants have been Moslems with even more education than their predecessors. However, a 1991 survey suggests that about half of Arab Americans identify themselves as Christians.

YOUNGER AND MORE EDUCATED

This article is based on the 1 percent Public Use Microdata Sample of the 1990 census. The sample is not large enough to look at Arabs by country of origin, but it does provide a broad look at the total Arab-American population.

The 1990 census found 870,000 Americans who list an Arab country among their top two ancestries. The census definition is not the only one, however, and it has not been consistent. Census records prior to 1920 lumped Arabs together with Turks, Armenians, and other non-Arabic-speaking people. Until recently, non-Syrian Asian Arabs were counted as "other Asians," while others were categorized as "other Africans." Palestinians, the main postwar group, were counted as refugees, Israelis, or nationals of their last country of residence. The current system doesn't capture everyone, either. Yvonne Haddad of the University of Massachusetts esti-

How many Arab Americans are there? The census counted 870,000, but some say 3 million.

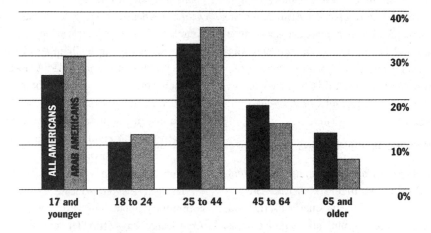

ARAB AMERICANS
ARE YOUNG...

Forty-eight percent of Arab Americans are aged 18 to 44, compared with 43 percent of all Americans.

(percent of Arab-American and U.S. population, by age, 1990)

AND
WELL-EDUCATED

Sixty-two percent of Arab Americans have been to college, compared with 45 percent of all Americans.

(percent of Arab-American and U.S. population aged 25 and older by educational attainment, 1990)

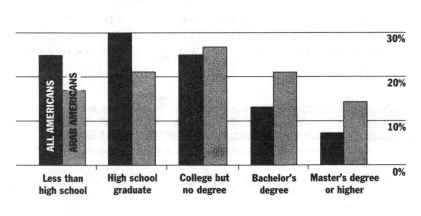

Source: 1990 census

grate. As a result, a large proportion of Arab Americans are in their childbearing years, and another large proportion are native-born children and teenagers.

As with many other minorities, Arab Americans are a geographically concentrated group. Over two-thirds live in ten states; one-third live in California, New York, and Michigan. They are also more likely than other Americans to live in metropolitan areas. Thirty-six percent of Arab Americans live in ten metros, led by Detroit, New York, and Los Angeles-Long Beach.

In general, Arab Americans are better-educated than the average American. The share who did not attend college is lower than average, and the share with master's degrees or higher is twice the average. Because a larger-than-average share of Arab Americans are highly educated people of working age, their work force rates are high. Eighty percent of Arab Americans

> **Eight in ten Arab Americans are employed; the national average is six in ten.**

aged 16 and older were employed in 1990, compared with 60 percent of all American adults.

ARAB-AMERICAN WORKERS

Sixty percent of Arab Americans work as executives, professionals, salespeople, administrative support, or service personnel, compared with 66 percent of the general American population. Arab Americans are more likely than average to work in sales and less likely to work in most other broad occupational categories, particularly administrative support and service jobs. Although many large companies are laying people off, Arab Americans may be better able to survive a changing economy. They are more likely than average to be entrepreneurs or self-employed (12 percent versus 7 percent).

Arab Americans hold different occupations in different cities. For example, 23 percent of those who live in Washington,

mates that if all 1990 census undercounts were corrected, the tally would run to more than 1 million Arab Americans.

Census data show that 82 percent of Arab Americans are U.S. citizens, and 63 percent were born in the U.S. Fifty-four percent of Arab Americans are men, compared with 49 percent of the total U.S.

population. This is partly due to the fact that men of all nationalities are more likely to immigrate first, while women tend to follow.

Arab Americans tend to be younger than the overall American population. Again, this is probably because younger people are more likely than older people to immi-

D.C. and Anaheim are executives, and 18 percent of those in Houston and Washington are professionals. Arab Americans are most likely to do sales work in Anaheim and Cleveland, while administrative support jobs are relatively more important in Bergen-Passaic, New Jersey, and New York City. Service jobs like education and health care are most important to Arab Americans in Cleveland and Boston.

In Detroit and Chicago, the above-mentioned mostly white-collar occupations only account for about half of Arab-American employment. In manufacturing-dominated Detroit, 16 percent of the Arab-American labor force works in precision, production, and craft occupations, or as machine operators and assemblers.

Only 35 percent of Arab Americans work in manufacturing, finance, and service industries, compared with 57 percent of all U.S. workers. Regardless of occupation, one in five Arab-American workers is engaged in the retail-trade industry, slightly higher than the 17 percent U.S. average. Of these, 29 percent work in eating and dining facilities, as everything from franchise managers to waiters. Eighteen percent work in grocery stores, 7 percent in department stores, and 6 percent in apparel and accessory outlets. Retail trade is the biggest employer of Arab Americans in every major metro except Boston—where a greater share are employed in health and educational services.

As occupation and industry vary, so does income. Among the ten metros with the most Arab Americans, median Arab-American household income in 1990 ranged from $32,300 in the Detroit metropolitan area to $53,600 in Washington, D.C. Median household income for all Arab-American households in 1990 stood at $39,100, compared with the U.S. average of $30,100.

Among the ten largest Arab-American metros, Arab Americans have above-average incomes in all but Detroit and Anaheim. Following D.C., the wealthiest Arab-American households are in Boston, Bergen-Passaic, and Los Angeles-Long Beach.

REACHING ARAB AMERICANS

Arab Americans are numerous, affluent, and often misunderstood. Like the gay population and Asian Americans, they suffer from stereotyping and negative press. Yet all are significant and distinct niche markets.

A glance through the advertising pages of Arab-American publications reveals a mix of specialized and mainstream products and services, such as medical and legal services, Middle Eastern foods, books, crafts, and jewelry, as well as "regular" videotapes, home electronics, travel, and restaurants. Like any other immigrant group, Arab Americans want to enjoy America's riches while preserving the important parts of their native culture.

The Arab-American community can be reached via Arabic-language radio, television, and print media, according to Abraham K. Osta, director of the Michigan American Arab Chamber of Commerce in Dearborn. "There must be six or seven TV stations broadcasting in Arabic in the Dearborn-Detroit area alone," he says. Arab-Net, an Arabic-language radio network, broadcasts in Detroit, Chicago, Los Angeles, Pittsburgh, and Washington.

The American Arab Chamber of Commerce provides a service called Arab-Link that helps businesses market to both Arab Americans and Arabs abroad. "We help companies devise marketing strategies, we help them formulate text and messages, we help them with translations, and we even help them buy media," says Osta.

"There is a need to educate the business community about how to deal with Arab Americans," says Osta. The media are the worst offenders when it comes to stereotyping Arab Americans, he says, but companies also make mistakes.

At the Chamber's 1993 annual banquet, one non-Arab guest surprised Osta by asking if women were permitted at this event. "The stereotype of Arab Americans says that women are not equal partners with men. It is simply not true. At any meeting we have, women comprise about half of the participants," he says.

Huntington Bank actively markets to Arab Americans. Almost the entire staff in

Arab Americans at Work

(percent employment in major institutions and top-five occupations for Arab Americans aged 18 and older for top-ten Arab-American metropolitan areas by population, 1990)

Retail trade is the biggest employer in nine of the top-ten metros for Arab Americans.

	Detroit, MI	New York, NY	Los Angeles-Long Beach, CA	Washington, DC-MD-VA	Chicago, IL	Boston, MA	Anaheim-Santa Ana, CA	Bergen-Passaic, NJ	Houston, TX	Cleveland, OH
INDUSTRY										
Manufacturing	9.8%	9.1%	13.2%	3.4%	14.5%	5.5%	10.1%	11.4%	7.7%	12.8%
Retail trade	25.1	19.6	16.7	18.3	16.5	20.2	26.7	17.0	16.8	23.9
Financial, insurance, and real estate	5.0	10.1	8.8	9.7	5.9	8.9	10.4	8.9	1.1	5.7
Health and educational services	7.2	13.0	9.3	11.1	8.3	21.2	3.1	7.6	12.3	15.2
Other services	5.5	6.4	4.9	10.1	4.8	6.1	3.8	3.9	10.3	2.9
TOP-FIVE OCCUPATIONS										
Executive/administrative/managerial	8.9%	15.4%	12.0%	22.9%	6.2%	17.6%	22.5%	14.9%	14.6%	7.4%
Professional specialty	6.8	11.1	14.8	18.0	10.5	14.7	6.5	13.4	18.2	12.5
Sales	15.2	14.9	16.7	13.3	14.5	11.8	23.8	10.6	14.7	19.9
Administrative support	12.3	15.2	11.8	13.3	12.9	12.6	15.0	15.6	9.1	9.9
Service (not household or protective)	7.2	7.3	5.0	5.2	5.4	9.9	2.9	7.2	7.8	11.7

Source: 1990 census

its East Dearborn branch speaks Arabic, according to Mary Short, vice president in charge of marketing at Huntington's headquarters in Troy. East Dearborn is an area heavily populated by people of Arabic descent, and the bank has successfully recruited many of its employees from the neighborhood. The bank advertises in Arabic-language publications and uses other media to reach its customers, but Short says that the best advertising is word-of-mouth recommendations from people who live and work nearby.

Last September, the Dearborn branch

Arab-Net broadcasts in Detroit, Chicago, Los Angeles, Pittsburgh, and Washington.

opened a small business service center in conjunction with Wayne State University. Wayne State has been working with minority business owners in other cities, but this new center represents its first outreach to the Arab-American community. Short says practically all of the branch's customers are self-employed and "doing a cash business."

Because Arab Americans are more likely than others to be entrepreneurs, business-to-business marketers would do well to learn more about this community. Last September, the American Arab Chamber of Commerce held a special conference for managers of Amoco Oil Company. "We talked about what to say and what not to say and gave an overview of generally acceptable behavior in the Arab-American community. Over 1,200 gas stations in the metro Detroit area are owned by Arab Americans. This is a large market for Shell, Amoco, Mobil, and all the others," says Osta.

The Chamber has recently released an *American Arab Directory*. It's the first publication to list Michigan businesses owned by Arab Americans or that cater to the Arab-American market. It also has a special export section that helps companies do business in the Middle East. After Canada and Mexico, the Middle East is Michigan's third largest export market.

Immigrants coming from Arab nations still represent less than 3 percent of all immigrants coming to the United States, but their numbers are growing. In 1992, more than 27,000 people from Arab nations immigrated to the United States— 68 percent more than those who came ten years earlier. These figures do not include Palestinians migrating from Israel or from the occupied territory. Among the 78,400 immigrants who arrived between 1990 and 1992, 17,500 are from Lebanon. That's more than one in every five recent Arab immigrants. People from Egypt (13,300) and Jordan (12,700) each account for about one in six Arab immigrants. Those coming from Syria (8,700) ranked fourth, accounting for one in nine recent arrivals. And Iraq (7,400) ranked fifth, making up less than one in ten immigrants. Although the order has changed somewhat, these same nations were also in the top five in 1982.

The fastest-growing Arab-immigrant group is from Sudan. While they accounted for only 675 immigrants in 1992, that's nearly nine times more than the number that arrived ten years earlier. The number of people coming from Qatar, Saudi Arabia, United Arab Emirates, and Yemen all grew more than fourfold between 1982 and 1992. But the largest of these rapidly growing segments, people from Yemen, accounted for just 2,100 immigrants in 1992. There were fewer than 600 immigrants from Saudi Arabia, fewer than 200 from the United Arab Emirates, and just 59 from Qatar. Other nations that have at least doubled the number of immigrants that they send to America include Algeria, Morocco, Tunisia, Bahrain, and Kuwait.

The economic and political instability of many Arab countries will spur continued growth in the Arab-American community. The newcomers will probably look much like their counterparts who are already here. Arab Americans are productive citizens, concentrated in a few geographic areas, and bound by a common heritage and language.

Businesses that want to reach Arab Americans should be aware that this is a sensitive market. They are tired of the negative press surrounding international issues. And they are tired of thoughtless portrayals in the media. Donald Bustany, president of the Los Angeles chapter of the American-Arab Anti-Discrimination Committee (ADC) told the *Dallas Morning News:* "Even with people of good faith, it takes awhile to turn attitudes around."

Several major mistakes were made in Disney's animated film *Aladdin,* according to the ADC. First of all, Aladdin sings a song about a "barbaric" country where he comes from. Secondly, while Aladdin and his Princess Jasmine speak like Americans, all the other Arabs speak with thick foreign accents. Third, the storefront signs in the mythical Arab land make no sense in Arabic or any other language. And finally, contrary to Islamic law, a guard threatens to cut off a young girl's hand for stealing food for a hungry child. Marketers can't afford to make these kinds of mistakes with these affluent, well-educated customers.

TAKING IT FURTHER

Samia El-Badry can be reached at P.O. Box 160728, Austin, TX 78716; telephone (512) 338-4011. The U.S. is home to a variety of Arab-American publications, including *Al-Wasat al-Arabi,* 3745 West Chapman Avenue, #206, Orange, CA 92668; telephone (714) 634-9588; *The Washington Report on Middle East Affairs,* Box 53062, Washington, DC 20009; telephone (800) 368-5788; and *ARAMCO WORLD,* 9009 West Loop South, Houston, TX 77096; telephone (713) 432-4000. To contact Arab-Net radio, telephone (301) 870-8700.

Several organizations provide information about Arabs, including Arab American Anti-Discrimination Committee, 4201 Connecticut Avenue, NW, Suite 500, Washington, DC 20009; telephone (202) 244-2990; Arab American Institute, 918 16th Street, NW, Suite 501, Washington, DC 20006; telephone (202) 429-9210; Arab Information Center, 747 Third Avenue, 35th Floor, New York, NY 10017; telephone (212) 838-8700; and the Michigan American Arab Chamber of Commerce, 2226 Garrison, Dearborn, MI 48124; telephone (313) 563-2222.

The Ethnic Factor: International Challenges for the 1990s

The process of better understanding the multiethnic character of America and the world involves the coordinated efforts of formal and informal education, which are influenced by public and private institutions and the community-based voluntary associations that are the building-blocks of society. This collection of articles addresses resistance to the challenges that are embedded in passionately held and politically potent traditions of ethnic opposition. The persistence of confusion, uncertainty, insensitivity, and violence toward and between ethnic groups is a sobering and stunning fact. Strategies for dealing with the tension and reality of bias are examined in this unit. Hatred and prejudice are frequently based on conscious manipulation of powerful images that profoundly shape personal and group identity. Exploring other societies is often a way of gaining fresh perspective on the American reality; differences and commonalities of the situations described in this unit are worth pondering.

Examination, for example, of the legacy of the civil rights laws crafted during the 1960s and the process of shaping a society grounded in exclusionary habits and institutions involves assessment on many levels—the social, the political, the ideological, and the economic. Even on the most basic level of public perception, most agree that progress has been made toward a society of equality and social justice, with increased hopes for decreased segregation in schools and neighborhoods. Yet disparities of these views among ethnic and racial groups indicate that uniformity and a shared sense of the past and present are not generally common. Attempting to overcome such gulfs of misunderstanding before they lead to more serious forms of conflict is among the great challenges of the present.

Novel approaches toward the peaceful reconciliation of conflict should be explored more thoroughly. For ex-

ample, unlike conflict between ethnic groups in the United States, conflict between the United States and Native Americans is regulated by treaties. The struggle over claims regarding the rights of nations and the interests of the U.S. government and its citizens is no longer at the margin of public affairs. Does the definition of this conflict as an issue of foreign and not domestic policy provide a meaningful distinction? Should the claims of ethnic groups in defense of culture, territory, and unique institutions be honored and protected by law and public policy?

Since the breakup of the Soviet empire, ethnicity has reoriented the international arena. New national claims as well as the revival of ancient antagonisms are fragmenting Europe. War, the systematic expression of conflict, and its aftermath are also occasions for the use and misuse of ethnically charged political rhetoric. The presence of a politically relevant past and the invocation of religious warrants for group conflict have indicated the need for new approaches to peacekeeping and educational strategies for meeting and transcending group differences. The critiques challenging multiculturalism, the educational controversy regarding which should be the dominant expressions of our human commonality, and the various values and virtues found in all ethnic traditions pose challenges for economically and socially turbulent times. Whether these moments are crises of growth or decline will be measured by a host of indicators. Which of these indicators are the most salient is, of course, another question, whose answer depends on our selective invocation of historical materials and ethnic symbols as guides for contemporary analysis.

Ethnic relations have erupted into warfare in Africa, where conflicts have shattered emerging states and thus challenged the hopeful myth of postcolonial renewal as well as the racial/ethnic myth of black solidarity. But Af-

rica's emerging countries are not alone: The Middle East, Central Europe, Canada, and the Balkans are additional venues of destructive conflict. Each of these simmering cauldrons—not melting pots—illustrates the stakes and consequences of unresolved conflict and distrust concerning land, religion, culture, leadership, and economic production and distribution. Each also shows the rewards and recognitions that fuel human passions, ambitions, and the will to dominate and to govern the affairs and destinies of various peoples that cohabit contiguous regions. Thus, the dramas of regional ethnic struggle and the growth of worldwide ethnic challenges to the constitution of human order itself are increasingly marked by episodes of blatant bigotry and intolerance. Fanatacism and zealotry impose themselves on the stage of history, which is rushing toward a new millennium. The threshold of hope that it promises for those who can recover and embrace the mystery of diversity waits to define the human condition in the twenty-first century.

Looking Ahead: Challenge Questions

International events frequently affect the United States. In what ways can such events affect ethnic populations?

Explain how the relationship of ethnic Americans to changes and challenges in the world arena provides strength or liability to American interests. Does conflict between ethnic interests and national interests present real or imaginary fears about our activities in international affairs? Explain.

How will increased immigration, technological advances, and a more competitive world market affect the relationships between ethnic groups?

Should the claims of ethnic groups in the United States in defense of culture, territory, and unique institutions be honored and protected by law and public policy?

Andrzej Szczypiorski: Poles and Germans

Interview: Agnieszka Englemann

The Polish author Andrzej Szczypiorski takes a close look at German-Polish history. The life and work of the 71-year-old Warsaw native have been shaped and influenced by traumatic experiences with Nazi Germany as well as a totalitarian Communist system.

Andrzej Szczypiorski has experienced the dark side of European history. Born in Warsaw in 1924, the son of a general secretary of the Social Democratic Party, he saw the Jewish ghetto in Warsaw go up in flames in 1943. One year later he fought in the Warsaw Uprising, after which he had to experience the horrors of the concentration camp at Sachsenhausen. "In my opinion, we are only alive when we are struggling," says this Polishman. But his struggle has not made him careworn. "Forbearance," he says, is his main character trait—but also his greatest failing.

Szczypiorski also put up resistance after the war. He was an unwelcome journalist under the Communist Polish regime, and, in 1968, "as the Communist powers became a fascist party also in theory," he distanced himself altogether from the political authorities. His most important book, "Mass for the Town of Arras" came from this period in time. The impetus for the work was the anti-Semitic campaign in Poland, which drove 20,000 Polish Jews to emigration. Szczypiorski transposed the events to the distant past of the French Middle Ages. Guilt and innocence, the situation and interrela-

tion of culprits, victims, and fellow travelers: these are his central themes. There is no article by or about this Polish author, no review of his work, no interview with him that does not bring up the question of the individual's dealing with totalitarian power.

Having joined the dissident movement, Szczypiorski was banned from publishing in the mid-1970s. His novels, essays, and stories could only appear in editions published underground or abroad. In December, 1981, Szczypiorski, who was co-organizer of the independent Congress of Polish Arts and member of the board of PEN, was interned at the Jaworza camp. His wife Ewa obtained his release six months later. Szczypiorski remained a member of the Solidarity movement and after the political changes in eastern Europe advanced to become an advisor on foreign affairs. He even spent two years in the senate, where he was an outstanding spokesman representing support for a decisively European, liberal democratic course.

Szczypiorski first drew greater attention in the West with the democratic breakthrough in eastern Europe. He became very popular in Germany in 1988 with his novel "The beautiful Mrs. Seiderman". The bestseller brought translations and publications of other works in its wake. True, he has retired from active politics, but his themes remain political: he is concerned above all with both the political malaise in a democratic Poland and the difficulties his country is having in finding direction. Another important topic for this

convinced European is Poland's path to integration within Europe, which in his opinion can only come about via Germany.

Szczypiorski, who works tirelessly for German-Polish dialogue, has been honored with numerous distinctions. In 1994, during official celebrations to mark the anniversary of German unity, he gave a much-noted address in Bremen. In January of this year, Andrzej Szczypiorski was distinguished with the highest honor that the Federal Republic can bestow, the Order of the Federal Republic of Germany, with Star, for his contribution over the years towards reconciliation between Germans and Poles. We spoke with the author in Warsaw.

Deutschland: Mr. Szczypiorski, how do you account for your great popularity in Germany?

Szczypiorski: I think that, to a certain degree, my books speak to the experience of German society. The imbroglios of the past between the Poles, the Germans, the Jews, and the Russians are also themes in my books. Perhaps it is interesting for Germans to look at how these imbroglios are seen from the perspective of Polish experience. In my book "Mass for the Town of Arras", I tried to depict the collective insanity in a society which is at the mercy of the pressure of ideological indoctrination. I wrote this book after the events in Poland of 1968, but of course it also refers, in no small way, to events in Nazi Germany. It also has something to do with

the events in the Communist world after 1945.

Deutschland: You recently received the Order of the Federal Republic of Germany. What does this honor mean to you?

Szczypiorski: I took this award as a sign of recognition; not for me, but vicariously for many Poles who in the past few years have worked for reconciliation with Germany. That the German nation acknowledged this fills me with great joy.

Deutschland: The course of your life predestined you to be the intellectual ambassador of Poland to Germany, and an advocate for Germany in Poland. Why did you opt for this role?

Szczypiorski: I did not take any deliberate decision in this direction. Life quite simply brought me to that point. If one can speak of any sort of conscious action taken on my part, then it should be seen within a certain context. As a very young person, in the Second World War, I was already convinced that not only the Germans were capable of atrocities. For example, I am of the view that the Holocaust, for which the Germans are to be blamed, was also dictated by the sordid dream Europe had been dreaming for 2,000 years. All of European Christendom is jointly responsible for the Holocaust, which was carried out by the Germans. In short, the atrocity, the fanaticism, the contempt for other people, thinking in totalitarian

From *Deutschland* magazine, April 1995, pp. 36-39. © 1995 by Frankfurter Societäts-Druckerei GmbH. Reprinted by permission of *Duetschland*, the magazine on politics, culture, business, and science.

categories, is a human and not only a German matter. Therefore, we must seek understanding between people. And in our own times it is once again the case that people in Europe are splitting themselves up into different peoples. We must and we should, whether we now want to or not, live with these peoples. And neither is it true that we always stood on a war footing with the Germans. We enjoyed long periods of fruitful and fervent cooperation. In other words, while not dividing up into nations, races, or groups, but trying only to see the individual person, I did something which was far from being my own invention, because it has been the task of literature since time immemorial. On the other hand, I was of the opinion, and still am, that we must somehow come to reconcile with and understand each other in order to go on living. What the Polish bishops did 25 years ago, for example, was a first important step. At that time, they wrote a letter to the German bishops, which said, in part: "We forgive, and ask for forgiveness." That was not only very Christian, it was also politically very clever. I try to make this a reality within the limited framework of possibilities open to me.

Deutschland: What does the fall of the Berlin Wall mean for Poland?

Szczypiorski: Poland is an occidental nation, a nation with Roman traditions. We belong to the west European family because of our Latin, Catholic tradition and centuries-long contacts. But geographically, we are in central Europe. But as far as our civilization is concerned, we belong to the West. The Berlin Wall created a situation in which we were cut off from the West. That is why the fall of the Wall means the opening up of the way to the West, the way to our "familial Europe." And that is also why

the fall of the Berlin Wall is a guarantee of Poland's independence. We are now the West, we are secure. In a situation in which the Germans are united and at the same time integrated into the rest of Europe, we, too, are integrating ourselves into the framework of Europe, which represents a political, economic, social, and psychological guarantee of our sovereignty both now, and over the coming years.

Deutschland: What can Poland and the other post-Communist states do to accelerate this process. Or are they just small players in all this entire complex process?

Szczypiorski: We are not small players. Over the course of the last six years, since the revolution, Poland has made an enormous leap in the direction of the West. The introduction of a democratic system and a free market was not a gift that the West gave us. We struggled for that ourselves, despite the small-mindedness and irresoluteness of the western world, which, because of fear, the Soviet Union had eating out of its hand. I remember the times when we were able to get passes and traveled to Bonn, Paris, New York, and London. People in those places thought we were crazy, because we wanted to destroy the status quo, because we wanted to oppose the Soviet Union. The Poles were the lunatics who ruined the West's good state of health. Nobody can tell us now, therefore, that we are passive. We made this revolution. Others also played major roles: Gorbachev, the Czechs, the Slovaks, the Hungarians, and there is no doubt about it, a certain role was played by the GDR. The West played practically no role at all in this entire process. Today we see the problems of integration in Europe. The powerful machinery of integration is beginning to falter, because the fear of the Soviet Union is no longer there. It

was this fear that held all the others together.

Deutschland: And how do the Polish view the reunified Germany, their western neighbor, today?

Szczypiorski: Germany now has obviously nothing in common with pre-war Germany. There are a few groups in Poland who still think about Germans in terms of clichés and stereotypes. The question of whether the Poles should be afraid of the Germans is one which always creeps into the debate. My answer is, no, the Poles are not afraid of the Germans. But this point is banal because the Poles are not afraid of anything or anyone, because in this regard they are a crazy people. But why should they be afraid? The Germans, who are integrating themselves into Europe, pose absolutely no threat whatsoever to their neighbors. Rather, the German government is the locomotive which is pulling the Polish in the direction of Europe – despite the many reservations of other west European partners. That is why I think that the maximal acceleration of the integration process should be one of the factors most intrinsically incorporated into a sensible Polish patriotism.

Deutschland: What is your general view on the near and distant future of Europe?

Szczypiorski: The vision of the near future is relatively simple. I hope that I will not be disappointed and I hope that I will experience it for myself. It is a vision of a Europe "under the one roof" of the European Union, to which Poles, Czechs, Slovaks, and Hungarians will also belong. I think that that can be realized within seven to ten years. This vision of Europe seems to me to be at hand, you only have to stretch out your arm to touch it. And the Europe of the distant future? I cannot really give an answer on that, because I have mis-

givings which are tied to the basic conflict of today's world – the North-South conflict, which the European Union is not solving, which it is not even occupied with at all.

Deutschland: You once said that history has so many faces that you cannot take them seriously. What do you mean by that?

Szczypiorski: That's simple. In every person's understanding, history depends on interpretations. As well as that, our relationship to the past is very selective. We take some factors into account, others we don't. As a result of this, the view of the past, the view of history of one's own people is always very subjective and dependent upon the experiences, the memory, the character, and the nature of each individual human being. On the other hand, life constantly compels us to make decisions, and it persistently pushes us to withstand the challenges it brings with it. For this reason, life is a hundred times more important than history.

Deutschland: In your books you propogate forgiveness. You believe in the good, even though you yourself have experienced evil. To what do you attribute this perspective?

Szczypiorski: That is why literature is there, to attenuate human fears. It should make people more tolerant. Hate is a feeling that destroys. Nothing comes from hate. Hate doesn't create anything. Only love is a creative feeling. The world came into existence out of love. But hate destroys not only that which I hate, it also takes its toll on me myself; it will burn me out, eat away at me, corrode and consume me; it will destroy me.

Deutschland: But how should people in everyday circumstances fight against the phenomenon of fanaticism?

Szczypiorski: There is one simple piece of advice: people should read books.

The Ends of History: Balkan Culture and Catastrophe

Thomas Butler

Thomas Butler is author of several books, including "Memory: History, Culture and the Mind," and "Monumenta Serbocroatica," a bilingual anthology of Serbian and Croatian texts.

Abuse of cultural memory—the manipulation of long-invalid past grievances to obtain present-day advantage—rules the day in the war-torn lands of Yugoslavia. Deliberate misreadings and misrepresentations of history are destroying the future in the Balkans.

The fundamental cause of Yugoslavia's terrible calamity is not just recent history, such as the infamous genocide by Croatians at the Jasenovac concentration camp during World War II. Nor is the cause rooted solely in the more distant chronicle of the Ottoman rule. Today's horrors are woven from strands of nothing less than the entire tapestry of history since the 6th-century Slavic invasion of the Balkans, with the subsequent division of Croats and Serbs between Catholicism and Orthodoxy and eventually Islam.

All these elements play a role in the minds of those destroying Bosnia. They are sick from history—from half-truths and ethnic prejudices passed from one generation to the next, through religion, political demagoguery, inflammatory tracts and even, through abuse of folk song and tales. More recently, the books of unscrupulous writers and the deliberately inaccurate speeches of unprincipled leaders have further contaminated the atmosphere.

Two years ago, at an international conference in Boston on cultural memory, I argued with an American scholar about the causes of the unfolding Yugoslav crisis. She felt that everything was traceable to 1941 and the Croatian killing of some 600,000 Serbs, Jews and gypsies at the concentration camp of Jasenovac. (Many of these Serbs were from the Krajina area of Croatia, which is now trying to merge with Serbia.) But I felt that the roots of the current conflict between Croats and Serbs ran much deeper, at least as far back as the schism between the Catholic and Orthodox Churches in 1054 A.D.

It appears we were both right. She, in that the immediate cause of the fighting between Serbs and Croats in Croatia was Serbian fear of another Jasenovac. When Franjo Tudjman, author of a book stating that Serbian losses were only one-tenth what they claimed, became president of Croatia, Serbs in Croatia saw this as a sign that they were not to expect fair and unbiased treatment in the new state. Tudjman did not offer them concrete guarantees that would have allayed their worries.

Although it was the Serbs in Krajina who provoked the outbreak of hostilities, over the long run the fighting between Serbs and Croats in Croatia and Slavonia has been fueled by culturally derived feelings of "otherness" between Orthodox Serbs and Catholic Croats. Orthodox-Catholic prejudice is a powerful force. A few years ago, I visited the Orthodox monastery of Iviron on Mount Athos, Greece. While I was attending the early morning liturgy, a monk approached and asked whether I was Orthodox or Catholic. When I replied "Catholic," he told me to "go outside and pray."

The Greek Orthodox Church, like Rome, has a long memory: In the young monk's mind, I was excommunicated. The Schism in 1054 A.D. and the plundering of Constantinople in 1204 A.D. by the Fourth Crusade are alive in the Orthodox mind of today and continue to affect Orthodox–Catholic relations, including those between Serbs and Croats. Some of the doctrinal differences between the two churches seem ludicrous today. Take for example the "filioque" controversy: according to the Roman Catholic Creed, the Holy Spirit "proceeds from the Father and the Son" (*et filioque procedit*), whereas the Orthodox Church claims that according to the original Nicene Creed (325 A.D.), the Spirit proceeds from the Father alone.

The difference had already threatened to split the Church in the 9th century, with pope and patriarch hurling anathemas at each other. This is not to say that Serbs feel justified in shelling Dubrovnik because they believe its inhabitants are schismatics, but rather that they are affected in their relations with the "Latini" by negative feelings of "otherness," the residue of doctrinal disputes of long ago. The sense of "otherness" is further exacerbated by the fact that the two peoples were ruled by different and opposing empires: the Croats by the Austro-Hungarian empire and the Serbs by the Ottoman.

As for Croatian and Serbian relations with Bosnia's Muslim population (who are actually Slavs), no one will deny that the Croats have the more harmonious dealings with their Islamic brethren. This may be because they see the Muslims as heretics, who can be saved through baptism. In fact, Tudjman was photographed a year ago, smiling benignly at the baptism of a group of Muslim children. This drove Bosnia's Muslim president, Alija Izetbegovic, into such a frenzy that he actually made a short-lived treaty with his arch-enemy, Serbia.

Serbs, on the other hand, take a different stance toward Muslims: They see them as *traitors,* as well as heretics. Scratch a Muslim, they believe, and you have a Serb whose ancestor went over to the Ottoman side four or five hundred years ago, in order to keep his land. The late novelist Mesa Selimovic, who was born and raised a Muslim but considered himself a Serbian writer, referred to himself and other Yugoslav Muslims as "renegades" in his autobiographical "Memories."

In a later edition he mentions that the lexicographer Abdulah Skaljic, a representative of the Reis-ul Ulema, the highest Islamic religious authority in Bosnia, objected to his use of the term "renegade" for those who had "taken the right road and the right faith."

(Actually, the adoption of the religion of the conqueror in order to maintain certain privileges such as land-holding was common not only to the Ottoman Empire. A similar situation existed in Ireland, where one or two brothers, with the agreement of the rest of the family, sometimes joined the Protestant church in order to preserve the family's land.)

In the Bosnian case, the situation is further complicated by the fact that great numbers of those who converted to Islam were members of a heretical Christian sect called "Bogomils" ["pleasing to God"]. They were threatened by the Inquisition, and some historians have written that they invited the Ottomans in (1463), rather than face invasion by a Hungarian army blessed by the pope.

From all this came the saying: "Bosnia fell with a whisper." It wasn't until the rise of nationalism in the last decades of the 18th century that these converts to Islam and their descendants were branded "traitors." Particularly in Yugoslavia, much of the bloodshed of the 20th century may be traced to such reinterpretations of cultural memory by 19th-century historians.

The Serbian "purification" (ciscenje) of Bosnian villages of Muslim inhabitants reminds me of a similar action, described by the 19th century Montenegrin poet Njegos in his "Mountain Wreath." He sings of the events leading up to an early 18th-century extermination of Muslims in Montenegro, directed by Danilo, the Orthodox prince bishop of Montenegro, and motivated by fear of contamination from within. The same paranoia may be found in Serbia today.

Even 20 years ago, long before today's civil war, such views were common. My Belgrade landlady told me then that the Albanians (Shiptars), who are mainly Muslim, were lighting bonfires at night on the hills around the city, signaling to each other. She voiced fear of their high birthrate—warning that they would inundate the Serbs, as they already have done in Kosovo, the "holy ground" of the Serbian medieval empire.

In recent years, I heard worried talk of how Islamic fundamentalism was sweeping Bosnia and of Saudi Arabian money being used to rebuild mosques and Muslim schools. I used to smile at such stories, as indicative of excessive Serbian anxiety about Muslims. But I was wrong. Obviously, Serbian extremists played on fears of a revived Islamic state in Bosnia as a way to spur their savage war. The fact that the Bosnian president, Izetbegovic, was the author of the Islamic Declaration, a 1970 tract calling for the moral renewal of Islam throughout the world—for which he was jailed by the Yugoslav communist government in the early 1980s—hardly reassured the Serbs.

This oppressive preoccupation with Muslims—Albanians in particular—is vividly illustrated in the war diary of a Serbian reservist from Valjevo, named Aleksandar Jasovic, published in a Belgrade journal this year. Jasovic served as a medic in the Serbian ranks in the fighting for Vukovar in Croatia in 1991. While his battery was shelling the Croats in the northeast, he recounts in his diary, he actually was preoccupied with fears about Kosovo far to the south—the cradle of the Serbian medieval kingdom and the scene of the Serbs' fateful loss to the Turks in 1389.

He writes of the Albanian Muslims, who because of a high birthrate and immigration from neighboring Albania now are a huge majority in Kosovo: "Their Sarajevo mother supports them!" Westerners may find the phrase obscure, but it illuminates what in the medic's mind seems the powerful, irrefutable and threatening connection between the Muslims of Bosnia and those of Kosovo.

Of Slav Macedonians, who also occupy a former Serbian medieval province, he comments: "The Macedonians are continuing to play the fool. The time is near when we'll have to protect Kumanovo too [the scene of a major Serbian victory in the First Balkan War, 1912.] The Serbs there are being threatened more and more, the Albanians are continuing to act in their usual fashion [and] we know all we need to know about the Slovenes and Croats. Europe is against us and everyone is against us."

Fear of encirclement by all-powerful enemies grips the medic. Not once does Jasovic ask himself whether his worries—and by extension, the worries of millions of other Serbs—are justified by the facts. Elsewhere he borrows an apocalyptic line from Njegos: "Let there be what there cannot be!" i.e., Serbia may lose these ancient provinces, but not without a fight to the end. Such thinking is at the heart of Serbian aggression and territorial aggrandizement. Will Kosovo and Macedonia be next on the list for "purification" and "ethnic cleansing"?

Is there any way out of the gyre of death and destruction in the Balkans? There may be, but the failure of diplomatic efforts up to now have shown that without more active U.S. participation, nothing will happen. Western Europe's leaders seem incapable of seeing that they should act forcefully—with military power, if needed—to force a ceasefire. For those untroubled by the daily murder of innocents in Sarajevo, Gorazde and other Bosnian towns, I should point out the danger to Europe's economy posed by the permanent immigration of 2 or 3 million Balkan refugees.

The U.S. offer of air and naval support for the U.N. relief effort is a first step, but even if this should bring about a ceasefire, we shall have to prepare ourselves to play a very strong role in the overall negotiations. Several European powers, particularly Britain, Germany, Italy and Turkey, seem immobilized, perhaps by their own past history of invasion or involvement in the Balkans.

If there is ever to be a healing, it may be that it can only begin with the establishment of a unique, continuing conference of Serbian, Croatian, Muslim and other historians, to arrive at a core of mutually-agreed upon statements regarding each group's history. Ideally, this multi-cultural convocation would face shibboleths regarding "enemy" ethnic groups, examine national memories for their accuracy and rationality and separate truth from prejudice. The mediation of Western experts will be vital, since Balkan scholars always seem biased in favor of their own group.

In examining the more documented history of the 20th century, responsibility will have to be accepted for the crimes of one nation against the other. For example, Serbs will have to admit their nation's guilt for the dictatorship of King Alexander in the 1920s and '30s, which undermined the pre-war Kingdom of Slovenia, Croatia and Serbia. In the same way, Croatia will have to come clean on the holocaust of Serbs at Jasenovac. Only the admission of guilt on one side, and the granting of forgiveness on the other, can start the healing process.

The same is true for the Christian relationship with the Muslims (the "Turks"). The Muslims need to admit that their ancestors abused and lorded it over the Christians for centuries. And the Serbs especially, while granting them forgiveness, must ask in turn for *their* pardon for recent savagery. We have precedents for such national confessions of guilt, in the West German acceptance of responsibility for Nazi crimes against Jews and recently (June 21) in the French intellectuals' call for their government to condemn, in the name of "the French collective memory," the Vichy government's persecution of Jews.

If such a healing process is to take place in the Balkans, it will be best to keep it out of the hands of religious leaders and politicians. The liturgy of reconciliation should be written by the poet, aided by others of good will. Thus the Yugoslavia that many of us in the West truly loved for its diversity may pass peacefully into history.

The state of Bosnia-Herzegovina

Yugoslavia, an invention of the 20th century, existed for centuries as several separate nations. In the current war within Bosnia-Herzegovina, ethnic Bosnian Serbs seek to join their land with Serbia, while Bosnian Muslims seek independence. The key players and the history:

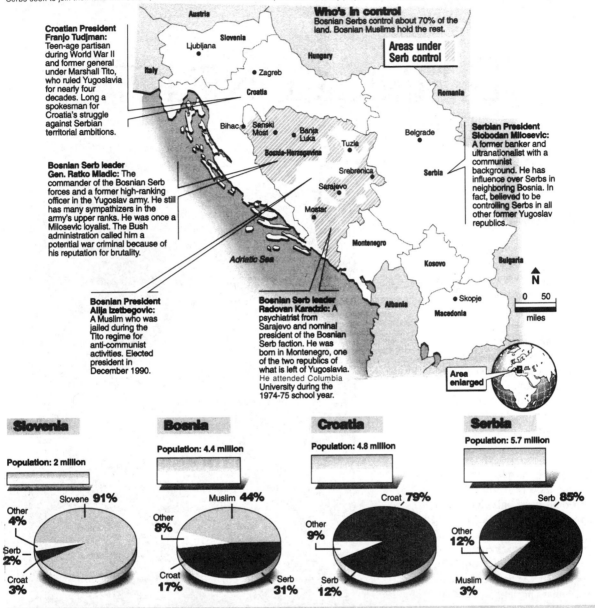

Croatian President Franjo Tudjman: Teen-age partisan during World War II and former general under Marshall Tito, who ruled Yugoslavia for nearly four decades. Long a spokesman for Croatia's struggle against Serbian territorial ambitions.

Bosnian Serb leader Gen. Ratko Mladic: The commander of the Bosnian Serb forces and a former high-ranking officer in the Yugoslav army. He still has many sympathizers in the army's upper ranks. He was once a Milosevic loyalist. The Bush administration called him a potential war criminal because of his reputation for brutality.

Bosnian President Alija Izetbegovic: A Muslim who was jailed during the Tito regime for anti-communist activities. Elected president in December 1990.

Who's in control
Bosnian Serbs control about 70% of the land. Bosnian Muslims hold the rest.

Areas under Serb control

Serbian President Slobodan Milosevic: A former banker and ultranationalist with a communist background. He has influence over Serbs in neighboring Bosnia. In fact, believed to be controlling Serbs in all other former Yugoslav republics.

Bosnian Serb leader Radovan Karadzic: A psychiatrist from Sarajevo and nominal president of the Bosnian Serb faction. He was born in Montenegro, one of the two republics of what is left of Yugoslavia. He attended Columbia University during the 1974-75 school year.

Area enlarged

Slovenia
Population: 2 million
- Slovene **91%**
- Other **4%**
- Serb **2%**
- Croat **3%**

Bosnia
Population: 4.4 million
- Muslim **44%**
- Other **8%**
- Croat **17%**
- Serb **31%**

Croatia
Population: 4.8 million
- Croat **79%**
- Other **9%**
- Serb **12%**

Serbia
Population: 5.7 million
- Serb **85%**
- Other **12%**
- Muslim **3%**

Roots and highlights of the latest Balkan War

June 28, 1389: Serb troops lose to Ottoman Empire in Battle of Kosovo Fields. Serbs begin saying they're chosen by God as 'the new Israel' and attach mythic and religious cloakings to recapturing Kosovo and uniting Serbs.

1918: From ashes of World War I rose a Slavic union, roughly the form of what became Yugoslavia.

Fall 1945: Yugoslavia formed under allied pressure under guerrilla leader Marshall Tito (Josip Broz, a Slovene-Croatian who believed in pan-Slavic communism).

May 4, 1980: Tito's firm one-man rule ends with his death. He's replaced by a weak collective.

May 1, 1991: The now-independent former Yugoslav republics of Slovenia

and Croatia sign a mutual defense agreement. War in Slovenia, from June 28 to July 8, 1991.

Jan. 15, 1992: European Community recognizes Croatia and Slovenia. A peace plan for Croatia, which sends U.N. troops to four areas held by ethnic Serbs, is agreed to after bloody fighting.

Feb. 29, 1992: Bosnia-Herzegovina declares independence. Bosnian Serbs declare a separate state and vow allegiance to Belgrade.

April 8, 1992: Serb forces in Bosnia begin seizing land. Sarajevo is shelled; civil war begins.

May 30, 1992: The U.N. votes sanctions against Serbia-dominated Yugoslavia, to begin in June.

June 11, 1992: U.N. peacekeepers arrive in Sarajevo. On July 10, a blockade goes up around what's left of Yugoslavia.

April 12, 1993: The United States, France and the Netherlands begin enforcing no-fly zone over Bosnia; Serbs attack Srebrenica.

June 18, 1993: U.S. soldiers arrive in Macedonia.

January 1994: British Lt. Gen. Sir Michael Rose takes command of U.N. Bosnia troops, vows 'more muscular' approach to delivering humanitarian aid.

February 28, 1994: U.S. F-16 planes shoot down four Serb aircraft bombing Muslim positions near Banja Luka in the first military action ever by NATO.

April 11, 1994: U.S. planes bomb Serbs attacking Gorazde. A second raid comes on April 12 and Muslim troops seize opportunity to attack Serbs in the area.

July 18, 1994: Muslim-led Bosnian government accepts peace proposal giving it and the Croats 51% of Bosnia, Serbs 49%. Bosnian Serbs, who hold more than 70%, reject the plan drafted by the United States, Russia and three other nations.

Oct. 28, 1994: Muslim-led Bosnian government forces go on the offensive against the Bosnian Serbs, making substantial gains in the Bihac area in northwest Bosnia. But on Nov. 6, the Serbs counterattack, triggering the latest round of fighting.

Sources: *The World Factbook;* Central Intelligence Agency; USA TODAY research

By Marty Baumann and Bob Laird, USA TODAY

ETHNIC CONFLICT

Andrew Bell-Fialkoff

Andrew Bell-Fialkoff, a former associate of the Center for the Study of Small States at Boston University, is completing his Ph.D. in ethnic conflict studies.

Lately one cannot open a newspaper or view the TV news without finding an item describing an attack on refugees in Germany or presenting the horrors of ethnic cleansing in the former Yugoslavia. Events such as these have stunned the civilized world. Aren't we supposed to have left such barbarity behind?

There is a common, widely held assumption that there is no place for ethnic nationalism in the modern world. Modernity and the concomitant urbanization, industrialization, and social mobility are deemed inimical to primordial attachments.

Clifford Geertz defined "primordial attachments" as those that "stem from being born into a particular religious community, speaking a particular language . . . and following particular social practices."[1]

In other words, all attachments engendered by ethnicity—those of kin, language, and custom—will gradually recede, lose their importance under the relentless assault of the all-pervasive modernity.

This assumption is based partly on the "liberal principle that people should be treated as individuals, and not as members of racial, religious, and other groups. . . . [Eventually] membership in ethnic groups must become increasingly irrelevant" and partly on the mistaken belief that increased economic and cultural integration of the global economy will diminish primordial attachments.[2]

■ A German Nazi poster, printed during World War II, meant to stimulate race hatred against both blacks and Jews.

Crudely put, if Serbs and Croats both like hamburgers they are less likely to kill each other.

That is why the recent explosion of nationalist passions in Europe and elsewhere caused such a shock. In fact, modernity is highly conducive to ethnic tensions. Nationalism was not an explosive issue when most people lived in small rural communities where everybody belonged to the same ethnic group. But in the modern world, people of different ethnic backgrounds are increasingly concentrated in huge urban agglomerations, and compete against each other in a presumably meritocratic society in a Hobbesian all against all.

The very fact that mobile society of-

This article first appeared in *The World & I*, July 1993, pp. 465-477. Reprinted with permission from *The World & I*, a publication of The Washington Times Corporation. © 1993.

fers a way to the top leads to fierce competition in which any weapon, but especially ethnic differences, lends itself to effective use. As Kautsky put it, "railways are the greatest breeder of national hatreds."[3] And airlines work even better, we may add.

CLASS AND ETHNICITY

The end-of-primordials assumption is shared by the Left, especially Marxists, but while liberals believe in the triumph of modernity, orthodox Marxists await the triumph of the working class.

To Marx, nationalism was part of the ideological superstructure arising on the foundations of economic self-interest. Like a true bourgeois, Marx was obsessed with monetary/economic relations of dominance and exploitation that reflected the ownership of the means of production. The main conflict pitted those who owned the means—the bourgeois—against those who did not—the proletariat. Everything else—culture, religion, ethnicity—was derivative.

Marx's hostility to nationalist movements also reflected his view that they served the interests of the middle classes and the bourgeoisie, diverting the proletariat from the really important task: the class struggle.

Actually, the relationship between nationalism and socialism was very complicated. In the nineteenth century they were allies in their struggle against autocracy and feudalism, at least in the semi-feudal Austrian, Russian, and Ottoman empires. Marx himself distinguished between national movements that were progressive, that is, all those struggling against czarist Russia and Austria, and those that were reactionary, for example, Croats who allied themselves with Vienna in 1848 out of fear of Hungarian centralism. This artificial distinction led to strange ideological somersaults: Romanians of Transylvania who, like Croats, sided with Vienna, were reactionary, while Romanians of Bessarabia fighting against St. Petersburg were progressive.[4]

Once the feudal order was defeated and the old empires collapsed, in 1917–18, nationalism and socialism parted company. Nationalism, for example, ethnic nationalism, tried to absorb socialism and quickly evolved into national socialism, which emphasized adherence to one's ethnic/racial group, whose economic

■ **Polish women being led to execution by German soldiers.**

and ideological life was to be developed along socialist principles.

Socialism, that is, class nationalism (as opposed to ethnic nationalism), emphasized devotion to one's class within one's ethnic entity. It tried to suppress (ethnic) nationalism in the belief that it tied the working classes to their capitalist exploiters, thus blunting the class struggle.

The most principled socialists, such as Rosa Luxembourg, always insisted that there was no place for nationalism in a socialist society. She was even willing to give up hope for Polish reunification because, once Austria, Germany, and Russia turned socialist, national oppression would disappear and nationalism itself would become meaningless.

Once the Bolsheviks came to power, however, they quickly realized that nationalist passions were a powerful tool, particularly in Russia, which transferred its religious zeal from Orthodox Christianity to orthodox Marxism. When in 1941 the German armies were approaching

Moscow, Stalin called for the defense of Mother Russia, not world socialism.

Contrary to commonly held opinion, communist ruling elites did not put nationalism on ice. Instead, they put it on the back burner, to be served to the presumably gullible public whenever an internal situation called for cohesion. They tried to domesticate it, to use it for their own purposes, as evidenced by government-inspired and -organized nationalist campaigns in virtually every socialist country, for example, Poland and Romania in the 1960s and repeatedly in Soviet Russia.

In the process, there occurred a nationalization of socialism that, in some aspects, moved it closer to the nationalist socialist mode. Thus, one hundred years after nationalism and socialism parted company, they joined hands again, this time with state socialism in the driver's seat.

Gradually, however, nationalism destroyed socialism from within and then slunk out of the old socialist skin. This is what happened in Eastern Europe in 1989. This is what accounts for nationalist virulence in the former communist countries.

NATIONAL SOCIALISM

While Marxism is a chiliastic movement striving for the yawning heights of a rational, scientific (perfect) society, fascism is representative of a whole class of antimodern ideologies that reject the anomie, the atomization and impersonal character, of modern society. It stresses social harmony, spiritual values, and cooperation that tilt it toward emphasizing primordial attachments, that is, ethnicity. Because "ethnicity ... implies affection based on intangible bonds and a belief in collective sustenance."[5]

That, incidentally, explains why, in a struggle of ethnic nationalism against class nationalism, ethnic nationalism always wins: It offers the additional comfort of kinship and affective ties, the warmth of community as opposed to impersonal class interests.

Fascism proclaims society's organic unity, which Marxist class struggle and liberal individualism have destroyed. Urban environment and industry, by their very nature, destroy human and social solidarity. Therefore, where modernity promotes conflict and individualism, fascism offers unity and mutual support. And unity based on ethnic community is all the stronger. This may be one of the main reasons for fascism's success: It promised support and solidarity to atomized, insecure, vulnerable masses. Communism did likewise but only to the working classes; fascism offered panacea to all.

Among things both movements share, none goes deeper than anti-Semitism. Marx, imbued with virulent German racism and Jew-hatred ("This Jewish Nigger Lassalle"[6]), redirected the hatred against an alien religious and ethnic group into the hatred of an economic class, the bourgeoisie. Jew the swindler and the moneybags became bourgeois-the-leech. Marx transferred the Jew-devil/Christian dichotomy of traditional anti-Semitism into a bourgeois/proletariat dichotomy. "Marx's invention of the 'bourgeoisie,'" wrote Paul Johnson, "was the most comprehensive of [the] hate-theories and it has continued to provide a foundation for all paranoid revolutionary movements, whether fascist-nationalist

or Communist-internationalist. Modern theoretical anti-Semitism [is] a derivative of Marxism."[7]

It is no accident that virtually all European communist countries have experienced periodic flare-ups of anti-Semitism: Russia repeatedly, Czechoslovakia in 1952–53 (largely Russian-inspired), Poland in 1967–68, and so forth.

ARE ETHNICITY AND NATIONALISM HERE TO STAY?

Attempts to define a nation are too numerous to be listed here. Perhaps the best known is that of Stalin, who listed four indispensable characteristics: a common language, a common territory, a common economic life, and a common mental makeup.[8]

However, one can always find ethnic groups that aspire to be called or to become full-fledged nations even though they lack one of these characteristics. Are Hispanics who barely speak English disqualified from being American? Do Transylvanian Hungarians cease being Hungarian because there is a stretch of Romanian ethnic territory that separates them from the bulk of their ethnic cousins? Was partitioned Poland no longer a nation? Wasn't Germany? And, of course "mental makeup" is too vague to be useful.

That is why many specialists despair.

"Thus I am driven to the conclusion that no 'scientific definition' of a nation can be devised; yet the phenomenon has existed and exists," wrote Seton-Watson.[9] And will continue to exist in the foreseeable future, we may safely add.

One of the most original explanations of why ethnicity is so persistent was provided by Pierre van den Berghe. It is based on notions derived from sociobiology and regards ethnicity as kin selection. "Ethnicity is common descent, either real or putative, but, even when putative, the myth has to be validated by several generations of common historical experience."[10] Ethnicity is thus perceived as something natural, rooted in the biological makeup of humankind. And favoring one's ethnic brothers (another kin term!) is part and parcel of any traditional social system.

This fact, of course, does not explain the many masks of nationalism. It was born in the struggle of the West Europe-

an middle class against feudal privilege and absolutism. Later, it was used by the state for colonial expansion and imperialism (the "bureaucratic nationalism," as Anthony Smith calls it.[11]) Meanwhile, as it expanded (or contaminated) multinational empires of Central and Eastern Europe, nationalism was adopted by the nascent intelligentsias of ethnic minorities who sought freedom and development through self-determination and secession. As it penetrated the lower social strata, nationalism merged with populism and xenophobia to support us against them and provide structure and cohesion that the uprooted masses lacked. In short, nationalism can put on any number of masks, which explains why it has "expanded and proliferated into the most powerful yet elusive of all modern ideologies."[12]

And there is no end in sight. The ideal of self-determination is now firmly established in the popular mind. Liberation movements of all kinds—ethnic, gay, women's, racial—have gained acceptance and respectability. Size no longer matters—Iceland, Luxembourg, and Malta proved that even very small states can be viable. Accession to economic unions, such as the European Community, gives even the smallest states access to huge markets. And successful conclusion of liberation struggles in former colonies gave a tremendous boost to ethnic political movements in the old countries in Europe.

Thus, smaller and more *ethnies*— the Basques and the Catalans, the Scots and the Flemings—are beginning to seek more autonomy and, eventually, independence, perhaps within a unified Europe.[13] And on it goes.

FROM VIENNA TO VERSAILLES

The gradual acceptance of the principle of self-determination can clearly be seen in the history of international congresses called upon to solve political problems after major wars.

Up until the nineteenth century, ethnicity got scant attention from statesmen and diplomats. As late as 1862, Lord Acton, in a flash of prescience, wrote that "nationality does not aim at either liberty or prosperity, both of which it sacrifices to the imperative necessity of making the nation the mould and measure of the

State. Its course will be marked with material as well as moral ruin."[14]

Only an absolutist state ruled by an established dynasty was recognized as an acceptable international partner. Thus, at the Congress of Vienna, the Great Powers upheld the legitimacy of dynastic empire and confirmed the partition of Poland with total disregard for ethnic sentiment. However, even mighty empires could not withstand the spread of new ideas, including the idea of popular sovereignty. When applied to nationality, the principle of popular sovereignty implied that ethnically alien government was illegitimate.

As ethnic nationalism gained momentum, European powers could no longer ignore it. The Greek war of independence, the conflict between Germans and Danes in Schleswig-Holstein, the Italian struggle for unification, Polish uprisings, all demanded settlement based on self-determination.

Once the Great Powers realized that they could not control or resist the rising tide of nationalism, they tried to use it for their own gain as, for example, Napoleon III used Italian struggle against Austria for his own purposes in 1859. At the Congress of Berlin in 1878 the Great Powers had to concede independence to various Balkan peoples who had broken away from the Ottoman Empire, but still felt free to carve up Bulgaria when it suited their interests.

It was only at the Paris Peace Conference of 1919 that the principle of nationality and self-determination was firmly established as the normative principle of a legitimate government. Thus, between 1814 and 1919 there occurred a major shift in the principle of settling international disputes. Since then, ethnicity has retained its importance.

Germany, Austria, and Turkey after World War I, Czechoslovakia in 1938, Romania in 1940, Yugoslavia in 1941—all lost territory or were dismembered along ethnic lines. (There are, of course, notable exceptions, as when Germany lost ethnically German territories after World War II, but even here populations were expelled to make sure that political and ethnic borders coincided.)

It was precisely for that reason (the lack of congruence between political and ethnic borders) that the settlement reached at Versailles proved so ephemeral: It left too many ethnic enclaves, too many ethnic problems unsettled.

SOLUTIONS: THE MELTING POT AND THE UNMELTABLE ETHNICS

Americans are probably most familiar with the notion of a melting pot. It could have developed only in a country of mass immigration, a country that had successfully absorbed millions of immigrants.

America, of course, is not unique in that sense. Other settler colonies—Canada, Australia, New Zealand, South Africa, to name a few—have also been settled in a similar pattern. And old countries like France after World War I also allowed and even promoted massive in-migration.

However, America has always been a classical land of immigration, so it is no wonder that the theory of assimilation and amalgamation of people of different ethnic stock was developed in this country. Basically, the theory postulated that assimilation was a four-stage process that included contact, competition, accommodation, and, finally, assimilation.

Since then the theory has been much tinkered with. For example, it has been suggested that white immigrants assimilate within large religious denominations. Some sociologists even ventured to predict that eventually large ethno-religious blocs of Protestants, Catholics, and Jews would develop.

The data on intermarriage seem to support this hypothesis. In the late 1970s, 40 percent of Jews and Catholics married outside their religion. And among certain ethnic groups high rates of intermarriage suggest the approach of complete meltdown: 70 percent for Germans and Irish, 50 percent for Poles and Italians, 40 percent for French Canadians.[15]

However, there are several cracks clearly visible in the melting pot. One is that ethnic identification often persists even after all ethnic peculiarities have been lost. America is full of Italians whose Italianness finds expression in eating pasta and Poles whose Polishness is limited to kielbasa.

Second, it takes two to assimilate. Acculturation, in other words, changes in observable behavior, can be accomplished by one actor. But assimilation, that is, absorption into the social structure of another group, is impossible without at least a tacit approval of the assimilating group.

In a country like Australia, which

■ **Croatian guards talk with an elderly man who is demanding the return of Baranya territory from Serbian occupation.**

was without significant racial minorities (until very recently), such assimilation may proceed relatively smoothly, but in the United States with its ethnic and racial diversity, complete amalgamation may have stalled, perhaps for good.

Does the melting pot work? There is no overall answer. We have to proceed country by country. In the United States, it worked for virtually all white immigrants although rates of assimilation and the degree of assimilation achieved vary from group to group. Some Asians, particularly second- and third-generation Japanese, have also achieved high rates of outmarriage. It is quite possible that they will eventually dissolve, like other immigrants, in the American stew.

The question is more problematic with black and Latino populations. Although rates of outmarriage have begun to increase among these groups as well, the presence of large Latino populations south of the border and the sheer numbers of the black minority (thirty million) make absorption more difficult.

So the verdict is still out. The important thing to keep in mind is that a melting pot can only work in a settler country where ethnic groups lack territoriality. Whenever the territorial dimension appears—as in Quebec—the melting pot would not work.

SWITZERLAND: THE ADVANTAGES OF APARTHEID

The exact opposite of a melting pot is the concept of apartheid, in other words, a complete legal and structural separation of constituent racial or ethnic groups.

Various approximations of apartheid, though best known as it was practiced in South Africa, can be found all over the globe, including Switzerland. (I can already see stares of incredulity on most readers' faces ... but wait.)

Even in South Africa, apartheid was never carried out to its logical extreme—the complete separation of racial groups from each other. In a developed industrial society dependent on cheap black labor that was impossible. So, even South Africa at the height of apartheid would not qualify as an example of pure apartheid. On the other hand, America, the classical land of a melting pot, never achieved complete melting. So, we have to keep in mind that we are talking about ideal types.

Now, Switzerland is far from being a land of apartheid in its pure form because all Swiss citizens are equal before the law (at least in theory). However, its major linguistic and religious groups do not mix, for each one has a canton or cantons of its own. And this fact allows me to call it, tongue in cheek, a country that practices apartheid.

Swiss indigenous population is highly heterogeneous, consisting of 75 percent German speakers, 20 percent Francophones, 4 percent Italians, and 1 percent Romansh. In terms of religious subdivisions, 58 percent are Protestant and 42 percent Catholic.

If we now take a closer look at the cantons, we will find that of the twenty-six cantons (actually, twenty-two cantons and four semicantons), twenty-three are more than 80 percent monolingual and in the other three the percentage of people speaking the main language does not dip below 60. What's more, in seventeen cantons, monolinguals amount to 95 percent. The same pattern can be observed in the distribution of religious denominations. In eighteen cantons religious majority exceeds 70 percent; nowhere does it fall below 53 percent.[16]

One may add that religion has not been a political factor in Switzerland since a brief civil war in 1847 that pitted the industrialized, liberal, largely urban northwest against the predominantly rural, conservative southeast. But even then, divisions cut across both major linguistic communities.

The same felicitous balance is found in terms of income distribution. Of the ten richest cantons, seven are German and three are French. And among the ten poorest ones there are seven German, two French, and one Italian (there is, however, a marked tendency for uneven income/religion distribution; thus, nine of the ten richest cantons are Protestant, nine of the ten poorest are Catholic, a clear indication of how Protestantism interacts with the spirit of capitalism).[17] In short, each canton has a large linguistic and religious majority, and this prevents fission based on language and religion.

A recently resolved problem in Jura is a hint of what might have happened if Swiss ethnic, linguistic, and denominational communities were mixed together. The territory, predominantly Francophone and Catholic, was attached to Bern by the Vienna Congress of 1814 as a compensation for the loss of a dependent territory. Its inhabitants never reconciled themselves to this gunpoint marriage. They continued to struggle against the imposition until, in a series of referenda conducted in the early 1970s, the Catholic part was allowed to secede and form a new canton, Jura. Protestants stayed with Bern.

Does Swiss apartheid work? Apparently it does. Will it work elsewhere? (Incidentally, the Swiss model has elicited much interest in South Africa, which quite possibly will try to follow the Swiss path, rather than the American, as a road to a multiracial, multiethnic society).

CONSOCIATIONALISM

Consociational or proportional democracy is a last-ditch arrangement when all alternatives are worse than a precarious balance.[18,19] Under consociationalism the constituent ethnic groups remain distinct for an indefinite period of time within one political system, but do not form separate administrative units.

Such a system requires stability and cultural pluralism. It also needs a cleavage between constituent groups (to reduce interethnic contact and, therefore, conflict and competition), absence of hegemony by one of the groups, attitudes favorable to all-inclusive coalition governments, and lack of external threat. It also helps if there is a limited interpenetration of the ethnies (this makes partition more difficult), some intermarriage (to prevent extreme polarization), and functional interpenetration at the governmental level (the more they share the less need they would feel to separate).

Actually, there are two kinds of consociationalism: One is political, that is, a situation where several political or spiritual families (e.g., Catholics, liberals and socialists) share power. Political consociationalism is fairly stable, as is evidenced in Austria or the Netherlands. The second kind is ethnic consociationalism, which is extremely unstable. Belgium gradually evolved toward a federalized tripartite system, while Lebanon (it would be more accurate to call it denominational, rather than ethnic, consociationalism) collapsed into chaos and civil war.

AUTONOMY

Among various solutions to ethnic problems the first one that comes to mind is autonomy. Usually, it means territorial autonomy, although there is also personal and corporate autonomy as well. In the less-known personal autonomy, the autonomous status applies to the minority individual no matter where he lives, as long as he is willing to be officially assigned minority status. The status is given to the individual on the basis of a personal declaration, government ordinance, or court decision based on language, origin, or a national characteristic. Ultimately, this form of autonomy is based on a personal decision of the individual.

Historically, corporate autonomy was tried in the Moravian compromise of 1905[20]; it was cut short by the collapse of Austria-Hungary in 1918, but theoretically, this solution is very promising because it combines personal choice with protection of minority rights and does not lead to the creation of rigid territorial units.

Entitlement programs in the United States (e.g., affirmative action, financial assistance to minority students, etc.) come very close to the model of corporate autonomy. In this instance, autonomous status is given to the minority as a whole, no matter where its representatives live, but the personal decision is lacking. An individual is assigned to his/her group on the basis of origin, language, or religion and enjoys all the advantages or disadvantages of a minority, but only on a corporate basis. This pattern is less flexible from the individual's standpoint, but it gives more organizational muscle to the minority group.

Finally, the best-known type of autonomy is territorial. It can be applied to those ethnic groups that live in compact territory with clearly marked borders. When such borders are lacking, things can get very complicated, as witnessed by German (and now Russian) ethnic enclaves scattered throughout much of eastern Europe.

Territorial autonomy has been tried many times and in many countries, often to satisfy aspirations toward self-determination by a small but strategically located ethnic minority whose complete separation would be detrimental to the interests of the larger state. However, federal autonomy often proved to be a stepping-stone toward a complete and final divorce. The Soviet Union and former Yugoslavia serve as good examples. Still, one has to keep in mind that in both cases autonomy was largely fictitious. Both states were ultimately held together by brute force.

What is usually overlooked, amid all the laments about fragmentation, is the fact that virtually all the newly established states aspire to join a united Europe. Thus, further unification of Europe, this time on the basis of voluntary association, rather than force, was impossible without the fragmentation of the old empires.

It is a dialectic that Marx had vaguely guessed, although he could not know that the new freedoms would bring the end of the proletarian hegemony. This was the ultimate victory of nationalism over its old ally.

NOTES

1. Clifford Geertz, *Old Societies and New States* (London: The Free Press of Glencoe, 1963), 109.

2. Arend Lijphart, "Political Theories and the Explanation of Ethnic Conflict in the Western World: Falsified Predictions and Plausible Postdictions," *Ethnic Conflict in the Western World.* Milton J. Esman, ed. (Ithaca and London: Cornell University Press, 1977), 53.

3. Karl Kautsky, *Neue Zeit* (1886), 522–5, cited in H.B. Davis, *Nationalism and Socialism*, (New York and London: Monthly Review Press, 1967), 142; ref. in A. Smith, *Nationalism in the Twentieth Century* (New York: New York University Press, 1979), 163.

4. Hugh Seton-Watson, *Nations and States* (Boulder, CO: Westview Press, 1977), 446.

5. Cynthia Enloe, *Ethnic Conflict and Political Development* (Boston: Little, Brown & Co., 1973), 67.

6. Paul Johnson, *Modern Times* (New York: Harper & Row, 1983), 117.

7. Johnson, *Modern Times*, 62.

8. Joseph Stalin, *Marxism and the National Question*, 1913.

9. Hugh Seton-Watson, *Nations and States*, 3.

10. Pierre van den Berghe, *The Ethnic Phenomenon* (New York: Elsevier, 1981), 16.

11. Anthony Smith, *Nationalism in the Twentieth Century* (New York: New York University Press, 1979), 169.

12. Smith, *Nationalism in the Twentieth Century*, 166.

13. A neologism borrowed from the French, now widely used by sociologists to denote a group that is ethnically, naturally, religiously, or otherwise distinct, so long as these groups claim ethnic particularity.

14. Lord Acton, "Essay on Nationality," reference in A. Smith, *Theories of Nationalism* (New York: Harper & Row, 1971), 9.

15. Pierre van den Berghe, *The Ethnic Phenomenon*, 228.

16. Pierre van den Berghe, *The Ethnic Phenomenon*.

17. Pierre van den Berghe, *The Ethnic Phenomenon*.

18. Arend Lijphart, *Democracy in Plural Societies* (New Haven: Yale University Press, 1977).

19. Gerhard Lehmbruch, "proporzdemokratie" Mohr, Tubingen, 1967.

20. Robert Kann, *The Multinational Empire* (New York: Columbia University Press, 1950), 194–5; and E.K. Francis, *Interethnic Relations* (New York: Elsevier, 1976), 98–99.

PASSIONS SET IN STONE

Jerusalem celebrates its 3,000th anniversary... but there's little celebration of the past, just fights about its future. Who will control it? Israelis? Palestinians? Ultrareligious Jews? No one?

PAUL GOLDBERGER

Paul Goldberger, the chief cultural correspondent for The Times, wrote "Reimagining Berlin" — about the city's identity crisis — for the Magazine in February.

'A PSYCHIATRIST COULD DO NOTHing to solve this city's problems — Jerusalem has no subconscious at all," Yehuda Amichai, Israel's most revered poet, remarked recently. "Everything is out in the open, even the infighting."

It was a sunny, intensely hot morning earlier this summer, and Amichai was sitting in his small cottage in Yemin Moshe, an exquisite neighborhood of 19th-century stone houses set along flower-bedecked walkways, not far from the center of Jerusalem. "Where else do you see Jews dressed like 19th-century Russians and Arabs dressed like Arabs and people in modern dress, all at each other?" he continued. "You could say that this city is an open madhouse. But its great accomplishment is that it has succeeded in not being a museum. It is heavenly and earthly together, and that is what will sustain it — the real life."

Life here had become startlingly real just minutes before: news had come through that Palestinian terrorists had bombed a bus near Tel Aviv. The bombing had shaken Amichai, and he broke off our conversation repeatedly to check the radio for the latest bulletins. In 1994, he went to Oslo with Yitzak Rabin, the Prime Minister, to read his poems when Rabin and Yasir Arafat were awarded the Nobel Peace Prize, and he knows that each new violent incident involving Palestinians threatens the whole peace process, precarious enough as it is. Everyone else in Jerusalem seems to know it too, which is why the Tel Aviv bombing shook this city nearly as much as the similar bombing a month later in one of Jerusalem's own buses — an act of terror that the Islamic resistance movement Hamas took responsibility for, and that killed 4 passengers and the bomber himself, and wounded 100 others.

Unlike Tel Aviv, whose identity as Israel's financial and cultural center is unlikely to be challenged, even by what Hamas called, in a statement describing the Aug. 21 attack, "a systematic military campaign," Jerusalem — its sense of itself and its future — hangs in the balance of world events. Uneasily united under Israeli rule since 1967, the city may again be divided, with a section turned over to Palestinian administration, much as the Gaza Strip and portions of the West Bank have already been. The 1993 agreement between Israel and the Palestine Liberation Organization specifies that negotiators will take up the question of Jerusalem's future in May 1996, and as that date approaches, every moment of stress between Israel and the Palestinians sends a vast shudder through the city. No item on the long Israeli-Palestinian agenda incites the emotional response that Jerusalem does, and Israelis are bitterly split between those who say that Jerusalem should be formally divided for the sake of peace and those who feel that giving up so much as a block of the city would be tantamount to ceding to the Palestinians Israel's most important national symbol.

JERUSALEM IS LIKE NO OTHER CITY ON earth, and the fact that it has no idea — or such different and strongly held ideas — of what its future will be is only a part of it. Nowhere else is there such a mix of the profound and the provincial. Paradoxically, the profound is easier to see: it is everywhere in the stones, in the overpowering presence of places sacred to three great religions, in the rhythm of hills and valleys that make half the city into an overlook, in the light so rich and golden that at dusk you could almost hold it in your hand. The provincial side is better hidden. It takes a bit of time here to discover that the capital of Israel, a city whose history goes back thousands of years, is a small town rife with political factionalism, a city that prides itself on its international presence but proves better than Chicago the axiom that all politics is local. The city is increasingly a set of neighborhoods fighting for their own interests; year by year, it seems, the fabled, sacred Jerusalem is less a whole than a set of distinct parts. And more and more it has become a battleground not only between Jews and Arabs, but between Jews and Jews.

These factional fights, along with the coming Israeli-Palestinian negotiations involving the city, have cast a pall over what was expected to have been a joyous, yearlong cultural festival, beginning this month, marking Jerusalem's 3,000th anniversary. The festival is going ahead, but without much enthusiasm from the city's Palestinians, who point out that what occurred 3,000 years ago was not the founding of the city, but King David's declaration of Jerusalem as the capital of the Jewish people. To the Palestinians — who number 167,000, or about 29 percent of the city's population of 570,000 — the festival is propaganda for the argument that the city belongs to the Jews, not to the Muslims or the Christians whose histories are also deeply bound up in it. And at best, the birthday is an arbitrary date: scholars are not sure precisely at what moment King David proclaimed Jerusalem his capital, and the timing for the cultural festival was set a few years back in the hope that it would provide a fitting climax to the final term of Teddy Kollek, the legendary Viennese-born liberal who had been Jerusalem's Mayor since 1965. What Kollek didn't count on was that he would lose his bid for re-election in 1993 and retire in some bitterness; the festival will now shine its spotlight on his very different successor, the sharply conservative Ehud Olmert.

The transition from Kollek to Olmert stands as an apt symbol of what has happened in Jerusalem in the last few years. Kollek turned Jerusalem from something of a sleepy backwater whose appeal was largely in its history into a city with a vibrant, international cultural presence. He helped found the Israel Museum, which marked its 30th anniversary this spring, and started the Jerusalem Foundation, which since 1966 has funneled more than $350 million in philanthropic gifts from around the world into the physical transformation of the city. A lover of architecture and urban design, Kollek set up an international advisory committee that included architects like Louis Kahn and Philip Johnson to advise the city on planning. And when the group recommended a tough line against high-rise building in Jerusalem, he went along with its wishes, throwing aside plans for highways and skyscrapers in the center of town and turning himself into a strong advocate of building in a way that would be consistent with the traditional spirit of the city.

Teddy, as he is referred to by everyone — an affectionate anomaly in this country where most politicians are sneeringly dismissed by their last names — is as well known outside Jerusalem as within it. Olmert is different: a pragmatic member of the conservative Likud Party, he set his sights on defeating Kollek by portraying him as old (Kollek is now 84) and out of touch. But the strategy worked less because of Kollek's weakness than because of Olmert's canny alliance with an increasingly powerful group in Jerusalem politics, ultrareligious Jews, known here as Haredim, literally "those who tremble," as with the awe of God. The throngs of Haredi sect members, with their black suits, beards, black hats and rigid devotion to rabbis who dictate when and how they can involve themselves in contemporary life, are the city's Jewish fundamentalists.

The heart of their community is in the twisted streets and ramshackle buildings of Mea Shearim, an old neighborhood in central Jerusalem that looks eerily like an Eastern European ghetto of a hundred years ago. The streets are narrow and there is virtually no play space for children, but room is somehow found for more than 50 small synagogues. Many of the Haredim themselves look as if they had just come off a street in 18th-century Poland or Lithuania, and until a few years ago they had seemed more a curiosity than a factor in Jerusalem's political life. But they are growing rapidly in number, thanks to immigration and to a

WHOSE JERUSALEM?

Last year, enrollment figures in Jerusalem showed that 52 percent of Jewish children under 10 were from ultrareligious families. Certain now that demographics are in their favor, the Orthodox are flexing political muscle as never before.

birthrate far above the city's norm. And with a total population of roughly 130,000, they have spread far beyond Mea Shearim to take over most of the neighborhoods on the northern side of Jerusalem. The Haredim average seven to eight children per family, and last year citywide school enrollment figures showed that 52 percent of Jewish children under 10 in Jerusalem were from ultrareligious families. Certain now that the demographics of the city are in their favor, the Haredim have begun to flex their political muscle as never before.

Their concerns are simple and direct: they want the city to provide money for their religious schools, and they want it to use the rule of law to protect their view of Judaism. To the Haredim, this means closing city streets and places of entertainment like movie theaters and restaurants on the Jewish Sabbath (when the ultrareligious are prohibited from driving cars or operating machinery) and limiting nonkosher restaurants. They can be fiercely intolerant of Jews who do not practice their style of Judaism — to the Haredim, Jews who have assimilated into modern society are the true heathens, far more so than non-Jews, who they tend to view with indifference. ("We are the goyim now," Yehuda Amichai says.)

Teddy Kollek dealt with the Haredim at a distance. Under him, the city banned Saturday traffic from Mea Shearim and adjacent neighborhoods, in an implicit trade for their keeping to themselves and out of politics. Sometimes the Haredim kept to the bargain; sometimes they did not — as when they threw rocks at cars driving near their neighborhoods on Saturday. Rock throwing still goes on from time to time, but that is the least of it. For the Haredim now constitute the single most potent bloc of voters in the city, and they no longer even pretend to remain quiet, studying Torah and leaving day-to-day governance to others.

Indeed, it is the Haredim who made Olmert, who is not himself ultrareligious, the Mayor of Jerusalem. On the day before the election the rabbis of the Haredi sects threw their support en masse to Olmert after he had agreed to offer high positions in his administration to ultrareligious politicians, among them Meir Porush, who until then had been running for Mayor himself. In exchange for Porush's withdrawal, Olmert became the head of a new coalition between the various ultrareligious parties and his own Likud. Porush became one of his deputy mayors, in charge of education; Chaim Miller, another Haredi, became a second deputy mayor, in charge of a new department of Haredi cultural affairs, and Uri Lupolianski, also a Haredi, became the senior deputy mayor and was given charge of the all-important area of city planning.

To Olmert, the new coalition was nothing more than a practical response to the demographic realities of the city. In the view of many of the city's liberal Jews, however, Olmert had turned over control of the city to the Haredim. These liberal Jews fear the Jerusalem of Teddy Kollek is dead. In the next century, they say, the city will be essentially the capital of Jewish fundamentalism.

JERUSALEM HAS ALWAYS BEEN A CITY OF SEParate and distinct neighborhoods, but never more so than today. The beginning of the intifada, or Palestinian uprising, in December 1987, sharply curtailed traffic between the Arab neighborhoods of East Jerusalem and the rest of the city, and even now, with the intifada largely over, there are few places in Jerusalem where Jews and Arabs are likely to meet. The central business district is almost entirely Jewish, while the markets in the Old City, the walled district that is the city's ancient heart, are almost entirely Arab. Haredim rarely leave their own neighborhoods except, these days, to go to City Hall.

It is not true, however, that there are no Jews in Arab areas. There are vast numbers of them, living not in old East Jerusalem but in new neighborhoods built by the Israeli Government in the last 25 years. When Israel won the Six Day War in 1967, it did not merely unite Jerusalem, it began to expand it. Satellite neighborhoods were built to establish a Jewish presence on formerly Jordanian land outside the city. The Jewish sections of this new Jerusalem have become so extensive that they leave the Arabs in control today of only 13.5 percent of East Jerusalem and the annexed areas, according to Sarah Kaminker, a planner and former member of the Jerusalem City Council.

This new Jerusalem — suddenly a metropolis — was not created simply by drawing a big circle; its borders were as skillfully drawn as a gerrymandered Congressional district, zigzagging around areas that had considerable Arab populations and including plenty of raw land for new Israeli neighborhoods, all so as to keep the voting population of the city heavily Jewish. And thus it remains. Although the city's Arab population once supported Kollek, it has withdrawn into itself since the intifada, and the level of voter participation, even among Arabs entitled to vote in the Jerusalem municipal elections, is small. Not surprisingly, the Arab indifference bothers the ultrareligious Jews of Jerusalem not at all — and not just because it leaves the way clear for them to play a larger role in local politics. It also points up a striking similarity between the two groups, who in some respects have an increasingly common vision of the city's future.

When Israel was established in 1948, its founding generation of Zionists was driven by a desire to create a utopian, largely socialist nation that would break away from the dark, dreary ghetto life of Eastern Europe; it would be Jewish, but not rigidly religious, and would substitute free intellectual inquiry for the doctrinaire Talmudic study of the past. There is little room for this Zionist dream in the minds of either the Haredim or the Palestinians. Some of the most zealous Haredim do not even recognize the Government of Israel, believing that a Jewish state is only appropriate after the coming of the Messiah. Even the ultrareligious who have come to see the benefits of political power have their hearts elsewhere — turned inward to their own small, closed communities. And the Palestinians, needless to say, never thought much of the Zionist dream in the first place. They dismissed its utopianism as hypocrisy, and saw it only as a naked grab for land that they believed was rightfully theirs.

The city's secular Jews, for their part, increasingly present another obstacle to the dream of an integrated city: prosperity. Half the people on the streets of West Jerusalem seem to have cellular phones in their ears. Israel's economy has been strong in the last few years, spurred on by the country's success in developing itself as the high-tech center of the Middle East, and the standard of living has grown by leaps and bounds. As the old Zionists die off, the modest, communal life they envisioned as the Israeli ideal has been replaced by something much richer, much more oriented to consumption, much more American. In a country that once had relatively few cars, the streets are now clogged with late-model Subarus, Volvos and Mercedes-Benzes. And there are more good restaurants, music clubs and movie theaters — plenty of which are open on the Sabbath — than ever before. Indeed, the proliferation of night life in Jerusalem, and the presence of so many more entertainment options on Saturday than there were even five years ago, is taken by some observers as a sign that the Haredi influence is exaggerated. But what it really indicates is that the secular community has changed its nature, and is much more interested now in having a good time.

The most conspicuous sign, at least architecturally, of this sea change in the life of secular Jerusalem is the Kenyon Jerusalem, the city's first shopping mall — a sprawling structure on three levels with vaulted skylights, covered parking and a central atrium — which opened last year in the southeast corner of the city. It is jammed with people, and except for the signs in the windows and the language an eavesdropper hears, it could be suburban Dallas. If the increasing presence of the Haredim, bustling about City Hall in their long black frock coats and black hats, is one symbol of the new Jerusalem, the mall is surely the other.

"When I first came here, there was an idealism," says Shula Navon, an American who immigrated to Jerusalem in 1965 and now runs a United States-based foundation here. "Life was difficult — you would save tinfoil because it was so expensive, you would only call the United States once a year, but it was passionate, intense, and you felt you were here for a purpose. Now everyone

has faxes and E-mail and two cars and you might as well be in a suburb of Boston."

URI LUPOLIANSKI, 44, WOULD NOT BE likely to have been the deputy mayor in charge of planning and building in a suburb of Boston. He would not have had that job in Jerusalem, either, had Olmert's victory last year not made him one of the most powerful Haredi politicians in the city. Lupolianski, a member of the United Torah Party, is a short, stout man with an easy manner and a round face out of which springs an endearing, satisfied smile and a medium-length black beard. He represents the new breed of Haredim, worldly and determined to operate within the sphere of the secular world — if not to change that world, then to extract as much as possible from it.

Lupolianski has not spent his life only studying Torah. Although he has no training in architecture and planning, he has been in public life in a sense since he founded Yad Sarah, Israel's largest volunteer organization, 20 years ago. Widely acclaimed for the support it provides for the aged and infirm, Jews and non-Jews alike, the organization was awarded the Israel Prize, the Government's highest civilian honor, last year, and it has made Lupolianski one of the few Haredim with a high profile in Israel's broader culture.

Lupolianski sees himself as a manager who once applied his talents to the problem of volunteerism and can apply them just as easily to the future of the physical city. In his view, the city is filled with competing populations who cannot live in proximity to one another and should not be forced to, and he makes no apologies for a planning strategy that presumes that neighborhoods will be totally segregated.

"There is a difference in mentality between Arabs and Jews, and I do not believe that they can live on top of each other," he explained when I visited him in City Hall. "Different populations have different needs — the Arabs will not build a lot of apartments on a plot of land and the Jews will. And then the religious families need different apartments from the secular Jews, bigger ones with room nearby for schools and synagogues they can walk to. You can't plan a neighborhood without knowing who it is being planned for."

Both Lupolianski and Mayor Olmert believe that the city can continue to grow beyond its current population, and say that it may reach as high as 850,000 in another decade. (Israel Kimhi, a senior researcher at the Jerusalem Institute for Israel Studies, a local think tank, foresees a population of 750,000 by 2010, still an increase of more than 30 percent.) To accommodate Jerusalem's continued expansion, the Mayor and his chief planner envision both more housing around the periphery and denser construction in the center, reversing Teddy Kollek's slowdown of high-rise construction.

"There is only a given amount of space we have—this is not Mexico or Australia," Lupolianski says. "You cannot make flat declarations like no skyscrapers. People say don't build in the east, that is where the Arabs are, don't build in the north because Arabs are there too, don't build in the west because that's where the green forests are, don't build in the south because there are too many political conflicts there, don't build up because it will ruin the skyline and don't build down because there are ancient graves. So where will the people live?"

About high-rises, he says: "If people come to me with proposals I will say all right, if you leave me some land, some open space on the street, for people. It's not appropriate for the Old City or Mea Shearim, but downtown—let them build."

Lupolianski's view of the city is pragmatic and down-to-earth; like many of the Haredim, he saves his emotions for religious matters. Not for him the romantic images of Jersusalem as the place where golden light dances upon ancient stones. He thinks in terms of numbers of housing units and of conflict resolution. At a recent hearing at City Hall, called to discuss a proposed restaurant to be added to a movie theater in the German Colony, a secular and rapidly gentrifying neighborhood that is known for cafes, restaurants and restored houses, Lupolianski was businesslike, even brusque, as he listened to neighbors objecting to the noise and disruption they allege the theater causes by remaining open on the Sabbath. Presiding at the head of a long table with a gavel and a can of Diet Coke, he cut off long-winded speakers, argued technicalities with the architect and acted generally like a teacher determined to put an unruly class in order.

What he did not do at any point was tip his hand and indicate sympathy for the neighbors, even though he might have been expected to support anyone determined to make it more difficult to do business on the Sabbath. But he is too savvy a politician to use up points on a minor issue in a neighborhood that is primarily secular. He saves his energy for more important battles—for example, the recent one he led to defeat an expansion plan by the Intel Corporation, which has a large factory in an industrial park on the northern side of Jerusalem. Lupolianski claimed that there were environmental risks to the high-tech manufacturing done by Intel, and successfully beat back the chipmaker's proposal. Few observers were convinced that Lupolianski, who until then had shown little interest in environmental issues, had turned green. What mattered to Lupolianski was the industrial park's proximity to the rapidly growing Haredi neighborhoods on the north side of the city, virtually all of which are in desperate need of more apartments—which could be built on the land Intel sought.

In my conversation with Lupolianski, he made no attempt to hide the fact that the housing problems of the ultrareligious are his first priority: "The need is greatest among the Haredim," he said. The land on which Intel had hoped to build is now likely to be used for housing for the ultrareligious, and while Intel continues to have facilities in Israel, it will locate its proposed new enterprise elsewhere, taking new jobs and investment away from Jerusalem.

THOSE JEWS IN JERUSALEM WHO ARE THE MOST religious tend to see the city in the most practical way, and nowhere in the city is this paradox more marked than at Ramat Polin, an extraordinary new neighborhood on the city's north side. Built in the 1970's to the designs of Zvi Hecker, one of Israel's most determinedly avant-garde architects, Ramat Polin was one of the few attempts by the national Ministry of Housing, which oversees the design and construction of Jerusalem's new neighborhoods, to break out of the standard architectural mold. Hecker created a "beehive"—a cluster of prefabricated, hexagonal units that were stacked in a manner that made for intriguing geometries but for little livability. The hexagonal shapes yielded internal spaces that were determinedly bizarre, with no vertical walls and a nearly overpowering sense of arbitrary and intrusive architectural presence.

Not surprisingly, the project was a failure: apartments went unsold, since few Israelis had any interest in being guinea pigs in an architect's ongoing experiment about rethinking the nature of domestic space. It was rescued financially—and filled to overflowing—only when an arrangement was made for one of the ultrareligious housing cooperatives to take it over, filling it with Haredi families who were eager for a roof over their heads, and cared not at all if that roof came down at a 15-degree angle. In fact, they seemed not to care much what the roof even looked like, or the walls, or much of anything else. They have turned Romat Polin into a kind of avant-garde shtetl. Open balconies are crowded with lean-tos, scrolled ironwork now decorates many of the windows and terraces and the pathways in front of these futuristic buildings are chock-full with men dressed in the 18th-century garb of the most traditional Haredim. Nowhere in Jerusalem, surely, is there as striking a contrast between the container and the people it contains.

Romat Polin is like a concert of difficult, atonal music for which tickets have been sold only to the tone-deaf. The Haredim are almost entirely without interest in esthetics, for theirs is a culture of words, not images. (Martin Weyl, the director of the Israel Museum, recalls a visit to the museum by one of the Haredi rabbis, itself a startling event, since the ultrareligious community has made no secret of its disapproval of the museum for showing contemporary art and images of women. But the rabbi, Weyl recalls, paid little attention to the pictures: he spent most of his time reading the labels, and looking at pictures that themselves contained writing.) At Ramat Polin, an unusual, highly personal notion of utopia was envisioned by an architect. The Haredim who live there give no indication of seeing this, or of perceiving Hecker's ideas at all. They see the buildings only in the most earthbound terms, blinkered by their obsession about a heaven of their own.

Heaven in one form or another is, of course, ever present in Jerusalem. It is there in the route Jesus took through the city to his crucifixion, the Stations of the Cross; it is at the Dome of the Rock, where the prophet Mohammed is said to have leaped toward the sky for his nighttime rendezvous with God, and it hovers over the Western Wall, the remnant of the foundations of the Second Temple and the most sacred shrine in Judaism. All three of these sacred sites are close upon one another in the Old City, and while they are deluged continually with both tourists and pilgrims, in their political status they are more like little countries than tourist attractions, for control over them has been the subject of two thousand years of struggle. Indeed, these sacred places are in one sense the most earthly realms of all, for in the long history of Jerusalem they have inspired as much war as peace.

Heaven intrudes upon Jerusalem in another way, too, in the recurring question of how much the whole city should itself resemble a perfect kingdom, or simply be allowed to look like other places. The British, who governed Jerusalem from 1917 to 1947, made a powerful gesture toward a higher Jerusalem when they decreed that all buildings had to be faced with Jerusalem stone, a local form of limestone with an exceptionally warm, golden hue. The rule remains in effect, lifted only for a short time in the 1930's when a stonecutters' strike led to the approval of several modernist buildings of stucco, and again briefly in the 1950's in the rush to build subsidized housing. This rule may be the most important single act of city planning ever in Jerusalem. The stone is an extraordinary material, rich and textured and almost magical in the glow of dawn and dusk in the city's heavy light, and it brings even the most mediocre architecture into a sense of wholeness with the city.

It is difficult to imagine what Jerusalem would be like without that stone. It turns the Old City into a single, glowing mass, and it saves the newer sections, with their waves of identical apartment blocks rolling over the hills, from total dreariness. Teddy Kollek said not long ago that he felt that "keeping the stone and keeping the city green" were his two greatest accomplishments so far as physical planning is concerned, and he is right—the city has numerous parks and open spaces, many of which were expanded and improved with the help of the Jerusalem Foundation. The area around the walls of the Old city, where buildings once went right up against the stone, has now been cleared and turned into a public open space as well, setting off the Old City with a slender belt of green. Construction is now moving ahead on one of the most ambitious projects of the Kollek era, Mamilla, a huge urban renewal project combining hotels, condominiums, retail space, parking and terraced open space in a mix of new and rehabilitated buildings in front of the Jaffa Gate, the prime entrance to the Old City. Designed by Moshe Safdie, Mamilla was initially to have been a huge complex that threatened to overpower the Old City beside it; after years of controversy,

the plan was scaled back to something smaller in scale, more pedestrian-oriented, and more likely to provide a comfortable bridge between the central business district and the Old City.

JERUSALEM, WHICH THE ISRAELIS CLAIM as their capital and like to suggest is synonymous with Jewish identity, was almost not a part of Israel in the first place. The founders of the state, including David Ben-Gurion, the first Prime Minister, accepted a 1947 United Nations proposal to partition Palestine into Jewish and Arab states that would have placed the city under international sovereignty. They agreed partly for practical reasons—they did not want to take on the United Nations at that stage—and partly because Jerusalem was never central to the dreams of the secular Zionists anyway. (Chaim Weizmann, the first President of Israel, called Jerusalem "a cursed city which has nothing in it," and also said, "As for the Old City, I would not take it even as a gift.") The Arabs rejected the partitioning plan and initiated what became Israel's war of independence, but even when the war was won in 1948, and the western sections of Jerusalem were in Israeli hands, the newly declared state of Israel still established its capital in Tel Aviv.

It was only a year later, in 1949, when the United Nations tried to move ahead on a plan to internationalize Jerusalem, that Israel had second thoughts and announced that Jerusalem would be considered its capital. (Most countries, including the United States, still do not recognize Israel's right to Jerusalem as a capital, and maintain their embassies in Tel Aviv.) Capital or not, Jerusalem in the years before 1967 had a profound sense of isolation from the rest of the country. The post-1948 borders were drawn in such a way as to make Jerusalem a kind of finger sticking into Jordanian territory, so the city's residents were surrounded on the north, east and south by Arabs.

Israel has controlled East Jerusalem for more than 28 years, but the difference in the condition of the two sides of the city is as striking, in some ways, as it was in 1967. Teddy Kollek was a passionate advocate of tolerance, and moved audiences around the world with his pleas for unity and concern for the Arab citizens of Jerusalem, but the fact is that his administration did relatively little to improve conditions on the Palestinian side of town. East Jerusalem was largely poor and depressed before the Six Day War, and it remains so today. While electricity and telephone service have been upgraded, it's probable that these things would have happened eventually even under the Jordanians, who controlled East Jerusalem along with the Old City until their defeat in the '67 war. The one major capital improvement made in the Kollek years in East Jerusalem—modernizing the sewer system—came only after an outbreak of cholera led to fears that disease in East Jerusalem could put the citizens of West Jerusalem in jeopardy.

Actually, making things better for West Jerusalem was the goal of most of the Kollek policies. The former Mayor was probably better at easing the concerns of liberal Jews that he was not doing enough for the Arabs than he was at caring for the Arabs themselves; since

1967, for example, according to a study by B'Tselem, the Israeli Information Center for Human Rights in the Occupied Territories, 64,880 housing units have been built in Jerusalem for Jews and only 8,800 for Palestinians. "Since the annexation of East Jerusalem in 1967, the Israeli Government has adopted a policy of systematic and deliberate discrimination against the Palestinian population in all matters relating to expropriation of land, planning and building," the B'Tselem study declared.

A report from this spring by the city government itself contains statistics that are just as damning: out of 900 sanitation workers, only 87 are assigned to East Jerusalem; out of 100 firefighters, only 14 are assigned to East Jerusalem. Mayor Olmert shows off the report as a sign of his predecessor's hypocrisy, and claims that he will do things differently. "Teddy could afford to do nothing for the Arabs—he was a liberal," Olmert says. "I am a right-wing conservative, so I will have to prove that I am concerned. So we are going to provide better services—it is incumbent upon us to show we can live with them equitably."

Sarah Kaminker, the former City Council member and, on the Israeli political spectrum, left of center, says, in reference to the Kollek years: "The government was absolutely brilliant in everything it did in East Jerusalem, because the policy was to isolate the Arabs and keep them quiet and yet appear to be treating them well. There are no master plans for a lot of Arab neighborhoods, and not even roads to connect the older villages with each other. All the new roads were built to connect the new Jewish neighborhoods to the center of the city."

The new neighborhoods were not of the city's own making, of course; they were a policy decision by the national Government, which was determined to create what came later to be called "facts on the ground"— irrefutable evidence of Jewish presence on land that had once belonged to Arabs. Yet Teddy Kollek endorsed the thrust of this policy, with its overwhelming bias in favor of Jewish residents of Jerusalem, and put the city's resources at its disposal. His passion for a unified city drove him to reject proposals shortly after the 1967 war to reconstitute the old municipal government of East Jerusalem and allow it to operate under the supervision of Israeli authorities, as the governments of many West Bank cities did—a system that would have meant that Jerusalem would have been governed by two separate entities, both reporting to the same national Government. Complex though it seems, such a plan could well have made the political life of the city easier today.

"I worked long and hard on that plan—I even kept the green chairs from the East Jerusalem council chamber in storage for four or five years," recalls Meron Benvenisti, a deputy mayor under Kollek, and now a writer, scholar and frequent critic of the Kollek administration. "But Teddy said he didn't want it. He demolished the legitimately constructed Arab municipality of East Jerusalem"—to assure that Jerusalem would be managed only by a single government, the Jewish government of West Jerusalem.

"NOBODY WANTS A GOOD GOVERNMENT— they only want their own government," Kollek says now. "We see this all over Africa—no country has as good a government as it did under the Dutch. But you can't go back." The comparison of the Israeli government of Jerusalem with the colonial governments of Africa is a startling and damning one, of course, and it points up precisely where Kollek is out of touch: he has no sense of the power of nationalist passions, and no understanding of the extent to which they could lead Palestinians, as they had led Africans, to be willing to forgo creature comforts in exchange for a sense of control over their own destiny. In his belief that the promise of parks, schools and health centers would suffice to keep the Palestinians happy, Kollek really did see himself as a kind of benign colonial ruler, not only over the Arabs but over many of the city's recently immigrated Jews, too. "The Jews coming here from the former Soviet Union, the Arabs, the ultrareligious Jews—none of them really know democracy," he says. "They think not of what they can do, only of what they need."

Kollek began during his administration to institute what he called a borough system to give neighborhoods some control over their own affairs by turning over management of certain city services, like street cleaning, to localities. But this was as much a means of holding back power as granting it, creating the illusion of broader participation in city government as a means of keeping the lid on dissatisfaction; the goal, as in Mikail Gorbachev's perestroika, was to preserve the existing system, not to undermine it. For Kollek was a committed, at least publicly, to the notion of Jerusalem's oneness throughout his 28 years in City Hall as much as he was in 1969, when he rejected any possibility of continued life for the government of East Jerusalem. "The Arabs have more freedom under us," he says. "A divided city is not a practical proposition."

And those in power in Jerusalem now, if they lack Kollek's colonialist slant, take an even harder line. "The city cannot be divided like Berlin," Uri Lupolianski says. Mayor Olmert says, "If Jerusalem is split, the city will be destroyed—it is a death penalty on the city." Palestinians, not surprisingly, offer no such dire predictions. They have nothing to lose from a change in Jerusalem's governance. Lacking any real control over any portion of Jerusalem, they can only describe the prospect of their getting it as assuring a future of tranquility and good feeling—something that, in truth, is no more likely to occur than the apocalypse feared by conservative Israelis.

"There is a division now between East and West Jerusalem—people from the east do not go to the west, and people from the west do not go to the east," says Faisal Husseini, the head of the Palestine Liberation Organization in Jerusalem. "What good is it to control some area if you cannot go there except with guns, and you cannot enjoy the life there? I think people want to enjoy life in Jerusalem, and not to have all this fighting go on. I accept that the west side of the city is under Israeli sovereignty if the east side is under Palestinian sovereignty. What they cannot say is that all of Jerusalem is under Israel's sovereignty."

Sovereignty has become a buzz word in Jerusalem. There have been dozens of proposals by politicians, political scientists, research institutes here and research institutes from around the world as to how some form of shared jurisdiction over Jerusalem might work. (One study counted 56 separate proposals for how the city might be governed.) Two distinct municipalities; one municipality with two separate governing bodies reporting to it; international sovereignty; Israeli sovereignty with special privileges for a Palestinian authority; a joint administration of an undivided city; shrinking the city to the pre-1967 borders; expanding it even beyond the current borders—all of these things have been proposed, so frequently that they have given rise to what Meron Benvenisti calls "the solution industry."

Most Palestinians continue to view East Jerusalem as the future capital of their future state, and the Israeli Government continues in its efforts to disabuse the Palestinians of such notions. Late last month, Israel ordered the closing of three Palestinian offices in East Jerusalem, claiming they were run by Yasir Arafat's government of Palestinian autonomy in violation of the peace agreement. The Israeli Government believes the P.L.O. is trying to establish its own "facts on the ground"—establishing a de facto government in the eastern sector of the city.

It is impossible to know at this stage how the negotiations between Israel and the Palestine Liberation Organization will resolve the status of Jerusalem. It is only clear that the negotiators in Oslo, where the timetable was set up in 1993, knew what they were doing holding Jerusalem for the end.

T HE ISRAELIS AND THE PALESTINIANS both believe that their past relationship to the city gives them a rightful claim on its future. And who can say otherwise? The most convincing Israeli argument against giving over a portion of Jerusalem to Palestinian control is how hard it would be to administer a city that was effectively part of two countries. Yet things are hardly working as they are, and it is possible that a Jerusalem under dual sovereignty could serve not as the model for conflict that it has been for so long, but as a model for harmony, as a reminder not of Israeli intransigence, but of Israeli generosity of spirit.

Israelis seem to be coming, gradually, to accept the notion that the only way to a permanent peace may be to give up total control over their capital. According to a public opinion poll conducted in May for the Israel-Palestine Center for Research and Information, 28 percent of Israeli Jewish adults say they are ready to accept some form of divided sovereignty over Jerusalem, so long as Israel could retain control over the Jewish neighborhoods in East Jerusalem. It is not a huge number, but more than had been widely believed. There appears to be an increasing number of Israelis who believe, as the architect Moshe Safdie puts it, "that it is time to separate the notion of sovereignty from the idea of a divided city. We have a divided city now in all but name—and maybe by giving up sovereignty over a portion of it, we could actually make it more united."

Safdie's paradox—that in division there may, in the end, be a truer unity—is an essential observation, for it cuts through much of the denial on both sides. The city is no more truly united today that it was before the 1967 war; it is unified only administratively, not socially, culturally or economically. A solution to Jerusalem's future must acknowledge this, even as it also acknowledges, as Israel Kimhi of the Jerusalem Institute says, "that we still have to manage planning, transportation, water, electricity and everything else together. This is a holy city, but people have to go to work each morning."

They have to go to work and not on a bus that might, one morning or the next, by carrying a suicide bomber. Last month's attack brought many Jerusalemites back to the terrible killing of February 1993 in Jeusalem's new East Talpiot neighborhood, set high on the ridge above the poor Arab village of Jabel Mukaber. A resident of East Talpiot was stabbed to death and another seriously wounded as they waited for a city bus, and the tragedy is marked in two ways: there is a monument at the bus stop, and there is now a high fence separating the Jewish settlement from the Arab village.

Jerusalem cannot afford more fences between its East Talpiots and its Jabel Mukabers. Taking them down will not be easy, especially in an atmosphere in which people wonder if and where there will be a next bomb. In the end, the solution for Jerusalem cannot be one that makes anyone terribly happy, because any solution that makes someone too happy will probably make someone else too unhappy, and things will be right back where they started. The political solution, whatever it turns out to be, will be one that people will live with grudgingly, not exuberantly. For what will save Jerusalem will not be a miracle, but the ordinary, slow dreary business of compromise, the acknowledgement by all sides that no one is going away, and that what is sacred to them is always going to belong, in part, to someone else. But what better lesson, in the end, could a holy place confer than that of understanding reality, and of seeing the sacred city as something more profound than an object to be held like a trophy won in battle?

"I am against the solution industry, because the solution is going to have to be ambiguous," Meron Benvenisti says. "I see neither redemption nor apocalypse, but a future in which Jerusalem will learn how to cope with friction, and develop a way of living with it—a future in which the city will become wise enough to live with ambiguity."

Understanding Cultural Pluralism

The increase in racial violence and hatred on campuses across the country is manifested in acts ranging from hateful speech to physical violence. Strategies for dealing with this problem on a campus include increased awareness through mandatory ethnic studies, the empowerment of targets of violence, and fostering social and cultural interaction in festivals, folk-arts fairs, and literary and political forums. Systematic knowledge about ethnic groups has not been a central scholarly concern. In fact, mainstream literary, humanistic, and historical disciplines have only recently begun to displace sociological attention to the pathologies of urban ethnicity as the primary contact and source of information and interpretation of ethnic traditions. The historic role that voluntary groups have played in the reduction of bias and bigotry also needs to be revalued and revitalized. Voluntary associations can take part in a host of state and local initiatives to improve intergroup relations. Schools and parents can help children understand commonalities and differences among and within ethnic traditions and groups. The incorporation of everyday experiences of families and a formal pedagogy rooted in accurate and locally relevant resources are essential building blocks for understanding diversity.

The reemergence of the discussion of race, ethnicity, and intelligence that is included in the selections found in this unit reveals the embeddedness of interpretive categories that frame the discussion and analysis of race and ethnic relations. The enormity of the educational effort that is required as we attempt to move beyond the ethnocentrism and racism that bred hatred and destructive relationships between persons and communities is revealed in a variety of ways. Philosophic reflection on the epistemological issues associated with explaining human variety is rarely invited. However, it is precisely at this intersection of social philosophy and science that the crucial breakthroughs in understanding are likely to appear. The continual mismeasures of intelligence and misreadings of meaning indicate the long-term need for critical reformulation of the very idea of race.

At this time a variety of ways of measuring the development of race and ethnic relations are imposing the accuracy of their claims. Evidence cited by claimants to such authoritative knowledge and the attendant public criterion of credibility point to the expectation of a spirited debate. This unit challenges us to rethink the assumptions, contradictions, and aspirations of social development models.

Looking Ahead: Challenge Questions

What signs have you seen of an increase in racist, anti-Semitic, anti-immigrant, and antiminority group acts that recent studies apparently confirm?

What explains the fact that large population studies confirm that, in the areas of ethnic, racial, and religious differences, Americans are more tolerant than ever?

Why do teenagers commit 80 percent of all bias-related acts?

What problems does conflict in ethnic and race relations pose for corporate and governmental institutions?

What media images of race and ethnicity are dominant?

What avenues are available for the authentic cultural resources of ethnic communities and traditions?

How can multiethnic expressions of traditions intersect with the breakdown of community and the isolationist tendencies related to individual and personal achievement?

How can the promotion of positive prototypes of ethnicity ever become as powerful as negative stereotypes?

How can dialogue among conflicting parties about dilemmas that are essential to technological and economic change enable us to share and shape the burden of social change?

Are national and local media a source of further exacerbation of race and ethnic relations? Explain.

Why should advocates of multicultural development and diversity argue for the following: (1) Fair and equal protection under the law? (2) The compilation of full and accurate data on the ethnic composition of the American population? (3) Corporate and governmental leaders who are focused on issues that have specific ethnic and racial significance?

What are the benefits if ethnic groups meet regularly with other ethnic groups and engage in friendly "what's your agenda" meetings?

Who, if anyone, benefits from the persistence of ethnic tension and conflict?

UNDERSTANDING AFROCENTRISM

WHY BLACKS DREAM OF A WORLD WITHOUT WHITES

GERALD EARLY

Gerald Early is director of the African and Afro-American Studies Program at Washington University in St. Louis.

The White man will never admit his real references. He will steal everything you have and still call you those names.

—Ishmael Reed,
Mumbo Jumbo (1972)

Furthermore, no one can be thoroughly educated until he learns as much about the Negro as he knows about other people.

—Carter G. Woodson,
The Mis-Education of the Negro (1933)

[Alexander] Crummell's black nationalism was marked by certain inconsistencies, but they derived from the inconsistencies and hypocrisy of American racism, rather than from any intellectual shortcomings on his part. It was impossible to create an ideology that responded rationally to an irrational system.

—Wilson Jeremiah Moses,
Alexander Crummell: A Study of Civilization and Discontent (1989)

IN A SPAN OF THREE WEEKS DURING THE EARLY SPRING semester of 1995, Angela Davis and bell hooks, two notable black leftist, feminist thinkers, visited the campus of Washington University in St. Louis, invited by different student groups. They were generally well received, indeed, enthusiastically so. But there was, for each of them during these visits, something of a jarring note, both involving black students.

Professor Davis, entertaining questions during a panel session after having spoken earlier on the subject of prison reform, was asked by a black woman student what she had to offer black people as a solution to their problems. The student went on to explain that she did not consider herself an African-American. She was simply an African, wishing to have nothing to do with being an American or with America itself. She wanted black people to separate themselves entirely from "Europeans," as she called white Americans, and wanted to know what Davis could suggest to further that aim.

Davis answered that she was not inclined to such stringent race separation. She was proud of being of African descent but wished to be around a variety of people, not just people like herself. Davis felt further that blacks should not isolate themselves but accept in partnership anyone who was sincerely interested in the cause of overthrowing capitalism, a standard and reasonable Marxist response to the "essentializing" of race in a way that would divert true political engagement "against the system." The student was visibly annoyed with the answer, which presumably smacked of "white" intellectualism.

Professor bell hooks, after her address on ending racism and sexism in America—love, I think, was the answer—was asked by a black woman student how feminism was relevant to black women. Hooks explained that feminism was not only for white women, that black women needed to read more feminist texts, even if some of them were racist. After all, Karl Marx was racist but he did give the world a brilliant analysis of capitalism. She had said in her speech how disappointed she was that her black women students at City College of New York were not inclined to embrace feminism, rejecting it as something white. She felt that these black women were unduly influenced by black male rappers who bashed feminism. The answer did not persuade or please the student.

From *Civilization*, July/August 1995, pp. 31-39. © 1995 by Gerald Early. Reprinted by permission.

Later that day, I heard many black undergraduates dismiss hooks's talk as not addressing the needs of black people, as being too geared to the white feminists in the audience. Some were disturbed that hooks would feel that they formed their opinions on the basis of listening to rap records. None of this was said, necessarily, with hostility, but rather with regret and a shade of condescension that only the young can so keenly and innocently express when speaking about the foolishness of their elders.

I recall a fairly recent incident where a black student, a very bright young woman, asked if, when doing research, one had to acknowledge racist books. I told her that a certain amount of objectivity was part of the discipline of being a scholar. Anger at unjust or inaccurate statements and assessments was understandable, but personalizing everything often caused a kind of tunnel vision where crude self-affirmation seemed to be the only fit end of scholarship. She responded that she would refuse to acknowledge racist sources, that if the book was racist, then everything it said was tainted and should be disregarded.

The attitudes of these students have been shaped by Afrocentrism, an insistence by a growing number of black Americans to see the world from an "African-centered" perspective in response to the dominant "European-centered" perspective to which they feel they have been subjected throughout their lives. Afrocentrism is many things and has many degrees of advocacy. It can range from the commercialism and pretense of the shallow holiday called Kwanza (no shallower, it should be said, than the commercialized celebration of Christmas) to the kente-cloth ads and nationalist talk that one finds in most black publications these days; from talk about racist European scholarship to a view that world culture is essentially African in origin and that Europeans are usurpers, thieves, and generally inferior. On the one hand, we have the recent cover story "Is Jesus Black?" in *Emerge*, an Afrocentric-tinged news magazine for the black middle class. The answer in this instance, of course, is clearly yes. (Obviously, this is grounds for competing claims between blacks and Jews; whatever can be said about Jesus' skin color or the religious movement that bears his name, there is no question that he was a Jew.) On the other hand, we have the first explicitly Afrocentric Hollywood Western in Mario Van Peebles's 1993 film *Posse*, a jumbled multicultural critique of white *fin de siècle* imperialism and the myth of how the West was won.

No doubt, Afrocentrists specifically and black folk generally found it to be a signal victory that in the recent television dramatization of the love affair between Solomon and Sheba, Sheba was played by a black actress and Solomon by a swarthy Hispanic. In the 1959 Hollywood film version of *Solomon and Sheba*, directed by King Vidor—who, incidentally, made the first all-black Hollywood film—Solomon was played by Yul Brynner and Sheba by Gina Lollobrigida. It is safe to say that the real Solomon and the real Sheba, if they ever existed, did not look remotely like any of the actors who ever played them. But whom we want them to look like is very important. The Afrocentrists will feel their triumph to be complete when black actors portray Beethoven, Joseph Haydn, Warren G. Harding, Alexander Hamilton, Hannibal, Abraham Lincoln, Dwight Eisenhower, Cleopatra, Moses, Jesus Christ and Saint Augustine. Many African-Americans are inclined to believe that any noted white with ambiguous ancestry must be black. They are also inclined to believe that any white with dark skin tones, one who hangs around blacks or who "acts black" in some way is truly black. At various times in my life, I have heard blacks argue vehemently that Madonna, Phoebe Snow, Keith Jarrett, Mae West, Ava Gardner and Dorothy Parker were black, even though they did not have a shred of evidence to support the claims. Blacks have always been fascinated by "passing," by the possibility that some whites are really black—"fooling old massa," so to speak.

AFROCENTRISM IS AN INTELLECTUAL MOVEMENT, a political view, a historically traceable evolution, a religious orthodoxy. It derives, in part, from Negritude and Pan-Africanism, which stressed the culture and achievements of Africans. Both movements were started by Africans, West Indians and African-Americans in response to European colonialism and the worldwide oppression of African-descended people. But Afrocentrism is also a direct offshoot of earlier forms of black nationalism, in which blacks around the world believed they had a special destiny to fulfill and a special consciousness to redeem. More important, Afrocentrism is a mood that has largely erupted in the last 10 to 15 years in response to integration or, perhaps more precisely, to the failure of integration. Many blacks who have succeeded in the white world tend to feel most Afrocentric, although I think it would be a mistake to see Afrocentrism purely as middle-class, since significant numbers of working-class blacks are attracted to some elements of it. The bourgeois, "midcult" element of Afrocentrism, nonetheless, is very strong. "Integrated" middle-class blacks see it as a demonstration of their race loyalty and solidarity with their brothers and sisters throughout the world, whether in American cities or on African farms. (It is worth noting the economic clout of the black middle class, which can be seen in the growing number of black Hollywood films and filmmakers, in new black magazines ranging from *Body and Soul* to *The Source* to *Upscale*, and in the larger audience for black books. It is the market power of this class that has given Afrocentrism its force as a consumer ideology.)

So the middle-class black, having had more contact with whites and their institutions, is expected to speak for and to other blacks. Afrocentrism, like Negritude and Pan-Africanism, is meant to be an ideological glue to bring black people together, not just on the basis of color but as the expression of a cultural and spiritual will that crosses class and geographical lines. As W.E.B. Du Bois wrote in 1940: "Since the fifteenth century these ancestors of mine and their other descendants have had a common history; have suffered a common disaster and have one long memory.... The real essence of this kinship is its social heritage of slavery; the discrimination and insults; and this heritage binds together not simply the children of Africa, but extends through yellow Asia and into the South Seas. It is this unity that draws me to Africa."

Louis H. Farrakhan, the head of the Nation of Islam, is probably the most familiar figure associated with Afrocentrism. (Muhammad Ali introduced Islamic conversion to an even bigger public, suffering greatly for his religious and political beliefs and becoming the most noted and charismatic dissident of his era. Ali's prodigious athletic abilities and his genial temperament succeeded in endearing him to the American public despite his religion. He never became a member of Farrakhan's sect.) Farrakhan is a fiery preacher, prone to making extreme statements, with a militant flair and a racist edge, that have the conviction of truth among some blacks. He especially exploits the idea that he is a heroic black man at grave risk for daring to tell the truth about the white man. (Malcolm X used this device effectively, too.) He is also a master demagogue who exploits the paranoia of his audience. But then, as a friend once said to me, "What black person isn't justified in being at least half-paranoid?"

Farrakhan has found three effective lines of entry among blacks, particularly young blacks, that draw on the Afrocentric impulse: First, that Islam is the true religion of black people. (This has led to a move among black Christian leaders to point out with great vehemence the African origins of Christianity, to make it, in effect, a black religion.) Second, that black people need business enterprise in their community in order to liberate themselves (an old belief among blacks, going back to at least the early part of the 19th century). And third, that Jews of European descent (what he calls "false Jews") are not to be trusted, a charge that exploits the current tension between blacks and Jews—and that Farrakhan has used to move into the black civil-rights establishment. All three positions enjoy remarkable support within the black middle class, a situation that has helped Farrakhan tap people's insecurities for his own purposes. The Nation of Islam may be famous for converting addicts and criminals, but above all, it wants, as all religions do, to win over the middle class, with its money, its respectability and its organizational know-how.

Whatever might be said of Farrakhan's importance as a political figure in the black community or in the United States, he is a minor figure in the development of Afrocentrism. His position in the history of Afrocentrism is similar to that of, say, Rush Limbaugh in the development of American conservatism. He is, like Limbaugh, a figure the media can use to give a sellable face and voice to a unique temper among a group of people. For both Limbaugh and Farrakhan represent an intense sentimentality in American life, a yearning for a fantasized, idealized past of racial grandeur and simplicity. This sentimentality appeals powerfully to the black middle class, which yearns for a usable, untainted past. This partly explains why Farrakhan and the Muslims can often be found speaking to black college students.

In thinking about the connection between class and nationalistic feelings, it should be recalled that in Harriet Beecher Stowe's 1852 novel, *Uncle Tom's Cabin,* the most light-complexioned blacks, the ones with the greatest skills, George, Eliza and Cassy, return to Africa at the novel's end to retrieve their degraded patrimony. It might be said that this is purely Stowe's own perverse vision, since some of the fiercest advocates for returning to Africa have been Martin Delany, Alexander Crummell and Marcus Garvey, all very dark men. Yet there is more than a little truth to the idea that class, caste and race consciousness are closely interwoven. Nationalism of whatever sort has almost always been an affair of a disaffected middle class. And until the 1920s, the black middle class in America was disproportionately made up of light-skinned people.

The paradox of the bourgeois aspect of Afrocentrism is that it rejects cosmopolitanism as being "white" or "Eurocentric." Yet Afrocentrism has no other way of seeing cosmopolitanism except on the "Eurocentric" model, so it tries to make Africa for black Americans the equivalent of what Europe is for white Americans: the source of civilization. Indeed, by trying to argue that Africa is the source of Western civilization, the Afrocentric sees the African, symbolically, as the mother of white Europe (just as the black mother, the mammy, is the mythic progenitor of the white South, or so Langston Hughes seemed to believe in his famous short story "Father and Son," which became his even more famous play, *Mulatto).* The African becomes, in this view, the most deeply cultured person on the planet, which matches his status as the oldest person on the planet, with the longest and deepest genetic history. In short, Afrocentrism becomes another form of the American apologizing for being American to people he imagines are his cultural superiors. Afrocentrism tries to mask a quest for American filiopiety behind a facade of African ancestor and culture worship.

I T WOULD BE EASY, ON ONE LEVEL, TO DISMISS AFROCENtrism as an expression, in white workplaces and white colleges, of intimidated black folk who are desperately trying to find a space for themselves in what they feel to be alien, unsympathetic environments. Seen this way, Afrocentrism becomes an expression of the low self-esteem and inferiority that blacks feel most intensely when they are around whites; their response is to become more "black," estranged from the environment that they find so unaccepting of them. The greatest psychic burden of the African-American is that he must not only think constantly about being different but about what his difference means. And it might be suggested that Afrocentrism does not solve this problem but merely reflects it in a different mirror. There is a certain amount of truth to this, especially at a time when affirmative action, which promotes group identification and group difference, tends to intensify black self-consciousness. And black people, through no fault of their own, are afflicted with a debilitating sense of self-consciousness when around whites. When whites are in the rare situation of being a minority in a sea of blacks, they often exhibit an abject self-consciousness as well, but the source of that self-consciousness is quite different. The white is used to traveling anywhere in the world and having his cultural inclinations accommodated. The black is neither used to this nor does he realistically expect it. The European exults in his culture while the African is utterly degraded by his. That blacks should want to free themselves from the white gaze seems not merely normal but essential to the project of reconstructing themselves as a people on their own terms. And the history of blacks in the United States has been an ongoing project—tragic, pathetic, noble, heroic, misguided, sublime—of self-reconstruction.

FOR BLACK PEOPLE TO FEEL UNIFIED, ANCIENT EGYPT HAD TO BE A

When it comes to black folk in America, the white man wants to say that if you have one-thirty-second portion of black blood, a mere drop of black blood, then you are black, no matter what your skin color. But when it comes to the ancient Egyptians, it doesn't matter if they have a drop of black blood, and we know that they had at least one-thirty-second portion of African blood. It doesn't matter how much African blood they have, they are still white. The white man wants to have his cake and eat it too. When it's convenient, he wants you to be black and when it's convenient, he wants you to be white. Either you're a nigger, because he thinks you're nothing. Or you're white, if you have done anything he's bound to respect. The white man wants to control all the definitions of blackness.

—A conversation with an Afrocentric friend

Afrocentrism, like a good many nationalistic ideologies, might be called the orthodoxy of the book, or more precisely, the orthodoxy of the books. Afrocentrism is an attempt to wed knowledge and ideology. Movements like Afrocentrism, which feels both its mission and its authority hinge on the revelation of a denied and buried truth, promote a fervent scholasticism, a hermeneutical ardor among true believers for compilations of historical minutiae on the one hand, and for grand philosophical tracts on the other. The former might be best represented by George G.M. James's *Stolen Legacy*, published in 1954, the latter by Mustafa El-Amin's *Al-Islam, Christianity, and Freemasonry* and *Freemasonry, Ancient Egypt, and the Islamic Destiny*. These books were not written by professional historians or by college professors. The fact that several classic Afrocentric texts have been written by amateurs gives Afrocentrism its powerful populist appeal, its legitimacy as an expression of "truth" that white institutional forces hide or obscure. At the same time, this leaves it vulnerable to charges of being homemade, unprofessional, theoretically immature and the like. It is one of the striking aspects of Afrocentrism that within the last 20 years it has developed a cadre of academics to speak for it, to professionalize it, to make it a considerable insurgency movement on the college campus.

There are several texts that might be considered the literary and intellectual cornerstones of the Afrocentrism movement. Molefi K. Asante, professor and chair of African-American studies at Temple University in Philadelphia, is credited with inventing the name "Afrocentrism" or "Afrocentricity" (although currently the term "Africentrism" is on the rise in certain quarters, probably because there is a group of black folk who, for some reason, despise the prefix "Afro," as if the word "Africa" itself were created by the people of the continent rather than by Europeans). Asante's very short books, including *The Afrocentric Idea*, published in 1987, and *Afrocentricity: The Theory of Social Change*, published in 1980, are frequently the starting points for people seeking a basic explanation of this ideology. As defined by Asante, Afrocentrism seems to take the terms and values of Eurocentrism—intense individualism, crass greed, lack of spirituality, warlike inclinations, dominance and racism, dishonesty and hypocrisy—and color their opposites black, giving us a view of black people not terribly different from the romantic racism of Harriet Beecher Stowe and other whites like her in the 19th and 20th centuries. I cannot recount the number of "race sensitivity" meetings I have attended where blacks begin to describe themselves (or those they perceive to be Africans) as more spiritual, more family-oriented, more community-oriented, more rhythmic, more natural and less combative than whites. All of which is, of course, a crock of nonsense, largely the expression of wishes for qualities that blacks see as absent from their community life now. But, thanks to Asante, this has become the profile of the African in the Afrocentric vision.

Martin Bernal's massively researched two-volume *Black Athena* (published in 1987 and 1991) is a popular title in Afrocentric circles, in large measure because Bernal, a professor at Cornell, is one of the few white scholars to take Afrocentrism seriously—William Piersen, Robert Farris Thompson and Andrew Hacker, in decidedly different ways, are others—and one of the few to write an academic treatise in its defense that forces whites to take it seriously too. (The irony that blacks still need whites, in some measure, to sell their ideas and themselves to other whites is not entirely lost on those who have thought about this.)

Black Athena supports three major contentions of the Afrocentrists: 1) ancient Egypt was a black civilization; 2) the Greeks derived a good deal, if not all, of their philosophy and religion from the Egyptians; 3) European historiography has tried strenuously and with clear political objectives to deny both. Bernal's book provoked a scathing attack by Mary R. Lefkowitz, a professor at Wellesley, who characterizes Afrocentrism as a perversion of the historiography of antiquity and a degradation of academic standards for political ends. Lefkowitz has also battled with Tony Martin, a cultural historian, barrister and Marcus Garvey specialist, who began using and endorsing the Nation of Islam's anti-Semitic *The Secret Relationship Between Blacks and Jews* (Vol. 1) in his classes on slavery at Wellesley. Martin responded in 1993 with his own account of the dispute, *The Jewish Onslaught: Despatches from the Wellesley Battlefront*, which elaborates his claims of Jewish racism and the hypocrisy of academic freedom.

Maulana Karenga, professor and chair of black studies at California State University at Long Beach, created the black philosophical code called the Kawaida, which was the inspiration for Kwanza and the seven principles (Nguzo Saba) that the holiday celebrates. The code contains a bit of Marxism to create a "theoretical" ambiance. Karenga is also author of the popular *Introduction to Black Studies*, used by many colleges in their introductory courses, despite its rather tendentious manner, which he tries to pass off as sharp-minded Marxism, and the fact that the book is weak on a good many aspects of African-American life and culture.

Perhaps the most popular Afrocentric text is Chancellor Williams's *The Destruction of Black Civilization: Great Issues of a Race from 4500 B.C. to 2000 A.D.* (published in 1987), an account of his exhaustive research trips to Africa. Although not directly trained in the study of African history, Williams studied under William Leo Hansberry, a history professor at Howard University and probably the leading black American authority on Africa during the 1930s, 1940s and 1950s. Hansberry did path-breaking work in an utterly neglected field, eventually becoming known as "the father of African studies" in the United States. (Scholars, until recently, did not think Africa had a "history." The continent, especially its sub-Saharan regions, had an "anthropology" and an "archaeology," folkways to be discovered and remains to be unearthed, but never a record of institutions, traditions, political ideologies and complex societies.) Williams also did research on African history at Oxford and at the University of London, where, because of colonialism, interest in the nature of African societies was far keener than in the United States. His book *The Re-Birth of African Civilization,* an account of his 1953–1957 research project investigating the nature of education in Europe and Africa, calls for Pan-African education of blacks in Africa and around the world. Williams concluded that "European" and "Eurocentric" education was antithetical, both politically and intellectually, to African interests, a common refrain in Afrocentrist thought.

Most Afrocentric scholars at universities today genuflect at the intellectual altar of Cheikh Anta Diop, a Senegalese humanist and scientist who began his research into African history in 1946, as the battle against European colonialism in Africa was beginning. Diop saw his mission as undermining European colonialism by destroying the European's claim to a superior history. He was tenacious in demonstrating that Africa had a "real" history that showed that Africans were the product of civilizations and not of the jungle. This claim to history was a sign to the African that he was an equal player in the family of man, and was essential to any demand for independence.

For Diop, it was not enough to reconstruct African history; it was also necessary to depict a unified Africa, an idea that, whether myth or fact, was considered ideologically crucial by the Pan-African movement to overthrow European imperialism. Like every other oppressed people, the African could face the future only if he could hark back to some version of his past, preferably a past touched with greatness. This could be done only by running African history and civilization through Egypt, the only African civilization that impressed European intellectuals. As jazz and cultural critic Stanley Crouch suggested, Egypt is the only African civilization that has monuments, a physical legacy that indicates history as understood in European terms. Thus, for black people in Africa to be unified, for black people around the world to feel unified, ancient Egypt has to be a "black" civilization and serve as the origin of all blackness and, even more important, all whiteness. We know from scientific evidence that Africa is the place of origin for human life. If it is also true that Egypt is the oldest civilization from which Europeans borrowed freely (Bernal makes a persuasive argument for the influence of Egypt on European intellectuals through the 19th century), then Africans helped shape Western culture and were major actors in history, not bit players in the unfolding drama of European dominance.

Diop's doctoral dissertation, based on the idea that Egypt was African and that European civilization was largely built on Egyptian ideas, was rejected at the University of Paris in 1951. The story goes that he was able to defend his dissertation successfully only in 1960 when he was accompanied into the examination room by an army of historians, sociologists and anthropologists who supported his views, or at least his right as a responsible scholar to express them. By then, with African independence in full swing, his ideas had a political currency in Africa as an expression of Pan-Africanism. And no one supported the idea of a unified Africa

more than Egypt's then-president, Gamal Abdel Nasser, probably the most powerful independent leader on the continent. Like Gandhi, Nasser called himself a black man, and he envisioned an Africa united in opposition to Israel and South Africa. It was a good moment for Diop to be saying what he was saying. At the 1956 Conference of Negro-African Writers and Artists in Paris, Diop was one of the most popular speakers, although black American James Baldwin was not much impressed with his thesis. (Admittedly, for Baldwin this was pretty new stuff.) For his part, Diop, a Marxist, thought the American delegation was blindly anticommunist and naively committed to the integrationist policies of the civil-rights movement.

Diop produced a number of volumes translated into English, some based on his dissertation. They include *The African Origin of Civilization: Myth or Reality, Civilization or Barbarism: An Authentic Anthropology* and *The Cultural Unity of Negro Africa.* For Diop, everything turned on establishing that ancient Egypt was a black civilization: "The history of Black Africa will remain suspended in air and cannot be written correctly until African historians dare to connect it with the history of Egypt." Moreover, Diop felt that the African could not remove the chains of colonialism from his psyche until he had a fully reconstructed history—in other words, until he had an unusual past. Diop was brilliant and clearly obsessed. His importance in the formation of African-American intellectual history does not depend on whether his historical theories are correct. (Although there is considerable debate about ancient Egypt—not surprising, since there is no documentation of the claim in the language of the people who lived there at the time—it is now conceded by virtually everyone that the Egyptians were a mixed-race people.) Diop's work transcends questions of historical accuracy and enters the realm of "belief." Much of what Diop wrote may be true (he had vast amounts of evidence to support his claims) but, as a Marxist, he was not motivated simply by the quest for positivistic, objective "truth." He wanted to use the supposed objectivity of scientific research for political ends.

DIOP BROUGHT TOGETHER THREE IMPORTANT elements in understanding the origins of Afrocentrism: first, the tradition of professional, politically motivated historical research that buttresses the claims of untrained, amateur historians; second, the explicit connection between knowledge of one's "proper" history and one's psychological and spiritual well-being; third, the connection between "proper" knowledge of one's history and the realization of a political mission and purpose. If European history functioned as an ideological and political justification for Europe's place in the world and its hope for its future, why shouldn't African history function in the same manner? This is the reasoning of the Pan-Africanists and Afrocentrists who see "proper" history as the version that is most ideologically and politically useful to their group. Diop's research supports the idea of a conspiracy among white historians to discredit or ignore black civilization. Without a "proper" knowledge of African history, Diop argues, blacks will remain politically impotent and psychologically crippled. These ideas have become the uncritical dogma of Afrocentrism. By the time Diop died in 1986, he had been virtually canonized by an important set of black American scholars who identified themselves as Afrocentric.

Diop is useful for Afrocentrism today not only because of his monumental research but because he was an African, thus linking Afrocentrism to Africa itself and permitting the black American to kneel before the perfect intellect of the "purer" African. But Diop's ideas about ancient black civilization in Egypt and the importance of fuller knowledge of its history had been advanced earlier by several African-American intellectuals, including W.E.B. Du Bois in his momentous book *Black Folk, Then and Now: An Essay in the History and Sociology of the Negro Race*, which appeared in 1939. Du Bois said he was inspired to write about the glories of the Negro past after hearing a lecture in 1906 at Atlanta University by the preeminent white anthropologist Franz Boas, debunker of racism and mentor of Zora Neale Hurston. Du Bois's work remains, despite the more richly researched efforts of Diop, Bernal and St. Clair Drake in *Black Folk Here and There* (published in two volumes in 1987 and 1990), the best and most readable examination of the subject. Indeed, his work must be seen in a larger historical context, dating back to the founding of the American Negro Academy in 1897, when he and other black intellectuals tried to organize themselves for the purpose of producing scholarship that defended the race and promoted race consciousness. Yet Du Bois's book is not the central work of the Afrocentric movement by a black American writer.

That book would be Carter G. Woodson's *The Mis-Education of the Negro*, originally published in 1933. Woodson, a Harvard Ph.D. in history who launched both the Association for the Study of Negro Life and History (1915) and Negro History Week (1926), was as obsessed with the reconstruction of the Negro past as Diop or Du Bois. He churned out dozens of books on virtually every aspect of African and African-American history. Some were wooden, opaque or just plain sloppy, and several are unreadable (even in the opinion of his assistant, the late, brilliant black historian Lorenzo Greene), indicating the haste with which they were composed. Even so, Woodson was a serious and demanding scholar. Greene thought of him, at times, as having the pious devotion of a Franciscan friar and the crotchety temper of an eccentric intellectual consumed by his work.

The Mis-Education of the Negro, although written by a man who endorsed Booker T. Washington and the Tuskegee method, was generally critical of black education. Black people, Woodson argued, were not being educated in a way that would encourage them to press their own political and economic interests or make them a viable social group in the United States. They were, in fact, being educated against their own interests, largely because their education was controlled by whites who saw advantage in giving blacks an inferior education. Moreover, Woodson made the explicit connection between "improper" education, including a lack of knowledge about the black past, and the psychological degradation of the Negro, his internalized sense of inferiority. In short, a white-controlled education led to Uncle Tomism and black sellouts, to a defective Negro who suffered from false consciousness, or, more precisely, "white" conscious-

ness. Some of this argument was restated in black sociologist E. Franklin Frazier's seminal 1957 work, *Black Bourgeoisie*. The black middle class was almost exclusively the target of this indictment—a fact that prompted that class to romanticize certain aspects of black lower-class life, particularly its antisocial and criminal elements, in an effort to demonstrate its solidarity with "authentic" black experience. This was true with the Black Panthers in the late 1960s and it continues with rap music today. Another consequence is that the black middle class insists on a degree of race loyalty that sometimes thwarts any critical inquiry that does not promote race unity.

Much of Woodson's argument resonates with blacks today because it seems to endorse the idea of Afrocentric schools and especially the idea that knowledge of a glorious African past would give black youngsters self-esteem, reduce violence and criminality in black neighborhoods, and lead to the spiritual and political uplift of black people. This is why history is actually a less important discipline to the rise of Afrocentrism than psychology. After all, the reconstruction of black history was always connected with the reconstruction of the black mind, a mind that existed before the coming of the white man—or at least a mind that could be free of the white man and his image of what black people were.

In some ways, the rise of Afrocentrism is related to the rise of "black psychology" as a discipline. The Association of Black Psychologists was organized in 1968, a time when a number of black professional offshoots were formed in political and ideological protest against the mainstream, white-dominated versions of their organizations. Somewhat later came the *Journal of Black Psychology*, given impetus by the initial assaults against black intelligence or pointed suggestions of black genetic inferiority by Richard Herrnstein, Arthur Jensen and others in the early 1970s; this was also the time of the first wave of court challenges against affirmative action. The black psychology movement argued for new modes of treatment for black mental illness, the medical efficacy of using black history to repair a collectively damaged black psyche, and the destruction of "Eurocentrism" and the values it spawned—from the idealization of white standards of beauty to the scientific measurement of intelligence—as totally inimical to the political and psychological interests of black people. Rationality, order, individualism, dominance, sexual repression as well as sexual license, aggression, warmaking, moneymaking, capitalism itself—all soon became "white values."

That all of this happened during the era of Vietnam War protests, when white Western civilization was coming under withering intellectual attack from the radical left, is not without significance. Radical white intellectuals, who otherwise had no more use for a black epic history than a white one, found the black version useful as a weapon against "Eurocentrism," which, as a result of the Vietnam War, they held in utter contempt. In short, Jean-Paul Sartre and Susan Sontag were as instrumental, albeit indirectly, in the formation of Afrocentrism as, say, the Black Power movement of the late 1960s or the writings of African psychiatrist Franz Fanon, whose *The Wretched of the Earth* became the revolutionary psychological profile of the oppressed black diaspora. Also occurring at this time was the

THE RECONSTRUCTION OF THE BLACK MIND, A MIND FREE OF THE WHITE MAN

movement on white college campuses to establish black studies programs, which provided a black intellectual wedge into the white academy. These programs, largely multidisciplinary, required an ideological purpose and mission to bind together the various disciplines, which is why many began to articulate some kind of Afrocentrism or, as it was called in the 1970s, "black aesthetic"—in other words, an ideological framework to give black studies a reason for being. When used to challenge the dominance of Western thought, Afrocentrism becomes part of a multicultural wave of complaint and resentment against the white man by a number of groups that feel they have been oppressed.

In an age of dysfunction and psychotherapy, no one can have greater claim to having been made dysfunctional by political oppression than the African-American, who was literally a slave; and no one can have a greater need for recourse to psychotherapy in the form of Afrocentrism. But what made the black psychology movement possible was the rise of the Nation of Islam, particularly the rise of Malcolm X.

The charismatic Muslim minister did two things. First, he forced the white mainstream press to take notice of black nationalism, Pan Africanism and the concept of African unity. Previously these ideas had been marginalized as ridiculous or even comic expressions of black nationalism, to be read by blacks in black barbershops and beauty salons as they thumbed through the Ripley's-Believe-It-or-Not-type work of the self-taught black historian J. A. Rogers (*One Hundred Amazing Facts About the Negro, Five Negro Presidents* and the like). Malcolm X revitalized the ideas of Marcus Garvey, the great black nationalist leader of the 1910s and 1920s, whose Universal Negro Improvement Association became, for a time, one of the most popular black political groups in America. Malcolm, like Garvey, felt that the Negro still needed to be "improved" but, unlike Garveyites, the Muslims did not offer costumes and parades but sober suits, puritanical religion, dietary discipline and no-nonsense business practices. Malcolm himself was also, by his physical appearance alone, a figure who would not be dismissed as a buffoon, as Garvey often was by both blacks and whites. According to Malcolm's *Autobiography,* his father had been a Garveyite as well as a wife beater who favored his lighter-skinned children. Malcolm's Islamic-based black nationalism, his sexual abstinence, which lasted from his religious conversion until his marriage a decade later, and his triumph over his own preference for lighter-skinned blacks and whites were all meant to demonstrate, vividly, how he superseded his father as a nationalist and how the Nation of Islam has superseded Garveyism.

Malcolm enlisted a body of enforcers, the feared Fruit of Islam, grim-faced men who, one imagines, were supposed to personify the essence of an unbowed yet disciplined black manhood. In this way, he dramatically associated black nationalism with a new type of regenerated black male. It was said in the black community, and may still be, that no one bothers a Muslim for fear of retribution from the Fruit of Islam. Certainly, there was a point in the development of the Fruit of Islam and the Nation itself in the 1960s and early 1970s (Malcolm was assassinated in 1965) when both were closely associated with racketeering and gangster activity. During this period, many East Coast mosques were among the most terrifying organizations in the black community.

Second, Malcolm, in his *Autobiography*, also managed to link the psychological redemption of the Negro with his reacquaintance with his history. The prison chapters of the *Autobiography* have become nearly mythic as a paradigm of black reawakening. Malcolm's religious conversion became, in a sense, the redemption of the black male and the rehabilitation of black masculinity itself. Lately, we have seen two major black male public figures who were incarcerated for serious crimes, Marion Barry and Mike Tyson, use the Malcolm paradigm to resuscitate their standing with the black public. The martyrdom of Malcolm gave this paradigm a blood-endorsed political heroism that has virtually foreclosed any serious criticism of either its origins or its meaning.

It is extraordinary to contemplate how highly regarded Malcolm X is in the black community today, especially in comparison with Martin Luther King. (When I wrote an article for *Harper's* that was critical of Malcolm X, I received three death threats.) Despite the fact that King's achievements were enormous—and that Malcolm left really nothing behind other than a book—King's association with integration, with nonviolence, even with Christianity has reduced him in the eyes of many blacks. When blacks in major cities, inspired by figures like Malcolm X and the romanticization of Africa that Malcolm's nationalism wrought, began to organize African-oriented celebrations, such as my aunts did in Philadelphia with the creation of the Yoruba-inspired Odunde festival in 1975, then Afrocentrism has succeeded not only in intellectual spheres but on the grass-roots level as well. Its triumph as the legitimation of the black mind and the black aesthetic vision was complete.

Afrocentrism may eventually wane in the black community but probably not very soon. Moreover, a certain type of nationalistic mood, a kind of racial preoccupation, will always exist among blacks. It always has, in varying degrees. Homesickness is strong among black Americans, although it is difficult to point to a homeland. What Afrocentrism reflects is the inability of a large number of black people to deal with the reality of being American and with the meaning of their American experience.

Stanley Crouch is right in pointing out that the Afrocentrist is similar to the white Southerner after the Civil War. To black nationalists, the lost war was the "war of liberation" led by black "revolutionaries" in the late 1960s, which in their imagination was modeled on the struggles against colonialism then taking place around the world. (The enslavement of the Africans, of course, was an earlier lost war, and it also weighs heavily on the Afrocentrist. He, like the white Southerner, hates the idea of belonging to a defeated people.) This imaginative vision of a restored and indomitable ethnicity is not to be taken lightly. In a culture as driven by the idea of redemption and as corrupted by racism as this one, race war is our Armageddon. It can be seen in works as various as Thomas Jefferson's *Notes on the State of Virginia*, David Walker's *Appeal to the Colored Citizens of the World*, Joseph Smith's *Book of Mormon*, D.W. Griffith's *Birth of a Nation* and Mario Van Peebles's *Posse*.

WHAT BLACKS DESIRE DURING THESE TURBULENT TIMES IS EXACTLY WHAT

WHITES WANT: THE SECURITY OF A GOLDEN PAST THAT NEVER EXISTED

TODAY, AFROCENTRISM IS NOT A MATURE POLITICAL movement but rather a cultural style and a moral stance. There is a deep, almost lyrical poignancy in the fantasy of the Afrocentrist, as there is in the white Southerner's. What would I have been had I not lost the war? The Afrocentrist is devoted to his ancestry and his blood, fixated on the set of traditions that define his nobility, preoccupied with an imagined lost way of life. What drives the Afrocentrist and the white Southerner is not the expression of a group self-interest but concern with pride and honor. One group's myth is built on the surfeit of honor and pride, the other on the total absence of them.

Like the white Southerner, the Afrocentrist is in revolt against liberalism itself, against the idea of individual liberty. In a way, the Afrocentrist is right to rage against it, because liberalism set free the individual but did not encourage the development of a community within which the individual could flower. This is what the Afrocentrist wishes to retrieve, a place for himself in his own community. Wilson Jeremiah Moses, a black historian, is right: Afrocentrism is a historiography of decline, like the mythic epic of the South. The tragedy is that black people fail to see their "Americanization" as one of the great human triumphs of the past 500 years. The United States is virtually the only country where the ex-masters and the ex-slaves try to live together as equals, not only by consent of the ex-masters but by the demand of the ex-slaves. Ironically, what the Afrocentrist can best hope for is precisely what multiculturalism offers: the idea that American culture is a blend of many white and nonwhite cultures. In the end, although many Afrocentrists claim they want this blending, multiculturalism will not satisfy. For if the Euro-American is reminded through this that he is not European or wholly white, the African-American will surely be reminded that he is not African or wholly black. The Afrocentrist does not wish to be a mongrel. He wants, like the Southerner, to be pure.

Afrocentrism is intense now because blacks are in a special period of social development in a nation going through a period of fearsome transition. Social development, by its nature, is ambivalent, characterized by a sense of exchange, of gaining and losing. Afrocentrism, in its conservatism, is opposed to this ambivalence and to this sense of exchange. What blacks desire during these turbulent times is exactly what whites want: the security of a golden past that never existed. A significant number of both blacks and whites want, strangely, to go back to an era of segregation, a fantasy time between 1920 and 1955, when whites felt secure in a stable culture and when blacks felt unified and strong because black people were forced to live together. Afrocentrism wants social change without having to pay the psychic price for it. Perhaps many black folk feel that they have paid too much already, and who is to say they are not right.

The issue raised by Afrocentrism is the meaning and formation of identity, which is the major fixation of the American, especially the black American. In a country that relentlessly promotes the myth of self-reliance because it is unable to provide any sense of security in a cauldron of capitalistic change, identity struggle is so acute because so much is at stake. Afrocentrism may be wrong in many respects, and it certainly can be stifling and restrictive, but some of its impulses are right. In a culture where information and resources of knowledge are the main levers for social and economic advancement, psychological well-being has become increasingly important as, in the words of one scholar, "a social resource," just as "social networks of care and community support [have become] central features of a dynamic economy." Black folk know, and rightly so, that their individual identities are tied to the strength of their community. The struggle over black identity in the United States has been the struggle over the creation of a true black community here. What integration has done to the individual black mind in the United States is directly related to what it has done to the black community. This is the first lesson we must learn. The second is that perhaps many black folk cling to Afrocentrism because the black *American* experience still costs more, requires more courage, than white Americans—and black Americans—are willing to admit.

In the U.S., a jury of one's peers usually decides guilt or innocence. But in a multiethnic society...

Whose Peers?

RICHARD LACAYO

JUST HOW CAREFULLY BALANCED DOES a jury have to be in order to render a fair verdict—not to mention one that the public will *believe* is fair? In language dating back to the Magna Carta, the English common-law tradition promises defendants a jury of their "peers." The U.S. Constitution mandates "an impartial jury," and American law requires that it be drawn from a representative cross section of the community.

None of those guarantees has been interpreted by U.S. courts to mean that defendants have a right to be tried by jurors of their racial or ethnic background. But in a society that is increasingly racially mixed, the pressure is on to fashion juries that look something like the panel of judges at an Olympic diving meet: one from this nationality, one from that.

The acquittal of four police officers in the first Rodney King trial raised havoc in large part because they were freed by a jury with no blacks, drawn from a California community with very few. In May the retrial of Hispanic police officer William Lozano, whose 1989 shooting of a black motorcyclist set off three days of rioting in Miami, was shuffled five times among three Florida cities in search of a "balanced" jury. Ultimately, a jury consisting of three whites, two Hispanics and one black acquitted Lozano..

Studies of trial outcomes show that in cases in which evidence of guilt or innocence appears to be clear, the ethnic and racial makeup of juries "doesn't seem to matter," says University of Iowa law professor Michael Saks. Many immigrants come from cultures in which anyone charged with a crime is presumed guilty, and they tend to apply this standard even to defendants of their own background. On the other hand, many are also deeply suspicious of authority because of their experience with prejudice or police harassment. Whatever the case, the presence of jurors who share the background of a defendant or plaintiff is useful in pointing out to other jurors cultural differences and confusions. Paul Igasaki, executive director of the Asian Law Caucus in San Francisco, recalls a recent lawsuit heard by a jury containing only one Asian American. The panel was puzzled by the failure of the plaintiffs to demonstrate sufficient passion over the damages they claimed to have suffered. More Asian Americans on the jury might have illuminated matters by pointing out that the plaintiffs came from a Chinese-Filipino culture that frowns upon public displays of emotion.

"We don't all see things in the same way," observes Beth Bonora of the National Jury Project, a trial consulting firm. "That's why the jury system exists in the first place." But how to arrive at the proper mix to ensure justice? The simplest step would be to expand the pool of potential jurors. The federal courts and nearly all states currently use the list of registered voters. Because minorities, among others, are underrepresented among voters, half the states and some of the federal courts add other lists, most commonly those of licensed drivers. That has problems too. Driver lists, for example, can underrepresent city dwellers, who are less likely to drive, but include ineligible nonresidents and noncitizens.

"We have the rhetoric of representativeness but not the reality," says Temple University law professor David Kairys. "We're not making the effort to get the results, and it is very easy to do." To remedy the underrepresentation of Hispanics in the Philadelphia jury pool, Kairys brought a court challenge earlier this year that led the city to begin drawing potential jurors from the welfare rolls.

Even when minorities are summoned in greater numbers, they often cannot serve because of economic hardship. Many work in low-wage jobs for employers who will not pay the salaries of absent workers. To remedy that, eight states require employers to pay at least part of the salary of workers who are called. As a way to tap into such deprived groups, courts in Hawaii and many other states now dismiss citizens who have not been added to a jury by the end of the first day of their duty, freeing them from the prospect of wasting weeks in the jury pool without serving.

The final fashioning of a jury comes in the courtroom. Though it has never established an obligation for courts to seat multiracial juries, the U.S. Supreme Court in recent years has made it harder to create all-white ones. In 1986 it limited the power of prosecutors to exclude jurors on the basis of race through the use of "peremptory challenges"—a procedure that allows lawyers to dismiss prospective jurors without explanation. Last year the court similarly restricted defense attorneys.

Even backers of multiracial juries have doubts about forcing courts to create them. "People are not knee-jerk voters in the jury room on the basis of their color," says Los Angeles Superior Court Judge Alexander H. Williams III. "If an African American commits a crime in a city that is all white, is there something wrong with him going to trial with a white jury? It's not a much further step to say that if I'm an African American, I have a right to representatives of my race on any jury that tries me."

Not much further at all; some advocates argue that just such a guarantee of minority representation should be part of the law. Sheri Lynn Johnson, a law professor at Cornell University who has written about jury composition, believes defendants should be guaranteed three members of their own racial group on a 12-member jury. "Race doesn't just influence cases like the Lozano and King cases, but most cases," she says.

If that is so, is the only solution an outright racial-quota system? And how finely would the jury need to be divided? Could Latinos in general judge other Latinos? Or would Cuban Americans be needed for the trial of Cuban Americans, Mexican Americans for other Mexican Americans and so on? If the goal is better justice and greater legitimacy, American juries certainly need to be more representative. But in a just society, the process of creating a true assembly of peers need not be reduced to a systematic gathering of the tribes.

—With reporting by Marc Hequet/St. Paul

The "Cultural" Defense

IN CONNECTICUT LAST APRIL, WITH FIVE friends from a Buddhist youth group assisting him, Binh Gia Pham doused himself with gasoline, flicked a lighter and exploded into flames. The 43-year-old immigrant was protesting attempts by the Vietnamese government to suppress Buddhism.

Pham's friends had recorded his death with video cameras, then promptly notified Connecticut police. "It was clear," says Sergeant Scott O'Mara, "that they did not think they had done anything wrong." The state saw things differently. All five were charged with second-degree manslaughter, for aiding a suicide, an offense that carries a maximum of 10 years in prison. Fortunately for the five, the judge ruled that Pham would have sacrificed himself "with or without" his friends and granted them probation.

New immigrants are often ignorant of U.S. laws, even as they hold tightly to values brought from their homelands. But business as usual in the old country can be a felony in the U.S.; conventional child-rearing practices there, for example, might be considered child abuse here. One result of the rising immigrant tide is the increasing use of "the cultural defense"—legal shorthand for courtroom attempts to explain the actions of foreign-born defendants by invoking the mores and taboos of their native countries. Defense attorneys use the tactic in two major ways: to persuade prosecutors to reduce charges and to encourage judges to exercise leniency at sentencing.

Courts and prosecutors approach the matter with some puzzlement. In 1990 J. Tom Morgan, now the district attorney of DeKalb County, Georgia, decided not to press charges of child molestation against a South American woman suspected of stroking her male toddler's genitals, having concluded that "this is the way her culture taught her to put healthy young boys to sleep." Four years earlier, however, he had brought a Somali woman to trial for allegedly performing a clitoridectomy, traditional in some parts of Africa, on her two-year-old niece. In 1989 Dong Lu Chen, a Chinese immigrant in New York City, hammered his wife to death because he suspected her of cheating on him. Feminists were outraged when Chen was sentenced to just five years' probation. But the judge had relied on an anthropologist's testimony about the seriousness of infidelity in Chinese culture and on the defense's contention that shame pushed Chen to an extreme act.

Should American jurists bend the rules to accommodate foreign cultures? Can judges and juries draw reliable conclusions about what the rules in those cultures might really be? Most jurists recognize that ignorance of the law has never been—and should not be—a basis for full acquittal. Yet in determining charges before trial and in sentencing afterward, U.S. law has always taken into account a wide array of factors that might shed light on the responsibility of the accused. That might be a useful—and defensible—basis for a cultural defense, but only after some well-defined guidelines are developed to help steer the courts through this vexing legal issue. —*By Richard Lacayo. Reported by Adam Biegel/Atlanta and John F. Dickerson/New York*

Color Blinded?

Race Seems to Play an Increasing Role in Many Jury Verdicts

Blacks Express Skepticism of the Justice System; Acquittals in the Bronx

The Issue of 'Nullification'

Wall Street Journal staff reporters Benjamin A. Holden in Los Angeles, Laurie P. Cohen in New York and Eleena de Lisser in Atlanta.

The evidence against Davon Neverdon seemed overwhelming.

Four eyewitnesses testified that they saw him kill a man in a robbery attempt. Two others said he told them he committed the crime. Even Mr. Neverdon was expecting to be convicted: He had offered to plead guilty in exchange for a 40-year sentence, a deal the prosecutor had rejected at the request of the victim's family.

But that wasn't how the Baltimore jury, which included 11 African-Americans, saw it. After 11 hours of deliberation, they acquitted the defendant, who is black. A note from the jury room before the July 28 verdict suggested an explanation for the contrarian result: "Race," the lone Asian-American juror informed the judge, "may be playing some part" in the jury's decision-making.

Commentators have warned during the yearlong ordeal of the O.J. Simpson case—which ended in not-guilty verdicts yesterday—that a juror's race doesn't dictate his or her verdict, and that evidence matters more than skin color.

But, increasingly, jury watchers are concluding that, as in the Neverdon case, race plays a far more significant role in jury verdicts than many people involved in the justice system prefer to acknowledge. And rather than condemn this influence, some legal scholars argue that it fits neatly into a tradition of political activism by U.S. juries.

The case of Darryl Smith in 1990 is a less celebrated, but perhaps more telling, example of how race can affect a criminal trial. After an all-black jury in Washington acquitted Mr. Smith of murder in March 1990, a letter from an anonymous juror arrived at the superior court there. The letter said that while most jurors in the case believed Mr. Smith was guilty, the majority bowed to holdouts who "didn't want to send anymore Young Black Men to Jail."

With as many as half of young black men under the supervision of the criminal-justice system in some cities, "African-American jurors are doing a cost-benefit analysis," says Paul Butler, a black criminal-law professor at George Washington University. Many black jurors have determined, he adds, that "defendants are better off out of jail, even though they're clearly guilty."

The phenomenon of race-based verdicts isn't limited to blacks, of course. In past years, all-white juries, particularly in the South, nearly always convicted blacks accused of crimes against whites, regardless of the evidence—while whites who raped or lynched blacks went free. In death-penalty cases, white jurors frequently refused to send whites to death row for murdering blacks. When Los Angeles police officers charged in the videotaped beating of Rodney King were acquitted Simi Valley, Calif., in 1992, many observers attributed the verdict to the fact that 10 of the jurors were white and none were black.

EMERGING PHENOMENON

But the willingness of many blacks, in particular, to side with African-American defendants against a mostly white-dominated justice system is a relatively new phenomenon with specific roots and ramifications, according to researchers who have analyzed recent jury verdicts.

At the simplest level, they say, minority jurors are merely drawing on their own life experiences, as jurors are expected to do, in evaluating evidence. Based on such experiences, they are quicker than whites to suspect racism on the part of police and prosecutors and thus more likely than whites to distrust the evidence they present. Indeed, a recent USA Today/CNN/Gallup Poll found that 66% of blacks believe the criminal-justice system is racist, compared with 37% of whites. This disparity inevitably affects deliberations.

But some black jurors are quietly taking a further, much more significant step: They are choosing to disregard the evidence, however powerful, because they seek to protest racial injustice and to refrain from adding to the already large number of blacks behind bars.

HIGH ACQUITTAL RATES

Most black jurors "understand how fine the line is between doing well and being on trial," says Thomas I. Atkins, a defense lawyer who is former general counsel of the National Association for the Advancement of Colored People. For many blacks, he says, "It's not enough to merely conclude that the right person is on trial and that the evidence is sufficient. You also have to prove that the right thing to come out of this trial is a conviction."

The race factor seems particularly evident in such urban environments as the New York City borough of the Bronx, where juries are more than 80% black and Hispanic. There, black defendants are acquitted in felony cases 47.6% of the time—nearly three times the national acquittal rate of 17% for all races. Hispanics are acquitted 37.6% of the time. This is so even though the majority of crime victims in the Bronx are black or Hispanic.

Although other jurisdictions generally don't break down conviction rates by race, overall figures for heavily black urban areas suggest that the Bronx phenomenon extends elsewhere. In Washington, D.C., where more than 95% of defendants and 70% of jurors are black, 28.7% of all felony trials ended in acquittals last year, significantly above the national average. In Wayne County, Mich., which includes mostly black Detroit, 30% of felony defendants were acquitted in 1993, the last year for which statistics were available.

Jury watchers point to a number of high-profile cases in recent years in which urban juries acquitted black defendants, despite what appeared to many observers to be strong evidence for conviction. These include the 1990 case of Washington Mayor Marion Barry, who was acquitted on all but one of 14 counts against him stemming from a sting operation in which the FBI and police videotaped him smoking crack cocaine; the string of acquittals of defendants charged with beating Reginald Denny during the Los Angeles riots in 1992; and the November 1988 Bronx acquittal of Larry Davis on charges of attempting to murder nine police officers.

After the verdict, Mr. Davis's lawyer, the late William Kunstler, acknowledge that there was "no question" that race influenced the jurors. But he said this had led to a just, rather than an unjust, verdict.

Some black lawyers and scholars argue that any defiance of what blacks perceive as a racist system falls within the tradition of so-called jury nullification—the rejection of the law in favor of the jurors' own views of justice. They note that this controversial power, which the U.S. Supreme Court explicitly affirmed 100 years ago, has played an important role at key times in U.S. history—and may be doing so again today.

During colonial times, for instance, jurors used the power to acquit colonial defendants of political crimes against the Crown. In the mid-19th century, Northern jurors kept the tradition alive by acquitting people who harbored runaway slaves, even though the law explicitly made this a crime. The constitutional prohibition against trying a person twice for the same crime protects the defendant in all such circumstances from having an acquittal overturned because the jurors didn't follow the law.

NATIONAL CRISIS?

Some jury-nullification advocates now say blacks are justified in using their jury-room vote to fight what they perceive as a national crisis: a justice system that is skewed against them by courts, prosecutors and racist police such as former Los Angeles Detective Mark Fuhrman.

"Jury nullification is power that black people have right now and not something Congress has to give them," Mr. Butler says. In a forthcoming law-review article, Mr. Butler even argues that in nonviolent crimes, black jurors should "presume in favor of nullification."

"Black people," he writes, "have a community that needs building, and children who need rescuing, and as long as a person will not hurt anyone, the community needs him there to help."

Not surprisingly, prosecutors vehemently disagree with such reasoning, which they see as undermining the rule of law. "It's terrible and sad that juries will base their opinions on race bias rather than the facts, but it happens every day," says Ahmet Hisim, the assistant state's attorney in Baltimore who lost the Neverdon case. "It's very bad for justice," he adds.

Mr. Hisim blames much of the problem on defense lawyers, whose "main ploy is to nullify juries for racial reasons," he says.

'MONEY AND SURVIVAL'

But some defendants are adopting race-based defense tactics themselves. Representing himself in an Atlanta trial last summer, Erick Bozeman openly pleaded with a jury to acquit him of serious federal drug charges because he is black. In his opening statement, he told jurors that the U.S. war on drugs was part of the same war on black people that "has existed in one way or another since African prisoners arrived in 1619 as slaves." He described his birthplace as "the urban war zone of South Central Los Angeles where the real law is money and survival" and his profession as that of a drug middleman, "a broker, just like Michael Milken and Ivan Boesky."

The case ended in a hung jury on the central charge, that Mr. Bozeman was a drug "kingpin," a crime punishable by life in prison. All three voting to acquit were black. Afterward, Judge Clarence Cooper, who is also black, privately told the jurors he was disappointed with the verdict, and he questioned their common sense.

As in the Neverdon case, the black jurors denied race was a factor in the verdict. Ulysses Garror, one of the jurors who voted for acquittal, says only, "There wasn't enough there to convict." But a white juror, Russell Snellgrove, now says, "These people, I hate to say this, it could have been a racial thing. They didn't come out and say it, but their arguments were such that it was apparent."

More prevalent than outright jury nullification is the greater tendency of many blacks to believe that police will falsify evidence and lie on the witness stand—factors that became major elements in the Simpson case. In this regard, African-American jurors are concentrating on the evidence, but filtering it, as any juror must, through their own perspectives.

'NOT JUST RACE'

Robert E. Kalunian, assistant public defender for Los Angeles Country, while agreeing that "race does affect jury deliberations," adds, "It's not just race. It's life experiences. Blacks are more likely to have been jacked by the police, and less likely to view police testimony with quite the same pristine validity as a white male from the suburbs."

Defense lawyers in urban areas with large black populations routinely attribute acquittals they have won to distrust of the police. "African-American jurors who live in communities where cops are the enemy don't have to be educated that police lie," explains Peter Kirscheimer, a onetime Bronx legal aid attorney who is now a federal defender in Brooklyn.

Many times, of course, a verdict may stem in part from jurors' evaluation of the evidence and in part from a broader, racially influenced desire to see certain defendants acquitted because circumstances make a conviction appear unfair to them.

This mix seemed to be at play in a gun-possession case in September in the same courthouse where the Simpson trial was in progress.

The stakes in the case were particularly high because defendant Byron Carter, 22 years old and black, had two prior convictions, and a conviction here would mean life in prison. Because it was a gun-possession case, the defense appeared to have an instant advantage. Jurors living in dangerous urban ares, recognizing a need to be armed in self-defense, are known to be particularly reluctant to convict for gun possession. Indeed, in the Bronx, 75% of such cases end in acquittals.

CONFLICTING CAMPS

Deliberating after a six-day trial, the jury of five blacks, three Hispanic-Americans, two whites and two Asian-Americans split instantly into two conflicting camps. Leading one side was Howard Anderson, the black 34-year-old jury foreman, who believed certain statements made by the two white arresting officers were transparently false. On the other side were Asian-Americans Ken Chan, 27, and Paul Wong, 35, who felt the police were more believable than the defendant, since he was a convicted felon. One of the two white jurors says he felt Mr. Carter was guilty but came to believe the evidence was sufficient.

The main issue for the panel was whether a young, urban black man would ever confess, as the police claimed that, "I'd rather be caught in this neighborhood by the police with a gun than caught otherwise without one." The two arresting officers, who didn't record the statement or obtain Mr. Carter's signature on a written version of it, claimed he had made the confession after they confronted him in a van that was parked too far away from the curb.

Mr. Carter testified at trial that he actually said: "Everybody and their mamma in this neighborhood got a gun." But he said he told the police that the weapon in question wasn't his. He also said the van was legally parked.

All of the black members of the jury immediately agreed that Mr. Carter's version of the statement was more consistent with urban slang than the police's, which was submitted as part of the alleged confession. After an initial discussion, the first ballot was 10–2 to acquit—with only Messrs. Chan and Wong seeking a conviction.

LITTLE AGREEMENT

The dissenters ultimately gave in, but not a lot of convincing was done: "We reached a unanimous verdict, but we still don't agree on the facts," Mr. Chan says.

The jury experience "showed me the reason so many people are being locked away," Mr. Anderson says. Jurors without experience dealing with inner-city black defendants "just sit there and look on them as criminals before the trial even starts."

After the verdict, several black jurors talked openly about the illogic of sending another young black man away to spend his life in jail for what they considered the "victimless" crime of possessing a .22-caliber handgun. But was this jury prepared to defy the law? Not quite, says black juror Troy Richardson.

The thought of voting to acquit regardless of the evidence "did enter my mind," says Mr. Richardson, "but I decided if the evidence says he's guilty, I'm going to send him away."

WHAT COLOR IS BLACK?

And what color is white? The markers of racial identity are every conceivable hue—and suddenly matters of ideology and attitude as much as pigmentation.

Tom Morganthau

Nearly 400 years after the first African came ashore at Jamestown—and 40 years after Rosa Parks launched the Montgomery bus boycott—Americans are still preoccupied with race. Race divides us, defines us and in a curious way unites us—if only because we still think it matters. Race-based thinking permeates our law and policy, and the sense of racial grievance, voiced by blacks and whites alike, infects our politics. Blacks cleave to their role as history's victims; whites grumble about reverse discrimination. The national mood on race, as measured by NEWSWEEK's latest poll, is bleak: 75 percent of whites—and 86 percent of blacks—say race relations are "only fair" or "poor."

But the world is changing anyway. By two other measures in the same NEWSWEEK Poll—acceptance of interracial marriage and the willingness to reside in mixed-race neighborhoods—tolerance has never been higher. The nation's racial dialogue, meanwhile, is changing so rapidly that the familiar din of black-white antagonism seems increasingly out of date. Partly because of immigration—and partly because diversity is suddenly hip—America is beginning to revise its two-way definition of race. Though this process will surely take years, it is already blurring our sense that racial identity is fixed, immutable and primarily a matter of skin color. What color is black? It is every conceivable shade and hue from tan to ebony—and suddenly a matter of ideology and identity as much as pigmentation.

The politics of racial identity are public and deeply personal. Twenty-eight years after the last state anti-miscegenation law was struck down, an interracial

NEWSWEEK POLL		
Are the numbers of immigrants entering the U.S. from each of the following areas too many, too few or about right? (percent saying too many)		
AREA	BLACKS	WHITES
Europe	36%	30%
Latin America	40%	59%
Africa	24%	35%
Asia	39%	45%

THE NEWSWEEK POLL, FEB. 1-3, 1995

generation is demanding its place at the American table. They are not the first biracial Americans; that honor belongs to youngsters who grew up in Colonial Jamestown. But they are the first to stake a claim to mainstream status, discomfiting in the process blacks and whites who are reluctant to reconsider familiar racial categories. They are aided by older cousins who, if nothing else, are changing the talk of the nation, producing powerful memoirs about life on the color line.

It is important to note, meanwhile, that the idea of race itself is now coming under attack by science. To scientists who have looked into the question, race is a notoriously slippery con-cept that eludes any serious attempt at definition: it refers mostly to observable differences in skin color, hair texture and the shape of one's eyes or nose. Considering the whole range of biological variation within the human species, these differences are at best superficial—and try as they will, scientists have been broadly unable to come up with any significant set of differences that distinguishes one racial group from another. ("The Bell Curve," a best-selling book by Richard Herrnstein and Charles Murray, revives the old controversy about black-white differences in intelligence, but surely does not settle it.) The bottom line, to most scientists working in these fields, is that race is a mere "social construct"—a gamy mixture of prejudice, superstition and myth.

This assault on racialist thinking is compounded by the visible results of 30 years of accelerating immigration from Latin America, the Caribbean and Asia. That trend, still continuing, has added approximately 18 million people to the American melting pot, most of whom are eligible to be labeled "persons of color." One obvious consequence is the prediction that Hispanics, now 25 million strong and nearly 10 percent of the population (blacks are almost 13 percent, and non-Hispanic whites are 74 percent), will be the nation's largest minority by the year 2010. But Latinos are neither a "race" nor an "ethnic group." They are a disparate collection of nationalities variously descended from Europeans, African slaves and American Indians. The new immigrants also include some 3.5

million Chinese, Japanese, Koreans, Filipinos, Vietnamese and Laotian Hmong. And hundreds of thousands of dark-skinned East Indians, Pakistanis and Bangladeshis—who, despite their color, are Caucasians.

Solidarity is hard to find. One third of African-Americans polled say that blacks should not be considered a single race.

All of this portends an era of increasing multiethnic and multiracial confusion: Diversity "R" Us. The question now is whether America's traditional concept of race is relevant to the nation's changing demographics—and the answer, almost certainly, is "no." Americans have long tended to take a "binary" approach toward race—to assume, based on our own historical experience, that only two races count and that skin color is the dividing line between them. This belief is rooted in what historians call the "one-drop rule," which is a relic of slavery and segregation. But as Harvard sociologist Orlando Patterson says, "The U.S. approach to racial identity has been most unusual. In much of the rest of the world, people make [social and class] distinctions based on gradations of color." Now, Patterson says, the arrival of millions of new immigrants from racially mixed societies is undermining the de facto consensus on the meaning of race in the American context. "We've had this large group of people coming from parts of Latin America . . . [who] don't consider themselves white or black," he says. "They don't want to play the binary game."

The demand for a more flexible view of race and ethnicity is not limited to immigrants—for many native-born Americans are refusing to play the binary game as well. Ramona Douglass of Chicago is the child of a multiracial couple: her mother was Sicilian-American and her father was half African-American and half Ogalala Sioux. Douglass says she is frustrated that native-born multiethnics are "invisible" to the rest of society. She is president of a group, the Association of MultiEthnic Americans, that is lobbying Washington to add a multiracial category to the questionnaire for the next

census. Currently, respondents are asked to choose between White, Black, Asian or Pacific Islander, American Indian, Eskimo or Aleut; and the catchall designator "Other." (The questionnaire provides a separate Hispanic/Spanish-origin box in addition to these racial categories.) Simply changing the census form, Douglass argues, would help to acknowledge the nation's increasing diversity "in a positive way."

This seemingly innocuous revision is fast becoming a hideously complicated issue. Federal officials are well aware that the census form forces millions of Americans to identify themselves as "Other," which sounds faintly diminishing. They are also aware that the current racial categories do not depict the nation's increasingly fluid demographics. "The problem is that the country is changing at a very rapid rate now, and the categories have not changed for the last 20 years," says Ohio Rep. Thomas C. Sawyer. "The [census] numbers may be precise, but they are precisely wrong. They do not reflect the reality of who people think they are." In 1990, census officials say, Americans used a write-in blank on the census form to identify nearly 300 "races," 600 Indian tribes, 70 Hispanic groups and 75 combinations of

NEWSWEEK POLL		
Should the U.S. Census add a multiracial category so people aren't forced to deny part of a family member's heritage by choosing a single racial category?	BLACKS	WHITES
Add category	49%	36%
Don't add	42%	51%
Should the U.S. Census stop collecting information on race and ethnicity?	BLACKS	WHITES
Should stop	48%	47%
Should not stop	44%	41%

THE NEWSWEEK POLL, FEB. 1-3, 1995

multiracial ancestry—including one person self-identified as "black/Hmong."

Viewed as a matter of individual choice, the census-form issue looks like healthy self-assertion for those who feel themselves confined by America's traditional beliefs about race identity. It is that—but it is also a potentially major political issue. If significant numbers of blacks and Hispanics begin to check the proposed multiracial box, that shift could trigger changes in census-based formulas

used to distribute federal aid to minorities. It could also undermine part of the Voting Rights Act that requires so-called minority districting for blacks and His-

NEWSWEEK POLL		
How important is it that voting districts be drawn so that blacks can obtain representation in elective office comparable to their numbers in the population?	BLACKS	WHITES
Somewhat or very important	92%	59%

THE NEWSWEEK POLL, FEB. 1-3, 1995

panics in congressional elections. And some speculate that it could lead to an expansion of affirmative action for previously ineligible minority groups.

All this remains so much speculation until (and unless) the census form is changed. But the demand for recognition by emerging multiethnic and multiracial groups is a clear rejection of the binary view of race and the one-drop rule as well. As such, it implicitly threatens the tradition of black solidarity on the long march toward social equality. Black intellectuals and political activists already recognize that possibility, and some are worried by the prospect of change. Since a great many black Americans can clearly claim to be biracial, the worst-case scenario is that black solidarity will slowly erode because of "defections" to multiethnic status. But not everyone agrees. "I don't think there are *any* political implications," says Bill Lynch, a former deputy mayor of New York. "It's no different from checking the 'Other' box."

And what if multiethnicity is the way out of our binary stalemate? Orlando Patterson, for one, takes exactly that view. "If your object is the eventual integration of the races, a mixed-race or middle group is something you'd want to see developing," he says. "The middle group grows larger and larger, and the races eventually blend." Patterson knows that whites are wary and that blacks are warier still. But he thinks the amount of social interaction between the races is already "surprising," and he insists there is "nothing fundamental" about American society to block the ultimate blending of black and white. All it requires is patience, faith—and a measure of good will.

With SUSAN MILLER, GREGORY BEALS *and* REGINA ELAM *in New York*

A Distorted Image of Minorities

Poll Suggests That What Whites Think They See May Affect Beliefs

Richard Morin

Washington Post Staff Writer
Mario A. Brossard, assistant director of Washington Post polling, contributed to this report.

A majority of white Americans have fundamental misconceptions about the economic circumstances of black Americans, according to a new national survey, with most saying that the average black is faring as well or better than the average white in such specific areas as jobs, education and health care.

That's not true. Government statistics show that whites, on average, earn 60 percent more than blacks, are far more likely to have medical insurance and more than twice as likely to graduate from college.

Most of those surveyed, regardless of race, also greatly overestimated the number of minority Americans in the United States. Most whites, blacks, Hispanics and Asian Americans said the black population, which is about 12 percent, was twice that size. Those whites with the most inaccurate ideas about the size of the minority populations were the most likely to say that further increases would be bad for the country.

"There is real meaning, substantive meaning in these numbers," said Richard Neimi, a political scientist at the University of Rochester who has studied the relationship between knowledge and attitudes. "People do misunderstand what the country is like. They overestimate. . . . And it is not a big leap to imagine that this may well affect the way people think about minorities, that it may lead to this idea that the country is being overrun."

These misperceptions were one finding of a recent national telephone survey sponsored by The Washington Post, the Kaiser Family Foundation and Harvard University, the first in a series of polls that will explore how much Americans know and how it may affect the way they think about themselves and their country. A total of 1,970 randomly selected Americans were interviewed, including 802 whites, 474 blacks, 352 English-speaking Asians, and 252 Spanish and English-speaking Hispanics. The remainder were of other races or declined to identify their race.

Overall, the survey found that Asian Americans generally were closer to whites on many but not all racial issues, while Hispanics were closer to black views.

Pessimism united the races. A majority said they feel the American Dream is fading for them and for their children. Good jobs, they said, are harder to find. So is decent housing. Schools are getting worse, not better. Those in America's growing black middle class said they felt particularly vulnerable, expressing fears that tough times and discrimination could wash away their gains.

Regardless of race, an overwhelming majority agreed that merit—not diversity—should decide who is hired, promoted and admitted to college. No such consensus emerged, however, about the value of integration in workplaces, neighborhoods and schools. Half of each group said it was important; half said it wasn't.

The sharpest divisions occurred in the way whites and blacks view the world. Simply put, a majority of whites said they believed that many blacks have achieved equality with whites on the cornerstone issues that gave momentum to the civil rights movement more than 30 years ago. Most blacks, in stark contrast, said they believe that racism and discrimination have been on the rise in the past decade.

For example, 68 percent of blacks surveyed said racism is "a big problem in our society today," but only 38 percent of whites agreed. Similarly, 71 percent of blacks said "past and present discrimination" was a major reason for the economic and social problems facing some African Americans today, but only 36 percent of whites thought this was true.

The gap is so wide that "it really seems that blacks and whites may as well be on two different planets," said Robert Blendon, a Harvard professor who an-

MISPERCEPTIONS ABOUT U.S. POPULATION

Poll

Q: What percentage of the U.S. population is...	White responses	Black responses	Asian responses	Hispanic responses	1992 census data
... WHITE?	49.9%	45.5%	54.8%	46.7%	74%
... BLACK?	23.8%	25.9%	20.5%	22.7%	11.8%
... HISPANIC?	14.7%	16.3%	14.6%	20.7%	9.5%
... ASIAN?	10.8%	12.2%	8.3%	10.8%	3.1%

NOTE: Response percentages are averages of the estimates made by those polled. Hispanics can be of any race. Percentages do not total 100 because other races are not shown.

SOURCES: Washington Post/Kaiser Family Foundation/Harvard University survey, U.S. Census Bureau

THE WASHINGTON POST

alyzed the poll's results. Blendon, who specializes in public policy and survey research, was a member of The Post/Kaiser Foundation/Harvard team that designed the survey.

The racial divide was clearly visible in longer follow-up interviews conducted with survey participants.

Merle Barone, 64, a white retired department store clerk living in Monroeville, Pa., said: "I just feel as though the white person is being blamed for everything that goes wrong with the African Americans. Nobody owes any of us anything. Let's get on with our lives and make the best of it. . . . Come on. Everything in the world can't be racial."

Whites "do not want to get it," said Kolima David Williams, 38, a black chemist in Lewisville, Tex. "The reason they don't acknowledge the problems is because then they would have to admit that the system is corrupt and that it's working for their benefit and then they would have to give up something they have and would have to share."

Whites and blacks in the survey tended to agree on what Congress should do—balance the budget, reform welfare, preserve programs that help children—but they disagreed about most issues relating directly to race.

The overwhelming majority of whites said blacks have an equal chance to succeed, that whites bear no responsibility for the problems that blacks face today, that it's not the federal government's role to ensure that all races have equal jobs, pay or housing.

In several key areas, the survey found, a majority of whites said blacks are as well or better off than whites. For example, 46 percent of whites said blacks on average held jobs of equal quality to those of whites, 6 percent said blacks had jobs that were "a little better" and another 6 percent said "a lot better." Conversely,

26 percent of the whites questioned said jobs held by blacks were a "little" worse than those held by whites, 15 percent said they were a "lot worse" and the remainder did not express an opinion.

Gloria Jean Smith, 46, a white nurse in St. Louis, said: "The percentage of black people that are middle class and the percentage of white people that are middle class I would say are equal."

For Smith, this perceived parity means that affirmative action programs are not necessary. "I'm against affirmative action," she said, "because there are just as many white people that would like to have a hand up as black people. I don't think it's a question of money from the government to help people achieve their goal. I think it has to come from their persistence, their dream, their determination and that is the only way that you can really make it and feel good about yourself."

Michael Dawson, a University of Chicago professor who has studied racial attitudes, said many whites in the survey seemed to believe that "we can't do anything, we shouldn't do anything because it runs counter to basic American values and, besides, there's nothing to do because there aren't really any differences between blacks and whites."

Blacks, on the other hand, appeared to believe "it is our duty as a people, under the egalitarian principles of the Declaration of Independence, to redress these differences" through government action, Dawson said.

Large majorities of all the races said the federal government did have a responsibility to make sure that minorities and whites receive equal treatment from the courts and police. They also agreed that the government should assure that all Americans receive equal health care. There was broad consensus that it is the government's job to ensure that all Americans receive equal educations.

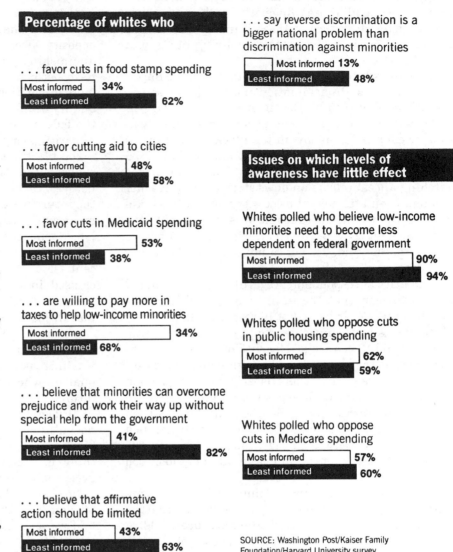

Poll

HOW PERCEPTIONS AFFECT ATTITUDES

***D**o perceptions influence how people think about issues? Yes, the survey results suggest. Respondents were asked whether the average black is faring better, worse or the same as the average white in six categories: income, jobs, housing, education, job security and access to health care, all areas where government statistics show the average white is faring better.*

Most informed
Definition: Those who gave correct answers to five or more questions.

Least informed
Definition: Those who gave incorrect answers to five or more questions.

Of the 870 whites interviewed, about 22 percent fell into the "most informed" category, 38 percent into the "least informed" group with the remainder somewhere in between.

Percentage of whites who

. . . favor cuts in food stamp spending
Most informed 34%
Least informed 62%

. . . favor cutting aid to cities
Most informed 48%
Least informed 58%

. . . favor cuts in Medicaid spending
Most informed 53%
Least informed 38%

. . . are willing to pay more in taxes to help low-income minorities
Most informed 34%
Least informed 68%

. . . believe that minorities can overcome prejudice and work their way up without special help from the government
Most informed 41%
Least informed 82%

. . . believe that affirmative action should be limited
Most informed 43%
Least informed 63%

. . . say reverse discrimination is a bigger national problem than discrimination against minorities
Most informed 13%
Least informed 48%

Issues on which levels of awareness have little effect

Whites polled who believe low-income minorities need to become less dependent on federal government
Most informed 90%
Least informed 94%

Whites polled who oppose cuts in public housing spending
Most informed 62%
Least informed 59%

Whites polled who oppose cuts in Medicare spending
Most informed 57%
Least informed 60%

SOURCE: Washington Post/Kaiser Family Foundation/Harvard University survey

---

But the consensus collapsed on the question of whether the government has a role in ensuring economic equality. Two-thirds of whites interviewed said the federal government had no responsibility to make certain minorities have jobs and incomes equal to whites, while 7 of 10 blacks surveyed said the federal government had an obligation to equalize outcomes as well as opportunity.

Whites stood alone in their view of black circumstances. Overwhelming majorities of African Americans said blacks were far worse off on each of these measures of economic well-being. Large majorities of Hispanics and Asian Americans too agreed that blacks were worse off than whites in terms of income, jobs, housing and education.

Whites who had not attended college were twice as likely to be misinformed about black circumstances than were whites who had continued their educations. But other factors proved to be only weakly associated or completely unrelated to knowledge levels. According to the survey, white men were as misinformed as white women, wealthy whites were only slightly more informed than lower-income whites and white Republicans surveyed were slightly more informed than white Democrats.

How whites saw black circumstances was closely tied to a range of beliefs and policy preferences. Two-thirds of whites—65 percent—who saw little difference between the social and economic conditions of blacks and whites also opposed additional federal spending to help low-income minorities. That compared with just 32 percent of those who knew that blacks on average still fared at least somewhat worse than whites on most measures of economic well-being.

Blacks and whites fundamentally disagreed over the causes of the problems facing some African Americans. Seven out of 10 blacks put discrimination and lack of jobs and education at the top of the list, followed closely by lack of jobs and education. "You look at homelessness, crime and all those things; it's a cycle, and racism can be factored into all of those things," said Nadine Etienne, 24, a black clerical worker living in Coconut City, Fla.

But many whites in the survey minimized the importance of any past discrimination and traced the source of black problems to blacks themselves, with 58 percent of whites citing the breakup of the black family as a major cause of problems in the black community.

"They're not disciplined," said Richard Oskin, 68, a retiree living in New Kensington, Pa. He described watching a local television news story about a teacher who had been attacked at a local school. "A black kid punched the teacher because he was told to go to the principal, and they were interviewing his mother on television. She said, 'He got in my boy's face.' She was defending him!"

A majority of respondents, regardless of race, shared a common fear: that the future looks bleaker rather than brighter. Nearly 6 out of 10 respondents said they felt further away from achieving the American Dream than they did 10 years ago. Nearly 8 of 10 said they are worried that they won't have enough money to get by.

"I don't believe that there is an American Dream anymore," said Kathy Brown, 47, an escrow mortgage officer living in East Long Beach, Calif. "It has been just blown apart. I mean the world has gone to hell in a handbasket. . . . Between drugs, gangs, crime on the rampage, there is no such thing as a nice neighborhood anymore."

"As far as going out and getting a job and staying there for 30 years, that don't happen anymore, like the way my father retired," said Marcus Lucero, 32, a machinist living in Niles, Mich. "Those jobs aren't there."

"There's really no decent jobs," said Violettia Dague, 27, a pillow maker living in Maquoketa, Iowa. "There's no decent housing and there's really no money. It's all gone before you even get it. It's costing more and more and more every year to send a kid to college. I'm going

to have one going in eight years and I don't even want to think about it."

Yet these shared anxieties push blacks and whites in opposite directions. Facing increased insecurity and diminishing prospects, the survey suggests that whites have become more hostile to minorities, fearful that more minorities would further erode their diminishing quality of life and far less sympathetic to attempts by the federal government to address problems that the minority poor face.

For blacks, the dimming of the American Dream suggests the need for more government intervention, not less. Blacks who expressed the most concern about the future were far more likely to favor strong government action to counter the economic and social problems facing minorities.

Overall, nearly half of those interviewed—47 percent—said that tension between the races had increased in the past 10 years, a view shared by 45 percent of all whites, 59 percent of the blacks and pluralities of Hispanics and Asian Americans.

Among the quarter of the sample who reported the most economic distress, 57 percent said racial tension was increasing compared with 39 percent among the quarter who reported the fewest worries about the future.

"It used to be pretty much a black and white thing; now it's Asian, it's Hispanic," said Calvin Harris, 39, a black maintenance worker living in Ray, Mich. "Everything is supposed to be equal now. Everyone is at everyone's throat fighting for jobs."

New arrivals to this country said they sensed the tension immediately.

"I want to melt into this country and participate in the life here, but it seems so hard," said Deborah Hsu, 20, a college student in Los Angeles who came to the United States from Taiwan just over a year ago. "People don't give me a chance to make friends with them or try to understand me and give me a chance to make friends with them. Nobody gives you a second chance. Everybody is just thinking about themselves."

THREE IS NOT ENOUGH

Surprising new lessons from the controversial science of race

Sharon Begley

To most Americans race is as plain as the color of the nose on your face. Sure, some light-skinned blacks, in some neighborhoods, are taken for Italians, and some Turks are confused with Argentines. But even in the children of biracial couples, racial ancestry is writ large—in the hue of the skin and the shape of the lips, the size of the brow and the bridge of the nose. It is no harder to trace than it is to judge which basic colors in a box of Crayolas were combined to make tangerine or burnt umber. Even with racial mixing, the existence of primary races is as obvious as the existence of primary colors.

Or is it? C. Loring Brace has his own ideas about where race resides, and it isn't in skin color. If our eyes could perceive more than the superficial, we might find race in chromosome 11: there lies the gene for hemoglobin. If you divide humankind by which of two forms of the gene each person has, then equatorial Africans, Italians and Greeks fall into the "sickle-cell race"; Swedes and South Africa's Xhosas (Nelson Mandela's ethnic group) are in the healthy-hemoglobin race. Or do you prefer to group people by whether they have epicanthic eye folds, which produce the "Asian" eye? Then the !Kung San (Bushmen) belong with the Japanese and Chinese. Depending on which trait you choose to demarcate races, "you won't get anything that remotely tracks conventional [race] categories," says

anthropologist Alan Goodman, dean of natural science at Hampshire College.

NEWSWEEK POLL		
Race relations in the U.S. are:		
	BLACKS	WHITES
Excellent	2%	1%
Good	10%	22%
Fair	45%	44%
Poor	41%	31%

THE NEWSWEEK POLL, FEB. 1-3, 1995

The notion of race is under withering attack for political and cultural reasons—not to mention practical ones like what to label the child of a Ghanaian and a Norwegian. But scientists got there first. Their doubts about the conventional racial categories—black, white, Asian—have nothing to do with a sappy "we are all the same" ideology. Just the reverse. "Human variation is very, very real," says Goodman. "But race, as a way of organizing [what we know about that variation], is incredibly simplified and bastardized." Worse, it does not come close to explaining the astounding diversity of humankind—not its origins, not its extent, not its meaning. "There is no organizing principle by which you could put 5 billion people into so few categories in a way that would tell you anything important about humankind's diversity," says Michigan's Brace, who will lay out the case against race at the annual meeting of the American Association for the Advancement of Science.

About 70 percent of cultural anthropologists, and half of physical

anthropologists, reject race as a biological category, according to a 1989 survey by Central Michigan University anthropologist Leonard Lieberman and colleagues. The truths of science are not decided by majority vote, of course. Empirical evidence, woven into a theoretical whole, is what matters. The threads of the argument against the standard racial categories:

• **Genes:** In 1972, population biologist Richard Lewontin of Harvard University laid out the genetic case against race. Analyzing 17 genetic markers in 168 populations such as Austrians, Thais and Apaches, he found that there is more genetic difference within one race than there is between that race and another. Only 6.3 percent of the genetic differences could be explained by the individuals' belonging to different races. That is, if you pick at random any two "blacks" walking along the street, and analyze their 23 pairs of chromosomes, you will probably find that their genes have less in common than do the genes of one of them with that of a random "white" person. Last year the Human Genome Diversity Project used 1990s genetics to extend Lewontin's analysis. Its conclusion: genetic variation from one individual to another of the same "race" swamps the average differences between racial groupings. The more we learn about humankind's genetic differences, says geneticist Luca Cavalli-Sforza of Stanford University, who chairs the committee that directs the biodiversity project, the more we see that they have almost nothing to do with what we call race.

• **Traits:** As sickle-cell "races" and epicanthic-fold "races" show, there are as many ways to group people as there are traits. That is because "racial" traits are what statisticians call nonconcordant. Lack of concordance means that sorting people according to *these* traits produces different groupings than you get in sorting them by *those* (equally valid) traits. When biologist Jared Diamond of UCLA surveyed half a dozen traits for a recent issue of Discover magazine, he found that, depending on which traits you pick, you can form very surprising "races." Take the scooped-out shape of the back of the front teeth, a standard "Asian" trait. Native Americans and Swedes have these shovel-shaped incisors, too, and so would fall in the same race. Is biochemistry better? Norwegians, Arabians, north Indians and the Fulani of northern Nigeria, notes Diamond, fall into the "lactase race" (the lactase enzyme digests milk sugar). Everyone else—other Africans, Japanese, Native Americans—forms the "lactase-deprived race" (their ancestors did not drink milk from cows or goats and hence never evolved the lactase gene). How about blood types, the familiar A, B and O groups? Then Germans and New Guineans, populations that have the same percentages of each type, are in one race; Estonians and Japanese comprise a separate one for the same reason, notes anthropologist Jonathan Marks of Yale University. Depending on which traits are chosen, "we could place Swedes in the same race as either Xhosas, Fulani, the Ainu of Japan or Italians," writes Diamond.

• **Subjectivity:** If race is a valid biological concept, anyone in any culture should be able to look at any individual and say, Aha, you are a . . . It should not be the case, as French tennis star Yannick Noah said a few years ago, that "in Africa I am white, and in France I am black" (his mother is French and his father is from Cameroon). "While biological traits give the impression that race is a biological unit of nature," says anthropologist George Armelagos of Emory University, "it remains a cultural construct. The boundaries between races depends on the classifier's own cultural norms."

• **Evolution:** Scholars who believe in the biological validity of race argue that the groupings reflect human prehistory. That is, populations that evolved together, and separately from others, constitute a race. This school of thought holds that blacks should all be in one race because they are descended from people who stayed on the continent where humanity began. Asians, epitomized by the Chinese, should be another race because they are the children of groups who walked north and east until they reached the Pacific. Whites of the pale, blond variety should be another because their ancestors filled Europe. Because of their appearance, these populations represent the extremes, the archetypes, of human diversity—the reds, blues and yellows from which you can make every other hue. "But if you use these archetypes as your groups you have classified only a very tiny proportion of the world's people, which is not very useful," says Marks, whose incisive new book "Human Biodiversity" (*321 pages. Walter de Gruyter. $23.95*) deconstructs race. "Also, as people walked out of Africa, they were differentiating along the way. Equating 'extreme' with 'primordial' is not supported by history."

Often, shared traits are a sign of shared heritage—racial heritage. "Shared traits are not random," says Alice Brues, an anthropologist at the University of Colorado. "Within a continent, you of course have a number of variants [on basic traits], but some are characteristic of the larger area, too. So it's natural to look for these major divisions. It simplifies your thinking." A wide distribution of traits, however, makes them suspect as evidence of a shared heritage. The dark skin of Somalis and Ghanaians, for instance, indicates that they evolved under the same selective force (a sunny climate). But that's all it shows. It does *not* show that they are any more closely related, in the sense of sharing more genes, than either is to Greeks. Calling Somalis and Ghanaians "black" therefore sheds no further light on their evolutionary history and implies—wrongly—that they are more closely related to each other than either is to someone of a different "race." Similarly, the long noses of North Africans and northern Europeans reveal that they evolved in dry or cold climates (the nose moistens air before the air reaches the lungs, and longer noses moisten more air). The tall, thin bodies of Kenya's Masai evolved to dissipate heat; Eskimos evolved short, squat bodies to retain it. Calling these peoples "different races" adds nothing to that understanding.

Where did the three standard racial divisions come from? They entered the social, and scientific, consciousness during the Age of Exploration. Loring Brace doesn't think it's a coincidence that the standard races represent peoples who, as he puts it, "lived at the end of the Europeans' trade routes"—in Africa and China—in the days after Prince Henry the Navigator set sail. Before Europeans took to the seas, there was little perception of races. If villagers began to look different to an Englishman riding a horse from France to Italy and on to Greece, the change was too subtle to inspire notions of races. But if the English sailor left Lisbon Harbor and dropped anchor off the Kingdom of Niger, people looked so different he felt compelled to invent a scheme to explain the world—and, perhaps, distance himself from the Africans.

Next time, census takers ought to carry palettes, too. *In 1990, Americans claimed membership in nearly 300 races or ethnic groups and 600 American Indian tribes. Hispanics had 70 categories of their own.*

This habit of sorting the world's peoples into a small number of groups got its first scientific gloss from Swedish taxonomist Carolus Linnaeus.

(Linnaeus is best known for his system of classifying living things by genus and species—*Escherichia coli, Homo sapiens* and the rest.) In 1758 he declared that humanity falls into four races: white (Europeans), red (Native Americans), dark (Asians) and black (Africans). Linnaeus said that Native Americans (who in the 1940s got grouped with Asians) were ruled by custom. Africans were indolent and negligent, and Europeans were inventive and gentle, said Linnaeus. Leave aside the racist undertones (not to mention the oddity of ascribing gentleness to the group that perpetrated the Crusades and Inquisition): that alone should not undermine its validity. More worrisome is that the notion and the specifics of race predate genetics, evolutionary biology and the science of human origins. With the revolutions in those fields, how is it that the 18th-century scheme of race retains its powerful hold? Consider these arguments:

• **If I parachute into Nairobi, I know I'm not in Oslo:** Colorado's Alice Brues uses this image to argue that denying the reality of race flies in the face of common sense. But the parachutists, if they were familiar with the great range of human diversity, could also tell that they were in Nairobi rather than Abidjan—east Africans don't look much like west Africans. They could also tell they were in Istanbul rather than Oslo, even though Turks and Norwegians are both called Caucasian.

• **DOA, male, 5′11″ . . . black:** When U.S. police call in a forensic anthropologist to identify the race of a skeleton, the scientist comes through 80 to 85 percent of the time. If race has no biological validity, how can the sleuths get it right so often? The forensic anthropologist could, with enough information about bone structure and genetic markers, identify the region from which the corpse came—south and west Africa, Southeast Asia and China, Northern and Western Europe. It just so happens that the police would call corpses from the first two countries black, from the middle two

Asian, and the last pair white. But lumping these six distinct populations into three groups of two serves no biological purpose, only a social convention. The larger grouping may reflect how society views humankind's diversity, but does not explain it.

• **African-Americans have more hypertension:** If race is not real, how can researchers say that blacks have higher rates of infant mortality, lower rates of osteoporosis and a higher incidence of hypertension? Because a social construct can have biological effects, says epidemiologist Robert Hahn of the U.S. Centers for Disease Control and Prevention. Consider hypertension among African-Americans. Roughly 34 percent have high blood pressure, compared with about 16 percent of whites. But William Dressler finds the greatest incidence of hypertension among blacks who are upwardly mobile achievers. "That's probably because in mundane interactions, from the bank to the grocery store, they are treated in ways that do not coincide with their self-image as respectable achievers," says Dressler, an anthropologist at the University of Alabama. "And the upwardly mobile are more likely to encounter discriminatory white culture." Lab studies show that stressful situations—like being followed in grocery stores as if you were a shoplifter—elevate blood pressure and lead to vascular changes that cause hypertension. "In this case, race captures social factors such as the experience of discrimination," says sociologist David Williams of the University of Michigan. Further evidence that hypertension has more to do with society than with biology: black Africans have among the lowest rates of hypertension in the world.

If race is not a biological explanation of hypertension, can it offer a biological explanation of something as complex as intelligence? Psychologists are among the strongest proponents of retaining the three conventional racial categories. It organizes and explains their data in the most parsimonious way, as Charles Murray and Richard Herrnstein argue in "The Bell Curve."

But anthropologists say that such conclusions are built on a foundation of sand. If nothing else, argues Brace, every ethnic group evolved under conditions where intelligence was a requirement for survival. If there are intelligence "genes," they must be in all ethnic groups equally: differences in intelligence must be a cultural and social artifact.

Scientists who doubt the biological meaningfulness of race are not nihilists. They just prefer another way of capturing, and explaining, the great diversity of humankind. Even today most of the world's peoples marry within their own group. Intramarriage preserves features—fleshy lips, small ears, wide-set eyes—that arose by a chance genetic mutation long ago. Grouping people by geographic origins—better known as ethnicity—"is more correct both in a statistical sense and in understanding the history of human variation," says Hampshire's Goodman. Ethnicity also serves as a proxy for differences—from diet to a history of discrimination—that can have real biological and behavioral effects.

In a 1942 book, anthropologist Ashley Montagu called race "Man's Most Dangerous Myth." If it is, then our most ingenuous myth must be that we sort humankind into groups in order to understand the meaning and origin of humankind's diversity. That isn't the reason at all; a greater number of smaller groupings, like ethnicities, does a better job. The obsession with broad categories is so powerful as to seem a neurological imperative. Changing our thinking about race will require a revolution in thought as profound, and profoundly unsettling, as anything science has ever demanded. What these researchers are talking about is changing the way in which we see the world—and each other. But before that can happen, we must do more than understand the biologist's suspicions about race. We must ask science, also, why it is that we are so intent on sorting humanity into so few groups—us and Other—in the first place.

Goin' Gangsta, Choosin' Cholita

Teens today "claim" a racial identity

Nell Bernstein

WEST MAGAZINE

Nell Bernstein is editor of YO! (Youth Outlook), *a Bay Area journal of teen life produced by Pacific News Service. Subscriptions: $12 young people/$75 supporter/yr. (6 issues) from Pacific News Service, 450 Mission St., Room 506, San Francisco, CA 94105.*

Her lipstick is dark, the lip liner even darker, nearly black. In baggy pants, a blue plaid Pendleton, her bangs pulled back tight off her forehead, 15-year-old April is a perfect cholita, a Mexican gangsta girl.

But April Miller is Anglo. "And I don't like it!" she complains. "I'd rather be Mexican."

April's father wanders into the family room of their home in San Leandro, California, a suburb near Oakland. "Hey, cholita," he teases. "Go get a suntan. We'll put you in a barrio and see how much you like it."

A large, sandy-haired man with "April" tattooed on one arm and "Kelly"—the name of his older daughter—on the other, Miller spent 21 years working in a San Leandro glass factory that shut down and moved to Mexico a couple of years ago. He recently got a job in another factory, but he expects NAFTA to swallow that one, too.

"Sooner or later we'll all get nailed," he says. "Just another stab in the back of the American middle class."

Later, April gets her revenge: "Hey, Mr. White Man's Last Stand," she teases. "Wait till you see how well I manage my welfare check. You'll be asking me for money."

A once almost exclusively white, now increasingly Latin and black working-class suburb, San Leandro borders on predominantly black East Oakland. For decades, the boundary was strictly policed and practically impermeable. In 1970 April Miller's hometown was 97 percent white. By 1990 San Leandro was 65 percent white, 6 percent black, 15 percent Hispanic, and 13 percent Asian or Pacific Islander. With minorities moving into suburbs in growing numbers and cities becoming ever more diverse, the boundary between city and suburb is dissolving, and suburban teenagers are changing with the times.

In April's bedroom, her past and present selves lie in layers, the pink walls of girlhood almost obscured, Guns N' Roses and Pearl Jam posters overlaid by rappers Paris and Ice Cube. "I don't have a big enough attitude to be a black girl," says April, explaining her current choice of ethnic identification.

What matters is that she thinks the choice is hers. For April and her friends, identity is not a matter of where you come from, what you were born into, what color your skin is. It's what you wear, the music you listen to, the words you use—everything to which you pledge allegiance, no matter how fleetingly.

The hybridization of American teens has become talk show fodder, with "wiggers"—white kids who dress and talk "black"—appearing on TV in full gangsta regalia. In Indiana a group of white high school girls raised a national stir when they triggered an imitation race war at their virtually all white high school last fall simply by dressing "black."

In many parts of the country, it's television and radio, not neighbors, that introduce teens to the allure of ethnic difference. But in California, which demographers predict will be the first state with no racial majority by the year 2000, the influences are more immediate. The California public schools are the most diverse in the country: 42 percent white, 36 percent Hispanic, 9 percent black, 8 percent Asian.

Sometimes young people fight over their differences. Students at virtually any school in the Bay Area can recount the details of at least one "race riot" in which a conflict between individuals escalated into a battle between their clans. More often, though, teens would rather join than fight. Adolescence, after all, is the period when you're most inclined to mimic the power closest at hand, from stealing your older sister's clothes to copying the ruling clique at school.

White skaters and Mexican would-be gangbangers listen to gangsta rap and call each other "nigga" as a term of endearment; white girls sometimes affect Spanish accents; blond cheerleaders claim Cherokee ancestors.

"Claiming" is the central concept here. A Vietnamese teen in Hayward, another Oakland suburb, "claims" Oakland—and by implication blackness—because he lived there as a child. A law-abiding white kid "claims" a Mexican gang he says he hangs with. A brown-skinned girl with a Mexican father and a white mother "claims" her Mexican side, while her fair-skinned sister "claims" white. The word comes up over and over, as if identity were territory, the self a kind of turf.

At a restaurant in a minimall in Hayward, Nicole Huffstutler, 13, sits with her friends and describes herself as "Indian, German, French, Welsh, and, um…American": "If somebody says anything like 'Yeah, you're just a peckerwood,' I'll walk up and I'll say 'white pride!' 'Cause I'm proud of my race, and I wouldn't wanna be any other race."

"Claiming" white has become a matter of principle for Heather, too, who says she's "sick of the majority looking at us like we're less than them." (Hayward schools were 51 percent white in 1990, down from 77 percent in 1980, and whites are now the minority in many schools.)

Asked if she knows that nonwhites have not traditionally been referred to as "the majority" in America, Heather gets exasperated: "I hear that all the time, every day. They say, 'Well, you guys controlled us for many years, and it's time for us to control you.' Every day."

When Jennifer Vargas—a small, brown-skinned girl in purple jeans who quietly eats her salad while Heather talks—softly announces that she's "mostly Mexican," she gets in trouble with her friends.

"No, you're not!" scolds Heather.

"I'm mostly Indian and Mexican," Jennifer continues flatly. "I'm very little…I'm mostly…"

"Your mom's white!" Nicole reminds her sharply. "She has blond hair."

"That's what I mean," Nicole adds. "People think that white is a bad thing. They think that white is a bad race. So she's trying to claim more Mexican than white."

"I have very little white in me," Jennifer repeats. "I have mostly my dad's side, 'cause I look like him and stuff. And most of my friends think that me and my brother and sister aren't related, 'cause they look more like my mom."

"But you guys are all the same race, you just look different," Nicole insists. She stops eating and frowns. "OK, you're half and half each what your parents have. So you're equal as your brother and sister, you just look different. And you should be proud of what you are—every little piece and bit of what you are. Even if you were Afghan or whatever, you should be proud of it."

Will Mosley, Heather's 17-year-old brother, says he and his friends listen to rap groups like Compton's Most Wanted, NWA, and Above the Law because they "sing about life"—that is, what happens in Oakland, Los Angeles, anyplace but where Will is sitting today, an empty Round Table Pizza in a minimall.

"No matter what race you are," Will says, "if you live like we do, then that's the kind of music you like."

And how do they live?

"We don't live bad or anything," Will admits. "We live in a pretty good neighborhood, there's no violence or crime. I was just…we're just city people, I guess."

Will and his friend Adolfo Garcia, 16, say they've outgrown trying to be something they're not. "When I was 11 or 12," Will says, "I thought I was becoming a big gangsta and stuff. Because I liked that music, and thought it was the coolest, I wanted to become that. I wore big clothes, like you wear in jail. But then I kind of woke up. I looked at myself and thought, 'Who am I trying to be?'"

They may have outgrown blatant mimicry, but Will and his friends remain convinced that they can live in a suburban tract house with a well-kept lawn on a tree-lined street in "not a bad neighborhood" and still call themselves "city" people on the basis of musical tastes. "City" for these young people means crime, graffiti, drugs. The kids are law-abiding, but these activities connote what Will admiringly calls "action." With pride in his voice, Will predicts that "in a couple of years, Hayward will be like Oakland. It's starting to get more known, because of crime and things. I think it'll be bigger, more things happening, more crime, more graffiti, stealing cars."

"That's good," chimes in 15-year-old Matt Jenkins, whose new beeper—an item that once connoted gangsta chic but now means little more than an active social life—goes off periodically. "More fun."

The three young men imagine with disdain life in a gangsta-free zone. "Too bland, too boring," Adolfo says. "You have to have something going on. You can't just have everyday life."

"Mowing your lawn," Matt sneers.

"Like Beaver Cleaver's house," Adolfo adds. "It's too clean out here."

Not only white kids believe that identity is a matter of choice or taste, or that the power of "claiming" can transcend ethnicity. The Manor Park Locos—a group of mostly Mexican-Americans who hang out in San Leandro's Manor Park—say they descend from the Manor Lords, tough white guys who ruled the neighborhood a generation ago.

They "are like our…uncles and dads, the older generation," says Jesse Martinez, 14. "We're what they were when they were around, except we're Mexican."

"There's three generations," says Oso, Jesse's younger brother. "There's Manor Lords, Manor Park Locos, and Manor Park Pee Wees." The Pee Wees consist mainly of the Locos' younger brothers, eager kids who circle the older boys on bikes and brag about "punking people."

Unlike Will Mosley, the Locos find little glamour in city life. They survey the changing suburban landscape and see not "action" or "more fun" but frightening decline. Though most of them are not yet 18, the Locos are already nostalgic, longing for a Beaver Cleaver past that white kids who mimic them would scoff at.

Walking through nearly empty Manor Park, with its eucalyptus stands, its softball diamond and tennis courts, Jesse's friend Alex, the only Asian in the group, waves his arms in a gesture of futility. "A few years ago, every bench was filled," he says. "Now no one comes here. I guess it's because of everything that's going on. My parents paid a lot for this house, and I want it to be nice for them. I just hope this doesn't turn into Oakland."

Glancing across the park at April Miller's street, Jesse says he knows what the white cholitas are about. "It's not a racial thing," he explains. "It's just all the most popular people out here are Mexican. We're just the gangstas that everyone knows. I guess those girls wanna be known."

Not every young Californian embraces the new racial hybridism. Andrea Jones, 20, an African-American who grew up in the Bay Area suburbs of Union City and Hayward, is unimpressed by what she sees mainly as shallow mimicry. "It's full of posers out here," she says. "When *Boyz N the Hood* came out on video, it was sold out for weeks. The boys all wanna be black, the girls all wanna be Mexican. It's the glamour."

Driving down the quiet, shaded streets of her old neighborhood in Union City, Andrea spots two white preteen boys in Raiders jackets and hugely baggy pants strutting erratically down the empty sidewalk. "Look at them," she says. "Dislocated."

She knows why. "In a lot of these schools out here, it's hard being white," she says. "I don't think these kids were prepared for the backlash that is going on, all the pride now in people of color's ethnicity, and our boldness with it. They have nothing like that, no identity, nothing they can say they're proud of.

"So they latch onto their great-grandmother who's a Cherokee, or they take on the most stereotypical aspects of being black or Mexican. It's beautiful to appreciate different aspects of other people's culture—that's like the dream of what the 21st century should be. But to garnish yourself with pop culture stereotypes just to blend—that's really sad."

Roland Krevocheza, 18, graduated last year from Arroyo High School in San Leandro. He is Mexican on his mother's side, Eastern European on his father's. In the new hierarchies, it may be mixed kids like Roland who have the hardest time finding their place, even as their numbers grow. (One in five marriages in California is between people of different races.) They can always be called "wannabes," no matter what they claim.

"I'll state all my nationalities," Roland says. But he takes a greater interest in his father's side, his Ukrainian, Romanian, and Czech ancestors. "It's more unique," he explains. "Mexican culture is all around me. We eat Mexican food all the time, I hear stories from my grandmother. I see the low-riders and stuff. I'm already part of it. I'm not trying to be; I am."

His darker-skinned brother "says he's not proud to be white," Roland adds. "He calls me 'Mr. Nazi.'" In the room the two share, the American flags and the reproduction of the Bill of Rights are Roland's; the Public Enemy poster belongs to his brother.

Roland has good reason to mistrust gangsta attitudes. In his junior year in high school, he was one of several Arroyo students who were beaten up outside the school at lunchtime by a group of Samoans who came in cars from Oakland. Roland wound up with a split lip, a concussion, and a broken tailbone. Later he was told that the assault was "gang-related"—that the Samoans were beating up anyone wearing red.

"Rappers, I don't like them," Roland says. "I think they're a bad influence on kids. It makes kids think they're all tough and bad."

Those who, like Roland, dismiss the gangsta and cholo styles as affectations can point to the fact that several companies market overpriced knockoffs of "ghetto wear" targeted at teens.

But there's also something going on out here that transcends adolescent faddishness and pop culture exoticism. When white kids call their parents "racist" for nagging them about their baggy pants; when they learn Spanish to talk to their boyfriends; when Mexican-American boys feel themselves descended in spirit from white "uncles"; when children of mixed marriages insist that they are whatever race they say they are, all of them are more than just confused.

They're inching toward what Andrea Jones calls "the dream of what the 21st century should be." In the ever more diverse communities of Northern California, they're also facing the complicated reality of what their 21st century will be.

Meanwhile, in the living room of the Miller family's San Leandro home, the argument continues unabated. "You don't know what you are," April's father has told her more than once. But she just keeps on telling him he doesn't know what time it is.

In the eighteenth century a disastrous shift occurred in the way Westerners perceived races. The man responsible was Johann Friedrich Blumenbach, one of the least racist thinkers of his day.

the Geometer of Race

STEPHEN JAY GOULD

Stephen Jay Gould, a contributing editor of Discover, *is a professor of zoology at Harvard who also teaches geology, biology, and the history of science. His writing on evolution has won many prizes, including a National Book Award, a National Magazine Award, and the Phi Beta Kappa Science Award. For* Discover's *November 1993 special section on ten great science museums, Gould wrote about the glass flowers at Harvard's Botanical Museum.*

INTERESTING STORIES often lie encoded in names that seem either capricious or misconstrued. Why, for example, are political radicals called "left" and their conservative counterparts "right"? In many European legislatures, the most distinguished members sat at the chairman's right, following a custom of courtesy as old as our prejudices for favoring the dominant hand of most people. (These biases run deep, extending well beyond can openers and scissors to language itself, where *dexterous* stems from the Latin for "right," and *sinister* from the word for "left.") Since these distinguished nobles and moguls tended to espouse conservative views, the right and left wings of the legislature came to define a geometry of political views.

Among such apparently capricious names in my own field of biology and evolution, none seems more curious, and none elicits more questions after lectures, than the official designation of light-skinned people in Europe, western Asia, and North Africa as Caucasian. Why should the most common racial group of the Western world be named for a mountain range that straddles Russia and Georgia? Johann Friedrich Blumenbach (1752–1840), the German anatomist and naturalist who established the most influential of all racial classifications, invented this name in 1795, in the third edition of his seminal work, *De Generis Humani Varietate Nativa* (On the Natural Variety of Mankind). Blumenbach's definition cites two reasons for his choice—the maximal beauty of people from this small region, and the probability that humans were first created in this area.

> *Caucasian variety.* I have taken the name of this variety from Mount Caucasus, both because its neighborhood, and especially its southern slope, produces the most beautiful race of men, I mean the Georgian; and because . . . in that region, if anywhere, it seems we ought with the greatest probability to place the autochthones [original forms] of mankind.

Blumenbach, one of the greatest and most honored scientists of the Enlightenment, spent his entire career as a professor at the University of Göttingen in Germany. He first presented *De Generis Humani Varietate Nativa* as a doctoral dissertation to the medical faculty of Göttingen in 1775, as the minutemen of Lexington and Concord began the American Revolution. He then republished the text for general distribution in 1776, as a fateful meeting in Philadelphia proclaimed our independence. The coincidence of three great documents in 1776—Jefferson's Declaration of Independence (on the politics of liberty), Adam Smith's *Wealth of Nations* (on the economics of individualism), and Blumenbach's treatise on racial classification (on the science of human diversity)—records the social ferment of these decades and sets the wider context that makes Blumenbach's taxonomy, and his subsequent decision to call the European race Caucasian, so important for our history and current concerns.

The solution to big puzzles often hinges upon tiny curiosities, easy to miss or to pass over. I suggest that the key to understanding Blumenbach's classification, the foundation of much that continues to influence and disturb us today, lies in the peculiar criterion he used to name the European race Caucasian—the supposed superior beauty of people from this region. Why, first of all, should a scientist attach such importance to an evidently subjective assessment; and why, secondly, should an aesthetic criterion become the basis of a scientific judgment about place of origin? To answer these questions, we must compare Blumenbach's original 1775 text with the later edition of 1795, when Caucasians received their name.

Blumenbach's final taxonomy of 1795 divided all humans into five groups, defined both by geography and appearance—in his order, the Caucasian variety, for the light-skinned people of Europe and adjacent parts of Asia and Africa; the Mongolian variety, for most other inhabitants of Asia, including China and Japan; the Ethiopian variety, for the dark-skinned people of Africa; the American variety, for most native populations of the New World; and the Malay variety, for the Polynesians and Melanesians of the Pacific and for the aborigines of Australia. But Blumenbach's original classification of 1775 recognized only the first four of these five, and united members of the Malay variety with the other people of Asia whom Blumenbach came to name Mongolian.

We now encounter the paradox of Blumenbach's reputation as the inventor of modern racial classification. The original four-race system, as I shall illustrate in a moment, did not arise from Blumenbach's observations but only represents, as Blumenbach readily admits, the classification promoted by his guru Carolus Linnaeus in the founding document of taxonomy, the *Systema Naturae* of 1758. Therefore, Blumenbach's only original contribution to racial classification lies in the later addition of a Malay variety for some Pacific people's first included in a broader Asian group.

This change seems so minor. Why, then, do we credit Blumenbach, rather than Linnaeus, as the founder of racial classification? (One might prefer to say "discredit," as the enterprise does not, for good reason, enjoy high repute these days.) But Blumenbach's apparently small change actually records a theoretical shift that could not have been broader, or more portentous, in scope. This change has been missed or misconstrued because later scientists have not grasped the vital historical and philosophical principle that theories are models subject to visual representation, usually in clearly definable geometric terms.

By moving from the Linnaean four-race system to his own five-race scheme, Blumenbach radically changed the geometry of human order from a geographically based model without explicit ranking to a hierarchy of worth, oddly based upon perceived beauty, and fanning out in two directions from a Caucasian ideal. The addition of a Malay category was crucial to this geometric reformulation—and therefore becomes the key to the conceptual transformation rather than a simple refinement of factual information within an old scheme. (For the insight that scientific revolutions embody such geometric shifts, I am grateful to my friend Rhonda Roland Shearer, who portrays these themes in a forthcoming book, *The Flatland Hypothesis*.)

BLUMENBACH IDOLIZED his teacher Linnaeus and acknowledged him as the source of his original fourfold racial classification: "I have followed Linnaeus in the number, but have defined my varieties by other boundaries" (1775 edition). Later, in adding his Malay variety, Blumenbach identified his change as a departure from his old mentor in the most respectful terms: "It became very clear that the Linnaean division of mankind could no longer be adhered to; for which reason I, in this little work, ceased like others to follow that illustrious man."

Linnaeus divided the species *Homo sapiens* into four basic varieties, defined primarily by geography and, interestingly, not in the ranked order favored by most Europeans in the racist tradition—*Americanus, Europaeus, Asiaticus,* and *Afer,* or African. (He also alluded to two other fanciful categories: *ferus* for "wild boys," occasionally discovered in the woods and possibly raised by animals—most turned out to be retarded or mentally ill youngsters abandoned by their parents—and *monstrosus* for hairy men with tails, and other travelers' confabulations.) In so doing, Linnaeus presented nothing original; he merely mapped humans onto the four geographic regions of conventional cartography.

Linnaeus then characterized each of these groups by noting color, humor, and posture, in that order. Again, none of these categories explicitly implies ranking by worth. Once again, Linnaeus was simply bowing to classical taxonomic theories in making these decisions. For example, his use of the four humors reflects the ancient and medieval theory that a person's temperament arises from a balance of four fluids (*humor* is Latin for "moisture")—blood, phlegm, choler (yellow bile), and melancholy (black bile). Depending on which of the four substances dominated, a person would be sanguine (the cheerful realm of blood), phlegmatic (sluggish), choleric (prone to anger), or melancholic (sad). Four geographic regions, four humors, four races.

For the American variety, Linnaeus wrote "*rufus, cholericus, rectus*" (red, choleric, upright); for the European, "*albus, sanguineus, torosus*" (white, sanguine, muscular); for the Asian, "*luridus, melancholicus, rigidus*" (pale yellow, melancholy, stiff); and for the African, "*niger, phlegmaticus, laxus*" (black, phlegmatic, relaxed).

I don't mean to deny that Linnaeus held conventional beliefs about the superiority of his own European variety over others. Being a sanguine, muscular European surely sounds better than being a melancholy, stiff Asian. Indeed, Linnaeus ended each group's description with a more overtly racist label, an attempt to epitomize behavior in just two words. Thus the American was *regitur consuetudine* (ruled by habit); the European, *regitur ritibus* (ruled by custom); the Asian, *regitur opinionibus* (ruled by belief); and the African, *regitur arbitrio* (ruled by caprice). Surely regulation by established and considered custom beats the unthinking rule of habit or belief, and all of these are superior to caprice—thus leading to the implied and conventional racist ranking of Europeans first, Asians and Americans in the middle, and Africans at the bottom.

Nonetheless, and despite these implications, the overt geometry of Linnaeus's model is not linear or hierarchical. When

Scientists assume that their own shifts in interpretation record only their better understanding of newly discovered facts. They tend to be unaware of their own mental impositions upon the world's messy and ambiguous factuality.

we visualize his scheme as an essential picture in our mind, we see a map of the world divided into four regions, with the people in each region characterized by a list of different traits. In short, Linnaeus's primary ordering principle is cartographic; if he had wished to push hierarchy as the essential picture of human variety, he would surely have listed Europeans first and Africans last, but he started with native Americans instead.

The shift from a geographic to a hierarchical ordering of human diversity must stand as one of the most fateful transitions in the history of Western science—for what, short of railroads and nuclear bombs, has had more practical impact, in this case almost entirely negative, upon our collective lives? Ironically, Blumenbach is the focus of this shift, for his five-race scheme became canonical and changed the geometry of human order from Linnaean cartography to linear ranking—in short, to a system based on putative worth.

I say ironic because Blumenbach was the least racist and most genial of all Enlightenment thinkers. How peculiar that the man most committed to human unity, and to inconsequential moral and intellectual differences among groups, should have changed the mental geometry of human order to a scheme that has served racism ever since. Yet on second thought, this situation is really not so odd—for most scientists have been quite unaware of the mental machinery, and particularly of the visual or geometric implications, lying behind all their theorizing.

An old tradition in science proclaims that changes in theory must be driven by observation. Since most scientists believe this simplistic formula, they assume that their own shifts in interpretation record only their better understanding of newly discovered facts. Scientists therefore tend to be unaware of their own mental impositions upon the world's messy and ambiguous factuality. Such mental impositions arise from a variety of sources, including psychological predisposition and social context. Blumenbach lived in an age when ideas of progress, and the cultural superiority of European ways, dominated political and social life. Implicit, loosely formulated, or even unconscious notions of racial ranking fit well with such a worldview—indeed, almost any other organizational scheme would have seemed anomalous. I doubt that Blumenbach was actively encouraging racism by redrawing the mental diagram of human groups. He was only, and largely passively, recording the social view of his time. But ideas have consequences, whatever the motives or intentions of their promoters.

Blumenbach certainly thought that his switch from the Linnaean four-race system to his own five-race scheme arose only from his improved understanding of nature's factuality. He said as much when he announced his change in the second (1781) edition of his treatise: "Formerly in the first edition of this work, I divided all mankind into four varieties; but after I had more actively investigated the different nations of Eastern Asia and America, and, so to speak, looked at them more closely, I was compelled to give up that division, and to place in its stead the following five varieties, as more consonant to nature." And in the preface to the third edition, of 1795, Blumenbach states

that he gave up the Linnaean scheme in order to arrange "the varieties of man according to the truth of nature." When scientists adopt the myth that theories arise solely from observation, and do not grasp the personal and social influences acting on their thinking, they not only miss the causes of their changed opinions; they may even fail to comprehend the deep mental shift encoded by the new theory.

Blumenbach strongly upheld the unity of the human species against an alternative view, then growing in popularity (and surely more conducive to conventional forms of racism), that each major race had been separately created. He ended his third edition by writing: "No doubt can any longer remain but that we are with great probability right in referring all . . . varieties of man . . . to one and the same species."

AS HIS MAJOR ARGUMENT for unity, Blumenbach noted that all supposed racial characteristics grade continuously from one people to another and cannot define any separate and bounded group. "For although there seems to be so great a difference between widely separate nations, that you might easily take the inhabitants of the Cape of Good Hope, the Greenlanders, and the Circassians for so many different species of man, yet when the matter is thoroughly considered, you see that all do so run into one another, and that one variety of mankind does so sensibly pass into the other, that you cannot mark out the limits between them." He particularly refuted the common racist claim that black Africans bore unique features of their inferiority: "There is no single character so peculiar and so universal among the Ethiopians, but what it may be observed on the one hand everywhere in other varieties of men."

Blumenbach, writing 80 years before Darwin, believed that *Homo sapiens* had been created in a single region and had then spread over the globe. Our racial diversity, he then argued, arose as a result of this spread to other climates and topographies, and to our adoption of different modes of life in these various regions. Following the terminology of his time, Blumenbach referred to these changes as "degenerations"—not intending the modern sense of deterioration, but the literal meaning of departure from an initial form of humanity at the creation (*de* means "from," and *genus* refers to our original stock).

Most of these degenerations, Blumenbach argued, arose directly from differences in climate and habitat—ranging from such broad patterns as the correlation of dark skin with tropical environments, to more particular (and fanciful) attributions, including a speculation that the narrow eye slits of some Australian aborigines may have arisen in response to "constant clouds of gnats . . . contracting the natural face of the inhabitants." Other changes, he maintained, arose as a consequence of customs adopted in different regions. For example, nations that compressed the heads of babies by swaddling boards or papoose carriers ended up with relatively long skulls. Blumenbach held that "almost all the diversity of the form of the head in different nations is to be attributed to the mode of life and to art."

Blumenbach believed that such changes, promoted over many generations, could eventually become hereditary. "With

Blumenbach upheld the unity of the human species against an alternative view, then growing in popularity (and surely more conducive to conventional racism), that each race had been separately created.

the progress of time," Blumenbach wrote, "art may degenerate into a second nature." But he also argued that most racial variations, as superficial impositions of climate and custom, could be easily altered or reversed by moving to a new region or by adopting new behavior. White Europeans living for generations in the tropics could become dark-skinned, while Africans transported as slaves to high latitudes could eventually become white: "Color, whatever be its cause, be it bile, or the influence of the sun, the air, or the climate, is, at all events, an adventitious and easily changeable thing, and can never constitute a diversity of species," he wrote.

Convinced of the superficiality of racial variation, Blumenbach defended the mental and moral unity of all peoples. He held particularly strong opinions on the equal status of black Africans and white Europeans. He may have been patronizing in praising "the good disposition and faculties of these our black brethren," but better paternalism than malign contempt. He campaigned for the abolition of slavery and asserted the moral superiority of slaves to their captors, speaking of a "natural tenderness of heart, which has never been benumbed or extirpated on board the transport vessels or on the West India sugar plantations by the brutality of their white executioners."

Blumenbach established a special library in his house devoted exclusively to black authors, singling out for special praise the poetry of Phillis Wheatley, a Boston slave whose writings have only recently been rediscovered: "I possess English, Dutch, and Latin poems by several [black authors], amongst which however above all, those of Phillis Wheatley of Boston, who is justly famous for them, deserves mention here." Finally, Blumenbach noted that many Caucasian nations could not boast so fine a set of authors and scholars as black Africa has produced under the most depressing circumstances of prejudice and slavery: "It would not be difficult to mention entire well-known provinces of Europe, from out of which you would not easily expect to obtain off-hand such good authors, poets, philosophers, and correspondents of the Paris Academy."

Nonetheless, when Blumenbach presented his mental picture of human diversity in his fateful shift away from Linnaean geography, he singled out a particular group as closest to the created ideal and then characterized all other groups by relative degrees of departure from this archetypal standard. He ended up with a system that placed a single race at the pinnacle, and then envisioned two symmetrical lines of departure away from this ideal toward greater and greater degeneration.

WE MAY NOW RETURN to the riddle of the name Caucasian, and to the significance of Blumenbach's addition of a fifth race, the Malay variety. Blumenbach chose to regard his own European variety as closest to the created ideal and then searched for the subset of Europeans with greatest perfection—the highest of the high, so to speak. As we have seen, he identified the people around Mount Caucasus as the closest embodiments of the original ideal and proceeded to name the entire European race for its finest representatives.

But Blumenbach now faced a dilemma. He had already affirmed the mental and moral equality of all peoples. He therefore could not use these conventional criteria of racist ranking to establish degrees of relative departure from the Caucasian ideal. Instead, and however subjective (and even risible) we view the criterion today, Blumenbach chose physical beauty as his guide to ranking. He simply affirmed that Europeans were most beautiful, with Caucasians as the most comely of all. This explains why Blumenbach, in the first quote cited in this article, linked the maximal beauty of the Caucasians to the place of human origin. Blumenbach viewed all subsequent variation as departures from the originally created ideal—therefore, the most beautiful people must live closest to our primal home.

Blumenbach's descriptions are pervaded by his subjective sense of relative beauty, presented as though he were discussing an objective and quantifiable property, not subject to doubt or disagreement. He describes a Georgian female skull (found close to Mount Caucasus) as "really the most beautiful form of skull which . . . always of itself attracts every eye, however little observant." He then defends his European standard on aesthetic grounds: "In the first place, that stock displays . . . the most beautiful form of the skull, from which, as from a mean and primeval type, the others diverge by most easy gradations. . . . Besides, it is white in color, which we may fairly assume to have been the primitive color of mankind, since . . . it is very easy for that to degenerate into brown, but very much more difficult for dark to become white."

Blumenbach then presented all human variety on two lines of successive departure from this Caucasian ideal, ending in the two most degenerate (least attractive, not least morally unworthy or mentally obtuse) forms of humanity—Asians on one side, and Africans on the other. But Blumenbach also wanted to designate intermediary forms between ideal and most degenerate, especially since even gradation formed his primary argument for human unity. In his original four-race system, he could identify native Americans as intermediary between Europeans and Asians, but who would serve as the transitional form between Europeans and Africans?

The four-race system contained no appropriate group. But inventing a fifth racial category as an intermediary between Europeans and Africans would complete the new symmetrical geometry. Blumenbach therefore added the Malay race, not as a minor, factual refinement but as a device for reformulating an entire theory of human diversity. With this one stroke, he produced the geometric transformation from Linnaeus's unranked geographic model to the conventional hierarchy of implied worth that has fostered so much social grief ever since.

I have allotted the first place to the Caucasian . . . which makes me esteem it the primeval one. This diverges in both directions into two, most remote and very different from each other; on the one side, namely, into the Ethiopian, and on the other into the Mongolian. The remaining two occupy the intermediate positions between that primeval one and these two extreme varieties; that is, the American between the Caucasian and Mongolian; the Malay between the same Caucasian and Ethiopian. [From Blumenbach's third edition.]

With one stroke, Blumenbach produced the geometric transformation from Linnaeus's unranked geographic model to the conventional hierarchy of implied worth that has fostered so much social grief ever since.

Scholars often think that academic ideas must remain at worst, harmless, and at best, mildly amusing or even instructive. But ideas do not reside in the ivory tower of our usual metaphor about academic irrelevance. We are, as Pascal said, a thinking reed, and ideas motivate human history. Where would Hitler have been without racism, Jefferson without liberty? Blumenbach lived as a cloistered professor all his life, but his ideas have reverberated in ways that he never could have anticipated, through our wars, our social upheavals, our sufferings, and our hopes.

I therefore end by returning once more to the extraordinary coincidences of 1776—as Jefferson wrote the Declaration of Independence while Blumenbach was publishing the first edition of his treatise in Latin. We should remember the words of the nineteenth-century British historian and moralist Lord Acton, on the power of ideas to propel history:

It was from America that . . . ideas long locked in the breast of solitary thinkers, and hidden among Latin folios, burst forth like a conqueror upon the world they were destined to transform, under the title of the Rights of Man.

FOR FURTHER READING

Daughters of Africa. Margaret Busby, editor. Pantheon, 1992. A comprehensive anthology of prose and poetry written by women of African descent, from ancient Egyptian love songs to the work of contemporary Americans. The collection features the work of Phillis Wheatley, the first black to publish a book of poetry in the United States.

Battling for Souls

As more blacks warm to Islam's emphasis on order, Protestant leaders scramble to make their traditional churches more appealing to young men

CARLA POWER
AND ALLISON SAMUELS

ISLAM IS SPREADING RAPIDLY among black Americans—not so much because of Louis Farrakhan, but because of men like Suetwedien A. Muhammed. Standing amid boarded-up buildings and graffiti in the East Germantown section of Philadelphia last week, the 31-year-old African-American says, "I know this area. I helped mess up this area." As a boy he sang in the Baptist church's choir, but as a teenager he spent a lot of time on neighborhood street corners. In 1975 he converted to Islam; by 1992 he had opened a small storefront mosque to help turn the neighborhood around. It offers a "homework association," a crime watch and a Big Brothers program for young black men—most, like him, converts from Christianity. "A lot of people leave church and go into the bars with their Sunday clothes on," Muhammed says. "We've been getting a fast fix in church, with the singing and the clapping. Then we come out and are faced with the same problems."

Although Christian ministers say their congregations aren't shrinking—and black evangelical numbers are growing slightly—some leaders are worrying about the church's ability to attract young people in the country's toughest neighborhoods. About one third of the 4 million to 5 million Muslims in the United States are African-Americans, and at its current rapid rate of growth, Islam will become the second largest religion in the United States by the year 2000. While still small compared with Christianity's overall numbers, the Muslim community's growth has been dramatic. In 1989, there were 2,000 declared Mus-

lims in the armed services. This year there are 10,000. In Philadelphia, the number of Muslim blacks has risen from 40,000 to 60,000 in five years. In Chicago, there were only a handful of mosques 20 years ago; today there are 30. And a third of all blacks in the federal prison system are Muslim; most of them converted after being locked up. The surge in interest in Islam—underscored by the prominent Islamic rhetoric at the Million Man March—is forcing mainstream Protestant churches to try new ways to put people in their pews. They realize that Islam's popularity is an indictment of their performance. "We've got a million black men in prison, and they're quickly becoming Muslims," says the Rev. Henry Lyons, leader of the National Baptist Convention, the largest organization of Baptists. "And we're standing by idly doing nothing."

In marketing themselves to black men, traditional African-American churches face two problems: Jesus is commonly depicted as white and most churchgoers are women. The growing interest in the African heritage of American blacks—from music to fashion to academics—has led some to view Christianity as a religion imposed on them by slaveholders. "Christianity is what kept the slaves in check in the first place," said 37-year-old Gwen Priestly, a media consultant in Los Angeles, who recently converted from Roman Catholicism to Islam. "That religion told them to be patient and to wait on the better life in heaven." As earthly conditions for black men have deteriorated, more of them have come to dismiss local churches as irrelevant. "The church was just too women-oriented for me," says Jason Gordon, a 21-year-old from Los Angeles who recently left the Baptist Church for

Islam—over his mother's strenuous objections. "Men my age didn't really seem to have an active place. And they do in Islam."

ISLAM IS PERCEIVED AS MORE COMpatible with Afrocentrism and, in some ways, as more masculine. Islamic clergy often emphasize that about a third of the slaves were shipped to America from Muslim countries. And since Islam rejects visual depictions of God, blacks can pray to a formless Allah instead of a blond, blue-eyed Jesus. Most important, Islam's emphasis on dignity and self-discipline appeals to many men in the inner city, where disorder prevails. Muslims are expected to pray five times a day, avoid drugs and alcohol and take care of their families. "Even the manner of walking is different," says Ghayth Nur Kashif, imam of a mosque in southeast Washington. When young men are first introduced to Islam, he says, many come in strutting—"swaying from side to side or walking with a little limp. In very short order the limp and swinging stops." In keeping with the notion that Islam is a full-time way of life, Islamic clergy also pay great attention to the worldly needs of men. Kashif's mosque offers classes not only in the Koran but in computer programming and typing.

Farrakhan may be the best-known "Muslim" leader, but the Nation of Islam has only 20,000 members. In fact, many Muslims don't think the Nation is actually Islamic. Among many differences, Orthodox Muslims believe Allah created all mankind; the Nation teaches that the white race resulted from a botched experiment by a mad black scientist named Yakub. Traditional Islam preaches racial harmony; the Nation advocates racial separatism.

72% of blacks—and **53%** of whites—think the call for black self-help at the Million Man March was a necessary step toward future integration.

Meanwhile, some churches—impressed with the Muslims' success—have tried to attract more black men by Africanizing Christianity. More ministers are wearing kente cloth on their vestments and playing African drums during services. At First A.M.E. Church in Los Angeles, a stained-glass image of a black Jesus was installed three years ago. Some Philadelphia churches now have images of Christ, Solomon and Moses depicted as black. The Rev. Ivan Hicks, assistant pastor of the Bright Hope Baptist Church, says he hopes to talk young men out of converting to Islam by showing them these images and saying, "You see those broad lips and that broad nose? Jesus looks just like you." And then he talks about Jesus as "a revolutionary, someone who was bringing liberation to the oppressed."

Churches, like mosques, are keen to emphasize outside-the-sanctuary selling points. At Bright Hope Baptist, they've started a Rites of Passage program in which elders mentor 14- to 18-year-olds in spiritual growth and African history. And even without dramatic changes in theological marketing, Protestant leaders believe that there's a limit to how much Islam can ultimately grow, given that the religion traditionally encourages women to wear Muslim garb and concentrate on child rearing. "Women aren't going to put up with all that veil stuff," says Herb Lusk, pastor of the Greater Exodus Baptist Church in Philadelphia.

If that's true, there may be a widening of the spiritual gender gap in the black community, with women going to churches and men to mosques. Religious leaders say that's not necessarily bad. The Rev. James Demus, of the Park Manor Christian Church in Chicago, says the battle for the hearts of young black men is not between Christianity and Islam, but between religion and the lure of the streets. "If they see the street gang as addressing their needs, they go there," he says. "If it's a church group, they go there. If it's Islam, they go there." The hope is that in religion, as in commerce, competition will raise the quality of all the services offered.

With STEVE RHODES *in Chicago and*
STEVEN WALDMAN

BRIDGING THE DIVIDES OF RACE AND ETHNICITY

The process of overcoming bias must begin in communities, where people interact and daily face the consequences of racial, ethnic and class antagonisms. Successful programs combine opportunities for face-to-face dialogue among individuals from diverse backgrounds with broad-based support and involvement of local organizations and governing institutions.

MARTHA L. MCCOY
ROBERT F. SHERMAN

Martha L. McCoy *is codirector of the Study Circles Resource Center, Pomfret, Connecticut.* **Robert F. Sherman,** *PhD was founding executive director of the Increase the Peace Volunteer Corps, 1991–94, Office of the Mayor, City of New York. He currently is a consultant to the National Funding Collaborative of Violence Prevention, New York, New York.*

What we ordinarily see as the fundamental elements of our identities —race, class, gender, religion, civic group membership, place of residence, language — too often constitute the very sources of our separateness and group antagonisms. Valuing our diversity while discovering our commonalities is essential to the cohesion and effectiveness of our communities and a realistic vision of civic renewal.

Democracy is most dynamic when community members work together and feel deeply that by doing so they can make a difference in their personal and collective lives. Physical separation based on race and class—the norm in most communities—is a powerful barrier to democratic practice.[1] It

> *Valuing our diversity while discovering our commonalities is essential to the cohesion and effectiveness of our communities*

also compounds misperceptions, fear, mistrust, and the belief that community concerns are "their issues" rather than "our issues."

These divisions and the attitudes they engender affect where we choose to live (and even whether we *can* choose), where we walk, the jobs we hold, how we are educated, the community projects we promote, and our beliefs about effectiveness.

As the dire consequences of these divisions become apparent, there are more frequent calls for people of different races to explore what they have in common.[2] This article describes specific examples of communities that have established institutions for genuine, effective interracial interaction. These examples demonstrate that communities can make a significant difference in the ways people view each other and work together. •

WHAT DIVIDES OUR COMMUNITIES?
WHAT CAN BRING US TOGETHER?

Recent evidence has demonstrated the persistence and even growth of corrosive and negative stereotypes held about others by almost every group in America. A recent wide-ranging public opinion survey conducted by the National Conference (formerly the National Conference of Christians and Jews) uncovered "two polar views of equality: white and non-white." Differing perceptions about the level of inequality in society lead people of different races not only to conflicting ideas about public policy but also to negative personal judgments about the members of other races.[3] Strengthening those perceptions is what Howard Gadlin has called a "structurally based antagonism between the races," the fact that "lack of agreement is structured into the very ways people of different races experience themselves."[4]

Our current institutions most often reflect rather than confront structurally based antagonisms. On the individual level, segregated neighborhoods and work places, as persistently divided as ever, do not offer a chance to challenge misperceptions. On the institutional level, creating opportunities for cross-group progress has not had the same priority as either maintaining the status quo or fighting for a single group.

How can our society — our communities — begin to counter this great rift? Honest, open dialogue is an essential first step.[5] Leaders and everyday community residents need the chance to confront their stereotypes, recognize and reduce prejudice, learn how to resolve conflict, and work together to develop interpersonal relationships.

In remarks to the 98th National Conference on Governance in 1992, Henry Cisneros argued that communities must *create* the structures for this human interaction: "In an age of diversity we will have to govern differently, we'll have to build communities differently. . . .Among our most important innovations must be those associated with creating 'mediating institutions' to resolve conflict — new hybrids of institutions where people can come to resolve differences, to hear each other, to

listen, to share ideas." And he went further, saying, "It's not good enough to leave this to chance. It's not good enough to hope that somehow in the random meetings of elites — the business elite and the minority elite gathering together at the museum cocktail party — that somehow we'll make contact, [and that this casual interaction] will somehow pass for civic dialogue."[6]

The National Conference survey cited above uncovered a "central willingness on the part of a sizable majority of the American people to give racial and religious and ethnic matters a front-and-center place in the priorities of the nation."[7] Yet, in spite of this readiness, citizens also recognize the lack of opportunities and encouragement to do this in their everyday lives and in the context of their communities. A recent study of Los Angeles conducted by the

---

Our current institutions most often reflect rather than confront structurally based antagonisms.

National Civic League showed that community members feel this absence of opportunity most keenly. They expressed the need for ongoing, respectful, neutral forums where they can meet with members of other racial and ethnic groups.[8]

CREATING INSTITUTIONS FOR
BRINGING PEOPLE TOGETHER

Cities and towns across the country are beginning to establish the kinds of bridges between people that lead to community change. Because of the scope of the challenge, these efforts require ongoing commitment, time and resources.

Many of these efforts utilize small-group, highly participatory, democratic discussions known as "study circles." The history of study circles in the United States goes back to the Chautauqua movement. Today, a growing number of public officials and community coalitions are using study circles as a way to engage citizens in dialogue and problem solving. Study circles are based on the idea that a democracy requires public spaces where people can build community, openly discuss important social and political issues, and find collaborative ways to address them.

Particularly on the issue of race relations, community-wide study circles have been a powerful vehicle for helping individuals view each other and their communities in a new light. By providing opportunities for safe, respectful dialogue, study circles on race offer a way for people to overcome stereotypes, learn about each other's cultures, and discover commonalities. They also provide a starting point for working together to address a range of other community issues. The Study Circles Resource Center supplied technical assistance and training materials for the projects presented below.

Lima, Ohio. The first of these community-wide efforts began in Lima, Ohio in 1992. When the first wave of Rodney King verdicts caused racial tensions to surface in this city of about 50,000 Mayor David Berger convened a multi-racial task force of clergy members to search for new ways to address the underlying causes of the tensions. At their first meeting, it became evident that even members of the clergy had rarely come together across racial lines for open dialogue. This prompted them to arrange such opportunities for the broader population of the city. It was then that the mayor's office and the Office of Continuing Education of The Ohio State University at Lima teamed up to initiate and organize the community-wide study circles.

At a kick-off meeting, the mayor, Ohio State Lima and task force members spoke to the clergy of the city, enlisting their support in recruiting study circle leaders and participants from their congregations. Ohio State Lima and the mayor's office trained the study circle leaders; the mayor's office coordinated the establishment of the circles, ensuring racial diversity in each by pairing black and white churches.

In the first phase of the program in Lima, nearly 1,000 community members participated in groups of about 10 to 15 members each, meeting for several two-

hour sessions.[9] Organizers, leaders and participants in the discussions were overwhelmingly enthusiastic, about both what they had learned and the experience of new interracial friendships and bonds. They also knew that they had formed new interracial networks for addressing community issues. Many participants have continued to meet socially, have extended their study circles, or have taken action together in the community as a result of their discussions.

> *... face-to-face contact among members of traditionally segregated groups — publicly visible to the neighborhood — can have the most far-reaching effects in promoting intergroup peace.*

An interdisciplinary team of researchers at Ohio State Lima has conducted studies revealing evidence of significant, positive attitude changes toward people of other races as a result of the study circles.[10]

Many of the first-phase study circle organizers and leaders now are reaching out to involve new organizations and individuals in a second round of study circles. "Allen-Lima Leadership," a community leadership-development organization in the city and surrounding county, teamed up with the mayor's office and Ohio State Lima at the beginning of 1994 to help organize businesses, neighborhood associations and schools to participate in the phase-two study circles. The mayor's office has formed a "study circle council," and continues to provide overall coordination for the effort, cementing this new avenue of connection between citizens and the municipal organization.

Lima's experience in promoting interracial dialogue is also having ripple effects in other communities. In an April 1994 conference at Ohio State Lima, organizers and leaders of the Lima program shared their experiences with community leaders from around the Midwest. Also in April, Ohio Governor George Voinovich featured the study circle program at a statewide conference of mayors and other community leaders.

Springfield, Ohio. In Springfield, the Department of Human Relations, Housing and Neighborhood Services, with the support of the city commission, has assumed active leadership in fostering dialogue. Selena Singletary, director of human relations, and Faye Flack, city commission member and assistant mayor, called together a core group of officials to expand dialogue on race to the broader community, involving government agencies, schools, colleges and universities, churches, and civic groups. Leaders from each of these sectors recruited study circle leaders and participants, and the Department of Human Relations held a training session for the study circle leaders.

In the first phase of the community discussions, about 300 community members participated, with a culminating community event on Martin Luther King Day, 1994. Because of the unique ways in which the study circles have addressed interracial issues in Springfield, the human relations department and the city commission now are planning a second round of study circles. Community leaders also have carried their program beyond their own city, sharing their organizing model at the April conference at Ohio State Lima and in discussions with community leaders around the country.

Activity elsewhere. As of mid-1994, study circle programs on race relations are beginning in Baton Rouge and New Orleans, Louisiana; Portsmouth, Virginia; Albuquerque, New Mexico; and Columbus, Ohio. Fifteen cities around the country are planning study circle programs. In many of these communities, the mayor's office or a city agency is taking the lead. Even where other community groups take the lead in coordinating the study circles, the city government usually lends its endorsement and involvement.

Each community-wide study circle program reflects a recognition that personal renewal and community change go hand in hand. Mayor Berger of Lima confirmed that connection when he said, "Participants come out of the discussions fundamentally changed. This city will never be the same."

BRINGING PEOPLE TOGETHER
IN THE METROPOLIS:
INCREASE THE PEACE VOLUNTEER CORPS

In the fall of 1991, following a summer of racial unrest and riots in the Crown Heights section of Brooklyn, New York Mayor David Dinkins initiated a program to attract and involve grass-roots participation in solving intergroup tensions in the city's neighborhoods. Housed in the mayor's office, the Increase the Peace Volunteer Corps (IPVC), during its 2½ years of operation, identified, trained and worked with nearly 1,500 volunteers who supplied input, time and attention to how different groups share large and complex neighborhoods, and the city as a whole.

IPVC rested on two fundamental principles. First, residents of particular neighborhoods, or members of a particular group, understand their own challenges in dealing with members of other groups (e.g., their own beliefs, histories, stereotypes, allies, barriers, etc.) better than do outsiders. Armed with the proper tools and training, group members or neighborhood residents themselves possess the greatest potential for resolving conflicts and easing intergroup tensions. Second, IPVC was based on the notion that face-to-face contact among members of traditionally segregated groups — publicly visible to the neighborhood — can have the most far-reaching effects in promoting intergroup peace.

IPVC enjoyed strong, city-wide support. A broad range of people from almost all neighborhoods reported similar reasons for stepping forward: to be close to Mayor Dinkins, who as New York's first African-American mayor symbolized hope for significant progress on race relations; to encounter a wide array of fellow New Yorkers whom they otherwise would have no opportunity to meet; to avail themselves of the free training offered by IPVC; to find outlets for strong desires to overcome apathy and become active in improving race relations in the city; and to protect their communities from crisis and street violence. Some volunteers chose to work in their own neighborhoods while others participated in city-wide task forces.

IPVC developed a 20-hour series of three highly interactive trainings, mandatory for membership, which were designed to ensure familiarity with basic subject matter and methods: multi-cultural sensitivity, conflict resolution and community organizing. The first two encouraged participants to examine their own backgrounds, stereotypes, orientations to conflict, and understanding of intergroup tensions, while teaching specific intervention skills. The final training, in community organizing, was a springboard into the activities of IPVC, teaching how to develop a collaborative intergroup project from the idea stage through implementation and evaluation. The trainings offered a shared experience and common bond for all members. An advanced training in neighborhood-based crisis response was offered to highly motivated volunteers from all parts of the city.

Groups of trained volunteers proposed projects to which a staff of nine in the mayor's office offered technical assistance and support. IPVC maintained that effective intergroup relations work can take a great variety of forms, and focus on a range of particular subjects, provided two fundamental rules are observed: Projects must 1) have *multi-group participation* and 2) result in *multi-group benefit*.

Interracial groups of community-based IPVC members designed and implemented a variety of pro-active projects, among them:

• Summer programming in local parks that aimed to break down the segregated use of park space. Youth video "speakouts" on race relations were viewed by hundreds of people, playground clean-ups were undertaken by integrated groups, and street fairs and festivals brought social service providers together to jointly inform residents of the various public services available in their communities.

• In Jamaica, Queens, a neighborhood serving as a transportation hub for 8,000 high school students each day, IPVC spearheaded a campaign along with neighborhood institutions to reduce racially motivated attacks by largely Caribbean-American customers on Asian-American small businesses. Arrest numbers, usually especially high during the Halloween season, were reduced in 1992, as were tensions in the community which had grown to an all-time high.

• In Staten Island, New York's most conservative borough, IPVC members sponsored the first-ever public forum on intergroup relations following the brutal bias beating of a gay man. The meeting was attended by 200 people, and was widely reported in the local press.

• In selected high schools, IPVC members developed a program to take groups of 20 students from different ethnic backgrounds on a series of field trips to each other's cultural institutions, with the aim of promoting intergroup appreciation and understanding.

• In high schools where highly publicized racial incidents had taken place, IPVC members and adults from the surrounding neighborhoods actively engaged students on issues of intergroup relations.

In addition to the initiatives listed above, city-wide task forces were formed around 15 issue areas, among them the following:

• A Black-Jewish dialogue group, which met on a monthly basis for close to two years.

• A theater group, called Theater for a Greater Peace, formed by 45 IPVC members, wrote and produced a play about neighborhood racial tension, "My Enemy, My Brother," which was performed to excellent reviews in community centers and even had an off-Broadway run.

• A Women's Issues task force arranged art shows and discussion meetings, and co-sponsored a major conference with the New York City Commission on the Status of Women on the many roles of women as peacemakers in homes, communities and the city.

IPVC's design exemplifies the two-pronged approach typical of the other programs discussed earlier: municipal sponsorship and involvement, and personal transformation through finding common ground with members from ordinarily segregated groups. The more visible the public sector leadership and the more sustained the work of individuals, the more widely effective the program. The model of people working across race and class lines to improve civic life can change the neighborhood and community-wide climate in very concrete ways.

FOSTERING DIALOGUE THAT BRIDGES BARRIERS: SOME FINAL NOTES

The programs described above offer hopeful signs that American society, community by community, can begin to span the divisions that prevent us from working together.

While these programs focused on race, the same mechanisms that foster interracial interaction can be applied across all lines of our society, including class. By deliberately involving people of *all* backgrounds in community planning, organizers communicate that everyone's participation is welcome and vital. For example, an additional benefit of the grassroots approaches of IPVC and the study circle examples was their inclusion of socio-economic diversity.

Programs of the type described here are most effective when they involve members of the community who do not readily or ordinarily participate. Widely held misperceptions of individuals of other races decreases everyone's desire and ability to work together in communities. Moreover, when racial divisions are intensified by people's alienation from the general community—as when poverty complicates racial segregation—finding ways to enlarge participation can be the greatest challenge.[11]

CONCLUSION

The enormity of the challenges of race and class must galvanize rather than paralyze us. The success of a wide-ranging renewal of our civic life and community governance practices will depend on discovering ways to create opportunities for people of all groups to come together. People across the

country "only will trust what they themselves can do in bonding with others experiencing similar problems, across racial and

The enormity of the challenges of race and class must galvanize rather than paralyze us.

ethnic barriers, [while working] specifically and concretely on thousands of projects together in neighborhoods, towns, villages, city blocks, ghettos, barrios, and cities. . . ."[12]

The models described in this article, while differing in details, offer important lessons for communities seeking to address and overcome racial and socio-economic barriers: 1) Large-scale, face-to-face dialogue among people of different racial and class groups is critical to reducing prejudice, learning how to communicate with one another, finding commonalities, and creating ways to work together on community issues. 2) The collaboration and support of racially diverse leaders from a broad spectrum of community organizations is essential for encouraging dialogue in the larger community. When community leaders themselves participate in constructive interracial dialogue, they provide decisive leadership to members of their own groups and to the community as a whole. 3) An institutional basis for fostering and carrying out interracial dialogue is fundamental to involving all races and all sectors of the community. The study circle programs and the Increase the Peace Volunteer Corps are two successful models for providing this essential structure.

Importantly, a mayor's office or a city agency is especially well positioned to encourage the involvement of the public and community organizations in dialogue, since public officials have high visibility. The institutional base is also necessary for coordinating and carrying out the many daily communication and coordination tasks that add up to personal change and community renewal. The effects of the models described here are far-reaching.

Beyond helping people communicate about what divides them they provide ongoing ways for diverse people to understand and take on all the community issues they hold in common. C ᴺR

NOTES

[1] This segregation of groups fosters an artificial and persistent sense that race and class are identical. Clarence Wood of the Chicago Human Relations Foundation is among those who have tried to tease this confusion apart, viewing poverty as an economic issue in need of economic remedies, and racism as a social issue in need of interpersonal remedies. See, Clarence Wood, *The Critical Chasm Between Racism and Poverty in Present-Day America* (Chicago: The Human Relations Council of Chicago, 1992).

[2] One of the most prominent of these calls is coming from Sheldon Hackney, chair of the National Endowment for the Humanities, in his proposal for a "national conversation" on American identity. See, Sheldon Hackney, "Organizing a National Conversation," *Chronicle of Higher Education*, 20 April 1994. Senator Bill Bradley of New Jersey also has called for dialogue on race in the context of communities. Consult the Congressional Record for his 26 March 1992 Senate floor statement, "Race and the American City."

[3] LH Research, *Taking America's Pulse: The National Conference Survey on Inter-Group Relations* (New York: The National Conference, 1994).

[4] Howard Gadlin, "Conflict Resolution, Cultural Differences and the Culture of Racism," *Negotiation Journal*, January 1994.

[5] There are many interesting writings on the requirements for productive interracial dialogue. For one very accessible text, see, William M. Boyd, "Can the Races Talk Together?," *Poynter Report*, Spring 1993.

[6] Henry G. Cisneros, "Valuing the Differences: Diversity as an Asset," remarks to the 98th National Conference on Governance, Los Angeles, California, November 13, 1992.

[7] *Taking America's Pulse*, p. 52.

[8] Derek Okubo et al., *Governance and Diversity: Findings from Los Angeles* (Denver: National Civic League **Press**, 1993), p. 24.

[9] The study circles moved from discussions of personal experiences to discussions of race in the greater society, to what can be done in the community. The study circles in this and other programs mentioned in this article use and adapt *Can't We All Just Get Along? A Manual for Discussion Programs on Racism and Race Relations*, 2d Ed. (Pomfret, Conn.: Study Circles Resource Center, 1994). Anyone interested in initiating a community-wide dialogue on race relations may contact the Study Circles Resource Center (SCRC) at (203) 928-2616. SCRC assists and tracks a growing network of communities conducting citizen-based dialogue on race relations and other community issues.

[10] Drawn from unpublished research by David Adams and George Handley; see, "Attitude Adjustment," *The Lima News*, 19 April 1994.

[11] Gary Orfield has elaborated on the "underclass problem": "The fundamental problem is that a large share of central-city, nonwhite children are growing up in settings which have no working links to the jobs and higher education necessary to success in American society. . . .In spite of billions of dollars invested in a variety of compensatory education, housing, and other programs to increase opportunity for inner-city communities, no city has developed a set of policies that have created genuine equal opportunity for young people in areas of concentrated segregation and poverty." (Source: *Newsroom Guide to Civil Rights* [Washington, D.C.: The Communications Consortium Media Center, 1994], p. 109.)

[12] *Taking America's Pulse*, p. 59.

Achuar peoples, 89
Acuna, Rudy, 116, 117
affirmative action, 12, 31, 32–33, 36, 118, 158–163, 168–170, 199, 200, 236; alternative principles of, 162–163; arguments about, 178; success of, 179
African People's Socialist Party, 117
Afrocentrism, 264; understanding, 234–241
Akaka, Daniel K., 11
Ak-Chin Indians, 89
Alaskan Native, 10–16
Alien and Sedition Acts of 1798, 43
alliance, Black-Jewish, 196–204
American Arab Chamber of Commerce, 209
American Arab Directory, 209
American Association for the Advancement of Science, 253
American Civil Liberties Union (ACLU), 36, 165
American Dream, 252; faith in, 180
American Enterprise Institute, 178
American Indians, 10–16, 101–105
American Jewish Committee, 197
American-Arab Anti-Discrimination Committee (ADC), 209
Amichai, Yehuda, 224, 226
anti-Catholicism, 45
Anti-Defamation League, 192
anti-immigrant, 45
antimiscegenation laws, 13, 140
anti-Semitism, 152, 201, 204, 212, 220; modern, as derived from Marxism, 220
anti-Zionism, 201, 203
apartheid, 222
Appiah, Kwame Anthony, 12
Arab American, demographics of, 205–209
Arafat, Yasir, 224, 231
Argentina, indigenous peoples of, 84
Armelagos, George, 254
Asante, Molefi Kete, 16, 237
Asian American, 128–129, 130–131; artists and writers, 139; immigration of, 44–52; interracial marriages and, 13
Asian Law Caucus, 242
Asian-Indian Americans, demographics of, 132–138
Association for MultiEthnic Americans, 248
Atkins, Thomas I., 245
Atlanta Compromise, 149
Australia, indigenous peoples of, 93
autonomy: corporate 223; territorial, 223
Aymara people, 89

Bakke, Alan, 28–29
Bakke decision, 27–31, 160, 162
Balkan culture, 214–216
Balkan War, 214–217; roots and highlights of, 217
Bangladesh, immgrants from, 132–138
Barry, Marion, 155
Bates, Daisy, 151
Bell Curve, The (Murray and Herrnstein), 179, 247, 255
Benvenisti, Meron, 230, 231
Berger, David, 267, 269
Berlin Wall, fall of, 213
Bernal, Martin, 237, 238
bigotry, 203
bilingualism: German edition of Texas laws and, 44; in schools, 51
bingo, American Indians and, 103
Bissoondath, Neil, 66–67
Black Power movement, 239
blacks, 6–9, 10–16, 178–180; Afrocentrism and, 234–241; cultural deficiencies of, 178; immigration and, 41, 148; interracial marriages and, 13; middle class, 178; Million Man March of, 152–154; real estate ownership and, 171–175; relationships of Jews with, 192–204; religion and, 264–265; separated institutions, 148–149; ten most dramatic events in history of, 148–151; wealth and, 179; whites and, 266–272
Blendon, Robert, 249, 250

Blumenbach, Johann Friedrich, 259–263
Boas, Franz, 239
Bolivia, indigenous peoples of, 84, 93
Bonora, Beth, 242
Bonsa-Herzegovina, 214–217; "purification" in, 215
Brace, C. Loring, 253, 254
braceros, 49
Brazil, indigenous peoples of, 84, 88
Bromley, Charles, 171, 173
Brown, et al. v. Board of Education of Topeka, 24–26, 31, 150, 164–167
Brues, Alice, 254, 255
Bunzel, John, 162

Calandra, John D., 187
California Civil Rights Initiative (CCRI), 158, 168
Canadian Indians, 88–89
Carter, Jimmy, 193
Castillo, Herberto, 117
Catholicism: discrimination and, 181–186; Orthodoxy division and, 214–216
Caucasian, 189; origin of term, 259–263
Cavalli-Sforza, Luca, 253
census, 10–16, 53–57, 101, 108–114, 132–138, 205–209
Census Bureau, 173
Chechnya, 81–82
Chiapas Indians, revolt of, against Mexico, 94–96
Chicano, 115–119
Chicano Art: Resistance and Affirmation (CARA), 116, 117
Chile, indigenous peoples of, 93
Chinese Exclusion Act, 48
Chinese, immigration of, 40, 44–45, 48, 49
Christianity, Islam and, 264–265
Cisneros, Henry, 174, 267
citizenship, definition of, and Dred Scott decision, 6–9
civil rights: effect of Immigration Reform Act of 1965 on, 161; legislation, 179
Civil Rights Act of 1866, Section 1981, 188–190
Civil Rights Act of 1964, 160; repeal proposed, 178; Title VII, 188
Civil Rights Act of 1968, 165
Civil Rights Commission, of the United States, 162
civilization, contrasted with culture, 71–73
Clinton Administration: Chechnya and, 81; housing segregation and, 174
Clinton, Bill, 64, 81, 152, 168
collaborative processes or problem solving, 72
Columbia, immigrants from, 109–114
Columbus, Christopher, 11, 84, 88, 116, 117–119
Communist Party, 118
concentration camps, 212
Congress of Polish Arts, 212
Congressional Black Caucus, 192–193
consociationalism, 222
conspiracy, "Jewish," 192
Constitution of the United States: Bakke decision and, 27–31; Brown v. Board of Education decision and, 24–26; Dred Scott decision and, 6–9, Plessy v. Ferguson decision and, 17–23
Cooper, Clarence, 246
Croatia, 214–216
Crouch, Stanley, 240
Crummell, Alexander, 236
Cuba, immigrants from, 50, 108–114
cultural diversity, limits of, 70–73

Daniel, G. Reginald, 12
Darwin, Charles, 261
Davis, Angela, 234
Delany, Martin, 236
DeMarco, Don, 172
Democratic Revolutionary Party (PRD), 117
Denton, Nancy A., 171
Department of Housing and Urban Development, 165
deportation, 68–69
desegregation, 32–33, 36; of schools, 164–167
Diamond, Jared, 254

Diaz, Angel, 115
Dinkins, David, 269
Diop, Cheikh Anta, 238
discrimination: anti-Catholic, 181–186; based on nationality, 187–191; lending industry and, 173; in real estate, 171–175
diversity, in U.S., 186; cultural, limits of, 70–73
Dole, Bob, 158
Dominican Republic, immigrants from, 109–114
Douglass, Frederick, 12, 149
Douglass, Ramona, 248
Drake, St. Clair, 239
Dred Scott v. Sandford, 6–9, 22
D'Souza, Dinesh, 178, 179
Du Bois, W. E. B., 12, 149, 150, 198, 235, 239
due process clause, of Fourteenth Amendment, 18, 26

Eastern Europeans, 181–186; immigration of, 46
Ecuador, 85, 88, 90–91, 109–114
education, of immigrants, 53–57, 58–62, 128, 132–138, 205–209
El Salvador, immigrants from, 109–114
emancipation, 149
English, immigration of, 42
"English Only" laws, 116, 145
entitlement programs, 223
entrepreneurship, 178
environmental issues, indigenous people and, 91–93, 97–100
Equal Employment Opportunity Commission (EEOC), 160
equal protection, under Fourteenth Amendment, 18, 20, 24, 26, 190
equality, economic, 251–252
Eritrea, 82–83
ethnic(s): categories in census, 10–16; conflict, 218–223; nationalism and, 218–223; white voters and, 181–186
ethnicity: devisiveness of, 266–272; new, 181–186
Eurocentric, 238, 239
European immigrants, Eastern and Southern, 181–186

Fiar Housing Act of 1968, 171
Farrakhan, Louis, 12, 152–154, 161, 192–193, 201, 202, 235–236, 264; biography of, 155–157
Feagin, Joe R., 179
Federal Homeowners Administration loans, 172
Filipino: diaspora, 139–145; immigration, 51
Flack, Faye, 269
Fourteenth Amendment, 18, 20, 24, 26, 27–31, 190
Free African Society, 149
Freedom Movement, 150–151
Freedom Rides, 151
Freud, Sigmund, 193, 194
Fruit of Islam, 193, 201
Fuhrman, Mark, 155, 245
Fund for an Open Society, 172

Gadlin, Howard, 267
Galster, George, 172
gambling, on Indian reservations, 103–105
Gandhi, Mahatma, 199
Garn, Stanley, 13
Garvey, Marcus, 156, 157, 236, 240
Geertz, Clifford, 218
gender preferences, 158
geometer, 259–263
Germans, immigration of, 41–44
Gingrich, Newt, 158
Gonzales, "Corky," 117
Gonzales, Nita, 117
Gould, Stephen Jay, 13
Graham, Hugh Davis, 161
Great Hunger, 44
Great Migration, 150
Great Society programs, 49
Greene, Lorenzo, 239

Guatemala, immigrants from, 109–114
Guinier, Lani, 12
Gypsies, 194–195, 214

Hacker, Andrew, 237
Hahn, Robert A., 15, 255
Hamas, 224
Hansberry, William Leo, 237
Haredim, 225–230
Herbert, Bob, 192
Herrnstein, Richard, 179, 247, 255
Hill, Anita, 178
Hisim, Ahmet, 245
Hispanic(s), 115–119; Americans, 108–114;
  Catholicism and, 122–125; census and, 10–11,
  14
Hitler, Adolph, 202
Hochschild, Jennifer L., 179–180
"holding five," 34–35
Holocaust, European Christendom as responsible
  for, 212
home ownership, blacks and, 171–175
Honduras, immigrants from, 109–114
hooks, bell, 179, 234, 235
Hoover Institution, 162
Huerta, Dolores, 117
Human Genome Diversity Project, 253
Hurston, Zora Neale, 239
Husseini, Faisal, 230
hypersegregation, defined, 171

Ice-T, 161
Igasaki, Paul, 242
illegal aliens, 40
immigration: arguments about, 63–65; history of,
  40–52; quotas for, 47–52; racism and, 40–52
Immigration Reform Act of 1965, 49; effect of, on
  civil rights, 161
Increase the Peace Volunteer Corps (IPVC), 269
India, immigrants from, 132–138
Indian Self-Determination and Education Act of
  1975, 80
indigenous people, 76–83; American, 79–80, 89,
  101–105; Canadian, 88–89, 91, 97–100;
  Chechen, 82–83; environmental issues and,
  91–93, 97–100; Eritrean, 82–83; Latin
  American, 89, 91; Mexican, 91, 94–96; regions
  of, 91; South American, 84–87, 91; successes
  of, 90–93
Inouye, Daniel K., 130
integration, 235
intergroup relations, 270
interracial: divisiveness of, interaction, 266–272;
  groups, 270; marriage, 11, 12, 13, 18, 221,
  247; percent in California, 258
intifada, 226
Inuit, 88–89, 97–100
IPVC, 270–271
Irish, immigration of, 41–45
Islam: in Bosnia, 215; Christianity and, 264–265
Israel, 199; founding of, 226
Italian American Institute, of City University of
  New York, 187–191
Italian American Legal Defense and Higher
  Education Fund, 187
Italian Americans, 187–191; immigration of, 46
Ivy League, 183
Izetbegovic, Alija, 215

Jackson, Jesse L., 36, 152, 157, 169, 193, 203
Jankélévitch, 193, 194, 198, 201, 203, 204
Jankowski, Martin Sanchez, 179
Japanese Americans, 130–131
Jasenovac concentration camp, 214, 216
Jefferson, Thomas, 152, 198
Jeffries, Leonard, 201
Jerusalem, 224–231
Jews: group and individual identities and, 183;
  relationships of blacks with, 192–204
Jim Crow laws, 12, 150, 198
Johnson, Lyndon B. 151, 160

Johnson, Sheri Lynn, 243
Johnson-Reed Act, 48
juries: all-black, 244; all-white, 244; multiracial
  243; race and, 242–243
jury nullification, 245

Kairys, David, 242
Kalmijn, Matthijs, 13
Kaminker, Sarah, 226, 230
Karadzic, Radovan, 217
Karenga, Maulana, 237
Katzen, Sally, 15
Kazan, Elia, 183
Kazin, Alfred, 195
Kimhi, Israel, 227
King, Martin Luther, Jr., 12, 36, 118, 150, 151,
  161, 198, 240
King, Rodney, verdict, 268
Know-Nothing movement, 45
Kollek, Teddy, 225–230
Koreans, immigration of, 50
Kunstler, William, 245
Kurds, 81

La Raza, 115–119
Landry, Bart, 173
Latinos, 115–119
Leadership Education for Asian Pacifics (LEAP),
  128
Lefkowitz, Mary R., 237
Lewontin, Richard, 253
liberalism: shoddy variant of, 198; Third Worldism
  versus, 198–204
Lieberman, Leonard, 253
Limbaugh, Rush, 236
Lincoln, Abraham, 45
Lincoln, C. Eric, 155, 157
Linnaeus, Carolus, 254–255, 260
Little Rock, Arkansas, 151
Loving v. Virginia, 13
Lummi tribe, 90
Lupolianski, Uri, 226, 227, 230
Luxembourg, Rosa, 219

Magida, Arthur, 156–157
mail-order brides, 144
Malcolm X, 12, 157, 198, 240
Marable, Manning, 118, 178
March on Washington (1963), 199
Marin, Patricia, 117
Marks, Jonathon, 254
marriage, interracial, 11, 12, 13, 18, 221, 247
Marshall, Thurgood, 150, 198
Martin Luther King Day, 269
Marx, Karl, 219, 220, 234
Mason, Jackie, 193
Massey, Douglas S., 171
McCarran-Walter Act, 48
McGovern, George, 185
MEChA (Movimiento Estudiantil Chicano de
  Aztlan, the Chicano Student Movement of
  Aztlan), 116, 117, 118
medical school admission, Bakke decision and,
  27–31
melting pot, 184, 221, 222
mestizo, 14, 85, 139
Metropolitan Strategy Group, 171
Mexican Americans, 109, 115–119, 120–121
Mexico, 94–96; immigrants from, 109–114;
  indigenous peoples of, 91
Mfume, Kweisi, 193
Miller, Chaim, 226
Million Man March, 152–154, 264; support of
  black middle class for, 153
Milosevic, Slobodan, 217
minorities: Eastern and Southern European,
  181–186; inaccurate view of, 249–252
Missouri v. Jenkins, 32–33
Mladic, Ratko, 217
Mongolian, origin of term, 259–263
Montagu, Ashley, 13, 255

Moses, Wilson Jeremiah, 241
Mothers of East Los Angeles, 117
Muckleshoot tribe, 90
Muhammad, Elijah, 155–157, 192
Muhammad, Khalid Abdul, 161, 192–193
mulatto, 12
multiculturalism, 186, 241; attack on, 178;
  Canadian, 66–67
Murray, Charles, 179, 247, 255
Muslims, 214–216; orthodox beliefs of, 264
Myanmar (Burma), Karen Nation in, 82–83

Namibia, indigenous peoples of, 91
Nassar, Gamal, 199
Nation of Islam, 117, 152–154, 155–157,
  192–193, 235–236, 240, 264
National Association for the Advancement of
  Colored People (NAACP), 150, 151, 193, 196,
  197, 245
National Chicano Moratorium Committee, 117
National Civic League, 267
National Conference, 267
National Jury Project, 242
National Organization of Women (NOW), 168
National Research Council, 171
nationalism, 139; black, 235; communism and,
  219–220; socialism and, 219–220; types of
  ethnic and class, 220
nationality: defined, 41; self-determination and, 221
Native Americans, 13, 119
naturalization, 6–9
Negritude, 235
Nei, Masatoshi, 13
Neimi, Richard, 249
Neverdon, Davon, 244
New Zealand, indigenous peoples of, 93
Niagara Movement, 150
Nicaragua, 91, 109–114
Nixon, Richard, 185
Njeri, Itabari, 15
Noah, Yannick, 254
Nobel Peace Prize, 224
"Not of Hispanic Origin," on census, 10–11
Nunavik, 97–100

octoroons, 12
official languages: of India, 136; of Paraguay, 85
Oliver, Melvin, L., 179
Olmert, Ehud, 225–230
"one drop of blood" rule, 10–16
Orfield, Gary L., 164

Pacific Islander, 10–16
Pacific Northwest Indians, 90
Pakistan, immgrants from, 132–138
Palestine Liberation Organization (PLO), 224, 231
Palestinians, 199–200, 205, 224–231
Palm Beach County, 165
Pan Africanism, 235, 240
Panama, immigrants from, 109–114
Paraguay, indigenous peoples of, 85
Paris Peace Conference of 1919, 221
Parks, Rosa, 150
Patterson, Orlando, 248
PEN, 212
People for the American Way, 193
Perk, Ralph, 185
Perot, Ross, 156
Peru, 85, 88, 93, 109–114
Petri, Thomas E., 10
Piersen, William, 237
Plessy v. Ferguson, 17–23, 24, 25, 150
polls: on affirmative action, 168–170; on
  economics and race, 249–252
Porush, Meir, 226
post-Communist states, 213
Powell, Colin, 152, 155, 156
Protestant sensibilities, 184
Puerto Rico, immigrants from, 109–114
Puyallup Indians, 89

quadroons, 12
Quichua peoples, 89

Raab, Earl, 183
Rabin, Yitzak, 224
race, 10–16, 247–248; affirmative action and, 158–163; "claiming" identity, 256–258; class as distinguished from, 179; classification, devised, 259–263; face-to-face dialogue on, 271; historical view of, 189; interracial acceptance and, 266–272; juries and, 242–246; preferences, 159–163; public sector hiring and, 158–163; riots, 49; science of, 253–255
racial categories, 259–263; census and, 10–16; genetic variations and, 13
racism, 178–180; dilemma of, 178; home ownership and, 171–175; immigration and, 47; study circle dialogues and, 267–269; view of, 249–250
Randolph, A. Philip, 198
Reagan administration, enforcement of fair housing laws and, 165
Refugee Act of 1980, 50
refugees, 48, 50, 68–69
Rizzo, Frank, 185
Robertson, Pat, 156
Rogers, J. A., 240
Roland Shearer, Rhonda, 260
Rosenthal, A. M., 192, 193
Roychoudhury, Arun K., 13
Rustin, Bayard, 198, 199, 201
Ryser, Rudolph, 78

Saks, Michael, 242
Salazar, Ruben, 115, 116
Sartre, Jean Paul, 184, 239
Sawyer, Thomas C., 10–16
Scelsa decision, 187–191
Scelsa, Joseph V., 187, 188
schools: magnet, 165–167; on military bases, 167; on work sites, 167; segregation of, 21, 24–26, 36
Scots, immigration of, 41–42
Sechelt Indians, 88–89
Secret Relationship Between Blacks and Jews, The, 192, 237
segregation: in accommodations, and *Plessy v. Ferguson*, 17–23; *Brown v. Board of Education* and, 24–26; hypersegregation and, 171; Jerusalem and, 88–89; real estate and home

ownership and, 171–175; in schools, and *Missouri v. Jenkins*, 32–33, 36
Selena, 120–121
self-determination, 76–83
Selimovic, Mesa, 215
Selling Illusions: The Cult of Multiculturalism in Canada, (Bissoondath), 66–67
"separate but equal," 17–23, 24–26
Serbia, 214–217
Shapiro, Thomas M., 179
Shining Path, 85–86
Shiwar peoples, 89
Shoshoni-Bannock Indians, 89
Simpson, O. J., verdict, 152, 244
Simpson-Mazzoli Act of 1986, 52
Singletary, Selena, 269
sit-ins, 151
skin color, 10–16, 21, 247–248, 253–255, 256–258, 261–262
slavery, 6–9, 17–23, 30, 178
Slavic American, 181–186
Smeal, Eleanor, 169
Smith, Darryl, jury verdict, 244
Smith, Michael Peter, 179
socialism, nationalism and, 219–220
Solidarity, 212
Sontag, Susan, 239
South American Indians, 84–87
sovereignty, of Jerusalem, 231
Spencer, Jon Michael, 16
states' rights, 6–9, 17–23, 198
Steele, Shelby, 168, 194, 195
Steinberg, Stephen, 179
study circles, and dialogues on racism, 267–269
Supreme Court: affirmative action, 32, 36; decisions of, 6–9, 17–23, 24, 25, 26, 32–33, 150, 189, 190; "holding five," 34–35
Szczypiorski, Andrzej, interview with, 212–213

Tagalog, 145
Taney, Roger Brooke, 6
Tejano, 120–121
Tel Aviv, 224
Third Worldism, liberalism versus, 198–204
Thirteenth Amendment, 17–23, 189
Thomas, Clarence, 36, 178
Thompson, Robert Farris, 237
Tribe, Lawrence, 36
Truman, Harry, 48
Tudjman, Franjo, 217

Tulalip tribe, 90
Turner, Nat, 149
Tuskegee method, 239

United Farm Workers of America, 140
United Nations, 76–83; Jerusalem and, 229
United Nations Working Group on Indigenous Peoples (UNWGIP), 76–83
Urban Institute, 172

van den Berghe, Pierre, 220
Venezuela, indigenous peoples of, 88
Veterans Administration loans, 172
Vietnam War, 49, 115, 239
Vietnamese, immigration of, 50
Voting Rights Act of 1965, 11, 13, 49, 160

Walters, Ronald, 168
war brides, 13
War Brides Act of 1945, 48
Ward, Lynn, 115
Warren, Earl, 24, 150
Washington, Booker T., 12, 149, 198, 239
Washington, George, 151
wealth, of blacks and whites, 179
Webster, Yehudi, 15
Weizmann, Chaim, 229
West, Cornell, 179
Wheatley, Phillis, 262
Wilder, Douglas, 12
Wilkins, Roger, 192
William, Chancellor, 237
Williams, David, 255
Wilson, Pete, 40, 158
Wilson, William Julius, 179
Woodson, Carter G., 239
World Bank International Monetary Fund, 144
World War II, 214
Wright, Richard, 196, 201

Yad Sarah, 227
Yanomami, 89
Young, Andrew, 193
Yugoslavia, 214–217

Zhirinovsky, Vladimir, 81
Zionism, 199

Credits/ Acknowledgments

Cover design by Charles Vitelli

1. Race and Ethnicity in the American Legal Tradition
Facing overview—Reproduced from the collections of the Library of Congress.

2. Immigration
Facing overview—Courtesy of Louis P. Raucci.

3. Indigenous Ethnic Groups
Facing overview—United Nations photo by Heidi Larson.

4. Hispanic/Latino Americans
Facing overview—United Nations photo by Christina D. Sagona.

5. Asian Americans
Facing overview—Photo by Pamela Carley.

6. African Americans
Facing overview—Reproduced from the collections of the Library of Congress.

7. The Ethnic Legacy
Facing overview—New York Convention and Visitors Bureau photo.

8. The Ethnic Factor
Facing overview—United Nations photo by S. Whitehouse.

9. Understanding Cultural Pluralism
Facing overview—United Nations photo by Y. Nagata.

PHOTOCOPY THIS PAGE!!!*

ANNUAL EDITIONS ARTICLE REVIEW FORM

■ NAME: _____ DATE: _____

■ TITLE AND NUMBER OF ARTICLE: _____

■ BRIEFLY STATE THE MAIN IDEA OF THIS ARTICLE: _____

_____

■ LIST THREE IMPORTANT FACTS THAT THE AUTHOR USES TO SUPPORT THE MAIN IDEA:

_____

_____

_____

_____

_____

_____

■ WHAT INFORMATION OR IDEAS DISCUSSED IN THIS ARTICLE ARE ALSO DISCUSSED IN YOUR
TEXTBOOK OR OTHER READING YOU HAVE DONE? LIST THE TEXTBOOK CHAPTERS AND PAGE
NUMBERS:

_____

_____

_____

_____

_____

_____

■ LIST ANY EXAMPLES OF BIAS OR FAULTY REASONING THAT YOU FOUND IN THE ARTICLE:

_____

_____

_____

_____

■ LIST ANY NEW TERMS/CONCEPTS THAT WERE DISCUSSED IN THE ARTICLE AND WRITE A SHORT
DEFINITION:

_____

_____

_____

_____

_____

*Your instructor may require you to use this Annual Editions Article Review Form in any number of
ways: for articles that are assigned, for extra credit, as a tool to assist in developing assigned papers, or
simply for your own reference. Even if it is not required, we encourage you to photocopy and use this
page; you'll find that reflecting on the articles will greatly enhance the information from your text.

ANNUAL EDITIONS: RACE AND ETHNIC RELATIONS 96/97
Article Rating Form

We Want Your Advice

Here is an opportunity for you to have direct input into the next revision of this volume. We would like you to rate each of the 57 articles listed below, using the following scale:

1. **Excellent: should definitely be retained**
2. **Above average: should probably be retained**
3. **Below average: should probably be deleted**
4. **Poor: should definitely be deleted**

Your ratings will play a vital part in the next revision. So please mail this prepaid form to us just as soon as you complete it.
Thanks for your help!

Annual Editions revisions depend on two major opinion sources: one is our Advisory Board, listed in the front of this volume, which works with us in scanning the thousands of articles published in the public press each year; the other is you—the person actually using the book. Please help us and the users of the next edition by completing the prepaid article rating form on this page and returning it to us. Thank you.

Rating	Article	Rating	Article
	1. *Dred Scott v. Sandford*		30. Configuring the Filipino Diaspora in the United States
	2. One Drop of Blood		31. 10 Most Dramatic Events in African-American History
	3. *Plessy v. Ferguson*		32. Leader Popular among Marchers
	4. *Brown et al. v. Board of Education of Topeka et al.*		33. An Angry "Charmer"
	5. *University of California Regents v. Bakke*		34. So You Want to Be Color-Blind
	6. High Court Loosens Desegregation's Grip		35. 40 Years after *Brown*, Segregation Persists
	7. As Deadline Nears, Court Leaders Pin Hopes on "Holding 5"		36. Affirmative Action: Four Groups' Views
	8. Court Grows Critical When Race, Law Intersect		37. Home Ownership Anchors the Middle Class: But Lending Games Sink Many Prospective Owners
	9. A Nation of Immigrants		38. America's Dilemma
	10. Census Bureau Finds Significant Demographic Differences among Immigrant Groups		39. The New Ethnicity
	11. The Foreign-Born Population: 1994		40. Italian Americans as a Cognizable Racial Group
	12. Is Latest Wave a Drain or Boon to Society?		41. The Other and the Almost the Same
	13. Pride and Prejudice		42. The Arab American Market
	14. Coping with Deportation—The Integration of Millions of Refugees		43. Andrzej Szczypiorski: Poles and Germans
	15. The Limits to Cultural Diversity		44. The Ends of History: Balkan Culture and Catastrophe
	16. 12th Session of UN Working Group on Indigenous Peoples		45. The State of Bosnia-Herzegovina: Roots and Highlights of the Latest Balkan War
	17. Paupers in a World Their Ancestors Ruled		46. Ethnic Conflict
	18. Struggling to Be Themselves		47. Passions Set in Stone
	19. Return of the Natives		48. Understanding Afrocentrism
	20. Why Did Chiapas Revolt?		49. Whose Peers?
	21. Towards Information Self-Sufficiency		50. Color Blinded? Race Seems to Play an Increasing Role in Many Jury Verdicts
	22. American Indians in the 1990s		51. What Color Is Black?
	23. Specific Hispanics		52. A Distorted Image of Minorities
	24. There's More to Racism than Black and White		53. Three Is Not Enough
	25. Born on the Border		54. Goin' Gangsta
	26. A Place of Our Own		55. The Geometer of Race
	27. Asian Americans Don't Fit Their Monochrome Image		56. Battling for Souls
	28. A Migration Created by Burden of Suspicion		57. Bridging the Divides of Race and Ethnicity
	29. Asian-Indian Americans		

(Continued on next page)

ABOUT YOU

Name _____ Date _____

Are you a teacher? ❏ Or student? ❏

Your School Name _____

Department _____

Address _____

City _____ State _____ Zip _____

School Telephone # _____

YOUR COMMENTS ARE IMPORTANT TO US!

Please fill in the following information:

For which course did you use this book? _____

Did you use a text with this Annual Edition? ❏ yes ❏ no

The title of the text? _____

What are your general reactions to the Annual Editions concept?

Have you read any particular articles recently that you think should be included in the next edition?

Are there any articles you feel should be replaced in the next edition? Why?

Are there other areas that you feel would utilize an Annual Edition?

May we contact you for editorial input?

May we quote you from above?

ANNUAL EDITIONS: RACE AND ETHNIC RELATIONS 96/97

BUSINESS REPLY MAIL

First Class   Permit No. 84   Guilford, CT

Postage will be paid by addressee

**Dushkin Publishing Group/
Brown & Benchmark Publishers**
Sluice Dock
Guilford, Connecticut 06437